HANDBOOK OF METADATA, SEMANTICS AND ONTOLOGIES

HANDBOOK OF METADATA, SEMANTICS AND ONTOLOGIES

editor

Miguel-Angel Sicilia

University of Alcalá, Spain

World Scientific

NEW JERSEY • LONDON • SINGAPORE • BEIJING • SHANGHAI • HONG KONG • TAIPEI • CHENNAI

Published by

World Scientific Publishing Co. Pte. Ltd.

5 Toh Tuck Link, Singapore 596224

USA office: 27 Warren Street, Suite 401-402, Hackensack, NJ 07601

UK office: 57 Shelton Street, Covent Garden, London WC2H 9HE

British Library Cataloguing-in-Publication Data
A catalogue record for this book is available from the British Library.

HANDBOOK OF METADATA, SEMANTICS AND ONTOLOGIES

ISBN 978-981-283-629-8

Typeset by Stallion Press
Email: enquiries@stallionpress.com

Printed in Singapore by Fuisland Offset Printing (S) Pte Ltd

PREFACE

Metadata in its different forms have become increasingly important in the last years. This is partly because metadata schemas are devised to bring structure to information on the Web, in an attempt to describe Web resources in a more homogeneous way. Also, metadata is the principal way of recording provenance information of Web resources in an explicit way. In consequence, metadata is critical both for interoperability and as a mean to improve search and assess intellectual property rights.

The proliferation of metadata schemas and ontologies of diverse kind offer a rich array of languages to describe and annotate Web resources. However, that diversity can turn into a problem as it has given rise to competing schemas, using different levels of formality and tailored for some particular uses. While standardization efforts are slowly making these converge, the task of a metadata expert is nowadays a challenge, as in many cases there are no clear criteria to decide which form and schema is better for a particular situation. The recent emergence of the Web of Linked Data has made this landscape even more complex, as vocabularies intended to be use to expose data in RDF form derive in some cases from previous metadata schemas, but in other cases are devised from scratch. And the use of Linked Data conventions represent a different approach to sharing metadata to previous practices mainly based on harvesting and interchange of XML files.

In consequence, information managers need to have a broad knowledge of what is available and what is more important, which are the key properties of a schema or metadata solution that makes it different from others. There is currently not any available corpus that compiles knowledge about metadata in a comprehensive way. That aim is currently hardly attainable due to the dynamic nature of the field and to the fact that its boundaries are still somewhat fuzzy. It is also challenging as a large part of the work in metadata is done by communities in particular domains, e.g. agriculture, environmental sciences, etc.

This book aims at providing an overview of metadata as practiced in a variety of different domains, and taking a plurality of perspectives. It does not aim to cover all the domains, schemas and techniques since that task would nowadays require an encyclopaedic approach. We hope that the book is useful as a reflection of the metadata field itself: heterogeneous and rich and at the same time complex. The selection of chapters was done via a process of peer review that took into account technical correctness and representativeness to the domain. The result is a somewhat fragmentary but highly representative overview of domains and topics on metadata. While some of the chapters may be to some extent not completely updated when the book is published, they are still appropriate vehicles to inform information managers so that they can drill down into more details using the book as a roadmap.

I believe the coming years would be exciting times for professionals and researchers involved in metadata, and I hope this book represents a modest contribution towards understanding metadata as a professional and technical discipline that stands in its own and requires specialized training and competence.

Miguel-Angel Sicilia

CONTENTS

CHAPTER I.1

METADATA RESEARCH: MAKING DIGITAL RESOURCES USEFUL AGAIN?

Miguel-Angel Sicilia

Department of Computer Science
University of Alcalá, Polytechnic building
Ctra. Barcelona km. 33.6
Alcalá de Henares(Madrid), Spain
msicilia@uah.es

The growth of the Web represents also one of its major challenges, as users face the problem of selecting the pages that are most relevant to their taskfrom a vast amount of information. Search engines and microdata are an example of a means towards the end of helping in better targeting search, but there is no universal perfect solution for all information needs. In addition, the last years have witnessed the emergence of the Web of Linked Data, fostered by the increasing adoption of openness as a paradigm for sharing information for the benefit of the commons. Microdata, linked data and other technologies are no other thing than different ways of using metadata to enhance information seeking, targeting and integration. Metadata thus is nowadays the fabric of the Web. Understanding the different forms and arrangements of metadata is in consequence a required skill for researchers and practitioners that aim at understanding and getting value from the Web.

Keywords: Metadata, Linked Data, microdata, terminologies

1. Introduction

"Metadata" has become a term frequently used both in academia and also in the professional context. As an indicator of its growing acceptance as a common concept, the Google Scholar service[1] estimates more than 1 million results when we formulate a query using only the term. The results' estimation

[1] http://scholar.google.com/

become more than 30 million if we use instead the non-specialized search service provided by Google. While the common usage of the term seems to be uncontroversial, there is an increasing heterogeneity in the ways metadata is defined, created, managed, and stored. This heterogeneity probably comes from the lack of a precise definition of metadata that captures the main elements behind the application of metadata technologies.

Metadata is commonly defined as "data about data", according to its etymology. While this definition cannot be considered false, it has the problem of covering too many things and at the same time capturing only part of the aspects that are considered important by researchers and practitioners working with metadata. Following such definition, if I write some data in a piece of paper about an interesting book from my local library, that is a piece of metadata. This naïve example actually can be used to raise several of the important questions revolving around metadata research. For example, for some people metadata only applies to digital information (and this is precisely the focus of interest we take here). Or for some others metadata needs to be formulated with some form of schema or structure that brings a level of standardization or homogeneous use across Web sites and systems.

Another problem with metadata as a concept is that it has been metadata and not meta-information the term that has reached widespread use. There is a conceptual distinction according to which data, information and knowledge are different but interrelated things (Zins, 2007). However, to follow the common use of the term, we refer here to metadata as a generic term of any kind of meta-information also.

Metadata existed many years before the Web was even conceived. However, with the Web metadata has been brought to the hearth of the architecture of cyberspace. Originally the Web was only made up of HTML pages following a simple interlinked structure. But it has evolved into something much more complex in which metadata mixes with the contents of the pages or is arranged as a layer of information that "points" to the resources described via URIs.[2] Also, HTML is not anymore the only way of describing information on the Web. XML first and RDF then, along with some microformats, are the main expression mediums for metadata today.

Understanding what is metadata and how it manifests today in the Web is a key skill for practitioners and researchers in a variety of domains. Here we attempt to succinctly delineate the main characteristics of metadata and the way metadata nowadays conforms a space of information that surrounds the Web.

[2] http://tools.ietf.org/html/rfc3986

The rest of this chapter is structured as follows. Section 2 briefly discusses the emergence of metadata as a differentiated area of inquiry. Then, in Section 3 a definition of metadata is provided with the aim of covering in a broad sense such inquiry area. Section 4 then discusses some particular kinds of metadata as illustrations of its diversity. Finally, conclusions and outlook are provided in Section 5.

2. Metadata as a research discipline

During the last years we have been starting to speak of "metadata research". People have started to define themselves as "metadata specialists" and there have been international projects that were basically "metadata aggregation" projects. But is there anything as a discipline or area of "metadata research?". This is difficult to say, as the discipline is not defined by any society or professional organization to our knowledge. While there exist a few scholarly journals that have "metadata" in the title, and conferences that explicitly deal with metadata, delineating the boundaries of the topic is a challenging effort.

It is also difficult to clearly define the object of metadata research. A possible tentative would be that of defining that object as to an engineering discipline. Engineering is the science of design and production, and in this case we aim at devising *information mechanisms* for a *better access* to information resources.

An information mechanism can be broadly defined as any technique or method (or sets of them) that provides an organization to other information resources. Having databases of XML records with DublinCore metadata[3] is such an information mechanism. It has a defined schema, a format of expression and a way to point to the original resources, e.g. using <dc:identifier>. The Linked Open Data approach in DBPedia is another example (Morsey *et al.*, 2012). In this case it is based on the RDF standard,[4] and also follows a set of conventions that make it available via dereferenceable URLs. Many different information mechanisms can be devised for the same or different purposes. And metadata research is about how to make these more effective and efficient for particular purposes.

The purposes are the "better access" part of the definition. For example, the Europeana digital library[5] is essentially a system built on top of the

---

[3] http://dublincore.org/

[4] http://www.w3.org/RDF/

[5] http://www.europeana.eu/

aggregation of metadata using primarily harvesting mechanisms, starting from the OAI-PMH protocol. Here the "better access" means several things, including (a) homogeneous presentation of cultural resource descriptions, (b) a single point of interaction for a large mass of content and (c) some form of quality control in the ingestion process. In this example, it becomes evident that information mechanisms are encompassing not only formats, schemas and database technologies but also approaches to quality, organizational issues. In general, they involve a socio-technical system with procedures, technologies, tools and people.

A further characteristic of metadata research that makes it challenging is that the evolution of the field takes place in the context of the social phenomenon of adopting particular schemas and practices. In that direction, the survival and spread of a particular metadata schema arguably depends to a large extent on its readiness to be easily implemented by the community of practitioners and researchers in that area. In consequence, there may be metadata schemas for a given purpose that are richer than others, but they are also more slowly accepted and used. This may be attributed to different causes, as the difficulty of implementing, how hard is to transition legacy metadata and the degree of openness and transparency of their curators, to name a few. This is a sort of "natural evolution" of schemas and practices that in some cases cannot be directly related to the technical merits of the different approaches. It related to the social nature of the Web (Berners-Lee *et al.*, 2006).

In consequence, it is difficult to say if metadata research is a scientific discipline in itself with its own theories, assumptions and corpus of commonly accepted knowledge. However, it is clear that metadata research is a field of inquiry that is evolving and growing, and concepts and practice get consolidated with the years. It is in consequence worth the effort looking at the evolution of metadata research and doing an attempt to identify its foundations.

3. Defining metadata

Greenberg (2003) defines metadata as "structured data about an object that supports functions associated with the designated object". Structure in metadata entails that information is organised systematically, and this is nowadays primarily achieved by the use of metadata schemas. The functions enabled can be diverse, but they are in many cases related to facilitating discovery or search, or to restrict access (e.g. in the case of licensing information) or to combine meta-information to relate resources described separately.

The main characteristic of metadata is its *referential* nature, i.e., metadata predicates about some other thing (even describing another metadata record). Such 'other thing' can be considered as 'anything' from the broadest perspective, but such a view could hardly be useful for bringing semantics to current information systems as the web. Then, we will restrict our discussion to digital resources of a diverse kind. In the scope of the current web, resources can be unambiguously identified by the concept of URI.

For metadata to become an object of scientific inquiry there is a need to make it measurable in its core attributes, beyond measures related to size or availability. Metadata then should be considered to be subject to assessment in several dimensions. They include at least the following:

— Quality
— Richness
— Interoperability

While these three aspects are not independent completely, they look at the problem of having better metadata systems from different angles. Current studies on metadata quality mainly deal with completeness of metadata records and in some cases with the degree of use of controlled vocabularies. However, there is little research on richness, i.e. the amount of useful information or possibilities of interlinking of metadata collections or systems. The problem of richness should be approached at two levels. At the schema level, there are still no metrics for assessing and comparing metadata schemas according to their expressivity and possibilities to convey more detailed information. At the record level, the problem becomes even more challenging, as the final richness depends on the schema, the completeness of the records and also some other aspects that are in many cases domain-dependent.

Interoperability should in theory be taken from granted in metadata systems, however, it is a matter of fact that there are differences. The problem of interoperability starts obviously at the syntactic level. In common, general-purpose metadata schemas, simplicity comes at the cost of reducing possibilities to integrate information. There is a sort of trade-off between using highly generic metadata schemas as Dublin Core and richness, as the latter often require more specificity and detail. In any case, syntactic issues are just the beginning of the problem, as semantic interoperability is the target of any metadata mechanism. Semantics should be enabled by the use of terminologies, ontologies or any other kind of Knowledge Organization System (KOS). These systems are maintained independently from metadata schemas, and thus metadata systems need to address change. Even thus a KOS like a thesaurus usually has a low change rate, they evolve with time, and metadata referencing the thesaurus need to be updated accordingly. This requires mechanisms for referencing external KOS that include some form of update for the terms used.

In general, quality, richness and interoperability can be considered the three main attributes desirable for any metadata collection. However, there is a need for considerable research effort in the direction of measuring these attributes to make schemas, systems, mechanisms and collection more reliably and objectively contrastable.

4. The different forms of metadata today

Metadata today can be found in many places, taking different forms and being layered in different ways. While we do not attempt to offer a comprehensive typology of metadata uses, it is useful to look at some particular forms of metadata that are representative of different ways of conceiving the layered approach to meta-information in the Web. Here we look at three common forms of metadata, pointing to their differences and how they may complement each other.

Many systems today expose their metadata in XML form. These include the large installation base of systems commonly used in institutional repositories as DSpace[6] or EPrints.[7] These systems usually implement also harvesting mechanisms based on the OAI-PMH protocol.[8] The combination of XML metadata, a common metadata schema as Dublin Core and an OAI-PMH endpoint establishes a baseline interoperability level that has been proven for the development of many aggregators, most of them thematic.

In a totally opposite end of the metadata spectrum we have microdata. Microdata is structured markup included inside HTML pages as a way to make them easier to be found by search engines. On June 2, 2011, Bing, Google, and Yahoo! announced the joint effort Schema.org. Schema.org ontologies are intended for the creation of microcontents targeted to improving indexing and search systems (Ronallo, 2012). Schema.org can be considered a KOS specifically targeted to providing a degree of semantic interoperability to microdata.

Microdata and XML metadata ready for harvesting are two widely used metadata mechanisms nowadays. However, from the viewpoint of many, the

[6] http://www.dspace.org/

[7] http://www.eprints.org/

[8] http://www.openarchives.org/pmh/

metadata system that better follows the original principles of the Web is Linked Data (Heathand Bizer, 2011). In Linked Data, the mechanism for identifying resources in the Web is given a prominent status, as URLs are supposed to represent resources and/or entities, and they should be dereferenceable, i.e. when used, they should deliver "useful information" that may eventually enable reaching other related information. The emphasis on relatedness is implemented using links. In the current practice of Linked Data, RDF is used as the implementation technology (the most common even though JSON-LD[9] is also a workable option now), and RDF links become the key fabric to create a "Web of Data". The concept of Linked Data is thus simple, but at the same time extremely powerful, and it overcomes limitations of microdata and XML-based harvested collections. However, Linked Data still relies in the agreement on using KOS by different communities and on using common vocabularies that enable a higher degree of semantic interoperability. In any case, the Web of Data is actually a Web of Metadata, in which the layering becomes evident. Dataset metadata for example expressed using VOID[10] or DCAT[11] leads to collection discovery, and in turn, inside the RDF in a given collection, one can navigate to others by following RDF links or using SPARQL queries.[12] While the current state of Linked Data has still some issues to solve, as the expression of complex data structures in an interoperable way, it provides the fundamental properties to build a coherent global system of metadata in the coming years.

The important aspect of any of the abovementioned metadata mechanisms is that they are built as an attempt to make the Web better for search, discovery and integration. They provide a way by which different systems can enhance the value they provide to their users (Lytras and Sicilia, 2007) by better organizing the vast space of information resources in the Web.

5. Conclusions and outlook

Metadata nowadays has become a subject of inquiry by itself. Its purpose is essentially making Web resources better described so that they can more easily be targeted to particular uses and they can be more easily integrated.

In the next years, the Web of Data will probably change the way metadata is shared towards a linked approach. However, the foundations of metadata

---

[9] http://json-ld.org/

[10] http://www.w3.org/TR/void/

[11] http://www.w3.org/TR/vocab-dcat/

[12] http://www.w3.org/TR/rdf-sparql-query/

research remain unchanged. Metadata is now a way of building layers of meta-information for the filtering, search and integration of information and data. It is not an organized effort, but rather a set of practices and technologies that evolve in parallel with the Web and that emerge from research and practice by the progressive adoption of practices and schemas in different communities.

Metadata research is now established and it will stay in the future as it represents a decoupled and distributed infrastructure for the Web. We can expect the field evolve into a more coherent, consistent and organized body of knowledge in the next years. For this to become a reality, researchers need to emphasize the use of empirical methods for measuring metadata quality and richness, so that schemas, approaches, systems and protocols can be contrasted in the most objective possible way. There is also a need for further research in metadata as a socio-technical system, in which producers and consumers of metadata are people, organizations and other systems. This approach is needed to understand the macro-level of the Web of Metadata. The interdisciplinary paradigm of Web Science (Berners Lee *et al.*, 2006) provides an adequate framework for approaching this particular view on metadata research.

References

Berners-Lee *et al.* (2006). "Creating a Science of the Web," *Sciences* 313(11), pp. 769–771.

Greenberg, J. (2003) 'Metadata and the world wide web', in Dekker, M. (Ed.): Encyclopaedia of Library and Information Science, pp. 1876–1888.

Heath T. and Bizer, C. (2011) Linked Data: Evolving the Web into a Global Data Space, ser. Synthesis Lectures on the Semantic Web: Theory and Technology. Morgan & Claypool.

Lytras, M. and Sicilia, M.A. (2007). Where is the value in metadata? *Int. J. Metadata Semant. Ontologies* 2(4), pp. 235–241.

Morsey, M., Lehmann, J., Auer, S., Stadler, C. and Hellmann, S. (2012). Dbpedia and the live extraction of structured data from wikipedia. Program: electronic library and information systems 46(27), pp. 157–181.

Ronallo, J. (2012) HTML5 Microdata and Schema.org. Code4Lib Journal.

Zins, C (2007). Conceptual approaches for defining data, information, and knowledge. *Journal of the American Society for Information Science and Technology* 58(4), 479–493.

CHAPTER I.2

METADATA TYPOLOGY AND METADATA USES

Eva Méndez

Dpto. Biblioteconomía y Documentación Universidad Carlos III de Madrid C/ Madrid, 128 (Office: 14.2.17), 28903 Getafe (Madrid), Spain
emendez@bib.uc3m.es

Seth van Hooland

Dép. des Sciences de l'Information et de la Communication Université Libre de Bruxelles Avenue F.D. Roosevelt 50, 1050, Bruxelles, Belgium
svhoolan@ulb.ac.be

This chapter provides an overview of metadata typologies and uses, clarifying why sometimes different approaches to metadata types and metadata uses could be misleading. We present a general overview of how metadata can be interpreted differently, and then elaborate specific typologies of metadata schemas, metadata schemes, and metadata elements. The second part of the chapter focuses on how these metadata schemas, schemes and elements, which are in a sense abstract constructions and containers, are being deployed by their user communities. Concluding, the analysis of concrete metadata uses discussed within the second part provides new refinements to the metadata types and vocabularies discussed in the first part.

1. Introduction

Empirical phenomena tend to question the rigid and fixed boundaries imposed by typologies [7]. Metadata are by nature empirical, as they document parts of our continually evolving environment. A systematic classification of metadata types and uses is therefore not definitive, and is destined to be outdated in a short time by the evolving character of how we create and use metadata. Metadata standards only exist as long as they are endorsed by a user community.

Furthermore, the current proliferation of different metadata models, schemas, formats, etc. throughout different application domains has made it increasingly difficult to obtain a general overview of metadata and how they are used. A victim of its own evolution and success, the term metadata is currently being used in by large variety of application domains, users and projects. These each give their own interpretation to what exactly metadata are, which results in different interpretations, meanings, uses and levels of expectation. Librarians identify metadata with their highly structured and professionally created catalogs, whereas many web designers consider metadata as keywords to be entered at the beginning of a html file (useless because the keywords that are included within the meta-name headers are no longer indexed by search engines due to spamming practices, although in the last three or four years metadata have come to be considered again as part of the SEO gameplan in new forms like tags and tagging practices). Many other forms of metadata exist to describe documents or data within specific disciplines or by the type of media (image, video, text, etc). Consistent use of metadata improves searching by bringing together records under common forms of names, titles, descriptions, subject headings, places, and so forth [5]. Even domains that have no direct relationship with bibliographic control or information retrieval have incorporated the term "metadata" within their discipline's argot to refer to the way that they want to describe and retrieve their specific information assets in a Web environment. The contemporary art scene for example has embraced metadata as an inspiration source and point of departure for exhibitions and art works.[1]

But even between the Library and Information Science and the Computer Science communities, which have been the main agents dealing with metadata for information discovery in the last 15 years, diverging definitions and interpretations of metadata occur. A majority of the metadata-related publications considered their machine readability as a key characteristic. But when converting paper-based library catalog cards to a database, by scanning and applying OCR techniques upon the images to convert them into structured machine-readable text, at which point can we start talking about metadata?

---

[1]The exposition Information/Transformation, held in Antwerp in 2005 was partly inspired by the groundbreaking work of Paul Otlet, one of the grounding fathers of information science, stood central. The cupboards with the catalog cards from his documentation institute also appeared in the exposition "Visionair Belgie", curated by Harald Szeemann in 2005.

This short overview of the widely varying ways of understanding metadata illustrates the necessity of this chapter, which offers a badly needed overview by clearly distinguishing metadata schemas, schemes and elements, based upon the current state of the art in metadata research. As the chapter will demonstrate, typologies can be drawn up from different perspectives, and we will therefore not offer one single overarching classification of metadata types. The different perspectives will allow a deeper understanding of the complexity behind the deceivingly simple terms of metadata and metadata types.

2. Typology of metadata

Scholars and practitioners need to ascribe types to things, to be sure that they can classify and tell apart kinds of "things" having a better understanding of them and of their variety and complexity. So we need to typify metadata, but also metadata schemas, metadata uses, metadata elements, and sometimes even metadata values, using or building up metadata schemes.

In our particular approach to metadata types, let us first point out that the common general and simple expression "types of metadata" includes different realities such as: types of metadata standards, types of metadata values, types of metadata functions and types of metadata elements regarding its function or main goal. If somebody asks "Which types of metadata do you know?", an expert might include in a single answer: Dublin Core; metadata for preservation; metadata for intellectual property rights; METS; metadata for geospatial information; AACR; metadata for describing music; FRBR; LOM; RDA; and RDF, mixing up different models, domains, uses, functions, formats and elements that come together in our individual understanding of metadata. Different ways of classifying metadata are related to different manners of classifying and aggregating digital data or digital assets.

To typify we need criteria. We also need to clarify that the simple term "metadata" and its simple definition "data about data" encompass a complex technical and intellectual infrastructure to manage and retrieve digital objects in different digital contexts, within different digital information systems and services. The criteria could be as diverse as the diversity of digital information management systems, and they could be applied to different metadata levels (records, agents, elements, schemas, and so on). Therefore, in this part of the chapter we will enumerate criteria that we can use to typify several aspects of metadata, then make our own classification based on current practices and approaches to metadata systems.

2.1. *Different approaches to classify metadata*

Metadata describe different attributes or properties of information objects, giving them meaning, context and organization in a standardized way. The first publications on metadata typologies appeared more than a decade ago, and studied metadata by analyzing the different functionalities supported by existing metadata elements. Recognition of the many uses and dimensions of metadata has led to the construction of a very broad typology. Most of the traditional categories refer to the functional use and intent of the metadata rather than to inherent qualities of the metadata schemas, the metadata elements or a perception of their values. We will discuss here several approaches to making metadata taxonomies, from different points of view, bearing in mind the complex construct of metadata systems and its evolution in the last 15 years.

We can use obvious criteria to typify metadata in a straightforward way. Accordingly we might classify metadata, mixing different levels (systems, practices, models, schemas, elements, records and trends) with seven criteria:

(a) Criterion 1: The **way of creation**, regarding the agent creating the metadata record.
   - Metadata created manually and Metadata created automatically. Or, Metadata created by humans and Metadata created by machines.
   - Metadata created by specialists and Metadata created by non-experts, including user-generated metadata in social tagging context.

(b) Criterion 2: The **moment of creation**. We can consider, at least: Metadata created at the same time as the resource and Metadata created after the object's creation or digitization.

(c) Criterion 3: The **way of storage**. We differentiate here, for example, embedded Metadata, maintained and stored within the object it describes, and stand-alone Metadata, created, maintained and stored independently of the object.

   If combine the moment of creation with the agent creating the metadata record and the way it is stored or recorded, we can state other different types of metadata, such as automatic metadata created within an object (e.g., EXIF metadata for still digital images); embedded metadata created manually when creating born-digital information objects; a database with automatically extracted metadata; an RDF metadata record created by an expert and linked by a "link rel" element in an XHTML object; metainformation encoded as microformats or in RDFa and many other options.

(d) Criterion 4: **Level of structure**. We can contemplate unstructured metadata, semi-structured metadata, and structured metadata. This criterion could be considered both at schema level and at records level. Some time ago, this criterion drove Mathew Dovey [13] to characterize three meta data schools: *the cataloging school, the structuralist school,* and the *data-structure school,* identified 10 years ago as a *fairly new school which sees XML as a universal language for defining data structures.* Now, even the bibliographic control or cataloging school, which lay down strict cataloging rules or MARC format, has been converted to the data-structure approach with metadata formats like MARCXML or MODS. So was the structuralist school, based on SGML metadata standards like TEI or EAD, who now also use an XML basis for defining and exchanging the semantic structure of the databases as well as the data content.

(e) Criterion 5: The **purpose** of the metadata: Metadata for general purposes (like Dublin Core) and Metadata for specific purposes (like domain oriented metadata, for example, FGDC/ISO19115 for geospatial information). This criterion is applicable at schema level, but if we apply it to the element level, we can also distinguish:

- Domain independent metadata: Those elements reflecting general properties of information objects, enabling the abstraction of representational details, such as, the file format, the type of document, the title, etc.
- Domain dependent metadata: The elements enabling a particular representation of domain information and knowledge, describing the information domain to which the underlying digital object belongs. This is for example the case of metadata elements (from a schema or even in a particular record) expressing the geographic coverage in a geospatial information system.

In this classification, we can also bear in mind the schemes level, i.e., those subject vocabularies to be applied for a particular domain, for example a gazetteer or a specific domain ontology.[2]

(f) Criterion 6: **Application**, i.e., what are the metadata used for. This is perhaps the loosest but most important criterion, since the main goal of metadata, whether considered as a theory or implemented in a functional system, is to make data useful. So any kind of metadata application can be included here, either at schema, record or element level. This criterion has been used by experts from Eric Miller in the 7th WWW conference [31] to the NISO. Miller recognized different metadata types

---

[2] *Cfr.* 3.2.

based on their application. Thus we can see metadata for: cataloging (items and collections), resource discovery, electronic commerce, intelligent software agents, digital signatures, content rating, intellectual property rights and privacy preferences and policies. Likewise, but six years later, the NISO identified metadata functions as a general manner to classify metadata, such as: resource discovery, organizing e-resources, facilitating interoperability, digital identification, and archiving and preservation [33].

From the last criterion, application or functionality, we can deduce two categories: Metadata for **resource discovery** and metadata for **resource use** [8]:

- Metadata for resource discovery: those data such as bibliographic records or electronic headers, either attached to the document (embedded) or stored separately (stand-alone), explicitly designed to enhance the resource's discoverability within large information stores.
- Metadata for resource use: data such as XML mark-up and database schema, which determine how a document can be used and manipulated.

Ahmed *et al.* [1] proposed other significant categories for metadata types based upon their intended use, application or specific purpose: metadata for annotations, for cross references, for cataloging and identification and for subject indexes. This classification is very much in accordance with the approach to metadata types that we are going to describe here. Let us pay more attention to the last two types:

- Metadata for cataloging and identification are the kind of metadata tending to associate specific properties and their values with whatever the metadata is about. For example a library catalog record for a book, giving its title, author, publisher, etc., i.e., information about the properties of the resource, which we can call **resource based metadata.**
- Metadata for subject indexes. These metadata refer to data which represent subjects and their interrelationships, and also usually designate specific information resources as belonging to these subjects. For example, a subject index to a library of books or to a collection of digital objects. When this kind of metadata is implemented in XML, they can look very similar to the resource based metadata described before, since the subjects can be modeled as properties of the information resources associated with them. However, they can be considered as distinct, and we will call them **subject based metadata**.

(g) Criterion 7: **Level of standardization**. Although every single metadata initiative is born with the objective of becoming a standard, we can also classify metadata models or schemas regarding the level of standardization they reached. There are then:

- *De jure* metadata standards are usually recognized at international or national level, and are metadata models or infrastructures that have achieved a formal approval by means of a standardization process and a standardization body. This is for example the case of ISO 15836-2008 (Dublin Core Metadata Element Set) or ISO 19115-2003 for metadata used for geographic information.
- *De facto* metadata standards, also known as PAS or Public Access Specifications, are standards dealing with one or several aspects of a metadata policy (elements, defined values, best practices etc.) that has achieved a dominant position in its field or geographic area.

But in general most of the metadata initiatives, before becoming *de facto* or formal standards are standards "by seduction", which means that a community, a project or a scientific domain adopts a certain model because it is useful, simple, extensible, flexible and so on.[3] Furthermore, analyzing standardization is crucial to deal with metadata as a whole system, not only studying standards' level of acknowledgment but also the different standardized dimensions. Digital information services involve different types of data/metadata standards to be considered [17, 39]:

- Standards for data structures (metadata formats/models or metadata element sets), that can be understood as "categories" or "containers" of data that make up a metadata record.
- Standards for data values (thesauri, controlled lists). These are the terms, names, and other values that are used to identify particular elements of a data structure.
- Standards for data content (cataloging rules and codes). These are guidelines for the format and syntax of the data values that are used to populate metadata elements.
- Standards for data format and technical interchange (metadata standards expressed in machine-readable form). This type of standard is often a manifestation of a particular data structure standard, encoded or marked up for machine processing, that can be properly called a metadata schema.

[3] This is, for example, what happened with Dublin Core Metadata Initiative (DCMI) in the 90's before it became a NISO standard (ANSI/NISO Z39.85-2001) or an ISO standard (ISO 15836-2003, second edition on February 15, 2009).

2.2. *Confronting metadata types to understand metadata systems*

The typology from the Metadata Information Services in the University of Melbourne applies simple criteria, like we did above, to categorize metadata [24]. They distinguish different types of metadata, in this case in a binary, simple, consistent, manner. This classification also mixes different levels to categorize metadata (record level, element level or schema/element set level):

(a) General *versus* specialist: Considering the Dublin Core (DCMES, Dublin Core Metadata Element Set) as generalist metadata because it is commonly used to describe resources across all domains, while on the other hand considering, for example, IEEE LOM as specialist metadata since it is designed for a specific community, in this case educational resources (learning objects).
(b) Minimalist *versus* rich: Minimalist schema elements tend to be generic in nature at a high level of granularity. They also tend to have a limited set of elements. General metadata are often minimalist in nature (e.g., DC simple used for OAI interoperability) with specialist metadata schemas being richer in the data collected. Minimalist schemas tend to describe objects in isolation either with very cursory or no relationship data included. Kartus identified rich metadata with bibliographic standards/formats proposing a comprehensive way of describing the world as viewed by a specific community.
(c) This binary classification reminds us of the minimalist/structuralist dichotomy discussed at the beginning of the Dublin Core, and the intelligent perception of the spectrum of resource description and the continuum of metadata that came up with the Canberra Qualifiers [38].
(d) Hierarchical *versus* linear: Hierarchical schemas are characterized by the nesting of elements and sub-elements, identifying and displaying relationships between them (e.g., IEEE LOM). A linear (flat) schema is characterized by the absence of element relationships. Each element is unique and defines a specific data element (e.g., DCMES).
(e) Structured *versus* unstructured: Metadata is considered to be structured when it complies with a set of rules or specifications for data entry and/or data structures. The structure of the elements and their attributes can be simple or complex.
(f) Machine generated *versus* human authored: Humans create metadata by writing descriptions of resources either in a structured or unstructured form. Computer applications can extract certain information from a

resource or its context. This may involve simply capturing information that is already available (the format of the file, or running an algorithm to determine the subject of a textual resource by counting keywords or by checking and analyzing pointers to the resource, like Google does).

(g) Embedded *versus* detached: While metadata has existed before the World Wide Web, it has taken on a special significance in the context of the online delivery of information. HTML can be used to record metadata (known as embedded metadata) as well as the instructions for rendering information on a web page. Detached metadata are what we classified above as "stand-alone" metadata, i.e., metadata stored in files separate from the resource.

This classification has also a unitary criterion known as "surface information", recognizing the direct availability of some useful information to manage the resource. Information that can be gathered by machines and converted into metadata is known as "surface" metadata and the process of gathering it is often known as "screen scraping". This process can be used to populate repositories with structured metadata, especially where the resources are uniformly marked-up and well-formed. Finally, Kartus recognizes "other types of metadata" including keywords, Google, tags, user created metadata, etc., acknowledging the usefulness of all of them, and current self-description mechanisms for social tagging and new trends to avoid "keyword stacking".

Just considering metadata types and reflecting all the criteria we have pointed out we could come up with an up to date classification of metadata from the current Semantic Web perspective.

3. An eclectic and integrated approach to metadata types from metadata vocabularies

The purpose of any metadata, (whether element or model), is to describe a property or set of useful properties of an information resource or object. However, we want to cover here the multidimensional nature of current metadata systems that we can generally name "metadata vocabularies". To explain this typology, we ought to state:

— Metadata models or formats allow us to express a set of properties of a resource, e.g., a subject. When those metadata formats are encoded in a standardized machine readable mark-up language, they are considered metadata schemas.

— A metadata scheme is a set of rules or terms for encoding the value of a particular metadata term. When a scheme is a subject vocabulary, encoded in a formal language (SKOS, OWL), it constitutes a subject based metadata system to represent a knowledge field.
— Both schemas and schemes involve metadata elements. Those metadata elements are currently grouped in metadata registries or synsets to improve semantic interoperability.

Several authors usually do not make a clear distinction between schemas/schemata and schemes [9, 19, 33] considering both as important metadata vocabularies.[4]

In the 1990's it was common to speak about "metadata formats" or "metadata models" to refer to a set of properties, expressed and defined in a standardized way, which served to describe a digital information object. Each description, applying that metadata format to a particular object, constituted a metadata record. For example, Dempsey and Heery grouped metadata formats into bands along a continuum of growing structural and semantic richness, which allowed them to identify shared characteristics of each grouping (Table 1).

When those metadata formats or models become not only standardized but also formalized in an RDF/XML schema, we start calling those models and metadata elements sets "schemas". DCMI Glossary has a meaningful entry "schema/scheme", defined as: *any organization, coding, outline or plan of concepts. In terms of metadata, a systematic, orderly combination of elements or terms.* The key issue is that when a declaration of metadata terms is represented in XML or RDF schema language, it could be considered strictly a schema. Schemas are machine-processable specifications which define the structure and syntax of metadata specifications in a formal way.

[4] Priscilla Caplan [9] recognizes that in common usage, the terms *scheme* and *schema* are used interchangeably to refer to sets of metadata elements and rules for their use. In her opinion, *schema* has another meaning in relation to computer database technology as the formal organization or structure of a database, and another specialized meaning in relation to XML. So, in the cited book, she uses the term *scheme* to refer to any set of metadata elements. However, we think that it is very useful and practical to differentiate schema and scheme, since in the Web — more and more semantic and more and more social — every set of metadata terms could be encoded as a formal schema, RDF/XML for metadata elements and RDF/SKOS/OWL for subject based terms belonging to different kinds of knowledge organization systems (e.g., thesauri, ontologies, and so on).

Table 1. Typology of metadata formats [12, 30].

	Band one	**Band two**	**Band three**
Characteristics	Full-text indexes Proprietary systems Basic structure	Simple structured formats De facto standards Generic formats	More complex structure Domain-specific formats Part of a larger semantic framework
Examples, formats	Proprietary formats HTML <META> tags	DC/DCMI IAFA RFC 1807 SOIF LDIF EdNA AGLS etc.	ICPSR CIMI EAD TEI MARC DC-AP DIG35 etc.

It is very difficult to think of a single metadata element or a single metadata value. In the current Semantic Web approach, we usually speak about schemas and schemes, and we assume that they are formalized in a machine-understandable way. That is why we want to typify metadata here in this sense. Schemas are sets of metadata elements and rules that have been previously stated for a particular purpose. Schemes are a set of rules for encoding information that supports a specific information domain. Nowadays schemas/schemata end schemes are commonly expressed in XML/RDF vocabularies, so we can call them, as a complete metadata infrastructure for current digital information services, **Metadata Vocabularies**. Thus we will substantiate our metadata classification starting from metadata vocabularies, which include: Metadata schemas; Metadata schemes and Metadata elements.

3.1. *Types of metadata schemas*

Referring to Kant and his treatise *Critique of the pure reason*, Jane Greenberg accentuates the importance of relying on observations and gathering practical experiences when elaborating metadata schemas [19]. In practice, current metadata schemata include not only the semantics of an entire element set but also the encoding of elements and structure with a mark-up language. Furthermore, we must point out two crucial criteria to take into account in order to categorize the complexity and variety of current metadata: the granularity and the information domain. We should also remark that in practice, every single metadata schema has the susceptibility to be or to become a standard, so the expression "metadata schema" is commonly interchangeable with the expression "metadata standard".

3.1.1. *Typology based upon the granularity of metadata schemas*

We can draw up a typology of metadata schemas based upon the hierarchical relations between different sets of metadata. This illustrates the Russian puppets syndrome when addressing the ever-extendibility of metadata:

— Global metadata schemas: Global metadata schemas are what we have called general purpose metadata [30, 39], or what Kartus [24] calls just general metadata, considering a schema as a set of elements. These global metadata schemas or schemata take on the role of providing crosswalks between different local metadata. The Dublin Core is the most well-known example. In theory, the minimal set of 15 Dublin Core elements could be used to natively describe cultural heritage resources, but in practice they do not offer sufficiently broad possibilities to fully describe a resource. The Open Archives Initiative Protocol for Metadata Harvesting (OAI-PMH) uses for example DC simple elements to map the fields from different content providers that have more or less the same semantic meaning to one single field.

— Local metadata schemas: With local metadata schemas we mean schemas that are specific and rich enough to grasp all of the information that needs to be recorded in order to fulfill the local needs of digital information service. Here for example, we can refer to the SEPIADES, which was specifically developed for digitized historical photographs. With its 400 elements, it proposes a very rich model, which also makes it difficult and costly to apply [26]. Another good example is the Europeana Semantic Elements [14], a metadata schema for the digital cultural or scientific objects included in the European Digital Library. Thus, local schemas are specific purpose metadata devoted to describe particular information objects within a very particular (local) project, either with a limited number of objects or with a huge amount of information resources.

— Container metadata schemas: Different metadata schemas are sometimes used for the management of all metadata in one single record. So-called container metadata standards offer a framework to simultaneously use different schemas, that each has their specific use. Container architectures are defended since the mid 90's in the 'Warwick framework' [27] for aggregating multiple sets of metadata, and of course in Resource Description Framework (RDF) which provides a mechanism to integrate different metadata schemas. However, the Metadata Encoding and Transmission Standard (METS) is currently the best-known container metadata schema. METS is a standard for encoding descriptive, administrative, and structural metadata regarding objects within a digital library. Concretely, this means that the same bibliographic record can both incorporate Online Information eXchange (ONIX, the metadata standard used by the book industry) information, which will be used by a publisher, and a Machine Readable Cataloging (MARC) description that will address the needs of a library.

— Conceptual metadata schemas: These schemas do not deliver a limited set of elements that can be immediately implemented within collection registration software, but provide rigorous definitions and a formal structure when working on the development of a metadata scheme and strategy. The Conceptual Reference Model from the International Committee for Museum Documentation (CIDOC-CRM) does exactly this for the cultural heritage sector, by providing definitions of concepts and relationships between concepts. CIDOC-CRM illustrates for example how the different concepts intervene during the acquisition of an object, such as an actor who can be the current or former owner of an object. This schema, which also indicates the cardinalities of the relationships between concepts, can be used to guide the design process of a collection registration database.

3.1.2. *Typology of metadata schemas based upon the application domain*

Web information is tacitly sectioned in a vertical way. Of course there are global search engines and very large digital libraries like Europeana, but more and more there are also different portals, digital libraries, and other digital information systems/services, where the objects you can find in there belong to a category, either subject-oriented or type-oriented. Moreover, metadata have evolved from several different communities, each with its own disciplinary background, objectives, and needs. There are as many metadata schemas as information domains you can find on the Web, however we are going to point out the most meaningful domains. In all these cases metadata schemas/standards are constituents of a more complex specific system infrastructure.

(h) **Metadata for Cultural Heritage**, applied to cultural objects and visual resources. Those are the schemas created to describe the information resources coming from memory institutions, mainly what we call Archives, Libraries and Museums (ALMs). Digital library is just a concept which embraces all digital collections, digital repositories, or just digital information services focusing on cultural of scientific digital content. In this huge information context there are a lot of early developed metadata schemas ranging from those that came from the librarian's domain to those built from archives and museums or arts and architecture domains. Some examples in this field are:

— Traditional cataloging standards converted into schemas like MARC21/MARCXML, or some newer ones like Metadata Object Description Schema (MODS) designed to meet the new digital objects requirements, to be able to carry selected data from existing MARC21 records and to enable the creation of original resource description ones.
— Metadata standards for Finding Aids, like Encoding Archival Description (EAD), which development started in 1993, first in SGML and then in XML, to encode encoding standard for machine-readable inventories, registers, indexes, and other documents created by archives, libraries, museums, and manuscript repositories to support the use of their holdings.
— The Text Encoding Initiative (TEI), started also in the early 90's for the representation of digital texts, includes a set of standards and guidelines to encode machine-readable texts, mainly in the humanities, social sciences and linguistics. Since 1994, the TEI have been widely used by libraries, museums, publishers, and individual scholars to present texts for online research, teaching, and preservation.
— Metadata schemas/standards for digital visual arts. Also in the early 90's appeared Categories for the Description of Works of Art (CDWA), more than a simple set of elements or a metadata schema. CDWA is a framework to build art-oriented information systems or services, including guidelines for the description of art objects and images. From visual resource collections VRA Core Categories was also developed, to allow visual databases to contain and associate both work records and image records, describing the manifestation of views of an object.

(i) **Metadata for geographic and geospatial information systems**. Geospatial information is another big domain to differentiate metadata schemas. Unlike many other information domains, where there are different schemas to describe domain information objects, metadata in this field have a clear protagonist: the Content Standard for Digital Geospatial Metadata (CSDGM), originally adopted for the Federal

Geographic Data Committee in 1994 and revised it in 1998, and usually known as FGDC, whose main elements were embraced by the international community, through the ISO metadata standard ISO 19115. Under this big tradition of metadata standardization, each nation can craft their own profile of ISO 19115 with the requirement that it include the 13 core elements in their particular schemas. For some specific purposes, geographic/geospatial information can be considered public sector information.

(j) **Metadata for public sector information and eGovernment**. It is difficult to define "public sector information" in the Web landscape. It includes the national administrative archival policies for eGovernment practices. For the European Commission,[5] public sector information is data produced and collected by public bodies that could be re-used or integrated into new products and services. This kind of information, this information domain, needs specific metadata schemas to manage those date helping the public administration's transactions and the access. Metadata schemas are in this domain very close to the information policies ranging for the earlier metadata standards like Government Information Locator Service (GILS) in the U.S.A., based on MARC, or AGLS in Australia, NZGLS in New Zealand and Management Information Resources for eGovernment (MIReG) in Europe, all based on Dublin Core. We can also find even more specific metadata infrastructures like INSPIRE for spatial public information in the EU, or the OECD metadata standard for government publications [18].

The development of interoperable infrastructures, like Interoperable Delivery of European eGovernment Services to public Administrations, Business and Citizens in Europe (IDABC) or initiatives like e-Gov in UK, demonstrate the different dimensions of metadata for e-Administration, including the semantics of metadata elements, syntax for encoding them, structure and context. Thinking of their application, metadata in eGov domain are needed to manage data and data sets, for privacy protection for rights management for digital preservation but also for record-keeping purposes, and they have also achieved a high level of standardization (ISO 23081).

(k) **Metadata for educational information systems**. Another big domain to analyze specific metadata schemas and standards is the educational/learning environment. As with geospatial information, educational systems encompass a set of diverse standards to guarantee interoperability

[5] See: http://ec.europa.eu/information_society/policy/psi/index_en.htm

within the domain. This complex collection of standards [like IMS (Instructional Management System) for example] includes metadata schemas or metadata models. Learning objects used and reused for educational purposes are a particular type of digital information objects, requiring particular types of metadata schemas to describe their education-specific properties. Learning Objects Metadata (LOM), developed by the IEEE Learning Technology Standards Committee is the main metadata schema in this field. LOM has a more complicated structure than many other schemas, and integrates every kind of metadata elements (descriptive, administrative, and technical elements [39]. Another kind of metadata standard in this field is Sharable Content Reference Model (SCORM), which is, more than a simple metadata schema, a reference model to achieve interoperability among learning content in different Learning Management Systems (LMS). The new more industrial eLearning environments use Common Cartridge (CC), a set of standards to enhance SCORM, attempting to provide support for all teaching and learning objects, paying special attention to interactive and collaborative environments. CC includes a metadata schema based upon Dublin Core's 15 elements, to describe the new needs of learning objects.

(l) The last type of metadata that we want to highlight is not a vertical application domain but a transversal one: **metadata for digital preservation/curation**. If we have a typology of metadata at element level,[6] all the metadata schemas include in their set administrative elements devoted to record preservation issues. Digital preservation and curation implies, much more than metadata, a broad range of systems and infrastructures designed to preserve the usable life of digital objects. Preservation metadata is a domain that supports all processes associated with digital preservation. Here the historic milestones for preservation metadata as a specific domain are OAIS (ISO 14721) as a reference model for Open Archival Information Systems and PREMIS (Preservation Metadata: Implementation Strategies).

The domain approach to digital information is more and more manifest throughout digital information services. Besides the big metadata schemas based upon a specific domain, there are many **application profiles**, which are data elements drawn from other metadata schemas, combined together and used for more specific or even local application domains,

[6] See: 3.3.

for example for public sector information [6]. There are also application profiles based on one schema but tailored for a particular information community, for example, DC Education Application Profile, which is the adaptation of a general purpose metadata schema (Dublin Core) to a particular purpose (Education). The level of specialization of a metadata application profile could be limited even to a local area or language, for example, the LOM national application profiles: LOM-FR and LOM-ES adapted for specific learning information systems in France and Spain, respectively. Sometimes the application profiles became a new formal schema of their own.

3.2. *Types of metadata schemes*

Metadata schemes might be considered, in a broad way, metadata content standards. Like cataloging rules [Anglo American Cataloging Rules (AACR), or Cataloging Cultural Objects (CCO), for instance], schemes describe a particular way to encode the metainformation describing a resource. In the case of schemes, they are also (like schemata) sets of terms or vocabularies, but only concerning the possible values a metadata element could have. As Joe Tennis defined them, metadata schemes are the range of values that can be provided for an assertion about a resource [34]. There are also standardized vocabularies which operate with metadata schemas to be applied to particular metadata elements, giving clues to encode their values. Date-time formats, authority lists, controlled vocabularies, etc. are examples of metadata schemes. An authority list, for instance, is a metadata scheme that could be applied to encode the values of a metadata element/term in a metadata schema, dealing with the resource's authorship, for example, the element "DC.Creator" in Dublin Core or "Author" in TEI Header or in another local metadata model.

Large-scale metadata content standards such as CCO include general instructions applicable to a metadata model or a set of its elements, while metadata schemes are specific vocabularies devoted to the values of a particular metadata element. Encoding schemes provide contextual information or parsing rules that aid in the interpretation of an element value. Such contextual information may take the form of controlled vocabularies, formal notations, or parsing rules. If an encoding scheme is not understood by a client or an agent, the value may still be useful to a human reader. Schemes could be called also "value spaces" [39], as the set of possible values for a given type of data.

3.2.1. *Typology based upon the coverage of the metadata scheme*

There are two types of schemes: Vocabulary Encoding Schemes (VES) and Syntax Encoding Schemes (SES).

SES (Syntax Encoding Schemes)

The Syntax Encoding Schemes are the value spaces, which indicate that the value of a particular element is a string formatted in accordance with a formal notation or standard, such as the ISO 8601 date–time format or W3CDTF, encoding "2009-07-20" as the standard expression of a date.

VES (Vocabulary Encoding Schemes)

VES are value-space structures to encode metadata elements' values, such as "subject" or what we classified before as **subject based metadata**. Those subjects can be modeled as properties and encoded in a formal *schema* (XML/RDF) like metadata schemas are. While schemas allow us to say that a particular resource has an attribute (e.g., a subject), a scheme allows us to make explicit what that subject is: The value of that attribute chosen from a collection of possible elements [e.g., all the words included in the Library of Congress Subject Headings (LCSH)].

Traditional approaches to schemes include here controlled vocabularies, organized arrangement of words and phrases used to index content and/or to retrieve content through browsing or searching. It typically includes preferred and variant terms and has a defined scope or describes a specific domain.

3.2.2. *Typology of metadata schemes based upon the application domain*

As with schemas, schemes could be classified as:

— General purposes schemes, including universal classifications like DDC, UDC, or generic subject heading lists like LCSH, etc.
— Specific purposes schemes, which include traditional metadata schemes like thesauri and other vocabularies applied to a specific information domain.

According with what we said speaking about the typology of metadata schemas based upon the application domain, there are also as many vocabularies encoded as metadata schemes as there are information domains on the Web. So we can find particular metadata vocabularies for cultural heritage, Union List of Artist Names (ULAN), Arts and Architecture Thesaurus (AAT), etc., or all the classifications and vocabularies that could be used in the

LOM/SCORM kingdom in educational information systems, having their own mechanisms for encoding those vocabularies like IMS Vocabulary Definition Exchange (VDEX).

Those schemes could be traditional thesauri, classification schemes and other knowledge organization systems, or new paradigms for subject-based metadata like ontologies and folksonomies, or traditional vocabularies encoded for the Semantic Web, following a formal *schema* like Simple Knowledge Organization System (SKOS). "Skosifying" traditional vocabularies is a common practice in the current metadata landscape. Most of the ontologies are domain oriented too and they divide the realm of knowledge that they represent into: individuals, classes, attributes, relations, and events. Folksonomies do not usually have a domain orientation and they do not have any kind of control. A folksonomy is a record with the labels, tags or keywords used by many people on the Web, usually not with particular purposes but general ones.[7] However there are some experiences using social tagging within a specific domain, like Steve Museum,[8] a systematic research project into how social tagging can best serve the museum community and its visitors.

If schemes are used to find, collocate, and identify items in Semantic Web applications like they are in catalogs, then we must be sensitive to the versioning of these schemes, and the changes affecting the values from them [34]. In some domains, schemes change even more rapidly than Decimal Dewey Classification, and in a distributed networked environment, managing the semantics of these changes is vital to the functioning and utility of these schemes.

3.3. *Types of metadata elements, element sets and registries*

The most traditional classifications of metadata types are based on metadata elements, assuming that every metadata schema/format has elements of similar types. Thus, almost every metadata handbook, from the traditional ones [3, 9, 25, 28, 32] to the most recent ones [39] distinguish the following types of metadata:

— Descriptive metadata elements allow the identification and the retrieval of a document, such as the creator, the title, or the subject. They are the metadata used for information discovery of digital resources.

[7] Studying folksonomies in deep surpasses the objectives of this chapter but should be mentioned because, in general, social tagging practices could bridge the gap between Web 2.0 and Semantic Web.

[8] Steve: The museum social tagging Project: http://www.steve.museum.

— Structural metadata elements facilitate storage, navigation and/or presentation of digital objects and electronic resources. They provide information about the internal structure of resources including page, section, chapter numbering, indices, and table of contents, and they also describe relationships among objects.
— Administrative metadata elements help to structure information regarding the management and conservation of a digital object/collection, such as the date and method of acquisition. These metadata are used for managing and preserving objects in a collection or repository, and they can also incorporate "meta-metadata", information regarding the metadata (such as the name of the indexer, and so on).

In general, metadata schemas and standards include these kinds of metadata (e.g., METS packages structural, descriptive, administrative, and other metadata with an information object or digital surrogate and indicates the types of relationships among the different parts of the current complex information objects). For practical purposes, the types and functions of metadata elements have been classified into these broad categories: descriptive, structural, and administrative. However, they do not have well-defined boundaries and often overlap. These typologies are important to understand the different functionalities supported by metadata elements, but in practice the different types blend into one another when using a specific metadata schema. Ingrid Mason for example distinguishes curatorial (keeping practices), semantic (terminology and documentation) and technical (web design and communication) metadata elements [29]. But EAD, which she classifies as a technical metadata schema, includes essential semantic information about the resource, whereas DCMES, which is classified as a semantic metadata schema, can also contain technical metadata elements. Furthermore, any metadata schema can classify their elements as different types of metadata. One of the most traditional categorizations in this sense is Dublin Core elements division who distinguish three groups for its metadata elements:

— Content elements, which includes: Title, Subject, Description, Source, Language, Relation and Coverage.
— Intellectual Property elements: Creator, Publisher, Contributor, Rights.
— Instantiation elements: Date, Type, Format and Identifier.

Gilliland adds three types of metadata elements to the traditional and acknowledged classification, including more specific types for administrative metadata (preservation and technical) and also use metadata, for those elements devoted to record the level and type of use. More particularly [17]:

— Preservation metadata are those related with the preservation management of collections and information resources, such as physical condition of the resource, actions and policies taken to preserve physical or digital versions of a resource, changes occurred during digitization processes and so on.
— Technical metadata are those related to how a system functions or metadata behaves, for example, hardware and software information, formats, compression ratios, etc. as well as authentication and security data.
— Use metadata are related to the level and type of use of collections and digital objects. Circulation records, use and user tracking, content reuse and multiversioning information, search logs and rights metadata are all examples of use metadata.

The complexity of metadata elements has led to new mechanisms to register the variety of elements in different schemas and application profiles, so that metadata format developers can list the specific metadata elements they have defined for particular uses. A registry makes available information on the authoritative version of a given format, as well as the data element definitions for the format. **Metadata schema registries** are databases of schemas that can trace an historical line back to shared data dictionaries and the registration process encouraged by the ISO/IEC 11179 [20]. The motivation for establishing registries came from domain communities, and from the knowledge management community. Examples of current registry activity include: the U.S. Environmental Data Registry (EDR), or the Australian Institute of Health and Welfare (AIHW), who have set up a National Health Information Knowledge base, both ISO 11179-compliant [23]. Metadata registries are used to guarantee that metadata elements are non-duplicates, precise, consistent, distinct and approved by a digital information community.

4. Metadata uses and users' communities

The first part of this chapter has given an overview of the complexity behind metadata and the different trends, typologies and standards currently available to structure their form and content. We have seen how several factors, such as the type of resource and the application domain, shape and influence the formation of metadata standards. However, the actual use of the metadata by the user's community is ultimately their reason for existing, and should therefore have a decisive impact on how metadata are created and maintained. As digital information systems/services are more and more vertical, more and more subject-oriented or community-oriented, so are their metadata.

The commonly accepted "fitness for purpose" definition of metadata quality [21], which states that metadata are of good quality if they fulfill the needs of their users, reflects the importance of monitoring the use of metadata to evaluate their quality. In light of the tremendous investments made to create and maintain metadata, it is of the utmost importance that these processes are in line with user expectations. As the second part of the chapter will demonstrate, identifying and monitoring the actual use of metadata is not a straightforward process.

4.1. *Taking into account the importance of user needs*

As long as metadata, under the form of traditional paper-based documentation or early 1980s and 1990s stand-alone bibliographic databases, remained within the safe boundaries of the organizations which produced them, users mostly had a direct and tangible contact with the metadata providers. But then came the web, which radically transformed the relationship between the metadata providers and — users, by liberating the latter from any time or space related constraints to consult the metadata. We found the first clear consideration of the role of users, in one of the main articles in the 90's, that we have already cited, *Metadata: A current view of practice and issues,* where Lorcan Dempsey and Rachel Heery wonder what type of things users, programs or people need to know about resources, which allowed them to substantiate the need for metadata and even to typify them. They consider different kind of users such as: the user as researcher; the user as consumer; the user as client; the user as information provider and even the user as parent, who may wish to know whether a server contains material which is likely to be unsuitable for his/her child to see. They finally point out a "future user" whose expectations they did not dare to describe [12].

The future user foreseen in the late 90's is already here. With the lowering of the barriers to consult metadata, the type of users also shifted from a restricted number of well-informed users to a far wider user community then originally envisioned by the metadata creators, which has made it increasingly difficult to provide a satisfying user-experience through one single interface.

Setting metadata loose, through the internet and their widening user base, has in some cases resulted in new user contexts for existing metadata. The biodiversity domain provides an excellent illustration of how metadata which previously might have had a strong local focus and user community can attract a wider interest on the internet. International collaborative efforts, such as the European Network for Biodiversity Information (ENBI), are currently building large metadata repositories by aggregating metadata of local institutions through portals. Existing metadata are thus repurposed in the context of the international research on global warming and its impact on biodiversity [36].

This example also illustrates how a widening audience brings new user needs to the fore, which are not always easy to foresee or even to detect. The user needs regarding cultural heritage for example have always been defined in general and vague terms. Even if the digitization of cultural heritage resources and their metadata has enormously facilitated their access, museums, libraries and archives are currently struggling to identify user needs. The report *Assessment of End-User Needs in IMLS-Funded Digitization Projects* [22], produced by the Institute of Museum and Library Studies (IMLS) offers an interesting overview on this problem area.

User needs have attracted attention on a research level and within individual projects, but the application of research outcomes and recommendations in the field remains problematic. User needs evaluation studies tend to make for example an abstraction of the massive presence of legacy metadata and the limited resources of institutions to adapt these existing metadata to a more user-friendly format. Metadata practitioners rarely have the occasion to start from scratch and build their metadata services completely centered on user needs. The next section will identify the existing user studies' methodologies, which will then be followed by an overview of emerging approaches which are adopting a more pragmatic approach by taking into account different constraints such as the presence of legacy metadata and the limited resources to make these conform to emerging standards.

4.2. *Use analysis methodologies*

The study and analysis of metadata uses has until now not been specifically tackled by a monograph or a significant number of articles. Recent and recommendable books on metadata [16, 39] marginally discuss the topic. The work of Diane Hillman regarding metadata quality has acknowledged the importance of evaluating how the quality of metadata corresponds to the user's expectations [21].

The literature regarding themes closely related to metadata, such as digital libraries and repositories that appeared shortly after 2000, has focused regularly on usability and the identification of user needs (e.g., Coleman and Sumner [10]). Information Architecture gleans interesting insights on how to involve users during the conceptual modeling of metadata creation software but also of metadata schemas.

Surveys are one of the most frequently used methods throughout different domains to obtain information from users on how they consult resources and whether their needs are met. Web-based forms and email greatly improve the speed and lower the costs of organizing surveys, but their effectiveness is still questionable. The experience of the Museum and Online Archives California (MOAC) project for example shows that only a limited set of data can be gathered regarding metadata use.

Direct interaction with users, either through face-to-face or telephone interviews, or through observation in a usability-testing environment, is also a recurring method. The work of Tonkin [35] on paper-based user modeling describes in detail a methodology on how to involve users in a hands-on manner during the development of standards and interfaces. However, the preparation, set-up and analysis of interviews and observations are very resource intensive. Additionally, the methods discussed above only deliver results which represent a "snapshot" of user needs at a very specific moment in time.

More automated means of capturing user needs are to be preferred, which can be run at any time at no extra cost. The outcomes of the analyses can be then monitored over time, allowing the discovery of trends and evolutions in user needs over periods of time. However, the interpretation of the log files is not always a straightforward process. The academic library community for example has developed standards such as the Counting Online Usage of NeTworked Electronic Resources (COUNTER) and the International Coalition of Library Consortia (ICOLC) to gather use data regarding the highly expensive electronic resources to which they offer access. The actual use of these standards the last two to three years has demonstrated a need for a clearer understanding of how one defines a "search", a "session" and starting from what moment a session time-out appears. Without a consensus on these key issues, the analysis of use statistics will not result in generic outcomes [4].

4.3. *Exploring new possibilities*

As the previous section demonstrated, no standard set of practices or methodologies exists to monitor the use of metadata. The following sections will explore two innovative approaches within this problem area, which offer an alternative to the more traditional and resource intensive methods such as user surveys and interviews [11]. Firstly, we will describe a prototype that was built into a collection management system to monitor in an automated manner the use of the different metadata fields. The users of the collection management system are offered a dynamic search interface in which they can intuitively customize which fields they want to query and in which order. The second novel method introduces the concept of "use-neutral" metadata, where we will focus on how third parties can build new services on top of existing metadata and thereby re-use them in a different context.

4.3.1 *Monitoring the use of metadata with the help of dynamic search interfaces*

Marketers and human–computer interaction specialists have been deducing information regarding the preferences of users by analyzing their behavior and actions through logfiles and tools such as heatmaps [2]. The success of popular web applications such as Facebook or Last.fm depends to a great extent on the intuitive manner in which these applications also gather information from their users. Facebook and Last.fm alike rely heavily on the analysis of use data to deliver a more personalized service. Last.fm tracks for example all of the music files played by the user, which allows Last.fm to fine-tune the user's profile and to offer extra features, such as the notification of concerts which take place around the home area of the user. The social networking site Facebook takes the same approach of aggregating use data in an unconscious manner from the user. The first time a user logs in, the application asks if it can import all of the e-mail addresses from different types of email accounts, and then checks which contacts are already on Facebook, which allows the new user to link in an automated manner to all of these contacts. Once a user is logged in, all of the actions undertaken on the platform are used to render the user's profile more detailed, and like in the Last.fm case, to offer customized features which consist in this case mainly of highly personalized marketing.

These two emblematic Web2.0 applications demonstrate how use data describing user needs and interests can be gathered in an automated manner, by relying on small actions performed by the users in an unconscious manner. The success factor of these platforms resides in how users can be persuaded to spend time customizing their profile, by clearly offering them an added-value service. We propose to adopt a similar approach to gather use data about how and which metadata fields are effectively used within a collection management database [37]. The previous sections already explained that users are not inclined to participate in initiatives such as surveys or questionnaires as these time-consuming activities are of no direct use to them. It is therefore crucial to offer a direct added value to users if we want them to interact with an application which will allow us to monitor their use of metadata.

Concretely, the idea behind the dynamic interface is that the user is confronted with a default search interface which can be very intuitively configured to the individual needs of the user. Inspired by the way blocks of information can be "dragged and dropped" on the iGoogle interface, this application gives the possibility to customize the search interface by adding, deleting and re-arranging the metadata fields/elements.

Behind the direct interest for users of having a customizable search interface, the collections manager has the possibility to monitor which metadata fields are actively being used within the database. The use data are collected in a seamless and automated way and allow monitoring of changes in user needs and perform statistical analyses over long periods of time. Currently, the dynamic interface is still in a prototype phase, but this tool will be included as a permanent feature within the next version of CollectiveAccess,[9] an open source collections management system, which is used by a wide diversity of heritage institutions throughout Europe and the United States.

Collection managers will be able to use the outcomes from the dynamic interface to judge the relevance of the different metadata fields, and to provide statistical backing when deciding on resource distribution for the creation and maintenance of metadata. As the case of use evaluation of electronic resources within the academic library world has demonstrated, the linking of statistics with management decisions is not straightforward and needs to be carefully put within a larger perspective. Nevertheless, metadata providers need to start experimenting with tools and methodologies which allow them to monitor the effective use of the metadata they produce by its user community. The dynamic interface presented above offers a first essential step in this direction.

4.3.2 *Considering software packages as a user group*

So far we have described how institutions are currently trying to adapt their descriptive practices as much as possible to fit the needs of their users.

[9] CollectiveAccess: http://collectiveaccess.org

A recent development, and something of a sidestep within this discussion is to adopt and radicalize the idea that an institution can never predict future user needs, and should therefore concentrate on offering data and metadata in a use-neutral manner. From a technical point of view, this approach has been catalyzed over the last years by the increasing availability of web services and the development of Application Programming Interfaces (APIs) which allow the linking of data and services in an automated manner between independent content- and service providers.

The overall idea behind these technologies is to facilitate the development of new services by third parties based upon existing data and metadata. Content- and metadata providers allow and even encourage users to "hack" their data and metadata by offering them a toolkit to re-use data and metadata for their specific needs. The outcomes of this approach have been labeled with the term "mash-ups", referring to the practice of dj's who create new music by mixing existing music from different sources [15].

Google Maps offers one of the most well-known and widely-used APIs and demonstrates how metadata can be enriched through a third-party service. The service is increasingly used to add a geographical component to the search- and browse interface of metadata providers. This feature allows users of the Coney Island History project[10] to intuitively browse through collections and to compare the actual situation of a site with historical images which display the former state of the site.

The reuse of existing metadata within another context can be illustrated with the widget of the Rijksmuseum in Amsterdam, which they launched in 2005. A widget is a light-weight application a user can install on his computer to perform a very specific and limited task. When launching the Rijksmuseum widget, the user is presented with a random artwork and its metadata from the collection database. Shortly after the launch of this widget, a student hacked the XML stream to offer a Rich Site Summary (RSS) feed that is now know as the informal museum feed of the Rijksmuseum. Another example of the reuse of metadata is given on the website www.chopac.org, which provides a tool to export the metadata attached to a record from the Amazon database to the MARC format.

5. Conclusions

We agree with Anne Gilliland [17] that the existence of many types of metadata will prove critical to the continued access to and utility of digital

[10] Coney Island History project: http://www.coneyislandhistory.org/development.

information, as well as the original objects and collections to which they relate. However, the Web has changed and information systems are more and more user-centered, so we must also change the criteria to typify metadata, and the metadata themselves, understood as standardized systems to organize digital information and create knowledge throughout the Information Society.

The Web has changed not only to a Web of different objects but to a complex Web of data, and so did the metadata. We therefore need more criteria to typify metadata, including the burgeoning user-generated metadata. In the current realm of linked data metadata usually needs to be able to be shared, exchanged and reused by different users for different purposes, including by automated systems.

The importance of user needs can be underlined by using the metaphor of the construction of a tunnel. The creation and management of metadata on the one hand, and their use by the public on the other hand, can be considered as both ends of where the construction of a tunnel starts. The goal is to meet in the middle and to have a perfectly coordinated match in order for the creation process of the tunnel to be a success. The same logic can be applied to the creation and management of metadata on the one hand and user needs on the other. The more the two are in line with one another the higher the quality of the metadata can be considered. The two innovative approaches which were discussed in the second half of this chapter hold the promise to foster the alignment of metadata with the user needs.

In this chapter we put together a reflective and thorough overview of metadata types and the criteria to classify metadata, but we also demonstrate that the most important issue in current metadata research is user-centered metadata approaches. Therefore, we could state the simplest classification of metadata ever: good metadata or bad metadata: writ large, the quality criterion to classify metadata systems, not only metadata elements.

References

1. Ahmed, K, *et al.* (2001). *Professional XML Meta Data.* Birmingham: Wrox Press.
2. Atterer, R and P Lorenzi (2008). A heatmap-based visualization for navigation within large web pages. In *Proceedings of the 5th Nordic conference on Human-computer interaction: Building bridges,* 407–410. Lund, Sweden.
3. Baca, M (ed.) (1998). *Introduction to Metadata: Pathways to Digital Information.* Los Angeles: J. Paul Getty Trust.
4. Blecic, DD, JB Fiscella, and SE Wiberley, Jr. (2007). Measurement of use of electronic resources: Advances in use statistics and innovations in resource functionality. *College & Research Libraries,* 68(1), 26–44.

5. Borgman, CL (2007). *Scholarship in the Digital Age: Information, Infrastructure and the Internet.* Cambridge, etc.: MIT Press.
6. Bountouri, L, *et al.* (2009). Metadata interoperability in public sector information. *Journal of Information Science,* 35(2), 204–231.
7. Bowker, GC (2006). *Memory Practices in the Sciences.* Cambridge, etc: MIT Press.
8. Campbel, G (2005). Metadata, metaphor and metonymy. *Cataloging and Classification Quarterly,* 40(3/4), 57–73.
9. Caplan, P (2003). *Metadata Fundamentals for All Librarians.* Chicago: ALA.
10. Anita Coleman and Tamara Sumner (2004). Digital libraries and user needs: Negotiating the future [online]. *Journal of Digital Information,* 5(3). Available at http://journals.tdl.org/jodi/article/view/119/123 [accessed on 20 July 2009].
11. Leeuw, ED, J How and D Dillman (eds.) (2008). *International Handbook of Survey Methodology.* New York: Psychology Press.
12. Depmsey, L and R Heery (1998). Metadata: A current view of practice and issues. *Journal of Documentation,* 54(2), 145–172.
13. Dovey, MJ (1999). "Stuff" about "Stuff" — the differing meanings of "Metadata". *Vine (Theme issue, 116: Metadata. Part 1),* 29(3), 6–13.
14. ESE (2009). *Specfication for the Europeana Semantics Elements. V. 3.1.,* 25/02/2009 [online]. Available at http://dev.europeana.eu/public_documents/Specification_for_metadata_elements_in_the_Europeana_prototype.pdf [accessed 20 July 2009].
15. Floyd, IR, *et al.* (2007). Web mash-ups and patchwork prototyping: User-driven technological innovation with Web 2.0 and open source software. In *Proceedings of the 40th Annual Hawaii International Conference on System Sciences,* 86–96.
16. Foulonneau, M and J Riley (2008). Metadata for digital resources: Implementation, systems design and interoperability. Oxford: Chandos.
17. Gilliland, AJ (2008). Setting the stage. In *Introduction to Metadata. Online Edition. Version 3.0* [online]. Los Angeles: J. Paul Getty Trust. Available at http://www.getty.edu/research/conducting_research/standards/intrometadata/setting.html [accessed on 20 July 2009].
18. Green, T (2009). We need publishing standards for datasets and data tables. *OECD Publishing White Paper* [online]. OECD Publishing. Available at http://dx.doi.org/10.1787/603233448430 [accessed on 20 July 2009].
19. Greenberg, J (2005). Understanding metadata and metadata schemes. *Cataloging and Classification Quarterly,* 40(3/4), 17–36.
20. Heery, R and H Wagner (2002). A metadata registry for the semantic web [online]. *D-Lib Magazine,* 8(5). Available at http://www.dlib.org/dlib/may02/wagner/05wagner.html [accessed on 20 July 2009].

21. Hillman, DI and EL Westbrooks, (eds.) (2004). *Metadata in Practice.* Chicago: American Library Association.
22. IMLS (2003). Assessment of end-user needs in IMLS-funded digitization projects. Institute of Museum and Library Services Technical report.
23. ISO 11179 (2009). ISO/IEC JTC1 SC32 WG2 Development/Maintenance. *ISO/IEC 11179, Information Technology — Metadata registries (MDR)* [online]. Updated: 2009-03-25. Available at: http://metadata-standards.org/11179/ [accessed on 20 July 2009].
24. Kartus, E (2006). Types of metadata [online]. In *Information Services Metadata.* University of Melbourne. Available at http://www.infodiv.unimelb.edu.au/metadata/add_info.html [accessed on 20 July 2009].
25. Kenney, AR, OY Rieger and R Entlich (2003). *Moving Theory into Practice: Digital Imaging for Libraries and Archives* [online]. Cornell University Library/Research Department, 2000–2003. Available at http://www.library.cornell.edu/preservation/tutorial/preface.html [accessed on 20 July 2009].
26. Klijn, E (ed.) (2003). *SEPIADES Recommendations for Cataloguing photographic collections* [online]. Amsterdam: European Commission on Preservation and Access.
27. Lagoze, C (1996). The warwick framework: A container architecture for diverse sets of metadata [online]. *D-Lib Magazine.* Available at http://www.dlib.org/dlib/july96/lagoze/07lagoze.html [accessed 20 July 2009].
28. LC (2005). Core metadata elements [online]. Washington, D.C.: *Library of Congress Digital Repository Development,* 1998–2005. Available at http://www.library.cornell.edu/preservation/tutorial/preface.html [accessed on 20 July 2009].
29. Mason, I (2007). Cultural information standards — political territory and rich rewards. In *Theorizing Digital Cultural Heritage: A Critical Discourse,* pp. 223–243. Cambridge, etc.: MIT Press.
30. Rodríguez, EM (2002). *Metadatos y recuperación de información: Estándares, problemas y aplicabilidad en bibliotecas digitales.* Gijón: Trea.
31. Eric Miller (1998). Using web metadata: The resource description framework [online]. *WWW7 Tutorial 04/10/1998.* Available at http://www.w3.org/People/EM/talks/www7/tutorial/part2/ [accessed on 20 July 2009].
32. Milstead, J and S Feldman (1999). Metadata: Cataloging by any other name. *Online,* January/February, 23(1), 24–31. Available at http://www.iicm.tugraz.at/thesis/cguetl_diss/literatur/Kapitel06/References/Milstead_et_al._1999/metadata.html [accessed on 20 July 2009].
33. Niso (2004). *Understanding Metadata* [online]. Bethesda: NISO Press. Available at http://www.niso.org/standards/resources/UnderstandingMetadata.pdf [accessed on 20 July 2009].

34. Tennis, JT (2007). Scheme versioning in the semantic web. In *Knitting the Semantic Web*, J Greenberg and E Méndez (eds.), 85–104. Binghamton, N.Y.: Haworth Press.
35. Tonkin, E (2009). Multilayered paper prototyping for user concept modeling (will be published in the DC conference proceedings of Korea).
36. Torres, RS, *et al.* (2006). A digital library framework for biodiversity information systems. *International Journal on Digital Libraries*, 6(1), 3–17.
37. Boydens, I et van Hooland S. (2011). Hermeneutics applied to the quality of empricial database. *Journal of Documentation*, 67(2), 279–289.
38. Weibel, S, R Iannella and W Cathro (1997). The 4th Dublin core metadata workshop report [online]. *DLib Magazine*. Available at http://www.dlib.org/dlib/june97/metadata/06weibel.html [accessed on 20 July 2009].
39. Zeng, ML and J Qin (2008). *Metadata.* New York, London: Neal-Schuman.

CHAPTER I.3

THE VALUE AND COST OF METADATA

Miltiades D. Lytras*

Department of Management Science and Technology
Athens University of Economics and Business
47A Evelpidon Str., 113 62 Athens, Greece
mdl@aueb.gr

Miguel-Ángel Sicilia[†]

Computer Science Department
University of Alcalá, Ctra. Barcelona km. 33.6 28871
Alcalá de Henares (Madrid), Spain
msicilia@uah.es

Cristian Cechinel[‡]

Computing Engineering Course
Federal University of Pampa
Caixa Postal 07, 96400-970, Bagé (RS), Brazil
contato@cristiancechinel.pro.br

* Dr. **Miltiadis D. Lytras** is a faculty member in both the Computers Engineering and Informatics Department (CEID) and the Department of Business Administration at the University of Patras. His research focuses on Semantic Web, knowledge management and e-learning, with more than 70 publications in these areas. He has co-edited 13 special issues in international journals and authored/edited six books. He is the founder of the Semantic Web and IS SIG in the Association for Information Systems (http://www.sigsemis.org). He serves as the Editor-in-Chief for three international journals, and as editor or EB member in seven other journals.

[†] Dr. **Miguel-Ángel Sicilia** obtained his degree in Computer Science from the Pontifical University of Salamanca, and his PhD from Carlos III University. He is currently associate professor at the Computer Science Department of the University of Alcalá. His research interests are primarily in the areas of the Semantic Web, learning technology, and human-computer interaction, with a special focus on the role of uncertainty and imprecision handling techniques in those fields.

[‡] M.Sc **Cristian Cechinel** is a professor of the Computer Engineering Course at the Federal University of Pampa. He obtained his bachelor's and master's degree in Computer Science from the Federal University of Santa Catarina, and he is currently taking his PhD in the field of metadata quality at the Computer Science Department of the University of Alcalá. Besides the Metadata subject, his research focuses on issues related to Learning Objects technologies and Artificial Intelligence.

The value and cost of metadata are highly dependent on the functions enabled by metadata inside systems and organizations. As the number of functions and the kinds of organizations that typically create and use metadata are extremely diverse, valuing and cost-justifying metadata turn out to be a difficult and multi-faceted task which involves several different aspects, such as, for instance, metadata language complexity, system target user population, metadata source and metadata quality. This chapter relates these aspects showing some typical cases of organizations using metadata, and then explores how metadata as an organizational asset can be framed in existing Information Systems theories.

1. Introduction

It is possible to define metadata as structured data about *other* data, created and managed to describe it in some way that can be used for a function *different* from the functions of the original data object.[1] There are several different uses for metadata, but one of the most common today is that of *enhancing information retrieval,* as an alternative or a complement to text-based retrieval algorithms [31] and formal bibliographic records [15].

Metadata can also be used to *restrict access* to some resources, in the case of metadata describing intellectual property rights, and to *locate people,* in the case of on-line contact systems. There are some e-business models [9] that also rely on metadata. For example, many systems doing some form of brokering — as product comparators or marketplaces — organize their competitive strategy in owning a database of metadata about the products or services of others, thus being able to *make decisions and recommendations* for their customers based on that additional meta-information. This is also the case of internal enterprise document systems where metadata-enhanced search supports the work of employees, and aids the processe of corporative decision making.

It is clear that metadata is a product that once created and properly managed becomes an asset for some *functions* that in turn produce some kind of *value* (see Fig. 1). Determining the value of metadata for a concrete organization (or for those inside the organization which use a metadata system) is a problem that requires clarifying these aspects of metadata use. If we consider metadata as a concrete kind of **Information Technology (IT)** artifact, then we could explore how existing **Information Systems (IS)** theories can be applied for valuing metadata. For example, if we take a cost-benefit approach for metadata assets, following the analysis of King and Schrems [23], we could

[1] Here we consider only metadata in digital form, which is subject to be used through communication technologies and is managed through software.

Fig. 1. Metadata as a product which delivers/carries value.

evaluate the contribution of metadata to the functioning of the organization in terms of cost or error reduction or improvements in the efficiency of the activities. However, once the procedures for creating the metadata are working, it is not so easy in most cases to assess the impact metadata is having. It is especially difficult to evaluate the contribution of metadata in monetary terms, since it might be the case that metadata created for one purpose can be found to be useful for a different one in the future (e.g., metadata could even under some conditions be sold under license even if it was not planned to be so). Furthermore, in the case of non-profit organizations, the value produced by delivering free services is not so easily measurable, and in many cases is related to the provision of "public service".

Thus, metadata value is in itself a difficult and multi-faceted concept, which requires further and deep inquiry. What seems evident is that the benefits of metadata depend on the kind of organization and function to be enabled, while the cost-side of metadata is more accessible.

This chapter is an extension of a previous paper entitled "Where is the value in metadata?" [24], and reports on some preliminary analysis of the different facets of metadata value and its dimensions. Our aim here is to stimulate debate and a more careful consideration of the value and the cost-side of metadata. The rest of this chapter is structured as follows. Section 2 discusses some relevant related reports (or essays) on the aspects of metadata value. Then, the different dimensions that influence notions of value in metadata and typical cases of organizations dealing with metadata are discussed in Sec. 3. Section 4 reports some issues regarding metadata costs, and Sec. 5 describes some IS theories and models which the authors believe that can be used to help valuing and cost-justifying metadata systems. Finally, Sec. 6 provides some conclusions and viewpoints about the topics discussed.

2. Aspects of metadata value

The definition for the concept of "value" varies according to the many sciences which use and study this field (anthropology, sociology, politics, psychology, etc). Here we deal with "value" as defined by Taylor [43] in the context of information systems as **something which increases information**

usefulness, and creates benefits to the systems users through production and distribution. Taylor also provides two perspectives for interpretations of value: (1) the value related to the content of information itself, and (2) the value of the service that provides that content of informationa.[2] As the provision of such systems always involves financial costs, the term "cost" will appear in our discussion often related to value (as it is the case of other papers in the field, such as, for instance, in Stvilia and Gasser [40]).

The literature on the different aspects of "metadata value" is scattered and scarce. However, different authors have reported on problems, solutions and techniques to enhance the value of metadata or to provide some support for justifying the investment in metadata. Here we report on some existing literature that deals with these aspects in some way.

Besemer [4] has recently discussed some aspects of how organizations could manage application metadata — that is, schemas related to the internal application of an enterprise. In that particular kind of metadata use, interoperability and software evolution can be used as the key measures for metadata value, thus approaching the evaluation in terms of Software Engineering. In the very different context of metadata for digital contents, Scheirer [37] mentioned a "technology transfer dilemma" related to metadata in digital music "although incremental advances in music information retrieval (MIR) technology will likely *offer* incremental benefits to consumers who wish to use digital music systems, it is difficult to find cost justification for deploying these systems".

Michener [29] approaches the value of metadata in the context of the sustained value of research outcomes. After providing the case for metadata in scientific publishing, he considers the perspective of increasing the metadata management benefit–cost ratio for the average scientist via incentives and enabling tools. Maxymuk [26] surveys metadata applications from the perspective of the preservation of documents, which is an example of a value-justification that relies on public or scientific interest, and not on the business perspective.

One of the key drivers in the deployment of metadata-related technology is the adoption of standards. There are a plethora of metadata schemas and specifications, but adoption takes time. An example of that is the adoption of IEEE LOM metadata [38]. However, there are protocols and standards that are quickly gaining widespread adoption and that are actually considered as an important feature in new deployments. An example of those standards is that of technologies for metadata interoperability [28].

[2] In our work, these perspectives are related to metadata and metadata systems respectively.

Another important aspect related to the value of metadata is metadata *quality*. For example, Stuckenschmidt and van Harmelen [41] have reported on tools to enhance specifically the value of metadata through a verification process. Robertson [36] considers that different settings and purposes require different types of metadata quality concepts. This adds another dimension on the complexity of metadata value, since the standard used for evaluation may be different in different application settings. Stvilia and Gasser [40] proposes a function for value-based metadata quality assessment based on the following quality dimensions: activity success or failure, cost and rework, amount of use and activity cost. Following Robertson's direction, the authors concluded that "end user's model for metadata quality could be significantly different from the model used by data providers", and "different end users may have different value functions for particular metadata".

3. Typology of metadata systems

Considering the elements required to set up a system that operates with metadata, and the definition of metadata as "structured data about an object that supports functions associated with the designated object" [18], it is possible to develop a typology of metadata systems with at least the following dimensions:

(1) *Functions* to be enabled by the description. For instance, "support data discovery, facilitate acquisition, comprehension and utilization of data by humans, enable automated data discovery, ingestion, processing and analysis" [29].
(2) *Languages* used for the schemas. Since metadata is "structured", there are several approaches to provide that structure, with different levels of normalization and formalization.
(3) *Quality* in the description of the objects of interest, which can be subject to metrics or evaluation processes.
(4) *Level of interoperability* of the applications that enable those functions.
(5) *Target user population* of the functions enabled by metadata. This varies from the general public (in the case of applications in the Web with unrestricted access) to applications that are internal to an organizational unit inside a single enterprise.
(6) The *source* of metadata. This varies from specialized metadata to public metadata creation, or even automatic metadata generation.

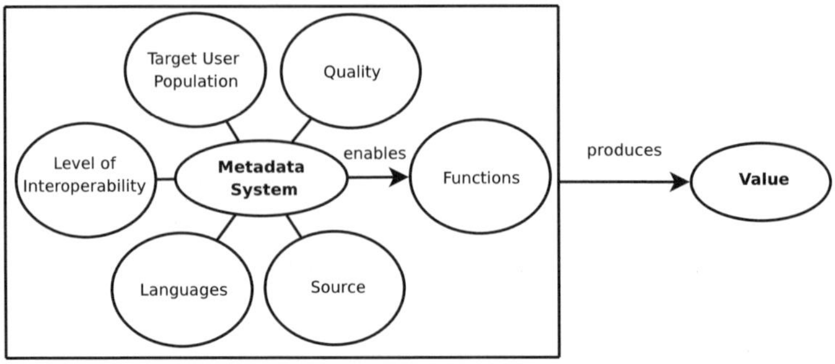

Fig. 2. Expanding views of metadata systems dimensions.

The dimensions specified expand existing views on the kinds of applications of metadata related strictly to functionalities, and are determinants of potential value models (see Fig. 2). For example, data discovery can be enhanced by using different languages, from *ad hoc* simple XML[3] to ontological schemas that are open and based on previous standards. Obviously, they are at the same level of functionality, but they widely differ in complexity, cost and interoperability, and they offer different possibilities in relation to the functionalities targeted.

The languages used for metadata schemas have an impact on the kind of technological framework implementing metadata systems. Most metadata schemas provide nowadays an XML mapping. However, there are richer languages as RDF or OWL that are used in the context of Semantic Web applications. Semantic Web technology [3] can be considered a specific case of metadata technology that uses formal knowledge representations in the form of ontologies [20]. The use of ontology-based annotations provides the added benefit of richer metadata schemas and the possibility of using automated reasoners. However, today this comes at the cost of increased complexity in the deployment of specialized technology. This is a clear case of the impact of the languages and schemas used in the economic assessment of metadata deployment.

The source of metadata is another important cost driver in metadata deployment. In some cases, metadata is created and maintained by expert or specialized staff, but in other cases, it is the general public that creates metadata as in the case of some Web 2.0 applications as tag or "folksonomy" systems. Some authors [6] consider the role of metadata specialized as a new role that differs from the classical ones. However, other authors emphasize

[3] http://www.w3.org/XML/

the typical problems of such systems. For example, Spiteri [39] considers that some additional recommendations and guidelines must be followed if folksonomies are wanted to be used in the context of libraries. In other direction, it is possible to create metadata automatically [19], but a careful examination of how this affects the quality of the resulting asset is required.

Table 1 gives an overview of typical kinds of metadata systems and their classification into the dimensions identified. The table describes only typical cases, and it should be considered with caution, since there the use and management of metadata widely differs among particular organizations.

Enterprise Information Systems (EIS) typically manage metadata for purposes of control and analysis. For example, metadata can be used to control the configuration management process of software, or it can be used for enhancing information retrieval in the mass of documents produced by the organization. The evaluation for those resources is typically formal, subject to organizational procedures. The cost and benefits in that case are related to providing support to some organizational functions. The case of an EIS enhanced with Semantic Web technologies is provided for comparison purposes.

Table 1 includes two cases of Web systems that could in principle target the public in general: publishers of open resources and social metadata systems (assuming payment is not required). In this case, the requirements for evaluation are typically less expensive, and in the case of publishers that rely on author fees or marketing ads, it will depend directly on concrete policies.

3.1. *Comparisons of metadata systems*

Figure 3 represents a comparison among three fictitious types of applications: an EIS, an **EIS enabled by Semantic Web technologies (ESWA)**, and the metadata system of a **publisher of open digital resources (PDR)**. This kind of analysis helps in appreciating differences and similarities between approaches. In the figure, it is clear that the use of Semantic Web technologies raises **language complexity (LC)** (it requires the use of richer, more complex metadata languages as OWL) and consequently the requirement for **spending resources (internal resources spent — IRS)** is increased. **Quality control (QC)** may follow similar procedures as in the case of a non-semantic EIS. The **target population (TP)** in both cases (the staff) is small if compared to a publisher of open resources. The contrast with the PDR is clear in that less internal resources are spent, less expensive control is required, but the population is much larger.

Table 1. Examples of metadata systems and their typical characteristics.

Type of metadata system	Functions enabled	Languages used	Quality and evaluation policy	Target user population	Resources invested	Sources of value
Enterprise Information System	Application interoperability, Document management, Dataanalysis	Relational database models	Formal evaluation as part of Information System Design.	Enterprise or departmental.	Development staff. Specialized metadata management software.	Increased application interoperability. Reduced maintenance costs. Increased utility of documents and data.
Library or Information Center	Online Public Access Catalog (OPAC). Information retrieval	Bibliographic Machine Readable Cataloging Format(MARC). Dublin Core	Formal, but the procedure depends on internal policies.	Library users	Specialized software. Technical staff	Increased effectiveness of information seeking and control.
Publisher of digital resources.	Information retrieval Citation Indexing	Open Archives Initiative (OAI). Formats for specialized publishing databases.	Formal by editors or reviewers.	Customers: Subscribers or buyers.	Specialized software. Technical staff	Improved information seeking resulting in increased sales.
Publisher of open digital resources	Information retrieval	Open Archives Initiative (OAI). RSS	Highly dependant on concrete policies.	Global	Technical staff.	Public service. Author fees. Online advertisement

(*Continued*)

Table 1. (*Continued*)

Type of metadata system	Functions enabled	Languages used	Quality and evaluation policy	Target user population	Resources invested	Sources of value
Information broker	Aggregation, comparison and selection of systems or products.	Specific APIs for concrete purposes	Formal, internal to the business.	Customers	Technical staff.	Improved item or service selection resulting in increased sales.
Social metadata system	Specialized (contacts, bookmarks, etc.)	RSS. Application spe cific.	None.	Registered users.	Maintenance of the system.	Public service. Online advertisement.
Enterprise Information System with Semantic Web technology	Application inter-operability. Document management. Data analysis. Intelligent processing.	Ontology languages (e.g., OWL) on top of RDF repositories	Formal evaluation as part of Information System Design. Requires specialized expertise	Enterprise or departmental.	Development staff. Specialized Semantic Web technology.	Increased application interoperability. Reduced maintenance costs. Increased utility of documents and data.

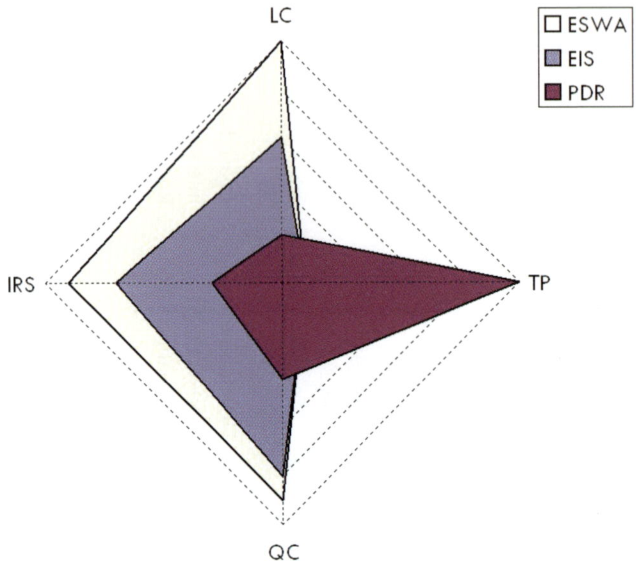

Fig. 3. Comparing approaches to metadata.

Comparisons as the one depicted in Fig. 3 would allow classifying different types of metadata systems. In principle, from a perspective of value, only systems that have a similar pattern (as ESWA and EIS) are comparable. For example, the "universal access to knowledge" that a PDR helps attaining can hardly be measured in the same terms as the increase of effectiveness of business operations typical of an EIS. The morale behind this analysis is that a collection of models for metadata value is required, which accounts for the dimensions provided in Table 1, and probably for others that could be found to have an impact on the economics of the design and maintenance of systems that deal with metadata.

4. Cost estimation of metadata

Metadata cost can be estimated by using parametric models, as done in other fields, by using past experience to build regression curves (or other kind of multivariate prediction models) that model the effort required to create or manage metadata for some given setting. Typical cost drivers for metadata include of course the volume of objects to be described, but also all the dimensions which compose the typology of metadata systems mentioned before.

Available information on metadata cost is mostly related with the costs involved in creating metadata records, or setting up a metadata solution. As mentioned before, the implementation of metadata solutions and its costs are strictly related with the kind of system and organization in which the solution will be used; however, there are some cost components that are commonly observed in most of the cases. Among the efforts towards establishing cost models for metadata, one can mention the **Lifecycle Information for E-literature (LIFE)** project,[4] in which metadata activities are considered as part of a lifecycle for digital materials. In this initiative, metadata costs per item are documented, so they can be used as a point of contrast for other projects. In fact, building databases of historical cost of metadata has the potential of becoming a powerful management tool, since at least the economic function for predicting effort required to create metadata for a digital collection could be reliably established. In a similar direction, there is also the **DMCI Global Corporate Circle Community**,[5] which aims "to develop a body of work which provides best practices, case studies and examples of how Dublin Core is implemented and its value to the organization. Examples can include what elements are used, how they are interpreted for the organization, values/controlled vocabularies developed and the **return on investment (ROI)** of metadata, specifically Dublin Core, for a company". Different resources can be found in the website of the circle, including a bibliography, reports on the activities of the group, and a list of the main components for the establishment of a metadata cost model, which are [13]: (1) infrastructure costs, (2) training and education, (3) application software, (4) consulting and personnel, (5) ongoing operations, (6) integration and process changes, (7) organizational changes, and (8) communications.

Some cost indicators about metadata can also be extracted from the context of digital preservation (or digital archives) and serve as a standpoint for the subject. In its 2005 report [11], the Digital Preservation Testbed of the National Archive of the Netherlands[6] differed the following indicators of costs that can be related to the context of metadata solutions: (1) cost of the digital repository and functionalities (physical space, hardware for the storage of the records, network facilities, and software), (2) personnel costs (staff required for designing and constructing the digital archive, the management of the system and cataloging), (3) costs of the acquisition of software for the preservation of the records (regarding issues as integrity and authenticity of the records), (4) costs of storage (interface with management system, migration and conversion of records), and (5) other factors, such as the number of

---

[4] http://www.life.ac.uk/

[5] http://dublincore.org/groups/corporate/

[6] http://www.nationaalarchief.nl/

users and supplementary storage requirements. Other important facts revealed in this report are that: (1) it costs more to add metadata for an existing document than to a new one; and (2) the "amount of work involved in adding metadata to each type of record, and in developing and testing the requisite information, varies with the type of the record".

Table 2 shows some costs involving multiple kinds of metadata records creation and metadata systems implementations.

The examples contained in the table 2 were mostly collected from companies presentations, prices catalogs and organization reports, and they rely highly on these contexts. The table helps to highlight the influence of some aspects previously mentioned in this chapter. For instance, the influence of language complexity can be observed in cases 2 and 3 in which the prices

Table 2. Some metadata costs examples.

N Description	Associated Cost	Context
1. Re-edition of Learning Object Metadata [10]	13,2 minutes or £2,60 per record	Learning Object Repository
2. Compact disc records[30] (shortest record of OCLC	15.75 minutes or $6.20 per record	Library or Information Center
3. Compact disc records [30] (fullest record of OCLC	37.25 minutes or $14.67 per record	Library or Information Center
4. Cataloguing a website [8]	$70.54 per website	Library or Information Center
5. Cataloguing serials [8]	$202.00 per serial	Library or Information Center
6. Adding metadata for a new email [11]	EUR 800.00 per batch of 2.000 emails	Digital Archives
7. Adding/editing metadata for an existent email [11]	EUR 4.900,00 per batch of 2.000 emails	Digital Archives
8. Adding metadata for a new spreadsheet [11]	EUR 1.600,00 per batch of 20 spreadsheets	Digital Archives
9. Adding/editing metadata for an existent spreadsheet [11]	EUR 5.100,00 per batch of 20 spreadsheets	Digital Archives
10. Average initial meta data solution for an organization [12]	$195.000,00–$275.000,00 per solution (involving software, employees and consultant)	Business Metadata Repositories

of metadata creation are significantly different depending on how complete metadata descriptions are, and the influence of quality control can be observed in cases 1, 6, 7, 8 and 9, in which the re-edition of bad-formed metadata is revealed as a costly issue.

Besides the aspects of metadata costs mentioned before, it is also possible to approach the issue of metadata cost estimation from the perspective of the costs of "not having a metadata solution". The IDC[8] has investigated the costs that organizations might have when the information they possess is not findable. In this study they developed three different scenarios [14] (time wasting searching, cost of reworking information, opportunity costs) and estimated that an enterprise with 1.000 knowledge workers" wastes at least \$2.5 to \$3.5 million per year searching for non-existent information, failing to find existing information, or recreating information that cannot be found", and the loss with potential additional incomes exceeds \$15 million per year. This kind of information is particularly interesting when it is needed to establish cost models to justify metadata investments in organizations, as it is the case with ROI approach.

5. Theories used in the analysis of metadata value

5.1. *Return on investment (ROI)*

ROI approach to metadata value faces the challenging problem of measuring the benefits of metadata. Tannenbaum [42] pointed it out in these words: "measuring the return on an organizations metadata solution investment, otherwise known as the ROI, requires the calculation of the specific investment cost, typically, quite tangible, as well as the projected savings or increased earnings, often quite intangible". This is a complex issue, and makes it difficult to apply cost–benefit analysis as for other kinds of IT investment [23]. However, it is possible to find some efforts towards establishing models (or parameters) to help measuring metadata ROI in organizations, or just to help identifying some focus for measuring it.

For instance, Mchugh [27] describes a simple model in which the relation between the maturity of the metadata and the business intent can be seen in business benchmarks, helping the company to establish business value. The model describes categories concerning metadata capability (varying from basic to advanced) and business benefits (such as, workgroup efficiency, workgroup effectiveness, enterprise agility and enterprise prescience). The

[8] International Data Corporation. More information at: http://www.idc.com.

resultant axis of this relation generates specific ROI metrics divided into three aspects: activities benchmarks (tasks performed by individuals), business process benchmarks (changes in the way business is conducted), and competitive benchmarks (strategic advantages). Those metrics are then used to measure the value of metadata and to progressively build/improve metadata capabilities. The author herself recognizes that the model is not perfect since it "implies linear development of metadata that is typical but not universal", but it depicts an interesting point of view on the subject.

Another example is given by David Marco [25] who addresses the metadata ROI approach specifically from the perspective of implementing metadata repositories for decision support systems. He provides a metadata ROI curve in which the metadata value increases in accordance with corporate value and metadata complexity. In this approach, metadata value corresponds to the value of the business solution which is provided by implementing the metadata repository. The key solutions to common business problems described by the author (in ascending order of value) are: data definition reporting, data quality tracking, business user access to metadata, decision support impact analysis, enterprise-wide impact analysis and metadata controlled systems. For each of these key solutions it is provided a list containing the business (or technical) values and their respective ROI measures.

Finally, some real cases showing metadata ROI were already internationally recognized by the *Wilshire Award for Meta Data Best Practices.*[9] Among these cases, one can mention the Intel Corporation metadata program (2004 award winner), and the Bank of Montreal Financial Group metadata management initiative (2006 award winner). Intel Corporation started its metadata program in 1998 as a strategy to improve information quality management, and it defined in its Program Life Cycle the following measures for value: time to market, headcount productivity, system end-of-life and hardware/software avoidance. After six years of metadata management, Intel claimed to be in a position of "extreme reuse, reduced time for design, and increased mapping to an enterprise meta-model" [22]. One of the results reported by Intel was that for every $1 invested by customers in using their metadata solution, $6 were saved through the reduction of development and sustaining costs. The Bank of Montreal Financial Group (BMO) has also presented some value indicators obtained through its metadata management into business. According to BMO [1], implementing metadata has brought

[9] The Wilshire Award is an annual award to organizations that demonstrate business benefits in implementing solutions based on metadata technologies. More information available at: http://www.wilshireconferences.com/.

significant avoidance of costs through the saving of both time and efforts. For instance, their project for improving branch/client interaction reduced in 20 times the number of days necessary to investigate the scope of program changes, and the program for improving customer information was capable of nearly eliminating the number of duplicate records (they stood at 20% by the time the project started) and increasing the percentage of record-perfection from 0% to 90–100%.

5.2. *Information systems research theories*

Besides ROI, it is also possible to explore other alternative theories of IS value that could be used for positioning metadata applications in the organizational context. Table 3 summarizes the main points of the following discussion. Of course, the examples mentioned do not exhaust the applicability of the existent theories, but are intended to serve as typical cases. It is also important to mention that some of these theories are interrelated and the

Table 3. Some theories or models used in IS and their applicability to the analysis of the value of metadata system.

IS theory or model	Application to metadata
RBV of the firm theory	Metadata can be considered a resource enabling competitive advantage. Customer-item related metadata is an example of this.
Social capital theory	Metadata can be seen as an enabler of social connections. Examples are social software (e.g., typical Web 2.0 applications), or online contact systems.
Transactive memory theory	Metadata as a way to store individuals memories in order to form an universal and collective body of knowledge.
Organizational Information Processing theory	Metadata and metadata management practices can be considered a way to develop mechanisms to reduce business uncertainty.
Knowledge creation theory	Metadata as a kind of explicit knowledge that describes other explicit knowledge.
Decision theory	Metadata as an infrastructure which helps decision making process.
Secondary document notion	Metadata provides layers of secondary documents which can be used for the evaluation of systems, as well as for tracking the processes of information development and management.

benefits of using one or another to value metadata can sometimes overlap. The **resource-based view (RBV)** of the firm [2] argues that firms possess resources, a subset of which enables them to achieve competitive advantage, and a subset of those that lead to superior long-term performance. Resources that are valuable and rare can lead to the creation of competitive advantage. This approach is useful at least in the cases in which metadata is maintained for customer relationship management, which is considered a key element of competitive advantage for Internet firms [35]. That kind of metadata includes customer preferences but also information on the items provided by the firm. This kind of *customer-item* information can be exploited for cross-selling, market segmentation and even re-structuring of the offering. Further, this can be applied equally to providers of on-line education or training, which might make use of metadata about past activities for improving the materials, strategies or for the purpose of targeting the offering to some learner profiles. The RBV has been applied to e-commerce [45] and it provides a promising direction for metadata projects, since it is metadata that in many cases makes unique electronic commerce systems. **Knowledge-based theories (KBT)** of the firm [17] extend the RBV model to emphasize the importance of knowledge assets. If we consider metadata as a form of information that has a significant potential to create knowledge, KBT frameworks could provide a good model for metadata justification.

In another direction, **social capital theories** [33] provide the ground for justifications of metadata that enables and strengthens social relations that have potential to facilitate the accrual of economic or non-economic benefits to the individuals. This covers many of the applications of technologies that follow the Web 2.0 approach. It is also a model for contact networks or for systems that use metadata for enhancing collaboration, as efforts of collective, open text creation like the Wikipedia. Similarly, **transactive memory theory** [44] offers the perspective of valuing metadata as a way to store individuals memories, impressions or/and information about a subject in order to form a universal and collective body of knowledge, or even to serve as an external memory aid for other individuals. This can be particularly perceived in Web 2.0 applications, but also in many other systems in which users and developers provide feedback/information about some product or content available.

Organizational Information Processing theory (OIPT) establishes that organizations need quality information to cope with environmental uncertainty and improve their decision making [16]. Metadata in this framework can be considered as a way to (1) develop buffers to reduce the effect of uncertainty, and (2) implement structural mechanisms and information processing capability to enhance the information flow and thereby reduce uncertainty. An example of the former might be that of gathering metadata about the resources of the firm (e.g., describing them to find common aspects) and about the users of the website. This improves the (explicit) knowledge of the firm about its assets and its context, and can be combined with data mining for finding valuable information. An example of structural mechanisms could be that of establishing metadata creation practices in commercial publishers — this enables a better control of the kind of contents that can be sold. Metadata can also be applied to competitors, thus helping in reducing uncertainty about the competitive setting [34].

Knowledge creation theories [32] can be used for metadata projects under the consideration that metadata is a particular kind of explicit knowledge about another explicit knowledge items. Under this view, metadata has a particular role inside the cycle of socialization, combination, internalization and externalization. It is a way of making accessible relevant explicit knowledge. Metadata can also be justified or valued from the point of view of **decision theory**. In this scenario, it can be considered as a fundamental piece of infrastructure inside data warehouse frameworks, providing information and supporting decision making processes inside organizations. For instance, metadata can contextualize data and provide definitions to business terms, avoiding misleading decisions occasioned by misunderstandings about the data signify [21].

In addition to the theories and models mentioned so far, metadata fits the notion of **secondary document** (in digital, structured form) in models of documentation that are found in Information Science [5]. In fact, metadata aims at providing layers of secondary documents that are defined according to known structured, formal schemas and that can be manipulated by software. Thus, models that evaluate information retrieval (as TREC evaluation sets[10]) can be used for the evaluation of systems that use metadata. They can be used to contrast them with non-metadata based solutions to provide figures on the improvement of effectiveness of search, which in turn could be translated into measures of potential benefit. Furthermore, metadata as secondary document can be used to track the development and management of information processes in order to attend demands of regulatory agencies [27].

Other theoretical frameworks are promising for framing metadata as a key resource. For example, **Informing Science** [7] provides a trans-disciplinary

[10] http://trec.nist.gov/

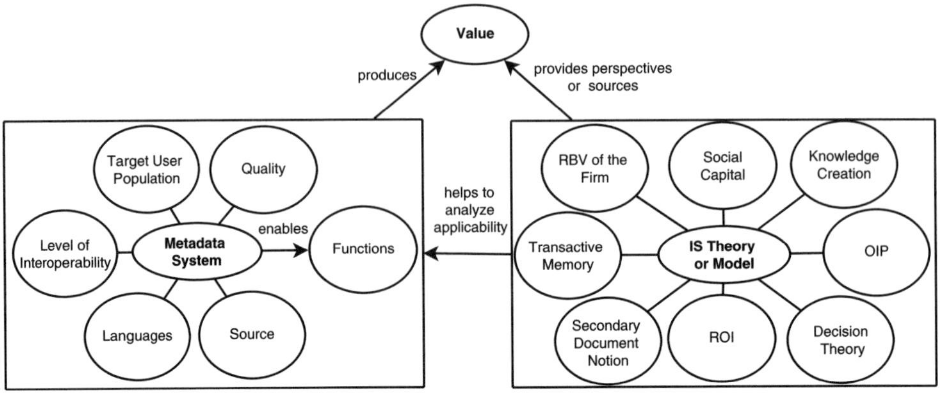

Fig. 4 IS theories helping on valuing metadata systems.

framework in which the focus is the effectiveness of information delivery. However, these theories are general and abstract, and they do not provide practical ways for the measurement of value in concrete figures. Figure 4 gives a general idea of the discussion presented in this section and its relations with the concepts presented throughout the chapter.

6. Final remarks

Metadata research needs to address the value justification of the investment in creating and managing metadata. As with any effort-intensive investment, managers and decision makers need clear cases regarding how metadata adds value to their business models in financial terms and competitive advantage, or how metadata enhances the services provided at no cost, in the case of non-profit organizations. However, the assessment of the value added by metadata is challenging and depends on the kind of organization and functions enabled by metadata. In addition, metadata languages, interoperability and required quality are factors that affect the cost of deployment of metadata solution. This chapter has reported the existence of scattered literature about metadata value, and has provided an analysis of the main aspects affecting the justification of investment on metadata. Nonetheless, this represents only an initial step in the search for business models and economic estimation techniques in the field of metadata. Further inquiry is required in several directions, and research papers on metadata applications should in some way address the concrete value aspects mentioned here. These include the gathering of historical data on the cost and resources spent in metadata projects and systems, the detailed examinations of economic models and their potential application to metadata deployments, and the categorization and clear differentiation of the different kinds of metadata systems. Future achievements in these areas would eventually lead to more systematic approaches to engineering metadata systems and understanding metadata as a critical asset that plays an important role towards enabling some functions.

References

1. Bank of Montreal Financial Group. Award submission for 2006 Wilshire award: The award for best practices in meta data management. Available at http://www.wilshireconferences.com/MD2006/BMO_Metadata_Award_Submission.pdf/ [accessed on 22 March 2009].
2. Barney, JB (1991). Firm resources and sustained competitive advantage. *Journal of Management*, 17, 99–120.
3. Berners-Lee, T, J Hendler and O Lassila (2001). The semantic web. *Scientific American*, 284(5), 34–43.
4. Besemer, D (2007). Netting value now from metadata management investments. *DM Direct Newsletter* March 2, 2007. Available at: http//www.information-management.com/infodirect/20070302/1076647-1.html [accessed on 22 March 2009].
5. Buckland, M (1997). What is a "document"?. *Journal of the American Society of Information Science*, 48(9), 804–809.
6. Calhoun, K (2007). Being a librarian: Metadata and metadata specialists in the twenty-first century. *Library Hi Tech*, 25(2), 174–187.
7. Cohen, E (1999). Reconceptualizing information systems as a field of the transdiscipline informing science: From ugly duckling to swan. *Journal of Computing and Information Technology*, 7(3), 213–219.
8. Crocker, MK (2004). Colorado state publications library. Available at http://www.cde.state.co.us/stateinfo/download/pdf/December_2004.pdf/ [accessed on 28 March 2009].
9. Currie, W (2004). *Value Creation from E-Business Models*. Burlington, MA: Elsevier.
10. Currier, S, J Barton, R O'Beirne and B Ryan (2004). Quality assurance for digital learning object repositories: Issues for the metadata creation process. *ALT-J: Research in Learning Technology*, 12(1), 5–20. ISSN 0968-7769.
11. Digital Preservation Testbed (2005). Costs of Digital Preserving (version 1.0). Nationaal Archief of the Netherlands. Available at http://www.

digitaleduurzaamheid.nl/bibliotheek/docs/CoDPv1.pdf/ [accessed on 27 March 2009].

12. Doane, M (2003). Metadata, search and meaningful ROI. Global Corporate Circle DCMI 2003 Workshop. Dublin Core Metadata Initiative. Avaiable at http://dublincore.org/groups/corporate/Seattle/Circles-Workshop-Papers/DC2003-Doane.ppt/ [accessed on 26 March 2009].
13. Doe, J (2006). Defining return on investment (ROI) for metadata environments. DCMI global corporate circle. Dublin Core Metadata Initiative. Avaiable at http://dublincore.org/groups/corporate/DC_ROIofMetadata.ppt/ [accessed on 27 March 2009].
14. Feldman, S and C Sherman (2001). The high cost of not finding information. IDC International Data Corporation.
15. Frumkin, J (2006). The death, and rebirth, of the metadata record rethinking library search. *OCLC Systems & Services*, 22(3), 164–165.
16. Galbraith, JR (1974). Organization design: An information processing view. *Interfaces*, 4(3), 28–36.
17. Grant, RM (1996). Toward a knowledge-based theory of the firm. *Strategic Management Journal*, (17), Winter Special Issue, 109–122.
18. Greenberg, J (2003). Metadata and the world wide web. In *Encyclopaedia of Library and Information Science*, M Dekker (ed.) pp. 1876–1888.
19. Greenberg, J, K Spurgin and A Crystal (2006). Functionalities for automatic metadata generation applications: A survey of metadata experts' opinions. *International Journal of Metadata, Semantics and Ontologies*, 1(1), 3–20.
20. Gruber, TR (1993). A translation approach to portable ontologies. *Knowledge Acquisition*, 5(2), 199–220.
21. Inmon, W H, B ONeil and L Fryman (2008). *Business Metadata: Capturing Enterprise Knowledge*. Burlington, MA: Elsevier. ISBN 978-0-12-373726-7.
22. Intel Corporation. Nomination submission for 2004 Wilshire award: The award for best practices in meta data management. Avaiable at http://www.wilshireconferences.com/webfiles/award/2004/winner-finalists.htm/ [accessed on 22 March 2009].
23. King, JL and EL Schrems (1978). Cost-benefit analysis in information systems development and operation. *Computing Surveys*, 10(1),
24. Lytras, MD and M Sicilia (2007). Where is the value in metadata? *International Journal of Metadata, Semantics and Ontologies*, 2(4), 235–241.
25. Marco, D (2000). *Building and Managing the Metadata Repository: A Full Lifecycle Guide*. New York: Wiley Computer Publishing John Wiley & Sons, Inc. ISBN: 0471355232.
26. Maxymuk (2005). Preservation and metadata. *The Bottom Line: Managing Library Finances*, 18(3), 146–148.

27. Mchugh, L (2005). Measuring the value of metadata. *Baseline Consulting.* Available at http://www.baseline-consulting.com/uploads/BCG_wp_MeasureValueMetadata.pdf/[accessed on 20 March 2009].
28. Medeiros, N (2006). Metadata in a global world. *OCLC Systems & Services,* 22(2), 89–91.
29. Michener, W (2006). Meta-information concepts for ecological data management. *Ecological Informatics,* 1(1), 37.
30. Miller, RM (2003). How much will it cost? Making informed policy choices using cataloging standards. *TechKnow,* 9(2). Available at http://www.olc.org/pdf/Techknow5.03.pdf/ [accessed on 24 March 2009].
31. Mohamed, K (2006). The impact of metadata in web resources discovering. *Online Information Review,* 30(2), 155–167.
32. Nonaka, I (1994). A dynamic theory of organizational knowledge creation. *Organization Science,* (5:1), 14–37.
33. Portes, A (1998). Social capital: Its origins and applications in modern sociology. *Annual Review of Sociology,* (24), 1–24.
34. Porter, ME (1979). How competitive forces shape strategy. *Harvard business review,* 57(2), 137–145.
35. Rajshekhar, RGJ, PR Lori, G Pendleton and RF Scherer (2005). Sustainable competitive advantage of internet firms: A strategic framework and implications for global marketers. *International Marketing Review,* 22(6), 658–672.
36. Robertson, RJ (2005). Metadata quality: Implications for library and information science professionals. *Library Review,* 54(4), 295–300.
37. Scheirer, E (2002). About this business of metadata. In *Proceedings of the 3rd nternational Conference on Music Information Retrieval* (ISMIR 2002), Paris.
38. Sicilia, MA, E García-Barriocanal, C Pagés, JJ Martínez and JM Gutiérrez (2005). Complete metadata records in learning object repositories: Some evidence and requirements. *International Journal of Learning Technology,* 1(4), 411–424.
39. Spiteri, LF (2007). Structure and form of folksonomy tags: The road to the public library catalogue. *Webology,* 4(2), Article 41. Available at http://www.webology.ir/2007/v4n2/a41.html [accessed on 29 March 2009].
40. Stvilia, B and L Gasser (2008). Value-based metadata quality assessment. *Library & Information Science Research,* 30(1), 67–74.
41. Stuckenschmidt, H and F van Harmelen (2004). Generating and managing metadata for Web-based information systems. *Knowledge-Based Systems,* 17(5–6), 201–206.
42. Tannenbaum, A (2001). Metadata solutions and their return on investment. Available at http://www.dbdsolutions.com/ [accessed on 15 July 2007].

43. Taylor, RS (1982). Value-added processes in the information life cycle. *Journal of the American Society for Information Science*, 33(5), 341–346.
44. Wegner, DM (1986). Transactive memory: A contemporary analysis of the group mind. In *Theories of Group Behavior*, M. B. & G. G. R. (eds.). pp. 185–205. New York: Springer-Verlag. Avaiable at http://www.wjh.harvard.edu/~wegner/pubs.htm/ [accessed on 23 March 2009].
45. Zhuang, Y and AL Lederer (2006). A resource-based view of electronic commerce. *Information & Management*, 43(2), 251–261.

CHAPTER I.4

METADATA QUALITY

Xavier Ochoa*

Via Perimetral Km. 30.5
Guayaquil — Ecuador,
xavier@cti.espol.edu.ec

The level of service that metadata-based systems could provide is directly influenced by the metadata characteristics. Several of these characteristics are encompassed under the concept of "quality". As important as it is for these systems, metadata quality is a poorly researched area due to its inherent complexness and subjectiveness. This section presents the main theoretical approaches to the definition of metadata quality and its multiple dimensions. It also presents and compares the most followed frameworks to estimate the quality of metadata records. To provide a real perception of the current status of metadata quality, this section also describe several manual and automated studies in real digital repositories. Full examples of how these studies are conducted are also provided. Finally, the section presents a selection of strategies and tools to evaluate the quality of metadata. The section closes with conclusions about the current state of research on metadata quality and perspectives for the future.

1. Introduction

Metadata is created and added to a piece of information in order to improve the functionality of a given system. For example, the shelf location is added to the bibliographic record to allow patrons of the library to retrieve the actual book; the educational context is added to the description of a learning object in order to facilitate the selection of the most adequate material for a given setting; the date of the last modification included in the

*Xavier Ochoa is professor of the Electric and Computer Engineering Faculty at Escuela Superior Politecnica del Litoral.

information about computer files enables users to perform advanced searches about recently altered documents. The performance of these metadata-based systems, therefore, heavily depends on the characteristics of the metadata [1,2]. Good quality metadata will make the system to work as expected, while bad quality metadata will often break the system. For example, a bibliographic record with a wrong shelf location would make almost impossible to retrieve the referred book; learning object metadata that is not clear about how the referred object can be used in an educational context would make it harder to reuse the material; if the last-modification information is lost when the files are copied, the user is no longer able to discriminate between current and old files. Due to this reliance on the characteristics of underlying metadata, many authors stress the importance of the study of metadata quality to understand the success or failure of metadata-based Information Systems [3,4].

Despite the wide agreement on the need to assure high quality metadata, there is less consensus on what high quality means and even less on how it should be measured. Traditionally, quality has been defined as the intrinsic degree of excellence of an object. Under this definition, a metadata record should possess an objective level of quality since its creation. This level is maintained unless there are changes to the metadata or the referred object. However, experience shows us that metadata quality does not only depends on the some objective internal characteristics of the record, but also on the needs and uses of a given community of practice. What for some communities is good quality metadata, for others is unusable information. For example, metadata records in japanese that are consider of high quality in japanese library settings, will be useless for U.S. library users, that in their majority cannot read japanese. Moreover, the metadata quality is also determined by the technical context where the metadata is used. For example, metadata about images usually do not contain title information. While image metadata could be of high quality in an image specific library, they can be considered incomplete in other type of libraries where the objects are found and presented based on their title. Due to this clear dependance on the final user and its context, more modern researchers consider the metadata quality as the capacity that it has to support the functional requirements of the system it is designed to support. This definition equals quality with "fitness for purpose" [5].

The first step to understand the effect of metadata quality in metadata-based Information Systems, is to establish the main functionalities for which metadata is used. Focusing in library systems, the International Federation of

Library Associations and Institutions (IFLA) identified four activities where metadata is involved [6]:

- To **find** relevant elements (e.g., search for all the articles belonging to specified time-period);
- To **identify** an element or discriminate between elements (e.g., to distinguish between two learning objects with the same title);
- To **select** the most appropriate elements (e.g., to select a version of the book that is available at the library);
- To **retrieve** or obtain access to the selected element (e.g., to provide the URL to the desired online resource).

Additionally to this four activities, modern metadata-based Information Systems has also new uses for the metadata:

- To **cluster** elements (e.g., recommend similar music based on song characteristics [7]).
- To **improve the efficiency** of the system (e.g., detect image duplication through a hash [8]).

The metadata quality is directly related to how well metadata facilitate these six activities. Understanding how different metadata characteristics affect how the user find, identify, select and retrieve the described elements and how they help or hinder the provision of extended or improved functionality is the main goal of current research on metadata quality.

2. Assessing and measuring metadata quality

In order to provide any practical value in the administration of metadata-based Information Systems, metadata quality at collection and record level should be assessed or measured. This type of assessments or measurements, however, presents three main difficulties. First, metadata quality is inherently multi-dimensional. There exist several independent characteristics of the metadata record that affect quality. For example, characteristics such as how complete a record is and the number of typographical errors it contains, both affect quality in different ways, being complete independent one from the other. Second, metadata quality is user and task dependent. The assessment or measurement made for one community of practice and system maybe is not valid for other community or even the same community using a different system. Finally, quality is not static. The aging of the record, the addition of new metadata records in the collection or the change in the usage patterns could affect how well the records enable the different functions of the systems. For example, metadata records describing dynamic objects, such as web pages, can easily become obsolete over time if the characteristics of the object changes from what is presented in the record.

As difficult, changing and subjective as metadata quality assessment and measurement could be, having a clear picture of the quality of each metadata record used in a metadata-based Information System allows its administrator to understand the current performance of the system, to plan new services, to focus quality-improving interventions and to set guidelines and recommendations for metadata creation and maintenance. In order to deal with the multidimensionality and to reduce subjectivity in the assessment of information quality, several researchers have developed quality evaluation frameworks. These frameworks define parameters that indicate whether information should be considered of high quality. Different frameworks vary widely in their scope and goals. Some have been inspired by the Total Quality Management paradigm [9]. Others are used in the field of text document evaluation, especially of Web documents [10]. Particularly interesting for metadata quality are the frameworks that have evolved from the research on library catalogs [5].

From these frameworks to assess metadata quality, four of them are presented in the following subsections. The selection was based on how specific they are for metadata, how often they have been used in real metadata quality studies and how current they are.

2.1. *Moen et al.*

In 1997, William Moen, Erin Stewart and Charles McClure were in charge of analyzing the quality of the metadata stored in the Goverment Information Locator Service (GILS) [11]. Given that at the time of the study there were no framework to assess metadata quality, they decide to explore the scientific literature in search of the different quality dimensions of metadata records. Unifying the opinion of six other metadata researchers (Ede, Heery, Mangan, Taylor, Xu and Younger), they proposed [23]. "assessment criteria": Access, Accuracy, Availability, Compactness, Compatibility, Comprehensiveness, Content, Consistency, Cost, Data Structure, Ease of Creation, Ease of Use, Economy, Flexibility, Fitness For Use, Informativeness, Protocols, Quantity, Reliability, Standard, Timeliness, Transfer and Usability. While the purpose of Moen *et al.* was not to describe in detail each one of these dimensions, this list define a first approach to define the different dimensions of metadata quality.

Being designed mainly as theoretical list of quality criteria, the main disadvantage of this framework is its applicability. The lack of concrete definitions of each one of the criteria, together with their large scope, makes almost impossible to use it as a guiding framework in practical applications. Even Moen *et al.*, in their study, condensed the 23 criteria into just three composed criteria (Accuracy, Completeness and Serviceability) in order to evaluate GILS metadata. Although this framework is unpractical for its use in real metadata studies, it was the first attempt to operationalize the definition of metadata quality in a set of measurable characteristics. It can be consider the source from where more modern frameworks are derived.

2.2. *Bruce and Hillman*

In 2004, with the purpose of re-ignite the discussion about metadata quality, Bruce and Hillman proposed a conceptual measurement framework [12]. This framework is based on seven quality criteria: Completeness, Accuracy, Conformance to Expectations, Logical Consistency and Coherence, Accessibility, Timeliness and Provenance. These criteria were derived from older Information Quality frameworks, in particular the Quality Assurance Framework (QAF). An explanation of these criteria follows:

- *Completeness*: A metadata instance should describe the resource as fully as possible. Also, the metadata fields should be filled in for the majority of the resource population in order to make them useful for any kind of service. While this definition is most certainly based in static library instance view of metadata, it can be used to measure how much information is available about the resource.
- *Accuracy*: The information provided about the resource in the metadata instance should be as correct as possible. Typographical errors, as well as factual errors, affect this quality dimension. However, estimating the correctness of a value is not always a "right"/"wrong" choice. There are metadata fields that should receive a more subjective judgement. For example, while it is easy to determine whether the file size or format are correct or not, the correctness of the title, description or difficulty of an object has much more levels that are highly dependent of the perception of the reviewer.
- *Conformance to Expectations*: The degree to which metadata fulfills the requirements of a given community of users for a given task could be

considered as a major dimension of the quality of a metadata instance. If the information stored in the metadata helps a community of practice to find, identify, select and obtain resources without a major shift in their workflow it could be considered to conform to the expectations of the community.

- *Logical Consistency and Coherence*: Metadata should be consistent with standard definitions and concepts used in the domain. The information contained in the metadata should also have internal coherence, which means that all the fields describe the same resource.
- *Accessibility*: Metadata that cannot be read or understood have no value. If the metadata are meant for automated processing, for example GPS location, the main problem is physical accessibility (incompatible formats or broken links). If the metadata are meant for human consumption, for example Description, the main problem is cognitive accessibility (metadata is too difficult to understand). These two different dimensions should be combined to estimate how easy is to access and understand the information present in the metadata.
- *Timeliness*: Metadata should change whenever the described object changes (currency). Also, a complete metadata instance should be available by the time the object is inserted in the repository (lag). The lag description made by Bruce and Hillman, however, is focused in a static view of metadata. In a digital library approach, the metadata about a resource is always increasing which each new use of the resource. The lag, under this viewpoint, can be considered as the time that it takes for the metadata to describe the object well enough to find it using the search engine provided in the repository.
- *Provenance*: The source of the metadata can be another factor to determine its quality. Knowledge about who created the instance, the level of expertise of the indexer, what methodologies were followed at indexing time and what transformations the metadata has passed through, could provide insight into the quality of the instance.

For a discussion on the rationale behind these parameters, the reader can consult the original article [12].

While this conceptual framework is too abstract to be used as-is to determine the quality of metadata collections, it is widely accepted as the reference metadata quality framework over which to improve or even operationalize [13]. The original purpose of fostering the discussion about metadata quality seems to be fulfilled as the original paper in which this framework is presented is the most referenced framework in current metadata quality research.

2.3. *Stvilia and gasset*

Parallel to the proposal of Bruce and Hillman, Stivilia and Gasset proposed, also in 2004, the use of their Information Quality Assessment Framework to the measurement of metadata quality [14]. This framework is rooted in a more theoretical approach to establish the different dimensions of information quality in general. The Stivilia and Gasset framework propose 38 dimensions divided into and three categories (Description taken from [14]):

- *Intrinsic IQ*: Some dimensions of information quality can be assessed by measuring attributes of information items themselves, in relation to a reference standard. Examples include spelling mistakes (dictionary), conformance to formatting or representation standards (HTML validation), and information currency (age with respect to a standard index date, e.g., "today"). In general, Intrinsic IQ attributes persist and depend little on context, hence can be measured more or less objectively.
- *Relational/Contextual IQ*: This category of IQ dimensions measures relationships between information and some aspects of its usage context. One common subclass in this category includes the representational quality dimensions those that measure how well an information object reflects some external condition (e.g., actual accuracy of addresses in an address database). Since metadata objects are always surrogates for (hence bear a relationship to) other information objects, many relational dimensions apply in measuring metadata quality (e.g., whether an identifier such as URL or ISBN actually identifies the right document; whether a title field holds the actual title). Clearly, since related objects can change independently, relational/contextual dimensions of an information item are not persistent with the item itself.
- *Reputational IQ*: This category of IQ dimensions measures the position of an information artifact in cultural or activity structure, often determined by its origin and its record of mediation.

Again, the reader can obtain more information about this framework consulting its most recent and polished version [15].

While not exclusive for metadata, some of the 38 dimensions of this framework has been successfully operationalized to measure the quality of metadata collections [4]. However, its theoretical complexness and continuous evolution has limited the re-utilization of the framework by the research community.

2.4. *Margaritopoulos et al.*

Margaritopoulos *et al.*, in 2008, presented one of the most recent and innovative metadata quality frameworks [16]. They proposed a Conceptual Framework for Metadata Quality Assessment based on a "court metaphor". This metaphor compares the quality of a metadata record with the quality of the testimony presented by a witness. The witness is asked to testify "the truth, the whole truth and nothing but the truth". This three requirements are translated into three metadata characteristics: Correctness, Completeness, and Relevance. In the word of its authors:

> The issue of defining the quality of the metadata of a resource can be approached by using the abstract of the oath a witness takes in the court when he/she swears to ...tell the truth, the whole truth and nothing but the truth... for the case he/she testifies. The quality of the testimony is assessed from its distance from the true fact (truth correctness of the testimony), the inclusion of all the possible aspects of the fact (whole truth completeness of the testimony) and the relation of the testimony with the case under examination (nothing but the truth relevance of the testimony). The representation of the resources in a repository with the facts of a case in court and the metadata describing the resources with the witnesses testimonies, leads to defining metadata quality as the resultant of their correctness, completeness, and relevance.

Their work discusses how these three characteristics should be enough to provide a quality assessment of any metadata collection. They also assert that some of the dimensions proposed in other frameworks such as provenance, authority, timeliness, etc. "constitute signs and trails implying quality and not indicators assessing quality itself" [16] and are not considered.

The simplicity is the main advantage of this framework, however, it is also its weakest point when its applicability is considered. The three quality characteristics are too abstract and it is an open exercise to the implementor how to translate them into measurable quantities. Margaritopoulos *et al.* present some theoretical examples of how this operationalization could take place. However, this framework has never been used in real quality evaluations.

2.5. *Framework selection*

The first question that arise after discussing the different frameworks is which is the most appropriated one to use for performing the quality assessment of a metadata collection. The most simple and broadly useful answer is: any of them. All the presented frameworks, if applied as their creators intended, would provide information about the strengths and weakness of the studied body of metadata. While they all differ in the quantity and name of the quality criteria or dimensions, those dimensions can be easily mapped between frameworks. For example, Stivlia *et al.* proposed a mapping between 21 of their quality dimensions and the seven dimensions of Bruce and Hillman [17]. A similar mapping is said to be possible between Bruce and Hillman seven dimensions and the three dimensions of Margaritopoulos *et al* [16]. A diagram combining the Stivlia *et al.* mapping, with a proposed mapping between Bruce and Hillman with Margaritopoulos *et al.* frameworks can be seen in Fig. 1.

From a pragmatical point of view, all the frameworks are equivalent, that is, end up measuring the quality of the metadata records. However, there exist a very important distinction between the different quality frameworks: the level of detail. The 38 dimensions of the Stivilia and Gasset framework are bound to produce a clearer picture of the quality of a metadata collection than just measuring the three dimensions of Margaritopoulos *et al.* On the other hand, obtaining a value for 38 dimensions is by far much more complicated than obtaining an assessment just for three dimensions. In a more detailed answer to the question presented in this subsection, the selection of the quality assessment framework depends on the compromise between the desired level of detail and the amount of resources available for the assessment. For example, if the evaluation will be conducted by experts in metadata management over a sample of records in order to provide a detailed picture of status metadata collection, the Stivilia and Gasset framework should be preferred. Alternatively, a study that will be conducted regularly by non-experts or automatic means over the whole collection require easier frameworks such as Bruce and Hillman or Margaritopoulos *et al.*

To have a better understanding of the selection process, the following section presents the decision of different real world studies of metadata quality concerning the frameworks and criteria used to assess the quality of metadata collections.

3. Quality Studies in metadata collections

The main purpose of establishing measurements and metrics of metadata quality is to analyze the contents of existing metadata collections such as digital libraries. As mentioned before, the quality of the metadata in these systems have a direct impact on their usability and performance. Several

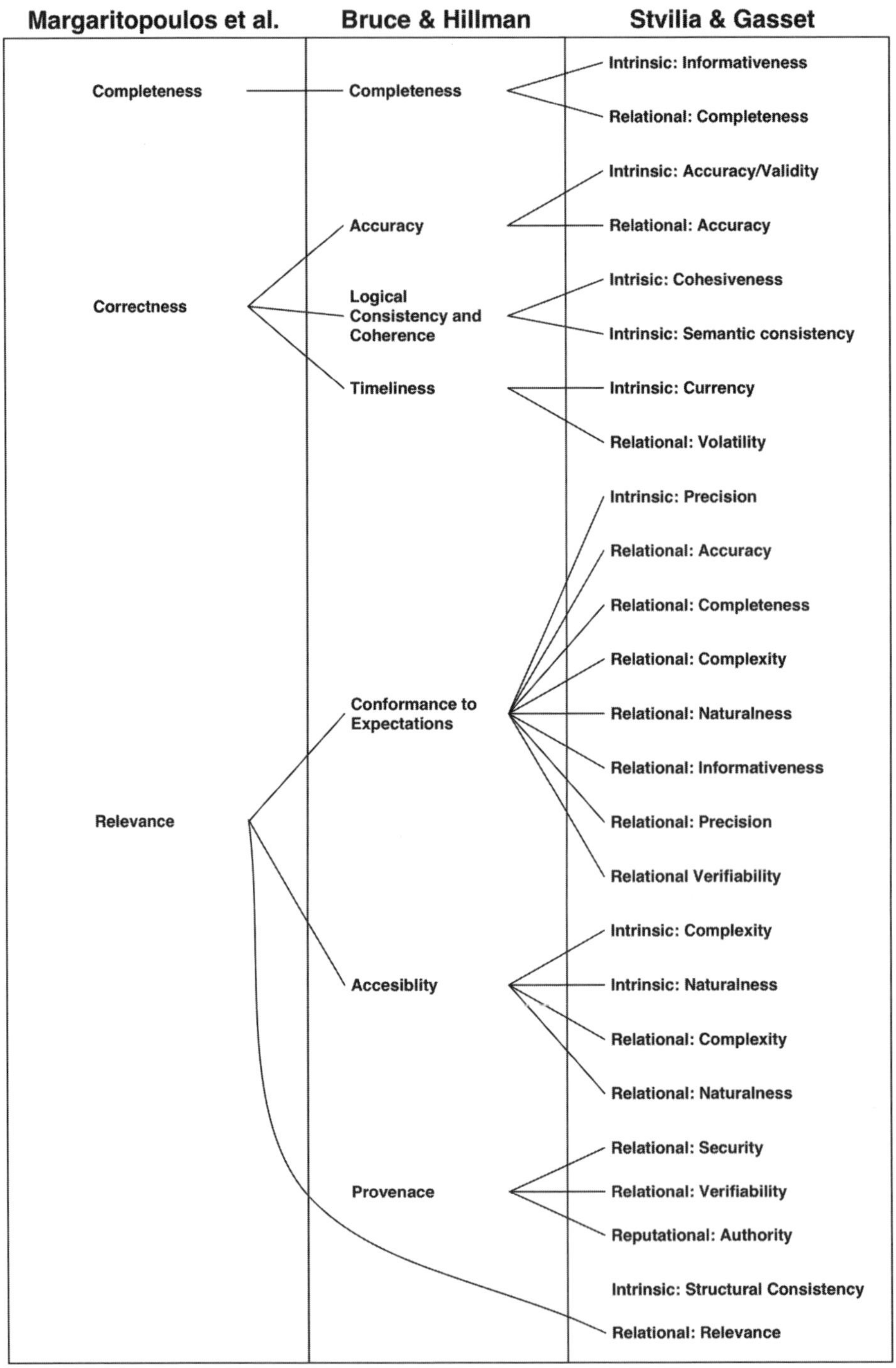

Fig. 1. Mapping between different metadata quality frameworks. (Some dimensions from the Stvilia and Gasset framework are repeated for clarity.

researchers have applied different measurement frameworks in order to gain insight on the metadata quality issues in diverse collections.

These metadata quality studies could be roughly divided into two main groups according to its methodology. Some of these studies can be called "Manual Studies". In the manual studies, metadata experts are assigned to manually evaluate a statistically significant sample of the metadata instances according to a predefined framework or set of quality criteria. This methodology is rooted in the quality assurance practices in library cataloguing [18]. Once the experts return their evaluations the values for the different criteria are averaged and an estimation of the metadata quality for the whole collection is inferred.

There are other metadata quality evaluations that can be considered "Automated Studies". The automated studies collect numerical and statistical information from all the metadata instances in the collection to obtain an estimation of their quality. The core of these studies are quality metrics, small calculations that can be performed by a computer based on the metadata, usage and contextual information about the collection. These studies obtain a basic estimation of the quality of each individual metadata instance without the cost involved in manual quality review. However, the perception of researchers is that they do not provide a similar level of "meaningfulness" as a human evaluation, although there is some evidence of the contrary [13].

The following subsections present several Manual and Automated Studies performed to real metadata collections together with a discussion of their main advantages and pitfalls. The selection was based on their representativeness in the field and to stress the diversity of objectives for this kind of studies.

3.1. *Manual studies*

Arguably the most influential metadata quality study in the realm of digital metadata was performed by Moen *et al.* during 1997 and 1998 over the U.S. Government Information Locator Service (GILS) [11]. Their objective was to establish a quality baseline for the metadata present in GILS and provide recommendations for metadata creation process. Using a framework developed by them for this study (explained in the previous section), they manually examined, in a first phase, 80 instances from the 5,000+ collection in order to validate the quality criteria. In a second phase, the quality of 83 instances was studied. The results of the study were summarized in three general areas: Accuracy, Completeness, and Serviceability. The main conclusions of the study point that most of the quality issues could be easy to remedy with appropriate guidance at creation time.

Greenberg *et al.* in 2001, published another manual study [19]. Its objective was to determine the ability of resource authors to create acceptable metadata. They asked six non-experts to create in total 11 metadata instances. These instances were evaluated by metadata experts. While the existence of quality frameworks is mentioned in the paper, their evaluation does not use any of them and prefers ad-hoc criteria based on the expertise of the evaluators to accept or reject the metadata fields. Although the weakness of this study, it is the first to suggest that non-expert authors can create good quality metadata that in some cases may is of better quality than metadata professionally produced.

Concerned with how "shareable" is the metadata between different collections belonging to a federation, Shreeves *et al.*, in 2005 studied some of the repositories of the Open Archives Initiative (OAI) [17]. They manually review 35 metadata instances from each of four selected collections (45,000+ instances in total). They selected a subset criteria from the Stivilia and Gasset framework: Completeness, Structural and Semantic Consistency and Ambiguity (a composite of relational precision, intrinsic naturalness and informativeness). They found that the main quality issue in federated collections is the consistency, specially if the metadata comes from different institutions with different guidelines.

Greenberg in 2004, performed a new study, this time focused on the quality comparison between two automatic generator of metadata [20]. Both generators were fed with the same 29 documents and the resulting metadata instances were evaluated by three experts. Again, Greenberg did not use any quality framework, but instructed the experts to grade the quality of each metadata field in the Dublin Core standard according to the application profile of the target application. The conclusion of this work suggest that automatic metadata generators have the potential to create useful metadata.

This manual studies, while useful, present three main disadvantages: (1) the manual quality estimation is only valid at sampling time. If a considerable amount of new resources is inserted in the repository, the assessment could be no longer accurate and the estimation must be redone. (2) Only the average quality can be inferred with these methods. The quality of individual metadata instances can only be obtained for those instances contained in the sample. (3) Obtaining the quality estimation in this way is costly. Human experts should review a number of objects that, due to the growth of repositories, is always increasing. The automate studies try to overcome these limitations.

3.1.1. *Example of a manual study*

As an example of the manual metadata quality studies, a real evaluation is presented. In order to assess the quality of the metadata generated by SAmgI [21], an automated system that extract metadata information from documents and their context, an experiment was set. In this experiment the metadata that SAmgI extracted from a set of project report documents was compared with existing manually generated metadata from the ARIADNE [22] repository. During the experiment, reviewers graded the quality of a set of instances sampled from both sources. For the manually generated metadata, 10 objects were randomly selected from the ARIADNE repository. For the automatically generated metadata, 10 report documents were randomly selected from a universe of 114 documents from which SAmgI extracted their metadata.

Following a common practice to reduce the subjectivity in the evaluation, a metadata quality framework was used. The selected framework was the one proposed by Bruce and Hillman [12], because it presented just seven quality dimensions to measure. The definitions of each were also available during the evaluation process. The experiment was carried out online using a web application. After logging in, the system presented the reviewer with the instructions. After reading the instructions, the reviewer was presented with a list of the 20 selected objects in no specific order. When the reviewer selected an object, its metadata record (in LOM [23] format) was displayed. The reviewer could then download the referred object or document for inspection. Once the reviewer has examined the metadata and the object, she was asked to rate the quality of the metadata on a seven-point scale (From Extremely low quality to Extremely high quality) for each one of the seven parameters. Only participants that grade all the objects were considered in the experiment.

The experiment was available for two weeks. During that time, 33 different participants entered the system, but only 22 of them completed successfully the review of all the 20 objects. From those 22, 17 (77%) work with metadata as part of their study/research activities; 11 (50%) were undergraduate students in their last years, 9 (41%) were postgraduate students and 2 (9%) had a Ph.D. degree. The reviews given by those 22 participants were the ones considered in this study.

Because of the inherent subjectivity in measuring quality, the first step in the analysis of the data was to estimate the reliability of the evaluation. In this kind of experiment, the evaluation could be considered reliable if the variability between the grades given by different reviewers to a metadata

Table 1.

Quality Parameter	ICC
Completeness	0.881
Accuracy	0.847
Provenance	0.701
Conformance to Expectations	0.912
Consistency & Coherence	0.794
Timeliness	0.670
Accessibility	0.819

instance is significantly smaller than the variability between the average grades given to different objects. To estimate this difference we use the Intra-Class Correlation (ICC) coefficient [24] which is commonly used to measure the inter-rater reliability. The average measure of ICC was calculated using the two-way mixed model, given that all the reviewers grade the same sample of objects. In this configuration, the ICC is equivalent to another widely used reliability measure, the Cronbachs alpha [25]. The results for each quality parameter is reported in the Table 1.

The only value that falls below the 0.7 cut-off value to be considered acceptable is the Timeliness parameter. In other words, the reviewers did not "agree" in the measurement of the timeliness. For the other parameters, the ICC suggest that the reviewers provided similar values and further statistical analysis could be performed.

The second step was to asses if there is a difference between the average grade given to automatically generated metadata instances and the average grade given to manually generated metadata. These average values are presented in Fig. 2. To statistically establish whether the difference between average values is real or a by-product of the natural variance, we proceed to apply a one-way ANOVA test. Our null hypothesis is that there is no difference between the grades given to automated and manual metadata. Our alternative hypothesis is that there is indeed a difference. While the automatically generated metadata instances seem to be, in average, graded 0.4 points higher than the manual ones, in most of the parameters (completeness, accuracy, conformance to expectations, consistency & coherence and accessibility), the null hypothesis cannot be rejected: The difference found may be just the consequence of random variability. The significant difference found in provenance value could be explained by the fact that all the automated metadata instances had the same origin, ProLearn project reports, but

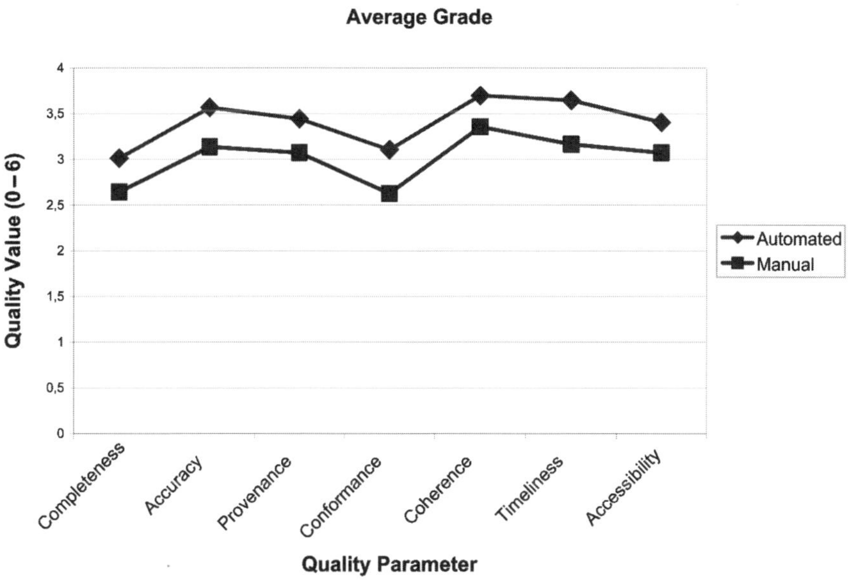

Fig. 2. Average quality grade for the different parameters.

cannot be generalized to other sources. While the timeliness parameter also shows a significant difference, the low value of reliability of this measure prevents to draw conclusions from it.

The main conclusion from this study is that there is no statistical difference between the quality grades given to a random sample of ARIADNE metadata instances and the ones produced automatically by SAmgI. That means that for the reviewers their quality is equivalent. We can introduce the automatically generated ones into ARIADNE without degrading the quality of the repository. These results could not be generalized to any kind of human generated metadata or any kind of automatically generated metadata. This evaluation only holds between ARIADNE metadata and the metadata for the ProLearn documents reports.

3.2. *Automated studies*

One of the first attempts of a systematic and automatic evaluation of the quality of digital metadata collections was performed by Hughes, in 2004 [26]. The objective of this work was to establish a quality score for each metadata instance present at the repositories of the Open Language Archives Community. The metrics used in this study were completeness (core elements per record, core element usage), vocabulary use (code usage, element and code usage), archive diversity (diversity by subject and diversity by type). With these metrics, Hughes computed a "star rating" for each repository, based on the quality score of its metadata. The result of work can be consulted live at http://www.language-archives.org/tools/reports/archiveReportCard.php. The main contribution of this paper was the creation of the first automated ranking system for data providers.

Following a different research question, Najjar *et al.*, also in 2005 [27], compared the metadata fields that are produced with the metadata fields that are used in searches inside the ARIADNE Learning Object Repository. They automatically measure the presence of values in the different fields of the 3,700 instances of Learning Object Metadata stored in ARIADNE. While their goal was not to measure the quality of the metadata records, they end up measuring how well the metadata present in ARIADNE supported its search functionality, one of the definitions of quality. An interesting finding of this study is that there is a large mismatch between the fields filled by the indexers and the fields used by searchers.

To the present, the largest metadata study has been conducted by Bui and Park [28] over more than one million instances of the National Science Digital Library (NSDL). Their objective was to determine the completeness of the Dublin Core instances present in the federation of repositories. Their main finding was that the most popular Dublin Core fields (title, identifier, author, descriptor) are present in more than 80% of the records. More exotic fields, such as coverage and relation, are only present in a small fraction of the records (less than 10%).

All the automated studies obtained a basic estimation of quality for each individual metadata instance without the cost involved in the manual quality evaluation. However, their level of "meaningfulness" is directly related with how comprehensive and complex is the set of calculated metrics. Given the exponential growth [29] of most repositories, automated studies, despise their problems, seems to be the only way in which quality evaluations could be performed.

3.2.1. *Example of an automated study*

As an example of the automated study, the evaluation perform using the metrics based on the quality frameworks in [13] is presented. In this study, the quality metrics were applied to two different sets of metadata. The first set was composed of 4426 LOM instances corresponding to an equal number of PDF Learning Objects provided in 135 courses in Electrical Engineering and Computer Science at the MIT Open Courseware site. These metadata have been manually generated by expert catalogers in the MIT OCW team [30]. The metadata downloading was performed on January 12, 2008. The second set of metadata was composed by LOM instances automatically generated from the same 4426 PDFs described in the first metadata set. The metadata was generated by only using the Text Content Indexer of SAmgI [21] that extracted and analyzed the text from the PDF files in order to fill the LOM fields. The fact that both instances refer to the same object enables the use of statistical tools to establish whether the difference between the average metric values for both sets is significant.

Ten metrics were applied to each metadata instance in both sets [13]. Once the values were obtained, a Paired *T*-Test was applied to measure whether the difference between the average values was statistically significant. The average value of metrics for each metadata set as well as the result of the Paired *T*-Test are reported in Table 2. All the metrics have a statistically significant different average value for the two sets. Also, the values obtained for metadata instances referencing the same learning object in the manual and automatic sets are not correlated. This independence let us discard the influence that the object itself have in the metadata quality measurement.

From the Average Quality (Qavg) values in Table 2, it can be concluded that, in general, the metrics found that the manual metadata set has higher quality than the automatic metadata set. A closer examination of the average of each quality metric reveals more information about the differences between both sets. The Completeness (Qcomp) and Weighted Completeness

Table 2.

	Average Metric Value			
Metric	**Manual**	**Automatic**	**Correl.**	**Paired T-Test (2-tailed)**
Qcomp	**0.49**	0.38	0.073	$t = 344$,df = 4425,Sig = 0.000
Qwcomp	**0.75**	0.41	0.182	$t = 232$,df = 4425,Sig = 0.000
Qaccu	0.59	**0.90**	0.191	$t = 107$,df = 4425,Sig = 0.000
Qcinfo	**0.93**	0.16	0.142	$t = 432$,df = 4425,Sig = 0.000
Qtinfo	**6.14**	5.9	0.029	$t = 10$,df = 4425,Sig = 0.000
Qcoh	**0.40**	0.26	−0.024	$t = 8$,df = 4425,Sig = 0.000
Qlink	0.22	**0.24**	0.103	$t = 3.5$,df = 4425,Sig = 0.001
Qread	**0.26**	0.11	−0.014	$t = 4.5$,df = 4425,Sig = 0.000
Qavg	**0.66**	0.47	0.115	$t = 210$,df = 4425,Sig = 0.000

(Qwcomp) metrics point that human experts filled more fields (and also more important fields) that the Samgl Text Content Indexer. This is an expected result given the limited amount of information that can be extracted by simple text analysis algorithms.

The automatic set has a better average value of the Accuracy (Qaccu) metric. This, however, does not mean that automatic metadata is more accurate than the manual one, but it is attributable to a measuring artifact. Qaccu is calculated measuring the semantic distance between the text in the metadata instance and the text in the original object. The fact that all the text in the automatic metadata instances is directly extracted from the object's text explains the high value of Qaccu for the automated metadata set.

Another expected result is that humans tend to select a richer set of categorical values than the simple automated algorithm. This is reflected in the average values of the Categorical Information Content (Qcinfo) metric. For example, where the Learning Resource type value for all the learning object is set to "narrative text" in the automated instances, the human experts classify the same objects as "problem statement", "lecture", "questionnaire", "slide", etc. When all the objects in the set have the same value, Qcinfo tend to be low.

An interesting result from the comparison is that the Textual Information Content (Qtinfo) of both sets is high and very similar. That means both instances, manual and automatic, contain long (and useful) descriptions. The manual ones were generated by humans; the automatic ones were obtained from text fragments of the original document. This finding implies that both metadata sets could have a similar level of performance (or quality) in learning object search engines that are based on text search in the metadata content.

The Coherence (Qcoh) and Readability (Qread) metrics are higher also for the manual metadata sets. Text written by humans is bound to be easier to read and more coherent than text fragments automatically obtained from the learning object itself. Also, the coherence between the title and the description in the automatic set is expected to be low because the automatic algorithm takes the title contained in the PDF metadata as the value for the Title field. Normally this title in the PDF metadata is just the name of the file.

Finally, another interesting result is the almost tie in the Linkage metrics (Qlink), which implies that the keywords manually added to the instances, and the keywords automatically generated have the same capability to link instances among them. This capability could be useful in search engine that use keywords as a way to discover new material (similar to the practice to use tags to link content).

This study comparing the quality metrics values of these two metadata sets suggest that human generated metadata is superior in several dimensions to the full text analysis of the documents. However, there are certain tasks (such as keyword generation and summary generation) where automatic metadata could be easily as good as its human generated counterpart.

4. Tools for metadata quality evaluation and assurance

As a side result of the research on metadata quality, especially on automated metrics, there are several tools that can be used over existing metadata collection in order to find and resolve several quality issues. This section presents an extensive, but by no means exhaustive, list of this tools together with some explanation of the scenarios where they can be more useful.

- *Visual Graphic Analysis*: Dushay and Hillman, in 2003, presented the use of a commercial product, Spotfire DecisionSite, a visual graphical analysis application, to evaluate the metadata quality characteristics of the NSDL collections (See Fig. 3). This tool imported the metadata instances as a comma separated file to produce a scatter plot visualization with the metadata fields on one axis and the metadata identifiers on the other. This representation allows to easily detect completeness issues. This can be considered the first and most basic automated tool to evaluate metadata quality. Nicholson *et al.* propose a similar tool, but based on the web.
- *Metadata Inspector*: One of the sub-project of the MIT SIMILE Project is called Gadget. It is an XML inspector than can be used to analyze large quantity of metadata instances given that it can be expressed as XML. Gadget is very useful for collection managers that want to understand not only the completeness of their metadata instance, but also the distribution of the different values among the metadata fields or elements (Fig. 5).
- *Treemap Metrics Visualization*: The metrics values can be used to create visualizations of the repository in order to gain a better understanding of the distribution of the different quality issues. For example, a treemap visualization could be used to answer different questions: Which authors or sources of metadata cause quality problems? How has the quality of the repository evolved over time? Which is the most critical problem of the metadata in the repository?, etc. An example of such visualization is presented by Ochoa and Duval [13]. The treemap represents the

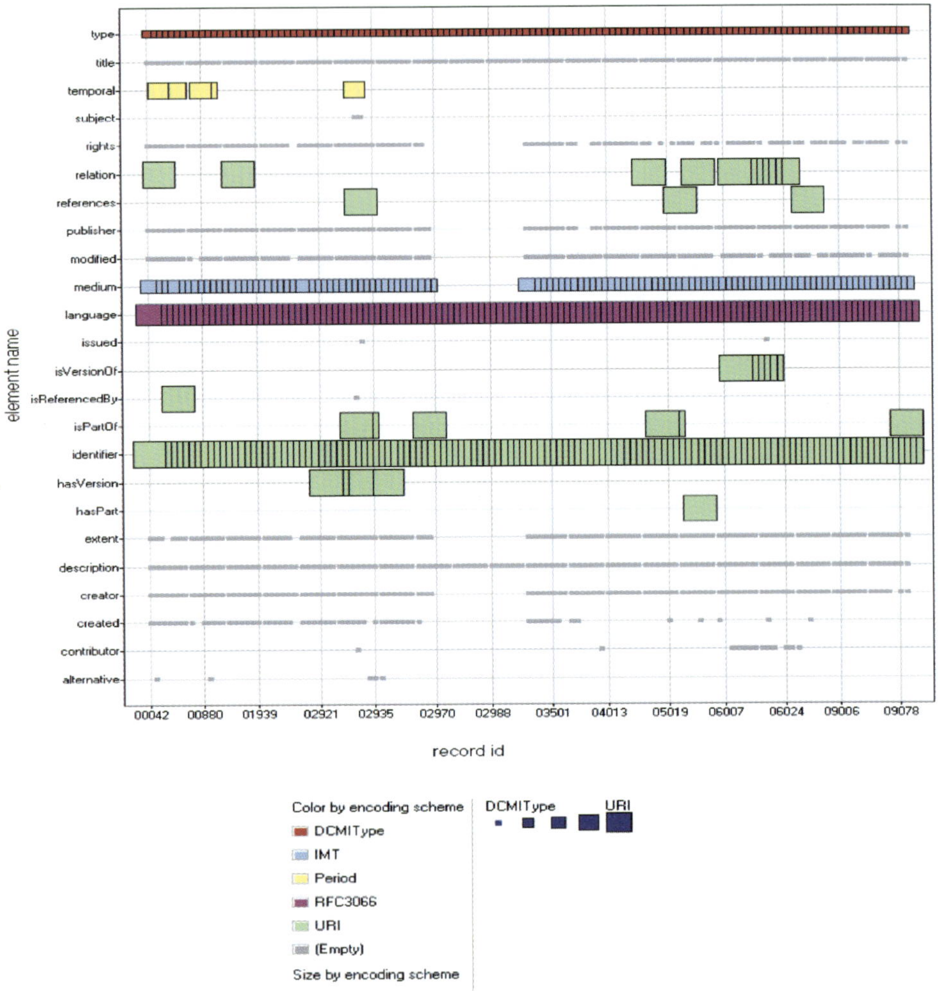

Fig. 3. Visual tool used by Dushay and Hillman to identify metadata problems. Taken from.

structure of the repository (Fig. 5). The global repository contains several local repositories and different authors publish metadata in their local repository. The boxes represent the set of metadata instances published by a given author. The color of the boxes represents the value of a given metric. This visualization helps to easily spot where an who produce problematic metadata.

- *Metadata Quality D-Space add-on*: A private company called @mire, has developed a plugin for D-Space repository that allow the fast correction of common metadata quality issues as incompleteness (through

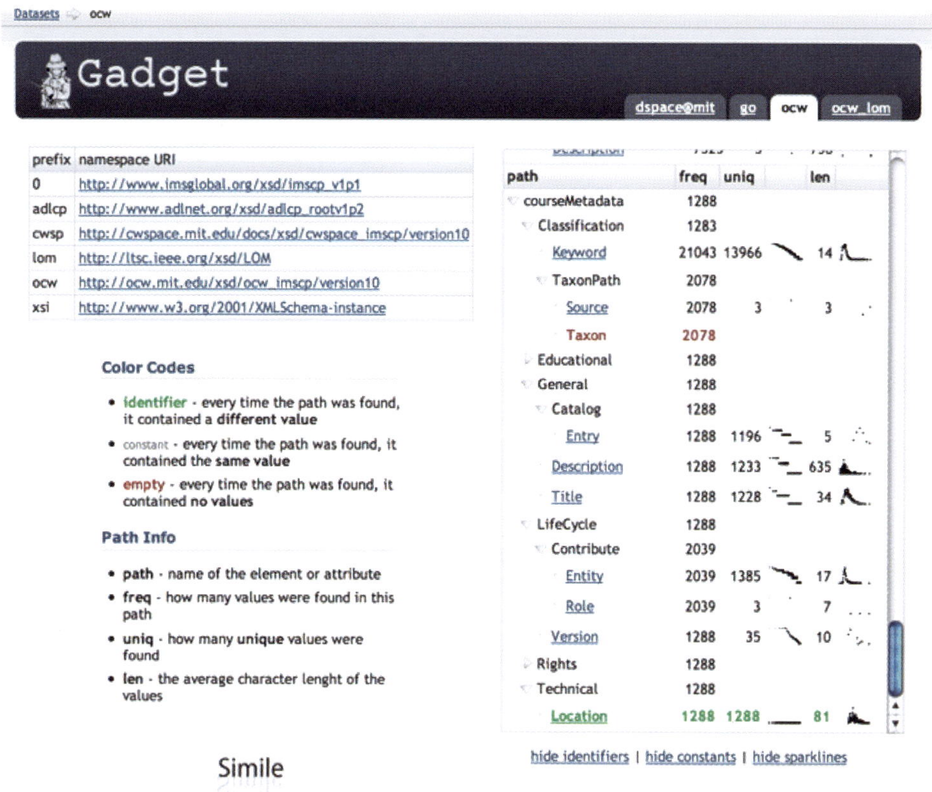

Fig. 4. Gadget, a XML inspector that can be used to analyze the quality of a metadata collection.

mass edition of instances) and detection of duplicates. While still not as useful as this kind of tools could be, it is one of the first addition to widely used metadata repository software that deals with quality issues.

Tools, such as the one described above, are usually considered as an afterthought of the conceptual research on metadata quality. It is, however, important to note that the main goal of metadata quality research should be the development of easy to use tools to prevent and correct metadata quality issues. Until then the different advances in frameworks and studies are simple research exercises with few practical implications in the functionality or performance of the digital metadata collections [13]. Interestingly enough, recent works point to the development of such kind of tools.

Fig. 5. A treemap visualization of the ARIADNE repository.

5. Conclusions and future perspectives

Quality of metadata it is a concept that if frequently cited as an important prerequisite to build several types of systems, from digital libraries to couple matching sites. However, the study of digital metadata quality it still in its infancy. There are some basic frameworks to measure it and some applications that use those frameworks to analyze quality problems, but, in general, metadata quality is an afterthought in most of existing systems.

In order to provide an adequate level of service, the metadata-based systems should integrate some kind of metadata evaluation. In most cases, given the amount of data to be analyzed, that evaluation should be automated by some mean, most easily, using metadata quality metrics. Unfortunately, these metrics are still under research and there are no agreement on a common or comparable set.

To conclude this section, a list of what the author think are the next steps to be taken in the field of metadata quality, are presented:

- *New metadata quality frameworks oriented to automatic processing:* Current metadata quality frameworks are deeply rooted in traditional, analog metadata. This metadata was meant to be consumed by humans and thus the quality characteristics considered in the frameworks were the ones that humans found important. Now, the metadata is mainly consumed and processed by automated software systems. It could be created or modified with each human interaction (corrections, annotations, tags, reviews, etc.) with the system. While it preserves some relation with its analog counterpart, digital metadata could not be measured with the same standards. New quality frameworks oriented to digital metadata and automatic processing should be developed.
- *Metadata aware tools:* The tools that are commonly used to manipulate documents have incorporated metadata services: long while ago. However, these services are too basic to be useful. For example, if a photo is copied from one document to another, the metadata of the photo (author, copyrights, date, etc.) are lost. Given that space restrictions are no longer an issue, storing the metadata, together with the actual object inside the documents formats could help to create smarter end-user tools.
- *Establishing a common data set:* Borrowing the idea that the TREC conference [31] initiated and in order to provide a better "measurement" of the quality of different metrics, the quality metrics should be applied to a known set of test metadata instances with an established and known value for different dimensions of quality. This is especially important to provide common ground to metrics proposed by different researchers. When applied to a common set, the prediction power of the metrics could be objectively compared and progress could be measured.

The main goal, however, of current research in metadata quality should be to hide its complexness from the end user. Electronics forms, asking for ten or more fields of metadata should exist no more. Metadata standards should be an issue for system implementors, not something in which author should be trained. Interoperability between system should be the common rule, not the exception. In other words, the main goal of metadata research should be to hide everything but the benefits.

References

1. Barton, J, S Currier and JMN Hey (2003). Building quality assurance into metadata creation: an analysis based on the learning objects and e-prints communities of practice. In *Proceedings 2003 Dublin Core Conference: Supporting Communities of Discourse and Practice — Metadata Research and Applications,* S Sutton, J Greenberg and J Tennis (eds.), pp. 39–48, Seattle, Washington. Available http://www.siderean.com/dc2003/201_paper60.pdf.
2. Beall, J (2005). Metadata and data quality problems in the digital library. *JoDI: Journal of Digital Information,* 6(3), 20. Available http://jodi.tamu.edu/Articles/v06/i03/Beall/.
3. Liu, X, K Maly, M Zubair and ML Nelson (2001). Arc — an oai service provider for digital library federation. *D-Lib Magazine,* 7(4), 12 Available http://www.dlib.org/dlib/april01/liu/04liu.html.
4. Stvilia, B, L Gasser and M Twidale (2006). Metadata quality problems in federated collections. In *Information Quality Management: Theory and Applications,* L Al-Hakim (ed.), pp. 154–158. Hershey, PA: Idea Group.
5. Ede, S (1995). Fitness for purpose: The future evolution of bibliographic records and their delivery. Catalogue & Index, 116, 1–3.
6. O'Neill, ET (2002). FRBR: Functional Requirements for Bibliographic Records; Application of the entity-relationship model to Humphry Clinker. *Library Resources & Technical Services,* 46(4), 150–159.
7. Whitman, B and S Lawrence (2002). Inferring descriptions and similarity for music from community metadata. In *Proceedings of the 2002 International Computer Music Conference,* pp. 591–598. Citeseer.
8. Wang, B, Z Li, M Li and W Ma (2006). Large-scale duplicate detection for web image search. *2006 IEEE International Conference on Multimedia and Expo,* pp. 353–356.
9. Strong, DM, YW Lee and RY Wang (1997). Data quality in context. *Communications of the ACM.* **40**(5), 103–110. Available citeseer.ist.psu.edu/strong97data.html.
10. Zhu, X and S Gauch (2000). Incorporating quality metrics in centralized/distributed information retrieval on the world wide web. In *Proceedings of the 23rd annual international ACM SIGIR conference on Research and development in information retrieval,* E Yannakoudakis, NJBMK Leong and P Ingwersen (eds.), pp. 288–295, New York, NY. ACM Press. Available citeseer.ist.psu.edu/zhu00incorporating. html.
11. Moen, WE, EL Stewart and CR McClure (1998). Assessing metadata quality: Findings and methodological considerations from an evaluation of the U.S. Government information locator service (GILS). In *ADL '98: Proceedings of the*

Advances in Digital Libraries Conference, TR Smith (ed.), pp. 246–255, Washington, DC, USA. IEEE Computer Society. ISBN 0-8186-8464-X.

12. Bruce, TR and D Hillmann (2004). The continuum of metadata quality: Defining, expressing, exploiting. In *Metadata in Practice,* D Hillmann (ed.), pp. 238–256. Chicago, IL: ALA Editions.
13. Ochoa, X and E Duval (2009). Automatic evaluation of metadata quality in digital libraries. *International Journal of Digital Libraries.* Available http://ariadne.cti.espol.edu.ec/xavier/papers/Ochoa-IJDL2009.pdf. (In Print).
14. Stvilia, B, L Gasser, MB Twidale, SL Shreeves and TW Cole (2004). Metadata quality for federated collections. *IQ,* 111–125.
15. Stvilia, B, L Gasser and M Twidale (2007). A framework for information quality assessment. *Journal of the American Society for Information Science and Technology.* 58(12), 1720–1733, (2007).
16. Margaritopoulos, T, M Margaritopoulos, I Mavridis and A Manitsaris (2008). A conceptual framework for metadata quality assessment. In *Proceedings of the International Conference on Dublin Core and Metadata Applications, DC-2008,* pp. 104–113.
17. Shreeves, SL, EM Knutson, B Stvilia, CL Palmer, MB Twidale and TW Cole (2005). Is "quality" metadata "shareable" metadata? the implications of local metadata practices for federated collections. In *Currents and Convergence: Navigating the Rivers of Change: Proceedings of the Twelfth National Conference of the Association of College and Research Libraries,* HA Thompson (ed.), pp. 223–237, Minneapolis, USA. ALA.
18. Chapman, A and O Massey (2002). A catalogue quality audit tool. Library Management, 23 (6–7), 314–324.
19. Greenberg, J, MC Pattuelli, B Parsia and WD Robertson (2001). Author-generated dublin core metadata for web resources: A baseline study in an organization. In *DC '01: Proceedings of the International Conference on Dublin Core and Metadata Applications 2001,* K Oyama and H Gotoda (ed.), pp. 38–46. National Institute of Informatics. ISBN 4-924600-98–9.
20. Greenberg, J (2004). Metadata extraction and harvesting. Journal of Internet Cataloging, 6 (4), 59–82.
21. Meire, M, X Ochoa and E Duval (2007). Samgi: Automatic metadata generation v2.0. In *Proceedings of the, ED-MEDIA 2007 World Conference on Educational Multimedia, Hypermedia and Telecommunications,* CMJ Seale (ed.), pp. 1195–1204, Chesapeake, VA AACE.
22. Duval, E, K Warkentyne, F Haenni, E Forte, K Cardinaels, B Verhoeven, R Van Durm, K Hendrikx, M Forte, N Ebel, *et al.* (2001). The ariadne knowledge pool system. *Communications of the ACM,* **44**(5), 72–78.

23. IEEE (2002). IEEE 1484.12.1 Standard: Learning Object Metadata (2002). http://ltsc.ieee.org/wg12/par1484-12-1.html, retrieved 2/04/2007.
24. Shrout, P and J Fleiss (1977). Intraclass correlations: Uses in assessing rater reliability. *Psychol Bull*, 86, 420–428.
25. Cronbach, L (1951). Coefficient alpha and the internal structure of tests. *Psychometrika*, 16 (3), 297–334.
26. Hughes, B (2004). Metadata quality evaluation: Experience from the open language archives community. In *Digital Libraries: International Collaboration and Cross-Fertilization: Proceedings of the 7th International Conference on Asian Digital Libraries, ICADL 2004,* Z Chen, H Chen, Q Miao, Y fu, E Fox and E Lim (eds.), pp. 320–329, Shangay, China. Springer Verlag. doi: http://www. springerlink.com/content/4kaxeu5p2fb2nac1. URL http://dx.doi.org/http://www. springerlink.com/content/4kaxeu5p2fb2nac1.
27. Najjar, J, S Ternier and E Duval (2003). The actual use of metadata in ariadne: an empirical analysis. In *Proceedings of the 3rd Annual ARIADNE Conference,* E Duval (ed.), pp. 1–6. ARIADNE Foundation.
28. Bui, Y and J-r Park (2006). An assessment of metadata quality: A case study of the national science digital library metadata repository. In *Proceedings of CAIS/ACSI 2006 Information Science Revisited: Approaches to Innovation,* 4 Mouk-dad (ed.), p. 13.
29. Ochoa X and E Duval (2009). Quantitative analysis of learning object repositories. IEEE *Transactions on Learning Technologies,* 2(3), 226–238. Available at http://ariadne. cti.espol.edu.ec/xavier/papers/Ochoa-TLT2009b.pdf. (In Print).
30. Lubas, R, R Wolfe and M Fleischman (2004). Creating metadata practices for MIT's Open-CourseWare Project. *Library Hi Tech,* 22(2), 138–143.
31. Harman, D (1993). Overview of the first TREC conference. In *SIGIR '93: Proceedings of the 16th annual interna-tional ACM SIGIR conference on Research and development in information retrieval,* R Korfhage, EM Rasmussen and P Willetl, pp. 36–47, New York, NY, USA. ACM Press. ISBN 0-89791-605-0. doi:http://doi.acm.org/10.1145/160688.160692.

CHAPTER I.5

ONTOLOGIES IN SYSTEMS THEORY

Emilia Currás

Profesora de Universidad
Universidad Autónoma de Madrid
Académica
emilia.curras@uam.es

The aim of this chapter is to apply Systems Theory — Systems Science — to Ontologies. The subject matter is given a modern context. The chapter contains a brief description of Systems Theory, which today has become what is known as Systems Science. Subsequently, Systems Science and systems are defined, as well as the links that are responsible for the correct function of a system, known as vectors. Ontologies will be discussed, along with their various definitions and characteristics. This chapter will be based on the premise that Ontology is a complex, conceptual, empirical classification system. An Ontology is structured like a system in which the principal and primary node is the word. A summary will be made of how this system should be constructed, concentrating on the vectors that help the system function. This will be illustrated with an example.

Keywords: Systems theory; systems science; ontologies; system; definitions of ontology; conceptual constructs; classification systems; computer science.

1. Preface

In recent times — or rather in recent years — the topic of Ontology has been raised in all kinds of different contexts. Our vision of the world has expanded in such a way as to make the old paradigms seem limited, incapable of explaining the world which we live in. Not only do these paradigms seem more limited, but also even in daily life in general, our actions and technical operations have moved away from what modern life actually means.

In order to place ourselves in the real, present-day world, a higher level of abstraction must be achieved. It is necessary to place ourselves a step above globalization in order to act on real and concrete cases. The Club of Rome's maxim, which attempts to consider problems or proposed questions from a point of view which consists of combining and globalizing them, in order to later apply particular solutions, is very helpful when it comes to reflecting on daily life.

The emergence of Ontologies has its foundations in this globalized way of seeing problems in order to apply concrete, practical solutions. A point has been reached where scientific evolution, and its consequent technology, has repercussions on the production of information. The information that has emerged is so extensive that the existing systems for dominating this information — until now considered to be classic and definitive — are not sufficient, and it is necessary to find alternative, more appropriate methods of controlling this information in order to match current requirements.

The problem that anyone who is handling information faces is finding fast, reliable, and efficient methods of storing and retrieving it. One speaks of professionals who manage information because, in fact, in the case of Ontologies it has not been those whose profession is information who have found the appropriate solutions. M.F. Peset [23] confirms this fact when she says that, in the construction of semantic webs and the instructions for their management, we documentalists have contributed very little. Once this misconception is recognized, it is necessary to confront the question and attempt to contribute what we can to the subject.

Therefore, Ontologies were the invention of computer specialists, who turned to philosophers in order to agree on an appropriate name for this subject [15], since the subject matter was classification, ontological, and etymological systems, based on the abstraction of concepts and objects (documents, L. M. Garshol [14]). That is where Ontologies come in, multiplying on a monthly and yearly basis. Indeed, in these recent years an issue of the magazine "El Profesional de la Información" ("The Information Professional") was published dedicated to Ontologies, which contained some important papers on this subject that are worth taking into account.

It could be said that without a doubt we are living in the Ontology Era.

2. Some notes on Systems Theory

Perhaps one way of getting to know and understand Ontologies is to study them from the perspective of Systems Theory, which is also very much in fashion these days.

Systems Theory has suffered the same modernization processes as the rest of the questions which concern us in the modern world. Systems Theory has had a theoretical foundation and scientific categorization added to it and consequently today we talk about Systems Science, which due to successive processes of conceptualization has become a kind of Systems Thinking, a Systems Philosophy even: the current culmination of the aforementioned process.

In order to orientate ourselves within this topic, of all the existing bibliography one clear and comprehensible definition of Systems Science (Currás [4]) has been chosen which deals with aspects of this topic that are relevant to this chapter:

> "[Systems Science is] *A body of doctrines, in accordance with predetermined paradigms, which studies the truth about things* (*or the world in which* we *live*), *organizing them into structures composed of structured units that show a mutual and simultaneous interrelation with each other and the environment in which they are found*".

From this definition it can be inferred that Systems Science can be comprehensively applied to Ontologies, as regards to structured units in simultaneous and mutual interrelation.

Information architectures, made up of structural units, in this case refer to systems, subject matter for the study of this Systems Science.

3. Systems

This section will begin with a discussion of **systems**.

Today, Systems Theory is applied to a wide range of activities, and the definitions of what might be classified as a system are abundant.

In selecting a definition of a system from the extensive existing bibliography on this subject, the following seems suitable for the purposes of this chapter (Currás [4]):

> "*A system is a group of independent entities which have an interrelation with each other and with the environment around them*".

This concise and simple definition adapts itself very well to the concept of Ontology which will be proposed in this chapter.

Another suitable definition in this case is that of Ouellet [21]:

> *which assumes, in every system, the supremacy of the whole over the part, taking into account the globalization issues which affect a group of relationships in interaction with the environment and the subject matter in hand.*

These definitions are suitable for application to Ontology since, moreover, the majority are based on the same principles and relationships, although these might be expressed in a wide variety of ways.

Every system's construction has its beginnings in an original and principal base element, denominated by Bertalanffly [1] as a **node** or **holon** (or complex node).

These nodes — or holons — can be simple, or unitary units, or subsystems of a certain complexity, which will again be based on a unitary primary node, the origin of the system under consideration. The nodes or holons can be found interacting through variables, parameters and transformables. The variables are defined as input vectors, output vectors or feedback loops, and are variable, as their name indicates. The parameters are the lines that show fixed relationships within the system, and the transformables are those lines, reciprocal or contradictory fluxes of movement, that can completely modify the original system.

There are a great variety of classes of systems which our different Ontologies can fit in to, according to the requirements of each case.

These brief thoughts on Systems Science will be sufficient for the purposes of the case in hand.

4. Ontologies

Once inside the world of Ontologies everything changes, due to the fact that we are entering the world of abstraction and empiricism. Our mentality needs to change in order to place ourselves a step above abstraction and globalization. Everything has different dimensions and conceptualizations, which seem to deal with the same problems, but perhaps seen from a different perspective.

Therefore, the terminology is transformed and a new language is used to describe the relevant content. Today we talk about classificatory fields, content domains, metadata, conceptual maps, relationals, epistemological combinations, as well as the organization of knowledge and learning, and even the organization of talent [18] and of Ontologies themselves.

According to Welty and Guarino [29], the word Ontology was coined by Rudolf Godenius in 1613. It derives from the philosophical concept of the same name, and was adopted by computer specialists who wanted to find a parallelism between "the study of what exists" (the domain of knowledge), with what "we assume exists", that is to say, the transformation of a natural language, reality, from a chosen domain, into a coded language which "we assume exists" in order to "achieve a coherent description of reality",

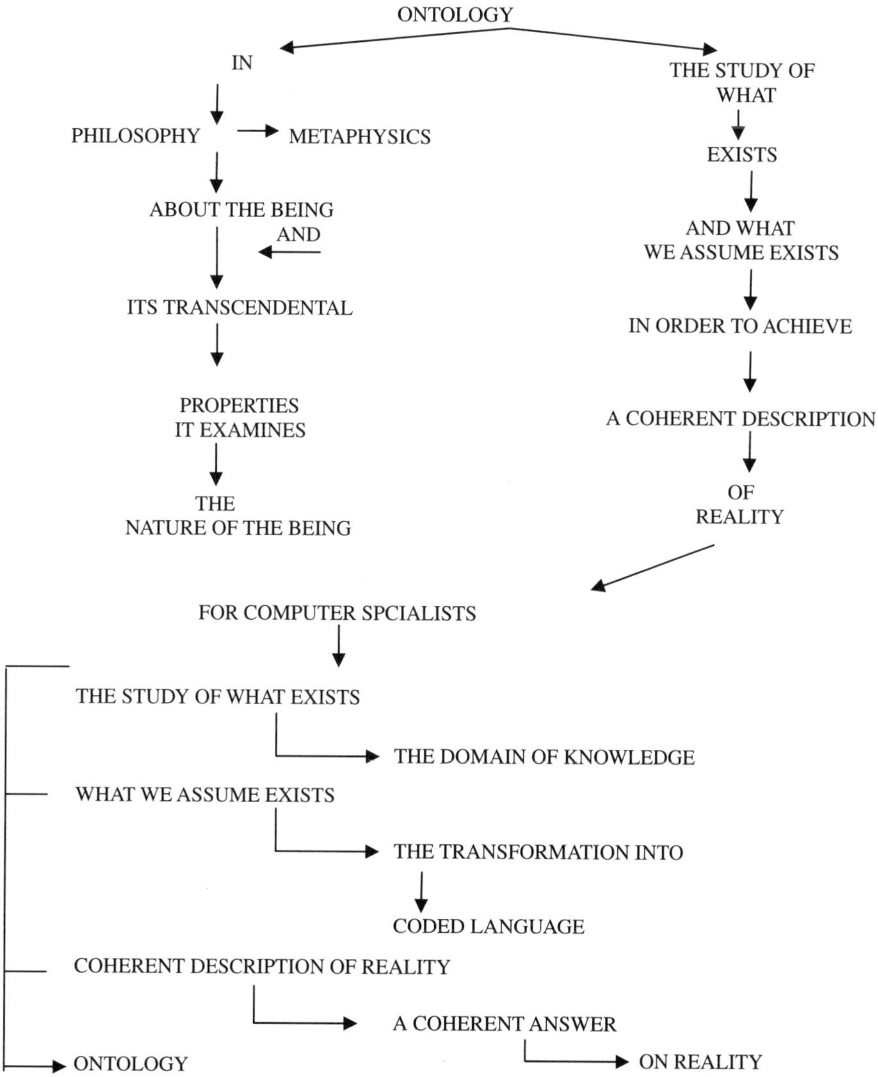

Fig. 1.

or rather, to be able to obtain from that domain a coherent "answer" about reality. See Fig. 1)

It was at the height of the 20th century that the term "Ontology" was first applied to the design of classification systems of a certain complexity: At the same time, Information Technology was developing to allow the construction of very sophisticated softwares. Vickery [28] accepts 1954 as the approximate date when the word "Ontology" was first mentioned within these fields of knowledge.

Vickery suggests that from 1997 there is a notable increase in this usage of the term. Nevertheless, it was around 1980 when it became accepted that the conceptualization of a domain was a necessary part of the knowledge acquisition process. In the 1990s, and above all from 1993 onwards, in the field of expert systems people began to accept the idea that when the sum knowledge in the mind of a human expert is codified, in some way it behaves like an expert computer system. In the conferences organized since 1996, frequent references to anthologies can be found. However, the real zenith has occurred in the last six or seven years. In 2005, I published a book on Ontologies, Taxonomies and Thesauri where this subject is discussed in depth.

Ontologies as systems can be classified according to the Fig. 2.

5. Definitions of Ontologies

Due to the numerous existing publications referring to Ontologies (see Bibliography), the number of definitions available is similarly high. The definitions quoted here are those that can be considered most appropriate for the application of the principles and practices of Systems Science.

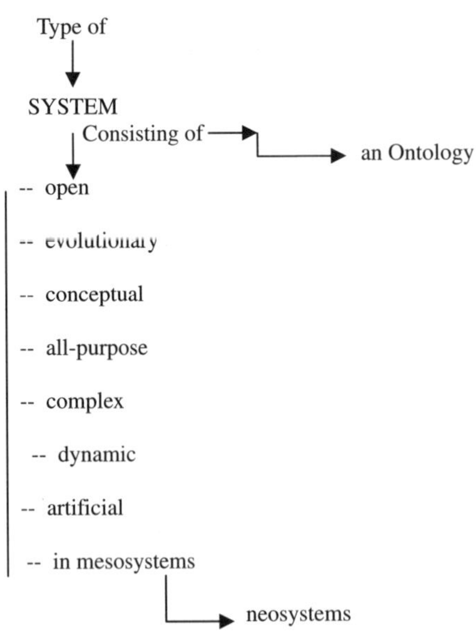

Fig. 2.

Amongst them those of:
Gruder (s. d.) (Gilchrist [15]), who defines an

Ontology as a formal and explicit specification of a shared conceptualization.

Lars M. Garshol [13], who places

Ontologies in the field of Computer Science as a model used to describe the world that consists of establishing a set of topics, properties, and relationships. A resemblance is established between the real world and the model created by Ontologies.

J. M. Moreiro [20], in a paper presented at the ISKO-Spain Conference (2007), defines an

Ontology as a structure where a system of concepts and the relationships between them within a certain domain are stored.

Javier García Marco [12], keen to find the philosophical angle within this field, tells us that:

Ontologies are a procedure based on first-order logic, developed in order to adequately encode the system of terms used in the aforementioned declarations (decision-making and task execution) in a way that adequately expresses the relationship between terms; that is to say, that they are tools used to construct conceptual systems, or in layman's terms, structured vocabularies in which the relationships between terms and other (applied) restrictions of meaning are made explicit.

For my part (Currás [6]), I consider an

Ontology as a systematic description of entities and their modalities, and the rules that permit the description of a specific model in agreement with the entities and processes that allow the description of "all" these entities and processes.

I cannot resist quoting a final definition by Garshol [13] where he describes an

Ontology as the culmination of an object classification process

The idea of comparing Ontologies with classification systems is not a new one. In fact, an

> *Ontology is, effectively, a system or method created in order to classify the content of a series of classes of information which helps in the storage process, and facilitates its retrieval in a computer system.*

6. Ontologies as a system

Using Ontologies as a base, a system within the field of Systems Theory can be constructed.

Firstly, two questions related to the concept of Ontology should be considered, which add particular connotations to this case. On the one hand, it is necessary to study a particular Ontology, isolated both in terms and classification; on the other hand, the set of all Ontologies should be also looked at, as a homogenous group, which are, perhaps, comparable to a general classification system such as a thesaurus or even as the Universal Decimal Classification (UDC).

6.1. *An Ontology as a system*

In order to be able to construct a system, it is necessary to start with a foundation element — a **node** — on which the whole building — the **system** — will be constructed and where the necessary relationships for the maintenance and proper function of this system will be established.

Using the general idea that Ontology is based on natural language as a starting point, the first node of the system will therefore be the **word**, maybe already converted into a **term**. Words are grouped into **phrases**, and these **phrases** into **thematic conceptualizations**. This is how the system is constructed.

This system is influenced by vectors, parameters and transformables, which are the factors that give a certain dynamism to the system. The fields of application of the constructed Ontology will be responsible for the fluctuations that the system experiences. In some cases it will be necessary to modify either some of the constructions or the whole conceptual apparatus. The introduction of a new field of knowledge or the suppression of an obsolete term modifies the whole system. In this way, the evolution of the aforementioned Ontology can be studied and foreseen in order to adapt it to the requirements for use in any given situation. (Fig. 3)

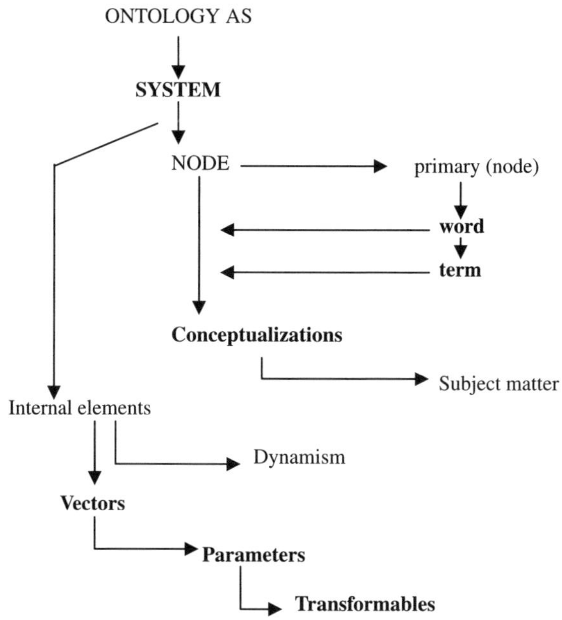

Fig. 3.

This system could be considered as open, evolutionary, conceptual, multi-purpose, complex, dynamic, artificial (man-made), and belonging to **mesosystems**, within **neosystems.**

In this system, the **vectors** will refer to the usual modifications that might take place in the Ontology in question: any addition or suppression of a term will modify the conceptual composition of the Ontology itself. Consequently, if one is dealing with the subject of education, for example, and the term "continuous" is added without taking this into account beforehand, the structural construct of the classifying unit will be modified. If it were as follows: "adult education", now the term "continuous" would have to be added to the word "education", with the necessity of accepting "continuous education" as a classifying unit. (Fig. 4)

For their part, the **parameters** will be determined by expansions: additions to the general themes of the Ontology in question. In the previous example, related to education, it could be said that the expansion of the topic to include certain schools would be a parameter, encompassing zones until now not taken into account (Fig. 5).

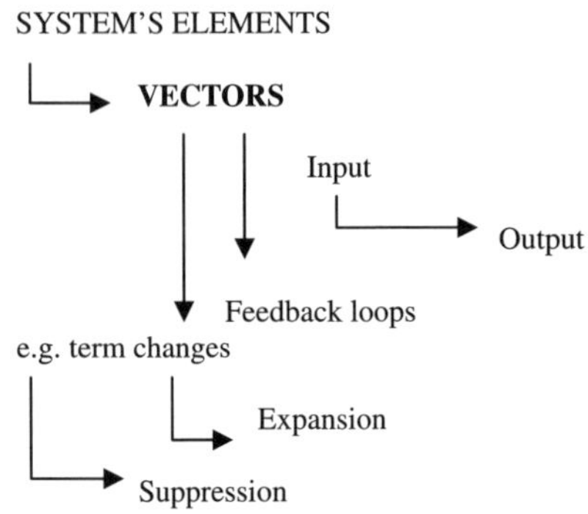

Fig. 4.

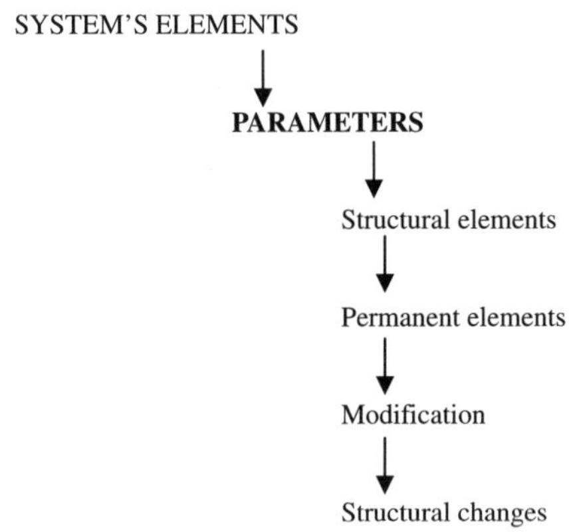

Fig. 5.

With regards to the **transformables**, which will modify the direction of the topic in question, in our example we would have to refer to a substantial change in the base topic and it could be taken as an example of a modification to the original source (Fig. 6).

6.2. *Ontologies as systems*

Now the term Ontologies will be used, in plural, to refer to that set of ontological units that constitute Ontologies as they are currently understood, that is to say, as a whole classification system.

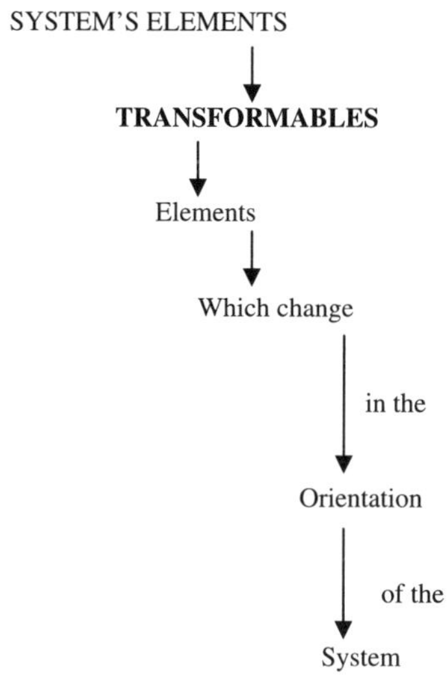

Fig. 6.

In Ontologies, the basic **node** will be the **word** once again, converted into a **phrase**, and eventually representing a **conceptual field**. However, the **holon** — a complex node which also forms a system — will be now used to form the desired Ontologies and which will consist of the very first conceptual construct which constitutes these Ontologies.

This is a much more complex system in which the relationships between holons are even more complicated again. Interrelations in two different directions will be established in which the input flows and output flows can have a bigger influence on the holons, and can eventually modify the whole system.

Supposing, for example, that Ontologies are constructed in order to solve the issue of a company's intranet. The knowledge fields are established (this will be the company's task), the interrelations and specifications for the individual case in hand are also established, and so everything appears to be working well. Moreover, these Ontologies have been passed on to another company in a similar field. Now the aforementioned company decides to extend the domains in which they have their business, which means adopting new conceptual topics, new terms (new words), and new interrelations. Logically, the existing constructed Ontologies must be modified, and this is where the vectors, parameters and transformables come into play, establishing new input and output vectors, as well as new feedback loops, fixed elements and perhaps transformables that will completely modify the Ontologies. Then the vectors are given values, the calculations are carried out on computer, and results are obtained which indicate in which way the Ontologies should be modified in order for the system to be operational again.

6.3. *A specific case*

It is not easy to mention a particular case, given that every situation or subject matter requires an extremely complex and specific treatment. Nevertheless, we shall take the risk, taking into account any possible omissions or modifications that could be applied to the example case in hand.

A topic with expansive dimensions will be used, that is, without specifying any particularities in each case.

Let us suppose that one is dealing with a company dedicated to documents computerization. Within the company as a whole, the following departments — amongst other factors — will have to be considered:

Management	Budget
Personnel	Resources
	Final products

For now fixed assets consumables, maintenance expenses, etc., will be disregarded; they will be included in the section on budget.

Note 1: Instead of "conceptual constructs", the more familiar and comprehensible term "classification units" will be used for our purposes in this field.

Therefore, the concept **management** would include the valid classification entities of:

— Management Organization
— Secretarial Staff

In the same way, within the **personnel** department the following valid classification entities would be considered:

— Personnel categories
— Salaries
— Holidays
— Sickness, etc.

Note 2: These classification entities will serve as examples for our purposes.

In the **budget** department, the aforementioned factors would be taken into account:

— Fixed assets
— Consumables
— Maintenance expenses
— Personnel expenses
— Resource acquisition
— Suppliers
— Type of documents to be acquired
— Magazine subscriptions, etc.

And in the case of the **final products** department, these factors would be considered:

— Types of final products
— Summary reports
— Alert services
— User Services, etc.

All this data can be summarized in order to construct the appropriate Ontology for a company dedicated to documents computerization (Fig. 6).

6.4. *Characteristics of the system*

In the ontology formulated and illustrated in Fig. 7, different questions arise, such as whether some of the classification units used as an ontological base affect any other classification units.

Thus, the classification unit "budget" affects all the other units. In the same way, "acquisition of resources" can modify "professional categories" and "consumable expenses", "fixed asset expenses" "type of final products" and various other categories.

The resulting **vectors** might be:

— Budget department (and all the other classification units, as above)
— Resource acquisition (again, with all the remaining classification units included)
— Final products department (including the classification units therein)

The variations of each of these vectors can produce alterations in any of the others, according to each case.

ONTOLOGY

Applied to a company dealing with the COMPUTERIZATION OF DOCUMENTS

- **Management** department
    - Management Organization
    - Secretarial staff, etc.
- **Personnel** department
    - Salaries
    - Holidays
    - Sickness, etc.
- **Budget** department
    - Fixed asset expenses
    - Consumable expenses
    - Maintenance expenses
    - Personnel expenses
    - Distribution of final products, etc.
- **Resources** department
    - Resource acquisition
    - Suppliers
    - Type of documents acquired
    - Magazine subscriptions, etc.
- **Final products** department
    - Summary bulletins
    - Alert services
    - User Services, etc.

Fig. 7.

The **parameters**, or "stable" elements, will have to be those that show almost no variations over (long) periods of time, such as:

— Management Organization
— Secretarial Staff
— User Service (its basic structure), etc.

And the **transformables**, which would require a radical change in the system, would be determined by variations in the type of:

— Resources
— Acquisition of documents, etc.

So, if the company in question dedicates itself to computerizing documents on mining engineering, and, due to modifications in market politics,

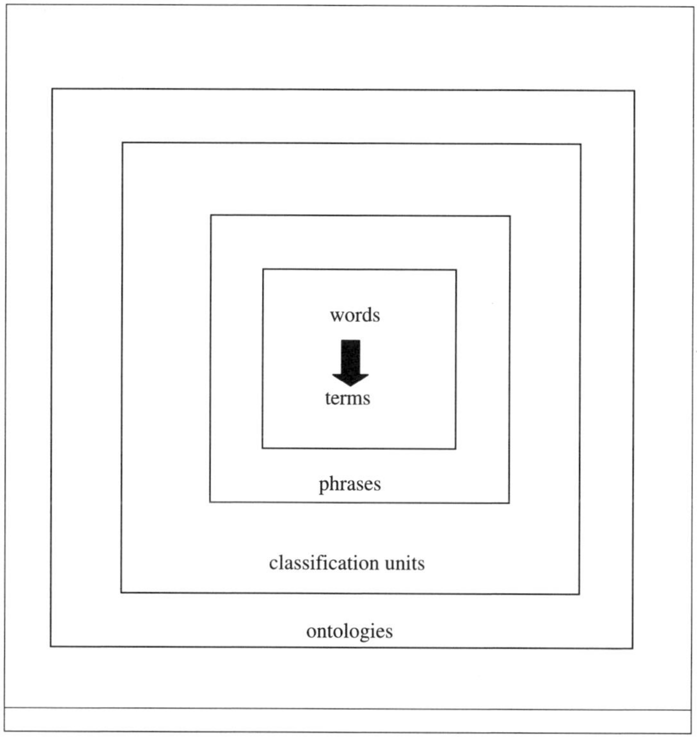

Fig. 8.

it decides to move on to metallurgical engineering products, logically a total change will be produced in certain aspects.

Figure 8 shows a diagram of these base Ontologies, applied to an unspecified company:

For this diagram to be applicable to the referred company, each of the squares should be filled in with the corresponding words, phrases, classification units, etc., until the specific Ontologies taken as an example had been fulfilled.

In order to complete this study, the causal and flow diagrams which best facilitated an understanding of the subject could be sketched.

7. Conclusion

There is no doubt that structuring an Ontology or various Ontologies referring to more or less concrete questions such as systems is a very complex matter which requires great attention to detail, and care in its production. All the relevant elements must be carefully determined and placed within the system that is being constructed, which is not an easy task.

Nevertheless, without a doubt the structuring of Ontologies based on systems units facilitates the study of subsequent variations or modifications, which it is necessary to carry out as you go along in order to achieve a better working order within the company as a whole, with the result — for example — that the company is more effective and productive from an economic point of view.

In this, Chapter I.5 of the book "Handbook of Metadata, Semantics and Ontologies" I have attempted to offer an alternative vision of what Ontologies can be in their theoretical–practical aspects.

Its objective is to present a systemic, complex aspect which can be applied to Ontologies construction.

References

1. Von Bertalanffly, L (1968). *General System Theory: Foundations, Development Application.* New York: Georges Braziller.
2. Von Bertalanffly, L (1979). *Perspectiva en la Teoría General de Sistemas.* Madrid: Alianza Universal.
3. Contreras, J and JA Martínez Comeche (2007). Las Ontologías: La Web Semántica. In *Ontologías y Recuperación de Información*, Septiembre 2007, Grupo Normaweb SEDIC, Universidad Complutense de Madrid, monografía.
4. Currás, E (1988). Implicaciones de la Teoría de Sistemas. In *La Información en sus Nuevos Aspectos. Ciencias de la Documentación*, pp. 140–168. Madrid: Paraninfo, ISBN 84-283-1600-7.
5. Currás, E (1999). Dialéctica en la Organización del Conocimiento. *Organización del Conocimiento en Sistemas de Información y Documentación*, 3, 23–43.
6. Currás, E (2005). *Ontologías, Taxonomía y Tesauros. Manual de construcción y uso.* Gijón: Trea S.L., ISBN: 84-9704-157-7.
7. Currás, E (2005). De las Clasificaciones a las Ontologías. In *Ontologías, Taxonomía y Tesauros. Manual de construcción y uso*, pp. 19–31. Gijón: Trea, S.L.
8. Currás, E (2005). Teoría de Sistemas aplicada a las Ontologías y a las Taxonomías. In *Ontologías, Taxonomía y Tesauros. Manual de construcción y uso*, pp. 319–320. Gijón: Trea, S.L.
9. Currás, E (2005). Estructura de las Ontologías. In *Ontologías, Taxonomía y Tesauros. Manual de construcción y uso*, pp. 36–42. Gijón: Trea, S.L.
10. Currás, E (2005). Los Tesauros en la Ciencia de Sistemas. In *Ontologías, Taxonomía y Tesauros. Manual de construcción y uso*, pp. 307–325. Gijón: Trea, S.L.

11. García Marco, FJ (2003). Desarrollo de ontologías orientadas a dominios específicos. In *Modelos y Experiencias. Retos y Perspectivas, VIII Encuentro sobre Sistemas de Información y Documentación,* Esquemas: pp. 11. Zaragoza: IBERSID.
12. García Marco, FJ (2007). Ontologías y organización del conocimiento: Retos y oportunidades para el profesional de la información. *El Profesional de la Información,* 16(6), 541–550.
13. Garshol, LM (2004). Research in action. Metadata? Thesauri? Taxonomies? Topic Maps! Making sense of it all. *Journal of Information Science,* 30(4), 378–391.
14. Garshol, LM (2006). *Ontology and Converter.* FML. Available at http://www.ontopia.net/topicmaps/materials/tm-vs-thesauri.html.
15. Gilchrist, A (2003). Thesauri, taxonomies and ontologies–An etymological note. *Journal of Documentation,* 59(1), 7–18.
16. Godenius, R, C Welty and N Guarino (2001). Supporting Ontological Analysis of Taxonomic Relationship. Available at http://citeseer.ist.psu.edu/452329.html.
17. Henrichs, N. *Information in the Philosophie.* In Grundlagen der praktischen Information und Dokumentation, (lecture), pp. 745–749.
18. Jericó, P (2000). *Gestión del Talento. Del Profesional con Talento al Talento Organizado.* Madrid: Pearson Education/Prentice may; Vedior.
19. Marín, R and B Martínez *et al.* (2003). El desarrollo de una ontología a base de un conocimiento enciclopédico parcialmente estructurado. Jornadas de tratamiento y recuperación de la información. Available at http://www.fiv.upv.es/jotri/Ponencias/Desarrollo.pdf.
20. Moreiro González, JA (2007). Definición de Ontología. In Evolución paralela de los Lenguajes Documentales y la Terminología, Ponencia presentada al Congreso ISKO-España, León, pp. 48.
21. Ouellet, A (1983). *L'èvolution Crèative: une aproche systèmique des valeurs.* Quèbec: Presses de l'Universitè du Quèbec.
22. Pedraza-Jiménez, R, L Codina and C Rovira (2007). Web semántica y ontologías en el procesamiento de la información documental. *El Profesional de la Información,* 16(6), 569–578.
23. Peset Mancebo, M. Fernanda: *Ontologías.* Available at mpeset@upvnet.upv.e
24. Rodríguez Delgado, R (1968). *Teoría general de Sistemas.* Apuntes de clase.
25. Rodríguez Delgado, R (1980). *Filosofía de Sistemas. Nuevo Paradigma Científico.* Ciclo de Conferencias sobre Teoría de Sistemas. Madrid: Universidad Complutense.
26. Sánchez-Jiménez, R and B Gil-Urdiciain (2007). Lenguajes documentales y ontologías. In *El Profesional de la Información,* 16(6), 551–560.
27. Vickery, BC (1996). Conceptual relations in information systems. *Journal of Documentation,* 52(2), 198–200.

28. Vickery, BC (1997). Ontologies. *Journal of Information Science*, 23(4), 277–286.
29. Welty, Ch. and Guarino, N (2001). Supporting ontological analysis of taxonomic relationship. Available at http://citeseer.ist.psu.edu/452329.html.

Publications Consulted

30. Bowen, PL, RA O´Farrell and FH Rohde (2004). How does your model grow? An empirical investigation of the effects of ontological clarity and application domain size on query performance. In *Proc. 2004 Int. Conf. Information Systems*, pp. 77–90. Washington, DC.
31. Christopoulou, E and A Kameas (2005). GAS ontology: An ontology for collaboratin among biquitous computing devices. *International Journal of Human-Computer Studies*, 62(5), 664–685. Available at LISA: Library and Information Science Abstract Database [accessed on 28 June 2007].
32. Cisco, SL and WK Jackson (2005). Creating order out of chaos with taxonomies. *Information Management Journal*, 39(3), 45–50. Available at LISA: Library and Information Science Abstract Database [accessed on 28 June 2007].
33. Currás, E (1989). *Dialectic Interaction in Science,* Actas Congrès Européen de Systémique, Association Française pour la Cybernétique, Économique et Technique, Lausanne (Suisse), *Ontologies in Systems Theory* 17. Octubre 1989, 1–11; e INICAE, 1990, 9(1), 5–17.
34. Currás, E (1991). *T(h)esaurus. Lenguajes Terminológicos.* Madrid: Paraninfo. ISBN: 84-283-1825-5.
35. Currás, E (1992). Information science–information as a dialectic interactive system. In *Cognitive Paradigms in Knowledge Organizatio*, pp. 419–431. Madras: Sarada Ranganathan Endowment for Library Science; (1995); Currás, E (1995). Information science–information as a dialectic interactive system. *IFID*, 20(1), 31–42.
36. Currás, E (1998). *Tesauros. Manual de Construcción y Uso.* Madrid: Kaher II S.A. ISBN: 84-605-7405-9.
37. Ferreyra, D (2003). *Las Ontologías en Relación con el Campo de la Documentación.* Argentina: Universidad Nacional de Misiones.
38. Gilchrist, A and P Kibby (2000). *Taxonomies for Business: Access and Connectivity in a Wired World.* London: TFPL.
39. Guerrero Bote, V and A Lozano Tello (1999). Vínculos entre las ontologías y la biblioteconomía y documentación. Representación y Organización del Conocimiento en sus distintas perspectivas: Su influencia en la recuperación de la información. In Organización del Conocimiento en Sistemas de Información y Documentación, IV Congreso ISKO-España, EOCONSID´99, MJ López Huertas and JC Fernández Molina (eds.), No. 4, pp. 25–31.

40. Krumholz, W (2004). Grenzen der physiologischen informationsverarbeitung des menschen. *Information–Wissenschaft und Praxis*, 55(5), 283–287.
41. La Ontología (2000). Available at http://elies.rediris.es/elies9/5-4.htm, pp. 1–13.
42. López Alonso, MA (2003). Integración de herramientas conceptuales de recuperación en la web semántica: Tesauros conceptuales, ontologías, metadatos y mapas conceptuales. VIII Encuentro sobre Sistemas de Información y Documentación: Modelos y Experiencias. Retos y Perspectivas. Zaragoza, IBERSID.
43. March, ST and GN Allen (2007). Ontological Foundations for Active Information Systems. *International Journal of Intelligent Information Technologies*, 3(1), 1–13.
44. Morán, O and HA Hassan. De una Ontología Empírica a una Ontología Objetiva, pp. 1–36. Available at http:/www.geocities.com/Athens/Delphi/6082/ontologia.
45. Moreira, A, L Alvarenga and A de Pavia Oliveira (2004). Thesaurus and ontology: Study of the definitions found in the computer and information science literature, by means of an analytical-synthetic method. *Knowledge Organization*, 31(4), 231–244.
46. Neelameghan, A and KN Prasad (eds.) (2001). *Content Organization in the New Millennium*. Bangalore, India: Sarada Ranganathan Endowment for Library Science.
47. Paducheva, EV (2007). Glagoly Interpretatsii: Taksonomiya i aktsional´nye klassy. Verbs denoting interpretation: Taxonomy and ontological categories. *Nauchno-Tekhnicheskaya Informatsiya*, Series 2(6), 28–34. LISA: Library and Information Science Abstract [accessed on 28 June 2007].
48. Poli, R. *Ontological Methodology*. Available at http://www.informatik.uni-trier.de.html.
49. Sánchez-Cuadrado, S and J Morato-Lara *et al.* (2007). De repente, ¿todos hablamos de ontologías. *El Profesional de la Información*, 16(6), 562–568.
50. Tramullas, J. *Agentes y ontologías para el tratamiento de la información: Clasificación y recuperación en Internet*. Available at http://tramullas.com/papers/isko99.pdf.
51. Uschold, M and M Gruninger (1996). Ontologies: Principles, methods and applications. *Knowledge Engineering Review*, 11(2), 93–136.

CHAPTER II.1

INTRODUCTION TO XML AND ITS APPLICATIONS

Laura Papaleo*,†

*IT Department, Provincia di Genova
P.le Mazzini, 2-16100 Genova, Italy
laura.papaleo@gmail.com
†Department of Informatics and Computer Science
University of Genova, Via Dodecaneso
35 16100 Genova, Italy
papaleo@disi.unige.it

Extensible Markup Language (XML) is a meta-language for defining new languages. Its impact on the modern and emerging web technologies has been (and will be) incredible and it has represented the foundation of a multitude of applications. This chapter is devoted to the presentation of XML and its applications. It provides an introduction to this wide topic, covering the principal arguments and providing references and examples.

1. Introduction

Extensible Markup Language (XML) is hugely important. It has been defined as *the holy grail of computing, solving the problem of universal data interchange between dissimilar systems* (Dr. Charles Goldfarb). XML is basically a handy format for everything from configuration files to data and documents of almost any type. The first version of XML became a W3C Recommendation in 1998, while its fifth edition has been declared recommendation, in 2008 [1].

XML is significant, but it is a hard subject to describe briefly in a chapter, since it describes a whole family of technologies and specifications. In 10 years, its success has been incredible and it has represented the foundation of a multitude of applications.

This chapter has the goal to present the XML meta-language, trying to give an overview of the most significant parts. We will describe the syntax to create XML documents and how we can structure them by defining specific grammars (DTDs and XML Schemas). We will also show how to render XML documents using *Cascading Style Sheet Language* (CSS) stylesheets and how to transform and render them with a family of XML-based languages (XSL, XSLT, and XPath). The end of the chapter will be dedicated to provide a snapshot of the "life" around XML, to let the reader understand the immense impact of XML in the actual technological world.

2. What extensible markup language (XML) is?

XML [1] is a simple, very flexible text format used for the description of marked-up electronic content. XML is classified as *extensible* because it allows the user to define the mark-up elements [2]. It is defined as a *markup language* because it allows to make explicit an interpretation of a text using a set of markup conventions (tags).

More exactly, XML is a *meta-language*, that is, a means of formally describing a language, in this case, a markup language. Today, XML is playing an important role in the exchange of a wide variety of data on the Web and elsewhere [1]. Generally speaking, XML's purpose is to aid information systems in sharing structured data, especially via the Internet, to encode documents, and to serialize data. XML, in combination with other standards, makes it possible to define the content of a document separately from its formatting, making it easy to *reuse* that content [2]. Most importantly, XML provides a basic syntax that can be used to *share* information between different applications and different organizations without using expensive and time-consuming conversion [3].

3. Origins of the extensible markup language

XML emerged as a way to overcome the shortcomings of its two predecessors, the *Standard Generalized Markup Language* (ISO 8879:1986 SGML) and the *HyperText Markup Language* (HTML) which are both restricted in some ways. Roughly speaking, HTML is too limited, while SGML is too complex. XML, instead, is a software- and hardware-independent light and simple tool for carrying information [4, 5].

The key point is that using XML, scientific organizations, industries and other companies, can specify how to store specific data in a machine-understandable form so that applications — running on any platform — can easily import and process these data. In the following subsections, we will briefly present SGML and HTML and we will outline their main differences with respect to XML. This will help the reader to understand why XML has been defined. Finally, we will shortly recall the history of the XML birth.

3.1. *Standardized generalized markup language — SGML*

The Standardized Generalized Markup Language (SGML, for short) — conceived notionally in the 1960s — 1970s, has been considered, since its beginning, the international standard for marking up data and it is an ISO standard since 1986, ISO 8879:1986. SGML has been defined as a powerful and XML with the main goal to semantic markup any type of content. This functionality is particularly useful for cataloging and indexing data [7]. SGML can be used to create an infinite number of markup languages and has a host of other resources as well.

Historically, it has been used by experts and scientific communities. However, SGML is really complex and expensive: adding SGML capability to an application could double its price. Thus, from the Web point of view, the commercial browsers decided not to support SGML.

Both SGML and XML are widely-used for the definition of device-independent, system-independent methods of storing and processing texts in electronic form. Comparing the two languages, basically, XML is a simplification or derivation of SGML, developed thinking at the emerging Web technologies [7].

3.2. *Hypertext markup language — HTML*

A well-known application of SGML is HTML, which is the publishing language of the World Wide Web. HTML defines a specific (finite) set of tags for structuring content and for publishing it over internet. HTML is free, simple and widely supported. Thousand of online tutorials, books and web portals exist describing the HTML language. In this section, we would like to concentrate on the main problems of the old versions of HTML, which have had certain significance in pushing the formalization of XML.

HTML has serious defects. The original thinking was to separate content from presentation, but the evolution of HTML lost this purpose (as for example due to the use of tags as `<em>` and `<font>`). Web pages began to be used for things that went wildly beyond the original concept, including multimedia (using the tag `<object>`), animation and many more. Thus, they started to become more containers of more fascinating objects (e.g., flash animations) than pages describing content, arising big problems in web searching performance. Also, browsers tried to be tolerant of incorrect web pages and this tolerance became a barrier to programmatic interpretation of published content, as for the use of HTML for structured data.

XML arose from the recognition that key components of the original web infrastructure — HTML tagging, simple hypertext linking, and hardcoded presentation — would not scale up to meet the future needs of the web [8].

Compared with HTML, XML has some important characteristics. First of all, XML is *extensible* so it does not contain a fixed set of tags. Additionally, XML documents must be well-formed according to a strict set of rules, and may be formally validated (using DTDs or XML Schemas), while HTML documents can contain errors and still the browsers render the pages as well as possible. Also, XML focuses on the *meaning of data,* not its presentation.

It is important to understand that XML is not a replacement for HTML. In most web applications, *XML is used to transport data,* while HTML is used to format and display the data for the Web. Additionally, thanks to XML, HTML evolved into XHTML [9] which is basically a reformulation of HTML (version 4) in XML 1.0.

3.3. *The birth of XML*

In 1996, discussions began which focused on how to define a markup language with the power and extensibility of SGML but with the simplicity of HTML. The World Wide Web Consortium (W3C) founded a working group [9] on this goal, which came up with XML, the *eXtensible Markup Language*. Like SGML, XML had to be not itself a markup language, but a specification for defining markup languages. Like HTML, XML was planning to be very simple to learn and clear in the syntax.

Since the beginning, the design goals for XML were clear to the working group and they can be summarized in the following 10 points:

(i) XML shall be straightforwardly usable over the Internet.
(ii) XML shall support a wide variety of applications.
(iii) XML shall be compatible with SGML.
(iv) It shall be easy to write programs which process XML documents.
(v) The number of optional features in XML is to be kept to the absolute minimum, ideally zero.
(vi) XML documents should be human-legible and reasonably clear.
(vii) The XML design should be prepared quickly.
(viii) The design of XML shall be formal and concise.

(ix) XML documents shall be easy to create.
(x) Terseness in XML markup is of minimal importance.

Over the next years, XML evolved: by mid 1997 The *eXtensible Linking Language* (XLL) project was underway and by the summer of 1997, Microsoft had launched the Channel Definition Format (CDF) as one of the first real-world applications of XML. Finally, in 1998, the W3C approved Version 1.0 of the XML specification as Recommendation. A new language was born reaching completely the planned goals. In 2008, the fifth edition of XML has been approved as W3C recommendation and the working groups on XML are still active.

4. XML documents: syntax

As we have seen, XML is a formal specification for markup languages. Every formal language specification has an associated syntax. In this section, we will briefly recall the syntax of XML documents. More details and information can be found in the XML specifications from W3C [1] or in books as [3, 4, 6].

An XML document consists of a *prolog* that includes an XML declaration and an optional reference to external structuring documents and the *body* consisting of a *number of elements* which may contain also *attributes*. These elements are organized in a hierarchical structure (a *tree*), meaning that there can only be one *root element*, also called the *Document element*, and all other elements lie within the root. In Fig. 1, we show an example of an XML document and the corresponding tree structure.

The first line of the prolog is the *declaration* (see Fig. 2) and it serves to let the machine understanding that what follows is XML, plus additional information such as the encoding. Other components that can be inserted in the prolog of an XML document as, for example, the associated schemas (either DTDs or XML Schema — see Secs. 6 and 7) or the attached stylesheets (in CSS or XSL — see Secs. 8 and 9).

XML document *body* is made up of elements (see Fig. 2). Each *element* is defined using two basic components *data* and *markup*. Data represents

```
<?xml version="1.0" standalone="yes" ?>
<message>
   <from> Robert </from>
   <to> Mario </to>
</message>
```

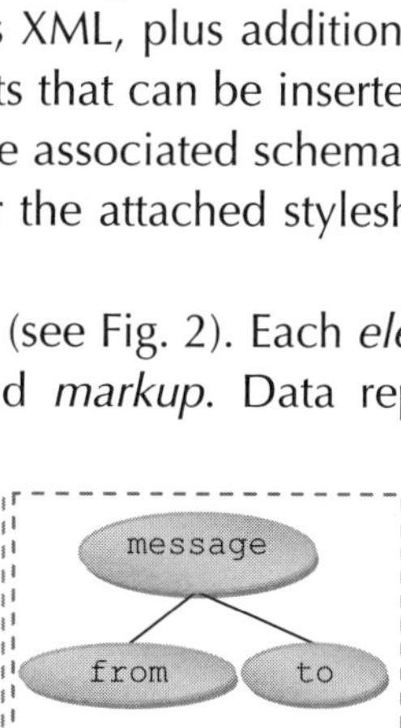

Fig. 1. An example of XML document (left) and the associate tree structure (right).

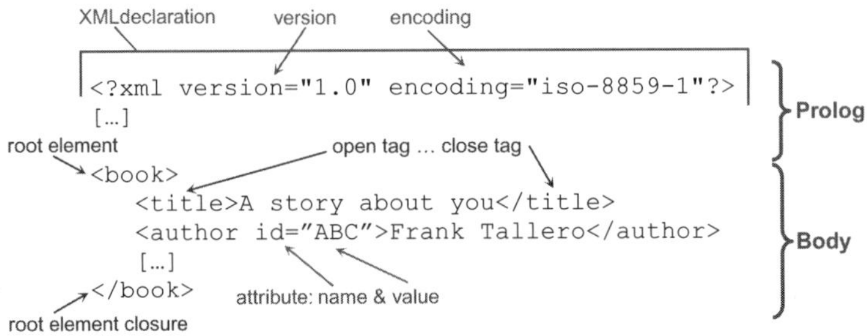

Fig. 2. An example of XML document. The prolog and the body are outlined as the root element. The image also shows the syntax for opening and closing a tag and the syntax for an attribute.

the actual content, thus the information to be structured. Markup, instead, are *meta-information* about data that describes it. What follows is an example for an element, structuring the information regarding a message body:

```
<message> This is the content </message>
```

For a reader who is familiar with HTML, the XML elements will be easy to understand, since the syntax is very similar. The markups are tags in the form `<tagName>...</tagName>`. Elements can also contain other elements and can have attributes. For the attributes, again, the syntax is very simple. Each attribute can be specified only in the element start tag and it has a *name* and a *value* and the value is enclosed strictly in double quotation-mark. Figure 2 shows an example of XML document outlining the prolog, the body, the elements and the attributes.

Empty elements do not have the closing tag `</tagName>`, instead, they have a "/" at the end. Code (4.1) represents an empty tag with attributes.

```
<book isbn="A234DX" />                                    (4.1)
```

When an element contains additional elements or attributes, it is defined as *complex*. In the following, we present two codes in XML of complex elements, structuring the same information:

```
<message>
  From Robert                                             (4.2)
  <to>Mario</to>
</message>
<message from="Robert">                                   (4.3)
<to>Robert</to>
</message>
```

In the years, different discussions are arisen within scientific and technical communities on when and why to encode information into attributes or as content in elements. There is not a specific rule and the choice depends on the designer. However, XML attributes are normally used to *describe* elements, or to provide additional information about elements. So, basically, *metadata* (data about data) should be stored as attributes, and that data itself should be stored as elements.

When necessary, comments can be inserted into an XML document. Their syntax is the same as for comments in HTML and it is the following:

```
<!-- This is a comment -->
```

An XML document can also contain *processing instructions.* Generally speaking, processing instructions encode application-specific data. The document declaration which opens every XML document is an example of a processing instruction. Processing instructions contain a target followed by data. Each instruction is enclosed in <? and ?> delimiters. The target identifies the application, and an application should ignore processing instructions for targets it does not recognize. Basically, processing instructions allow to enter directives into a XML document which are not part of the actual content, but which are passed up to different ad-hoc applications.

An XML document can use also *entities.* It could be easier to think of entities as a macro for programmers, or as aliases for more complex functions. A single entity name can take the place of a whole lot of text. An example of entity is showed below:

```
<!ENTITY myname "Laura">
```

Once defined, an entity can be recalled in the content of the document using the syntax "`&myname;`" and the following is a piece of XML code showing how to use the entity `myname`.

```
<details> My name is &myname; </details>
```

Finally, in a XML document *CDATA elements* can be used. A CDATA element tells the XML parser not to interpret or parse characters that appear in the section. An example is the following, where the content is parsable, even though it contains an unparsable character (the ampersand):

```
<hobbies><![CDATA[Singing & Swimming]]></hobbies>
```

4.1. *Well-formed XML documents*

Unlike HTML, which allows to create documents with errors in the structure which will be still rendered in a browser, XML has strict rules and a XML document must be correctly structured in order to be machine-understandable. The XML specification prohibits XML parsers from trying to fix and understand malformed documents. All a conforming parser is allowed to do is report the error.

Thus, an XML document must be *well-formed*. According to W3C, a well-formed XML document is defined as a document that:

- has at least one element.
- contains a unique opening and closing tag that enclose the whole document, called the root element.
- has all the elements with the closing tag, or empty elements correctly written.
- has all the tags and attributes names written accordingly to the case-sensitive rule, that is, for example that the tag `<name>` cannot be closed with `</Name>`. In other words, elements and attribute names may be any case chosen, as long as they are consistent.
- has all the elements properly nested, i.e., there must be an opening and a closing tag and the tags cannot overlap. For example if the tag `<name>` has been opened after the tag `<person>`, it must be closed before.
- has all the attribute values always quoted correctly.

These are the most important constraints for the well-formdness, but they are far to be a complete list: the XML Specifications [1] provides all the necessary details.

Well formed XML documents simply markup content with descriptive tags. This means that there is not the necessity to describe or explain what the chosen tags mean. We will see in Secs. 6 and 7 how DTDs and XML Schemas can define the meaning of the tags and can force the structure.

5. Namespaces

In XML, element names are defined by developers. This means that different organizations can use the same tag to markup content with different semantics. But XML has been invented also to allow interoperability and data exchange among different organizations so there must exist a way to combine several XML sources without ambiguity.

XML namespaces are used for providing uniquely named elements and attributes in an XML instance [13]. They are defined by a W3C recommendation called Namespaces in XML. As defined by the W3C, an XML namespace is a collection of XML elements and attributes identified by an Internationalized Resource Identifier (IRI); this collection is often referred to as an XML *vocabulary* [14].

Using namespaces, name conflicts can be solved thus allowing the correct integration among data. This means that, if each vocabulary has given a namespace then the ambiguity between identically named elements or attributes can be resolved.

Namespaces are declared as an attribute of an element by using the xmlns name attribute in the start tag of the element. It is not mandatory to declare namespaces only at the root element; rather it could be declared at any element in the XML document. A namespace has a scope which begins at the element where it has been declared and applies to the entire content of that element, unless overridden by another namespace declaration with the same prefix name [15]. A namespace is declared as follows, that can be read as binding the prefix *"myname"* with the namespace *http://www.whatever.com*:

```
<someTag xmlns:myname="http://www.whatever.com" />
```

So, the namespace declaration has the following syntax. `xmlns:prefix="URI"`. A Uniform Resource Identifier (URI) [3, 16] is a string of characters which identifies an Internet Resource. The most common URI is the Uniform Resource Locator (URL) which identifies an Internet domain address. Another, not so common type of URI is the Universal Resource Name (URN). Note that the URI is not actually read as an online address; it is simply treated by an XML parser as a string. Note also that, the empty string, though it is a legal URI reference, cannot be used as a namespace name.

A specific namespace identifies a *collection of names*. This collection can be made of element names, as in the case of the standard XHTML [9] or it can be a collection of attribute names, as in the case of XLink [17]. A namespace can collects names of properties (e.g., FOAF [18]) or can describe a set of functions, as it is the case for the XPath 2.0 Data Model [19].

6. Structuring XML documents: document type definition

As we said before, using XML, any developer can create his own well-formed documents in freedom, without any restriction or specific template rules on how to organize the tags. But, in case of organizations in which the XML documents must follow a specific grammar to be sharable and usable (as in the case of technical reports, e-commerce transactions, workers details), tools for describing the *shape* of all specific-topic XML documents are necessary [20].

The purpose of *Document Type Definition* (DTD) is exactly this. They provide a framework for validating XML documents by defining the legal building blocks of XML documents [3]. Basically, a DTD outlines what elements can be in an XML document and the attributes and sub-elements that they can take. Thus DTDs allow different organizations to create shareable data files.

A DTD can be part of the XML document, or it can be referred to by the XML document. In the first case, we call it an *inline* DTD while in the second case it is called *external* and it is a simple text file with ".dtd" extension.

DTDs embody a small syntax that can be mastered quite quickly. This syntax has several important components but can be summed into two essential structures, which are the *element* and the *attribute*. In the following subsections, we will describe the syntax used for these two types of declarations.

6.1. *Element declarations*

Element declarations describe the allowable set of elements within the document, and specify whether and how declared elements (and character data) may be contained within each element.

Recall that (Sec. 4) elements in XML documents can enclose other elements, can be empty, can contain content or can be mixed (containing content and other elements). In a DTD, the possible declarations for elements are the following:

- <!ELEMENT element-name (child1,child2,...)>, for an element containing other elements.
- <!ELEMENT element-name EMPTY>, for an empty element.
- <!ELEMENT element-name (#PCDATA)>, for an element containing directly content.
- <!ELEMENT element-name (#PCDATA|child1|otherchild1)*>, for a mixed element.
- <!ELEMENT element-name ANY>, for defining an element for which no further details are provided.

Additionally, a DTD must specify, by using special characters, how the elements can appear (i.e., in a given order) and if they can be repeated.

Table 1. A table indicating the special character to formalize repetitions and order when defining elements in a DTD.

Term	Meaning
,	Separates members of a sequence list and indicates sequential use of all members
|	Separates members of a choice list and requires use of one and only one member
+	Indicates a required and repeatable occurrence
*	Indicates an optional and repeatable occurrence
?	Indicates an optional occurrence

Specifically, the character "," defines an order, "|" defines alternatives (*either...or*), "()" group elements, "*" indicates any number (zero or more), "+" means at least once (one or more) and "?" marks for optional (zero or one). If there is no *, + or ?, the element must occur exactly one time.

For example, in case of XML documents describing books, with a title, multiple authors and different chapters, the definition of the element book will be the following:

```
<!element book (title,author+,chapter+)>
```

where we define that the element book can contain only other elements (not directly content) and, specifically a title (`title`), then one or more authors (author+) and successively one or more chapters (`chapter+`).

6.2. *Attribute-list declarations*

In the DTD, XML element attributes are declared with an `ATTLIST` declaration. Attribute-list declarations name the allowable set of attributes for each declared element, including the type of each attribute value, if not an explicit set of valid value(s) [22]. An attribute declaration has the following syntax:

```
<!ATTLIST elementName attributeName Type defaultValue>
```

There are the following attribute types: `CDATA` (Character set of data), `ID`, `IDREF` and `IDREFS`, `NMTOKEN` and `NMTOKENS`, `ENTITY` and `ENTITIES`, `NOTATION` and `NOTATIONS`, listings and `NOTATION`-listings. These data types are listed in Table 2.

A default value can be used to define whether an attribute must occur (`#REQUIRED`) or not (`#IMPLIED`), whether it has a fixed value (`#FIXED`), and which value should be used as a default value ("...") in case the given attribute is left out in an XML tag.

Table 2. A table showing the possible type of an attribute in a DTD declaration.

Value	Explanation
`CDATA`	The value is character data
`(eval|eval|..)`	The value must be an enumerated value
`ID`	The value is an unique id
`IDREF`	The value is the id of another element
`IDREFS`	The value is a list of other ids
`NMTOKEN`	The value is a valid XML name
`NMTOKENS`	The value is a list of valid XML names
`ENTITY`	The value is an entity
`ENTITIES`	The value is a list of entities
`NOTATION`	The value is a name of a notation
`xml:`	The value is predefined

6.3. *Valid XML documents: including DTDs into XML*

The document type declaration, which is situated after the XML declaration, is a mechanism for naming the document type to which a document complies and for including its definition. Valid XML documents must declare the document type to follow so that editors, browsers or converters can read the DTD to understand the template structure.

Well-formed documents can also include a document type declaration and include markup declarations in its external subset but are not required to do so. The document type declaration names the document type by making reference to the root element of the document. It can make reference to an external DTD, called the *external DTD subset*, include the DTD internally in the *internal DTD subset* or use both. Document type declarations take the general form [22]:

```
<!DOCTYPE NAME SYSTEM "file">
```

An XML document which must be compliant with respect to a DTD has the attribute `standalone` in the XML declaration set to `yes`. This means that the very first line of a document which follows a specific DTD will be the following:

```
<?xml version="1.0" standalone="no" [...] ?>
```

A XML document is defined to be *valid* if it is a *well-formed* document and it is conforms to the rules of a given Document Type Definition (DTD).

DTD

```
<!ELEMENT message (from,to+,body) >
<!ELEMENT from #PCDATA >
<!ELEMENT to #PCDATA >
<!ELEMENT body #PCDATA >
<!ATTLIST message reply (yes|no) "no" >
```

Valid XML document

```
<?xml version="1.0" standalone="no"
                    encoding="iso-8859-1"?>
<!DOCTYPE message SYSTEM "message.dtd">
<message reply="yes">
  <from>Laura</from>
  <to>John</to>
  <to>Robert</to>
  <body>this is the message body</body>
</message>
```

Fig. 3. A DTD modeling the structure of XML documents containing messages and a valid XML document with respect to the given DTD.

Valid XML documents offer much more to the document process than their well-formed counterparts. Document authoring, processing, storage and display are made easier because documents exist in a structured environment.

In the following, Fig. 3, we show an example of DTD and a valid XML document with respect to it.

7. Structuring XML documents: XML schemas

DTDs have been inherited by XML from its predecessor SGML, and were a good way to get XML started off quickly and give SGML people something familiar to work with. Nevertheless it soon became apparent that a more expressive solution that itself uses XML was needed.

First of all, DTDs do not make use of XML syntax. Second, DTDs have no constraints on character data, meaning that if a character data is allowed, any character data is allowed. Also, for DTDs, there is not a good support for schema evolution, extension, or inheritance of declarations. For what concern elements and attributes, DTDs provide too simple attribute value models, since enumerations are clearly insufficient, they provide a too simple ID attribute mechanism and allow only default values for attributes, not for elements.

XML Schema (second edition), which became a W3C recommendation in 2004, offers a rich and flexible mechanism for defining XML vocabularies, in alternative to DTDs. The main differences between DTDs and Schemas are that the second are written in XML syntax and that are always external documents. The XML Schema specification is divided into three specifications:

- *XML Schema Part 0: Primer* [23], which intends to provide a description of the XML Schema facilities and of the language
- *XML Schema Part 1: Structures* [24] and *XML Schema Part 2: Datatypes* [25] which provide the complete normative description of the XML Schema language.

To describe all the characteristics of the XML Schema language is out of the scope of this chapter, since a book by itself would be necessary. Here, we will outline the properties of the language providing explicative examples. The reader can refer to the online specifications [26] or to the available books on this topics [6, 22] to have more details.

An XML schema (called also XSD) is an XML document. It starts with the document declaration and continues by opening the root element `<schema>` and by defining the specific namespace. Within this root element all the specifications are defined. The schema ends closing the root element `</schema>`, as any well-formed XML document. Thus, in an XSD file (a simple text file with extension ".xsd"), the skeleton is the following:

```
<?xml version="1.0"?>
<xsd:schema xmlns:xsd=http://www.w3.org/2001/XMLSchema>
      [… body of the schema …]
</xsd:schema>
```

The body of the schema contains element declarations. There exist four main schema elements:

- `xsd:element` declares an element and assigns it a type.
- `xsd:attribute` declares an attribute and assigns it a type.
- `xsd:complexType` defines a new complex type.
- `xsd:simpleType` defines a new simple type.

This means that elements are declared using the element `xsd:element`, and attributes are declared using the `xsd:attribute` element. XML Schema provides a set of 19 primitive data types (e.g., boolean, string, decimal, date, time, dateTime, gYear, gDay, and NOTATION). They can be used directly in an element or attribute definition, as the examples below

```
<xsd:element name="name" type="xsd:string" />
<xsd:attribute name="age" type="xsd:integer" />
```

The two tags `xsd:complexType` and `xsd:simpleType` are used, instead, to define *new types*. Simple declarations define elements that do not have any children or attributes and can only contain text, while complex declarations describe elements that can have children and attributes as well as text.

The declarations are not themselves types, but rather an association between a name and the constraints which govern the appearance of that name in documents governed by the associated schema [22]. The following is an example of an XSD portion defining an element "`book`" of a user-defined complex type "`bookType`". Any sub-elements in the `bookType` definition is a simple element of type `string` or a number (`gYear`). The element `<xsd:sequence>` identifies a sequence of elements.

```
<xsd:element name="book" type="bookType"/>
<xsd:complexType name="bookType">
  <xsd:sequence>
      <xsd:element name="title" type="xsd:string"
         minOccurs="1" maxOccurs="1"/>
      <xsd:element name="author" type="xsd:string" />
      <xsd:element name="year" type="xsd:gYear" />
  </xsd:sequence>
</xsd:complexType>
```

XSD documents have more possibilities than DTDs for expressing cardinalities on elements belonging to a specific type. In a DTD repetitions and order can be given using special characters (Sec. 5) such as * or +. XSD uses the attributes `minOccurs` and `maxOccurs` to define cardinalities. In the example above, the directive says that the element "`title`" will occur only one time within the element "`book`". Also, it is possible to define a complex type inside the element that will use it (if it will be used only for that specific element). In this case, the complex type is called *anonymous* and the syntax will be the following:

```
<xsd:element name="book">
  <xsd:complexType>
      [... complex type definition ...]
  </xsd:complexType>
</xsd:element>
```

If necessary, XSD documents allow to derive new simple types from existing types, by using the `xsd:simpleType` element. It basically defines a subtype. The *name* attribute assigns a name to the new type, by which it can be referred to in a `xsd:element` type attributes. Different type of elements can be used to define the subtype. In particular:

- An `xsd:restriction` child element derives by restricting the legal values of the base type.
- An `xsd:list` child element derives a type as a white space separated list of base type instances.
- An `xsd:union` child element derives by combining legal values from multiple base types.

In the following, we present an example in which a new simple type (animal) is defined as enumeration of possible string values (dog or cat) and an element (webby) is defines of type animal.

```
<xsd:simpleType name="animal">
  <xsd:restriction base="xsd:string">
     <xsd:enumeration value="dog"/>
     <xsd:enumeration value="cat"/>
  </xsd:restriction>
</xsd:simpleType>
<xsd:element name="webby" type="animal" />
```

In the following, we provide an example of XML Schema to define the structure of XML documents which must follow the grammar defined by the DTD in the section before

XML Schema

```
<?xml version="1.0"?>
<xsd:schema
     xmlns:xsd=http://www.w3.org/2001/XMLSchema>
<xsd:element name="message" type="messageType"/>
  <xsd:complexType name="messageType">
    <xsd:sequence>
      <xsd:element name="from" type="xsd:string"
        minOccurs="1" maxOccurs="1"/>
      <xsd:element name="to" type="xsd:string"
        minOccurs="1" maxOccurs="unbounded"/>
      <xsd:element name="author" type="xsd:string" />
      <xsd:element name="body" type="xsd:string"
        minOccurs="1" maxOccurs="1"/>
    </xsd:sequence>
     <xsd:attribute
       name="reply" type="xsd:boolean" default="no"/>
  </xsd:complexType>
</xsd:element>
</xsd:schema>
```

To complete this section, we recall that there is a multitude of tools for validating and editing schemas in XSD on the net, open source or commercial. To have an idea the reader can visit the *XML Schema Working Group* website at W3C [26].

8. Rendering XML documents via CSS

As we have said in the previous sections, XML is born to *structure content*, not to display it. This means that, if an XML document is displayed in a browser it will be showed as text, without any formatting (actually some browsers support the user by showing the tree structure of the document, but nothing more). See, for example Fig. 4(a). This is perfectly in line with the main goals of XML.

Anyway, there is a way in which the web representation of an XML document can be improved. Basically, a CSS stylesheet can be applied similarly to what can be done (and must be done) with HTML files.

CSS is a language used to describe the presentation (that is, the look and formatting) of a document written in a markup language [27, 28, 29]. A CSS document is basically constituted by a set of rules that must be applied to elements in the reference file. A rule consists of two parts: a *selector* and a *declaration*, with the syntax:

```
selector {property1:value; property2:value;}
```

The *selector* is the reference to the element in the file that must be rendered and the *declaration* is that part of the rule that sets forth what the effect

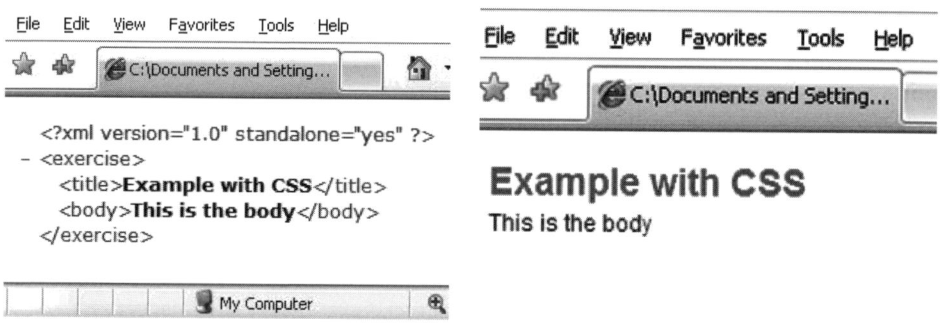

(a) (b)

Fig. 4. (a) An example of an XML document and how it is rendered in a browser. No specific formatting is applied. (b) The same XML document with a CSS stylesheet applied.

will be. The following is an example of rule applied to an element `H1` in a HTML page.

```
H1 {color:black;}
```

CSS2 (Cascading Stylesheet Level 2) defines around 120 properties and for all of them, different values can be assigned. For a tutorial on CSS/CSS2 see, for example [28] or the last specification at [29].

CSS/CSS2 stylesheet can be easily added to HTML documents using the `link` element which create a link to the external stylesheet. In XML it is possible to attach external stylesheets by means of the `xml-stylesheet` processing instruction, which must be placed in the prolog of the XML document. The syntax is the following:

```
<?xml-stylesheet href="thestyle.css" type="text/css"?>
```

Just as with the `link` element of HTML, there can be multiple `xml-stylesheet` processing instructions, meaning that is it possible to attach multiple stylesheets to an XML document. The possible attributes are *type*, *medium* and *title*, so that each stylesheet can have a local name (title), can be applied if the display medium is of a given type (print, screen..) and it has a specific type (usually text/css).

To show how to attach a CSS stylesheet to an XML document, we provide here a very simple example. Given the following XML code, it will be rendered in a browser as showed in Fig. 4(a).

```
<?xml version="1.0" standalone="yes" ?>
<exercise>
  <title>Example with CSS</title>
  <body>This is the body</body>
</exercise>
```

By adding the processing instruction for including a CSS stylesheet (named *style1.css*), the resulting XML code will be

```
<?xml version="1.0" standalone="yes" ?>
<?xml-stylesheet href="style1.css" type="text/css" ?>
<exercise>
  <title>Example with CSS</title>
  <body>This is the body</body>
</exercise>
```

The CSS file contains the following simple rules, one for the element `exercise` (thus it applies to the element and all its children), one for the element `title` and another for the element `body`. The results of applying style1.css to the XML document is showed in Fig. 4(b).

```
exercise        { font-family:Arial }
title           { display:block; color:red;
                  font-size:14pt;
                  font-weight:bold }
body            { color:black; font-size:12px }
```

Note that, even if the tags are no more visible in the browser window, the entire XML document is freely readable looking at the code of the page. Also, the way in which the information are presented follows strictly the order in which they have been modeled in the XML document (as in the case of simple HTML pages). Suppose, for example, that the initial XML document was related to a list of books for a library, it is impossible to show them in an alphabetic order, if the books have not been inserted in that order. Additionally, if part of the content has been modeled inside attributes, there is no way to access to the attributes values and to show them in the rendered page. These are some of the limitations of CSS (CSS2) in the context of XML documents. An immediate observation is that XML is not a replacement of HTML, thus, for creating web pages, HTML (or — better — XHTML) is more than enough. XML exists for *structuring data* and means for modifying, transforming and interrogating this data are necessary.

In the following section, we will show how XSL and XSLT support this type of functionalities.

9. Transforming and rendering XML documents: XSLT, XPath, XSL-FO

XSL is a family of recommendations for defining XML document transformation and presentation [30]. *Extensible Stylesheet Language* (languages) has the main goal to create stylesheets. Basically, an XSL engine uses these stylesheets to transform XML documents into other documents, and to format the output according to specific formatting templates. The XSL family consists of three main sub-languages:

- *XSL Transformations* (*XSLT*) [31] which is an XML-based language for transforming XML documents into other XML documents (even XHTML);
- the *XML Path Language* (*XPath*), [19] which is an expression language used by XSLT to access or refer to parts of an XML document;

- *XSL Formatting Objects* (*XSL-FO*), [32] which is an XML vocabulary for specifying formatting semantics (that can be used instead of CSS).

In the following subsections, we will briefly review the three languages, with simple examples that will support the reader in understanding how the transformation and rendering operations work on XML documents. The topic, however, is too large to be condensed in a single section of a chapter. Thus, we suggest the reader to consult books on these topics [33, 34] or the W3C online specifications [31].

Since XML documents can be represented as trees, in XSL, usually, the input document is called the *source tree*, and the output document the *result tree*.

9.1. *XSL transformations (XSLT) and the XML path language (XPath)*

XSLT is a powerful language for transforming XML documents into something else that can be an HTML document, another XML document, a Portable Document Format (PDF) file, a Scalable Vector Graphics (SVG) file, a flat text file, or most anything possible [34]. The general idea is that, an XSLT stylesheet defines the rules for transforming an XML document and the chosen XSLT processor does the work and produces the output.

XSLT relies on a technology called *XPath*. The XPath language allows XSLT identify nodes (elements, attributes, and other objects) in XML documents, as well as it provides functions for performing calculations [33].

To understand how XSLT works, we start from a XML document and we apply a XSLT template to transform the content of this document in a HTML page. The input XML document is the following:

```
<?xml version="1.0" standalone="yes" ?>
<TitleBook>This title will become H1</TitleBook>
```

It is a very simple document, with only the root element `TitleBook` which contains directly the content, with no other sub-elements. The objective of the XSLT transformation we are going to produce, is to take the content in the element `TitleBook` and to put it inside an `H1` tag of a HTML page.

Recall that an XSLT transformation file is, first of all, an XML document, thus it follows the same syntax of any other XML. Also, in order to "use" the

XSLT language we have to define the appropriate namespace. The skeleton of transformation file will be:

```
<?xml version="1.0" standalone="yes" ?>
<xsl:stylesheet version="1.0"
     xmlns:xsl="http://www.w3.org/1999/XSL/Transform">
<output method="html"/>
  [… other directives …]
</xsl:stylesheet>
```

The first line is the XML declaration, the second defines the root element `<xsl:stylesheet>` and the XSLT namespace (prefix `xsl:`) with the official W3C URI `http://www.w3.org/1999/XSL/Transform`. The third line, instead, provides a directive on the output method, namely HTML. As any well-formed XML, the stylesheet ends with the root element closing tag, in this case, `</xsl:stylesheet>`.

The other necessary directives are few and simple. First of all we need to intercept the root element and we need to apply a stylesheet template on it, taking the content associate and rewriting it as content of the HTML tag H1.

For doing this, we use the following code:

```
<xsl:template match = "/" >
  <html><body>
     <h1><xsl:value-of select = "TitleBook" /></h1>
  </body></html>
</xsl:template>
```

Basically, we define a *template* and we apply it to the XML portion which is described in the attribute `match`. In this case XPath language is used to intercept the desired element. In the example, the expression "/" identifies the root element (similarly to what we can do in a file system). There are different possible XPath expressions the can be used which allow to fetch every element, entity or attribute in the document. Table 3 provides a selection of XPath expressions [35].

Once the root element (node in the source tree) has been selected, we "extract" the content using another XSLT directive `<xsl:value-of…>`. It has an attribute `select` which contains another XPath expression. In the case of the example, we extract the content inside the element `TitleBook`. Finally, by putting the necessary HTML tags and the `h1` tag "around" the extracted content, we create the web page.

Taking a XSLT processor (even the modern browsers support this feature) and giving in input both the XML and the XSLT documents, it interprets the

Table 3. A selection of XPath expressions, divided into node oriented, sign oriented and Boolean.

Name	Return value
Node-Set-oriented	
`last()`	Number (of elements)
`count(node-set)`	Number of nodes in node-set
`name(node-set?)`	First node name in node-set
Sign oriented	
`concat(string,string*)`	Sequence of arguments
`starts-with(string,string)`	True if first string begins with second one
`contains(string,string)`	True if first string includes second one
Boolean	
`not()`	True if argument is not true
`true()/false()`	True/not true

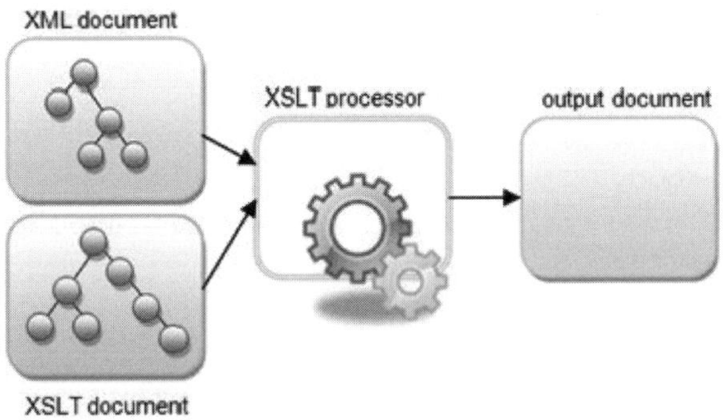

Fig. 5. One or more XML documents with one or more XSLT transformations are passed to the XSLT processor which builds the output document.

XSLT directive and creates the new HTML page. Actually, XML, XSLT, and XPath are correctly supported by the following browsers: Mozilla Firefox 3, Internet Explorer 6+, Google Chrome, Opera 9 and Apple Safari 3+.

The operational schema of an XSLT transformation is the one presented in Fig. 5.

The element `<template>` is the main element of a XSLT document. The number of elements (directives) it can contain is very high. We provide here some examples to let the user understand the power of the language.

A template can be iteratively applied to elements in the XML document using different tags, as, for example `<xsl:for-each ...>`. This is the case of a loop for each element satisfying the XPath expression inside the attribute

Table 4. Few examples of elements in XSLT for capturing, choosing content in XML documents, as well as defining templates of transformations on the basis of specific conditions.

Element syntax	Meaning and notes
<xsl:if test="..."> ... </xsl:if>	Yes or No conditions The condition is inside attribute test
<xsl:variable name="type" select="@type"/>	Allows a variable to be declared name is the variable name. It can be referred to later with $name select is the value of the variable
<xsl:when test="..."> ... </xsl:when>	Yes or No conditions test specifies criteria for entering the if
<xsl:choose> ... </xsl:choose>	Multiple choices No attributes
<xsl:for-each select="..."> ... </xsl:for-each>	Creates a loop which repeats for every match. select designates the match criteria
<xsl:apply-templates/>	Specifies that other matches may exist within that node; if this is not specified any matches will be ignored If select is specified, only the templates that specify a match that fits the selected node or attribute type will be applied. If mode is specified, only the templates that have the same mode and have an appropriate match will be applied
<xsl:text> a text </xsl:text>	Outputs the tag content
<xsl:value-of select="$s"/>	Outputs a variable Select specifies the variable

select of the <xsl:for-each ...> tag. For example the following code applies a template, selecting the content of each paragraph inside a chapter in the input XML document:

```
<xsl:template match="chapter">
  <xsl:for-each select="paragraph">
    <xsl:value-of select=".">
  </xsl:for-each>
</xsl:template>
```

Table 4 presents a set of elements for XSLT to provide an idea of the main functionalities.

9.2. *XSL formatting objects XSL-FO*

XSL Formatting Objects (or Flow Objects) [32], or XSL-FO, is a XML-based markup language which describes the formatting of XML data for output to screen, paper or other media. Thanks to XSL-FO it is possible to produce, for example, documents in PDF format, RTF or even PS, starting from an input XML document. XSL-FO covers the basic presentation requirements for a wide range of display devices, including reflow or repagination for palmtop devices, and for the accessibility requirements that are now mandated by governments.

XSL-FO is used inside XSLT transformations. As described in the above subsection, an XSLT transformation take an XML document (source tree) and gives the directive to produce a result tree (the work is done by the processor, which interprets the directives). Once transformed, the operation of *formatting* — done by the XSL processor — interprets the result tree looking at the formatting objects contained into the directives specialized with the XSL-FO language.

The XSL-FO language was designed for paged media, thus the concept of *page* is an important part of its structure, and the formatting objects it provides give significant expressive power in dealing with how information is displayed on a page.

So, basically, XSL-FO documents are XML files with output information, usually stored in files with `.fo` or `.fob` extension. They contain two required sections: (i) the first section details a list of named page layouts; (ii) the second section is a list of document data, with markup, that uses the various page layouts to determine how the content fills the various pages. The skeleton of an XSL-FO document is the following:

```
<?xml version="1.0"?>
<fo:root xmlns:fo="http://www.w3.org/1999/XSL/Format">
  <fo:layout-master-set>
     <fo:simple-page-master master-name="A4">
        <!-- Page template goes here -->
     </fo:simple-page-master>
  </fo:layout-master-set>

  <fo:page-sequence master-reference="A4">
        <!-- Page content goes here -->
  </fo:page-sequence>
</fo:root>
```

As for the other XML-based languages described before, a XSL-FO document starts with a root element `<fo:root>` containing the appropriate namespace declaration, namely "`http://www.w3.org/1999/XSL/Format`". Two main elements are successively declared:

- `fo:layout-master-set` which contains the collection of definitions of page geometries and page selection patterns.
- `fo:page-sequence` which contains the definition of information for a sequence of pages with common static information.

The interpretation of the two main elements above it the following: when the formatter reads the XSL-FO document, it creates a page based on the first template in the `fo:layout-master-set`. Then it fills it with content from the `fo:page-sequence`. When it has filled the first page, it instantiates a second page based on a template, and fills it with content. The process continues until the formatter runs out of content [22].

9.3. *Page formatting*

The page templates are called *page masters*. Each defines a general layout for a page including its margins, the sizes of the header, footer, and body area of the page, and so forth. XSL-FO 1.0 defines exactly one kind of page master, the `fo:simple-page-master`, which represents a rectangular page. The `fo:layout-master-set` contains one or more `fo:simple-page-master` elements that define master pages.

For example, we present in the following portion of XSL-FO code a `fo:layout-master-set` containing one `fo:simple-page-master`. It contains a single region, the body, into which all content will be placed.

```
<fo:layout-master-set>
  <fo:simple-page-master master-name="…"
      page-height=".." page-width=".." […]>
      <fo:region-body/>
  </fo:simple-page-master>
</fo:layout-master-set>
```

9.4. *Page sequence management*

In addition to a `fo:layout-master-set`, as we said before, each formatting object document contains one or more `fo:page-sequence elements`. In this case, the XSL-FO specifies the sequence of pages, where each page has an associated page master that defines how the page will look. Each page sequence contains three child elements in this order:

(i) An optional `fo:title` element containing inline content that can be used as the title of the document.
(ii) Zero or more `fo:static-content` elements containing the for every page.
(iii) One `fo:flow` element containing data to be placed on each page in turn (in case of pagination).

The following is an example of code for defining the pages sequence:

```
<fo:page-sequence master-reference="chaps">
  <fo:static-content flow-name="…">
     <fo:block text-align="outside" …>
        Chapter
        <fo:retrieve-marker
                  retrieve-class-name="chapNum"/>
        <fo:leader leader-pattern="space" />
        <fo:retrieve-marker retrieve-class-name="chap"/>
        <fo:leader leader-pattern="space" />
        Page
        <fo:page-number font-style="normal" />
        of
        <fo:page-number-citation ref-id='end'/>
     </fo:block>
  </fo:static-content>
  <fo:flow flow-name="…">
     <fo:block>
        <!-- Output goes here -->
     </fo:block>
  </fo:flow>
</fo:page-sequence>
```

In the example, the sequence of pages is defined for chapters in a book and the portion of document gives directives for the rendering of the chapter numbers, the page number and other information.

9.5. *Formatting objects*

The vocabulary of formatting objects supported by XSL-FO represents the set of typographic abstractions available. Some of them are very similar to properties that can be found in CSS. For example, it is possible to enrich text with character-level formatting. There exist several properties control font styles — family, size, color, weight, etc. The following is an example:

```
<fo:block font-family="Times" font-size="14pt">
  This text will be Times of size 14pt!
</fo:block>
```

Other formatting objects are specialized to describe the output on different media (pagination, borders and so on). Each formatting object class represents a particular kind of formatting behavior. For example, the `block` formatting object class represents the breaking of the content of a paragraph into lines [32, 37]. The following is an example:

```
<fo:block line-height="1.0" text-align="justify">
  Example of a justified formatted block.
  The space between lines is 1.0.
</fo:block>
```

Another example is the `list-item` formatting object which is a box containing two other formatting objects, namely `list-item-label` and `list-item-body`. The first one (`list-item-label`) is basically a box that contains a bullet, a number, or another indicator placed in front of a list item, the second one (`list-item-body`) is a box that contains the text of the list item.

Tables, lists, side floats, and a variety of other features are available. These features are comparable to CSS's layout features, though some of those features are expected to be built by the XSLT even before the application of XSL-FO, if necessary.

To conclude this section, we outline that there is a multitude of processors which are able to interpret the XSL family of technologies. The reader can refer to the official XSL web page at W3C for a complete list [30].

10. Conclusions and outlook

In this chapter, we have provided an introduction to XML, presenting its main goals and trying to focus on the great impact it had in the development of the modern Web Technologies. We outlined how XML is a meta-language for defining new languages potentially on every application domain.

We provided notions on the syntax and the ways in which organizations, companies and institutions can structure the content of XML documents by using DTDs and XML Schemas. We reviewed also how XML documents can be rendered, using CSS stylesheets and how they can be transformed and rendered using XSL/XSLT, which are powerful XML-based languages for creating directives to deal with XML documents.

It can be easily understood, by simply searching on the web the "XML" word, which is the incredible impact of XML in scientific and industrial scenarios. It has been proved to be a powerful mean to allow interoperability and to improve communications among business entities, which has emerged to be a real necessity thanks also to the evolution of the Web. Looking at the W3C home page, it is clear how many different technologies have been developed upon or around XML. Several working groups and activities have been defined and are active in many different topics related to XML.

In the context of this book, the Semantic Web Activity is maybe the most interesting [38]. The Semantic Web is a web of data, as the reader will discover in the other chapters of this book. This activity includes different recommendations, most of them designed on XML, as for example:

- Resource Description Framework (RDF) [12] is an XML text format that supports resource description and metadata applications.
- GRDDL [40] is a mechanism for gleaning resource descriptions from dialects of languages. It introduces markup based on existing standards for declaring that an XML document includes data compatible with the Resource Description Framework (RDF) and for linking to algorithms (typically represented in XSLT), for extracting this data from the document.
- The Web Ontology Language OWL [39] is a semantic markup language for publishing and sharing ontologies on the World Wide Web. OWL is developed as a vocabulary extension of RDF and is derived from the DAML+OIL Web Ontology Language.
- SPARQL query language for RDF, which can be used to express queries across diverse data sources [41].

However, for sake of completeness, we would like to remember that there are many other standards and on-going works of XML-based languages, as for example:

- XHTML: This is the XML-version of HTML 4.0 [9].
- Chemical Markup Language (CML): CML is used for molecular information management [10].

- Simple Object Access Protocol (SOAP): A protocol that is object based and used for information exchange in a decentralized and distributed environment [11].
- Synchronized Multimedia Integration Language (SMIL, pronounced "smile"). SMIL 3.0 defines an XML-based language that allows authors to write interactive multimedia presentations.
- Scalable Vector Graphics (SVG), is a language for describing two-dimensional graphics and graphical applications in XML.
- XML Query (XQuery), is a standardized language for combining documents, databases, Web pages and almost anything else.
- WSDL: Web Service Description Language. An XML format for describing XML web services, including the type definitions, messages and actions used by that service. The WSDL document should tell applications all they need to know to invoke a particular web service.

Acknowledgments

I would like to thank all the authors of existing books and online tutorials on XML who, being also on the web, allow to spread the knowledge on this powerful technology.

References

1. Extensible Markup Language (XML) 1.0 Fifth Edition (2008). W3C Recommendation, T Bray, J Paoli, CM Sperberg-McQueen, E Maler and F Yergeau (eds.). Available at www.w3.org/TR/REC-xml/
2. XML. Wikipedia, the free encyclopedia. Available at http://en.wikipedia.org/wiki/XML [accessed on 2009].
3. St. Laurent, S (1999). *XML: A Primer.* Foster City: M&T Books.
4. Bryan, M (1998). An introduction to the extensible markup language (XML). *Bulletin of the American Society for Information Science,* 25(1), 11–14.
5. Introduction to XML. W3Schools. Available at www.w3schools.com/XML/ [accessed on 2009].
6. Møller, A and MI Schwartzbach (2006). *An Introduction to XML and Web Technologies.* Reading: Addison-Wesley. ISBN: 0321269667.
7. Attipoe, A and P Vijghen (1999). XML/SGML: On the web and behind the web. *InterChange: Newsletter of the International SGML/XML Users' Group,* 5(3), 25–29.
8. Bosak, J (2003). The birth of XML: A personal recollection. Available at http://java.sun.com/xml/

9. XHTML™ 1.0 The Extensible HyperText Markup Language (Second Edition) A Reformulation of HTML 4 in XML 1.0 (2002) W3C Recommendation. Available at www.w3.org/TR/html/
10. Rust, PM and HS Rzepa (1999). Chemical markup, XML, and the world wide web. Basic principles. *J. Chem. Inf. Comput. Sci.*, 39, 928–942.
11. SOAP Version 1.2 Part 0: Primer (Second Edition) (2007). W3C Recommendation. Available at www.w3.org/TR/soap/
12. Resource Description Framework (RDF) (2004). W3C Recommendation. Available at www.w3.org/RDF
13. XML namespace. Wikipedia, the free encyclopedia. Available at http://en.wikipedia.org/wiki/XML_namespace [accessed on 2009].
14. Namespaces in XML 1.0 (Second Edition) (2006). W3C Recommendation. Available at www.w3.org/TR/xml-names/
15. Srivastava, R. XML schema: Understanding namespaces, oracle. Available at www.oracle.com/technology/pub/articles/srivastava_namespaces.html
16. Uniform Resource Identifier. Wikipedia, the free encyclopedia. Available at http://en.wikipedia.org/wiki/Uniform_Resource_Identifier
17. XML Linking Language (XLink) Version 1.0 (2001). W3C Recommendation, Available at www.w3.org/TR/xlink/
18. FOAF Vocabulary Specification 0.91 (2007). Namespace Document OpenID Edition. Available at http://xmlns.com/foaf/spec/
19. XML Path Language (XPath) Version 1.0 (1999). W3C Recommendation. Available at www.w3.org/TR/xpath
20. Maler, E. Guide to the W3C XML Specification ("XMLspec") DTD, Version 2.1. Available at www.w3.org/XML/1998/06/xmlspec-report-v21.htm [accessed on 2009].
21. XML Core Working Group Public Page. Available at www.w3.org/XML/Core/ [accessed on 2009].
22. Harold, ER (2001). *XML Bible*, 2nd edn. New York, NY, USA: John Wiley & Sons, Inc.
23. XML Schema Part 0: Primer Second Edition (2004). W3C Recommendation, DC Fallside and P Walmsley (eds.). Available at www.w3.org/TR/xmlschema-0/
24. XML Schema Part 1: Structures Second Edition (2004). W3C Recommendation, HS Thompson, D Beech, M Maloney and N Mendelsohn (eds.). Available at www.w3.org/TR/xmlschema-1/
25. XML Schema Part 2: Datatypes Second Edition (2004). W3C Recommendation, PV Biron, K Permanente and A Malhotra (eds.). Available at www.w3.org/TR/xmlschema-2/
26. The XML Schema Working Group (2001). Available at www.w3.org/XML/Schema

27. Cascading Style Sheets Home Page (2009). Available at www.w3.org/Style/CSS/
28. Lie, HW and B Bos (1999). Cascading Style Sheets, designing for the Web, 2nd edn. Reading: Addison Wesley. ISBN 0-201-59625-3.
29. Cascading Style Sheets Level 2 (CSS 2.1) Specification (2009). W3C Candidate Recommendation, B Bos, T Çelik, I Hickson and HW Lie (eds.). Available at www.w3.org/TR/REC-CSS2.
30. The Extensible Stylesheet Language Family (XSL). Available at http://www.w3.org/Style/XSL/
31. XSL Transformations (XSLT) Version 2.0 (2007). W3C Recommendation. Available at www.w3.org/TR/xslt20/
32. Extensible Stylesheet Language (XSL) Version 1.1 (2006). W3C Recommendation. Available at www.w3.org/TR/xsl/
33. Fitzgerald, M (2003). *Learning XSLT.* O'Reilly Press. ISBN 10: 0-596-00327-7.
34. Tidwell, D (2008). XSLT, 2nd edn., Mastering XML Transformations. O'Reilly Press. ISBN 10: 0-596-52721-7.
35. Kay, M (2000). *XSLT Programmer's Reference.* Birmingham: Wrox Press.
36. Holman, GK (2002). What Is XSL-FO. Available at www.xml.com/pub/a/2002/03/20/xsl-fo.html
37. How to Develop Stylesheet for XML to XSL-FO Transformation (2007). Antenna House, Inc. Available at www.antennahouse.com/XSLsample/howtoRC/Howto-develop-en-2a.pdf
38. The Semantic Web Activity, W3C. Available at www.w3.org/2001/sw/
39. The Web Ontology Language OWL, (2004). W3C Recommendation. Available at www.w3.org/TR/owl-ref/
40. Gleaning Resource Descriptions from Dialects of Languages (GRDDL) (2007). W3C Recommendation. Available at www.w3.org/TR/grddl/
41. SPARQL Query Language for RDF (2008). W3C Recommendation. Available at www.w3.org/TR/rdf-sparql-query/

CHAPTER II.2

ONTOLOGIES AND ONTOLOGY LANGUAGES

Sinuhé Arroyo

Information Engineering Research Unit, University of Alcalá de Henares
Ctra. Barcelona km 33,6. 28871, Alcalá deHenares, Madrid, Spain
sinuhe.arroyo@alu.uah.es

Katharina Siorpaes

STI Innsbruck, University of Innsbruck
ICT - Technologie Park Innsbruck,2nd Floor, Technikerstraße 21a, 6020 Innsbruck, Austria
katharina.siorpaes@sti2.at

In the first part of this chapter, we give a general overview of the most relevant existing approaches to modeling metadata, namely, controlled vocabularies, taxonomies, thesaurus and ontologies. Later the discussion focuses around ontologies, paying careful attention to explaining various key aspects such as the relation between ontologies and knowledge bases, the difference between light and heavy weight ontologies, and the main ontological commitments. Finally, the most relevant semantic web languages currently available are presented. Doing so, a thorough review of RDF, OWL and WSML is provided, where their main variants, underlying formalisms and main applicability are carefully reviewed.

1. Introduction

During the last years the Web has undergone an immense development. However, there are still open issues that limit the further explosion of the Web. From a technical point of view there are mainly two limitations to the impact the Web will have in our world. On the one hand, the computing power could place a burden on the capabilities and realization of new ideas and applications. On the other hand, it is the expressiveness of the formalism subjacent to computer science itself that could limit its expansion and impact. Yet, neither of them seems to currently pose a major obstacle. Actually, computing power continues to grow year after year challenging the limits of physics. Conversely, new ever demanding applications are developed that challenge and push forward the expressiveness and capabilities of computers.

It is precisely in the context of further advancing the expressiveness of the formalisms subjacent to computer science that the concept and idea of the Semantic Web has been conceived. Roughly speaking, the current Web defines a system of interlinked, hypertext documents running over the Internet mainly characterized by the static and syntactic nature of the information codified. This means that only the human reader can understand and intelligently process the contents available. Therefore, current Web technology is only able to exploit but very little of the information available. Also the information processing capabilities of modern computers are not brought to their full potential. They are used solely as information rendering devices, which present content in a human-understandable format.

In order to rise above these limitations, more expressive approaches are required that exploit all the capabilities computers and computer science can offer. The Semantic Web has precisely these objectives. The Semantic Web is the next generation of the WWW where information has machine-processable and machine-understandable semantics. The Semantic Web is an evolving extension of the Web in which content can be expressed not only in natural language, but also in a form that can be understood, interpreted and used by software agents, thus permitting them to find, share and integrate information more easily. In short, this novel technology brings structure to the meaningful content of the Web, being not a separate Web, but an augmentation of the current one, where information is given a well-defined meaning.

The core concept behind the Semantic Web is the representation of data in a machine interpretable way. Ontologies facilitate the means to realize such representation. They characterize formal and consensual specifications of conceptualizations, providing a shared and common understanding of a domain as data and information machine-processable semantics, which can be communicated among agents (organizations, individuals, and software) [7]. Ontologies put in place the means to describe the basic categories and relationships of things by defining entities and types of entities within its framework.

Ontologies bring together two essential aspects that are necessary to enhance the Web with semantic technology. Firstly, they provide machine processability by defining formal information semantics. Secondly, they provide machine–human understanding due to their ability to specify conceptualization of the real-world. By these means, ontologies link machine processable content with human meaning using a consensual terminology as connecting element [7].

It is the case that certain ontological aspects such as the relation to knowledge bases, the differences between lightweight and heavyweight ontologies or understanding the meaning of using or extending an ontology, the so-called ontological commitments are not always clear to the user. Therefore, additional clarification is required and we aim at providing it in this chapter.

Currently, a number of technologies exist that enable modeling and authoring ontologies, the Semantic Web Languages. These languages offer different levels of expressivity and inference capabilities based on the logic formalism used. Choosing the right one for the intended application domain is sometimes a question of balance between the former factors and the availability of tools. In this book chapter, we provide a review of the most relevant ones with the aim of trying to alleviate this problem.

In detail, this chapter is organized as follows. Section 2 explores the concepts and ideas behind metadata glossaries. The most relevant paradigms are carefully depicted with the aim of showing their different pros and cons, while evolving towards the concept of ontology. Section 3 introduces relevant ontology languages, i.e., Resource Description Framework (RDF), Web Ontology Language (OWL), Web Service Modeling Language (WSML), and Simple Knowledge Organization System (SKOS). Doing so, we examine their main features, applications and core characteristics. Finally, Chapter 4 concludes outlining the results of this work.

2. Metadata glossary: from controlled vocabularies to ontologies

In this section we portrait the main characteristics and differentiating aspects of controlled vocabularies, taxonomies, thesauri and ontologies. The aim is to provide the reader with the understanding required to assess the usage and application of each paradigm.

2.1. *Controlled vocabularies*

A controlled vocabulary is a finite list of preferred terms used for the purpose of easing content retrieval. Controlled vocabularies consist of pre-defined,

Fig. 1. Dog in the Wikispecies taxonomy.[3]

authorized terms, which is in sharp contrast to natural language vocabularies that typically evolve freely without restrictions. Controlled vocabularies can be used for categorizing content, building labeling systems or defining database schemas among others. A catalog is a good example of a controlled vocabulary.

[1] Screenshot from http://species.wikimedia.org/wiki/Dog

2.2. *Taxonomies*

The discipline taxonomy refers to the science of classification. The term has its etymological root in the Greek word *taxis,* meaning *order* and *nomos,* with the meaning of *law* or *science.*

In our context, taxonomy is best defined as a set of controlled vocabulary terms. Each individual vocabulary term is known as *taxa.* Taxa identify units of meaningful content in a given domain. Taxonomies are usually arranged following a hierarchical structure, grouping kinds of things into some order (e.g., alphabetical list).

A good example for a taxonomy is the Wikispecies[2] project, which aims at creating a directory of species. In the "Taxonavigation" the path in the taxonomy leading to the species is depicted. This is visualized for the example of the species dog in Fig. 1.

2.3. *Thesauri*

The term *thesaurus* has its etymological root in the ancient Greek word *θησαυρός,* which evolved into the Latin word *thesaurus.* In both, the cultures, thesaurus meant *storehouse* or *treasury,* in the sense of repository of words.[3] A thesaurus is therefore similar to a dictionary with the difference that it does not provide word definitions, its scope is limited to a particular domain, entry terms are single-word or multi-word entries and that it facilitates limited cross-referencing among the contained terms, e.g., synonyms and antonyms [17, 23].

A thesaurus should not be considered as an exhaustive list of terms. Rather they are intended to help differentiating among similar meanings, so that the most appropriate one for the intended purpose can be chosen. Finally, thesauri also include scope notes, which are textual annotations used to clarify the meaning and the context of terms.

In a nutshell, a thesaurus can be defined as a taxonomy expressed using natural language that makes explicit a limited set of relations among the codified terms.

The AGROVOC Thesaurus [1] developed by the Food and Agriculture Organization of the United Nations (FAO) is a good example of a thesaurus.

---

[2] http://species.wikimedia.org

[3] *Glossary, language reference book, lexicon, onomasticon, reference book, sourcebook, storehouse of words, terminology, treasury of words, vocabulary* or *word list* are all synonyms to thesaurus.

2.4. *Ontologies*

In philosophy, ontology is the study of being or existence. It constitutes the basic subject matter of metaphysics [23], which has the objective of explaining existence in a systematic manner, by dealing with the types and structures of objects, properties, events, processes and relations pertaining to each part of reality.

Recently, the term ontology was adapted in computer science, where ontologies are similar to taxonomies in that they represent relations among terms. However, ontologies offer a much richer meaning representation mechanism for the relationships among concepts, i.e., terms and attributes. This is the reason because they are, nowadays, the preferred mechanism to represent knowledge.

There exist numerous definitions of ontology. One of the earliest was that of Neches who in his work *Enabling Technology for Knowledge Sharing* [15], published in 1991 provided the following definition:

"An ontology defines the basic terms and relations comprising the vocabulary of a topic area as well as the rules for combining terms and relations to define extensions to the vocabulary".

In 1993, Gruber [9] provided one of the most widely adopted definitions of Ontology.

"An ontology is an explicit specification of a conceptualization".

Gruber's definition was further extended by Borst in 1997. In his work *Construction of Engineering Ontologies* [4] he defines ontology as follows.

"Ontologies are defined as a formal specification of a shared conceptualization".

Studer, Benjamins and Fensel [20] further refined and explained this definition in 1998. In their work, the authors defined an ontology as:

"a formal, explicit specification of a shared conceptualization.

Formal: *Refers to the fact that an ontology should be machine-readable.*

Explicit: *Means that the type of concepts used, and the restrictions on their use are explicitly defined.*

Shared: *Reflects the notion that the ontology captures consensual knowledge, that is, it is not the privilege of some individual, but accepted by a group".*

***Conceptualization**: Refers to an abstract model of some phenomenon in the world by having identified the relevant concepts of that phenomenon.*

2.4.1. *Ontologies and knowledge bases*

The relation between ontologies and knowledge bases is a controversial topic. It is not clear whether an ontology can only contain the abstract schema (example: concept Person) or also the concrete instances of the abstract concepts (example: Tim Berners-Lee). When drawing a clear line between abstract schema definitions and the instance level, one runs into the problem that in some cases instances are required in order to specify abstract concepts. An example that illustrates this problem is the definition of the concept "New Yorker" as the concept of persons living in New York: in this case, the instance "New York" of city is required in order to specify the concept.

A number or authors have tackled this problem and identified the limits and relationships among existing definitions.

Guarino and Giaretta in their work *Ontologies and Knowledge Bases: Towards a Terminological Clarification* [13] placed the basis for clarifying the relationship among ontologies and knowledge bases by portraying an ontology as a logical theory.

"A logical theory which gives and explicit, partial account of a conceptualization".

Guarino [14] further narrowed his own definition in 1998, clearly pin pointing that an ontology is comprised by a set of logical axioms and that it is an engineering artifact.

"A set of logical axioms designed to account for the intended meaning of a vocabulary".

Two definitions, the first one provided by Bernaras *et al.* [1], and the second one by Swartout [21], clearly identify the relationship between ontologies and knowledge bases.

"An ontology provides the means for describing explicitly the conceptualization behind the knowledge represented in a knowledge base" [1].

"An ontology is a set of structured terms that describes some domain or topic. The idea is that an ontology provides a skeletal structure for a knowledge base" [21].

2.4.2. *Lightweight vs. heavyweight ontologies*

Depending on the axiomatization richness of ontologies one can distinguish between heavyweight and lightweight ontologies. Those that make intensive use of axioms to model knowledge and restrict domain semantics are referred to as heavyweight ontologies [7]. On the other hand, those ontologies that make scarce or no use of axioms to model knowledge and clarify the meaning of concepts in the domain are referred to as lightweight ontologies. Lightweight ontologies are a subclass of heavyweight ontologies, typically predominantly a taxonomy, with very few cross-taxonomical links (also known as "properties"), and with very few logical relations between the classes. Davies, Fensel *et al.* [24] emphasize the importance of such lightweight ontologies:

> *"We expect the majority of the ontologies on the Semantic Web to be lightweight. [...] Our experiences to date in a variety of Semantic Web applications (knowledge management, document retrieval, communities of practice, data integration) all point to lightweight ontologies as the most commonly occurring type."*

2.4.3. *Ontological commitments*

Generally speaking, ontologies are engineering artifacts that provide the domain vocabulary plus certain assumptions regarding the meaning of the vocabulary [14]. They are used by the participants in a given interaction to communicate. This communication can only be effective if participants have previously committed to use common ontologies. This is, if their use of the vocabulary is coherent and consistent with that specified in the shared ontology.

Ontological commitments are therefore agreements to use a shared vocabulary in a coherent and consistent manner [12]. They guarantee consistency, but not completeness of an ontology. This involves making as few claims as possible about the world being modeled, as well as giving the parties committed freedom to specialize the ontology as required [7].

Gruber [11] defines five ontological commitments:

Clarity: An ontology should communicate effectively the intended meaning of defined terms. Definition should be objective. Definitions can be stated on formal axioms, and a complete definition (defined by necessary and sufficient conditions) is preferred over a partial definition (defined only by necessary or sufficient conditions). All definitions should be documented with natural language.

Minimal encoding bias: The conceptualization should be specified at the knowledge level without depending on a particular symbol-level encoding.

Extendibility: One should be able to define new terms for special uses based on the existing vocabulary, in a way that does not require the revision of the existing definitions.

Coherence: An ontology should be coherent: that is, it should sanction inferences that are consistent with the definitions [...]. If a sentence that can be inferred from the axioms contradicts a definition or example given informally, then the ontology is incoherent.

Minimal ontological commitments: Since ontological commitment is based on the consistent use of the vocabulary, ontological commitment can be minimized by specifying the weakest theory and defining only those terms that are essential to the communication of knowledge consistent with the theory.

3. Ontology languages

The following section provides a complete review of the most relevant ontology languages currently available, namely, RDF(S), OWL, WSML, and SKOS. For completeness reasons, we also briefly summarize the early language OIL and DAML+OIL.

3.1. *Resource description framework*

The RDF is a general-purpose language for representing information about resources in the Web [5]. Resource Description Framework Schema (RDFS) provides the means for defining the semantics of RDF modeling primitives. The combination of RDF and RDFS is commonly known as RDF(S). RDF(S) is not considered semantic language *per se*, but rather, a general purpose language for describing metadata on the Web [7].

RDF(S) data model provides a syntax-neutral way of representing expressions based on the use of binary relations. The language is based on the idea that the things have properties which have values, and that resources can be described by making statements, that specify those properties and values [6]. RDF(S) uses the concepts of *subject, object* and *predicate*, grouped in triples, to refer to the different parts of a statement. In a nutshell, subjects identify the resource the statement is about; predicates point the characteristic of the subject specified by the statement; and objects name the value of the property referred by the predicate. For example in the statement below:

www.ontogame.org *has an* ***author*** *whose value is* ***Katharina Siorpaes***

"***www.ontogame.org***" is the subject, the predicate is the word "***author***" and the object is the phrase "***Katharina Siorpaes***".

Notably, RDF(S) is enhanced with a reification mechanism that enables the definition of statements about statements. The language offers a good repertoire of ontology modeling primitives including sub-classing relationships that can be readily used to represent subsumption. Consequently it can be stated that the language is expressive enough for its intended purpose.

3.2. *Web ontology language*

The OWL [15] is an ontology language that evolved from the DAML+OIL language. It comprises three language variants, namely, OWL Lite, OWL DL and OWL Full, that offer different expressivity and reasoning capabilities.

3.2.1. *OWL Lite*

The OWL Lite is the least expressive and logically complex variant. It is intended for users needing a classification hierarchy and simple constraints. Cardinality constraints are supported, but only permit use of the values 0 and 1. Rapid language adoption is achieved by way of tool development and the easiness to migrate from thesauri and other taxonomics.

3.2.2. *OWL DL*

The descriptions logic variant OWL DL provides maximum expressivity while keeping full computational completeness and decidability. This variant imposes certain restriction on the use of the language constructs, e.g., a class can not be instance of another class.

3.2.3. *OWL Full*

OWL Full offers maximum expressiveness with no computational guarantees, i.e., completeness and decidability, combined with the syntactic freedom of RDF.

3.3. *Web Service modeling language*

The WSML [22] provides a formal syntax semantics for the Web Service Modeling Ontology (WSMO). WSML is based on different formalisms, namely, Description Logics, First-Order Logic and Logic Programming.

WSML provides a meaningful choice of variants able to accommodate the requirements of the application and targeted application domain. These are WSML-Core, WSML-DL, WSML-Flight, WSML-Rule, and WSML-Full.

The WSML family of languages provides a human-readable syntax and two additional ones, namely, XML, RDF, plus a mapping to OWL for the exchange among machines.

3.3.1. *WSML-Core*

WSML-core builds on top of the OWL Lite, which is a restricted version of OWL Lite, consequently making it fully compliant with this OWL subset.

The formalism used, precisely meets the intersection of Description Logic and Horn Logic (without function symbols and without equality), extended with data type support. The language provides the means to model classes, attributes, binary relationships (class hierarchies and relation hierarchies) and instances.

Due to the fact that it has the least expressive power of all the WSML family languages, WSML-core offers the most favorable computational characteristics, therefore making it the preferred language for practical applications.

WSML-Core is extended, both in the direction of Description Logics and in the direction Programming with WSML-DL and WSML-Flight respectively [9].

3.3.2. *WSML-DL*

WSML-DL extends syntactically and semantically WSML-Core to a fully fledged Description Logic paradigm, namely, SHIQ, thereby covering the part of OWL can be implemented efficiently.

WSML-DL extends WSML-Core by way of providing a less restrictive syntax. In this direction, most of the limitations on the use of WSMD-DL syntax are those derived from the use of Description logics.

3.3.3. *WSML-Flight*

WSML-Flight provides a powerful language that extends WSML-Core in the direction of Logic Programming. It provides a rich set of modeling primitives for attributes, such as value constraints and integrity constraints. WSML-Flight is semantically equivalent to Datalog with inequality and (locally) stratified negation. It incorporates a fully-fledged rule language, while still allowing efficient decidable reasoning.

3.3.4. *WSML-Rule*

WSML-Rule extends WSML-Flight in the direction of Logic Programming, providing a fully-fledged Logic Programming language. It supports the use of function symbols and unsafe rules and does not restrict the use of variables in logical expressions.

3.3.5. *WSML-Full*

WSML-Full unifies all WSML-DL and WSML-Rule variants under a common First-Order umbrella with non-monotonic extension of WSML-Rule.

3.4. *Simple knowledge organization system*

The SKOS[4] initiative focuses on the development of specifications for supporting knowledge organization systems, such as thesauri, folksonomies, and lightweight ontologies. Wilson, Brickley and colleagues [27] describe SKOS core, which is an RDF vocabulary that can express content and structure of concept schemes. Concept schemes include thesauri, classification schemes, glossaries, taxonomies, and ontologies — i.e., all kinds of controlled vocabulary. SKOS core is a very lightweight meta-model that describes just the minimal set of classes and properties that are necessary to express knowledge in simple structures, such as taxonomies.

As an RDF vocabulary SKOS allows very flexible use with other RDF vocabularies in case SKOS does not cover requirements of specific domains.

SKOS core contains the most important elements in order to specify controlled vocabularies. The most important elements in SKOS are concepts as units of thoughts, comparable to classes known in OWL that are enriched with labels. Furthermore, SKOS provides the expression of semantic relationships, such as "broader", "narrower" or "related". Additionally, SKOS allows usage of constructs for mapping of concepts — may it be fuzzy or exact. SKOS extensions are intended to facilitate the declaration of relationships between concepts with more specific semantics.

[4] http://www.w3.org/2004/02/skos/

3.5. *OIL, daml+oIL*

Fensel, Van Harmelen and colleagues [25] describe OIL which aims to express semantics on the Web, built on RDFS. It combines XML syntax, modeling primitives from the frame-based knowledge representation paradigm, and the formal semantics and reasoning support of description logics approaches. Besides the XML syntax, there is also OIL's presentation syntax. However, OIL is not an evolving language any longer as it was superseded by Daml+OIL [26]. DAML+OIL uses elements of XML as well as RDF. It adds elements from frame-based systems based on description logics. It was superseded by the OWL family of languages.

4. Conclusions

This chapter has reviewed the existing approaches to modeling metadata and the up-to-date most relevant semantic web languages. In detail controlled vocabularies, taxonomies, thesaurus and ontologies have been carefully reviewed with the aim of providing the reader with the understanding required to assess the uses and applications of each paradigm. As ontologies are the most complete of all the approaches presented, the discussion in the following section was centered on various issues relevant to this novel technology. In short, we discussed the relation between ontologies and knowledge bases, the difference between lightweight and heavyweight ontologies, and the main ontological commitments. Finally, the work focused on depicting the up-to-date most relevant semantic web languages. A thorough review of the most relevant languages has been provided with an attempt to provide a general understanding of each initiative, so that the most suitable formalism can be chosen. We also cover the latest development that of lightweight ontologies and semantics, which is covered by the SKOS initiative.

Acknowledgments

This work has been supported by EU-funded research project LUISA (*Learning Content Management System Using Innovative Semantic Web Services Architecture*), code FP6–2004–IST–4 027149 and by the Austrian BMVIT/FFG under the FIT-IT Semantic Systems project myOntology (grant no. 812515/9284).

References

1. Food and Agriculture Organization of the United Nations (FAO) (1980). *AGROVOC Thesaurus.* Available at http://www.fao.org/aims/ag_intro.htm.
2. Arano, S (2005). *Thesauruses and ontologies.* Available at http://www.hipertext.net/english/pag1009.htm
3. Bernaras, A, I Laresgoiti and J Corera (1996). Building and reusing ontologies for electrical network applications. In *Eurpean Conference on Artificial Intelligence (ECAI'96),* W Wahlster (ed.), Budapest, Hungary, pp. 298–302. Chichester, United Kingdom: John Wiley and Sons.
4. Borst, WN (1997). *Construction of Engineering Ontologies.* Centre for Telematica and Information Technology, University of Tweenty. Enshede, The Netherlands.
5. Brickley, D and RV Guha (eds.) (2004). RDF Vocabulary Description Language 1.0: RDF Schema. W3C Recommendation. 10 February.
6. Manola, F and E Miller (eds.) (2004). RDF Primer. W3C Recommendation. 10 February. Available at http://www.w3.org/TR/2004/REC-rdf-primer-20040210/.
7. Fensel, D (2001). *Ontologies: Silver Bullet for Knowledge Management and Electronic Commerce.* Berlin: Springer-Verlag.
8. Gómez-Pérez, A, M Fernandez-Lopez and O Corcho (2004). *Ontological Engineering.* Italy: Springer. ISBN: 978-1-85233-551-9.
9. Grosof, BN, I Horrocks, R Volz and S Decker (2003). Description logic programs: Combining logic programs with description logic. In *Proc. of the Twelfth International World Wide Web Conference (WWW 2003),* pp. 48–57. ACM.
10. Gruber, TR (1993). A translation approach to portable ontology specifications. *Knowledge Acquisition,* 5(2), 199–220.
11. Gruber, TR (1993). Toward principles for the design of ontologies used in knowledge sharing. In *International Workshop on Formal Ontology in Conceptual Analysis and Knowledge Representation,* N Guarino and R Poli (eds.), Padova, Italy. (Formal Ontology in Conceptual Analysis and Knowledge Representation). Deventer, The Netherlands: Kluwer Academic Publishers.
12. Gruber, TR and G Olsen (1994). An ontology for engineering mathematics. In Fourth International Conference on Principles of Knowledge Representation and Reasoning, J Doyle, P Torasso, Sandewall (eds.), Bonn, Germany, pp. 258–269. San Francisco, California: Morgan Kaufmann Publishers.
13. Guarino, N and P Giaretta (1995). *Ontologies and Knowledge Bases: Towards a Terminological Clarification.* In Towards Very Large Knowledge Bases: Knowledge Building and Knowledge Sharing (KBKS'95), N Mars (ed.), University of Twente, Enschede, pp. 25–32. The Netherlands: IOS Press.
14. Guarino, N (1998). *Formal Ontology in Information Systems.* In *1st International Conference on Formal Ontology in Information Systems (FOIS'98),* N Guarino (ed.), Trento, Italy, pp. 3–15. The Netherlands: IOS Press.

15. McGuinness, DL and F van Harmelen (2004). OWL Web Ontology Language Overview. W3C Recommendation. 10 February. Available at http://www.w3.org/TR/2004/REC-owl-features-20040210/#s1.
16. Neches, R, R Fikes, T Finin, T Gruber, R Patil, T Senator and WR Swartout (1991). Enabling technology for knowledge sharing. *AI Magazine,* 12(3), 36–56.
17. National Information Standards Organization (NISO) (2003). (ANSI/NISO Z39.19-2003, 2003: 1). Available at http://www.niso.org/home.
18. RuleML. http://www.ruleml.org/
19. Slype, GV (1991). *Langages d`indexation: conception, construction et utilisation dans les systemes documentaires.* Fundación Germán Sánchez Ruipérez. Madrid, p. 198.
20. Studer, R, VR Benjamins and D Fensel (1998). Knowledge engineering: principles and methods. *IEEE Transactions on Data and Knowledge Engineering,* 25(1–2), 161–197.
21. Swartout, B, R Patil, K Knight and T Russ (1996). Toward distributed use of large-scale ontologies. In *Proceedings of 10th Knowledge Acquisition for Knowledge-Based Systems Workshop,* Banff, Canada.
22. Toma, I (ed.), J de Bruijn, H Lausen, R Krummenacher, A Polleres, L Predoiu, M Kifer, D Fensel, I Toma, N Steinmetz and M Kerrigan (2007). *D16.1v0.3 The Web Service Modeling Language WSML.* WSML Working Draft. Available at http://www.wsmo.org/TR/d16/d16.1/v0.3/20070817/23.
23. Wikipedia. www.wikipedia.org
24. Davies, J, D Fensel, et al. (eds.) (2002). *Towards the Semantic Web: Ontology-driven Knowledge Management.* England: Wiley.
25. Fensel, D, F Van Harmelen, *et al.* (2001). OIL: An ontology infrastructure for the Semantic Web. *IEEE Intelligent Systems,* 16(2), 1366–1371.
26. Horrocks, I and F Van Harmelen (2001). Reference description of the DAML+OIL Ontology Markup language. Technical report.
27. Wilson, MD, D Brickley, *et al.* (2005). SKOS core: Simple knowledge organisation for the Web. *International Conference on Dublin Core and Metadata Applications.*

CHAPTER II.3

TOPIC MAPS

Piedad Garrido Picazo

Department of Computer Science and Systems Engineering
Ciudad Escolar s/n Teruel 44003
piedad@unizar.es

Jesús Tramullas

Department of Librarianship and Information Science
Ciudad Universitaria s/n Zaragoza 50009
tramullas@unizar.es

Topic Maps, and their XTM specification, have been revealed as a powerful tool especially designed to describe and organize digital information resources in the last decade. The availability of the ISO standard, and its specialization and revision, reflect the importance of the description scheme, as well as their gathering market and the increasing number of users. The standard specifications have been widely discussed in the specialized bibliography, but a deeper study about the available software collection tools that allow Topic Maps implementation is needed. This work, starting from the Topic Maps definition, details the current available management tools, and comments the integration of Topic Maps with other metadata schemes.

1. Introduction

The purpose of this chapter is to show the main developments in Topic Maps management tools. To do this, it is necessary to establish the context and foundations of Topic Maps, as well as to explain how they have been integrated in the software tools functionalities that made their implementation possible. Thus, we pretend to identify the main trends, research and development areas, emerging questions, and the most interesting experiences. According to this approach, the main objectives are:

- To analyze the Topic Map concept, its historical development, and the XTM specification as a reference framework for the selection and presentation of software tools.
- To detail the most important proprietary and free software tools.
- To present alternative metadata schemes, as well as tools that make its integration possible.

2. Topic maps

Over a very short period of years, the Topic Maps paradigm has gone from being almost an anonymity to becoming an important element in conferences, electronic journals and international congresses on XML. Such was its importance since its first appearance in public at *XML Europe 2000* in Paris, that specific international congresses on the theme have been subsequently created which, in recent years, have been covered in publishing houses, such as Springer (*Lecture Notes*), or the monograph of reference on the theme [1]. Furthermore, it has been acknowledged as a standard in ISO standard 13250:2003 Information Technology — SGML Applications — Topic Maps, where a detailed description of it is included, and a specification, XTM (*XML for Topic Maps*, available at http://www.topicmaps.org/xtm/), which is now available as version 2.0.

It is not easy to distinguish between what has been efficiently developed and proved, what pertains to future conjectures, or what has been paralyzed at a given time. The aim of this subsection is to provide a broad vision of the current state of the art in the world of Topic Maps by looking at their definition, motives, historic origin and development, and by analyzing the hardware and software technologies implied. Their application in various knowledge fields will be covered and other alternatives of information organization will be analyzed in order to conclude by reviewing what advances in terms of information visualization have been achieved.

2.1. *Definitions*

Topic Maps are included within a class of objects currently identified as *knowledge webs*. A knowledge web is a network of interconnected ideas whose skeleton does not simply comprise ideas but, and most importantly, also the way in which these ideas are organized and interrelated. This generic term encompasses conceptual maps, semantic networks, cluster maps, mental maps, circle diagrams, flow charts and Topic Maps, and it is not only limited to these, but also to other approaches and techniques which attempt to apply knowledge to the Web and to make the human mind much more intelligent [2].

To obtain information about knowledge webs of an introductory nature, the following authors, among others, are taken as references [3,4,5]. These authors analyze the power of language, the impacts that the various uses of language have on society and what the human being has been learning in 500 years of research about knowledge webs and cognitive processes.

The definitions of the term Topic Maps coincide, in that it is a standard for the organization, representation and management of knowledge. This is obvious in the different definitions and interpretations of the term which researchers and developers alike have provided over the years. For example, Biezunsky and Hamon consider that "A Topic Map is functionally equivalent to multi-document indexes, glossaries, and thesauri" [6]. In the first version of ISO standard 13250, a Topic Map is defined as:

> *a) A set of information resources regarded by a topic map application as a bounded object set whose hub document is a topic map document conforming to the SGML architecture defined by this International Standard, b) Any topic map document conforming to the SGML architecture defined by this International Standard, or the document element (topic map) of such a document, c) The document element type (topic map) of the topic map document architecture (ISO 13250, 1999, p. 5)*

In 2002, Steve Pepper and Piotr Kaminsky interpreted it, respectively, as:

> *"Since the basic model of semantic networks is very similar to that of the topics and associations found in indexes, combining the two approaches should provide great benefits in both information management and knowledge management, and this is precisely what the new topic map standard achieves. By adding the topic/occurrence axis to the topic/association model, Topic Maps provide a means of "bridging the gap", as it were, between knowledge representation and the field of information management"* [7].
>
> *"Due to its rich structure and peculiar terminology, the Topic Maps metamodel is often misunderstood by people with a background in simpler metamodels, but seems to fit well into the world view of librarians and other information workers"* [8]

More recently, Park [9] defines it as:

> *"A topic map is a set of topics and associations between them. A topic map may exist in either interchangeable syntax and/or ready-to-use form. When a topic map exists in the serialized form of interchange syntax, it is*

entirely possible for redundant elements (for example, XTM <topic> elements) to interchange the same subject. However, when the topic map is in ready-to-use form, topic merging should take place, and one topic should represent one and only one subject. The creators of Topic Maps determine the subjects of topics. For each topic, they assert some set of topic characteristics (in other words, they create associations in which topics play roles)"

But of them all, the definition which ought to be highlighted is that of Charles F. Goldfarb, the developer of markup languages and of SGML, who defines Topic Maps as *The GPS of the information universe* [10].

Topic Maps allow digital documents to be organized, navigation through the semantic relations connecting them, and linguistic structures to be used as search "probes" in the conceptually rich contexts to be obtained [11].

In short, Topic Maps are an instrument which represents the conceptual structure of the information contained in the website. For this very reason, the greater the contribution to the knowledge representation of this kind of structures, which encompass visual aspects, semantic webs and text, the more powerful they will be if considered jointly than each one being considered separately. What is true, however, is realizing that incorporated semantics will never replace linear text. Instead, it will accompany it on its way forward and will increase its potential since text will continue to supply pleasant items like detailed descriptions and creative expressions as far as objects and people are concerned.

2.2. *Motivations*

In a broad sense, the main motives which justify the appearance of this international standard are the following:

(i) To grade the content or the information contained in the topics. The basic objective is to enable navigational tools, such as indexes, cross-references, citation systems, glossaries, etc., which, in turn, act as criteria and principles of information organization.

(ii) To create navigation characteristics while creating interfaces that simulate thesauri, ontologies, knowledge bases, etc., and which address topics that provide the effect of merging already structured information bases.

(iii) To create specific views for different user profiles; this information filtering process could prove most useful in managing multilingual documents, in the management of access modes depending on the security criteria used, for the delivery of partial views depending on either user profiles or knowledge domains, etc.

(iv) To structure unstructured information objects.

(v) The Topic Maps merging mechanism may be considered an external markup mechanism in the sense that an arbitrary structure is imposed on the information, although its original format remains unaltered.

(vi) To construct significant and alternative search strategies which allow the information required to be recovered.

3. Historical development

Work on Topic Maps began in 1991 when the Davenport Group was founded by a group of Unix systems suppliers and editors which sought the means to make the exchange of technical documentation among computers possible.

On the one hand, clients are pressuring documentation suppliers to improve the self-consistency of printed documentation. They were not only aware of the inconsistent use of terms in the documentation which came with their systems, but also of the books published on this matter, and they concentrated on defining *DocBook* (available at http://www.docbook.org) which focused on the content of manuals. This is a DTD format, a direct application of the SGML/XML standard, and may be used to document any kind of material, especially computer programs. Its structure reflects a monograph abstraction. On the other hand, systems suppliers wanted to include the X-Windows-based independent generation of documentation, created under license by publishers like O'Reilly. This task, a seemingly clear one at the beginning, did not prove so easy to solve. One of the main problems that they came up against was how to supply master indexes for their independent maintenance since the technical documentation which the system suppliers added to the system manuals was constantly undergoing changes. In the words of Steve Newcomb, co-editor of the standard along with Michel Biezunski:

> *"That first inspiration [...] was that indexes, if they have any self-consistency at all, conform to models of the structure of the knowledge available in the materials that they index. But the models are implicit, and they are nowhere to be found! If such models could be captured formally, then they could guide and greatly facilitate the process of merging modelled indexes together. But how to express such models?"* [12]

The first attempt to solve this problem was known as *Standard Open Formal Architecture for Browsable Electronic Documents* (SOFABED) [13]. Providing master indexes proved so complex and interesting that, in 1993, a new group was created, *Conventions for the Application of HyTime* (CapH), with which the sophisticated hypertext characteristics would apply in the ISO standard 10744:1997 — *Information Technology — Hypermedia/Time-Based Structuring Language*, better known as the HyTime standard. HyTime was published in 1992 to extend *Standard Generalized Markup Language* (SGML) ISO standard 8879:1986 — Information Processing — Text and office systems — Standard Generalized Markup Language), and had both multimedia and hyperlink characteristics. CapH activity was welcomed by the *Graphic Communications Association Research Institute* (GCARI Institute), now called IDEAlliance (Official website http://www.idealliance.org/). After a lengthy review among the various possibilities offered to extend the hyperlink navigation model, the CapH group elaborated the SOFABED model and called it Topic Maps. Around 1995, the model had matured to such an extent that it was accepted by the ISO/JTC1/SC18/WG8 work group as a basis to develop a new international standard. The Topic Maps specification was finally published as the ISO/IEC 13250:2000 standard — *Information Technology — SGML applications — Topic Maps.* (Electronic version available at http://www1.y12.doe.gov/capabilities/sgml/sc34/document/0129.pdf)

Once understood, the model became widespread to include the electronic equivalents of other elements originating from the printing field, which act as an aid for the navigation tasks carried out by the user, for example, tables of contents, glossaries, thesauri and cross-references [14].

During the initial phase, the model that ISO standard ISO/IEC 13250 presented comprised two groups of elements:

- Topics, and
- Relationships among these topics (presently known as associations).

As the project developed, it was necessary to introduce a supplementary construction which would filter domains, language and security, and would control versions (*facets*). This characteristic was not considered in the standard, but was included in version 1.0 of the XTM specification. This approach was soon to be replaced by one that was more elegant and powerful, and one based on the scope notion which enabled Topic Maps to be capable of incorporating different views of the universe of discourse, and also different languages for certain users in specific contexts without any loss of its facility of use, and without any danger of it becoming an *infoglut*.

The ISO syntax associated with Topic Maps is very open but rigorously restricted at the same time, thanks to the fact that the syntax is expressed as a set of architectural forms. These forms are templates with structured elements, and the ease with which these templates are used is the central theme of ISO/IEC 10744:1997 — *Information Technology — Hypermedia/Time-Based Structuring Language*. Those ISO standard 13250-based applications may freely subclassify the types of elements supplied by the definition of the types of elements provided by the ISO standard syntax. Furthermore, the names of the types of elements, attributes, etc., may be freely renamed, which is why ISO standard 13250 uses the requirements of editors and other potential users to manage the source code developed in order to implement efficient searches for information resources.

Nonetheless, the appearance of XML, and the fact that it was accepted as the Web's *lingua franca* to exchange information in documents saved in different formats, gave way to a less flexible need and to a less deterministic syntax, as far as users were concerned, and to the development of web-based applications. This objective, which was met without any loss of either the expressiveness or part of the federated power that the Topics Maps paradigm provides its users and authors, is precisely the purpose of the XTM specification (*XML for Topic Maps*).

The XTM (Official web site http://www.topicmaps.org/xtm/) initiative emerged when ISO standard 13250 was published for the Topic Maps specification. TopicMaps.org, an independent organization, was founded for the purpose of creating and publishing the XTM 1.0 specification as soon as possible. In less than a year, TopicMaps.org was set up, and the nucleus of the XTM specification became available as version 1.0. The development of the final XTM 1.0 version was completed on 2 March 2001 [15]. This specification was admitted by ISO, and was incorporated into the standard via a Technical Reform in October of the same year. In May 2002, the second edition of the standard was approved and published, and was included as ISO standard 13250:2003 — *Information Technology — SGML applications-Topic Maps* (Available at http://www1.y12.doe.gov/capabilities/sgml/sc34/document/0322_files/iso13250-2nd-ed-v2.pdf) which also incorporated the XML syntax in its Annex C. After finalizing the first version of the specification, TopicMaps.org was incorporated into the technical organization *Organization for the Advancement of Structured Information Standards* (OASIS), an international non-profit association which addresses the development, convergence and adoption of *e-business* standards. Presently, ISO is reviewing the second version of the XTM specification for its subsequent publication.

4. Software and developed technologies

Topic Maps/XTM implementation, as a tagging process, can be carried out using a simple text editor. Nevertheless, it's obvious that it is necessary to have tools which offer advanced possibilities and functionalities in order to make use of the whole potential that this scheme offers. During the last decade, two different emerging solutions can be identified:

- Proprietary software developed by software consulting companies, and joined by some of the most important authors on this field.
- Free Software, as a result of collaborative projects, and research results from academia.

4.1. *Commercial software for services and information management*

The tools for Topic Maps, on which information has been collected over these years of research into the theme, were initially developed by a group of firms dedicated to the creation of products and services which offered added value for information management processes. Their common objective was to simplify the way content was organized to subsequently facilitate its reuse and access.

Since its origins until the present-day, almost all the software available in the market for the user has been written in Java. Among these, *Omnigator* by the firm Ontopia, is worth emphasizing as it offers an online demo for consultation purposes (Available at http://www.ontopia.net/omnigator/models/index.jsp), and *Intelligent Topic Mapper* (ITM) T3 of Mondeca (Available at http://www.mondeca.com/index.php/en/intelligent_topic_manager). Both products will be detailed in the following paragraphs.

Table 1 contains a list of firms which incorporate this international standard into all the products and services they offer to their clients and users. All these firms started out with Topic Maps either to develop products which offered certain services or to participate in projects which enabled their products to develop.

Infoloom developed the *Topic Map Loom* technology, under Michel Biezunski, which was tested over a four-year period. The objective was to facilitate the creation and maintenance of Topic Maps. With this tool, users create their own Topic Maps and apply them to a set of information for the purpose of creating a navigatable screen output. The minutes of the European Congress on XML 2000 (http://www.gca.org/papers/xmleurope2000/) on

Table 1. Firms that work with Topic Maps.

Firm	Web
Infoloom	http://www.infoloom.com/
Ontopia	http://www.ontopia.net/
Empolis	http://www.empolis.com/
RivCom	http://www.rivcom.com
Mondeca	http://www.mondeca.com/
Cogito Ergo XML	http://www.cogx.com/
Networked Planet	http://www.networkedplanet.com/
Intelligent Views	http://www.i-views.de/web/
USU-The Knowledge Businness Company	http://www.usu-ag.com/english/index.html
Moresophy	http://www.moresophy.com/
Kalido	http://www.kalido.com/
Innodata Isogen	http://www.innodata-isogen.com/
CoolHeads	http://www.coolheads.com/index.htm
Semantext	http://www.semantext.com

CD-ROM were developed with this tool. It offers a clear example of a consistent Topic Map in a set of linked HTML sites in terms of the topic concept that it refers to.

For the time being, it is still a static solution for an automatic process to obtain a Topic Map. Its creation process has to be taken up again from the beginning should changes take place in its structure. InfoLoom offers an implementation reference at the web site http://www.quid.fr

Ontopia is a Norwegian firm specialized in developing Topic Maps-based applications. This firm had close ties with STEP Infotek, founded by Steve Pepper, which was also in the same Topic Maps-based application development market. It began to construct an open-source engine about Python, which is currently known as *tmproc,* and it allows a Topic Map to be created simply and automatically. This may be downloaded from the Ontopia web site (Available at http://www.ontopia.net/software/tmproc/). This firm also supplied two other products in 2000: *Atlas^{TM} Engine* and *Atlas^{TM} Navigator.*

It has presently developed two specific packs which work directly with the creation, navigation and visualization of Topic Maps. These products are the *Topic Map Starter Pack* (a set of materials and tools for users to create their own Topic Maps), and *Ontopia Knowlege Suite* (OKS) with applications like *Ontopia Topic Map Engine, Ontopia Navigator Framework, Ontopia Web Editor Framework,* and an example applications pack developed with this suite: *Omnigator* (browser), *Vizigator* (a graphic visualizer of associations) and *Ontopoly* (the creation of Topic Maps from ontologies).

STEP UK, nowadays known as Empolis, is a firm with ample experience in the SGML/XML field. Originally, its intention was to develop techology for Topic Maps whose components were as follows:

- A Topic Map engine developed in Java.
- A set of classes and interfaces capable of creating, handling and storing Topic Maps-based structures.
- Importing and exporting Topic Maps requests.
- A Topic Maps merger.
- Scalable storage: Gigabytes of information in Topic Maps.
- Structures of stored multidimensional data to supply a simple interaction with the user with a rapid set up.
- API development documentation.
- Selection of persistent models (Oracle, SQL Server, OO, …)
- Examples of applications, e.g., rendering HTML/WEB of information related to a Topic Map.
- *XLink* integration (handling all the *topics, associations* and *facets* as *Xlinks*).

Presently this firm is consolidated as an information-processing firm in the logistics sector, and it has two research projects underway which completely focus on the knowledge management field:

(i) The European SEKT Project (*Semantic Enabled Knowledge Technologies,* http://sekt.semanticweb.org/), which is part of the 6th Framework Program within strategic actions: semantic-based knowledge systems, whose purpose it is to provide computers with the ability to supply useful information which has been adapted to the context of the user's search where the user is a firm or an individual.
(ii) The SWAP (http://swap.semanticweb.org) project, which is partially subsidized by the European Union, and based on the combination of semantic web technology (Topic Maps, ontologíes) and *peer-to-peer* computing.

The *X2X* engine was part of the Topic Map engine developed by STEP (now known as Empolis) which acted as a technological solution to permit integration with *XLink*. It consisted in the implementation of a directioning mechanism which followed the Topic Map concept. *X2X* allowed links to be created, managed and handled. Its main characteristic was that a link could be created between information documents and information resources without changing the source or destination documents to be linked. Therefore, there was no need to insert links within the document contents as this scalable technology connected different information resources without taking their location into account.

Thanks to the *X2X Datafetcher* component, it is currently possible to access software tools with contents like *Astoria* and *Documentum*. Its operation is based on links which may be authorized by any application, and which is able to create an XML document. *XLink* is an XML application, which means that all the *XLink* documents are XML documents. After creating an *Xlink* document, we move on to *X2X* so that the information relating to the link may be added to the *X2X LinkBase* (see Fig. x).

As the Fig. 1 illustrates, the *X2X Linkbase* component is a persistant information repository used to store links. It may be implemented into a database management system which supports JDBC/ODBC, and which consequently enables information to be linked without having to bear in mind its location. For this purpose, it uses a Java API for the interface socket. The access route toward functioning is guaranteed thanks to the *X2X* engine. Besides, *X2X* runs under a server that listens to links. It is at this time that requests are processed by using the aforementioned API. As seen, the potential integration has no limits, and it may be stated that the power of *X2X* lies in its free interface and in API.

With *X2X Linkbase Explorer*, all the linked information, which is authorized and registered in the *Xlink* documents, along with the link objects created by API, may be used to represent the nodes, which in turn allows the

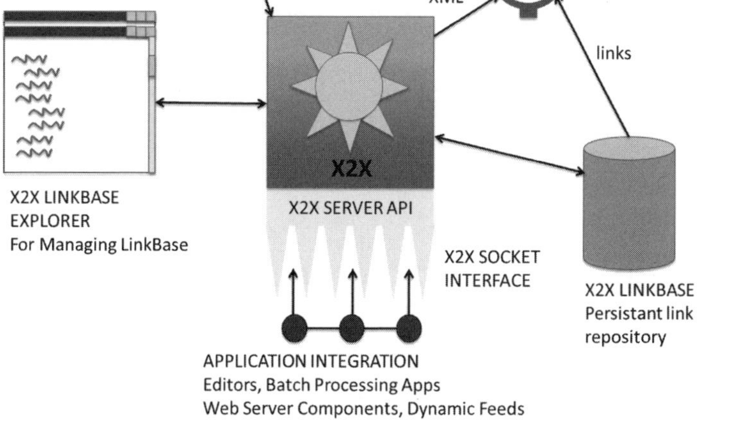

Fig. 1. Integration of engine *X2X* into an application.

user to navigate, erase and repair the link structures without affecting the integrity of the destination files.

The *X2X LinkManager* component is used to generate XML, HTML or SGML information. Links may be solved by means of simple hyperlinks, or by constructing documents made up of object resources. *X2X* was developed in Java and was fundamentally implemented with the link concept, which was understood as that defined by the last draft of the W3C proposal on *Xlink*. By way of conclusion, *X2X* is a technology capable of:

- Linking resources without having to make changes in them.
- Constructing new dynamic documents from a *LinkDocument* template.
- Establishing real two-way links among resources.
- Linking structured information with unstructured information.
- Managing large information repositories linked in an efficient centralized manner.
- Linking resources stored in a wide variety of information repositories.
- Creating links by using any application that creates *Xlink* documents.

Mondeca S.A. was founded around the year 2000 by a group of advertising software developers. It supplies software solutions to large firms, mainly in the pharmaceutical and tourism sectors. It has specialized in the management of content organization, automated knowledge representation, taxonomies and ontologies. For these purposes, it applies semantic metadata management to these solutions. This firm participated in the XTM authoring group. During its early days, it created a tool called *Knowledge Index Manager* (KIM). Presently, its research development is known as *Intelligent Topic Manager* (ITM, available at http://www.mondeca.com/index.php/en/news/mondeca_announce_itm_t3). This is a solution for organizations which work with large volumes of data. Its key elements are:

(iii) Organization management of metadata, taxonomies and ontologies.
(iv) Management of knowledge repositories.
(v) Federation and organization of distributed heterogeneous contents.

Cogitative Technologies is a consultancy firm working with XML, XSLT, Topic Maps, RDF, Java, C++, Visual Basic, Python, Perl, Relational Database Management Systems developed with Windows 32 bits, Linux and XWALT platforms (*XML Web Applications Template Library*). Nikita Ogievetsky, the firm's Chair, was a founder member and cooperator at the XTM Authoring Group, and is also a current member of IdeAlliance.

Networked Planet is a firm with ample experience in developing and working with the Topic Maps standard. It was set up in 2004, and its software applications focus on the development and processing of tools and specific applications for the Microsoft.NET platform. This firm's leading product, *TMCore05,* is a set of tools which permits NET programmers to create scalable applications using Topic Maps with robust, persistent storage in multiuser environments. This engine covers all the specifications of the standard, and also offers APIs flexible web services which easily process the XTM specification syntax, thus permitting a rapid development of applications, as well as a flexible presentation with this platform. It has one drawback; it is used with proprietary products and is limited to free software licenses at the most. Therefore, the source code will never be available.

With regard the software developed by the firms Intelligent Views, USU-The Knowledge Business Company, Moresophy, Kalido and Innodata Isogen, no technical information is available about their developments. Therefore, the interesting option of grouping them with some brief remarks as to the products and services they are known to offer was considered. The first firm of this group has developed a technology platform under the name *K-Infinity.* It offers knowledge management solutions based on knowledge networks which enable the user to consult intelligent semantic searches on the various information sources to be interrogated, and it offers new ways to navigate through the data. The second of these firms develops and distributes products and solutions toward comprehensibly integrating corporate knowledge into business processes and applications. The search technology it uses, with an international patent, is known as *USUKnowledgeMiner,* and is in charge of condensing information by relating knowledge to the user's context [16]. The third firm uses a neuronal network approach with *indexador L4* for data mining as a support to import and export Topic Maps by adjusting to the XTM specification with its professional editing. The fourth firm centers on key information management in the Web environment. It stands out for its capacity to produce a native output in the Topic Maps standard. Kalido MDM provides a method which is run by a totally automated business model that not only supports data-enriched definitions, but is the only information management product which provides configurational workflows that automatically detect invalid data so that the person in charge of business security may either correct them or reject them [17]. The last firm of this group, Innodata Isogen, contributes to improve the way in which the firm that contracts its services creates, manages and distributes information. It is a versatile firm within the Topic Maps field as its technology adapts to almost all the existing suppliers in the market that work with such matters. This firm also develops tailor-made applications based on this standard.

Coolheads supplies technical services which include production services with the Topic Maps standard by using the *Topic Map Loom* technology which Michel Biezunski developed. This firm is a pioneer in topic Map-related services which use the so-called *Versavant* engine (http://www.versavant.org/). The Topic Maps developed with this technology are of a self-described kind, and are ideal for supporting collaborative knowledge management activities. They also include information and indexes from various sources of knowledge. This technology works with Apache 2.0. An example of its use may be found in the Canadian IEML initiative (*Information Economy Meta Language,* available at: http://www.ieml.org/).

Semantext is an application prototype developed to demonstrate how ISO/IEC 13250:2000 standard may be used to represent semantic networks. These networks are in charge of constructing blocks of Artificial Intelligence Applications such as inference systems and expert services. This constructs a knowledge basis from a Topic Map in the form of a semantic network. It is written in Python, an independent platform, and it uses many already existing tools such as the Python user's graphic interface library, Python DLLs, and the processor for Topic Maps *tmproc.* Its user interface is simple and intuitive for working with Topic Maps-related information. Eric Freese, who developed it, was also a founder member of topicmaps.Org, and his research field's center on the analysis, specification, design, development, testing, implementation, integration and management of database systems and information technologies as far as businesses, educational engineering and government organizations are concerned.

Plug-in *RivComet,* developed by the firm Rivcom, is used to convert a Topic Map into an interactive visualization format which works with browsers like Internet Explorer or Mozilla Firefox. *RivComet's* basic function is applying the format and performance of XML documents. It receives one or several XML documents and a predominant stylesheet, then it generates the HTML code which may be shown in the browser, plus the behavior code which will determine what would happen if the user interacted with the page as it presently stands.

RivComet may control the documents presented thanks to stylesheets in order to determine what areas of the screen are active and what format they will adopt (for instance, command keys, text squares, or hyperlinks); specifying what would happen when the user clicks on or keys into an active area; controlling whether the information that the user has keyed in refers to the contents on the main page so that a sychronization task is carried out in such a way that the actions performed in a window do not affect the behavior of the rest. *RivComet* is capable of creating triggers in real time using XML information to show the specific content of a document. *RivComet* changes active styles without having to reload the document, and applies different styles to the various information sections.

As seen, the products detailed throughout this section present advanced technical specifications which use the latest technologies, such as *Java 2 Enterprise Edition* (J2EE), BEA WebLogic, IBM Websphere, Oracle Application Server, JBoss, PostgreSQL, XML, etc. Behind them we come across products like Empolis' *K42,* or *Bravo,* a collaborative tool based on Empolis' K42, designed by Global Wisdom.

4.2. *Free software for information services and management*

This section presents a set of free software tools and technologies to work with Topic Maps. Unlike the commercial software which is mostly developed in Java, in this sphere there is software also developed in Perl, Python, Ruby, Ajax, etc. Given the large amount of developments, the option taken was to provide a description of the most interesting and complete projects, products or technologies, and these have been arranged into categories in terms of engines, metadata, editors, browsers, stylesheets, subject-centering computing and other solutions.

4.2.1. *Engines*

In this section, what is actually being referred to when the compilation of a set of engines working with the Topic Maps standard is mentioned is the logic field and the inference systems whose main objective is to find a way to extract new knowledge from existing knowledge.

The inference system is in charge of extracting conclusions from a set of rules, premises or axiomas which are basically based on two approaches: the first encompasses those inference systems based on logic orders; the second is based on problem-solving methods using specialized algorithms which infer in expert *ad-hoc* solution systems. Table 2 presents the most relevant engines that work with Topic Maps.

As indicated in the previous section, *Semantext* is a Topic Maps-based application which demonstrates how to construct semantic networks based on this standard. It supports creations, modifications and navigations with Topic Maps. It also includes an inference system based on the rules integrated into the Topic Map component which allows specialized consultations to be made in the knowledgebase with a view to being able to interpret the knowledge stored. The 0.72.1 version supports the XTM specification.

Table 2. Engines which work with Topic Maps.

Tool	URL	Authoring
Semantext	http://www.semantext.com/	Eric Freese
TM4j	http://tm4j.org/	Kal Ahmed
Gooseworks	http://www.gooseworks.org/	Jan Alfermissen
TMapi	http://www.tmapi.org/	Proyecto TMAPI
ZTM	http://sourceforge.net/projects/ztm/	Lars Marius Garshol
TinyTM	http://tinytim.sourceforge.net/	Stefan Lischke
Perl XTM	http://search.cpan.org/dist/XTM/	Robert Barta
XTM4XMLDB	http://sourceforge.net/projects/xtm4xmldb	Stefan Lischke
QuaaXTM	https://sourceforge.net/projects/quaaxtm/	Johannes Schmidt
JTME	http://thinkalong.com/jtme/jTME.html	Jack Park
K-Discovery	http://gcc.upb.de/	Stefan Smolnik
TMproc	http://www.ontopia.net/software/tmproc/	Geir O. Grønmo

Presently, it has solved certain tasks which were pending in its first versions, for example, natural language processing, weighted associations, extending the variety of output formats, and what is known in the SGML community as *groves-based* implementation. It seeks access and how to handle documents of many kinds. Its complexity lies in the fact that a grove engine has to be capable enough to generate a report by using the components of a word processor, a spreadsheet, and a relational database, for example.

TM4J is the name of a project which includes a set of Java-programmed tools for the robust development of open-source applications for the creation, handling, web publication and visualization of Topic Maps. The project currently under way consists of the following subprojects, of which the first constitutes the central point, which is why it has inherited its name.

(i) *Motor TM4J*: A Topic Maps processing engine written in Java. It supports the Tolog consultation language, it imports and exports XTM, LTM syntax, and persistence in a wide variety of databases.
(ii) *TMNav*: A Java/Swing desktop application for navigation by Topic Maps.
(iii) *Panckoucke:* A library for the abstract creation of Topic Maps graphic representations.
(iv) *TM4Web*: A code to integrate the TM4J engine in application frameworks, such as Apache´s Cocoon (http://cocoon.apache.org/) and Struts projects (http://www.roseindia.net/struts/struts-projects.shtml. The storage of XTM information is carried out in either the memory or an object-oriented database known as Ozone (http://tm4j.org/ozone-backend.html).

Gooseworks Toolkit (GwTk). This supplies most of the construction blocks to assemble various kinds of Topic Map applications: command line tools, plug-ins for web browsers, etc. Under the Apache license, GwTk may be used as an extension of the most well-known scripting languages, e.g., Python, Ruby and Perl. These two subprojects were still in force, but their status is presently unknown:

(i) *TmTk* (*Topic Maps Toolkit*): This is an RM implementation (available at http://www.isotopicmaps.org/rm4tm/RM4TM-official.html). It included a development library to construct Topic Maps applications based on persistent graphs, an XTM processor, and a set of command lines to work with Topic Maps. The graph obtained could be interrogated using STMQL (*Subject-based Topic Map Query Language*)
(ii) *mod_topicmaps* (*apache module*) was a model for an Apache web server to supply a Topic Map-based graphic interface service with a REST architecture style [18].

TMapi is a programming interface to access and handle information stored in a Topic Map. The aim of this project is to obtain a common API so that all the developers can simply and functionally integrate it into their own developments under any platform by adjusting it to the standard. Some of the developments which use this component are: the aforementioned *TM4j; tinyTM*, a reduced implementation of this library which contains a *parser* and a *serializer* to write and interpret files which adjust to the XTM specification 1.0, and it is even possible to convert these files into RDF and LTM; and *XTM4XMLdb*, another free development which incorporates the *TMapi* component to work with Topic Maps and native databases in XML, such as *eXist* (http://exist.sourceforge.net/) or *Apache Xindice* (http://xml.apache.org/xindice/), among others.

ZTM is a development so that Topic Maps and the Zope content manager can work combined. Basically, the idea is to import the content of a specific Topic Map to the internal Zope structure, the *Content Management Framework* (CMF), which contains its own labels.

Perl XTM is a Topic Maps creation engine which supports the XTM specification 1.0, and is programmed in Perl.

QuaaXTM is a small-sized engine to access and process the information found in a Topic Map. It was developed with the TMAPI graphic interface, and with API which was implemented in the PHP programming language. Its information repository is stored in the InnoDB tables in the MySQL relational database management system. It mainly centers on merging Topic Maps and supports TMDM. Its drawbacks are evident as its development mainly supports the community of PHO software developers, so the user requires knowledge about computing and must master English. Its main advantage is that its license is GNU/GPL.

JTME is a persistent engine used for importing and exporting Topic Maps with the XTM specification version 1.0 [19]. It achieves persistence thanks to its relational database management system in Java, known as HypersonicSQL (http://sourceforge.net/projects/hsql/). JTME uses the *author's xtm,* a specific pack for working with Topic Maps and Java whose behavior is similar to *Enterprise Java Beans* (EJB).

The *K-Discovery* knowledge management system centers on work with Topic Maps in collaborative environments. This environment has several components which are the result of the doctoral dissertation by Stefan Smolni [20]:

(i) An engine which aims at collaborative work based on Topic Maps.
(ii) A modeler for collaborative work based on Topic Maps. This is a graphic tool to develop, configure and maintain Topic Maps templates.
(iii) A browser aimed at collaborative work and based on Topic Maps, which has an online demo available.

To complete this section, it is necessary to remember that Ontopia also has an engine for working with Topic Maps known as tmproc, whose most recent version dates back to October 2000. It is programmed in Python, and its main drawback is that some of its versions only operate with a specific Java platform known as Jython (available at http://www.jython.org/Project/index.html). This is a free software under a copyright license which may be consulted on the Ontopia website.

4.2.2. *Editor, browsers and visualizers*

This section, which looks at editors, browsers and visualizers working with Topic Maps, presents the most outstanding editors, browsers and visualizers. Some of these tools support the creation and are considered editors. Others allow navigation through topics, once the conceptual structure has been created, and through the relationships established among the topics, and they operate as a browser to facilitate the users with access to the information they require. Other tools enable a graphic visualization of information based on complex data structures, such as graphs, hyperbolic trees, etc., in such a way that the software acts as a tool to visualize documents. Table 3 presents a compilation of software which, as we will go on to detail, even allows to perform three operations with a single software tool in certain cases.

Topic Map Designer is an environment which includes an author's tool to create Topic Maps, a browser and a visualizer. It supports ISO standard 13250:2003, and exports to the XTM specification 1.0, but does not support the definition of the <*scope*> characteristic.

Wandora is an environment with which Topic Maps-based knowledge is extracted, managed and published [21]. The advantages it offers are that imports may be done in various formats, it converts pdf, jpg, html, bibtex files and some database files (MySQL and HSQL) into Topic Maps, it possesses a tool to provide statistics about associations, and it also offers different graphic forms of visualization. It also has its drawbacks; it only works with Topic Maps and with their set of metadata, so the user must have knowledge about Topic Maps. Furthermore, it only works with relational database management systems. Besides, the Information Recovery (IR) process works with the management system that it works under.

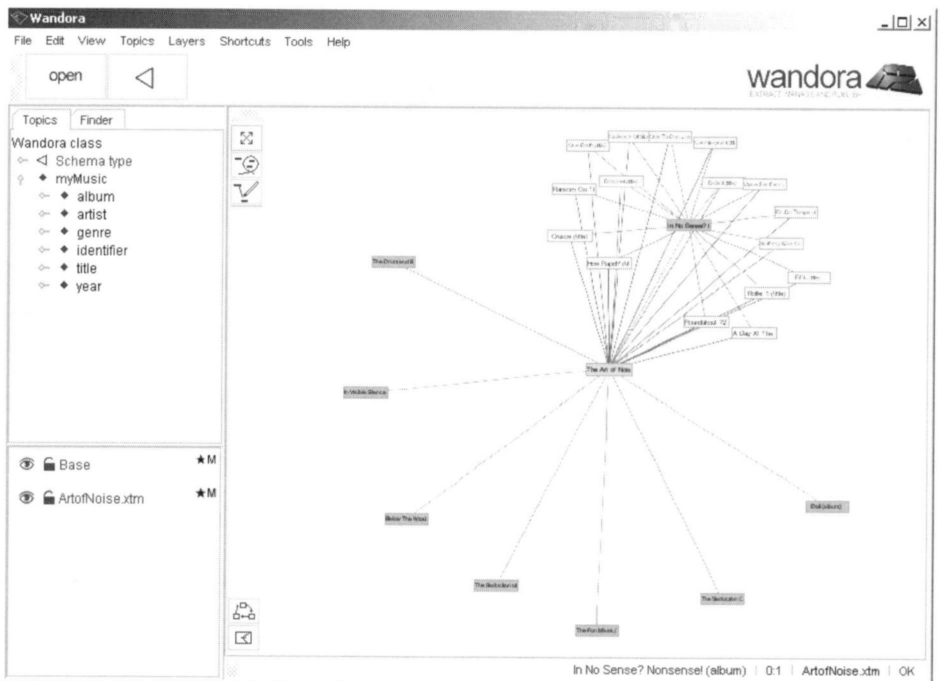

Fig. 2. Visualizing a Topic Map with Wandora.

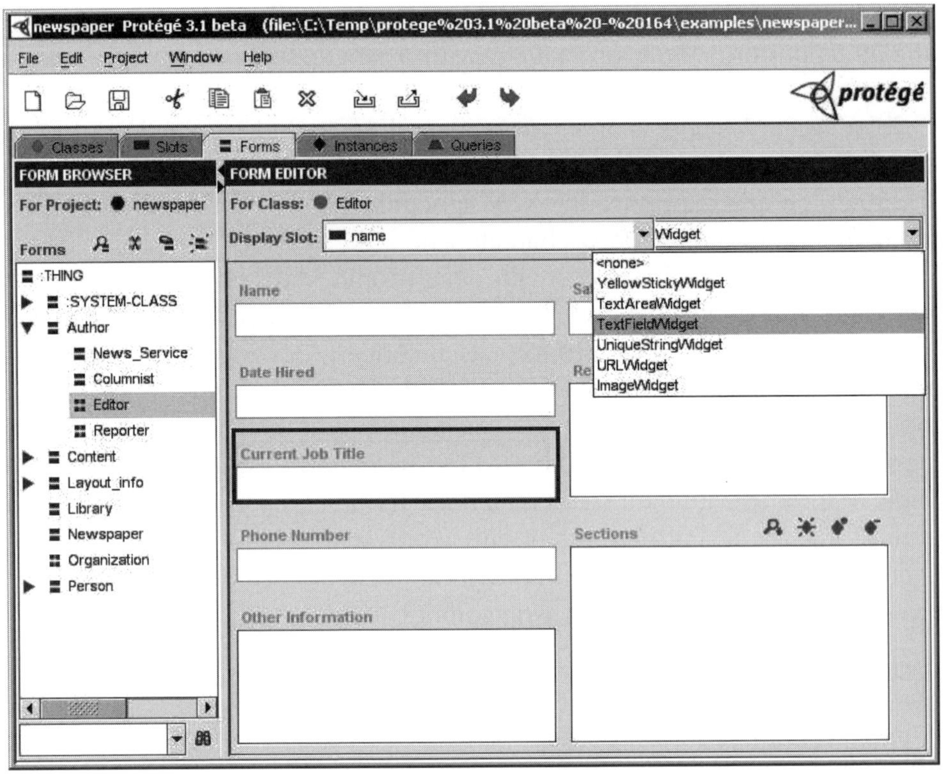

Fig. 3. Protegé's form editor.

Tmtab is a plug-in developed for *Protegé* which permits the construction of an ontology that may be exported to the XTM syntax. A practical example of such is considered in [22].

TM4L is presently being used as an *e-learning* platform based on ISO standard 13250:2003 regarding Topic Maps [23]. It is an author's tool for the creation, maintenance and use of didactic software with ontological awareness. One of its advantages is that it may be used as either a platform for the integration of online didactic resources or a Topic Maps development tool. Based on *TMAPI* and *TM4j*, which were mentioned in the previous section, it even enables a Topic Map to be visualized with the *TM4L Viewer* [24].

Ceryle is a free software tool to help users, for example writers, journalists, researchers or students, with how they organize their personal project information. It supports multimedia-type information and includes a note editor, a document viewer, a text editor, a database, a search option for complete texts, and a graph-based information visualizer [25]. However, problems arise when a topic containing a large amount of information is integrated into the visualization. Its future developments center on overcoming this kind of problems by providing its visualizer with the capacity to visualize subgraphs within the graph, for example.

Topicns is an author's tool which enables the creation of Topic Maps with browsers Mozilla Firefox and Opera. It is a Client/Server application based on the REST architecture [26] and it depends on Apache 2, MySQL and PHP 4 environments to operate correctly. Its main advantage is that once it has the suitable environment to operate in, it is very simple to use as the user does not need to have any in-depth knowledge of the Topic Maps paradigm. It has some drawbacks; it depends on a relational database management system, on some browsers which, although they are free, are specific for a certain community of users, and its functional nature purely centers on creating a Topic Map. By using this tool as a basis, other tools have come about such as *Topicns Wiki* [27], a user-friendly Topic Maps editor based on collaborative work which was presented at the 2nd edition of the International Conference on Topic Maps Research and Applications (Leipzig, Germany, 2007) or TMRA *Workshop*.

ATop is a Topic Maps editor and browser programmed in Java under the NetBeans 3.6. development platform. Its last version dates back to 2005, and this tool has been integrated into more complex systems to manage a respository of images for melanoma cases in [28, 29].

TMView is a visualization tool based on *i-Disc*, which is capable of visualizing and navigating with small-sized Topic Maps [30].

5. Metadata

On the one hand, the section on metadata presents alternative labeled languages to the syntax offered by this international standard and its corresponding XTM specification for the creation, development and maintenance of Topic Maps. On the other hand, it presents a compilation of tools which generate Topic Maps on the basis of the structures content, such as XSLT, DTDs, documents generated by office automation software packs, MP3 files and information from native XML databases.

AsTMa, and *Linear Topic Map notation* (*LTM*), are families of alternative languages to the syntax offered by ISO standard 13250:2003 and the XTM specification for the creation, development and maintenance of Topic Maps. The first family was elaborated at Bond University, Australia, where Robert Barta was in charge. It is a language with a somewhat complex syntax if the user is not familiar with it, but one that creates, maintains, restricts and consults

Topic Maps. The second syntax, developed by Lars Marius Garshol [31], is a simple user-oriented linear notation system. Despite being maintained by Ontopia, and unlike the other products or services developed by this firm, only the authoring reserves the right in the case of LTM, which means that users are free to use whatever they consider appropriate for their professional and/or academic developments.

Cogitech has a range of stylesheets, known as XSLT stylesheets, to transform DTDs in XML into Topic Maps. This DTD transformation process was designed to convert the description and syntax of an XML or SGLM document into XTM. In this way, it is able to work with tools that are already in the market and which were designed by firms like Empolis, Infoloom, Ontopia, etc.

Stefan Mintert is the person who designed xtm2xhtml, an XSLT program which transforms XHTM into XTM. This program is distributed under a free non-commercial license.

DTDdoc generates DTDs documentation. It is an XML-based application which operates as a console and uses the following parameters. If a run is done with the command line, parameter — f, which refers to format, the generator is capable of producing the output documentation in the HTML, DocBook or XTM formats. Note that it is necessary to install the *tmproc* engine with the last case for a correct operation. This DTD transformation process was designed to convert the structure description and the XML or SGML document syntax into XTM.

OpenSHORE SMRL Metaparser is a syntactic analyzer which transforms file contents, derived from OpenOffice, KOffice, Microsoft Office and DocBook, etc., into output formats, for instance, XTM, XHTML, SHORE XML, etc. It is based on the *Semantic Markup Rule Language* (SMRL) specification, which is a specification language to extract knowledge with a semantic load, such as the relationships between concepts. Its main drawback is that it works with documents that the user has had to previously structure, so an average knowledge of computer programming is needed for them to be integrated into a tool. Among its advantages, however, is its *Common Public License* (*CPL*) for its source code and binaries, and all the tools with or under which it works belong to the free software community.

Metadata Extraction Framework (MDF) is an environment for the automatic development of metadata generation. It was proposed by Kal Ahmed, and is distributed with an open-source license. It is combined with a simple approach to create reusable modules that are capable of processing metadata with implementation by using the Java programming language.

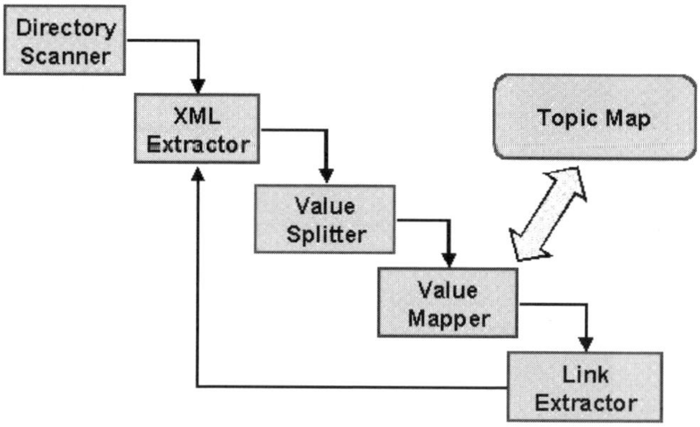

Fig. 4. MDF architecture.

The environment was designed with the idea of performing searches for information resources in such a way as to extract and wash metadata to finally obtain a Topic Map with the metainformation, which proved interesting. It works well with varying information, MP3 files, Word documents and the contents of XML-native databases. The process chain is that shown in Fig 4.

Its main disadvantage is its data model. Basically, it consists in a set of property-value pairs, which means that relationships cannot be represented directly. Therefore a mapping process from this data model to Topic Maps is complex and inflexible. This problem was overcome by applying RDF to the data model to autogenerate Topic Maps [32]. This, on the one hand, means that work is no longer done with a set of property-value pairs, but with a short list of values (property, value, owner) to allow more complex metadata to be handled and to facilitate the representation of relationships. On the other hand, it reuses the module developed with other tools using RDF, and enhances any existing compatibility between both technologies. Its architecture and its behavior is based on a set of files which:

- Compile,
- Divide into individual items,
- Parse each item heading to extract useful metadata,
- Process some of the metadata, for instance, those which may be decomposed into several values,
- Map the result in a Topic Map,
- Merge into the ontology and finally, export it to the XTM specification.

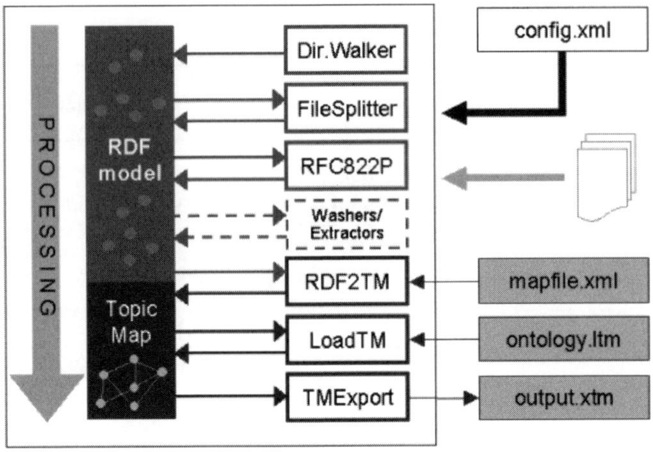

Fig. 5. MapMaker architecture.

6. Conclusions and outlook

As it has been demonstrated throughout the analysis and compilation presented in this chapter, if we have a conceptual metadata schema which correctly describes online information, such as Topic Maps, we solve two important issues. On the one hand, the structures definition, and on the other hand, the meanings of the managed information.

Moreover, as a result of the analysis of the selected tools, as well as the different specifications which support Topic Maps, we consider that Topic Maps provide added value to the Information Retrieval process since not only do they provide relevant information, but also allow that user has available the whole knowledge structure which contains the information he wanted to find. Furthermore, chapter showed that the selection of the proper technology to work with Topic Maps information not only must account for technical basis, but also other important issues since a lot of tools with different kinds of licenses are available, and they cover practically all the tasks regarding online information management.

To conclude this section, it is important to say that current trends in the use of tagging languages for online information managing allow us to state that a wider study of a collection of tagging languages, apart from Topic Maps and their different specifications, could be developed. These include Resource Description Framework (RDF), Ontology Web Language (OWL), Darpa Agent Markup Language (DAML), Ontology Inference Encoding and Transmission Standard (OIL), Metadata Object Description Schema (MODS), Darwin Information Typing Architecture (DITA), etc. All these languages are generally based on XML. Moreover, most of them are combinable, but they also have multiple overlapping possibilities, specifically, in content definition. Nevertheless, as some authors mentioned [33], the combination of some of the above-mentioned specifications, such as XTM and DITA would be as putting together a jigsaw puzzle, without any overlap. For that reason, we strongly recommend the use of Topic Maps since they provide all the item information.

References

1. Park J and S Hunting (2003). *XMLTopic Maps: Creating and Using Topic Maps for the Web.* Addison-Wesley.
2. Berners-Lee, T, J Hendler and O Lassila (2001). The Semantic Web. *Scientific American.* Available at http://www.sciam.com/2001/0501issue/0501berners-lee.html.
3. Postman, N (1993). *Technopoly: The Surrender of Culture to Technology.* New York: Vintage Books.
4. Sobel, D (2000). *Galileo's Daughter.* New York: Penguin Books.
5. Fisher, KM, J-H Wandersee and D Moody (2000). *Mapping Biology Knowledge.* Boston, MA: Kluwer Academic Publishers.
6. Biezunski, M and C Hamon (1996). A topic map of this conference´s proceedings. In *GCA International Hytime Conference,* 3. Seattle. Available at http://www.infoloom.com/IHC96/mb214.htm.
7. Pepper, S (2002). Lessons on applying Topic Maps. The XMLPapers, Ontopia. Available at http://www.ontopia.net/topicmaps/materials/xmlconf.html.
8. Kaminsky, P (2002). Integrating information on the semantic web using partially ordered multi hypersets. Available at http://www.ideanest.com/braque/Thesis-web.pdf.
9. Park (2003). *XMLTopic Maps: Creating and Using Topic Maps for the Web,* p. 542. Addison-Wesley.
10. Rath, HH (2003). *White Paper: The Topic Map Handbook.* Germany: Gütersloh. Available at http://www.empolis.com/download/docs/whitepapers/empolistopicmapswhitepaper_eng.pdf.
11. Pérez, MC (2002). Explotación de los córpora textuales informatizados para la creación de bases de datos terminológicas basadas en el conocimiento. *Estudios de Lingüística Española (ELiEs),* 18. Available at, http://elies.rediris.es/elies18/.
12. Pepper, S (2003). Euler, topic maps, and revolution. In *Proceedings Conference XML Europe, 1999,* Granada. Available at http://www.infoloom.com/tmsample/pep4.htm.

13. Rath, HH (2003). *White Paper: The Topic Map Handbook,* p. 45. Germany: Gütersloh. Available at http://www.empolis.com/download/docs/whitepapers/empolistopicmapswhitepaper_eng.pdf.
14. Pepper, (1999).
15. Biezunsky, M (2001). XML Topic Maps: Finding Aids for the Web. *IEEE Multimedia.,* 8(2), 104–108.
16. Khöler, A, A Korthaus and M Schader (2007). (Semi)-automatic topic map generation from a conventional document index. *Knowledge Sharing and Collaborative Engineering.*
17. Sheina, M (2007). Kalido releases third generation of MDM product. *CDR online Journal.* Available at http://www.cbronline.com/article_news.asp?guid=95572222-F6C6-491E-991B-7BF18BD80C74.
18. Fielding, R (2000). Architectural styles and the design of network-based software architectures. Dissertation of the their thesis to obtain the doctor of philos in Inform and Computer Science, University of California, Irvine.
19. Park, J (2001). *jTME: A Java Topic Map Engine. Cover Pages.* Available at http://xml.coverpages.org/ni2001-03-22-b.html.
20. Smolni, S and L Nastansky (2002). K-discovery: Using topic maps to identify distributed knowledge structures in groupware-based organizational memories. HICSS. In *Proceedings of the 35th Annual Hawaii International Conference on System Sciences,* 7–10, 966–975.
21. Kivelä, A (2007). *Topic Maps, Wandora ja kourallinen julkaisuprojekteja.* Presentation held in XML Finland meeting, November. Available at http://www.wandora. net/wandora/download/other/wandora_xml-finland.pdf.
22. Garrido, P (2004). *Topic Maps: normativa, aplicaciones y herramientas,* InfoDig Información Digital. Dpto. Ciencias de la Documentación, Universidad de Zaragoza. Available at http://tramullas.com/jaca/gescon/contenidos/textos/Garrido.pdf.
23. Dicheva, D and C Dichev (2006). TM4L: Creating and browsing educational topic maps. *British Journal of Educational Technology — BJET,* 37(3), 391–404.
24. Dicheva, D, C Dicehv and D Wang (2005). Visualizing topic maps for e-learning. In *Workshop on Applications of Semantic Web in E-Learning,* Kaohsiung, 950–951.
25. Murray, A (2007). *Class Topic Map Processor.* Manual de Ayuda del proyecto Ceryle.
26. Fielding, 2000.
27. Cerny, R (forthcoming). Topicns wiki: A collaborative topmapping. In *Scaling Topic Maps.* Springer. (In press)
28. Grammatikopoulos, G, A Papastergiou, A Hatzigaidas, Z Zaharis, P Lazaridis, D Kampitaki and G Tryfon (2006). Providing a sophisticated TM software tool to

support development of a TM-based system for managing melanoma cases images. In *Proceedings of the 5th WSEAS Int. Conf. on Data Networks, Communications & Computers*, Bucharest, 81–86.

29. Papastergiou, A, A Hatzigaidas, Z Zaharis, G Tryfon, K Moustakas and D Ioannidis (2007). Introducing automated melanoma detection in a topic map based image retrieval system. In *Proceedings of the 6th WSEAS International Conference on Applied Computer Science*, Hangzhou, 452–457.
30. Hoffman, T, H Wendler and B Froehlich (2005). The i-Disc — A tool to visualize and explore topic maps. In *Eurovis 2005: Eurographics/IEEE VGTC Symposium on Visualization*, 45–52.
31. Garshol, LM (2002). The Linear Topic Map Notation: Definition and Introduction, Version 1.2, Ontopia. Available at http://www.ontopia.net/download/ltm.html.
32. Pepper, S (2002). The Ontopia MapMaker: Leveraging RDF to autogenerate Topic Maps. The XML Papers, Ontopia. Available at http://www.ontopia.net/topicmaps/materials/MapMaker.pdf.
33. Gelb, J (2008). DITA and Topic Maps: bringing pieces together. In *Proceedings of the Topic Maps International Conference*, Oslo Available at http://www.topic-maps.com/tm2008/gelb.pdf.

CHAPTER II.4

METHODOLOGIES FOR THE CREATION OF SEMANTIC DATA

Tobias Bürger

PAYBACK GmbH
Theresienhöhe. 12
80339 München, Germany
tobias@biasbuerger.com

Elena Simperl and Christoph Tempich

Detecon International GmbH
Oberkasseler Str. 2
53227 Bonn, Germany
elena.simperl@sti2.at
Christoph.Tempich@detecon.com

This chapter is meant as an overview of the current state of the art in the area of knowledge engineering, with a particular focus on the methodologies describing how the process of creating ontologies and, more general, semantic content, should be performed in a rigorous and controlled manner. We introduce the most important methodologies proposed in the past years in this field, and the tool environments supporting their application. As a result of this survey we identify open issues and possible directions of research and development which are likely to lead to a mainstream adoption of the methodologies, and thus encourage the industrial takeup of semantic technologies.

1. Introduction

Ontologies, as a means for a shared understanding of knowledge and a way to represent real-world domains, are a core technology for the effective development of high-qualitative knowledge-based systems [1]. In particular they are facing a growing popularity with the emergence of the Semantic Web; besides providing standard Web-suitable representation languages such as RDF(S) and OWL [2–4], the Semantic Web community also encourages the development of methods and tools to build, maintain and reuse ontologies [5–8], and algorithms to manage them in terms of matching, alignment and integration [8, 9]. Due to the challenging and resource-intensive nature of ontology engineering processes special attention has also been paid to automatic methods, such as those based on the linguistics-based acquisition of domain-specific knowledge from document corpora [10] which assist humans during the operation of these processes. The sum of all the activities previously mentioned is referred to as *ontology engineering* [7].

Ontologies can be used as a vocabulary for describing Web resources in a machine-understandable way, a task which is typically referred to as *annotation*. A number of methodologies describing the process of annotation of various types of resources like textual documents, images, graphics, or videos, were proposed in the last years. Some of these methodologies are accompanied by software environments which allow the mechanization of specific annotation-related tasks; most notably for text or semi-structured data, automatic means to create semantic annotations are seen as a viable alternative, in terms of costs, to human-driven approaches.

The goal of this chapter is to present state-of-the-art process-driven methodologies for the creation of semantic content, i.e., ontologies, as well of semantic annotations based on ontologies. We will survey several of the most outstanding approaches that emerged in the last years in the fields of ontology engineering and semantic annotation, and will present tools supporting the operation of semantic content-creation processes and the application of their associated methodologies. For a consistent classification of works surveyed we employ the terminology introduced by Gómez-Pérez *et al.* in [7], which is based on the IEEE standard for software development [11]. It differentiates between *management, development-oriented* and *supportive* ontology-engineering activities. The first category includes control and quality assurance activities which can be observed across engineering disciplines. Development-oriented activities strictly relate to the process of creating an ontology, while support activities aim at aiding the engineering team in this endeavor by means of the documentation and evaluation of specific stages of the development process, or by extracting relevant ontological knowledge from external (semi-structured) resources. A similar classification can be applied to activities carried out within semantic annotation processes. In this case we can distinguish between general-purpose *management* activities, *development* activities related to the generation of semantic metadata and its maintenance, and, finally, *support* activities which cover the documentation and evaluation of the results, as well as their refinement through complementary automatic information extraction techniques.

It is commonly accepted that process-driven methodologies cannot be applied efficiently without adequate tool support. Therefore our chapter also includes an overview of the most popular ontology-engineering and semantic-annotation environments which can be utilized to carry out specific activities within the surveyed methodologies or at least facilitate these activities.

An analysis of open research and development issues in the fields of ontology engineering and semantic annotation concludes the survey.

2. Ontologies

In this chapter we adhere to a broad understanding of the term "ontology", which, most notably, does not impose any specific restrictions on the level of formality of an ontological model. According to Gruber an ontology is an *explicit, formal specification of a shared conceptualization* [12]. This definition emphasizes several important characteristics of an ontology [13]:

- It is formal and explicit. This means that an ontology is represented using a formal language, in other words, a language with a machine-understandable semantics, and that it uses types of primitives (such as concepts, properties, attributes, axioms) which are explicitly defined.
- It is shared. An ontology mirrors a common understanding of the modeled domain, being the result of a consensus achieved within a (potential) community of ontology users.
- It specifies a conceptualization. An ontology is used to model some domain of the world. This implies that an ontology is responsible for a specific view upon the corresponding domain, reflected in certain simplifications, abstractions, omissions or other modeling decisions.

Alternative ways to define ontologies usually highlight only a subset of the aforementioned aspects. A logics-centered view is held by Guarino: An ontology is a *logical theory which gives an explicit, partial account of a conceptualization* [14, 15]. This definition, though sharing several commonalities with the one from Gruber [12], reduces ontologies to logical structures, thus excluding conceptual models which do not commit to a logically precise theory. Furthermore it emphasizes the contextual nature of the represented knowledge, by defining ontologies as partial account of reality. The shared aspect is not (explicitly) taken into consideration.

A wide range of definitions concentrate on the content of ontologies from an engineering perspective. Emerged from the knowledge based systems' community, these definitions consider an ontology as a means to specify a hierarchically structured vocabulary of a particular domain and the rules for *combining the terms and relations to define extensions of the vocabulary* [16]. Ontologies are then used as schemas for building knowledge bases in order to simplify the integration and reuse of these systems. The consequences of this engineering-oriented view upon ontologies are twofold: they implicitly give hints on the mandatory content of ontologies and on the ways to build them: ontologies consist of concepts/terms, relations, rules etc., while concepts and relations might be organized in taxonomies. Accordingly, in order to build an ontology, a knowledge engineer has to specify its vocabulary and has to proceed by identifying concepts, organizing them in a hierarchy and linking them by means of relationships and constraints. Furthermore, it is explicitly stated that ontologies are intended to be reused and shared among software applications, a fact which has not been explicitly taken into account by the logics-centered approaches like the one by Guarino [14].

Given the multitude of application scenarios and the complementary points of view with respect to the exact meaning of ontologies we currently assist at a "mitigation" of the original definitions towards a more interdisciplinary, unified understanding of the term. Since ontology-like conceptual models have a long-standing tradition in computer linguistics (thesauri), database design (ER diagrams), software engineering (UML diagrams, object models), libraries (controlled vocabularies) or eCommerce (product taxonomies, business rules), a recent trend in identifying whether a certain conceptual structure is or is not an ontology is to enumerate the mandatory conditions for the former [17]. In order to distinguish ontologies from other (related) conceptual structures Uschold and Jasper introduced two criteria [17]:

- An ontology defines a vocabulary of terms.
- An ontology constrains the meaning of the domain terms by indicating how ontology concepts are defined and are inter-related to a specific domain structure.

2.1. *Types of ontologies*

A further attempt to clarify the partially divergent views upon ontologies was to classify them by various dimensions like formality [18] or scope [14]:

Formality: Uschold and Grüninger distinguish among four levels of formality [18]:

- *Highly informal*: The domain of interested is modeled in a loose form in natural language.
- *Semi-informal*: The meaning of the modeled entities is less ambiguous by the usage of a restricted language.
- *Semi-formal*: The ontology is implemented in a formal language.
- *Rigorously formal*: The meaning of the representation language is defined in detail, with theorems and proofs for soundness or completeness.

Most of the currently available (Web) ontologies belong to the second and third category. A further classification scheme by Wand and Weber differentiates between three levels of formality [19]: informal, semi-formal, and formal ontologies. Again, most of the currently available sources usually associated to the word ontology can be assigned to the category of *semi-formal* models. Lastly, McGuinness introduced an *ontological continuum* specifying a total order between common types of models [20]. This basically divides ontologies (or ontology-like structures) in *informal* and *formal* as follows:

- *Informal models* are ordered in ascending order of their formality degree as *controlled vocabularies, glossaries, thesauri* and *informal taxonomies.*
- *Formal models* are ordered in the same manner: starting with *formal taxonomies,* which precisely define the meaning of the specialization/generalization relationship, more formal models are derived by incrementally adding *formal instances, properties/frames, value restrictions, general logical constraints, disjointness, formal meronimy* etc.

In the first category we usually encounter thesauri such as WordNet [21], taxonomies such as the Open Directory[1] and the ACM classification[2] or various eCommerce standards [1]. Most of the available Semantic Web ontologies can be localized at the lower end of the formal continuum (that is, as formal taxonomies), a category which overlaps with the semi-formal level in the previous categorizations. However, the usage of Semantic Web representation languages does not guarantee a certain degree of formality: while an increasing number of applications are currently deciding to formalize

[1] http://www.dmoz.org
[2] http://www.acm.org/class/1998/

domain or application-specific knowledge using languages such as RDFS or OWL, the resulting ontologies do not necessarily commit to the formal semantics of these languages. In contrast, Cyc [22] or DOLCE [23] are definitively representative for the so-called heavyweight ontologies category, which corresponds to the upper end of the continuum.

Scope: According to [14], ontologies can be classified into four categories:

- *Upper-level/top-level ontologies* which describe general-purpose concepts and their properties. Examples of upper-level ontologies are the Top-Elements Classification by Sowa [24], the Suggested Upper Level Merged Ontology SUMO [25] or the Descriptive Ontology for Linguistic and Cognitive Engineering DOLCE [23].
- *Domain ontologies* which are used to model specific domains such as medicine or academia. A typical example in this area is the Gene Ontology [26].
- *Task ontologies* which describe general or domain-specific activities.
- *Application ontologies* which are to a large extent instantiations of domain ontologies having regard to particular application-related task ontologies and application requirements.

Other authors mention an intermediary category called *core ontologies*, which cover the most important concepts in a given domain. For example, the Semantic Network in UMLS[3] contains general medical concepts such as disease, finding, syndrome, thus being a core medical ontology. Others differentiate between *application domain* and *application task ontologies* [27]. The former instantiates general-purpose domain knowledge to particular application constraints, while the latter corresponds, similar to the *application ontologies* introduced by Guarino [14], to a combination of domain-relevant declarative and procedural knowledge.

A last category of ontologies, which was not covered by the classifications mentioned so far, are the so-called *meta-ontologies* or (knowledge) *representation ontologies*. They describe the primitives which are used to formalize knowledge in conformity with a specific representation paradigm. The Frame Ontology [28] or the representation ontologies of the W3C Semantic Web languages RDFS and OWL.[4] are well-known examples from this category.

---

[3] http://semanticnetwork.nlm.nih.gov/

[4] http://www.w3.org/2000/01/rdf-schema, http://www.w3.org/2002/07/owl last visited in May, 2006

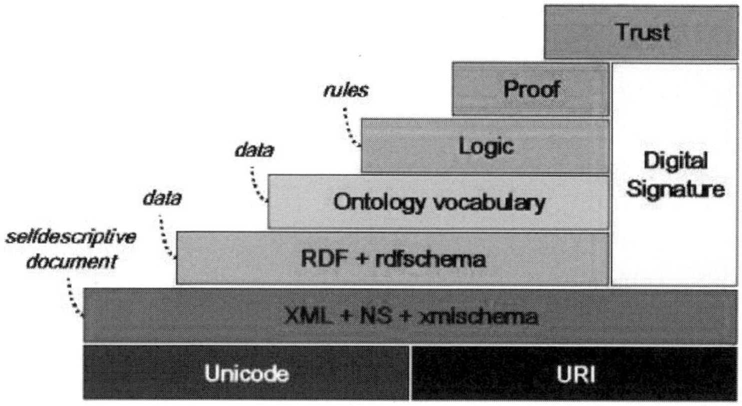

Fig. 1. High-level architecture of the Semantic Web.

2.2. *Representation languages for ontologies*

The Semantic Web is built on XML-based syntaxes which use URIs to uniquely identify Web resources (*cf.* Fig. 1). Resources include not only common Web documents, but any entity represented within a computer system (such as persons, physical objects, or even RDF statements) and are described by machine-processable metadata. Metadata is a collection of RDF statements of the type (*subject, predicate, object*), whereas the three fields can be individually referenced by means of URIs. This enables RDF to represent simple statements about resources as a graph of nodes and edges representing the resources, and their properties and values, respectively. The next layers in the Semantic Web language architecture add logically more expressive ontologies (e.g., OWL) and support for rules (for example SWRL [29]). RDF(S) provides a vocabulary for describing classes, their relations and properties of RDF resources. RDF(S) and OWL are used to formalize common vocabularies for metadata — OWL allows even equivalence definitions between resources — thus increasing interoperability among applications. Besides that, they re-define Web resources in terms of classes and properties with a well-formed semantics, which can be exploited by reasoners to generate implicitly formalized knowledge automatically. OWL is divided into three sub-languages, in order to maximize the trade-off between usability (with respect to expressivity) and computational properties (since more expressivity is achieved only at the expense of feasible computational properties). For simple knowledge representation tasks which involve classical subsumption, equivalence and restricted cardinality axioms, ontology engineers are provided with the OWL Lite language. This language is expected to cover most of the expressivity needs in current Semantic Web applications, while offering efficient computational support. The OWL DL language extends the expressivity of the former one, while still providing feasible properties with respect to decidability. The OWL Full language is compatible to RDFS, thus being extremely powerful with respect to its expressivity. However, it does not guarantee decidable computational features. OWL is complemented by SWRL, a rule-based knowledge representation formalism, which adds even more expressive power to OWL, but in the same time requires advanced reasoning capabilities to deal with the twofold (i.e., Description Logics and Rules) representation paradigm induced by OWL/SWRL knowledge bases.

2.3. *The usage of ontologies in information systems*

many different types of applications use ontologies to a various extent as a conceptual backbone. Jasper and Uschold [30] distinguish four different types of ontology-based systems:

Neutral Authoring: An enterprize with many applications can use a common ontology as the semantic core for all its data structures. The idea is to translate an ontology into different target application formats and use it as a basis for further development. Although the initial effort for the ontology development might be significant, the enterprize gains advantages in the form of reusable knowledge artifacts, increased maintainability and long-term knowledge retention.
Common Access to Information: Views are an established way to facilitate information integration if the information is modeled according to different data schemas (*cf.* [31]). An ontology can represent a global view. Many standardization efforts are underway to create uniform descriptions for, e.g., product data. As ontologies enable detailed descriptions of the semantics underlying different data sources, they can be used to check their consistency. This area is particulary interesting for the application of ontologies to describe Web services.[5]
Ontology-based Specification: The specification of software is another application field for ontologies. Requirements can be characterized and specified using ontologies. Following the ideas of the Model-Driven Architecture promoted by the OMG,[6] ontologies can support the validation

[5] cf. http://www.w3.org/Submission/WSMO/ or http://www.w3.org/Submission/OWL-S/
[6] http://www.omg.org/mda/

and verification of software [32]. Due to the formal specification of an ontology, changes in the model can be directly propagated to the implementing software.

Ontology-based Search: An ontology can provide an abstract description for various information repositories and thus assist search. It can support site organization, navigation and browsing, thus enabling structured, comparative, and customized search. Semantic search gains from the exploitation of the encoded generalization/specialization information and the sense disambiguation provided by an ontology. Taking, for instance, product search ontologies offer configuration support and auto-completion. In this case complex features requests from customers are characterized in the ontology to the level of detail necessary to select from the available products. Another example is multimedia retrieval. Here ontologies can be used to represent the content of the multimedia resources, providing a basis for keyword, or more complicated, searches.

Although ontologies are beneficial for a number of scenarios there is one major obstacle to their fast and wide spread adoption in information systems: It is complicated and time consuming to build and maintain ontologies. The process to develop ontologies has therefore attracted ongoing attention and a number of methodologies were proposed to organize the ontology engineering process in a systematic manner.

3. Semantic metadata

The term "semantic metadata" refers to machine-processable annotations of information (or Web) resources captured using RDF. In the context of the Semantic Web "annotation" is understood as the process of assigning terms from an ontology to a resource (e.g., to a text document, Web page, image, or video) or a part of a resource (e.g., to a sentence, word, or spatial/temporal region of a multimedia item). According to [33], the semantics of annotations can be characterized as follows:

- *Decoration*: Annotations are simply commentaries to resources.
- *Linking*: Annotations are a mechanism to provide link anchors.
- *Instance Identification*: Annotations make an assertion about a resource, in other words, the resource annotated is identified as an instance of a particular ontological primitive.
- *Instance Reference*: Here the assertion is made about the subject of a resource, not about the resource itself.

- *Aboutness*: Annotations establish a loose association between ontological concepts and information resources.
- *Pertinence*: In this case the association is a weak ontological extension, in other words, the annotation encodes additional information which is not subject of the resource itself.

Several enabling technologies for semantic annotation have emerged in the last decade. Languages for embedding RDF to existing Web content were designed within the W3C. RDFa (Resource Description Framework attributes)[7] defines several attributes that can be used to annotate markups encoded in an XML based language with semantics. The semantic content is extracted through pre-defined simple mappings. Alternatives to RDFa worthwhile to be mentioned are eRDF (embedded RDF) and microformats.[8] Complementarily Gleaning Resource Descriptions from Dialects of Languages (GRDDL) defines a markup format which allows one to create RDF data from traditional Web content (XHTML, HTML) through XSLT.[9] Other tools extract RDF from Wikipedia, databases, digital libraries, contributing, around seven years after the publication of the seminal paper about the Semantic Web by Tim Berners-Lee *et al.* [34], to the emergence of impressive amounts of RDF data publicly available on the Internet for further usage. The most prominent example in this context is, arguably, DBPedia, a data set of more than 200 million RDF triples extracted from Wikipedia, predominantly its English version.

4. Methodologies

When semantic content, be that ontologies or instances thereof, is created, it is obvious that a number of steps must be followed, in some particular order, in order to ensure that the results are delivered in a reasonable time frame, at a reasonable quality level and with reasonable costs. This process involves several actors, including domain experts, knowledge engineers and tool developers, who work in collaboration to deliver a specific semantic artifact in accordance to a set of user requirements. In order to ensure the operationalization of the underlying process in terms of results, labor and duration, significant efforts have been spent in the Semantic Web community to understand the life cycle of semantic content and to design methodologies providing descriptions of the process through which user needs are translated into semantic artifacts.

[7] http://www.w3.org/TR/xhtml-rdfa/

[8] eRDF: http://research.talis.com/2005/erdf/wiki/Main/RdfInHtml, microformats: http://microformats.org/

[9] http://www.w3.org/TR/grddl/

In general a methodology can be defined as *a comprehensive, integrated series of techniques or methods creating a general systems theory of how a class of thought-intensive work ought be performed* [35]. In particular a methodology includes a description of the process to be performed and of the participants/roles involved in the process, assigns responsibilities to activities and people and gives recommendations in the form of best practices and guidelines. It can be related to a specific process model, which provides additional details on the order and relationships between activities foreseen by the corresponding life cycle. In analogy to other engineering disciplines, notably Software Engineering, methodologies in the area of semantic content creation typically use models such as the Waterfall model by Royce [36], Boehm's spiral model [37] or some form of agile development.

In the following we describe several of the most prominent methodologies in the fields of ontology engineering and semantic annotation.

4.1. *Methodologies for the creation of ontologies*

Ontology engineering methodologies can be divided into two main categories, depending on the setting in which they can be applied in:

- *Centralized ontology engineering*: The ontology engineering team is concentrated in one location. Communication between team members occurs in regular face-to-face meetings. This setting is more relevant for the development of ontologies for a specific purpose within an organization.
- *Decentralized ontology engineering*: This setting is more relevant in the Semantic Web context or in other open, large-scale distributed environments. The ontology engineering team is composed of individuals dispersed over several geographical locations and affiliated to different organizations. Communication within the team is typically asynchronous. The ontology provides a lingua-franca between different stakeholders or ensures interoperability between machines, humans, or both.

Examples for methodologies which belong to the first category are IDEF5 [38], METHONTOLOGY [39], or the OTK methodology [40]. IDEF5 and METHONTOLOGY describe the generic ontology design process. As compared to the process model introduced in IDEF5 and METHONTOLOGY, OTK does not foresee any additional tasks or activities, but rather integrates the ontology engineering process into a more comprehensive framework for the creation of knowledge management applications which rely on ontologies.

4.1.1. *IDEF5*

IDEF5 is an ontology engineering methodology which supports the creation of ontologies for centralized settings [38]. It is well-documented as it originates and is applied by a company. The methodology is divided into five main activities: *Organize and Define Project, Collect Data, Analyze Data, Develop Initial Ontology* and *Refine and Validate Ontology.* The organization and definition activity defines the managerial aspects of the ontology development project. During the collect data activity the domain analysis is performed and knowledge sources are determined and exploited. The result of the analyze data activity is a first conceptualization of the domain. In the following activities the ontology engineers start defining so-called *Proto-Concepts* which are high level concepts characterizing the domain. These are refined with relations and axioms. The Proto-Concepts are later refined until the validation results in an ontology which meets the requirements defined in the beginning. Even though ontology evolution is supported by means of the extension of Proto-Concepts, decentralized development and issues around partial autonomy are not supported by IDEF5.

4.1.2. *METHONTOLOGY*

METHONTOLOGY belongs to the more comprehensive ontology engineering methodologies as it can be used for building ontologies either from scratch, reusing other ontologies as they are, or by a process of re-engineering them [39]. The framework enables the construction of ontologies at the knowledge level, such as, the conceptual level, as opposed to the implementation level. The framework consists of: identification of the ontology development process with the identification of the main activities, such as, evaluation, configuration, management, conceptualization, integration, or implementation; a life cycle based on evolving prototypes; and the methodology itself specifies the steps for performing the activities, the techniques used, the outcomes and their evaluation. The process to build an ontology for centralized ontology based systems is described in detail. However, METHONTOLOGY does not provide guidance for decentralized ontology development and does not focus on post development processes.

4.1.3. *OTK methodology*

The OTK methodology divides the ontology engineering process into five main steps. Each step has numerous sub-steps, which require a main decision to be taken at the end and which results in a special outcome [40]. The phases are *Feasibility Study, Kickoff, Refinement, Evaluation* and *Application & Evolution*. The sub-steps of the, for instance, *Refinement* are "Refine semi-formal ontology description", "Formalize into target ontology" and "Create prototype" etc. The documents resulting from each phase are, e.g., for the *Kickoff* phase an "Ontology Requirements Specification Document (ORSD)" and the "Semi-formal ontology description". The documents are the basis for the major decisions that have to be taken at the end in order to proceed to the next phase, for instance, whether in the *Kickoff* phase one has captured sufficient requirements. The phases *Refinement – Evaluation – Application – Evolution* typically need to be performed in iterative cycles. In a nutshell, the OTK methodology completely describes all steps which are necessary to build ontologies for centralized knowledge management systems.

Requirements from decentralized settings were the main drivers for the definition of the HCOME and DILIGENT ontology engineering methodologies which are explained in the following.

4.1.4. *HCOME*

In [41], the authors present a very recent approach to ontology development. HCOME, which stands for *H*uman-*C*entered *O*ntology Engineering *Me*thodology, supports the development of ontologies in a decentralized fashion. HCOME introduces three different spaces in which ontologies can be stored. The first one is the `Personal Space`. In this space users can create and merge ontologies, control ontology versions, map terms and word senses to concepts and consult the top ontology. The evolving personal ontologies can be shared in the `Shared Space`. The shared space can be accessed by all participants. In the shared space users can discuss ontological decisions based on the IBIS [42] model. After a discussion and agreement the ontology is moved to the `Agreed space`. HCOME does not provide a detailed description of the process steps to follow in order to reach agreement among the participants.

4.1.5. *DILIGENT*

DILIGENT is an ontology engineering methodology addressing the requirements of a distributed knowledge management scenario [43]. DILIGENT distinguishes five main stages which are interactively repeated. Those are the central build, local adaptation, central analysis, central revision and local update. A board comprising ontology engineers starts the process by building a small initial ontology which is distributed to the users. The users are allowed to locally adapt the shared ontology in order to comply with changing business requirements. The changes done by users serve as an input for a next version of the shared ontology. A board of ontology engineers and users updates the shared ontology in the central analysis and revision stage. The users locally update their shared ontology to the new version. In this way the shared ontology responds to emerging requirements, while the process allows for cost savings through small set up costs in comparison to a central approach.

A major issue in DILIGENT relates to the consensus building process, because the heterogeneous knowledge models created by the users should be partly integrated into the shared ontology. DILIGENT supports the consensus building process extending an existing argumentation model and adapts it to the requirements of ontology engineering discussions. It suggests a restricted set of argument types, thereby offers a systematic guidance for the discussions. As a result, the agreement process becomes more structured and traceable. Although the methodology has been tested in distributed knowledge management scenarios only the setup is similar to the requirements found in the Semantic Web.

Ontology engineering methodologies which were propsed recently concentrate even more on the decentralized aspects. There, the question of how to apply Web 2.0 paradigms and technologies in order to facilitate the development of community-driven ontologies has received particular attention. While solutions to this question have not yet matured into full-fledged methodologies, they indicate the direction in which the field is moving.

4.1.6. *Wiki-based ontology engineering*

Wiki-based ontology engineering aims at a separation of fully formalized ontology development and the development of concept trees and the like. Semantically enhanced Wiki engines support the conceptual phase of the ontology engineering process. This phase is performed by all stake-holders using the Wiki as a collaborative tool. Concepts are not only defined and described by a restricted team of experts, instead this part of the process is open for everyone interested in the results. Afterwards a formally extended version of the concept tree is built based on the resulting concept descriptions. This approach is particularly suitable for companies which intend to establish and define a company wide glossary while at the same time defining a common data model for application integration.

4.1.7. *Ontology engineering games*

Another interesting approach to knowledge elicitation is presented in [44]. There, games are developed in order to find shared conceptualizations of a domain. During the game, players describe images, text or videos. Users get points if they describe the content in the same way. Their input is formalized and translated into OWL.

4.1.8. *Tagging for ontology engineering*

Tagging is a very successful approach to organize all sorts of content on the web. Users tag, i.e., add short descriptions to their bookmarks, photos, articles, weblogs and other kinds of content. Based on that, so-called folksonomies evolve. Tags often describe the meaning of the tagged content in one term. Based on this observation, Braun *et al.* introduced a tagging-based ontology engineering methodology in [45]. The methodology introduces a four step process starting with Emergence of ideas, Consolidation in Communities, Formalization and Axiomatization. A tagging tool is used to support this process.

4.2 *Methodologies for the creation of semantic annotations*

This chapter will focus on methodological aspects of semantic annotation, which provide best practices and guidelines about how annotation of resources should be performed. This includes primarily the human-related aspects of the process; most notably for non-textual resources, annotation is still carried out manually to a large extent, thus being associated to significant costs. This is a consequence of the limitations of current techniques for multimedia understanding and methodologies are one of the means to lower the associated costs by enabling a systematic, controlled operation of annotation projects.

First manual annotation frameworks, which specified the annotation process and the components and interaction needed, were proposed around year 2000. Examples of such frameworks include Annotea [46] and CREAM [47], which were primarily implemented for the annotation of Web pages. Annotea specified an infrastructure for the annotation of Web-based resources, with a particular emphasis on the collaborative use of annotations. The format of the annotations is RDF. XML or HTML documents can be annotated using XPointer[10] for the location of parts of documents. CREAM is very similar to Annotea, while claiming to be more generic with respect to the supported types of documents that can be annotated.

[10] http://www.w3.org/TR/xptr/

Putting aside the user-friendly interfaces for concept and resource selection, early annotation tools provided very limited process support. Amaya [48] or OntoMat [47] provide basic features such as drag-and-drop lists of ontology concepts which can be used to annotate text markups. VAnnotea applies the same principle to multimedia content. More advanced tools include Information Extraction and Natural Language Processing techniques to suggest annotations to the user. S-CREAM applies Machine Learning to derive suggestions for annotations from past annotations, whilst M-Ontomat-Annotizer [49] supports multimedia annotation by extraction of low-level features to describe objects in images. The recently released K-Space Annotation Tool (KAT),[11] a major re-design of M-Ontomat-Annotizer includes plugins to analyze content, to browse ontologies, to edit annotations. KAT can be extended via its plugin architecture to include further analysis or annotation methods.

Process support is available, for instance, in Opas [50]. The tool implements a semi-automatic concept suggestion method based on previous annotations and on the common practices of the user. An initial automated suggestion is confirmed or altered by the user. This approach motivates especially novice users, while increasing the quality of the annotations by enforcing concepts to use.

A system explicitly targeting cross-media annotations is the AktiveMedia tool [51]. AktiveMedia provides easy to use drag-and-drop interfaces and semi-automatic concept selection. Another approach worthwhile to be mentioned is the SA-Methodology [52], whose aim is to support users in the process of manual annotation by providing aid in the selection of adequate ontology elements and in the extension of ontologies during annotation time. The Element Selection part includes a set of components for the selection of ontology elements based on semantic techniques. The key idea is to help the user in finding adequate ontology elements by using semantic retrieval techniques and by automatically proposing ontology elements that could be relevant for annotating a specific resource. The Element Addition consists of two components enabling a collaborative and work-embedded ontology engineering approach. These components allow the insertion of missing elements to ontologies at annotation time, and semi-automatic classification.

Last, but not least annotation approaches such as OntoTube [53], Peekaboom [54] or ListenGame [55] hide the complexity of the annotation process behind entertaining games. They are based on the ideas formulated by Louis van Ahn in [56].

[11] http://www.uni-koblenz.de/FB4/Institutes/IFI/AGStaab/Research/kat

4.2.1. *Automatic annotation methods*

Automated methods are mainly applied to bootstrap the creation of annotations for large document collections. These methods are sometimes based on the availability of small user-generated training sets which are used to derive semantic annotations from resources. Popular approaches include the Armadillo system which can be used to annotate large Web document collections. It makes use of adaptive information extraction techniques by generalizing annotated examples provided by the user. A similar approach is followed by SemTag [57] which is known to have produced the largest annotated document collection up to date. Furthermore, the KIM platform generates metadata in the form of named entities (i.e., persons, locations) in text-based resources.

4.2.2. *Work-embedded annotation methods*

Finally, methods exist which are being integrated in the authoring process of the annotations that are being generated. Early approaches include the Amaya browser which implements the Annotea framework and allows to annotate Web pages during their creation and viewing. A newer approach for integrated Web page annotation is WEESA [58]. WEESA extends XML-based Web development methods to include RDF based annotations in the creation process which are used to generate semantic summaries of Web pages available at run-time. Further examples include AktiveMedia which enables the creation and annotation of cross-media documents, the commercial tool OntoOffice[12] which can be used to annotate Microsoft office documents or the newer MyOntology Word plugin.[13]

5. A selection of tools

Tools for ontology engineering[14] and annotation[15] are meanwhile available and many overviews of them exist [59, 60]. This section briefly presents some of the most prominent ones.

---

[12] http://www.ontoprise.de

[13] http://www.myontology.org/semantics4office/

[14] Comparison and lists of ontology engineering tools, http://protege.stanford.edu/doc/users.html\#related

[15] List of annotation tools, http://annotation.semanticweb.org

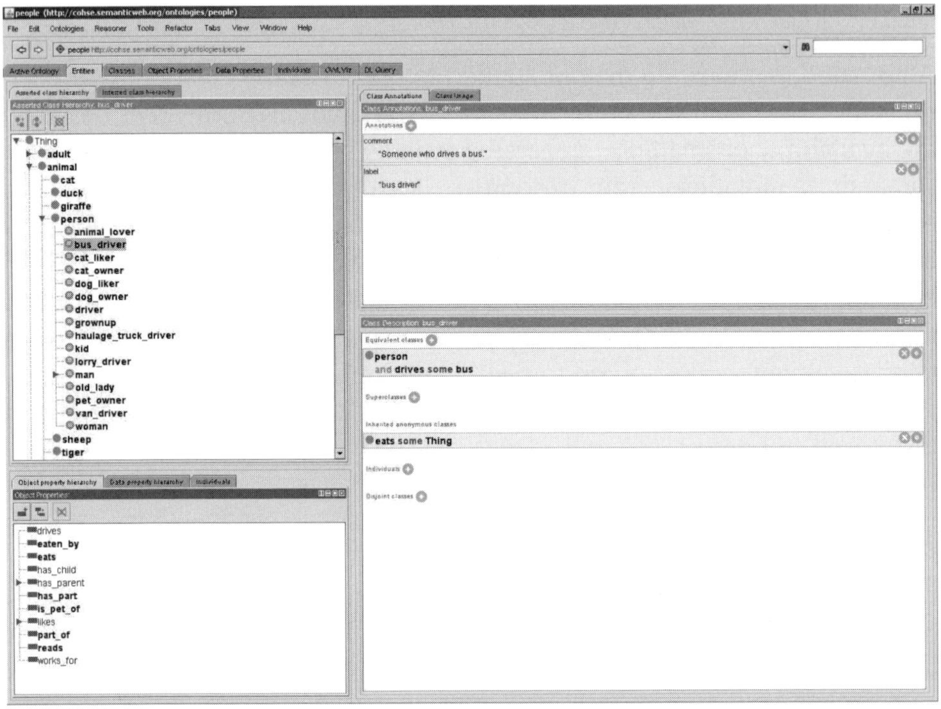

Fig. 2. Editing ontologies using Protégé.

5.1. *Ontology engineering tools*

Traditional ontology engineering: Protégé[16] (*cf.* Fig. 2) is probably the most well-known ontology engineering environment amongst many. Protégé is open source and, amongst others, supports the creation, visualization or maintenance of ontologies by many sub-tools and plug-ins which are publicly available.[17]

A commercial ontology engineering environment is provided by TopQuadrant: the TopBraid Composer which is part of the TopBraid Suite[18] (*cf.* Fig. 3). Besides similiar features for OWL ontologies as Protege, it supports more sophisticated ontology and RDF visualization features, data integration based on Mashups (i.e., the integration of geographical or calendar data), or RDFa and GRDDL support. The Maestro edition furthermore supports features like XML and RDF/OWL roundtripping or the creation of

[16] http://protege.stanford.edu
[17] http://protege.cim3.net/cgi-bin/wiki.pl?ProtegePluginsLibraryByType
[18] http://www.topquadrant.com/topbraid/composer/

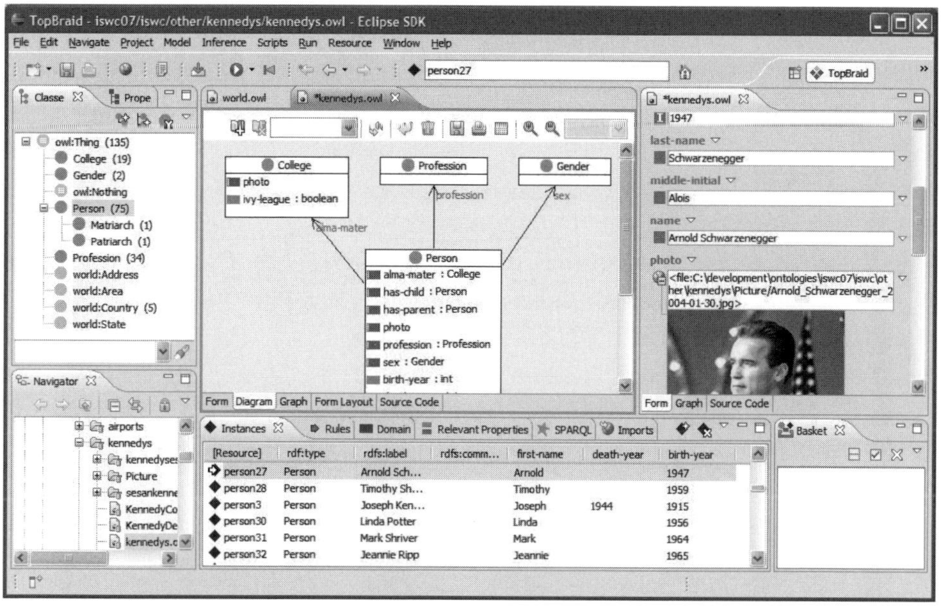

Fig. 3. TopBraid composer (http://www.topquadrant.com/).

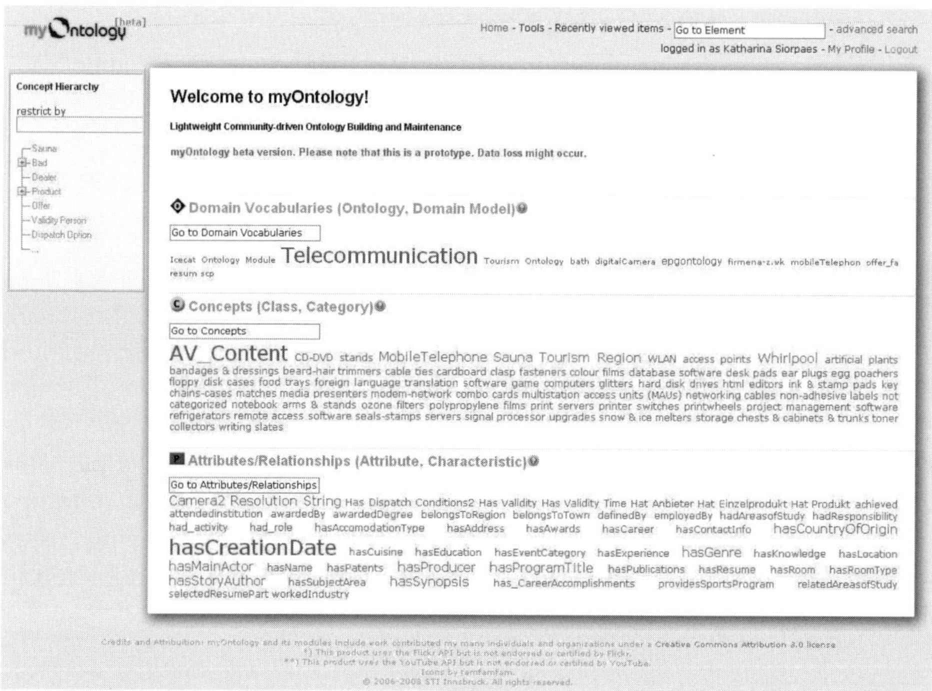

Fig. 4. Wiki-based ontology engineering using myontology.

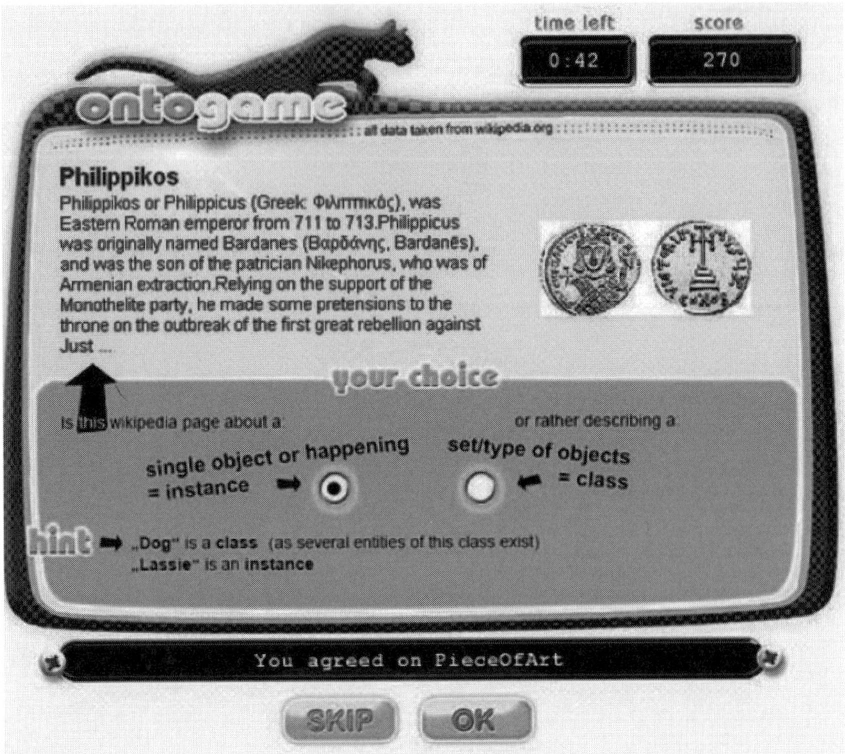

Fig. 5. OntoGame: players have to agree on ontological choice [44].

semantic server pages which are similar to java server pages and allow the embedding of SPARQL queries into web pages.

Wiki-based ontology engineering: MyOntology[19] is a novel approach to ontology engineering which combines popular Web 2.0 and social software approaches. As depicted in Fig. 4, it enables the creation, modification and discussion about items of an ontology using a Wiki.

Game-based ontology engineering: OntoGame [53] is motivated by Louis van Ahn's games with a purpose and hides the complexity of ontology engineering tasks behind game-based approaches. While playing, users are asked to describe and classify content from Wikipedia as depicted in Fig. 5.

[19] http://www.myontology.org/

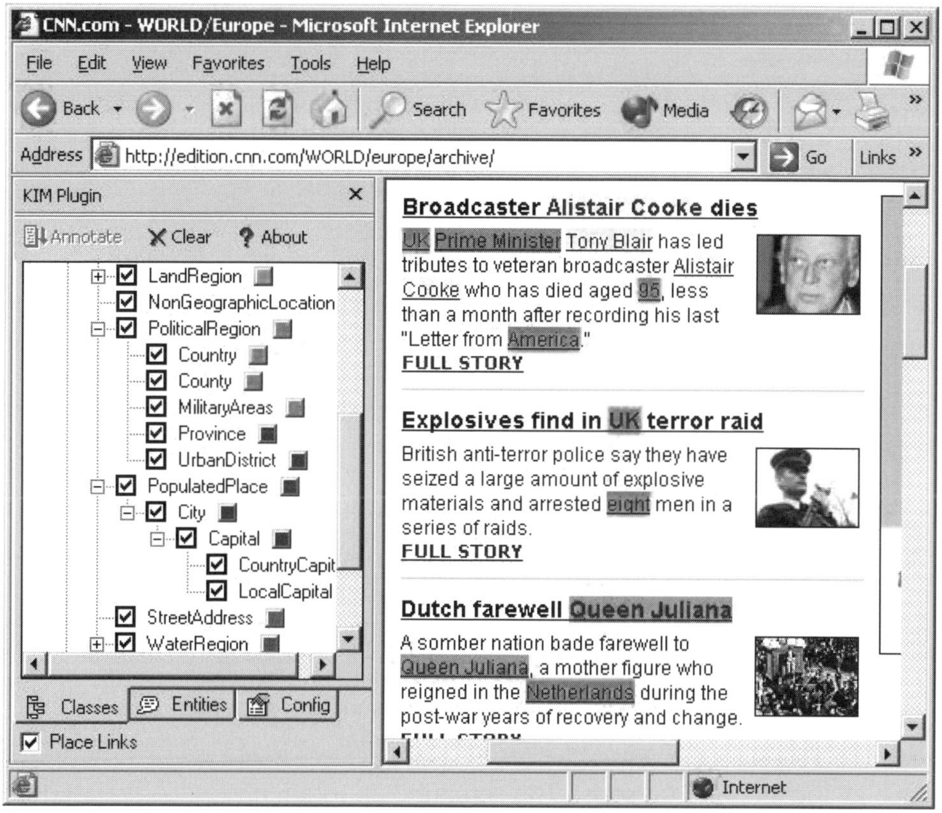

Fig. 6. Annotation of web pages with KIM.

5.2. *Annotation tools*

In this subsection annotation tools trying to cover different document types (text, Web pages, multimedia) and novel orthogonal approaches, i.e., game-based annotation, are introduced. While traditional approaches to annotation focus on text-based annotation and automation, more recent ones acknowledge the fact of subjectivity of annotations, annotations of hidden facts and end-user motivation.

Text annotation: The Knowledge and Information Management (KIM)[20] platform (*cf.* Fig. 6) applies an automated annotation approach and uses information extraction techniques to annotate large Web-based resource collections. Annotations are automatically generated for named entities

[20] www.ontotext.com/kim

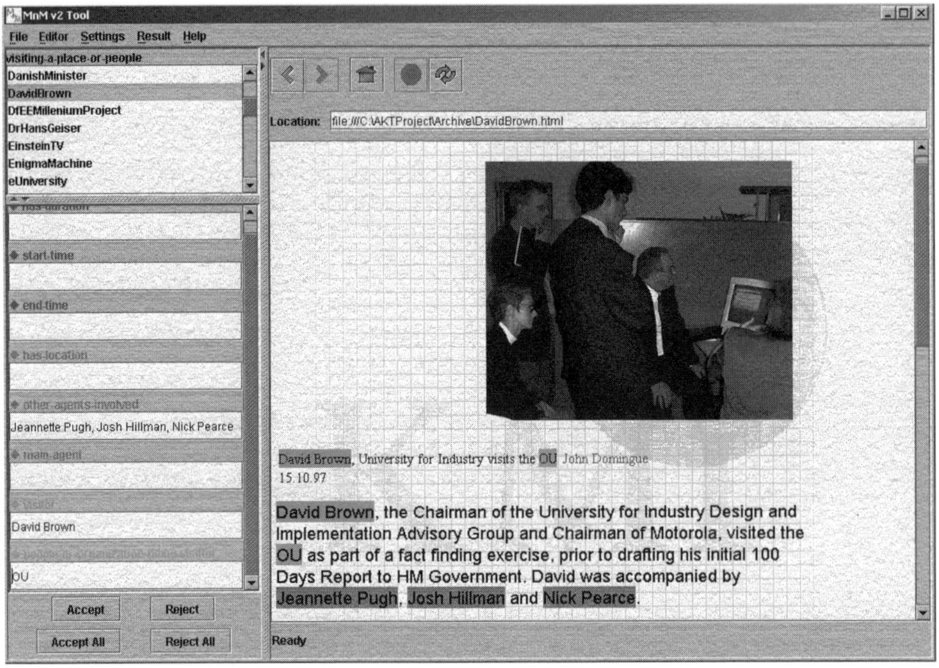

Fig. 7. MnM: results of the automatic extraction.

(such as locations of persons). The semantic annotation process is based on a pre-built ontology called KIMO and a knowledge base which contains a numerous amount of entities consisting of locations and organizations.

Another popular approach is provided by the MnM application [61] (*cf.* Fig. 7). MnM is based on manual annotations of a training corpus and uses wrapper induction and NLP techniques to generate rules that can be used to extract information from a text-based document collection.[21]

Web page annotation: Two applications that can be used to annotate Web pages in an integrated way are SMORE [62] and WEEKA. SMORE (*cf.* Fig. 8) was developed in the Mindswap project at the University of Maryland.[22] It allows to annotate Web pages via drag-and-drop and to create new HTML pages in the included HTML editor. Concepts, properties and relations can be assigned to resources via drag and drop. Furthermore SMORE enables the extension of ontologies in the ontology browser which is part of the system.

[21] http://kmi.open.ac.uk/projects/akt/MnM/
[22] http://www.mindswap.org/2005/SMORE/

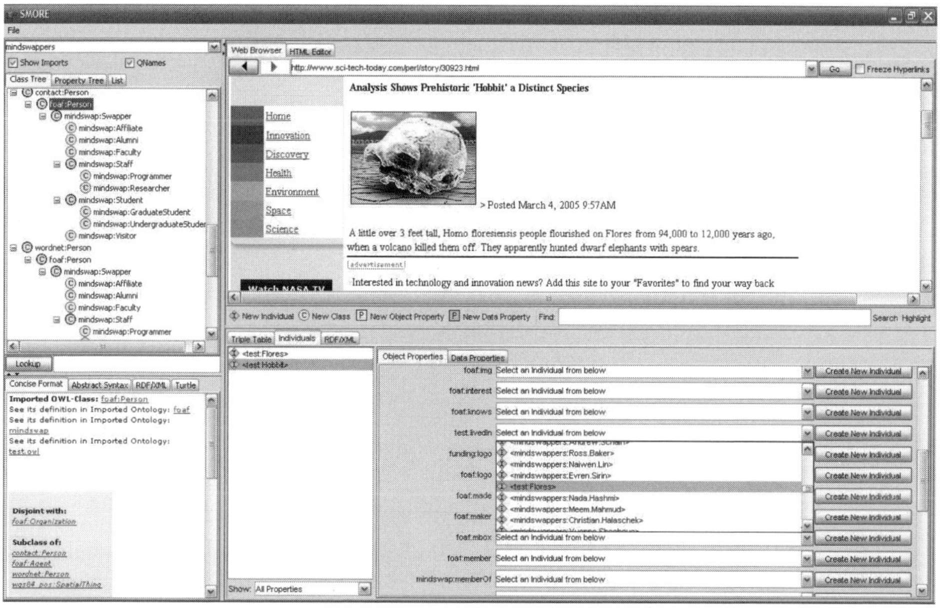

Fig. 8. Creation and markup of web pages in SMORE.

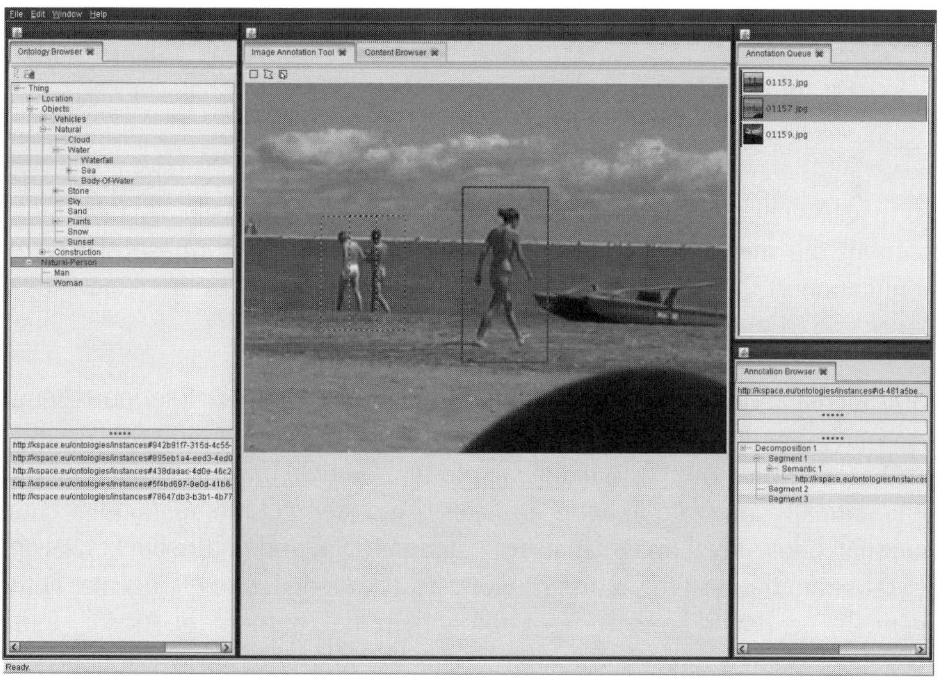

Fig. 9. The K-space annotation tool (KAT).

Fig. 10. The aktive media annotation tools as used by photocopain.

Another approach to annotate Web pages is WEESA,[23] which extends popular XML-based Web engineering methodologies. WEESA takes into account the metadata generation during the design-time phase of a Web application. It makes use of stylesheet transformations to both create HTML pages and RDF-based metadata descriptions from XML files.

Multimedia annotation: The K-SPACE Annotation Tool (KAT)[24] supports semi-automatic low-level feature extraction and semantic annotation (*cf.* Fig. 9).

Photocopain [63] especially exploits context information to semi-automatically annotate images. It makes use of camera metadata, GPS data, automated low-level image analysis, calendar data, and finally Flickr tags are used to train the system. In order to let user acknowledge or change the automatically generated annotations, Photocopain makes use of the Aktive Media Annotation tool to present the annotations to the user as shown in Fig. 10.

[23] http://www.infosys.tuwien.ac.at/weesa/

[24] http://www.uni-koblenz.de/FB4/Institutes/IFI/AGStaab/Research/kat

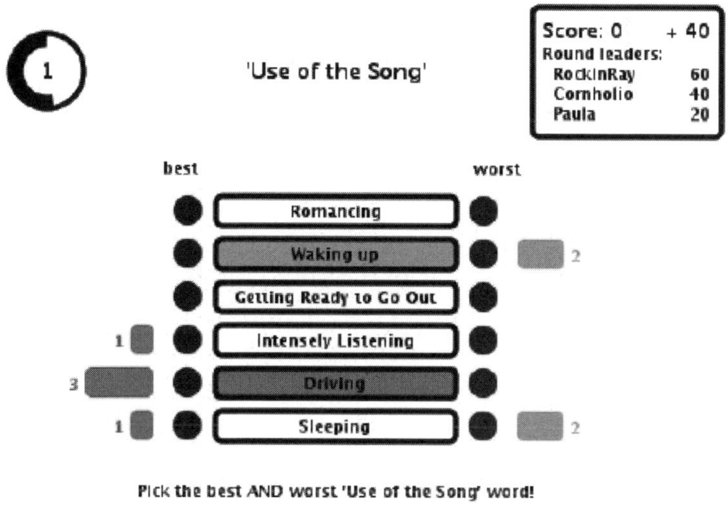

Fig. 11. ListenGame: players select best and worst words to describe a song.

Game-based annotation: Recent approaches for the creation of semantic content hide the process of content creation behind games. One example is ListenGame (LG) [55]. ListenGame (*cf.* Fig. 11) acknowledges the fact that automatically gathered information about music or artists is generally of low quality. It is a multi-player web-based game which was designed to collect associations between audio content and words. The semantic information collected is used to train an automated music annotation system. During the game players listen to a piece of music, select good and bad semantic labels and get realtime feedback on the selection of all other players. LG also supports the free assignment of keywords to songs.

6. Conclusions

The availability of a critical mass of semantic content, be it business relevant, widely-accepted ontologies, or machine-understandable annotations of Web pages and multimedia resources, is generally accepted as being one of the core ingredients for the wide adoption of semantic technologies. It is therefore understandable that in the past decade the question of how to create semantic content, ontologies as well as semantic meta-data, effectively and efficiently has received considerable attention in several areas related to semantic technologies, from ontology engineering, ontology learning and ontology population, to the semantic annotation of multimedia and Web service resources. The result is a maturing inventory of techniques and tools, which primarily aim at a complete (or at least partial) mechanization of the semantic content generation and management tasks, as a means to lower costs and improve productivity. Whilst the quality of such (fully) automated approaches has constantly improved, it is still far from outweighing the manual effort invested. This holds in particular when it comes to the creation of meta-data for non-textual resources, or the development of shared ontologies, tasks which are human-driven because of their very nature. At the other end of the (automation) spectrum ontology development environments such as Stanford's Protégé, TopQuadrant's TopBraid Composer, Altova's SemanticWorks®, or myOntology, to name only a few, offer a variety of features for humans to comfortably build ontologies, and to create semantic meta-data as instances of these ontologies — provided, of course, that humans are willing to participate in the semantic content authoring process at all. Whilst some of these tools have reached a user base of several tens of hundreds of users, a figure which is surely impressive if compared to other knowledge representation tools created in the last 20 years, they are still far away from reaching the same level of popularity as the most prominent Web 2.0 knowledge sharing platforms. User participation is not at the core of ontology development environments, their focus being rather on knowledge representation and process support.

Bridging the gap between human and computational intelligence is thus one of the core open issues in the current semantic content authoring landscape. What is needed are methodologies, methods and tools optimally exploiting the two in order to enable the creation and management of massive amounts of high-quality semantic content in an economical manner, consequently providing one of the core building blocks currently needed to enable the wide uptake of semantic technologies. At the core of this vision are means to stimulate the human participation in the creation of ontologies and in the annotation of Web resources of various kinds (images, videos, graphics etc), and techniques to integrate the results of human-driven content authoring tasks with (existing) approaches typically focusing on automatic processing. A first step in this direction was made with proposals such as OntoGame with promising results. Another relevant aspect which has so far received little attention is the integration of ontology engineering in the broader context of Enterprise Information Management. In an enterprise ontology, engineering must be part of other initiatives such as the enterprise architecture, IT governance, application integration or business intelligence. Best practices and guidelines are still missing for this area.

This means that extended investigations on wider range of activities related to ontology engineering and semantic annotation and targeting specific sectors and corporate settings are still required to give full particulars on the subject.

References

1. Fensel, D (2001). *Ontologies: A Silver Bullet for Knowledge Management and Electronic Commerce.* Springer.
2. Hayes, P and B McBride (2004). Rdf semantics. Available at http://www.w3.org/TR/rdf-mt/.
3. Brickley, D and RV Guha (2004). RDF Vocabulary Description Language 1.0: RDF Schema. Available at http://www.w3.org/TR/rdf-schema/.
4. Patel-Schneider, PF, P Hayes and I Horrocks (2004). Owl web ontology language semantics and abstract syntax. Available at http://www.w3.org/TR/owl-absyn/.
5. Cristani, M and R Cuel (2005). A survey on ontology creation methodologies. *International Journal of Semantic Web and Information Systems,* 1(2), 49–69.
6. Fernández-López, M and A Gómez-Pérez (2002). Overview and analysis of methodologies for building ontologies. Knowledge Engineering Review, 17(2), 129–156. ISSN 0269-8889. doi: http://dx.doi.org/10.1017/S0269888902000462.
7. Gómez-Pérez, A M Fernández-López and O Corcho (2004). *Ontological Engineering — with examples form the areas of Knowledge Management, e-Commerce and the Semantic Web.* Advanced Information and Knowledge Processing. Springer.
8. OntoWeb European Project (2002). Technical roadmap (Deliverable D.1.1.2 OntoWeb EU-IST-2000-29243).
9. Sekt Integrated Project (2004). State of the Art Survey on Ontology Merging and Aligning (Deliverable D4.2.1 Sekt EU-IST Integrated Project (IP) IST-2003-506826 SEKT).
10. OntoWeb European Project (2003). A survey of ontology learning methods and techniques (deliverable d1.5 ontoweb eu-ist-2000-29243).
11. IEEE Computer Society (1996). IEEE Standard for Developing Software Life Cycle Processes. IEEE Std 1074–1995.
12. Gruber, TR (1995). Toward principles for the design of ontologies used for knowledge sharing. *International Journal of Human-Computer Studies,* 43(5/6), 907–928. ISSN 1071–5819. doi: http://dx.doi.org/10.1006/ijhc.1995.1081.
13. Studer, R, VR Benjamins and D Fensel (1998). Knowledge engineering principles and methods. *Data and Knowledge Engineering,* 25(1/2), 161–197.
14. Guarino, N (1998). Formal ontology and information systems. In *Proceedings of the 1st International Conference on Formal Ontologies in Information Systems FOIS1998,* pp. 3–15. IOS-Press.

15. Guarino, N and P Giaretta (1995). *Ontologies and Knowledge Bases: Towards a Terminological Clarification,* Vol. Toward Very Large Knowledge Bases, pp. 25–32. IOS Press.
16. Neches, R, RE Fikes, T Finin, TR Gruber, T Senator and WR Swartout (1991). Enabling technology for knowledge sharing. *AI Magazine,* 12(3), 35–56.
17. Uschold, M and R Jasper (1999). A framework for understanding and classifying ontology applications. In *Proceedings of the IJCAI1999, Workshop on Ontology and Problem Solving Methods: Lessons Learned and Future Trends.*
18. Uschold, M and M Griininger (1996). Ontologies: Principles, methods and applications. *Knowledge Engineering Review,* 11(2), 93–155.
19. Wand, Y and R Weber (2002). Information systems and conceptual modelling: A research agenda. *Information Systems Research,* 13(4), 363–376.
20. McGuinness, DL (2002). Ontologies come of age. In *Spinning the Semantic Web: Bringing the World Wide Web to Its Full Potential.* MIT Press.
21. Miller, GA (1995). WordNet: A lexical database for English. *Communications of the ACM,* 38(11), 39-41.
22. Reed, SL and DB Lenat (2002). Mapping Ontologies into Cyc (White Paper). Available at http://www.cyc.com/doc/white-papers/mapping-ontologies-into-cyc-v31.pdf.
23. L. of Applied Ontology (2005). DOLCE: A Descriptive Ontology for Linguistic and Cognitive Engineering. Available at http://www.loa-cnr.it/DOLCE.html.
24. Sowa, JF (1995). Top-level ontological categories. *International Journal of Human-Computer Studies,* 43(5/6), 669–685. ISSN 1071-5819. doi: http://dx.doi. org/10.1006/ijhc.1995.1068.
25. Pease, A, I Niles and J Li (2002). The suggested upper merged ontology: A large ontology for the semantic web and its applications. In *Working Notes of the AAAI-2002 Workshop on Ontologies and the Semantic Web.*
26. Gene Ontology Consortium (2000). Gene ontology: Tool for the unification of biology. *Nature Genetics,* 25, 25-30.
27. Klinker G, C Bhola, G Dallemagne, D Marques and J McDermott (1991). Usable and reusable programming constructs. *Knowledge Acquisition,* 3(2), 117-135.
28. Gruber, TR (1993). A translation approach to portable ontology specifications. *Knowledge Acquisition,* 5, 199–220.
29. Horrocks, I, PF Patel-Schneider, H Boley, S Tabet, B Grosof and M Dean (2004). Swrl: A semantic web rule language combining owl and ruleml. Available at http://www. w3. org/Submission/S WRL/.
30. Jasper, R and M Uschold (1999). A framework for understanding and classifying ontology applications. In Proceedings of the 12th Workshop on Knowledge Acquisition, Modeling and Management KAW1999.

31. Ullman, JD (2000). Information integration using logical views. *Theoretical Computer Science*, 239(2), 189-210.
32. Uschold M and M Gruninger (2004). Ontologies and semantics for seamless connectivity. *SIGMOD Rec*, 33(1), 58-61. ISSN 0163-5808.
33. Bechhofer S, L Carr, C Goble, S Kampa and T Miles-Board (2002). The semantics of semantic annotation. In *TO CHECK*.
34. Berners-Lee T, J Hendler and O Lassila (2001). The semantic web. *Scientific American*, 284(5), 34-43.
35. IEEE Computer Society (1990). IEEE Standard Glossary of Software Engineering Terminology. IEEE Std 610.121990.
36. Royce, WW (1987). Managing the development of large software systems: Concepts and techniques. In *ICSE '87: Proceedings of the 9th international conference on Software Engineering*, pp. 328–338. Available at http://portal. acm.org/citation. cfm?id= 41801.
37. Boehm, B (1998). A spiral model of software development and enhancement. *Computer*, 21(5), 61–72.
38. Benjamin, PC, C Menzel, RJ Mayer, F Fillion, MT Futrell, P DeWitte and M Lingineni (1994). Ontology capture method (IDEF5). Technical report, Knowledge Based Systems, Inc., (1994).
39. Fernández, M, A Gómez-Pérez and N Juristo (1997). Methontology: From ontological art towards ontological engineering. In *Proceedings of the AAAI1997 Spring Symposium on Ontological Engineering*, pp. 33–40.
40. Sure, Y, S Staab and R Studer (2002). Methodology for development and employment of ontology based knowledge management applications. *SIGMOD Record*, 31(4), 18–23.
41. Kotis, K and GA Vouros (2005). Human-centered ontology engineering: The HCOME methodology. *Knowledge and Information Systems*, 10(1), 109–131.
42. Kunz W and H W J Rittel (1970). Issues as elements of information systems. Working Paper 131, Institute of Urban and Regional Development, University of California, Berkeley, California.
43. Tempich, C (2006). Ontology engineering and routing in distributed knowledge management applications. PhD thesis, Universität Karlsruhe (TH), Universität Karlsruhe (TH), Institut AIFB, D-76128 Karlsruhe.
44. Siorpaes, K and M Hepp (2008). Games with a purpose for the semantic web. *IEEE Intelligent Systems*, 23(3), 50–60.
45. Braun, S, A Schmidt, A Walter, G Nagypal and V Zacharias (2007). Ontology maturing: A collaborative web 2.0 approach to ontology engineering. In *Workshop on Social and Collaborative Construction of Structured Knowledge (CKC) at 16th International World Wide Web Conference (WWW 2007).*

46. Kahan, J, M-J Koivunen, E PrudHommeaux and R Swick (2001). Annotea: An open rdf infrastructure for shared web annotations. In *Proceedings of the 10th International World Wide Web Conference (WWW 2001).*
47. Handschuh, S and S Staab (2002). Authoring and annotation of web pages in cream. In *Proceedings of the 11th International World Wide Web Conference (WWW 2002).*
48. Quint, V and I Vatton (1997). An introduction to amaya. W3C NOTE 20-February-1997.
49. Bloehdorn, S, K Petridis, C Saathoff, N Simou, V Tzouvaras, Y Avrithis, S Handschuh, Y Kompatsiaris, S Staab and M Strintzis (2005). Semantic annotation of images and videos for multimedia analysis. In *Proceedings of CHECK!, co-located with EWSC 2005.*
50. Vehvilinen, A, E Hyvnen and O Alm (2008). A semi-automatic semantic annotation and authoring tool for a library help desk service. In *Proceedings of the Multimedia Metadata Management Workshop co-located with ESWC 2008.*
51. Chakravarthy, A, F Ciravegna and V Lanfranchi (2007). Cross-media document annotation and enrichment. In *TO CHECK.*
52. Bürger, T and C Ammendola (2008). A user centered annotation methodology for multimedia content. In *Poster Proceedings of the European Semantic Web Conference 2008.*
53. Siorpaes, K and M Hepp (2008). Ontogame — weaving the semantic web using games. In *Proceedings of the European Semantic Web Conference 2008.*
54. von Ahn, L, R Liu and M Blum (2006). Peekaboom: A game for locating objects in images. In *ACM CHI.*
55. Turnbull, D, R Liu, L Barrington and G Lanckriet (2007). A game-based approach for collecting semantic annotations of music. In *Proceedings of ISMIR 2007.*
56. von Ahn, L and L Dabbish (2004). Labeling images with a computer game. In *ACM CHI.*
57. Dill S, N Eiron, D Gibson, D Gruhl, R Guha, A Jhingran, T Kanungo, K McCurley, S Rajagopalan, A Tomkins, J Tomlin and J Zienberer (2003). A case for automated large scale semantic annotation. *Journal of Web Semantics,* 1(1), 115–132.
58. Reif G, H Gall and M Jazayeri (2005). Weesa — web engineering for semanitc web applications. In *Proceedings of the 14th International World Wide Web Conference,* pp. 722–729.
59. Uren, V, P Cimiano, J Iria, S Handschuh, M Vargas-Vera, E Motta and F Ciravegna (2006). Semantic annotation for knowledge management: Requirements and a survey of the state of the art. *Journal of Web Semantics,* 4(1), 14–28.
60. Obrenovic, Z, T Burger and R Troncy (2007). Multimedia semantics: Tools and resources. Multimedia semantics incubator group report, W3C.

61. Vargas-Vera, M, E Motta, J Domingue, M Lanzoni, A Stutt and F. Ciravegna (2002). Mnm: Ontology driven semi-automatic and automatic support for semantic markup. In *Proceedings of the 13th International Conference on Knowledge Engineering and Management (EKAW 2002)*, pp. 379–391.
62. Kalyanpur, A, J Hendler, B Parsia and J Golbeck (2003). Smore — semantic markup, ontology, and rdf editor. Technical report, University of Maryland.
63. Tuffield, M S Harris, D Duplaw, A Chakravarthy, C Brewster, N Gibbins, KO Hara, F Ciravegna, D Sleeman, N Shadbolt and Y Wilks (2006). Image annotation with photocopain. In *Proceedings First International Workshop on Semantic Web Annotations for Multimedia (SWAMM 2006)*.

CHAPTER III.1

METADATA AND ONTOLOGIES IN E-LEARNING

Manuel E. Prieto Méndez

Escuela Superior de Informática, Universidad de Castilla-La Mancha
Paseo de la Universidad. 4, 13071 Ciudad Real, España
manuel.prieto@uclm.es

Víctor H. Menéndez Domínguez

Facultad de Matemáticas, Universidad Autónoma de Yucatán
Periférico Norte. 13615, 97110 Mérida, Yucatán, México
mdoming@uady.mx

Christian L. Vidal Castro

Departamento Sistemas de Información, Universidad del Bío-Bío
Collao 1202, Concepción, Chile
cvidal@ubiobio.cl

This work aims to provide an overview of knowledge representation in e-Learning and concretely, the use of metadata and ontologies to express semantics in educational content. The chapter begins by describing relevant metadata standards for interoperability and reuse of educational resources Developments are also presented in relation to the development of ontologies to improve the use of resources in e-Learning. Emphasis is placed on the methods, representation languages, tools and types of ontologies developed or in use. Thus, the chapter provides guidelines for a semantic approach in E-Learning.

1. Introduction. e-Learning, metadata and ontologies

Learning support systems have been developed since the mid-twentieth century with high and low progress, with milestones, disappointments and major contributions. These systems have generally been based on the intention of answering the question: How can we improve the learning of people with support of computers and communication facilities?

There is still no conclusive answer although many efforts from the point of view of Educational Science, Psychology, and various areas of Computer Science.

We can identify three main periods in the development of this field:

- First: Characterized by Programmed Instruction and large scale computers.
- Second: Personal Computers, adaptability and courseware.
- Third (current): Group work, Internet and socialization.

Networks, Internet, the work in client–server mode and the new mark-up languages, together with the advances with standards, are additional elements that promote changes in current Computer-aided Learning Systems.

They provide both an opportunity for worldwide distribution, a mechanism for information dissemination and new ways for collaboration and interaction between people.

Cognitive psychology and the availability of new interfaces have enabled to raise the importance of social work and group learning. Recent contributions of Object Technology and Software Engineering allow the standardization of digital learning resources to be reusable and interoperable.

Instructional Design also attempts to establish widely used and symbolically represented specifications. In this sense, ontologies can, for instance, represent not only content domains but knowledge about student's learning styles or teaching techniques also.

It is likely that the latter concepts that form the main ideas of e-Learning are causing a further change if anything more spectacular than in previous years. Learning Objects and their repositories; Learning Management Systems; Metadata and Ontologies are concepts and technologies currently driving the growth and development of e-Learning.

Learning Objects and Metadata have come to offer a way to encapsulate knowledge and to use it in learning in standard, interoperable and reusable manners. Metadata and ontologies are fundamental for the advancement of e-Learning environments.

2. Metadata in e-Learning

2.1. *Fast review of concepts evolution*

In recent years, metadata are increasingly important in e-Learning. They will be most useful when the new standards become more stable. Starting from simple content descriptions to the definition of complex semantic structures, metadata are essential for many processes in e-Learning, such as reusability and knowledge sharing.

With well-defined metadata structures, contents can be presented in an efficient manner in terms of time and organization. At same time, metadata must be consistent with instructional requirements of students, teachers, or software agents. Many research works are focusing on the use of metadata with other forms of knowledge representation to improve e-Learning processes [1].

Metadata initial use was intended to describe structural aspects of instructional resources such as format, size, location, creation date, etc.

As in other areas of computing, the need of content representing in e-Learning resources, gives rise to the incorporation of semantic metadata. Current examples of metadata include keywords, descriptions, titles, annotations, comments, and links. Repositories and Learning Management Systems are benefiting from metadata for selection and presentation of resources [2,3].

Due to the nature of use of the instructional resources, metadata should cover educational aspects such as descriptions of instructional objectives, contexts of use, cognitive requirements, and many other issues with instructional relevance.

Normally, metadata are stored using a compact and encoded structure in some standard or specific format as XML or RDF. Metadata can be stored in an external document or be embedded within the resource. Many organizations have been involved in defining these kinds of patterns. The Dublin Core standard is widely used to describe digital resources.

In the case of e-Learning, diverse specification proposals have been made. In modern e-Learning, a Learning Object may be considered as the basic unit of reusability and sharing. A Learning Object is structured by an instructional resource and its metadata [4]. Metadata for Learning Objects are receiving special interest in the early years of the 21st century. Nowadays the Leaning Object Metadata (IEEE-LOM) is the generalized standard for e-Learning resources.

2.2. *Main metadata specifications*

Next sections describe the main specifications developed for the description of instructional resources. For each one, a brief overview and their main characteristics are given.

2.2.1. *Dublin core metadata terms and dublin core educational model*

The Dublin Core metadata standard [5] emerges as an initiative for the description of any digital document. Their use is widespread in today's Web.

Its name comes from the first workshop (Dublin, Ohio, USA, 1995) which defined the basic set of the standard (core). It was formalized in 2003 as the ISO Standard 15836-2003. Since 2007, it composes ANSI/NISO Standard Z39.85-2007 and IETF RFC 5013.

This standard is the results of the Dublin Core Metadata Initiative (DCMI). DCMI is a non-profit group integrated by many international public and private organizations, whose purpose is to establish metadata standards for interoperability and support of business models. Its proposals aim to facilitate the search, sharing and managing digital information, ensuring than results are independent of any commercial interest or technical mastery.

The DCMI Metadata Terms [6] is the greatest contribution of this group. Management and maintenance are its main activities. Another is the definition of Application Profiles that describe and guide the implementation processes of Dublin Core Metadata for specific contexts.

Dublin Core aims to be easy to create and maintain, enabling a common understanding of the metadata's semantics. It supports Application Profiles for better information's representation according to particular needs of knowledge domains.

The Dublin Core standard defines a set of 15 metadata elements that constitute the **Simple Dublin Core level**. These metadata describe the document's content, the intellectual property and the information for instantiation. Those sets of metadata are gray colored in the Table 1.

The **Qualified Dublin Core level** includes tree additional metadata elements (*audience, provenance*, and *rightHolder*) to Simple Dublin Core level. Also defines a set of qualifiers that clarify the semantic representation of resources for easy retrieval. These attributes refines metadata descriptions and are limited to certain elements that may be having associated vocabularies or natural language descriptions. There are two types of qualifiers (shown in the Table 1):

- *Element Refinements.* These qualifiers clarify the meaning of an element, making it more specific. For example, metadata *title* can be refined with element *alternative* to indicate a subtitle.
- *Encoding Schemes.* These qualifiers establish schemes that allow a better interpretation of the element's value. Generally, they have controlled vocabularies and formal notations (such as ISO 3166 for the representation of country's names with two characters).

In Dublin Core each element is optional and can be repeated. There is no specific order of appearance. Its content may be governed by encoding

Table 1. Dublin core standard (simple core and qualified level).

Type	Element	Element refinements	Encoding schemes
Content	title	alternative	
	subject		LCSH, MESH, DDC, LCC, UDC
	description	Table of contents, abstract	
	source		URI
	language		ISO 639-2, RFC 3066
	relation	isVersionOf, hasVersion, isReplacedBy, replaces, isRequiredBy, requires, isPartOf, hasPart, isReferencedBy, references, isFormatOf, hasFormat, conformsTo	URI
	coverage	spatial, temporal	DCMI-Point, ISO 3166, DCMI-Box, TNG, DCMI-Period, W3C-DTF
Intellectual property ghts	creator publisher contributor rights	accessRights, license	URI
Instantiation	date	created, valid, available, issued, modified, date-Accepted, dateCopy righted, dateSubmitted	DCMI-period, W3C-DTF
	type		DCMI-typeVocabulary
	format	extent, medium	IMT
	identifier	bibliographicCitation	URI
	audience	mediator, educationLevel	
	provenance		
	rightHolder		

schemes and controlled vocabularies, or be open to text descriptions in natural language.

The Dublin Core standard provides a set of guidelines for implementation in XHTML, XML and RDF, which allows the resources interoperability [7].

Table 2. Equivalences between DC-Ed and IEEE-LOM.

DC-Ed Element	IEEE-LOM Equivalent
subject	1.5 keyword 9 classification with 9.1 purpose = "Discipline" or "Idea"
relation	7:relation
relation (conformsTo)	9 classification with 9.1 purpose = "Prerequisite", "Educational Objective", "Skill Level", "Competency".
type	5.2 learningResourceType
audience	5.5 intendedEndUserRole
audience (educationLevel)	5.6 context, 5.7 typicalAgeRange, 9 classification with 9.1 purpose = "Educational Level" or "Skill Level".
audience (mediator)	5.5 intendedEndUserRole
instructionalMethod	5.10 description, 9 classification with a local vocabulary term defined for 9.1 purpose

In 1999, the DCMI established a group to define an application profile module emphasizing those properties useful for the Education. The main idea was to describe instructional resources considering the context where it should be used [8]. Another purpose was to provide recommendations in order to represent the IEEE-LOM using DCMI.

The DC-Ed Model [9] proposes an initial set of elements that describe resources in terms of their use in the teaching and learning processes. For each of them, it suggests the use of controlled vocabularies and the equivalent IEEE-LOM metadata (Table 2).

Currently, it is been discussed the inclusion of additional elements provided by the IEEE-LOM, that can not be mapped in DCMI as 5.1 *interactivityType*, 5.3 *InteractivityLevel*, and 5.9 *TypicalLearningTime*.

2.2.2. *IEEE Learning object metadata (IEEE LOM)*

While Dublin Core allows describing any digital document, it has no metadata describing instructional aspects in documents containing learning resources. IEEE Learning Object Metadata [10] (IEEE-LOM) is generally accepted standard for describing learning resources and Learning Objects specifically.

IEEE-LOM is based on integrating the work of several groups involved in e-Learning as ARIADNE, IMS, Dublin Core and IEEE-LTSC, its main promoter. Any person or institution can be integrated into the working groups of the IEEE-LTSC and therefore be able to contribute to the creation or modification of proposals or standards that are the responsibility of the group.

The IEEE-LTSC aims to develop technical standards, recommended practices and guidelines for learning technologies. It covers both technology (tools, technologies, components), and design methods. These integrated elements promote development, management and interoperability of components and Computer Based Instructional systems.

Originally, IEEE-LOM takes elements from other specifications such as IMS LRM and Dublin Core. Since 2002, IEEE-LOM conforms IEEE 1484.12.1, IEEE P1484.12.2, IEEE P1484.12.3, and IEEE P1484.12.4 standards.

IEEE-LOM has the purpose to define a structure for interoperable descriptions of Learning Objects. This allows the search, evaluation, acquisition and use of Learning Objects by manual or automatic methods. It promotes the interoperability between classification systems. Defines a simple and extensible standard to be adopted and implemented as best as possible.

IEEE-LOM provides a framework for the representation of metadata instances for Learning Objects. It defines a hierarchical structure consisting of nine categories and 68 items (Table 3). Each category contains items that can store values for different elements. Its structure is flexible enough to incorporate new metadata, as well as to define controlled vocabularies for their values.

All IEEE-LOM elements are optional and may even be repeated. For each element, the standard defines:

- The metadata's name (Table 4).
- The number of elements or values that can contains.
- If necessary considering the order of values or not.
- The data type that store (Table 5).
- The recommended space of values or controlled vocabulary defined by another standard.

It is possible to extend vocabularies or create a new one. In any case is necessary to define a set of specifications (you must indicate the source) and consider term-matching with the already defined vocabularies. IEEE-LOM extensions are allowed for the case of new semantics and not only for name change.

The standard establishes a framework for XML or RDF storage structure, although other representations can be used. IEEE-LOM also establishes a

Table 3. IEEE-LOM categories description.

Category	Description
general	Provides an overview of Learning Object. Their values are relative to the object as a whole. Contains 10 sub-elements. Some of these are *title, language, description and keyword.*
lifeCycle	It combines all the features and data related to the development process of Learning Object as current status and process participants. It contains six sub-elements. The metadata *version, status, contribution* and *date,* belong to this category.
metaMetadata	Provides information about metadata defined for the instance, who developed the instance, when or references used. Contains nine sub-elements. Some of its elements are *role, entity* and *metadataScheme.*
technical	Describes technical requirements and technological characteristics of the resource. Contains 12 sub-elements. Examples of metadata are *format, size, location, requirements.*
educational	Describes the object in instructional and pedagogical terms. It contains 11 sub-elements. Metadata *interactivityType, learningResourceType, semanticDensity, context* are examples of its elements. There may be multiple instances of the class.
rights	It describes the intellectual property rights and conditions of use of the resource. Contains three sub-elements such as *cost* and *descriptions.*
relation	It brings together the elements that establish the relationship of a Learning Object with other objects. It contains six sub-elements. Examples are metadata *entity, kind* and *description.* The relationships are allowing *isPartOf, isReferencedBy, requires,* etc. There may be multiple instances of the class to define multiple relationships.
annotation	Give feedback about the Learning Object, mainly educational, as well as who and when the recording was made. It contains three elements such as *entity* and *description.* There may be many entries for the same Learning Object.
classification	Describes the Learning Object on a classification scheme. It contains eight elements as *taxon, description, keyword, purpose.* Having multiple instances of this class, you may classify the same object using different schemes.

standard mapping with Dublin Core Simple, which allows exchange mechanisms between both standards (Table 6).

2.3. Other specifications

Numerous organizations have developed extensions or variations of previously existing specifications. Most of these extensions are based on the

Table 4. Elements and categories in IEEE-LOM.

Category	Elements
1 general	1.1 identifier: 1.1.1 catalog, 1.1.2 entry; 1.2 title; 1.3 language; 1.4 description; 1.5 keyword; 1.6 coverage; 1.7 structure; 1.8 aggregationLevel
2 lifeCycle	2.1 version; 2.2 status; 2.3 contribute: 2.3.1 role, 2.3.2 entity, 2.3.3 date
3 metaMetadata	3.1 identifier: 3.1.1 catalog, 3.1.2 entry; 3.2 contribute: 3.2.1 role, 3.2.2 entity, 3.2.3 date; 3.3 metadatScheme; 3.4 language
4 technical	4.1 format; 4.2 size; 4.3 location; 4.4 requirement: 4.4.1 orComposite: 4.4.1.1 type, 4.4.1.2 name, 4.4.1.3 minimumVersion, 4.4.1.4 maximumVersion; 4.5 installationRemarks; 4.6 otherPlatformRequirements; 4.7 duration
5 educational	5.1 interactivityType; 5.2 learningResourceType; 5.3 interactivityLevel; 5.4 semanticDensity; 5.5 intentedEndUserRole; 5.6 context; 5.7 typicalAgeRange; 5.8 difficulty; 5.9 typicalLearningTime; 5.10 description; 5.11 language
6 rights	6.1 cost; 6.2 copyrightAndOtherRestrictions; 6.3 description
7 relation	7.1 kind; 7.2 resource: 7.2.1 identifier: 7.2.1.1 catalog, 7.2.1.2 entry; 7.2.2 description
8 annotation	8.1 entity; 8.2 date; 8.3 description
9 classification	9.1 purpose; 9.2 taxonPath; 9.2.1 source; 9.2.2 taxon; 9.2.2.1 id; 9.2.2.1 entry; 9.3 description; 9.4 keyword

Table 5. IEEE-LOM data types.

Type	Description
LangString	Represents one or more strings in a particular language. May contain translations or semantic equivalences. Defines the language used in the chain and the chain itself.
DateTime	Set a point in time and the description of that item. The dimension of this point can be between one year and one second.
Duration	Set a time interval and its description. From years until seconds.
Vocabulary	Define a collection of values and sources for those values.
CharacterString	Define a character collection.

IEEE-LOM. The following are some important application profiles. For each one is indicating variations and extensions carried out.

2.3.1. *Educational network Australia application profile (Edna)*

The EdNA metadata application profile 1.1 [11] is the Australian proposal for the interoperability of search and resource management. It pretends to

Table 6. Equivalences between Dublin Core and IEEE-LOM.

Dublin Core	IEEE-LOM
identifier	1.1.2 entry
title	1.2 title
language	1.3 language
description	1.4 description
subject	1.5 keyword or 9 classification if 9.1 purpose = "discipline" or "idea"
coverage	1.6 coverage
type	5.2 learningResourceType
date	2.3.3 contribute.date if 2.3.1 role = "Publisher"
creator	2.3.2 entity if 2.3.1 role = "Author"
otherContributor	2.3.2 entity 2.3.1 role
publisher	2.3.2 entity if 2.3.1 role = "Publisher"
format	4.1 format
rights	6.3 description
relation	7.2.2 description
source	7.2 resource if 7.1 kind = "IsBasedOn"

facilitate the incorporation of metadata to resources in the Australian Education and Training network.

It uses the Dublin Core standard elements (DC) for resource description. It also includes elements of the Australian Government Locator Service (AGLS) and specific aspects of the Australian community of Education and Training. Some of the administrative metadata (AD) can be generated by Content Management Systems. They proposed 14 new elements and three refinements to Dublin Core standard (Table 7).

Because of these additions and modifications it defines new vocabularies and refinements. Edna keeps the essence of Dublin Core, in the sense that the elements are optional and may be repeated. Edna supports storage schemes based on XML, RDF and XHTML.

2.3.2. *Gateway to educational materials application profiles (GEM)*

The Gateway to Educational Materials project (GEM) [12] aims to define a set of metadata, and uses procedures that improve internet access to educational resources for students and teachers in the United States, this includes repositories of federation, states, universities as well as various Internet sites.

Table 7. EdNa elements.

Element	Element refinements	Coments
DC.subject		There is a new vocabulary (edna-kla)
DC.type		It incorporates new vocabulary (edna-document, edna-curriculum, edna-event)
DC.coverage		There is a new vocabulary (edna-spatial)
EDNA.audience		Uses controlled vocabularies (edna-audience, edna-sector, edna-UserLevel, Ev-audience, agls.audience) to describe the resource target
EDNA. categoryCode		Uses the controlled vocabulary edna-resource to indicate the resource's category
EDNA.collection		Uses the controlled vocabulary edna-collection to establish the type of project that owns the aggregated set of metadata records
EDNA.review		
EDNA.reviewer		
EDNA.version		
AGLS.availability		It uses X500 scheme
AGLS.function		It uses business function schemes and KAAA AGIFT
AGLS.mandate	act, case, regulation	Establishes a new element and its associated qualifiers. Defines a URL that describes a warrant
AD.approver		
AD.date	accepted, archive, display	Uses the DCMI-Period W3C-DTF schemes
AD.provider		
AD.provenance		
AD.submitter		

Based on Dublin Core standard, there are new qualifiers (GEM) added to the base elements (DC) considering specific needs for certain domains (Table 8). In addition, several controlled vocabularies have been developed that replace or extend existing ones. An important feature is the character of the elements and their qualifiers that may be optional, conditional, mandatory, recommended and repeatable. GEM define several Application Profiles by the filled elements (Gateway lite, full Gateway GEM).

Table 8. GEM elements.

Element	Refinements	Comment
DC.subject		Sets new controlled vocabularies (GEM-S, ERIC)
DC.relation	hasBibliographicInfoIn, isChildOf, isContentRatingFor, isDataFor, isDerivedFrom, isOrderInfoFor, isOverviewOf, isParentOf, isPeerReview, isRevisionHistory For, isSiblingOf, isSiteCriteria, isSponsoredBy	Incorporates new qualifiers
DC.publisher	onlineProvider	Incorporates a new qualifier
DC.contributor	MARC_Annotator, MARC_Artist, MARC_Author, MARC_Cartographer, MARC_Composer, MARC_Creator, MARC_Editor, MARC_Interviewee, MARC_Interviewer, MARC_Narrator, MARC_Photographer, MARC_Reviewer, MARC_Sponsor	Define new qualifiers to describe the contributor
DC.rights	priceCode	It incorporates a new qualifier and the corresponding controlled vocabulary (GEMpriceCode)
DC.date	placedOnline, recordCreated	Incorporates new qualifiers with the same schema (W3CDTF)
DC.type		Establishes a new controlled vocabulary (GEMType)
DC.format	platform	
DC.identifier	publicID, sid, sdn	
DC.audience	age, beneficiary, prerequisites	Incorporates new qualificadores and controlled vocabularies (GEM-BEN, GEM-LEVEL, GEM-MED)
GEM.cataloging	catalogingOrganization, cataloging Tool, individualCataloger	
GEM.duration		
GEM.resources		
GEM.instructionalMethod	assessment, grouping, teachingMethods	Adds a new element with its qualificadores and controlled vocabularies (GEM-AM, GRO GEM, GEM-TM)
GEM.standards		

2.3.3. *CanCore learning resource metadata initiative (CanCORE)*

The CanCore initiative [13] is maintained by several organizations in Canada, and includes a description of instructional resources to improve search and retrieval for teachers and students. It provides recommendations and guidelines to facilitate the implementation and interoperability of the initiative with other existing specifications (such as DublinCore or UKLOM).

It focuses primarily to establish simplifications of IEEE-LOM standard to make easier the implementations, depending on the context. For example, it defines criteria for which some metadata are more important than others (some metadata are important for search, others are required for results presentation, some elements can be generated automatically or manually) (Table 9).

Table 9. CanCORE elements.

Elements	Search	Displaying results	Automatic generation	Manual generation
1.1.2 entry			Yes	
1.2 title	Yes	Yes		Yes
1.3 language	Yes	Yes		Yes
1.4 description	Yes	Yes		Yes
1.5 keyword	Yes	Yes		Yes
1.8 aggregationLevel		Yes		Yes
2.1 version				Yes
2.3.1 role		Yes		Yes
2.3.2 entity	Yes	Yes		Yes
2.3.3 date				Yes
3.1.1 catalog			Yes	
3.1.2 entry			Yes	
3.2.1 role			Yes	
3.2.2 entity			Yes	
3.2.3 date			Yes	
3.3 metadatScheme			Yes	
3.4 language			Yes	
4.1 format	Yes	Yes	Yes	
4.2 size		Yes	Yes	
4.3 location		Yes	Yes	

(*Continued*)

Table 9. (*Continued*)

Elements	Search	Displaying results	Automatic generation	Manual generation
4.6 otherPlatformRequirements		Yes		Yes
4.7 duration				Yes
5.2 learningResourceType	Yes	Yes	Yes	
5.3 interactivityLevel		Yes		Yes
5.5 intentedEndUserRole	Yes	Yes		Yes
5.6 context	Yes	Yes		Yes
5.7 typicalAgeRange	Yes	Yes		Yes
5.9 typicalLearningTime		Yes		Yes
5.11 language				Yes
6.1 cost	Yes	Yes		Yes
6.2 copyrightAndOtherRestrictions		Yes		Yes
6.3 description				Yes
7.1 kind			Yes	
7.2.1.1 catalog			Yes	
7.2.1.2 entry			Yes	
8.1 entity				Yes
8.2 date			Yes	
8.3 description				Yes
9.1 purpose			Yes	
9.2.1 source			Yes	
9.2.2 taxon			Yes	
9.2.2.1 id			Yes	
9.2.2.1 entry	Yes	Yes		Yes
9.4 keyword	Yes	Yes		Yes

2.3.4. *LOM-ES*

LOM-ES v1.1 [14] is the version of IEEE-LOM for the Spanish educational community. It is the result of a joint work of several government agencies and educational institutions. And defines a specific metadata schema or Application Profile.

It includes several modifications over the standard IEEE-LOM (Table 10), mainly in the form of new elements (for example 5.12 *cognitive Process* and 6.4 *access*), as extensions to the predefined vocabularies (by example the vocabulary of 5.2 *LearningResourceType*) especially at the educational

Table 10. LOM-ES elements added to IEEE-LOM standard.

Element	Description
1.4 description	The specification uses a cataloging format that stores the resources characteristics based on vocabulary rather than with free text.
5.2 learningResouceType	Establishes a new controlled vocabulary for types: media systems, information representation, knowledge representation systems, application software, service and educational content.
5.5 intentedEndUserRole	Define four instances of this element with values collected from four vocabularies related to the type of learner, the groups, educator and expert.
5.6 context	Define three instances of this element that collect values from three vocabularies related to the place of execution, support, and modality.
5.10 description	Define a cataloger to keep three instances of this element which reflects the prior knowledge, teaching objectives and the type of knowledge (using a vocabulary).
5.12 cognitiveProcess	This new feature uses a controlled vocabulary to indicate the cognitive processes involved in the teaching process.
6.4.access 6.4.1.accessType 6.4.2.description	These new elements describe the restrictions that govern access to digital resources.

category. An important difference is in the nature of the elements defined as mandatory (such as *title, description, coverage*), recommended (such as *keyword, contribution, location*) or optional (such as *requirements, notes, cost*).

It also includes specifications for maintaining the performance, and interoperability semantic accordance with IEEE-LOM in their categories and elements.

2.3.5. *Other learning object's metadata specifications related*

Standards and specifications previously presented, try to describe the contents and use of learning resources to enable reusability and interoperability between repositories and Learning Managements Systems.

Generally, their elements are incorporated into other specifications as UK Learning Object Metadata Core (UK-LOM) [15], Australia New Zealand Learning Object Metadata (ANZ-LOM) [16], Korea Educational Metadata (KEM) [17], EUN Learning Resource Exchange Metadata Application Profile (LRE) [18].

Those proposals make it possible to create learning resources that motivate assessment, management, mentoring, collaborative activities, etc.

Before ending this section, it seems appropriate to clarify two specifications widely used in e-Learning: SCORM and IMS-LD. First, they are not proper metadata specifications. They mainly define learning experiences, using learning objects or resources, establish action sequences and in some case actors and politics.

Sharable Content Object Reference Model (SCORM) [19] specification consists of standards for content packaging in order to create hierarchical structures that are interchangeable, defines a protocol for communication between user and LMS, like one for the record of the actions undertaken by the user. SCORM uses the IEEE-LOM in its content aggregation model to describe the learning resources.

A similar idea applies to the IMS-Learning Design (IMS-LD) specification [20] that uses IEEE-LOM for describing instructional resources into its IMS-CP content packaged specification [21,22]. IMS-LD specifies a modeling language to define instructional activities and describe activities, actors, methods, acts, roles, resource and relationship between them.

3. Ontologies in e-Learning

3.1. *A brief review of ontologies in e-Learning*

Due to the current importance of ontologies in e-Learning, it is useful to know some existing ontological models in this area. For this, a study based on reports appeared in literature have been made. We used the methodology proposed by Kitchenham [23]. This methodology includes stages of planning, development and publication. Obtained results were adapted to the purposes of this publication.

3.2. *Taxonomy of e-Learning ontologies*

Before starting the study description, it should be presented a summary of the results of a preliminary work establishing a classification of knowledge models used in e-Learning.

There are different views and concepts to understand and classify ontologies. Some are restricted to philosophical or linguistic approaches. Here we focus on computational approaches and particularly in points of view regarding processing of semantic information and the knowledge related to e-Learning.

According to Van Heist [24], ontologies can be classified according to the amount and type of structure conceptualization:

- *Terminological Ontologies* that specify terms used to represent knowledge in certain universe of discourse. They are often used to unify vocabulary in a given field.
- *Information Ontologies* specify the storage information structure in databases. They offer a standardized framework for information storage.
- *Knowledge Modeling Ontologies* specify knowledge conceptualizations. They contain a rich internal structure and are usually tailored to the particular use of the knowledge they describe.

According to this view, Terminological Ontologies are of interest in e-Learning as they allow unifying terms and relations between them, in particular referring to the content knowledge. But *Knowledge Modeling Ontologies* are particularly important because they allow the expression of models, theories and techniques of Pedagogy and Behavioral Sciences.

M. Uschold *et al.* [25] provided three dimensions for ontologies:

- *Formality*: Referred to the formality degree of the language used to express concepts. (Highly informal ontology; Structured informal ontology; Semi-formal ontology and Rigorously formal ontology).
- *Purpose*: This refers to the intended use of ontologies. (Ontologies for inter-personal communications; Ontologies for interoperability between systems; Ontologies for systems engineering).
- *Subject*: To express the nature of the objects characterized by the ontology. (Domain ontologies, Task, method or problem-solving and Ontology representation or meta-ontologies).

Steve *et al.* [26] distinguish three main types of ontologies:

- *Domain ontologies,* which represents the relevant expertise in a domain or subdomain (Medicine, Engineering, Education ...).
- *Generic ontologies,* which are represented by general concepts.
- *Representational ontologies,* which specify the conceptualizations that underlie knowledge representation formalisms. They are also called meta-ontologies to top-level ontologies.

To these three types, Guarino [27] adds the ontologies that have been created for a specific task or activity:

- Task ontologies.

This classification is important in e-Learning. Meets several criteria and types of knowledge commonly used in applications for instruction and learning. Generic, domain and task models are appropriate to describe various situations.

However, the reality of current developments in e-Learning suggests considering some alternatives. After conducting a preliminary study of existing ontologies in our field, five categories were established. They differentiate and specialize domain, generic and task models according to the real use in e-Learning applications and models:

- Domain or content ontologies.
- Pedagogical ontologies.
- Ontologies on e-Learning resources.
- e-Learning content management ontologies.
- Ontologies on e-Learning administration.

3.3. *Objectives and methodology of the review*

The aim of the study is to identify published works related to the implementation of ontologies for e-Learning according to previous classification. The information sources used were the web search engine of the IEEE Digital Library, the ACM Digital Library, and ISIKnowledge Library as well as gray literature.

The following generic search string was used and adapted to the syntax of each searcher when necessary:

((e-learning or e-learning) and (ontologies or ontology) and
(development or built or support or endure or sustain))

Specifically criteria were defined for the inclusion and exclusion of papers retrieved:

- *Inclusion Criteria*: Papers that show implemented ontologies related to some aspect of e-Learning. The following aspects were considered: domain or content ontologies for e-Learning, pedagogical ontologies, ontologies on e-Learning resources, e-Learning content management ontologies, ontologies on e-Learning administration and other ontologies in e-Leaning. Ontologies must be described at least for his name, description and minimally documented in English or Spanish.
- *Exclusion Criteria*: Papers that show ontologies not implemented, which are not identifiable or do not present minimal technical documentation.

Table 11. Form used in the study.

Source General Information	
Title:	Knowledge Puzzle
Reference:	A. Zouaq, R. Nkambou, C. Frasson: Knowledge Puzzle. Interdisciplinary Journal of Knowledge and Learning Objects (IJKLO), 3: 135–162, 2007
Abstract:	Knowledge Puzzle, is an ontology-based platform designed to facilitate domain knowledge acquisition from textual documents for knowledge-based systems. First, the Knowledge Puzzle Platform performs an automatic generation of a domain ontology from documents' content through natural language processing and machine learning technologies. Second, it employs a new content model, the Knowledge Puzzle Content Model, which aims to model learning material from annotated content. Annotations are performed semi-automatically based on IBM's Unstructured Information Management Architecture and are stored in an Organizational Memory as knowledge fragments.
Paper URL:	http://ijklo.org/Volume3/IJKLOv3p135-162Zouaq.pdf
Technical Information	
Methodology used in development:	N/R
Tools used in development:	Protegé
Representation language:	OWL
e-Learning Ontology Taxonomy Class	
Pedagogical Ontologies; Ontologies on e-Learning Resources; e-Learning Content Management Ontologies.	

An initial selection was performed analyzing title, abstract and key-words. To improve selection, there was analyzed the paper's complete text.

The information collected from ontologies, initially included educational aspects and uses reported in practice. However, due to lack of published information, it was decided not to include them. Table 11 shows an example of the form used for collecting information from each paper.

3.4. *Results*

The search turned up 24 articles specifically referring to ontologies developed within the field of e-Learning. The full list of obtained results can be found at http://www.face.ubiobio.cl/~cvidal/full-list.pdf. Because several ontologies were referenced by more than one paper, we chose the one that best referenced the ontology.

The recovered information was summarized in the follow aspects: the paper's reference, the paper's URL and the ontology's URL when available.

Technical information is also displayed, as the methodology and tools used in construction and the ontology's representation language. When this information has not been reported, is indicated by N/R. Finally, each ontology was classified according to the above proposed taxonomy.

3.5. *Analysis of results*

Results are analyzed in terms of the construction methodology, the use of design tools, the used representation language and the ontology's classification referenced in each paper.

Note that most of papers do not deliver information about methodology used in construction. The analysis of the available information indicates that the method most used to guide the construction of ontologies is Ontology Development 101 [28] with the 17% of use (see Table 12). This methodology is a simple guide for building ontologies [29]. It is noteworthy that 13% of the jobs used, according to its own description, an ad-hoc approach.

Regarding to the representation language, the most used is OWL [30] (see Table 13). The 47% of the works reported its use. This number increases to 59% if we consider the works that uses OWL as single or as a complement to a second language.

Furthermore, 44% of the selected articles reported the use of Protégé [31] as the ontology design tool. Table 14 gives details this information.

Ontologies found were classified according to the taxonomy as outlined above and Table 15 was constructed with this results. It should be noted that ontologies could be classified in more than one category.

According the results, most of the ontologies are related to the representation of learning resources and content management.

Most of these ontologies are represented in the OWL language and designed with Protégé. This is possible due to the ease of OWL code

Table 12. Methologies used in the construction of ontologies.

Metodology used	Quantity
N/R	15
Ontology development 101	4
Ad-hoc methodology	3
OntoSpec	1
Methontology	1

Table 13. Ontologies representation languages.

Representation Language	Quantity
OWL	11
RDF	4
DAML+OIL	1
CycL+OWL	1
KIF	1
HOZO+OWL	1
OWL+SWRL	1
WSML	1
XTM	1
UML	1
OIL	1

Table 14. Ontologies design tools.

Tool used	Quantity
Protegé	10
N/R	10
OilEd	1
Ontololingua	1
Topic Maps	1

Table 15. Ontologies classified.

Ontology Type	Quantity
Domain or Content Ontologies	1
Pedagogical Ontologies	9
Ontologies on e-Learning administration	6
e-Learning Content Management Ontologies	14
Ontologies on e-Learning Resources	19

generation and the numerous extensions in the form of plug-ins and APIs available for programming. The vast majority of studies do not report information about the methodology used, except in cases where their concerns using Ontology Development 101. Noteworthy is the low number of domain ontologies developed specifically for use in e-Learning.

3.6. *An instructional design ontology*

Finally, we briefly describe an ontology [32] that supports the sequencing of Learning Objects. This ontology (LOSO), that can be classified as an Ontology on e-Learning Resources, was created with the intent to support the generation of sequencing strategies for LOs. In the terminology of Instructional Design, sequencing is the activity of gathering and combining individual Learning Objects so that they have instructional meaning. The generation of the Instructional Design Strategy (IDS) is performed according to an Instructional Requirement (IR), which indicates for example, if one require active or passive learning; cognitive style of students as well as the educational context, among other information.

All information associated with the IR and other items, are stored in the ontology. A view of the classes and relations that make up the ontology can be seen in Fig. 1. A central concept of the model, is ID_Strategy that represents the instructional strategy responding to a Instructional_Requirement, related to a specific Instructional_Context. The ID_Strategy relates Learning_Resource, Learning_Activity and Psicopedagogical_resource.

LOSO was built with Protégé using an adaptation of Methontology [33] that includes elements of the Semantic Web techniques and automatic knowledge acquisition. OWL was used as representation language with Semantic Web Rules Language (SWRL). OWL allows building hierarchies of concepts and defining them through a axioms language for reasoning and interpretation. SWRL adds an additional layer of expressiveness allowing the definition of inference rules in these models [34].

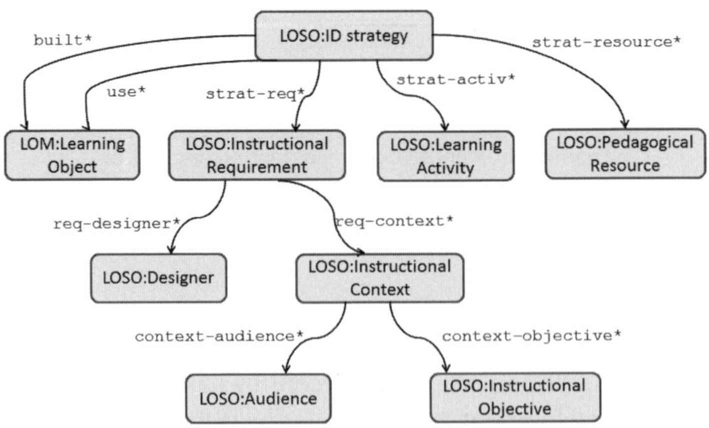

Fig. 1. Fragment of classes and relations in LOSO.

As an example, there is a sequencing rule obtained from the ontology. This rule, derived from the application of data mining techniques to an LO repository, defines the group of active objects as "highly active and interactive objects for the learner". These are mainly resources drill and practice. They have a high semantic density and average level of complexity regarding the use of LO. This rule is expressed in SWRL as follows:

LOM : learningObject (?lo) ∧
LOM : hasAggregationLevel (?lo, "1") ∧
LOM : hasStructure (?lo, "atomic") ∧
LOM : hasEducationalInformation (?lo, ?x) ∧
LOM : isIntendedForContext (?x, "higher education") ∧
LOM : hasDifficulty (?x, "easy") ∧
LOM : hasInteractivityLevel (?x, "very low") ∧
LOM : hasInteractivityType (?x, "expositive") ∧
LOM : hasSemanticDensity (?x, "medium")
→ LOSO : LOGroup (?lo, LOSO : very-pasive)

Rules were implemented using the Protegé SWRLTab plugin, with the Jess [35] rules machine. Implementation of such rules, allows support activities related to LO sequencing and therefore, to facilitate the construction of learning resources in e-Learning environments.

References

1. Puustjärvi, J (2006). *The Role of Metadata in E-learning Systems, Web-based Intelligent E-learning Systems.* Technologies and Applications, Z Ma (ed.), pp. 235–253. USA: Information Science Publishing.
2. Prieto, M, V Menendez, A Segura and C Vidal (2008). *A Recommender System Architecture for Instructional Engineering,* Lecture Notes in Computer Science, SB Heidelberg (ed.), pp. 314–321. Berlin: Springer-Verlag.
3. Segura, A, C Vidal, V Menéndez, A Zapata, M Prieto (2009). Characterizing metadata in learning object repositories. In *Proceeding of MTSR 2009 — Third International Conference on Metadata and Semantics Research,* Milán, Italia.
4. Wiley, D (2000). The instructional use of learning objects. Bloomington, AECT. Available at http://reusability.org/read/ [accessed on January 2008].
5. DCM, Dublin Core Metadata Initiative. Available at http://www.dublincore.org/about/ [accessed on May 2009].
6. DCMI, Dublin Core Metadata Initiative (2008). DCMI Metadata Terms. Available at http://www.dublincore.org/documents/dcmi-terms/ [accessed on April 2009].

7. DCMI, Dublin Core Metadata Initiative (2008). Encoding Guidelines. Available at http://www.dublincore.org/resources/expressions/ [accessed on April 2009].
8. DCMI-Ed, Dublin Core Metadata Initiative Education Community. Available at http://dublincore.org/groups/education/index.shtml [accessed May 2009].
9. DCMI-Ed, Dublin Core Metadata Initiative Education Community (2007). DC-Education Application Profile. Available at http://dublincore.org/educationwiki/Working_20Draft_20of_20DC_2dEd_20Application_20Profile/ [accessed on May 2009].
10. IEEE-LTSC, Learning Technology Standards Committee (2002). IEEE Standard for Learning Object Metadata. Available at http://ltsc.ieee.org/wg12/files/LOM_1484_12_1_v1_Final_Draft.pdf [accessed April 2008].
11. Edna, Educational Network Australia. Edna metadata standard (2002). Available at http://www.edna.edu.au/edna/go/resources/metadata/pid/261/ [accessed on February 2009].
12. GEM, Gateway to Educational Materials (2004). GEM project documentation. Available at http://www.thegateway.org/about/documentation [accessed on April 2009].
13. CanCore Initiative. Guidelines (2004). Available at http://www.cancore.ca/en/guidelines.html [accessed on April 2009].
14. AENOR, Asociación Española de Normalización y Certificación. Perfil de Aplicación LOM-ES V 1.0 (2008). Available at http://www.aenor.es/desarrollo/normalizacion/normas/fichanorma.asp [accessed on February 2009].
15. CETIS, Centre for Educational Technology Interoperability Standards (2008). UK LOM Core. Available at http://zope.cetis.ac.uk/profiles/uklomcore/ [accessed on February 2009].
16. The Learning Federation and E-standards for Training (2008). ANZ-LOM, Metadata Application Profile. Available at http://www.thelearningfederation.edu.au/verve/_resources/ANZ-LOM.pdf [accessed on February 2009].
17. KERIS, Korea Education & Research Information System (2004). Korea Educational Metadata (KEM) Profile for K–12. Available at http://www.keris.or.kr/datafiles/data/RM2004-22.pdf [accessed on April 2009].
18. EUN, European School Net (2007). The EUN learning resource exchange metadata application profile. Available at http://lre.eun.org/sites/default/files/pdf/AppProfilev3p0.pdf [accessed on August 2009].
19. ADL, Advanced Distributed Learning (2004). SCORM: Sharable Course Object Reference Model 2004 3rd Edition Documentation Suite. Available at http://adlnet.org/ADLDOCS/Other/SCORM_1.2_PDF.zip [accessed on December 2008].
20. IMS Global Learning Consortium (2003). IMS Learning Design. Available at http://www.imsglobal.org/learningdesign/ [accessed on January 2009].

21. IMS Global Learning Consortium (2004). IMS Content Packaging. Available at http://www.imsglobal.org/content/packaging [accessed on January 2009].
22. IMS Global Learning Consortium (2006). IMS Meta-Data Version 1.3. Available at http://www.imsglobal.org/metadata/#version1.3 [accessed on January 2009].
23. Kitchenham, B (2004). Procedures for performing systematic reviews (Joint Technical Report). Software Engineering Group, Department of Computer Science, Keele University and Empirical Software Engineering National ICT Australia Ltd.
24. Van Heist, G, T Schreiber and B Wielinga (1997). Using explicit ontologies in kbs. *International Journal of Human-Computer Studies*, 46, 183–292.
25. Uschold, M and M Grüninger (1996). Ontologies: Principles, methods and applications. Knowledge Engineering Review, 11, 2.
26. Steve, G, A Gangemi and D Pisanelli. Integrating Medical Terminologies with ONIONS Methodology. Available at http://saussure.irmkant.rm.cnr.it [accessed on February 2009].
27. Guarino, N (1998). Formal ontologies and information systems. Guarino, N. (ed.). Proceedings of FOIS'98, Trento, Italy, 6–8 June. Amsterdam: IOS Press.
28. Noy, N and D McGuinness (2001). Ontology Development 101: A Guide to Creating Your First Ontology. *Knowledge Systems Laboratory*, March, 1–25.
29. Cristani, M and R Cuel (2004). Methodologies for the Semantic Web: State-of-the-art of ontology methodology Column of SIGSEMIS Bulletin. Theme: SW Challenges for KM. 1, 2.
30. OWL Web Ontology Language Reference. Available at http://www.w3.org/TR/2003/PR-owl-ref-20031215/ [accessed on December 2008].
31. Protegé. Ontology Tool. Available at http://protege.stanford.edu/ [accessed on January 2008].
32. Vidal, C (2009). Diseño y Construcción de Ontologías en e-Learning. Una aplicación a la secuenciación de Objetos de Aprendizaje. Master's thesis. University of Castilla-La Mancha. España.
33. Fernández-Lopez, M, A Gómez-Pérez and N Juristo (1997). METHONTOLOGY: From Ontological Art towards Ontological Engineering. *Spring Symposium on Ontological Engineering of AAAI*, Stanford University, California.
34. O'Connor, MJ, R Shankar, S Tu, C Nyulas, A Das (2008). Developing a Web-Based Application using OWL and SWRL. *AAAI Spring Symposium,* Stanford, CA, USA.
35. O'Connor, M, H Knublauch, S Tu, B Grosof, M Dean, W Grosso, MA Musen (2005). Supporting rule system interoperability on the semantic web with SWRL. *Fourth International Semantic Web Conference (ISWC2005)*, Galway, Ireland.

CHAPTER III.2

METADATA AND ONTOLOGIES FOR HEALTH

Gianluca Colombo,*,† Daniele Merico*,‡ and Michaela Gündel*,§

*Department of Computer Science, Systems and Communication (DISCo), Universita di Milano-Bicocca (UNIMIB)
Ed. U14, Viale Sarca 336, Milan, Italy
†giacolos@gmail.com
‡daniele.merico@gmail.com
§Michaela.Guendel@gmail.com

The availability of information technology solutions for data storage and elaboration offers great opportunities to clinical medicine, but requires mastering the complexity of biomedical data.

Biomedical ontologies are often perceived just as a tool for terminological standardization useful for the exploitation of the electronic medium (for queries, statistical analysis, etc.). However, the topics posed by the electronic health records development to the bio-ontologies design also cover more conceptual and epistemological matters; primarily, the need to offer to the clinical user a view of the clinical data compatible with his mental model and work organization. For this reason a more articulated perspective must be adopted to highlight the foundational concepts and perspectives involved into the bio-ontology commitments. Such a critical inquiry over the roles and scopes of ontologies and metadata modeling for health, can be then profitability applied to the description and analysis of the existing general purpose medical ontologies, disease classifications, terminologies and data transmission standards.

1. Introduction

The notion of *electronic health record* (EHR)[1] [41,49, 50] is of primary importance to the field of medical informatics. A patient interacting

[1] *Electronic Medical Record* (EMR) is often used as a synonym of EHR.

with a healthcare institution typically undergoes a process of information collection, generation and elaboration; these information items (i.e., *clinical features*) span different areas, such as identification and demographics, medical findings, life style, health history; they are organized into a general structure, the *health record*, which is instantiated for every patient; therefore, health records of different patients differ by values, rather than by content. The importance of that information corpus predates the computer revolution, when health records were stored in a paper medium. As a matter of fact, the availability of health records enables an array of essential functions, such as clinical activity (diagnosis, treatment, and prognosis), research, and administrative tasks [41].

The availability of information technology solutions for data storage and elaboration offers great opportunities to clinical medicine, but requires mastering the complexity of biomedical data; moreover, different tasks often pose specific issues. In this chapter, we will first address how clinical data are used, and how different applications cast different needs on data modeling; second, what challenges must be addressed by ontological modeling in the clinical field; finally, we will briefly review publicly available ontologies and terminologies.

2. How clinical data are used

This section is devoted to briefly describe how clinical data are used by users or applications, and what the implications for their modeling are. Four broad groups can be identified, with different needs and perspectives:

— Data access in the daily clinical practice;
— Decision support systems;
— Clinical trials, association studies, translational research;
— Administration and management;
— Document management and cooperative work support.

2.1. Data access in the daily clinical practice

In the first place, the health record is meant to be accessed by the clinician, in order to retrieve essential information required by his daily activity with patients.

The typical interaction with the health records is on a by-patient basis, rather than on a by-field basis; that is, the clinician is often more interested in the value of several fields from the health record of the same patient, rather than in the value of one or few fields across different patients.[2]

The preference for the patient-based access mode also explains why clinicians largely resort to fields with natural language (NL) content to summarize the patient status in an expressive and intuitive way. The opposite access mode (on a field-basis) is more common for other use cases, such as in clinical trials and association studies.

The challenge here is to meet both these objectives:

(a) Maximize the exploitation of the electronic medium (for queries, statistical analysis, etc.);
(b) Offer to the clinical user a view of the data being meaningful, intuitive, and compatible with his mental model and work organization.

2.2. *Decision support systems*

Intensive attempts were initially made by the Artificial Intelligence community to reproduce the decision processes performed by the human clinical expert throughout the daily clinical practice (diagnosis, treatment, prognosis); success would have granted, on the practical side, a significant reduction in health care costs, and, on the theoretical side, a set of tools and paradigms for an even more ambitious modeling of mental processes. Such ambitious ends were never completely met, and the efforts have been progressively shifted to supporting the activity of the human expert, rather than replacing it, hence the term *Clinical Decision Support Systems* (CDSS) [56]. Examples are:

— *Real-time monitoring systems,* which trigger an alert when a health parameter of the patient goes out of range;
— *Checking systems,* which verify that all the steps of a standard procedure are accomplished.

[2] For instance, a clinician may first record the patient's symptoms and signs on admission, and schedule a first array of exams; when the exam results are available, he will need to enter them into the health record, then go back to the symptoms and signs previously stored, consider other patient's data (e.g., demographics and medical history), and eventually formulate an initial diagnostic hypothesis. Considering another example, when the clinician formulates the treatment, he may have to check for the patient's drug intolerances.

Even when looking for *similar cases* (i.e., patients with a clinical profile similar to the one under examination), the health record is still accessed mostly on a by-patient basis. This use-case is usually triggered by the encounter of a clinical case not fitting into the clinician's experience, or the established guidelines (for diagnosis, treatment, etc.).

In order for the EHR data to be used by a CDSS, they must be in a machine operable format, and not simply in a human user-readable format. This requisite is transversal to several use-cases beyond CDSS; specifically hard challenges are posed by information extraction from NL, and feature extraction from image data.

2.3. *Clinical trials, association studies, translational research*

Clinical trials, association studies and translational research require the use of clinical data in a context other than the clinical practice; the final end is not the healthcare of a single patient, but rather the discovery or testing of some biomedical relation or property, of general interest and validity in the medical domain. The relations and properties assessed in these studies contribute to the implementation of Evidence-Based Medicine (EBM), which is the use of available evidence from systematic research in the clinical practice[3] [51]. Specifically,

- *Clinical trials* consist in the testing of a drug or medication device, checking for its safety for the patients' health, and for its efficacy as a treatment (e.g., Is aspirin a good treatment for influenza?);
- *Association studies* are performed to identify correlations between (a) one (or more) clinical feature, including the genetic make-up of individuals, and (b) a clinical or pre-clinical disease state, or disease progression behavior (e.g., is the sodium level in the diet associated to hypertension? Is low-meat diet slowing the progression of prostate neoplasm from benign to malignant?);
- *Translational research* refers to the combination of biological research, at the molecular and cellular level, to clinical ends (e.g., identification of biomolecular disease markers for breast cancer).

Clinical trials and association studies present similar requisites:

- Cluster the patients into groups with common clinical conditions (i.e., segmentation);
- Large cohorts are necessary to grant statistical reliability; due to the rising costs of patient enrollment into ad-hoc cohorts, integration of existing data silos is an appealing solution; however, it is also prone to flaws and biases, unless the content of different resources is aligned on a semantic basis, preserving the meaning and the methodological coherence.

[3] "The practice of evidence based medicine means integrating individual clinical expertise with the best available external clinical evidence from systematic research" [51].

Translational research [52] is a broader term, generally referring to studies that connect the clinical realm to biomolecular research; specific types of clinical trials and association studies (e.g., phenotype–genotype associations) are included as well. The common denominator here is the existence of discrepancies between the clinical and biomolecular domain [8], typically in terms of:

— *Methodology*: Clinical medicine is committed to curing disease and preserving human health; it is subject to very tight constraints in the way the object of study can be investigated and sampled (e.g., Alzheimer cannot be diagnosed extracting a sample from the patient's brain, and then performing an array of lab tests); on the contrary, biomolecular research is committed to the elucidation of biological mechanisms, and can exploit experimental designs causing the death or disability of non-human organisms (e.g., systematic gene deletion is used to identify genes essential for the organism's survival);
— *Structural granularity*: Biomolecular research principally operates at the level of molecules and cells, with a special accent laid on the genetic information encoded by nucleic acids; clinical medicine spans all organization levels, with traditional practice operating mainly at the organ and organ system level;
— *Target organism*: Clinical medicine is devoted to the human organism, whereas biomolecular research largely exploits model organisms (e.g., yeast, fly, mouse), exhibiting variable levels of similarity to homo sapiens in terms of biological structures and processes.

Modeling frameworks supporting translational research must address these challenges, providing a bridge between the two disciplines [8].

2.4. *Administration and management*

Other tasks supported by the computational treatment of clinical data do not conform to the perspective of medical practice and research. We mention a few examples:

— *Billing*, that is the activity of automatically generating financial transactions or documents in relation to medical examinations;
— *Statistics* for the management and administration departments of health institutions, for insurance companies, for public health policy makers, for the national and international census offices.

The former use-case typically involves the attachment of financial codes or data to examinations and treatments, hence acting as an extension of the electronic health record, without significantly altering its structure. The latter use-case typically involves the attachment of disease codes to patients, according to existing classification systems; this operation resembles the clustering of patients into groups described for association studies and clinical trials, although the classification criteria adopted in the two cases rely on different perspectives.

2.5. *Document management and computer supported cooperative work*

Document management refers to document retrieval, indexing and cooperative document manipulation. *Computer-supported cooperative work* (CSCW) [53,54] enables different experts to share resources, exchange messages, and coordinate their work. Document management and computer-supported cooperative work are often grouped together under the broader concept of knowledge management [KM-08], a term we explicitly did not use to avoid confusion with other tasks.

The challenges posed to clinical data modeling by these tasks mostly resemble the challenges already encountered for other usage groups. The additional modeling challenges posed by these applications mostly fall outside the realm of the electronic health record.

2.6. *Final remarks*

In this chapter, the focus will be on ontologies and meta-data supporting applications obeying to a common perspective, that is *clinical practice and research*; therefore, we will not consider applications related to management, administration or other extra-clinical use-cases.

The term *clinical modeling* will be used throughout the text to refer to (a) the computer representation of clinical features, and specifically (b) the development of ontological models and meta-models supporting the previous task.

3. The Contribution of ontologies to clinical modeling

Apparently, the *data* have a central role in health applications: data are transferred from existing records when a patient is admitted, they are generated *ex-novo* during the diagnostic profiling, they are accessed and elaborated during the formulation of the diagnosis, prognosis and treatment, or during the execution of other tasks; data from different repositories need to be integrated and inter-operated to enable certain applications.

However, data themselves do not provide any explicit model of their semantics and the rationale of their organization [42]. Ontologies, intended as formal representations of entities and their inter-relations, enable to overcome those limitations. Biomedical ontologies are often perceived just as a tool for terminological standardization; however, a more articulated perspective will be adopted here. This section introduces and discusses foundational concepts and perspectives on ontology design.

3.1. *Ontologies by domain-specificity*

A major distinction in ontology design is between domain-dependent and domain-independent ontologies.

Among domain-independent ontologies, an Upper Ontology is committed to representing universal categories and relations (such as time, space, movement, object, etc.). The aim of Upper Ontology is to provide a foundational model, generally valid in different domains, and thus constitute a shared ground among different domain-specific ontologies [10]. There is a harsh debate concerning the feasibility of Upper Ontology [7, 9, 43], considering whether it is really possible to provide a single model with universal validity, and what is the best suited one among different proposals. Other efforts in domain independent ontologies are devoted to the formal properties of relations (e.g., transitivity), rather than providing an all-encompassing model of reality. These contributions are valuable for the design of the ontology metamodel [44].

3.2. *Ontologies by scope and purpose*

The target domain is not a sufficient criterion to determine the design of an ontological model, as different purposes and views can lead to diverging design solutions. Without exhausting all the possibilities, we specifically consider two possible views: *language* (or descriptive) and *concepts* (or prescriptive) [44]. In language-oriented ontologies (i.e., *terminologies*) the accent is laid on the catalog of the terms used in a domain, their interrelations, and their synonyms; typical applications are content indexing for document retrieval, information extraction, data integration based on terminological matching [12]. Concept-oriented ontologies are committed to represent conceptualizations, which are grounded onto a variable mix of explicit knowledge (e.g., a scientific theory) and implicit knowledge (e.g., individual experience, community practices, etc.). The two perspectives are not mutually exclusive, in the sense that a conceptual ontology can be extended by a terminological base, linking every class in the ontology to a set of linguistic terms; the critical point is that not all the applications interacting with a terminology necessarily require an exhaustive treatment of the underlying concepts [45].

3.3. *Meta-modeling and knowledge sources*

In the Computer Science arena, ontology is conceived as a model of a specific domain, aimed at providing a general representation of the entities belonging to it. Beyond the representational artifact itself, more theoretical questions concern the inner nature of any representational act [7, 9]:

— What cognitive models is it grounded onto?
— What is its purpose?

Is that sort of enquiry totally irrelevant to the computational applications of ontology? The answer is no. Reasoning by analogy, such questions set a topic to ontology quite similar to the one posed by the meta-modeling to the software engineering. In software engineering the term "meta-modeling" is the set of building blocks and rules used to build models. In the Ontology field, a meta-model is better conceived as the characterization of the criteria that guide a taxonomical arrangement of entities. As a consequence, the meta-modeling task in the ontology design mainly refers to the formal representation of those cognitive models and schemes that explicitly or tacitly drive humans in classifying entities into categories of entities.

In spite of the unsolvable dichotomy between realism and conceptualism in the ontology debate [46], the critical point here is that explicitly modeling the classification criteria (i.e., the meta-modeling issue) brings in the knowledge factor.

Despite the effort for defining a standard semantic, experts seem in fact to resist to any attempt of homogenization. Partly, this is due to practical problems, but there are also theoretical reasons why this is not easily accepted and not even desirable. In fact, lots of cognitive and organizational studies show that there is a close relationship between knowledge and identity. Knowledge is not simply a matter of accumulating "true sentences"' about the world, but it is also a matter of interpretation schemes (e.g., paradigms [57], contexts [58], mental models [59], perspectives [60], which allow people to make sense of what they know. All these mental structures identify different knowledge sources that are an essential part of what people know, as each of them provides an alternative lens through which reality can be read.

Knowledge sources can be divided into two extremes:

— General domain knowledge: This knowledge form is shared among a large number of subjects who, in that sense, speak the same language and think according to the same models; in addition, this knowledge form is usually encoded in a pre-formal way in manuals and other written documents. In the case of the medical domain, anatomy is typically part of the general knowledge, as it is object of total agreement among different medical experts.
— Community-specific knowledge: This knowledge form is held by the members of a smaller community of experts, and may reveal significant discrepancies when compared to the knowledge detained by another community [16], even when concerning the same domain of reality; in addition, this knowledge form is often implicitly encoded, and only partially captured by written documents [55].

Under an IT perspective, the fast proliferation of numerous local ontologies, often grounded on unrelated knowledge models, is a major factor hindering data exchange, system inter-operability and resource integration [1, 2]. Specifically, the misalignment among these models is neither on the syntactic/formal language level (*cf.* the success of OWL-DL [17,18]), neither on a purely terminological basis; the major problem is in the absence of a common meta-model [44] and design methodology [6, 15].

The solution to overcome this problem is not the radical elimination of local ontologies, and replacement with a one-fits-all model; indeed, some of the local ontologies actually capture valuable aspects of the knowledge schemes, specifically characterizing local communities and institutions [47]. A more reasonable scenario entails, on a global level:

— The establishment of a (global) Reference Ontology, composed by modular and orthogonal sub-ontologies;
— The establishment of common ontology design methodology and meta-model (e.g., OBO, for more details refer to Chapter 5); and, on the local level:
— The reception of as many elements as possible from the Reference Ontology, the meta-model and the design methodology, to the extent they fit into the local needs.

Even in case of incomplete alignment, a partial mapping between the local ontologies and the Reference Ontology can be very probably established, supporting integration tasks.

In such a scenario, the establishment of global resources is typically the result of a community effort, enacting a profitable osmosis between the modeling experiences at the local and global level.

4. Modeling issues in the clinical domain

This section is devoted to the specific issues posed by clinical features to ontology design. The focus is laid on the aspects connected to the clinical practice and research; aspects strictly related to management, administration and census will not be addressed.

The term *clinical indicator* identifies any clinically-relevant[4] patient feature, computationally represented as a field of the health record; the term indicator is preferred to datum, as it does not already imply the computational representation; their modeling is addressed in the firs sub-section, *Modeling Clinical Indicators.* The assessment of the clinical indicators leads to the progressive characterization of the patient's clinical state. Modeling clinical indicators *per se* does not enable to explicitly represent why the clinical indicators are assessed, nor their inter-relations in defining clinical states, or their relations to the world of biomedical research[5]; these issues are addressed in the second sub-section, *Making Sense of Clinical Indicators: Modeling Clinical States.*

4.1. *Modeling clinical indicators*

A clinical indicator can refer to different aspects of the patient; such differences are important for the modeling activity. A non-exhaustive but representative list is:

— *Personal identification* (e.g., name and surname, social insurance number);
— *Demographics* (e.g., age, education, ethnic group);
— *Life-style* (e.g., diet, smoking, alcohol consumption);
— Elementary, common-use *biometrics* (e.g., weight, height);
— *Vital parameters* (e.g., body temperature, pressure, pulse);

[4] By the term *clinically relevant,* we relate to the health state of the patient.
[5] In other words, these elements cannot be represented in a *data-model,* they require an *ontological model.*

— *Signs*, which are assessed by the medical doctor through a direct examination of the patient (e.g., pallor, swollen lymph nodes);
— *Symptoms*, which are self reported by the patients (e.g., headache, confusion);
— *Lab tests*, which are usually performed on a *sample*,[6] and which can be further grouped into genetic, biochemical, biomolecular, cellular, histological, etc... (e.g., hemoglobin level, blood leukocitary formula, blood group);
— *Instrumental recordings* (e.g., electrocardiogram);
— *Imaging* (e.g., MRI);
— *Expert reports*, further elaborating instrumental recordings or imaging, usually formulated in natural language (for instance, the radiologist's report[7]);
— Undergoing or past *treatment* (e.g., drug treatment: active ingredient and dose schedule; prostheses: ball and cage artificial heart valve);
— *Family history* (e.g., father died of myocardial infarction);
— *Diagnosis*, referring to an aspect or the whole clinical condition of the patients; these can be expressed by a short textual description, and/or by categorical values from disease classification systems (e.g., Diabetes Mellitus Type-2).

Different aspects need to be handled when modeling clinical indicators and their values, which can be summarized as:

— *Data type*: numerical (e.g., number of daily smoked cigarettes: 8), categorical (e.g., sex: male, female), serial code (e.g., social insurance number: 123-456-789), free text (e.g., "The absence of symptoms implies a benign lesion."), multimedia (e.g., a picture);
— *Scale or metric* (e.g., height: meters; cognitive function: Rancho Level of Cognitive Functioning Scale);
— *Time-dependence*, as the same indicator can be assessed multiple times;
— *Normality range*: normality ranges are usually applied to determine whether an indicator has a clinically abnormal value (e.g., normal body temperature, measured in the armpit, is between 35°C and 37°C);
— *Methodology and instrumental technology*: In this category, we include the procedure followed by the medical expert to perform the clinical assessment (e.g., temperature measurement: rectal) and the information

[6] A sample is a limited portion of the patient's body (e.g., a blood sample).
[7] E.g. "Appearances are consistent with a sessile osteochondroma of the proximal humeral diaphysis involving the medial cortex. The absence of symptoms implies a benign lesion."

relative to the measure device itself (e.g., CT-scan technology: electron beam; CT-scan device manufacturer: Siemens); additional methodological issues arise when instrumental results are elaborated using some formal and reproducible method (e.g., an algorithm encoded in a software tool) or are interpreted by an expert; the latter case introduces and additional problem of subjectivity;

— *Dependence on pre-conditions*: A specific issue with methodology is the existence of pre-conditions for the validity of the indicator determination (e.g., blood pressure higher than the reference threshold translates into);
— *Degree of objectivity or subjectivity*: The latter can be interpreted in a negative sense, implying lack of standardization, or in a positive sense, intending the contribution of the expert's implicit knowledge to problem solving;
— *Granularity and inter-dependence of clinical states*: Every indicator, with its specific value in the patient, can be regarded as a component of the global state; indicators with a more global scope (e.g., diabetes mellitus type-2) usually rely on aggregation of narrower indicators (e.g., fasting glycemia), and the application of normality ranges (e.g., over-simplifying the case, influenza is diagnosed when temperature is $T > 38°C$, the patients reports a general sense of malaise, and he has runny nose and/or sore throat); the dependence on the context can be analytically broken down into relations to other indicators, but only with a varying degree of completeness; the harder cases occur when these relations are established through implicit cognitive heuristics of the medical expert;
— *Directly observed or inferred*: Indicators may reflect to a different extent the "pure" observation[8] of some physical reality or the inferential processes[9] guiding the diagnostic activity (relying on medical theory, guidelines and best practices, personal experience); indicators belonging to the personal identification, life-style and demographics typically have no interpretative content, whereas the final diagnosis has the maximal interpretative content; this issue is strictly connected to the *subjectivity/objectivity* issue, as the inference criteria may be explicit/objective to a variable extent;

[8] No observation is truly *pure*: What is observed depends on a theory specifying what is relevant, and how it is observed influences the result. In addition, human contributions, such as instrument calibration, or discarding meaningless values, are often hidden behind apparently objective data.
[9] The *inferential process* mentioned here is intended as a human cognitive process.

— *Granularity of physical structures*, stratified at different scales of the organism organization (e.g., molecule, intracellular or extracellular structure, cell or extracellular matrix, tissue, organ, system, individual, population).

What are the issues to be tackled in this rich data landscape? As far as the semantics are concerned, as in the definition of an ontological model, certain properties of clinical data can pose serious criticalities. Granularity of structure, granularity of state and methodology will be systematically addressed in the next sub-section. Here we will consider the impingement of these issues on clinical data integration; the conclusion will be that an explicit ontological modeling of clinical states is required to resolve integration problems.

4.1.1. *A data integration toy problem*

Consider the case of two minimal health records, stored in two different databases; for simplicity, we will treat every database as a flat list of fields; for the same reason, we jointly present the database fields and the example values for two imaginary patients; the field names are designed as to express the maximal semantic, though this is not always the case with real world databases.

Database 1:

Patient X1:
Lesion.presence.MRI.1 = y
Lesion.side.MRI.1 = Left
Lesion.Stenosis.Coaxiality.1 = y
Stenosis.presence.CTA.1 = y
Relevant.Stroke.Lesion.1 = y

Database 2:

Patient X2:
Lesion.presence.CT.2 = y
Lesion.side.CT.2 = Right
Stenosis.presence.CTA.2 = y
Stenosis.side.CTA.2 = Right
Relevant.Stroke.Lesion.2 = y

Clearly, the database content itself does not give any idea of the reason why these different indicators are collected, what are their inter-relations, and what is their degree of granularity in assessing the patient's state. Even if an explicit semantic model is not developed, it is always possible to use the semantics of the indicators to attempt a direct matching of the fields. The diagnostic process behind these toy databases is the following:

1. Assess the presence and side (left, right) of a brain lesion using a suitable diagnostic method, such as Computed Tomography (CT) or Magnetic Resonance Imaging (MRI) brain imaging;
2. Assess the presence and side of a carotid stenosis using a suitable diagnostic method, such as Computed Tomography Angiography (CTA);
3. If the lesion is present, and it is co-localized with the stenosis, then a relevant stroke lesion is present.

On that basis, we can establish the following mappings between indicators, and the relative clinical states identified:

Lesion.presence.MRI.1 = y/n	Lesion.presence.CT.2 = y/n
Lesion.side.MRI.1 = Left/Right	Lesion.side.CT.2 = Left/Right
Stenosis.presence.CTA.1 = y/n	Stenosis.presence.CTA.2 = y/n
Relevant.Stroke.Lesion.1 = y/n	Relevant.Stroke.Lesion.2 = y/n

Albeit satisfactory, we have at least two residual problems:

— Coaxiality is differently defined in the two databases, in one case giving the sides of lesion and stenosis, in the other case giving the side of the lesion and the value of coaxiality;
— The presence of a stroke lesion, as reported in the database, depends on the value of other indicators, and we may want to establish a method for consistency checking;
— Lesion.presence is assessed using different techniques in the two databases; in this case the techniques are equivalent, though that may not hold for other cases, hence requiring a more sophisticated handling of methodological coherence[10];

Of course, these problems can be efficiently resolved using ad-hoc procedures.

Another solution, superior in terms of generality, is to explicitly define a conceptual model (which is an intuitive and semi-formal analogue of an

[10] For instance, only the entire expression: Lesion.presence.CT.2 = y AND Medical-History, PastStrokeLesion = n may be equivalent to Lesion.presence.MRI.1 = y.

ontological model) for aggregate clinical states — in this case, limited to the assessment of a relevant lesion:

Relevant.Lesion = y	:=	Stenosis.Presence = y AND Lesion.Presence = y AND Coaxiality = y
Relevant.Lesion = n	:=	Stenosis.Presence = n OR Lesion.Presence = n OR Coaxiality = n

And then map the actual database fields to the aggregate clinical states of the model above:

Coaxiality = y	:=	Lesion.Stenosis.Coaxiality.1 = y OR (Stenosis.side.CTA.2 = Right AND Lesion.side.MRI.2 = Right) OR (Stenosis.side.CTA.2 = Left AND Lesion.side.MRI.2 = Left)
Lesion.Presence = y	:=	Lesion.Presence.MRI.1 = y OR Lesion.Presence.CT.2 = y
Lesion.Presence = y	:=	Stenosis.Presence.CTA.1 = y OR Stenosis.Presence.CTA.2 = y

The latter approach is more general, as the clinical state model can be defined once for all, and can be then re-used to integrate different databases complying with that model; further advantages are in terms of readability and re-use.

4.2. *Making sense of clinical indicators: Modeling clinical states*

As stated in the introduction of this section, the assessment of the clinical indicators (i.e., instantiating the value of the indicator) leads to the progressive characterization of the patient's *clinical state*.[11] In other domains, a state is defined by the value of a set of parameters; specifically, in the clinical domain:

- Not all the possible combinations of indicators form relevant states;
- There are clinical states holding general validity, recognized in many different patients (typically, canonic diseases); these will be termed *prototypal* clinical states.

[11] The notion of *clinical phenotype* is highly similar to clinical state. *Phenotype* is a notion typically used in biology, in opposition to genotype, and defined as an *observable state*. Since the notion of clinical state is as general as possible, it includes the genotype as well, and thus is not equivalent to clinical phenotype.

The clinical indicators represented in the EHR are assessed during the diagnostic activity, and the follow-up after the treatment. A patient is typically admitted after reporting symptoms, or abnormal values in periodic screenings, that suggest a potential threat to his health. The clinician consequently formulates an array of initial hypotheses, which are evaluated performing additional exams. A final diagnostic hypothesis is eventually formulated, often referring to a prototypal state. The collection of clinical indicator values in the EHR reflects this process. Clearly, the diagnostic activity is characterized neither by the systematic assessment of all possible indicators, nor by the assessment of randomly picked ones; in this sense, the make-up of clinical states rationally mirrors the theory and experience guiding the diagnostic process.

Prototypal clinical states are typically represented as classes, i.e., universals, and organized into classifications (e.g., hypertension, intended as a state of abnormally high blood pressure, is a condition common to many different patients; different instances of hypertension will have specific values of blood pressure). The recognition of these prototypal states in the patients enables to cluster them into groups, as required by association studies and clinical trials.

A *clinical state ontology* (CSO) has the purpose of explicitly modeling how and why clinical indicators are aggregated to form clinical states. The criteria guiding the identification of universals and their inter-relations in clinical state ontology depend upon the factors identified in Sec. 3.3, i.e., knowledge sources (globally-valid or community-specific) and applicative use. Let's consider a specific example to evaluate the interplay of such factors. The *TOAST classification* [3, 4] defines a group of ischemic stroke prototypal states,[12] and it is broadly adopted in cerebrovascular medicine. These definitions are used as *guidelines* for the diagnostic activity, i.e., they are treated as best practices for stroke diagnosis, under the paradigm of EBM.[13] They are also used in clinical trials and association studies. For different applications, however, different specializations of such categories are typically developed; for instance:

— Clinical practice always takes place in the context of a specific healthcare institution; hence, different institutions can define more stringent

[12] The *stroke* itself is an accident (a sudden and critical disturbance in the blood vessels supplying blood to the brain), hence it may be apparently incorrect to treat ischemic stroke types as *states*. However, the TOAST defines ischemic stroke types on the basis of (1) probatory strength of symptoms, signs, and other evidences for the stroke; (2) anatomical location of the stroke; (3) mid/long-term disease causing the stroke (such as large arthery atherosclerosis, cardioembolism, small vessel disease), In that sense, a stroke type is a characterization of the patient's state. For more details, please refer to [KER-08].

[13] *Cf.* Subsec. 2.3.*Clinical Trials, Association Studies, Translational Research.*

criteria, implement additional diagnostic assessments, or use experimental treatments [48]; all these factors may lead to the local definition of specialized prototypal states;

— In the case of translational research related applications, such as genotype–phenotype associations studies, the final end is not diagnosis and treatment, but the identification of biomarkers or causal determinants of disease states; hence, if the TOAST is used in this context, certain classificatory aspects may be prioritized over others[14]: etiopathological mechanisms of the disease typically play a primary role, enabling to define patient groups with homogenous genetic predispositions [48].

4.2.1. *Clinical state granularity and mereology*

A *Clinical State Ontology* (CSO) is committed to representing prototypal clinical states of different granularity (i.e., scope, specificity), depicting their inter-relations, the relations to clinical indicators, and the relations to medical domain entities (such as anatomical parts, therapeutic interventions, etc.). In this sense, a CSO is a mereological deconstruction of prototypal clinical states [43]: The CSO entities can be typically used as *building blocks* for customized clinical states, intended as specialized versions of the prototypal ones, or even totally new.[15] This feature grants flexibility to local needs, and inter-operability among different local sites. In addition, a CSO can be suitably extended to support the bridging to biomolecular research (as discussed with more details in Sec. 4.2.3).

The minimal clinical state represented by a CSO can be defined to correspond to a single clinical indicator:

— If the indicator is *categorical*, the corresponding minimal clinical state is generated by the combination of the clinical indicator with its value (e.g., Stenosis = present → PresenceOfStenosis);

— If the indicator is *numerical*, the corresponding minimal clinical state is generated by the combination of the clinical indicator with a normality range or threshold (e.g., SystolicBloodPressure = 120, SystolicBloodPressure.threshold = 100, → HighSystolicBloodPressure);

[14]Three criteria often guide disease classification in the general clinical field:

— *Symptomatology,* in terms of symptom/sign severity or quality;

— *Etiology,* i.e., the causing agent or structural anomaly (including risk factors);

— *Anatomy,* i.e., the anatomical part affected.

[15]However, a change in the underlying paradigm would probably require a significant restructuring of the ontology. Here, the term *paradigm* is used informally, with a broad scope.

— If the indicator is more complex, as in the case of time-series recordings or multimedia, either it is reduced to an elaborated indicator conforming to the previous types, either a more sophisticated range or threshold criterion is defined.

As we briefly introduced above, deconstructing aggregate clinical states into more elementary clinical states, moving across the granularity dimension, implements a *mereological* model. For instance, referring once again to the cerebrovascular domain, an Atherosclerothic Ischemic Stroke can be decomposed into two parts: the Ischemic Stroke (a cerebrovascular accident), and the durative etiological factor Atherosclerosis (a circulation disease). Identifying these two parts is useful, as the Ischemic Stroke unit is also a part of Cardioembolic Ischemic Stroke [48].

In this model, the relations connecting clinical states are partonomical, but can be specified to render the rationale for the state aggregation; referring to the previous example, it is natural to think Atherosclerosis as the *cause* of Ischemic Stroke. Additional non-state entities need to be present in the ontology as well, such as Anatomical Parts; these entities will be connected to states by specific non-partonomic relations [48].

An important question naturally arises: Does the decomposition of a clinical state into the value of atomic indicators (formally represented as an axiom in formal KR languages) equal to a diagnostic rule? The answer is no. As a matter of fact, the axioms are not used to infer the occurrence of aggregated states given the atomic states as inputs; they can rather be used as a consistency check, or to integrate resources with granularity misalignments.

4.2.2. *Handling the granularity of organic structures and processes*

Organisms are organized into hierarchical levels. That property holds for structures and processes.[16] As stated in the previous sub-section, to fully deconstruct clinical states it is necessary to introduce non-state entities, referring to organic parts (e.g., anatomy) and physiological processes. These entities are typically the object of the general biomedicine knowledge, shared

[16]The separation between *structures* and *processes* is one of the principal themes in ontological meta-modeling. The terms are used here informally, as a very detailed discussion would be required to address the feasibility of such distinction within the domains of medicine and biology.

between medicine and biology,[17] and could be suitably represented by autonomous, orthogonal ontologies connected to the Clinical State Ontology.

4.2.3. *Towards a bridge between the clinical and biomolecular domains*

The great challenge for translational research is to translate the study of biomolecular structure and processes into disease pathophysiology, enabling improved disease classification, more powerful diagnostic and prognostic methods, more targeted and personalized therapies with maximal efficacy and minimal side-effects. Establishing a bridge between the clinical and biomolecular domains is a standing challenge for ontological modeling and information systems. A promising strategy is offered by the connection of clinical states to the underlying biomolecular processes and structures. A prototypal application of this strategy can be found in [48], and a greater effort by the NCBO and OBO communities is under way [61].

4.2.4. *The clinical state as a foundational concept*

In this section, the notion of Clinical State was assumed as a natural foundational concept, playing a pivotal role in the development of ontological models for clinical features. However, that is not a common tenet in the field of general-purpose medical ontologies and terminologies, which often do not have a single foundational concept; it is rather a more recently emerging pattern in the biomedical community [61], deemed very promising by the authors, also in relation to their previous research experience.[18]

In the next section, devoted to the description of existing medical ontologies, terminologies and standards, we will critically analyze to what extent the notion of clinical state is rendered and is influential for the ontology design.

5. Publicly-available general-purpose ontologies and terminologies

The principles of general purpose ontologies and terminologies have already been described in Sec. 3. This section is subdivided into general purpose medical ontologies, general purpose disease classifications, general purpose

[17] In opposition to clinical states used in daily clinical practice, which may have no direct correspondence in biology.

[18] Cfr http://www.bioontology.org/wiki/index.php/Clinical_Phenotypes

terminological bases and data transmission standards and is designed to provide an overview on the respective topics.

A large number of knowledge bases, which are often heterogeneous, exists today. A topical problem today still is the question how to integrate the different ontologies and terminologies that exist, which includes also those that are used in data transmission standards. The problem itself and an approach to solve it is described in [39]. Work on ontological and terminological integration is ongoing. Usually, knowledge bases are constructed by different work groups independently from each other. It happens that the same concept is described by several work groups, but with a different level of granularity, with different views of the world or just using different namings or languages. Thus, the challenge is to align the semantics contained in these heterogeneous sources. The better a presentation is defined in terms of semantics, the better can the concepts and relations be understood, integrated and thus used by others.

The Unified Medical Language System (UMLS) (see Sec. 5.3.2) tackled this challenge, integrating the various concepts while at the same time maintaining the different views on the concepts. Semantic types (high-level concepts) were introduced to which concepts of individual ontologies can be mapped. This helps to have a common semantics for the knowledge bases that are to be integrated with each other. In the Open Biomedical Ontologies (OBO) project [http://www.obofoundry.org/], which is an effort to create a set of interoperable reference ontologies for Biomedicine together with a set of design principles, an approach based on providing a general common semantic was chosen: the Basic Formal Ontology (BFO), contains high-level concepts (the SNAP and SPAN ontologies for continuant and occurrent concepts, respectively) and a set of agreed-upon relations is used [Relation Ontology (RO)], that are extended by participating ontologies. This builds the ground for a basic common semantic in the various participating ontologies.

The integration of ontologies is of great importance, not solely to make different systems that are built on a different ontological basis inter-operable, but also owing to the current trend to use concepts from existing ontological bases when constructing a new ontology, directly integrating them in the newly built knowledge base.

In the medical domain, the data that is dealt with is mostly highly sensitive, as it contains very personal information on the patients, such as in Electronic Health or Medical Records. This data is largely contained in clinical databases, the information in which needs to be mapped to knowledge bases to make the resulting information inter-operable with other systems. Due to the fact that this sensitive data is often located in databases at different locations, there needs to be a method of storing and transmitting this information in a secure, reliable and semantically well-described way.

5.1. *General purpose medical ontologies*

Examples of general purpose ontologies in the medical domain include SNOMED-CT and *Open*GALEN. Whereas the scope of SNOMED-CT in health care is especially to model clinical data, i.e., to assist in annotating Electronic Health and Electronic Medical Records, *Open*GALEN has the more general scope of being a reference for the integration of healthcare systems of different kinds.

5.1.1. *SNOMED-CT*

The development of SNOMED-CT and descriptions on it can be found in [5, 27–29]. "SNOMED-CT" stands for "Systematized Nomenclature of Medicine — Clinical Terms" and is a merger of SNOMED-RT (short for "Reference Terminology") by the College of American Pathologists (CAP) [http://www.cap.org] and the United Kingdom's National Health Service's (NHS) [http://www.nhs.uk] Clinical Terms version 3, also called the Read Codes CTV3. Today, the International Health Terminology Standards Development Organization (IHTSDO) [http://www.ihtsdo.org/] is responsible for the development of SNOMED-CT, for quality issues and the distribution of the terminology.

Work on this merger started in 1999, the first version of SNOMED-CT was released in 2002. SNOMED-RT is a terminology for healthcare in basic sciences, the laboratory field and specialty medicine and contains more than 120,000 concepts which are interrelated among each other. The CTV3 is a terminology system for storing primary care data of patient records in a structured way, it contains around 200,000 interrelated concepts. The semantic definitions and relations in both were created via automatic processing and manual curation. The CAP SNOMED-RT was accredited by ANSI, the American National Standards Institute [http://www.ansi.org].

The aim of the SNOMED-CT terminology of health and healthcare related terms is to provide a global and broad multilingual hierarchical terminology for the encoding, the storage and the retrieval of health-related and disease-related information. It is designed to be used by computer applications for the consistent and unambiguous representation of information relevant to clinical data to be used for electronic health records (EHR) and decision-support (DS) systems, enabling semantic interoperability, regardless of the type of technology used. It contains around 280,000 active concept codes, 730,000 descriptions/terms and 920,000 relationships [29].

The ontology is based on description logic and applies the use of existential restrictions on relations. SNOMED-CT's meta model is based on the modeling of patient data and clinical information, linked to information contained in the respective patient's EHR.

Thus, top-level classes in SNOMED-CT include [35] (examples are given in brackets): *clinical finding* (which contains the disease sub-hierarchy), *procedure* (such as excision of intracranial artery), *observable entity* (left ventricular end-diastolic pressure), *body structure* (mitral valve structure), *organism* (*bacillus anthracis*), *substance* (insulin), *pharmaceutical/biological product* (diazepam), *specimen* (cerebroventricular fluid cytologic material), *event* (earthquake), *social context* (middle class economic status), *situation with explicit context* (family history), *qualifier value* (mild) and more.

Classes can be assigned to four different types of relationships, the most important with regard to the meta-model being the defining relationships *IS-A* (for generating the hierarchy) and "attribute" relationships, such as *Finding site*, *Severity*, or *Associated* with sub-relations *After*, *Due to* and *Causative agent*, and others, for the modeling of clinical indicators. Furthermore, there are so-called "cross maps" included that link SNOMED-CT to other terminologies and classifications, such as ICD-9 or ICD-10 (see Sec. 5.2.1.), and also standards such as DICOM and HL7 (Sec. 5.4) are supported.

Considering these concepts included and the underlying modeling of relations with the use of existential qualifiers, SNOMED-CT can provide a basis for modeling clinical states. Providing clinical indicators, it contains concepts and relations that can be used to model a clinical state ontology (CSO) by aggregating the existing clinical indicators to form the clinical states. The cross-mappings to important standards such as the ICD disease classification and data transmission standards are valuable additional information in this context. Work to align SNOMED-CT to BFO upper-level concepts has started [40] which, when finalized, will make it an ontology that is compatible with the other OBO ontologies.

For browsing SNOMED-CT, tools such as the SNOB desktop browser (http://snob.eggbird.eu/) or the CLUE browser (http://www.clininfo.co.uk/clue5/download_clue5.htm) can be used. To use SNOMED-CT it is necessary to obtain a license from IHTSDO.

5.1.2. *Open-Galen*

*Open*GALEN is an open-source description-logic based medical ontology and is provided by the *Open*GALEN Foundation [http://www.opengalen.org]. It is part of the "General Architecture for Languages, Encyclopedias and Nomenclatures in Medicine" (GALEN) technologies, which originated from the GALEN Program and the GALEN-In-Use Project, both financed by the European Union.

A description on the GALEN project is given on the *Open*GALEN website [20] and in various publications, such as [19]. The aim of *Open*GALEN is not to provide an all-comprising terminology of medicine, but to make a sufficient amount of existing knowledge about concepts in medicine available for healthcare professionals dealing with computer-based systems and providing a possibility to integrate healthcare systems of various kinds. One example is the mapping of a clinical entry to a concept and to the most appropriate ICD code. To enable this, a model is provided that contains the building blocks from which the concepts can be generated.

The *Open*GALEN medical ontology, also called "Common Reference Model" [19], was developed in the description logic language GRAIL (short for "GALEN Representation and Integration Language").

The meta-model in GALEN consists of four parts. The first part is an upper-level ontology which describes the sorts of concepts and how these concepts can be assembled together to form more detailed concepts. Such concepts are *Phenomenon* (e.g., *Process, RiskFactor, StateOrQuantity,* ...) and *Modifier-Concept* (such as *InvestigationResult, ExaminationFinding, Observation,* ...). The second part is the Common Reference Model. It contains, for instance, concepts on human anatomy, physiology, pathology, symptomatology and pharmacology. It contains definitions, descriptions and constraints. The third and fourth part are additional extensions to the building blocks needed for special sub-domains in medicine, such as surgery, and a further model that defines concepts which are formed from those contained in the Common Reference Model and the extensions.

An important concept in GRAIL is the "Model of Parts and Wholes" [21]: semantic links, such as part-whole relations (also called "partonomies"), which according to the authors play a crucial role in modeling medical concepts, can be organized hierarchically, can be inherited and declared transitive. The consequence of this is that a formal representation of statements such as " 'parts of parts of a whole' are 'parts of the whole'" [21] is possible.

Especially in its Modifier and Phenomenon concepts, *Open*GALEN contains diverse clinical indicators. Also, a modeling of several clinical states is included in its *PathologicalPhenomenon* category. The concept of *IschaemicStroke* can be taken as an example: It is modeled as a *PermanentCentralNeuropathy* with the restrictions to be a consequence of some *CerebralIschaemia,* to have an abnormality status of *NonNormal,* to have a pathological status of *pathological,* to be permanent and to have a *LocativeAttribute* of *CentralNervousSystem.* Its mappings to ICD codes provide a further advantage. However, as far as known to the authors, there does not exist an alignment to BFO and the OBO efforts yet, which would be an important criterion for choosing an ontological base for the appropriate modeling of a new clinical states ontology.

The latest version of the ontology is that of 2005, but work is continuing. For *Open*GALEN, there is an online browser available at http://browse.opengalen.org/.

5.2. *General purpose disease classifications*

Examples of systems that classify diseases which will be described below are the ICD and the Disease Ontology. The ICD, as a classification system of disease, provides codes for disease which are broadly and mainly used for the compilation of mortality statistics and billing purposes. The Disease Ontology integrates the ICD codes (and others, such as SNOMED and the UMLS) in its terminology and provides a means to look up those codes for diseases in an automated way. IDO models biomedical and clinical aspects of infectious diseases and provides a common framework for more refined IDO extensions for the infectious disease sub-domains.

5.2.1. *ICD-9-CM and ICD-10*

The International Classification of Disease (ICD) by the World Health Organization (WHO) [http://www.who.int] is a means to classify disease and health problems to form the basis for storage and retrieval of such data [14].

The first version of the ICD, at that time called "International List of Causes of Death", was compiled in the 1850s. The WHO assumed the responsibility for the ICD in 1948.

Being a standard classification system in diagnostics, it is used for clinical and epidemiological purposes, and WHO Member States use it to compile their mortality and morbidity statistics. The use of the same classification system by the Member States forms the basis for comparisons of statistical data between the different states. A new version of the ICD is created approximately every 10 years to account for advances made in medicine, and the current ICD is ICD-10. As explained in [26], the main differences between ICD-9 [13] and ICD-10 [14] are an increased detail level for many conditions, a transfer of conditions inside the classification (i.e., moval of conditions to different chapters), replacement of numeric codes by alphanumeric codes (e.g., "E10-E14" instead of "250"), a modification of the coding rules and tabulation lists.

The acronym "CM" (e.g., "ICD-9-CM") stands for "clinical modification". ICD-CMs are used for the classification of morbidity (versus "classification of mortality") data from records of patients inside the clinic and outside as well as physician offices [NCHS-01]. There are also other country-specific versions of the ICD.

The ICD-10, version 2007, contains a total of 22 chapters including 12,420 codes organized into subclasses. The chapters categorize diseases into subclasses such as infectious and parasitic diseases, diseases of the nervous system, of the circulatory system, of the respiratory system, of the digestive system and further, and also include classifications according to external causes, factors influencing health status and more. As it became obvious that coding the diseases in a general way alone did not meet all the needs of statistical coding, the so-called dagger–asterisk system [36] was introduced in ICD-9 and continued in ICD-10. Using the dagger–asterisk system it became possible to assign two codes to the same diagnostic statement. The dagger constitutes the primary code and represents the generalized disease, whereas the asterisk (*) codes are optional and describe the manifestation of the underlying disease in a special organ or site.

Although the ICD classification with its clinical modifications is mainly used for statistical purposes, its encoding of diseases, symptoms and external causes and factors is very close to information contained in patient records. It is neither an ontology nor one of clinical states and not conformant to the OBO principles, but describes a large set of clinical indicators and might thus be appropriate as a cross-reference to create a clinical state ontology.

The ICD-10 can be browsed at the WHO site at http://www.who.int/classifications/apps/icd/icd10online/. To obtain a copy of the current version of ICD, it is necessary to obtain a license.

5.2.2. *Disease ontology*

As reported on the project website [11], the Disease Ontology was developed in collaboration with the NUgene Project [http://www.nugene.org/] at the Center for Genetic Medicine of the US Northwestern University [http://www.cgm.northwestern.edu/] and is a controlled medical vocabulary. It can be downloaded for free from the project website.

Its objective is to provide a mapping of human disease types and disease conditions to medical codes and concepts contained in classification schemes and medical billing codes such as ICD-9CM (see Sec. 5.2.1.), SNOMED and others, thus relieving clinicians from looking up the individual codes in the coding booklets manually. To get access to medical vocabularies, the Disease Ontology integrates a subset of the Unified Medical Language System (described in detail in Sec. 5.3.2). In doing so, much of the work that gets necessary to update the vocabularies is left to the UMLS.

The Disease Ontology, version 33 Revision 21, contains around 15.000 concept nodes and is primarily based on freely available UMLS vocabularies [11]. Although it is called an "ontology", it is more a classification schema, as it basically contains objects ordered in a hierarchy that are assigned an ID, that have a name and database cross-references. The term *Cerebral Infarction* (subclass of *Cerebrovascular Disorders*) for instance has the ID *DOID:3526*, has cross-references to the corresponding ICD-9CM and UMLS codes and has several synonyms taken from SNOMED-CT.

Being primarily a classification system that includes mappings to other resources, it does contain clinical states via its mappings, but without referring to the clinical indicators that describe and define the clinical states.

To view the Disease Ontology, a tool such as OBO-Edit [http://geneontology.sourceforge.net/] can be used.

5.3. *General purpose terminological bases*

In the following, an overview on MeSH and the UMLS is provided, being terminologies of wide-spread application. Whereas MeSH is mainly used to annotate publications, such as abstracts in PUBMED, thus supporting activities such as text mining, the UMLS contains a metathesaurus, i.e., a thesaurus of thesauri that also includes MeSH and provides mappings between them to enable semantic interoperability between the concepts contained in the various source vocabularies.

5.3.1. *MeSH (Medical Subject Headings)*

MeSH *(Lipscomb CE, 2000)* is a medical thesaurus developed at the US National Library of Medicine (NLM) [http://www.nlm.nih.gov/].

An electronic copy of MeSH can be downloaded without charges from the NLM after completing a Memorandum of Understanding.

Its first publication took place in 1960, with subsequent revisions until to date. It is used for the annotation and thus faster and more efficient retrieval of abstracts in MEDLINE/PUBMED [http://www.ncbi.nlm.nih.gov/sites/entrez], for an NLM database for cataloging books, documents and audiovisual materials and it can be helpful in knowledge discovery approaches, such as text mining.

MeSH contains a controlled vocabulary using a set of descriptors which are organized hierarchically with cross-references linking to metadata and related terms (e.g., annotations and synonyms). Descriptors may be located at different subtrees in the hierarchy and have a separate tree number for each of their locations in the MeSH tree. Tree numbers may change when MeSH is updated. The 16 most general headings contain concepts such as anatomy, diseases, chemicals and drugs, psychiatry and psychology, health-care and more. The hierarchy is composed of 11 levels in total, with terms increasing in granularity the deeper the term is located inside the hierarchy.

As reported in [22], in the 2008 edition of MeSH, there are 24,767 descriptors included and an additional 172,000 headings contained in a separate thesaurus, the Supplementary Concept Records. MeSH is updated and curated by a specialized staff at the NLM. Qualifiers [23] are used in MeSH together with descriptors for indexing and cataloging abstracts and are used to group together abstracts that are about a specific aspect of a subject. In total, there are 83 qualifiers and not all of these qualifiers are allowable for all descriptors. The descriptors have a list associated to them containing their allowable qualifiers. For example, it would not make sense to use the qualifier "administration & dosage" with descriptors stemming from the "Anatomy" subtree.

Thus, although MeSH was not explicitly modeled to organize clinical terms, the nature of medical publications, the cataloging of which it was created for, resulted in a large number of clinical terms being present inside MeSH that might eventually be usable to annotate clinical states. These concepts are mainly included in the "Anatomy [A]" and "Diseases [C]" sections of MeSH as clinical states usually concern an anatomical part and a disorder by which this anatomical part is affected. To model clinical states, also the "Chemicals and Drugs [D]" and the "Analytical, Diagnostic and Therapeutic Techniques and Equipment [E]" headings are certainly of interest as these concepts can be used to describe further how the clinical state of a patient is being treated and how and what techniques it was diagnosed with.

MeSH can be browsed online at http://www.nlm.nih.gov/mesh/MBrowser.html.

5.3.2. *UMLS (Unified Medical Language System)*

The Unified Medical Language System (UMLS) was developed by the US National Library of Medicine and is a repository of biomedical vocabularies [24]. It consists of the UMLS Metathesaurus, the Semantic Network, the SPECIALIST Lexicon and various software tools that can be used to access and use the sources.

UMLS is free of charge for research purposes, however, obtaining a license is required.

Its objective is to contribute to the interoperability of biomedical resources by providing a common terminological basis for the vocabularies included in the UMLS, covering "the entire biomedical domain" [24]. The aim is to "facilitate the development of computer systems that behave as if they 'understand' the meaning of the language of biomedicine and health" [25].

These vocabularies include clinical repositories (such as SNOMED-CT (see Sec. 5.1.1)), model organisms, anatomy, genome annotations, biomedical literature (e.g., MeSH (see Sec. 5.3.1)), genetic knowledge bases and other sub-domains (e.g., ICD-9-CM and ICD-10 (see Sec. 5.2.1)).

As described in [24] and [25], the UMLS Metathesaurus is the core UMLS component containing inter-related biomedical and health concepts, their different names and relations between them. It includes more than 100 source vocabularies. The UMLS is a graph, consisting of concepts from the source vocabularies, which have synonyms and are inter-connected using relations inherited from the source vocabularies or created for the scope of the Metathesaurus. Each concept contained in the Metathesaurus is categorized by the assignment of semantic types that are contained in the Semantic Network. While the Metathesaurus contains the information about the concepts, the Semantic Network contains additional information on the categories or semantic types that can be assigned to those concepts and relationships that may exist between these semantic types. Today, the Semantic Network contains 135 semantic types and 54 relationships. Examples of semantic types are *organisms, anatomical structures* or *biologic function*, examples of semantic relations linking them together are *isa, physically related to, functionally related to* and others.

The semantics of the concepts and relations contained in the source vocabularies are preserved; if different views of a concept are contained in the source vocabularies, also those are preserved in the Metathesaurus. For this reason, when applying the Metathesaurus, it is necessary in some contexts to restrict it to those vocabularies needed for the respective application and exclude those that would be counter-productive. Furthermore, the Metathesaurus also contains most external cross-references contained in the source vocabularies, such as pointers to GenBank [http://www.ncbi.nlm.nih.gov/Genbank] entries.

The tools included in the UMLS are MetamorphoSys (to exclude specific vocabularies which are not suitable for the specific application), lvg (based on the SPECIALIST lexicon and including some hand-coded rules, it can be used for natural language processing purposes such as generation of lexical variants) and MetaMap (extraction of Metathesaurus concepts from text, available as a web service). Metamorphosys can be installed using the installation DVD or downloaded from the resources mentioned in http://www.nlm.nih.gov/research/umls/meta6.html (although installation via DVD should be preferred owing to the size of the files needed).

The added semantics in the UMLS compared to that already contained in its source vocabularies mainly lies in the semantic types defined in the Semantic Network, which are high-level types. These do add additional knowledge to the concepts in the source ontologies but seem to be too high-level to effectively contribute to the creation of a clinical states ontology.

5.4. *Data transmission standards*

When electronic systems for dealing with healthcare related data emerged, there were no common standards on how this should be dealt with. Thus, different techniques and methods were implemented, resulting in heterogeneity between systems. Data were spread on systems, often saved in heterogeneous formats and without a common structure. This made it necessary to create widely accepted standards to enable the different systems to communicate and share information among each other, especially with the advent of the Electronic Health Record (EHR).

HL7 and DICOM are two such standards and are described in the following twosections. Whereas the HL7 standards aim at harmonizing the exchange of electronic health information such as EHR and administration, the scope of DICOM is to provide interoperability in the exchange of medical imaging data and complete documents. Both standards use vocabularies or standardized terminologies, respectively, thus containing semantic information.

5.4.1. *HL7*

An introduction and a description of Health Level Seven (HL7) is provided on the HL7 website [33] and in [34]. HL7 is a non-profit and volunteer standards organization for clinical and administrative data that develops specifications such as HL7 v2.x, v3.0 (messaging standards), HL7 RIM (a conceptual standard) and HL7 CDA (a document standard). The words "Level Seven" in the name of HL7 stand for the uppermost layer in the International Organization for Standardization's Open System Interconnection (ISO OSI) layer model, the application layer that deals with the exchange of data, identification of communication partners, user authentication, data syntax and privacy issues. HL7 is a standard for exchanging, retrieving, integrating and sharing electronic health information and achieving interoperability between different systems used in patient administration, laboratory procedures, electronic health records and others.

HL7 as a global organization has its headquarter in Michigan, US. It has affiliated country-specific organizations that have adopted the HL7 standards and apply them to particular healthcare domains. Affiliated organizations exist in more than 30 countries worldwide.

To obtain access to HL7 standards it is necessary to be a paying member of either HL7 or one of its national affiliated member organizations.

HL7 originated in 1987 to generate a standard for hospital information systems. Version 1.0 described the content and its structure, but was never implemented operationally. Versions 2.x were issued in 1988, the development of version 3.0 was initiated around 1995 and first published in 2005.

The messaging standards HL7 v2.x (a collective name for the various versions 2.x produced) aim at providing a standard for work flows and interoperability. The Arden Syntax for Medical Logical Modules (MLMs) [http://cslxinfmtcs.csmc.edu/hl7/arden/] is used to represent for instance contraindication alerts, treatment protocols or diagnosis scores. Health personnel can create MLMs, and information systems can use these modules directly which contain enough information for the system to make a medical decision, e.g., alerting a physician when a patient might be developing a certain disease state (see also Sec. 2.2.).

With the Clinical Document Architecture (CDA) in 2000, XML encoding was introduced. The Clinical Document Architecture defines an XML-based architecture for exchanging clinical records and makes documents both human readable and machine readable. The semantic basis of the CDA is defined in the Reference Information Model (RIM) and the vocabularies for terms that are used in HL7 standards to ensure semantic interoperability between systems sending and receiving messages. This way, the HL7 seeks to pave the way for common standards resulting in interoperability for supporting Electronic Health Records.

The RIM is an information model that is shared among domains and contains semantic and lexical information for the relations that exist between the fields inside an HL7 message. The RIM and its Unified Service Action Model (USAM) constitute a shared information model for Electronic Medical Records (EMR) and decision support (DS), thus proposing an approach to bridge the gap between EMR and DS. The underlying concepts are explained in [38]. The USAM is a simplification of the RIM and covers its clinical and ancillary parts, i.e., orders, service events, results, master files, scheduling and patient care. All clinical events are generalized under the class *service action*, which can be *medication, observation, procedure, condition node* and *transport*. The concept *action mood* stands for whether an action is *factual, possible, intended, ordered,* and so on. Typed *service relationships* serve to connect two services, indicating their *generalization* or *specialization (whole-part)*, their *precondition, postcondition* or *revision*.

However, there is criticism on the coherence of the RIM [37], for instance regarding its implementation and benefits of interoperability, its usability in specialist domains, its scope, documentation and definitions included. To go into this in detail would be beyond the scope of this chapter, the reader is referred to the publication cited above.

HL7 is ANSI [http://www.ansi.org] and ISO [http://www.iso.org] accredited and collaborates also with other Standard Development Organizations (SDOs), such as DICOM (see Sec. 5.4.2.).

5.4.2. *DICOM*

Digital Imaging and Communications in Medicine (DICOM) [30] is a standard for medical informatics for the storage, the transmission, the handling and the printing of medical image data, independent of the manufacturer of the device. An introduction is given in [32], and [32]. The main objectives are to globally create interoperability and an increased work flow efficiency between imaging and other systems. The primary areas of functionality of DICOM at the application level are the transmission and persistence of complete objects, such as images and documents, the query and retrieval of those objects, work flow management, quality and consistency of image data and performance of some specific actions, such as printing images on film [31]. Healthcare sectors that are addressed include cardiology, dentistry, endoscopy, mammography, orthopedics, pathology and more. DICOM is also considered to be an important standard for the eventual integration of imaging data into Electronic Health Records (EHR).

The free-of-charge DICOM standard was initiated by a collaborative committee consisting of the American College of Radiology (ACR) and the National Electrical Manufacturers Association (NEMA) in 1983. The first version of the standard, known as ACR-NEMA, was published 2 years thereafter. The first versions consisted of a standardized terminology, information structure and encoding of files, and version 3.0 which was issued in 1993 also included a standard for communicating image data in digital format. DICOM is constantly developed further and new updated editions are issued on a regular basis.

DICOM widely uses other standards, such as an upper layer protocol (ULP) to be used over the internet standard TCP/IP, thus ensuring that any two systems employing the DICOM standard can communicate with each other. Also standards like JPEG, JPEG 2000, or such issued by CEN, the European Committee for Standardization [http://www.cen.eu], are adopted and integrated. Furthermore, there is close collaboration with HL-7 (see also Sec. 5.4.1.) and integration also of other standards is in place. For the actual encoding of data, a DICOM data format is used.

DICOM was approved as a reference standard by ISO and CEN. The DICOM standard is applied in hospitals worldwide and is believed to spread even further [31], among other reasons due to an increasing need for standards with regard to the EHR.

Acknowledgments

A big thank you goes to Kai Kumpf, a former teacher in the ontological field and work colleague of one of the authors, for his valuable hints especially on sub Chapter 5.

References

1. Garcia-Remesal, M, V Maojo, H Billhardt, J Crespo, R Alonso-Calvo, D Perez-Rey, F Martin and A Sousa (2004). ARMEDA II: Supporting genomic medicine through the integration of medical and genetic databases. In *Bioinformatics and Bioengineering* (BIBE), 19–21 May 2004. *IEEE Computer Society* (2004), 227–234.
2. Beneventano, D, S Bergamaschi, F Guerra and M Vincini (2003). Synthesizing an integrated ontology. *IEEE Internet Computing*, 7(5), 42–51.

3. Adams, HP Jr, BH Bendixen, LJ Kappelle, J Biller, BB Love, DL Gordon and EE Marsh 3rd (1993). Classification of subtype of acute ischemic stroke, definition for use in a multicenter clinical trial, TOAST. Trial of Org 10172 in acute stroke treatment. *Stroke*, 24, 35–41.
4. Goldstein, LB, MR Jones, DB Matchar, LJ Edwards, J Hoff, V Chilukuri, SB Armstrong, RD Horner and J Bamford (2001). Improving the reliability of Stroke subgroup classification using the Trial of ORG 10172 in Acute Stroke Treatment (TOAST) criteria (Commentary). *Stroke*, 32, 1091–1097.
5. Donnelly, K and SNOMED-CT (2006). The advanced terminology and coding system for eHealth. *Stud Health Technol Inform*, 121, 279–290.
6. Bodenreider, O, B Smith, A Kumar and A Burgun (2007). Investigating subsumption in DL-based terminologies: A case study in SNOMED CT. *Artificial Intelligence in Medicine*, 39(3), 183–195.
7. Guarino, N and R Poli (1994). *Formal Ontology in Conceptual Analysis and Knowledge Representation*. Dordrecht: Kluwer Academic Press.
8. Bard, SY and JBL Rhee (2004). Ontologies in biology: Design, applications and future challenges. *Nature Reviews Genetics*, 6(5), 213–222.
9. Fielding, JM, J Simon, W Ceusters and B Smith (2004). *Ontological Theory for Ontological Engineering, Biomedical Systems Information Integration. KR*, 114–120.
10. Gomez-Perez, A, O Corcho-Garcia and M Fernandez-Lopez (2003). *Ontological Engineering*. New York: Springer-Verlag.
11. Disease ontology — NUgene Project. Available at http://diseaseontology.sourceforge.net/
12. Spasic, I, S Ananiadou, J McNaught and A Kumar (2005). Text mining and ontologies in biomedicine, making sense of raw text. *Brief Bioinform*, 6(3), 239–251.
13. ICD9-CM. Available at http://www.icd9cm.net/icd/default.asp
14. Available at http://www.who.int/classifications/icd/en/
15. Rector, A, J Rogers and W Solomon (2006). Ontological and practical issues in using a description logic to represent medical concept systems: Experience from GALEN. *Reasoning Web*, Springer Verlag, 197–231.
16. Palma, P, B Llamas, A Gonzàlez and M Menàrguez (2006). Acquisition and representation of causal and temporal knowledge in medical domains. *KES*, 1284–1290.
17. Baader, F, D Calvanese, DL McGuinness, D Nardi and PF Patel-Schneider (eds.) (2003). *The Description Logic Handbook: Theory, Implementation, and Applications*. New York, NY, USA: Cambridge University Press.
18. Web Ontology Language. Available at http://www.w3.org/TR/owl-guide/
19. Rector, A L, JE Rogers, PE Zanstra, E Van Der Haring (2003). OpenGALEN: Open source medical terminology and tools. *Proc AMIA Symp*.

20. OpenGALEN: Background and GALEN Model. Available at http://www.opengalen.org [accessed on 24 May 2008].
21. Rogers, J and A Rector (2000). *GALEN's Model of Parts and Wholes: Experience and Comparisons.* AMIA 2000 — Proceedings of the Annual Symposium of the American Medical Informatics Association. CA, November 4–8, 2000, pp. 714–718. Philadelphia, PA: Hanley & Belfus.
22. US National Library of Medicine: Fact Sheet — Medical Subject Headings (MeSH®) (2007). Bethesda. Available at http://www.nlm.nih.gov/pubs/factsheets/mesh.html [accessed on 24 May 2008].
23. US National Library of Medicine: Medical Subject Headings — Qualifiers (2007). Bethesda. Available at http://www.nlm.nih.gov/mesh/topsubscope2008.html [accessed on 24 May 2008].
24. Bodenreider, O (2004). The Unified Medical Language System (UMLS): integrating biomedical terminology. *Nucleic Acids Research,* 32, 267–270.
25. US National Library of Medicine: Unified Medical Language System — About the UMLS® Resources (2008). Available at http://www.nlm.nih.gov/research/umls/about_umls.html [accessed on 24 May 2008].
26. US National Center for Health Statistics (nchs): International Classification of Diseases — 10th Revision (ICD-10 brochure) (2001). Available at http://www.cdc.gov/nchs/data/dvs/icd10fct.pdf [accessed on 25 May 2008].
27. Spackman, KA and G Reynoso (2004). Examining SNOMED from the perspective of formal ontological principles: Some preliminary analysis and observations. *KR-MED,* 72–80.
28. Stearns, MQ, C Price, KA Spackman and AY Wang (2001). SNOMED clinical terms: Overview of the development process and project status. *Proc AMIA Symp,* pp. 662–666.
29. Spackman, K (2007). SNOMED clinical terms fundamentals. *International Health Terminology Development Organization,* 14 December. Available at http://www.ihtsdo.org/uploads/media/SNOMED_Clinical_Terms_Fundamentals.pdf
30. NEMA. Available at http://dicom.nema.org/ [accessed on 27 May 2008].
31. NEMA (2008). DICOM Strategic Document, Version 8.0, April 11, 2008.
32. NEMA (2007). Digital Imaging and Communications in Medicine (DICOM) — Part 1: Introduction and Overview.
33. HL7. Available at http://www.hl7.org/ [accessed on 29 May 2008].
34. Hammond, WE (1993). Health Level 7: A Protocol for the Interchange of Healthcare Data. In *Progress in Standardization in Health Care Informatics,* D Moore, C McDonald and J Noothoven van Goor (eds.). Amsterdam: IOS Press.
35. College of American Pathologists: *SNOMED Clinical Terms ® User Guide January 2007 Release,* 2007. Available at http://www.ihtsdo.org/fileadmin/user_upload/Docs_01/Technical_Docs/snomed_ct_user_guide.pdf

36. Smedby, B, O Steinum and M Virtanen (2004). Use of the dagger-asterisk system in the ICD-9 and ICD-10 and their national clinical modifications. Who Family of International Classifications Network Meeting, Whofic/04.079. Nordic Centre for Classifications in Health Care, Uppsala University, Sweden. Available at http://www.nordclass.uu.se/WHOFIC/papers/reykjavik79.pdf
37. Smith, B and W Ceusters (2006). HL7 RIM: An Incoherent Standard. In: Ubiquity: Technologies for Better Health in Aging Societies. *Proceedings of MIE2006,* A Hasman, R Haux, J van der Lei, E De Clercq, FHR France (eds.). IOS Press.
38. Schadow, G, DC Russler, CN Mead and CJ McDonald (2000). Integrating Medical Information and Knowledge in the HL7 RIM. *Proc AMIA Symp.,* 764–768. Available at http://www.amia.org/pubs/symposia/D200803.PDF
39. Lee, Y, K Supekar and J Geller (2006). Ontology integration: Experience with medical terminologies. *Computers in Biology and Medicine,* 36(7–8), 893–919.
40. Hogan, WR (2008). Aligning the top level of SNOMED-CT with basic formal ontology. *Nature Precedings,* doi10.103/npre.2008.2373.1, 2008.
41. Ohmann, WK (2009). Future developments of medical informatics from the viewpoint of networked clinical research. *Methods of Information in Medicine,* 48(1), 45–54.
42. Shankar, RD, SB Martins, MJ O'Connor, DB Parrish, AK Das (2006). Towards semantic interoperability in a clinical trials management system. *International Semantic Web Conference,* 901-912.
43. Smith, B, W Ceusters, B Klagges, J Köhler, A Kumar, J Lomax, C Mungall, F Neuhaus, A Rector and C Rosse (2005). Relations in biomedical ontologies. *Genome Biology,* 6(5), R46.
44. Smith, B, W Kusnierczyk, D Schober and W Ceusters (2006). Towards a reference terminology for ontology research and development in the biomedical domain. *KR-MED,* 57–65.
45. Smith, B and C Rosse (2004). The role of foundational relations in the alignment of biomedical ontologies. In *Medinfo,* M Fieschi, *et al.* (eds.), pp. 444–448. Amsterdam: IOS Press.
46. Smith, B (2004). Beyond concepts: Ontology as reality representation. In *Proceedings of the International Conference on Formal Ontology in Information Systems (FOIS 2004),* pp. 73–84. IOS Press.
47. Smith, B *et al.* (2007). The OBO foundry: Coordinated evolution of ontologies to support biomedical data integration. *Nature Biotechnology,* 25(11), 1251–1255.
48. Colombo, G, D Merico and G Mauri (2008). Reference ontology design for a neurovascular knowledge network. *Metadata and Semantics Research,* Springer.
49. McLendon, K (1993). Electronic medical record systems as a basis for computer-based patient records. *J AHIMA,* 64(9), 50, 52, 54–55.

50. Mantas, J (2002). Electronic health record. *Stud Health Technol Inform*, 65, 250–257.
51. Sackett, DL, WM Rosenberg, JA Gray, RB Haynes and WS Richardson (1996). Evidence based medicine: What it is and what it isn't. *BMJ*, 312(7023), 71–72.
52. Woolf, SH (2008). The meaning of translational research and why it matters. *JAMA*, 299, 211–213.
53. Grudin, J (1994). Computer-supported cooperative work: Its history and participation. *Computer*, 27(4), 19–26.
54. Weerakkody, G and P Ray (2003). CSCW-based system development methodology for health-care information systems. *Telemed J E Health*, 9(3), 273–282.
55. Sicilia, JJ, MA Sicilia, S Sánchez-Alonso, E García-Barriocanal and M Pontikaki (2009). Knowledge representation issues in ontology-based clinical knowledge management systems. *International Journal of Technology Management*, 47(1–3), 191–206.
56. Miller, RA (1994). Medical diagnostic decision support systems — past, present, and future: A threaded bibliography and brief commentary. *Journal of American Medical Informatics and Association*, 1(1), 8–27.
57. Kuhn, T (1970). *The Structure of Scientific Revolutions*. Chicago: University of Chicago Press.
58. Benerecetti, M, P Bouquet and C Ghidini (2000). Contextual reasoning distilled. *Journal of Theoretical and Artificial Intelligence (JETAI)*, 12, 279–305.
59. Johnson-Laird, PN (1983). *Mental Models: Towards a Cognitive Science of Language, Inference, and Consciousness*. Cambridge, MA: Harvard University Press.
60. Boland, J and RV Tenkasi (1995). Perspective making and perspective taking in communities of knowing. *Organizational Science*, 6(4), 350–372.
61. Available at http://www.bioontology.org/wiki/index.php/Clinical_Phenotypes http://bimib.disco.unimib.it/index.php/SSFW09

CHAPTER III.3

AGRICULTURAL KNOWLEDGE ORGANIZATION SYSTEMS: AN ANALYSIS OF AN INDICATIVE SAMPLE

Nikos Palavitsinis and Nikos Manouselis

Agro-Know Technologies
17, Grammou Str. 15265, Athens, Greece
{palavitsinis, nikosm}@agroknow.gr

The agricultural domain contains multiple different topics that are extensively researched, thus producing a great amount of data and information. The need of efficient organization of this material favors the use of Knowledge Organization Systems (KOSs). The present study carries out an online survey of KOSs that are being used in the agricultural domain so that a representative sample is collected. Then, an analysis of their characteristics is conducted and the main findings regarding the identified KOSs are presented, aiming to provide an initial insight to existing agricultural KOSs and their intended applications.

1. Introduction

Knowledge Organization Systems (KOSs), encompass all types of schemes for organizing information and promoting knowledge management. They have been introduced to reduce the ambiguity of natural language when describing and retrieving information. KOSs include classification schemes that organize materials at a general level, subject headings, which provide more detailed access and authority files that control variant versions of key information. They also include less-traditional schemes, such as semantic networks and ontologies [9, 22]. KOSs are being applied increasingly to Web site architecture and in interfaces to Web databases [12].

The agricultural domain includes various different topics with subjects varying from plant science and horticulture, to agricultural engineering and agricultural economics. These different subjects are extensively researched by scientists all over the world, thus producing a great amount of data. The abundance of information available online, favors the need of organization of the produced knowledge in relevant areas. Whenever a user needs to seek information agriculture, the task of retrieving accurate results becomes troublesome. Additionally, with the quick development of the World Wide Web, the information resources become continuously more available. Zillman [23] identified more than 135 online resources on diverse agricultural topics. Another study shows that China only has about more than 14.000 large agricultural web sites [21]. The volume of available information creates an information overload to the users that consume time and effort in order to find and access sources of interest.

The use of knowledge representation schemes, such as KOSs, helps users find easier relevant information that they are looking for. The reason behind the use of KOSs is that different people may use different words for the same concept or employ different concepts to refer to the same scientific terms. To this end, KOSs may improve access to (mostly digitally) stored information, by offering structured ways to represent and model it [16]. For example, universities (i.e., Oregon State University,[1] Cornell University[2]), government portals with agricultural content (i.e., Australia,[3] Canada[4] and United States[5]), agricultural portals & libraries (i.e., Organic.Edunet,[6] AGRICOLA[7]) and commercial websites (i.e., GreenWeb, Aqualex) use KOSs to organize the content they make available. A prominent example of an agricultural KOS is AGROVOC that is available in 20 languages and is being downloaded approximately 1,000 times per year (information retrieved on December 2010).

This chapter collected and analyzed a characteristic sample of online KOSs that facilitate representations of information related to topics of the agricultural domain. This study follows a previous one [11] that focused on the Environmental Domain KOSs. The previous analyzed mainly glossaries, thesauri and ontologies related to Environmental Sciences. This additional analysis aims to complement the findings of the previous study by examining KOSs that belong to a more extended domain.

A similar survey was conducted by Shiri [13] which aimed at evaluating the types of KOS systems and tools that have been utilized in governmental

[1] http://food.oregonstate.edu/
[2] http://www.plantpath.cornell.edu
[3] http://www.anbg.gov.au/
[4] http://sis.agr.gc.ca/
[5] http://soils.usda.gov/
[6] http://www.organic-edunet.eu
[7] http://agricola.nal.usda.gov

and academic digital collections in Canada. Our study has a broader geographical coverage though focusing on the agricultural domain. Through this initial analysis we hope to provide some first overview of the development of agricultural KOSs while having no intention to claim that this is an exhaustive survey. Building on the approach of Shiri [13], this chapter will provide some basic statistical data about the sample of the identified agricultural KOSs (origin, use, topics covered, etc.), rather than focus on the implementation issues (such as systems utilizing the KOSs). We focus on KOSs that can be fully found online: that is, their whole structure and content (and not only some terms), are openly accessible online.

2. Setting the context

In order to define the exact agricultural topics of the agricultural domain to be covered in the context of this chapter, a study of subject classification headings that are used from various agricultural publishers has taken place. The different subject headings that came out of this search were more than 25, covering a broad aspect of topics. Cross checking results from over nine sources, we decided to keep the headings referenced in most of them trying to include commonly covered topics. The subject headings that had less occurrences were therefore left out. Table 1 depicts the different sources and the final selection of the subject headings finally selected as covering the majority of topics in the agricultural domain.

The relationships among the topics identified above are not examined, since in each source, they were classified in different ways. For example, in some cases veterinary science was on the same conceptual level as animal science, both of them classified under the agricultural domain. In other cases, veterinary science was classified under biology whereas animal science was classified under agriculture. Nevertheless, for the needs of this study only an indicative and wide enough list of relevant topics was needed.

3. Survey of agricultural KOSs

3.1. *Methodology*

After deciding on the specific topics to be covered, an online research and identification of relevant KOSs has taken place. Apart from generic search engines (such as Google — www.google.com, Yahoo — www.yahoo.com, Bing — www.bing.com), the method engaged also included websites of agricultural publishing houses, agricultural research projects and websites dedicated to agricultural research. The results retrieved from searching with

Table 1. Subject headings frequently used to describe the topics that belong to the agricultural domain.

Source	URL	Final selection of terms
College of Agricultural Sciences (Penn State)	http://agsci.psu.edu	1. Food Science
Science.gov	www.science.gov	2. Animal Science
Directory of Open Access Journals (DOAJ)	www.doaj.org	3. Plant Science
Elsevier	www.elsevier.com	4. Aquaculture
Wikipedia	http://en.wikipedia.org	5. Soil Science
Access to Global Online Research in Agriculture	www.aginternetwork.org	6. Veterinary Science
Glanzel & Schubert (2003)	N/A	7. Horticulture
United Nations Department of Public Information Thesaurus Classification System	http://unic.un.org/	8. Agricultural Engineering 9. Agricultural Economics
Common European Research Classification Scheme (CERIF)	www.arrs.gov.si	10. Forest Science 11. Crop Science

the subject headings listed in Table 1, were documented and are being presented in the Table 2. Overall, a sample of 88 agriculture-related KOSs has been collected.

The first category of agricultural KOSs identified concerned *glossaries*. These are defined as a list of terms, usually with definitions. The terms may be from a specific subject field or those used in a particular work. The terms are defined within that specific environment and rarely have variant meanings provided [10]. In total, 49 glossaries, available online (see Table 2) were identified, covering various topics ranging from Food Science to Agricultural Economics. The presence of glossaries was the biggest one compared to the presence of the other KOSs that were found in the sample. This might be explained by the fact that glossaries pre-existed other KOSs (ontologies, taxonomies, etc.), and are also easier to construct in the sense that the creator does not have to identify relationships between terms, but merely list all the terms having to do with a specific topic, in an alphabetical order.

Another category of KOSs in the sample, have been *taxonomies*, i.e., schemes that partition a body of knowledge and define the relationships among the pieces. It is used for classifying and understanding the body of knowledge. Only seven agricultural taxonomies have been identified through this survey, mostly covering the topics of Plant Science, Soil Science and Animal Science.

Table 2. Glossaries/dictionaries available online.

No	Name	Topic	URL
1	Glossary of College of Health and Human Sciences, Oregon State University	Food Science	http://food.oregonstate.edu/glossary/
2	FAO Glossary of Biotechnology for Food and Agriculture	Food Science	http://www.fao.org/biotech/index_glossary.asp
3	Food — Info Glossary	Food Science	http://www.food-info.net/uk/glossary.htm
4	Animal Nomenclature and Terminology	Animal Science	http://www.agroweb.bf.uni-lj.si/nomenklatura.htm
5	MAGUS: Multilingual Animal Glossary of Unveiled Synonyms	Animal Science	http://www.informatika.bf.uni-lj.si/magus.html
6	Botany and Paleobotany Glossary	Plant Science	http://www.enchantedlearning.com/subjects/plants/glossary/indexg.shtml
7	Common Names of Plant Diseases	Plant Science	http://www.apsnet.org/online/common/
8	Wildflower Glossary	Plant Science	http://www.first-nature.com/flowers/~wildflower-glossary.asp
9	On-Line Glossary of Technical Terms in Plant Pathology	Plant Science	http://www.plantpath.cornell.edu/glossary/Glossary.htm
10	Aquatic, Wetland and Invasive Plant Glossary	Plant Science	http://plants.ifas.ufl.edu/glossary
11	Roses Glossary	Plant Science	http://www.hortico.com/info/glossary1.htm
12	Online Glossary to Plant Disease Control	Plant Science	http://plant-disease.ippc.orst.edu/glossary.cfm
13	Garden Web Glossary	Plant Science	http://glossary.gardenweb.com/glossary/
14	Fungi of Australia Glossary	Plant Science	http://www.anbg.gov.au/glossary/webpubl/fungloss.htm
15	Plant Morphology Glossary	Plant Science	http://www.csupomona.edu/~jcclark/classes/bot125/resource/glossary/index.html
16	UCMP Glossary	Plant Science	http://www.ucmp.berkeley.edu/glossary/glossary.html
17	A Short Botanical Glossary	Plant Science	http://www.anbg.gov.au/glossary/croft.html
18	Wildflower Glossary	Plant Science	http://www.wildflowerinformation.org/Glossary.asp
19	The virtual field herbarium Plant Characteristics Glossary	Plant Science	http://herbaria.plants.ox.ac.uk/vfh/image/index.php?glossary=show
20	Illustrated Glossary of Plant Pathology	Plant Science	http://www.apsnet.org/education/Illustrated-Glossary/default.htm

(*Continued*)

Table 2. (*Continued*)

No	Name	Topic	URL
21	Aquatic, Wetland and Invasive Plant Glossary	Plant Science	http://plants.ifas.ufl.edu/glossary
22	Tropical Plant Glossary	Plant Science	http://www.tropica.com/plant_print.asp
23	FAO Aquaculture Glossary	Aquaculture	http://www.fao.org/fi/glossary/aquaculture /
24	Aqualex Glossary	Aquaculture	http://www.aqualexonline.com/
25	Fish Farming Glossary	Aquaculture	http://www.aquaculture.co.il/getting_started/glossary.html
26	ez Aquaculture Glossary	Aquaculture	http://www.greatlakesbiosystems.com/cms/ez-aquaculture-glossary.html
27	FAO Fisheries Glossary	Aquaculture	http://www.fao.org/fi/glossary/default.asp
28	FAO Aquaculture Glossary	Aquaculture	http://www.fao.org/fi/glossary/aquaculture/default.asp?lang=en
29	Glossary of Soil Science Terms	Soil Science	http://nesoil.com/gloss.htm
30	Soil Microbiology Terms Glossary	Soil Science	http://cropsoil.psu.edu/sylvia/glossary.htm
31	Glossary of Terms in Soil Science	Soil Science	http://sis.agr.gc.ca/cansis/glossary/
32	Glossary of Veterinary Terms	Veterinary Science	http://www.bmd.org/health/glossary.html
33	Glossary Danish Veterinary and Food Administration	Veterinary Science	http://www.greenfacts.org/glossary/def/dvfa.htm
34	Glossary of Horticulture Terms	Horticulture	http://extensionhorticulture.unl.edu/Glossary/Glos saryA.shtml
35	ABCD Glossary	Horticulture	http://www.colostate.edu/Dept/CoopExt/4DMG/Glossary/glossary.htm
36	Ohio State University Department of Horticulture & Crop Science Glossary	Horticulture	http://hcs.osu.edu/plantfacts/glossary/edit.htm
37	GreenWeb's Gardening Glossary	Horticulture	http://boldweb.com/gw/index.php?option=com_content&task=view&id=29&Itemid=25
38	Glossary of Botanical terms	Horticulture	http://theseedsite.co.uk/botany.html
39	Paleobotany Glossary	Horticulture	http://www.ucmp.berkeley.edu/IB181/VPL/Glossary.html#parenchyma-c
40	Botanical.com / Glossary	Horticulture	http://www.botanical.com/botanical/mgmh/comindx.html
41	Dictionary of Botanical Epithets	Horticulture	http://www.winternet.com/~chuckg/dictionary.html
42	Agricultural engineering in development Glossary	Agricultural Engineering	http://www.fao.org/docrep/009/ah637e/AH637E30.htm

(*Continued*)

Table 2. (*Continued*)

No	Name	Topic	URL
43	Glossary of Terms for Agriculture, Agricultural Economics and Precision Farming	Agricultural Economics	http://ikb.weihenstephan.de/en/glossary/#English
44	Glossary of Australian Agricultural and Farm Business Terms	Agricultural Economics	http://www.agwine.adelaide.edu.au/agribus/agribus/resources/glossary/l.html
45	Glossary of Crop Science Terms Crop Science Society of America	Crop Science	https://www.crops.org/publications/crops-glossary
46	Multilingual Glossary Forest Genetic Resources	Forest Science	http://iufro-archive.boku.ac.at/silvavoc/glossary/af35_0en.html
47	Fire Effects Information System Glossary	Forest Science	http://www.fs.fed.us/database/feis/glossary.html
48	National Forestry Database Glossary	Forest Science	http://nfdp.ccfm.org/glossary_e.php
49	VLT Forestry Glossary	Forest Science	http://www.vlt.org/forestry_glossary.html

Table 3. Taxonomies available online.

No	Name	Topic	URL
1	Germplasm Resources Information Network (GRIN) Taxonomy of Plants	Plant Science	http://www.ars-grin.gov/cgi-bin/npgs/html/index.pl
2	The International Plant Names Index	Plant Science	http://www.ipni.org/ipni/plantnamesearchpage.do
3	Taxonomy of Flowering Plants	Plant Science	http://www.colby.edu/info.tech/BI211/Families.html
4	Plant Taxonomy	Plant Science	http://www.kingdomplantae.net/plantae.php
5	Natural Resources Conservation Center Soil Taxonomy	Soil Science	http://soils.usda.gov/technical/classification/
6	Mammal Species of the World	Animal Science	http://www.bucknell.edu/MSW3/
7	Marine Mammals of the World	Animal Science	http://nlbif.eti.uva.nl/bis/marine_mammals.php?menuentry=zoeken

As far as ***classifications*** are concerned, they are known to provide ways to separate entities into buckets or relatively broad topic levels. Some examples provide a hierarchical arrangement of numeric or alphabetic notation to represent broad topics [11]. Few agricultural ones could be found online, with five of them covering the topics of Plant Science (two classifications), Veterinary, Science, Forestry and Soil Science (one classification each) (see Table 4).

Ontologies are an explicit specification of a conceptualization. The term "conceptualization" is defined as an abstract, simplified view of the world,

Table 4. Classifications available online.

No	Name	Topic	URL
1	Plant Classification Thesaurus	Plant Science	http://plants.usda.gov/classification.html
2	Classification of Flowering Plant Families	Plant Science	http://theseedsite.co.uk/class2.html
3	ICOMANTH Classification	Soil Science	http://clic.cses.vt.edu/icomanth/classify.htm
4	ATCvet Classification	Veterinary Science	http://www.whocc.no/atcvet
5	CABI Classification	Forestry	http://www.cabi.org

Table 5. Ontologies available online.

No	Name	Field	URL
1	Plant Ontology Project	Plant Science	http://www.plantontology.org/docs/otherdocs/poc_project.html
2	Plant Anatomy & Development Ontology	Plant Science	http://irfgc.irri.org/pantheon/index.php?option=com_content&task=view&id=20&Itemid=37#germ-plasm_ontology
3	Fishery Ontology Service	Aquaculture	http://aims.fao.org/website/AOS-:-Registries
4	General Germplasm Ontology Ontology	Crop Science	http://irfgc.irri.org/pantheon/index.php?option=com_content&task=view&id=20&Itemid=37#germ-plasm_ontology
5	Taxonomic Ontology	Crop Science	
6	Phenotype and Trait Ontology Ontology	Crop Science	
7	Structural and Functional Genomic Ontology	Crop Science	

which needs to be represented for some purpose. It contains the objects, concepts, and other entities that are presumed to exist in some area of interest, and the relations that hold among them [8]. Surprisingly, our online survey resulted in only seven ontologies on the subjects of Plant Science (two ontologies), Aquaculture (one ontology) and Crop Science (four ontologies) (see Table 5).

Finally, a popular type of KOSs are *thesauri* which refer to a collection of terms along with some structure or relationships between them. There are a number of relationships that might be represented in a thesaurus, including broader/narrower terms and associated or related terms [1]. Overall, 11 thesauri were identified during the course of our search covering topics such as Food Science (three thesauri), Aquaculture (two), Soil Science (two), Veterinary Science (two) and Agricultural Economics (two) (see Table 6).

Table 6. Thesauri available online.

No	Name	Field	URL
1	FSTA Thesaurus	Food Science	http://www.foodsciencecentral.com/fsc/ixid14698
2	LANGUAL — The International Framework for Food Description	Food Science	http://www.langual.org
3	Food Science & Technology Abstracts Vocabulary Database	Food Science	http://ds.datastarweb.com/ds/products/datastar/sheets/fvoc.htm
4	ASFA Thesaurus (ASFA Aquaculture Abstracts)	Aquaculture	http://www4.fao.org/asfa/asfa.htm
5	Aqualine Thesaurus	Aquaculture	http://www.csa.com/factsheets/aqualine-set-c.php
6	Multilingual Thesaurus of Geosciences	Soil Science	http://en.gtk.fi/Geoinfo/Library/multhes.html
7	Soil Science Society of America Thesaurus	Soil Science	https://www.soils.org/publications/soils-glossary
8	Australian Governments' Interactive Functions Thesaurus (AGIFT)	Veterinary Science	http://www.naa.gov.au/records-management/create-capture-describe/describe/classification/agift/000238.htm
9	Government of Canada Core Subject Thesaurus	Veterinary Science	http://www.vocabularyserver.com/cst/index.php?tema=6289
10	Irandoc Thesauri	Agricultural Economics	http://thesaurus.irandoc.ac.ir
11	UK Archival Thesaurus (UKAT)	Agricultural Economics	http://www.vocabularyserver.com/ukat/index.php?-tema=350

Table 7. Glossaries, ontologies and thesauri on agriculture in general.

	Name	KOS Type	URL
1	AGRICOLA	Thesaurus	http://agricola.nal.usda.gov
2	The IRIS Keyword Thesaurus	Thesaurus	http://iris.library.uiuc.edu/~iris/thesaurus.html
3	UNESCO Thesaurus	Thesaurus	http://www2.ulcc.ac.uk/unesco/terms
4	AGROVOC Thesaurus	Thesaurus	http://aims.fao.org/en/website/Search-AGROVOC/sub
5	GEMET Thesaurus	Thesaurus	http://www.eionet.europa.eu/gemet/concept?langcode=en&cp=193
6	Semantic Web for Earth and Environmental Terminology	Ontology	http://gcmd.nasa.gov/records/SWEET-Ontology.html
7	CanSis Glossary	Glossary	http://sis.agr.gc.ca/cansis/glossary/index.html
8	New Mexico State University Agriculture Glossary	Glossary	http://aces.nmsu.edu/news/aggloss.html
9	AGROTHESAURUS for Flora and Fauna	Glossary	http://www.agroweb.bf.uni-lj.si/geslovnik.htm

In the process of conducting the online search, we have also identified several KOSs that may be classified under more than one topic areas, since they generally cover agricultural topics. These cases were documented separately in Table 7 and are treated in the context of this chapter as general KOSs, rather than focused on a specific field. In this category, five thesauri were identified, along with one ontology and three glossaries.

Tables 2 to 7 are summarized in Table 8, to provide a general view on the Agricultural KOSs that could be found online. From a first glance it can be observed that overall, the total number of the glossaries prevails, as 52 out of the total of 87 KOSs, are glossaries. Thesauri follow with 16 occurrences, while ontologies are limited to eight, taxonomies to seven and classifications to four cases respectively. This difference is mainly attributed to the presence of a large number of "Plant Science" glossaries available that create a difference in favor of the Plant Sciences field specifically but also for glossaries in general.

Figures 1 and 2 that follow clearly depict the differences between KOSs as well as between specific topic areas. In Fig. 1, it can be noted that the majority of KOSs identified were glossaries, with 52 cases. Thesauri, with less than one third of the occurrences, 16 are the second most frequent KOS used in

Table 8. Overview of KOSs per subject heading.

	Glossary	Ontology	Thesaurus	Taxonomy	Classification	Sum
Food Science	3	0	3	0	0	6
Animal Science	2	0	0	2	0	4
Plant Science	17	2	0	4	2	25
Aquaculture	6	1	2	0	0	9
Soil Science	3	0	2	1	1	7
Veterinary Science	2	0	2	0	1	5
Horticulture	8	0	0	0	0	8
Agricultural Engineering	1	0	0	0	0	1
Agricultural Economics	2	0	2	0	0	4
Agriculture in General	3	1	5	0	0	9
Crop Science	1	4	0	0	0	5
Forest Science	4	0	0	0	1	5
Total	**52**	**8**	**16**	**7**	**5**	**88**

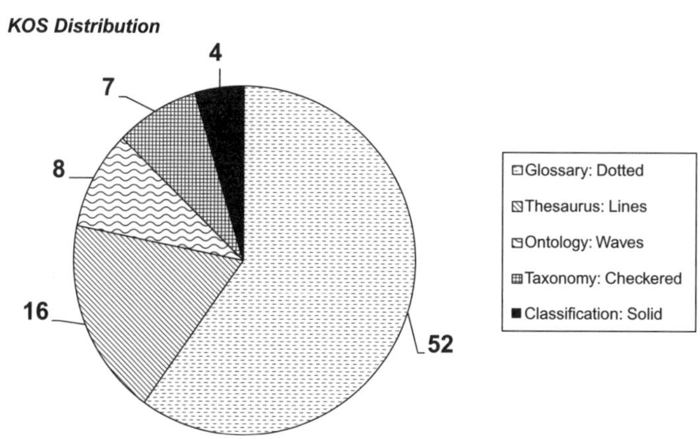

Fig. 1. KOS distribution for all the different fields examined.

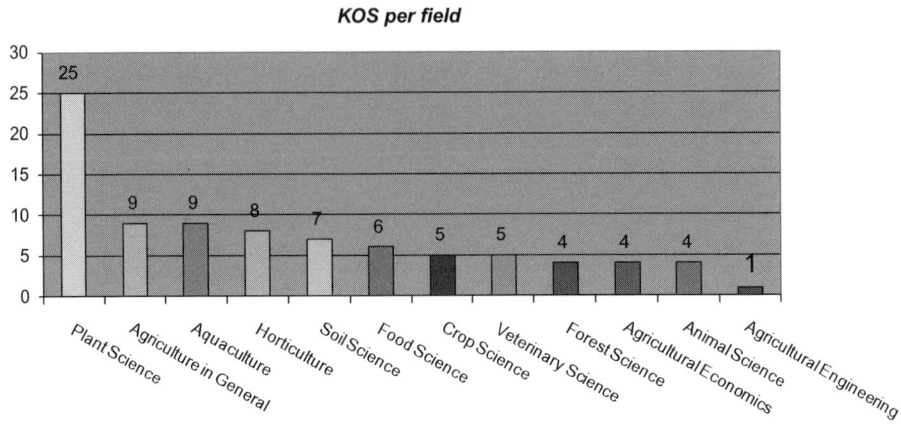

Fig. 2. Number of KOS in each different field.

the agricultural domain. Ontologies were used in eight cases, followed by taxonomies with six appearances and finally classifications with five.

Looking into the agricultural topics covered in this study, it is concluded that Plant Science is the subject heading with the highest number of identified KOS; most of them being glossaries. Nine KOSs addressed agriculture in general and nine more aquaculture.

Horticulture and Soil Science complete the five more frequent subject headings in the sample, summing up to 51 KOSs out of a total of 87 identified. Food Science, Crop Science and Veterinary Science are equally represented whereas Forest Science, Agricultural Economics and Animal Science, follow with four occurrences. Agricultural Engineering is lagging behind with only one case of one identified KOS.

Analyzing the KOSs depending on their launch date, it was seen that for 24 out of 87 (almost 28%), it was not possible to identify their date of launch. The total period for which data is available, covers the year 1994 to 2009. In order to analyze this data, the dates of launched are grouped into three distinct periods. The first period concerns 1994 to 1999 (prior to 2000), the second one lasts from 2000 to 2004 while the last one starts on 2005 until today.

Figure 3 presents the number of KOSs that were deployed online during the aforementioned periods. As it can be noted, there is a significant increase in the number of KOS launched from 2000 until 2004, in comparison to the ones launched prior to 2000. The KOSs launched from 2005 until today are almost the same compared to the total of KOSs launched from 1996 to 2004

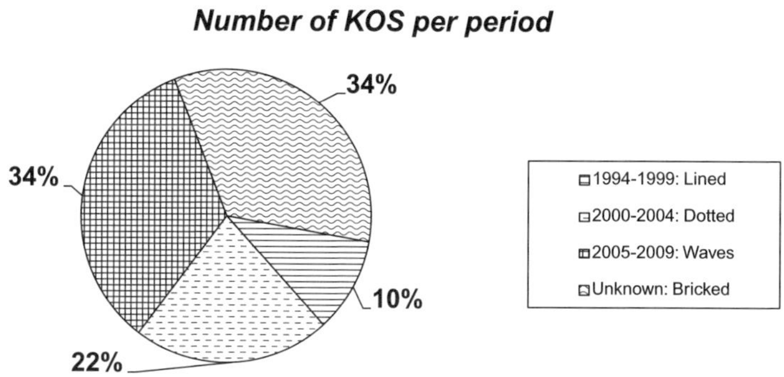

Fig. 3. KOS distribution per period of launch.

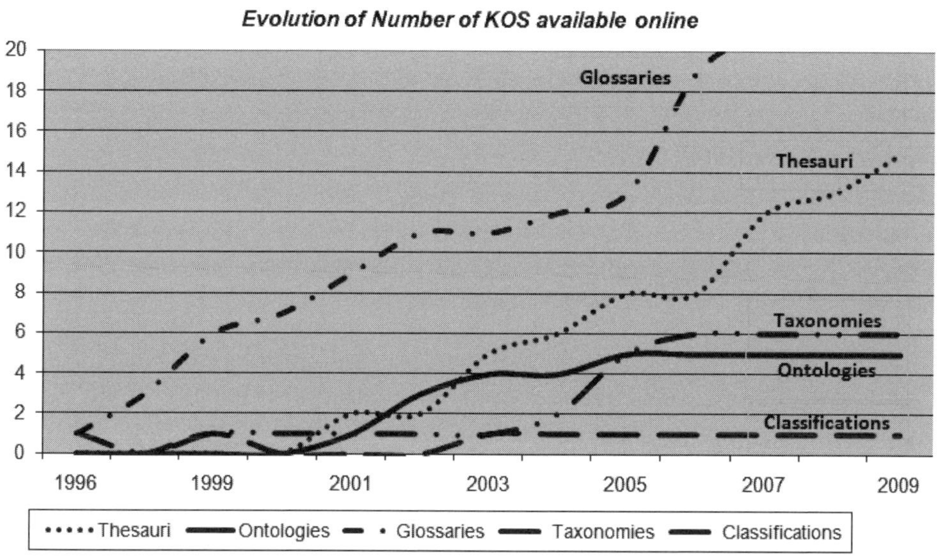

Fig. 4. Online deployment of KOSs (chronologically ordered).

(34% against 32%). The number of KOSs for which it was not possible to define a date of launch is also big, adding up to 34%. This fact undermines the outcomes from this figure, since a great deal of cases (29 KOSs) could not be assigned to a year.

Figure 4 shows the evolution of KOSs that were available online each year, starting from 1996 until 2009. This figure shows that around 2006 a great number of glossaries went online, while the launch of thesauri throughout the whole period shows a steady rate of increase (ranging from one to three

Table 9. Geographical coverage of the KOSs identified (refers to the country of origin).

Region	No of thesauri	No of ontologies	No of glossaries	No of taxonomies	No of classifications	Total
United States	3	2	23	5	1	34
International	6	3	6	1	1	17
United Kingdom	3	1	2	—	1	7
Canada	1	—	5	—	—	6
Australia	1	—	3	—	—	4
Slovenia	—	—	2	—	—	2
Netherlands	—	—	1	1	—	2
Israel	—	—	1	—	—	1
India	1	—	—	—	—	1
Germany	—	—	1	—	—	1
Finland	1	—	—	—	—	1
Denmark	—	1	—	—	—	1
Norway	—	—	—	—	1	1
Unknown	—	1	8	—	—	9
Total	16	8	52	7	4	87

thesauri per year). Ontologies have a relative small presence in this figure but nevertheless they seem to be deployed mainly from 2001 until 2005. Taxonomies were also deployed online mainly from 2004 to 2006, whereas Classifications where deployed online after 2002.

Table 9 that follows shows the geographic distribution of the KOS identified in different countries around the world.

As the previous table indicates, United States is represented by 34 KOSs, dominating the Agricultural Domain with 39% of the KOSs coming from institutions and organizations based outside Europe, and mainly in the United States of America. Seventeen KOSs were identified as international thus coming from international organizations and institutions that do not cover specific regions but on the other hand, concern wider areas and many countries.

United Kingdom (seven), Canada (six) and Australia (four) follow and along with the aforementioned cases they sum up to a total of 68 out of 87 KOSs. The rest KOSs identified come from Slovenia, Netherlands, India, Israel, Germany, Denmark, Norway and Finland, whereas another nine were not classified in any category. The amount of unclassified KOSs is not significant related to the total number of KOSs, so the results here are considered as representative of the actual situation.

When examining not only the regions but also the specific KOSs per region, it is noted that glossaries that are available online, mainly come from the United States, thesauri come from International organizations whereas ontologies are equally distributed between the two.

4. Conclusions & directions of research

The present chapter attempts to identify and briefly analyze a sample of online KOSs in the field of Agriculture. Nevertheless, all the offline KOSs are not presented in the chapter, whereas the search on the online KOSs cannot be considered exhaustive. On the contrary, taking into account the limitations of the research, the produced results can offer an initial insight on the Agricultural KOSs that are deployed online. The main outcomes of this chapter can be summarized as follows:

- Most KOSs available online were glossaries. Thesauri are used in a more restricted scale while ontologies, taxonomies and classifications were pretty limited in their use.
- Removing the extreme cases, (Plant Science and Agricultural Engineering) all the other fields follow more or less an equal distribution with small deviances in the total number of KOS identified (from four to nine).
- United States and especially educational institutions based there, are dominating the online KOSs that are available in the Agricultural Domain. Adding all the KOSs that come from European countries, the sum can barely reach half of the KOSs in the United States.
- Glossaries are mainly originated from United States, with almost 45% of them (23 out of 52) coming from institutions and organizations based overseas. Thesauri come mainly from International organizations and initiatives (6 out of 16) and secondly from the United States and United Kingdom (3 out of 17 each), whereas ontologies come mostly from International organizations with three occurrences. Finally, taxonomies come mostly from United States based organizations with five out of seven taxonomies coming from United States. No specific pattern was retrieved for classifications.
- Chronologically, the number of KOSs that are made available online is increasing. More specifically, from the total of nine KOSs made available prior to 2000 we reached 19 KOSs deployed from 2000 to 2004 and 29 KOSs that were made available online from 2005 until today.

- Analyzing the online presence of KOSs per year, it is seen that numerous glossaries have went online during the last few years, whereas thesauri are increasing in a steadier rate of one, two or three thesauri per year. Ontologies were mainly deployed from 2002 to 2005 and taxonomies from 2003 to 2006. No specific trend was retrieved for classifications.

As regards to the future directions of research, a more in-depth analysis of the KOSs available online in the Agricultural Domain is needed. The online search should be extended to include an exhaustive list of all the online KOSs available. Additionally, a survey on the offline KOSs would be useful in order to identify ways of deploying useful KOSs that are currently offline, in online systems taking advantage of their potential.

Among the limitations of this paper, we can identify the fact that the search was only conducted online thus leaving out of this discussion a number of popular KOSs that are widely used in agricultural science.

Based on this preliminary work, further analysis of Agricultural KOSs can take place, focusing on the particular application areas where they are used, the tools (e.g., repositories) that they support, and the type of information that they are used to represent and store. More specifically, we would be interested to extend this work by including more characteristics/attributes of the Agricultural KOSs. Furthermore, it would be interesting to examine the interoperability and harmonization of Agricultural KOSs. Studying how existing KOSs can describe agricultural information a harmonized way, so that projects that utilize different KOSs can exchange data or incorporate data from other initiatives would be of great value.

Acknowledgments

The work presented in this chapter has been funded with support by the European Commission, and more specifically the projects ECP-2006-EDU-410012 "Organic.Edunet: A Multilingual Federation of Learning Repositories with Quality Content for the Awareness and Education of European Youth about Organic Agriculture and Agroecology" of the eContentplus Programme and "agINFRA: A data infrastructure to support agricultural scientific communities Promoting data sharing and development of trust in agricultural sciences" of the FP7 programme, Research Infrastructures, Capacities Programme Objective INFRA 2011 1.2.2: Data infrastructures for e-Science.

References

1. Bechhofer, S and C Goble (2001). Thesaurus construction through knowledge representation. *Journal of Data & Knowledge Engineering*, 37, 25–45.
2. Chan, LM and ML Zeng (2002). Ensuring interoperability among subject vocabularies and knowledge organization schemes: A methodological analysis. 68th IFLA Council and General Conference, 18–24 August 2002, Glasgow. Available at http://archive.ifla.org/IV/ifla68/papers/008-122e.pdf [accessed on 10 February 2010].
3. Chandrasekaran, B, JR Josephson and VR Benjamins (1999). What are ontologies and why do we need them? *IEEE Intelligent Systems*, 14(1), 20–26.
4. Common European Research Classification Scheme (CERIF). Available at http://www.arrs.gov.si/en/gradivo/sifranti/inc/CERIF.pdf
5. Garshol, LM (2004). Metadata? Thesauri? Taxonomies? Topic Maps! Making sense of it all. *Journal of Information Science*, 30(4), 378–391.
6. Given, LM and HA Olson (2003). Knowledge organization in research: A conceptual model for organizing data. *Journal of Library & Information Science Research*, 25(2), 157–176.
7. Glänzel, W and A Schubert (2003). A new classification scheme of science fields and subfields designed for scientometric evaluation purposes. *Scientometrics*, 56(3), 357–367.
8. Gruber, TR (1993). A translation approach to portable ontology specifications, knowledge acquisition. *Special issue: Current Issues in Knowledge Modelling*, 5(2), 199–220.
9. Hodge, G (2000). *Systems of Knowledge Organization for Digital libraries. Be-yond Traditional Authority Files*. Washington, DC: The Council on Library and Information Resources.
10. Olson, HA and JJ Boll (2001). *Subject Analysis in Online Catalogs*. Englewood, CO: Libraries Unlimited.
11. Palavitsinis, N and N Manouselis (2009). A survey of knowledge organization systems in environmental sciences. In Information Technologies in Environmental Engineering, *Proceedings of the 4th International ICSC Symposium*, IN Athanasiadis, PA Mitkas, AE Rizzoli and J Marx-Gómez (eds.). Berlin Heidelberg: Springer.
12. Rosenfeld, R and P Morville (2002). *Information Architecture for the World Wide Web*, 2nd edn. Sebastopol, CA: O'Reilly.
13. Shiri, A (2006). *Knowledge Organization Systems in Canadian Digital Library Collections*. Available at http://www.cais-acsi.ca/proceedings/2006/shiri_2006.pdf [accessed on 22 December 2009].

14. Staab, S *et al.* (2001). Knowledge processes and ontologies. *IEEE Intelligent Systems*, 16(1), 26–34.
15. Staab, S and R Studer (eds.) (2004). *Handbook on Ontologies*. Verlag, Berlin Heidelberg New York: Springer.
16. Tudhope, D and ML Nielsen (2006). Introduction to knowledge organization systems and services. *New Review of Hypermedia and Multimedia*, 12(1), 3–9.
17. United Nations Department of Public Information Thesaurus (UNBIS). Available at http://unhq-appspub-01.un.org/LIB/ DHLUNBISThesaurus.nsf
18. Uschold, M and M Gruninger (1996). Ontologies: Principles, methods and applications. *Knowledge Engineering Review*, 11(2), 93–155.
19. Van Assem, M, V Malaise, A Miles and G Schreiber (2006). A method to convert thesauri to SKOS. In *Proceedings of the Third European Semantic Web Conference (ESWC'06)*, Lecture Notes in Computer Science.
20. Wielinga, BJ, A Th Schreiber, J Wielemaker and JAC Sandberg (2001). From thesaurus to ontology. In *Proceedings 1st International Conference on Knowledge Capture*, Y Gil, M Musen and J Shavlik (eds.), Victoria, Canada, pp. 194–201, 21–23 October 2001. New York: ACM Press.
21. Xie, N and W Wang (2009). Research on agriculture domain meta-search engine system. *IFIP International Federation for Information Processing*, Vol. 294; In *Computer and Computing Technologies in Agriculture II, Volume 2*, D Li and Z Chunjiang (eds.), pp. 1397–1403. Boston: Springer.
22. Zeng, ML and LM Chan (2004). Trends and issues in establishing interoperability among knowledge organization systems. *Journal of the American Society for Information Science and Technology*, 55(5), 377–395.
23. Zillman, MP (2009). Agriculture resources on the internet. Available at http://whitepapers.virtualprivatelibrary.net/Agriculture%20Resources.pdf [accessed on 23 December 2009].
24. Hepp, M (2007). Ontologies: State of the art, business potential, and grand challenges. In *Ontology Management: Semantic Web, Semantic Web Services, and Business Application*, M Hepp, P De Leenheer, A de Moor and Y Sure (eds.), pp. 3–22. Boston: Springer.
25. Zeng, M and L Chan (2003). Trends and issues in establishing interoperability among knowledge organization systems. *Journal of the American Society for Information Science and Technology*, Available at http://portal.acm.org/citation.cfm?id=986356 [online published 16 December 2003].
26. Tudhope, D and T Koch (2004). New applications of knowledge organization systems: Introduction to a special issue. *Journal of Digital Information*, 4(4). Available at https://journals.tdl.org/jodi/article/viewArticle/109/108 [27 January 2010].

CHAPTER III.4

METADATA AND ONTOLOGIES FOR BIOINFORMATICS

E. Blanco

Department de Genètica
Universitat de Barcelona
Av. Diagonal 643,
08028 Barcelona, Spain
eblanco@ub.edu

The post-genomic era is producing an enormous volume of data. Efficient applications and protocols are necessary in Bioinformatics to deal with this information. One of the most-challenging goals is the integration of knowledge extracted from different biological databases. Emerging ontologies in Molecular biology are very promising tools to provide sequence annotation standards that can be shared among genome annotation projects. The Gene Ontology (GO) is the most popular vocabulary to assign biological functions to genes, accordingly to evidence obtained from literature or computationally inferred. GO characterization of gene products is now an essential step of each genome annotation pipeline. Genome curators can use, in addition, auxiliar ontologies to describe biological sequences and alignments. The Open Biomedical Ontologies (OBO) consortium, a joint effort of bioinformatics and biomedical communities, has recently defined a common framework to standardize the ontologies developed in different fields. This chapter provides a comprehensive description of GO and other similar ontologies to annotate genome products.

1. Biological background

The instruction manual of every individual is stored on its genetic material. Cells contain one identical copy of the genome, which is the repository of information necessary to produce and regulate the proteins of the organism. Proteins are basic constituents of life, playing multiple biological roles on most cellular processes (e.g., enzymatic catalysis, molecular recognition or structural function). Chromosomes are basically large pieces of DNA in which genes are discontinuosly located within intergenic regions. Genes, which code for proteins, are the main components of genomes. However, important regulatory elements that control gene expression and genome structure can be found along the genome as well. Thus, genes are simple containers of protein-coding information, while gene products (proteins) play essential functions in the organisms [1].

The sequence of many genomes has been already obtained. For instance the genomes of human [2, 3], chimpanzee [4], mouse [5], chicken [6], and the fruit fly [7], among others, are publicly accessible through the main genome browsers on the internet (ENSEMBL [8], UCSC [9], NCBI [10]). Many other genome sequencing projects (animals and plants), in addition, will be completed in the future. Once the sequence is obtained, a team of experts (curators) is in charge of annotating, manually and computationally, the genome. The result is a catalogue of elements (e.g., genes and regulatory signals), which includes interactions between them and their biological functions. These elements tend to be evolutionarily conserved among different species, whereas non-functional regions accumulate multiple mutations. Comparative genomics, therefore, is very useful to extract novel knowledge from the comparison of the sequence of several genomes [11, 12]. Because of experimental and computational improvements, genome assemblies and annotations are periodically updated by different groups. Updates are independent, so several annotation releases are usually available for the same genome sequence assembly [8].

Bioinformatics is an interdisciplinary field involving biology, computer science, mathematics and statistics that analyzes biological sequence data and genome content to predict the location, the function and the structure of genes and proteins [13]. Bioinformaticians deal with many different problems: genome assembly and annotation [14, 15], database management and search [16,17], sequence comparisons [18, 19], phylogenetic analysis [20, 21], comparative genomics [22], gene prediction [23], gene regulation networks [24], protein-protein interaction [25], protein structure modeling [26] or RNA secondary structure prediction [27].

Sequence analysis is essential to tackle most problems in bioinformatics. For instance, genes are sequences of nucleotides that code for proteins [28], transcriptional regulatory elements are DNA motifs that control gene expression [29], and proteins are sequences of amino acids that adopt particular tridimensional structures to play specific biological functions [30]. Sequence alignments are very useful tools to infer novel knowledge for a sequence from another one that was previously annotated, under the assumption that similar sequences play similar functions [13]. There are different types of sequence alignments: global or local (to compare complete sequences or only fragments of them), pairwise or multiple (to align two or more sequences).

Genomes contain thousands of genes and each gene product can play multiple biological functions in different species. Obviously, many of these functions are still unknown. Once the earlier genome sequencing projects were completed, the need for a non-ambiguous and efficient gene functional annotation system was, therefore, evident. The Gene Ontology [31] was the first successful attempt to coordinate at a genomic level the unification of biological knowledge that world-wide researchers had about the genes and their products (see [32] for a historical review). Using a very simple set of metadata rules to establish the basic relationships among terms, the GO consortium provided a dictionary of abstract biological functions which incoporated no information about particular genes or genomes. Thus, the same GO term that defines a particular function in one organism can be used to annotate equivalent genes in other species. Several complementary ontologies appeared to provide support in other bioinformatic problems such as the Sequence Ontology (SO) [33]. Because of the lack of standards to produce ontologies, the Open Biomedical Ontologies consortium (OBO) [34] has been created to provide a uniform framework to integrate the mutiple ontologies that have proliferated nowadays.

2. The gene ontology (GO)

A large fraction of genes is conserved in different species. Approximately 80% of mouse genes have a counterpart in the human genome [5]. Novel biological knowledge about one organism can be therefore inferred from the comparison with others. Thus, new functions for one gene can be elucidated from the annotations available for the ortholog in other species. Current systems of nomenclature for genes and proteins are, however, historically divergent [6]. The gene name, in many cases, was derived from the function of the gene product (e.g., enzymes), or from the phenotype observed in the mutant form (e.g., genes in *Drosophila melanogaster*). The overwhelming amount of data incorporated to the biological databases in the final stages of initial genome sequencing projects produced even more confusion.

The Gene Ontology (GO), a collaborative international effort, was conceived in 2000 to integrate consistent information for different gene products that might be processed by automatical systems to infer novel knowledge [31].

The GO consortium was a joint project initially coordinated by three different model organism databases: *Drosophila melanogaster* (Flybase [35]), *Saccharomyces cerevisiae* (*Saccharomyces* Genome Database [36]) and mouse (Mouse Genome Informatics project [37]). GO ontologies are open in the sense that they can be distributed without any constraint and license, being receptive to modifications established in the community debates [34]. The output of the GO project (vocabularies, annotations, database and tools) are, therefore, in the public domain [38].

Most repositories for plant, animal and microbial genomes make use of GO to annotate their genes and proteins. Current state of genes and GO annotations in several model organisms, as of May 2008, is shown in Table 1. Over 200,000 genes from about 30 genomes have been manually annotated on the basis of the results reported in 52,000 scientific journal articles [39]. In total, more than 11 million annotations that associate gene products and GO terms, including manual and electronic annotations, are available [34].

2.1. *Three GO ontologies*

An ontology comprises a set of well-defined terms with well-defined relationships that describe all entities in an area of reality. Ontologies are therefore tools to organize information and to turn data into novel knowledge. The mission of the GO consortium, as defined in 2000 [31], is "to produce a structured, precisely defined, common, controlled vocabulary for describing the roles of genes and gene products in any organism". In detail, the GO project has three major goals [38, 40]: (1) to compile a comprehensive structured vocabulary of terms that describe key domains of molecular biology;

Table 1. Current annotations in GO (May, 2008). Data extracted from `http://www.geneontology.org/GO.current.annotations.shtml`

Species	Gene products annotated	Annotations	Non-electronic annotations
A. Thaliana	35,596	108,366	79%
C. elegans	13,772	81,234	45%
D. melanogaster	12,408	69,540	77%
G. gallus	16,581	61,169	3%
H. sapiens	35,551	183,795	32%
M. musculus	18,126	154,630	42%
O. sativa	52,082	64,119	100%
S. cerevisiae	6,348	77,649	49%

(2) to annotate biological objects using these terms; (3) to provide a centralized public resource to access these vocabularies and other software tools developed to deal with GO terms and annotations.

One important feature of the GO is the independence between ontologies and annotations. The GO consortium defines the terms and their relationships in the vocabularies, while curators of model organisms are the responsible for characterizing genes with GO terms in these genomes. The GO consists of three independent and non-overlapping ontologies: biological process, molecular function, and cellular component. These ontologies represent the basic information domains that are necessary to annotate information about the universe of genes and proteins in all living forms [40]:

Biological process (BP): 13,916 terms [39].

Biological objective to which a gene or gene product contributes. It often involves a chemical or physical transformation [31]. The terms "developmental process", "growth" or "metabolic process" are included in the BP ontology.

Molecular function (MF): 7,878 terms [39].

Biochemical activity (including binding to ligands or structures) of a gene product. It describes only what is done, without specifying where or when this event actually occurs [31]. Examples of MF terms are "catalytic activity", "transcription regulator activity" or "transporter activity".

Cellular component (CC): 2,007 terms [39].

The place in a cell where a gene product is active. Some CC terms are "organelle", "nucleus" or "extracellular region".

The BP, MF and CC ontologies provide independent attributes that characterize genes and gene proteins. The one-to-many relationship (1 gene to N GO terms) allows to express that a particular protein may function in several processes, play diverse molecular functions, and participate in multiple interactions with other proteins, organelles or locations in cells.

2.2. *GO structure*

Each GO term is an accessible object that has a unique identifier to be used as a database cross-reference to annotate genes in the genome databases (relationships between terms are not reflected in their GO identifiers). Each term is defined using the Oxford Dictionary of Molecular Biology [41] and other biological resources such as SWISS-PROT [42].

The three GO ontologies are structured vocabularies in which GO terms are connected to constitute Directed Acyclic Graphs (DAGs) that represent a network [40]. Relationships between parents and children nodes of this network are established using the "is a" or "part of" functions. The "is a" type describes specific instances of more general terms (e.g., "nucleus" -GO:0005634- is an instance of "intracellular membrane-bounded organelle" -GO:0043231-). The "part of" type refers to components of higher level concepts (e.g., "cell growth" -GO:0016049- is part of "regulation of cell size" -GO:0008361-). Each node can be a child of one or more than one parent. Thus, DAGs are more flexible structures, in comparison to hierarchical trees, to capture biological reality [40]. The three ontologies which are under development in the Gene Ontology are grouped into a single node "all". The GO entry of the MF term "transcription factor activity" (GO:0003700) is shown in Fig. 1.

Members of the GO consortium group may contribute to revisions of the ontologies. However, severe rules and standards must be followed in order to ensure the consistency of updated versions. The basic working principles are [40]: (1) the pathway from a child term to its top-level parent(s) must be true; (2) terms should not be species specific. They should be applied to more than one taxonomic class or organism; (3) GO attributes must be accompanied by appropriate citations.

2.3. *Annotating gene products*

Once the catalog of genes is elaborated, curators can provide a functional annotation for many of them according to the information available in the literature and other resources. The association between each gene and a set of GO terms must be accurately performed in order to ensure the correctness of the process. Association files are updated on each genome database, independently of the GO releases. The annotation of a gene product to one ontology is independent of the available annotations for the same gene in the other two ontologies [40].

Each GO annotation includes four pieces of information: the gene identifier, the GO term(s), the type of evidence supporting the association and a reference for that evidence. The functional annotation of the MYC human oncogene is shown in Table 2. The evidence code indicates how the annotation of a particular term for a gene was defined in the cited reference from

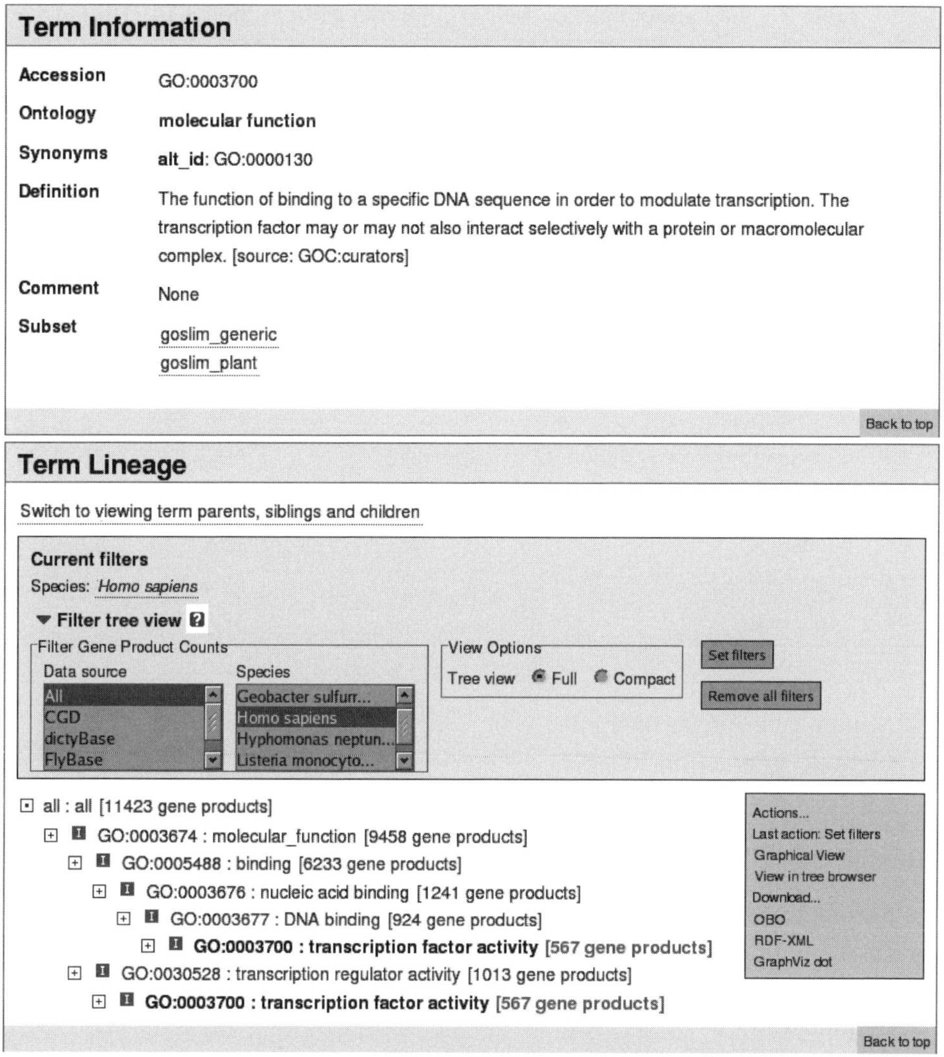

Fig. 1. Excerpt from the entry GO:0003700 in AmiGO.

PUBMED [10]. No measure of the quality of the annotation can be inferred, however, from this information. The GO evidence codes are divided into five categories:

(1) Experimental evidence inferred from:

Experiment (EXP)
Direct assay (IDA)
Physical interaction (IPI)

Table 2. GO annotation of the MYC human gene in the NCBI [10].

Ontology	Annotation	Evidence	PubMed
MF	DNA binding	NAS	2834731
MF	protein binding	IPI	9308237
MF	transcription factor activity	TAS	9924025
MF	transcription factor activity	IEA	
BP	cell cycle arrest	TAS	10962037
BP	cellular iron ion homeostasis	TAS	9924025
BP	positive regulation of cell proliferation	IDA	15994933
BP	regulation of transcription from RNA polymerase II promoter	TAS	9924025
BP	regulation of transcription, DNA-dependent	NAS	2834731
BP	regulation of transcription, DNA-dependent	IEA	
CC	nucleus	IDA	15994933
CC	nucleus	NAS	2834731
CC	nucleus	IEA	

Mutant phenotype (IMP)
Genetic interaction (IGI)
Expression pattern (IEP)

(2) Computational analysis inferred from:

Sequence or structural similarity (ISS)
Sequence orthology (ISO)
Sequence alignment (ISA)
Sequence model (ISM)
Genomic context (IGC)
Reviewed computational analysis (RCA)

(3) Author statement:

Traceable author (TAS)
Non-traceable author (NAS)

(4) Curator statement:

Inferred by curator (IC)
No biological data available (ND)

(5) Inferred from electronic annotation (IEA)

Evidence codes are manually assigned by curators, except IEA annotations which are provided by automated methods without curator revision. Several evaluation procedures to assess the accuracy and integrity of the huge volume of annotations in the genome databases have been published [43, 44]. Communication between GO contributors is actively promoted through Curator Interest Groups [45] that implement multiple mechanisms to manage content changes in the ontologies. Moreover, different activities to educate curators, such as "GO annotation camps" [45], are organized to improve the quality of annotations.

2.4. *GO tools and applications*

In order to uncover novel relationships, biologists can interrogate biological databases for genes which are associated to certain GO categories. Typically, GO annotations are helpful to characterize groups of genes that show similar expression patterns. Functional information can also be inferred between orthologous forms of a gene in different species. In general, GO analysis is an essential step in the basic protocol to fully understand the results of more complex experiments. Lomax [46] classified the most common ways of querying GO in:

Using a GO term:

To find the genes that are associated to one or more GO terms (e.g., a subset of the ontology) in one genome. The GO browser AmiGO [38] is the most popular application to perform simple queries about the three ontologies. Graphical views/tree views of the DAG that implements the ontology can be also displayed. AmiGO output for the GO term "Transcription factor activity" is shown in Fig. 1. More sophisticated tools are available to manipulate, create or maintain ontologies in the context of the OBO project (e.g., OBO edit, see Sec. 2.6).

Using one or more individual genes:

To show detailed information (GO associated terms) for a particular gene in one or more species. GO annotations for genes are usually accessed through major genome browsers (ENSEMBL [8], UCSC [9], NCBI [10]). AmiGO can be also used to browse gene association files, allowing to see the annotations for gene products of each species. It is important to mention that GO annotations are still in progress for most genomes, so many genes are still lacking from functional information. Comparative functional analysis in several species might be helpful in these situations. The GO annotation of the MYC human gene as provided by the NCBI Entrez [10] is shown in Table 2.

Using a gene list:

To obtain a subset of GO terms that characterize a list of genes that are physically clustered in a genome [50] or show similar expression patterns in microarrays [51]. Most available tools work in a similar way. First, the GO terms associated to these interesting genes are annotated. Next, a reference set (e.g., all genes in the microarray or in the genome) is also functionally annotated. Then, those GO categories that are statistically enriched in the set of interesting genes are selected. Finally, a feasible hypothesis that can explain the existence of such groups of genes is constructed from these over-expressed categories [46]. Many applications have been developed to implement this basic protocol (see Fig. 2 for some examples). However, there are many drawbacks and limitations in these approaches that must be still addressed (see [52, 53] for a comprehensive review).

The functional annotation of a group of genes (e.g., a genome or a microarray experiment) can be graphically visualized. GO slims are high-level views of each of the three ontologies that can be used to make comparisons of GO term distributions [38]. In Fig. 3, the *D. melanogaster* genome has been characterized using a GO slim that contains the first level of BP ontology terms (May, 2008).

2.5. *The Sequence Ontology (SO)*

The raw output of genome projects is the sequence of every chromosome. Sequences, however, are useless without the annotations that indicate the position of genomic elements (e.g., genes). These elements must be characterized using specific features. For instance, genes are constituted of two types of pieces (exons and introns). Boundaries between exons and introns are defined by biological signals or motifs (splicing signals). In addition, internal exons code for proteins (CDSs), while initial and terminal exons can contain untranslated regions (UTRs). Introns do not contain protein-coding information (see [54] for further information on gene structure). A gene constituted of five exons (introns are not shown) is graphically displayed in Fig. 4 (Top).

Coordinates and features of genomic elements are entered in biological databases using ambiguous formats that are often incompatible. In order to facilitate the exchange, comparison and management of this information, the Sequence Ontology (SO) provides a standardized set of terms and definitions for describing the features and attributes of biological sequences [33].The SO is designed for the markup of gene annotation data, which can be distributed in combination with other formats such as GFF

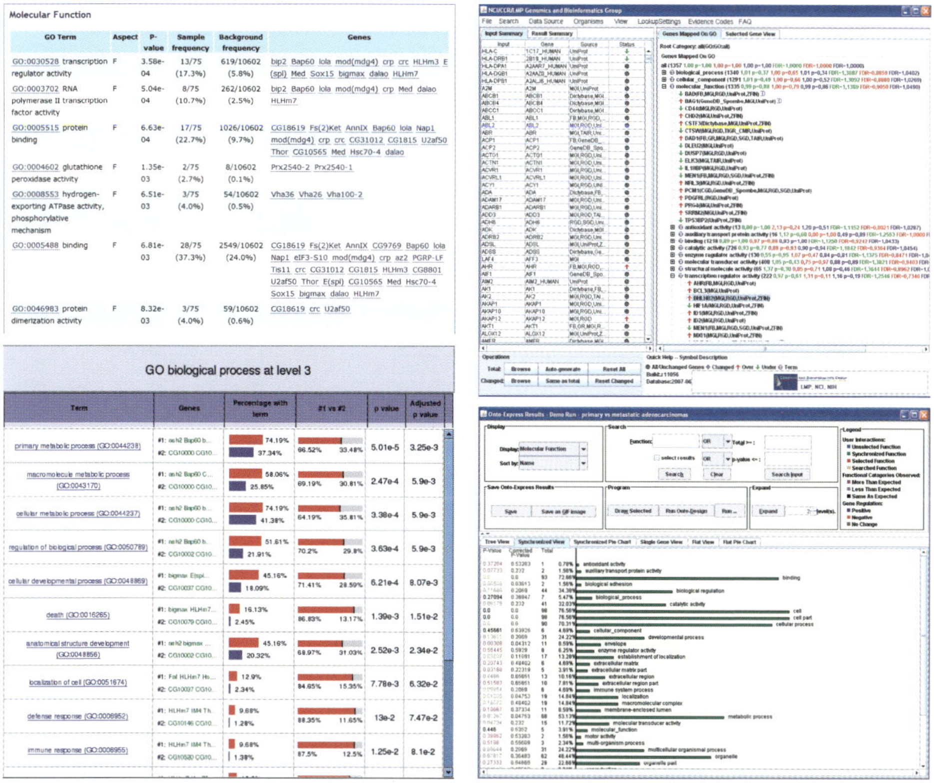

Fig. 2. Several tools to analyze gene expression data. (Top) Go Term Enrichment tool [39] and GOMiner [47]. (Bottom) FatiGO [48] and Onto-Express [49].

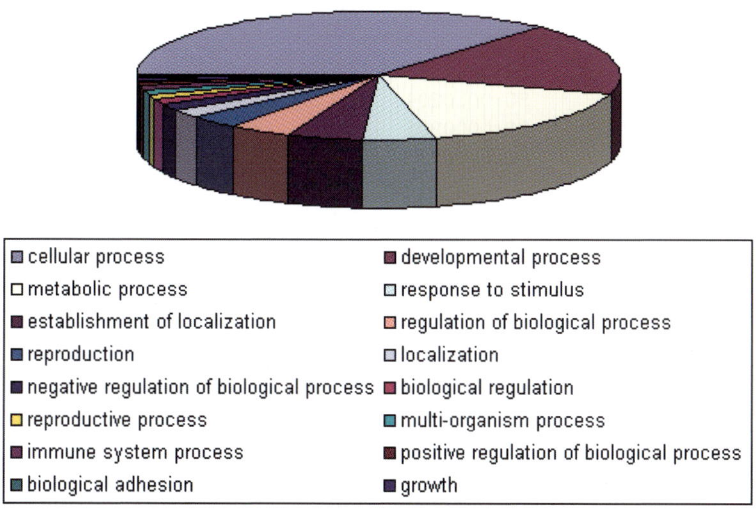

Fig. 3. GO silm (BP, first level) of the fruit fly genome [7].

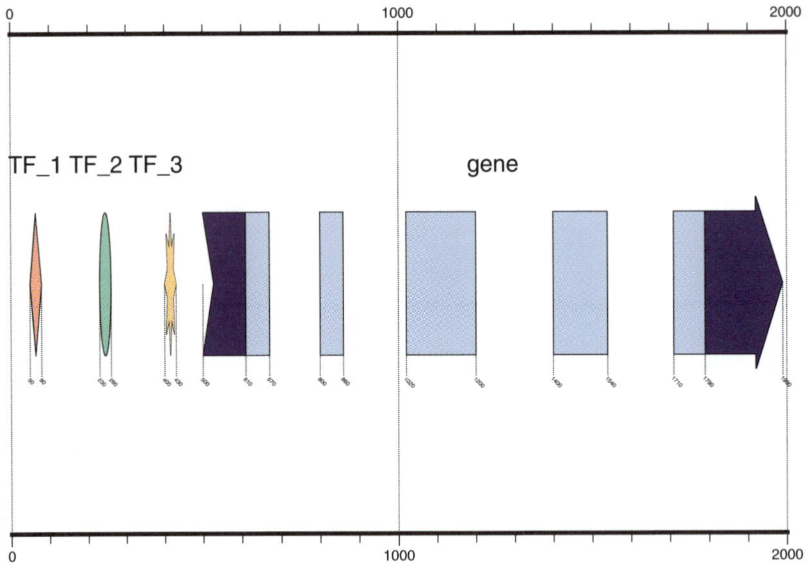

#GENE								
chr21	predictor	SO:0000204	500	610	.	.	.	gene
chr21	predictor	SO:0000316	611	670	.	.	.	gene
chr21	predictor	SO:0000316	800	860	.	.	.	gene
chr21	predictor	SO:0000316	1020	1200	.	.	.	gene
chr21	predictor	SO:0000316	1400	1540	.	.	.	gene
chr21	predictor	SO:0000316	1710	1790	.	.	.	gene
chr21	predictor	SO:0000205	1791	1990	.	.	.	gene
#TFs								
chr21	predictor	SO:0000235	50	80	.	.	.	TF_1
chr21	predictor	SO:0000235	230	260	.	.	.	TF_2
chr21	predictor	SO:0000235	400	430	.	.	.	TF_3
# SO terms								
CDS		SO:0000316						
five_prime_UTR		SO:0000204						
three_prime_UTR		SO:0000205						
TF_binding_site		SO:0000235						

Fig. 4. A canonical protein-coding gene and its regulatory region. (Top) Graphical representation obtained with the program gff2ps [55]. (Bottom) The gene described in GFF format.

(http:// www.sanger.ac.uk/Software/formats/GFF/GFF_Spec.shtml). Thus, a subset of SO terms, known as Sequence Ontology Feature Annotation (SOFA), has been selected to be used in genome annotation pipelines [33]. There are two basic types in SOFA: "region" (a genomic sequence of any length) and "junction" (boundary or space between two regions). The SO implements three relationship types: "kind_of" for instances of elements (e.g., "enhancer is a kind_of regulatory_region"), "derives_from" for relationships of process, (e.g., "EST derives_from mRNA") and "part_of" for components (e.g. "exon is a part_of a transcript"). Annotators are recommended to label their data using terms corresponding to terminal nodes in the ontology. A gene is described in GFF format in Fig. 4 (Bottom). Gene features are characterized using SO terms.

SO-compliant software can take advantage of SO properties to improve searching and querying tasks, and facilitate automatic validation of annotation data [33]. In contrast to GO, SO incorporates new analysis modes. For instance, extensional mereology (EM) operators such as "difference" and "overlap" can be used to ask questions about gene parts in different sets (e.g., alternative splicing in the *D. melanogaster* genome, see [33] for further information).

Sequence comparisons can be very useful to highlight conserved domains in proteins or motifs in regulatory regions from different species. However, comparison between results obtained using several sequence alignment programs is difficult because of the lack of common format standards. The Multiple Sequence Alignment Ontology (MAO) is designed to improve data integration between different alignment protocols to facilitate the construction of high quality multiple alignments. Thus, efficient knowledge extraction and presentation methods can be implemented for the biologists [56].

2.6. *The (OBO)*

Since the publication of the Gene Ontology [31], many other ontologies proliferated in separate life-science communities. These vocabularies, however, were independently designed due to the lack of a unifying framework. Thus, integration and comparison between different bodies of data was even more difficult. The Open Biomedical Ontologies (OBO) consortium was created in 2001 to become "an umbrella body for the developers of life-science ontologies to achieve that the data generated through biomedical research form a single, consistent, cumulatively expanding, and algorithmically tractable whole" [34].

The OBO contains over 60 ontologies (see Table 3) that evolve using the same principles successfully applied in the development of GO: open design, modular development, community debates and common systems of identifiers. The OBO Foundry has, therefore, provided a set of orthogonal guidelines used to reform existent ontologies and to create new vocabularies. OBO ontologies form DAGs with terms connected by edges (relationships), which

Table 3. Some of the OBO Foundry candidate ontologies [34].

Ontology	Prefix	URL
Common Anatomy Reference Ontology	CARO	`http://www.bioontology.org/wiki/index.php/CARO:Main_Page`
Disease Ontology	DO	`http://diseaseontology.sourceforge.net/`
Gene Ontology	GO	`http://www.geneontology.org/`
Foundational Model of Anatomy	FMA	`http://sig.biostr.washington.edu/projects/fm/index.html`
Multiple Alignment Ontology	MAO	`http://bips.u-strasbg.fr/LBGI/MAO/mao.html`
Ontology for Biomedical Investigations	OBI	`http://obi.sourceforge.net/index.php`
Phenotypic qualities	PATO	`http://www.bioontology.org/wiki/index.php/PATO:Main_Page`
Plan Ontology	PO	`http://www.plantontology.org/`
Protein Ontology	PRO	`http://pir.georgetown.edu/pro/`
Relation Ontology	RO	`http://www.obofoundry.org/ro/`
Sequence Ontology	SO	`http://www.sequenceontology.org/`
Systems Biology	SBO	`http://www.ebi.ac.uk/sbo/`

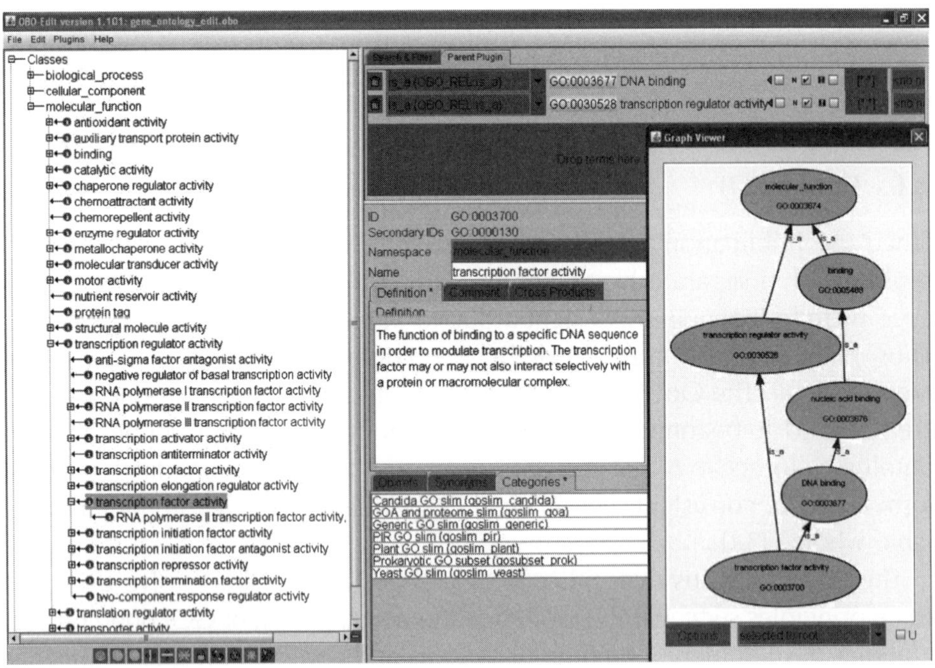

Fig. 5. Visualizing the entry GO:0003700 in OBO-edit.

are defined in the OBO Relation Ontology (RO) [57]. These vocabularies are distributed as files following the OBO format (including the three GO ontologies). Several software tools are available to manage the OBO ontologies such as the OBO-edit [58] or the Obol formal language [56]. The OBO-edit application is the standard tool to design new ontologies under the OBO standards [39]. Moreover, this program can be used to visualize and modify existent vocabularies. For instance, the GO term "transcription factor activity" (GO:0003700) is shown in Fig. 5, as displayed by the OBO-edit application.

References

1. Alberts, B, A Johnson, J Lewis, M Raff, *et al.* (2002). *Molecular Biology of the Cell*, 4th edn. Garland publishing. ISBN 0815332181.
2. Lander, E, L Linton, B Birren, C Nusbaum, *et al.* (2001). Initial sequencing and analysis of the human genome. *Nature*, 409, 860–921.
3. Venter, J, M Adams, E Myers, P Li, *et al.* (2001). The sequence of the human genome. *Science*, 291, 1304–1351.
4. Sequencing, TC and A Consortium (2005). Initial sequence of the chimpanzee genome and comparison with the human genome. *Nature*, 437, 69–87.
5. Waterston, R, K Lindblad-Toh, E Birney, J Rogers, *et al.* (2002). Initial sequencing and comparative analysis of the mouse genome. *Nature*, 420, 520–562.
6. Hillier, L, W Miller, E Birney, W Warren, *et al.* (2004). Sequence and comparative analysis of the chicken genome provide unique perspectives on vertebrate evolution. *Nature*, 432, 695–716.
7. Adams, M, S Celniker, R Holt, C Evans, *et al.* (2000). The genome sequence of *Drosophila Melanogaster. Science*, 287, 2185–2195.
8. Flicek, P, B Aken, K Beal, B Ballester, *et al.* (2008). Ensembl 2008. *Nucleic Acids Research*, 36, D707–D714.
9. Karolchik, D, R M Kuhn, R Baertsch and GP Barber (2008). The UCSC Genome Browser Database: 2008 update. *Nucleic Acids Research*, 36, D773–D779.
10. Wheeler, D, T Barrett, D Benson, S Bryant, *et al.* (2008). Database resources of the national center for biotechnology information. *Nucleic Acids Research*, 36, D13–D21.
11. Miller, W, K Makova, A Nekrutenko and R Hardison (2004). Comparative genomics. *Annual Review of Genomics and Human Genetics*, 5, 15–56.
12. Margulies, E and E Birney (2008). Approaches to comparative sequence analysis: Towards a functional view of vertebrate genomes. *Nature Reviews Genetics*, 9, 303–313.
13. Mount, D (2004). *Bioinformatics: Sequence and Genome Analysis.* Cold Spring Harbor Laboratory Press, 2nd edn. ISBN 0879697121.

14. Istrail, S, G Sutton, L Florea, A Halpern, *et al.* (2004). Whole-genome shotgun assembly and comparison of human genome assemblies. *PNAS*, 101, 1916–1921.
15. The ENCODE Project Consortium (2007). Identification and analysis of functional elements in 1% of the human genome by the ENCODE pilot project. *Nature*, 447, 799–816.
16. Stein, L (2003). Integrating biological databases. *Nature Reviews Genetics*, 4, 337–345.
17. Altschul, S, W Gish, W Miller, E Myers and D Lipman (1990). Basic local alignment search tool. *Journal of Molecular Biology*, 215, 403–410.
18. Needleman, SB and CD Wunsch (1970). A general method to search for similarities in the amino acid sequence of two proteins. *Journal of molecular biology*, 48, 443–453.
19. Smith, T and M Waterman (1981). Identification of common molecular subsequences. *Journal of Molecular Biology*, 147, 195–197.
20. Feng, D and R Doolittle (1987). Progressive sequence alignment as a prerequisite to correct phylogenetic trees. *Journal of Molecular Evolution*, 25, 351–360.
21. Fitch, W and E Margoliash (1967). Construction of phylogenetic trees. *Science*, 155, 279–284.
22. Ureta-Vidal, A, L Ettwiller and E Birney (2003). Comparative genomics: Genome-wide analysis in metazoan eukaryotes. *Nature Reviews Genetics*, 4, 251–262.
23. Brent, M (2005). Genome annotation past, present, and future: How to define an ORF at each locus. *Genome Research*, 15, 1777–1786.
24. Davidson, E, J Rast, P Oliveri, A Ransick, *et al.* (2002). A genomic regulatory network for development. *Science*, 295, 1669–1678.
25. Ideker, T. and A Valencia (2006). Bioinformatics in the human interactome project. Bioinformatics, 22, 2973–2974.
26. Moult, J, K Fidelis, A Kryshtafovych, B Rost, *et al.* (2007). Critical assessment of methods of protein structure prediction — Round VII. *Proteins: Structure, Function, and Bioinformatics*, 69, 3–9.
27. Mathews, D (2006). Revolutions in RNA secondary structure prediction. *Journal of Molecular Biology*, 359, 526–532.
28. Blanco, E and R Guigó (2005). Predictive Methods using DNA Sequences. In *Bioinformatics: A Practical Guide to the Analysis of Genes and Proteins*, pp. 115–142. New York, USA: John Wiley & Sons Inc., ISBN 0-471-47878-4.
29. Fickett, JW and W Wasserman (2000). Discovery and modeling of transcriptional regulatory regions. *Current Opinion in Biotechnology*, 11, 19–24.
30. Berman, H, J Westbrook, Z Feng, G Gilliland, *et al.* (2000). The protein data bank. *Nucleic Acids Research*, 28, 235–242.
31. The Gene Ontology Consortium (2000). Gene Ontology: Tool for the unification of biology. *Nature Genetics*, 25, 25–29.

32. Lewis, S (2004). Gene Ontology: Looking backwards and forwards. *Genome Biology*, 6, 103.
33. Eilbeck, K, S Lewis, C Mungall, M Yandell, *et al.* (2005). The Sequence Ontology: A tool for the unification of genome annotations. *Genome Biology*, 6, R44.
34. Smith, B, M Ashburner, C Rosse, J Bard, *et al.* (2007). The OBO Foundry: Coordinated evolution of ontologies to support biomedical data integration. *Nature Biotechnology*, 25, 1251–1255.
35. Wilson, R, J Goodman, V Strelets and The FlyBase Consortium (2008). FlyBase: Integration and improvements to query tools. *Nucleic Acids Research*, 36, D588–D593.
36. Hong, E, R Balakrishnan, Q Dong, K Christie, *et al.* (2008). Gene Ontology annotations at SGD: New data sources and annotation methods. *Nucleic Acids Research*, 36, D577–D581.
37. Eppig, JT, JA Blake, CJ Bult, JA Kadin and the Mouse Genome Database Group (2007). The Mouse Genome Database (MGD): New features facilitating a model system. *Nucleic Acids Research*. 35, D630–D637.
38. Gene Ontology Consortium (2004). The Gene Ontology (GO) database and informatics resource. *Nucleic Acids Research*, 32, D258–D261.
39. Gene Ontology Consortium (2008). The Gene Ontology project in 2008. *Nucleic Acids Research*, 36, D440–D444.
40. The Gene Ontology Consortium (2001). Creating the Gene Ontology resource: Design and implementation. *Genome Research*, 11, 1425–1433.
41. Cammack, R, T Atwood, P Campbell, H Parisha, T Smith, J Stirling and F Vella, (Eds.) (1997). *Oxford Dictionary of Biochemistry and Molecular Biology*. Oxford: Oxford University Press, ISBN 0198529171.
42. Boeckmann, B, A Bairoch, R Apweiler, M Blatter, *et al.* (2003). The SWISS-PROT protein knowledgebase and its supplement TrEMBL in 2003. *Nucleic Acids Research*, 31, 365–370.
43. Dolan, M, L Ni, E Camon and J Blake (2005). A procedure for assessing GO annotation consistency. *Bioinformatics*, 21, i136–i143.
44. Buza, T, M Fiona, M McCarthy, N Wang, *et al.* (2008). Gene ontology annotation quality analysis in model eukaryotes. *Nucleic Acids Research*, 36, e12.
45. Gene Ontology Consortium (2006). The Gene Ontology (GO) project in 2006. *Nucleic Acids Research*, 34, D322–D326.
46. Lomax, J. (2005). Get ready to GO! a biologist's guide to the Gene Ontology. *Briefings in bioinformatics*, **6**, 298–304.
47. Zeeberg, B, W Feng, G Wang, M Wang, *et al.* (2003). GoMiner: A resource for biological interpretation of genomic and proteomic data. *Genome Biology*, 4, R28.

48. Al-Shahrour, F. R Daz-Uriarte and J Dopazo (2004). Fatigo: A web tool for finding significant associations of gene ontology terms with groups of genes. *Bioinformatics*, 20, 578–580.
49. Draghici, S, P Khatri, P Bhavsar, A Shah, *et al.* (2003). Onto-Tools, the toolkit of the modern biologist: Onto-Express, Onto-Compare, Onto-Design and Onto-Translate. *Nucleic Acids Research*, 31, 3775–3781.
50. Spellman, P and G Rubin (2002). Evidence for large domains of similarly expressed genes in the *Drosophila* genome. *Journal of Biology*, 1, 5.
51. Schena, M, D Shalon, R Davis and P Brown (1995). Quantitative monitoring of gene expression patterns with a complementary dna microarray. *Science*, 270, 467–470.
52. Dopazo, J (2006). Functional interpretation of microarray experiments. *OMICS*, 10, 398–410.
53. Khatri, P and S Draghici (2005). Ontological analysis of gene expression data: Current tools, limitations, and open problems. *Bioinformatics*, 21, 3587–3595.
54. Zhang, M (2002). Computational prediction of eukaryotic protein-coding genes. *Nature Review Genetics*, 3, 698–709.
55. Abril, JF and R Guigo (2000). gff2ps: Visualizing genomic annotations. *Bioinformatics*, 8, 743–744.
56. Thompson, J, S Holbrook, K Katoh, P Koehl, *et al.* (2005). MAO: A Multiple Alignment Ontology for nucleic acid and protein sequences. *Nucleic Acids Research*, 33, 4164–4171.
57. Smith, B, W Ceusters, B Klagges, J Kohler, *et al.* (2005). Relations in biomedical ontologies. *Genome Biology*, 6, R46.
58. Day-Richter, J, M Harris, M Haendel. The Gene Ontology OBO-Edit Working Group and S Lewis (2007). OBO-Edit — an ontology editor for biologists. *Bioinformatics*, 23, 2198–2200.
59. Mungall, C (2004). Obol: Integrating language and meaning in bio-ontologies. *Comparative and Functional Genomics*, 5, 509–520.

CHAPTER III.5

METADATA AND ONTOLOGIES FOR MECHANICAL OBJECTS' DESIGN AND MANUFACTURING

Fabio Sartori* and Stefania Bandini†

Department of Computer Science
Systems and Communication, University of Milan–Bicocca
v.le Sarca 336, 20126 Milan (ITALY)
**sartori@disco.unimib.it*
†bandini @disco.unimib.it

In this chapter a conceptual and computational framework for the development of Knowledge–Based Engineering tools is presented. The framework is based on the adoption of ontologies and metadata as effective methods to represent the different levels of competence owned by expert designers of complex mechanical objects. After a brief review of literature on this topic, the Chapter gives a complete overview of the approach, explaining how it can be used to represent functional, procedural and experiential knowledge necessary to accomplish a mechanical object design task. Moreover, the Chapter describes a framework application case study, namely the IDS project, to support expert designers working for Fontana Pietro SpA, an Italian enterprise leader in the development of dies for automotive industry.

1. Introduction

The aim of this Chapter is to provide a methodological approach to the development of decision support systems for supporting experts involved in the design and manufacturing of complex mechanical objects, in the research field named Knowledge–Based Engineering (KBE). The chapter will focus on the industry world, trying to describe how Knowledge Management

* Corresponding author.

can be integrated with other disciplines and methods like CAD/CAM, FEM analysis and so on typically adopted in the mechanical domain.

Several tools have been proposed as Knowledge–Based Engineering applications (see e.g. the MOKA project [1]), providing software environments for automating repetitive engineering tasks [2]. Knowledge Based System applications have the big potential to reduce costs related to repetitive engineering tasks, but require strong efforts to collect, represent and formalize the necessary knowledge.

The knowledge of this meaningful literature addressed the choices of our position on the activity of domain knowledge modeling and representation, taking into account its nature, its use and the sharing of conceptual categories, instead to force into a predefined theoretical model the knowledge coming from the field. In our experience, we had the possibility to tackle different problems related to the mechanical domain, which allowed us to identify three main distinct kinds of knowledge involved in it:

- Functional knowledge [3], related to the representation of what kind of function is performed by each part of the object;
- Procedural knowledge [4], related to the representation of the order of steps in the design of an object;
- Experiential knowledge, related to heuristics coming from the stratified knowledge of the company on the domain, and increased through the experience of the professionals belonging to the Unit (but never formalized).

Functional knowledge is captured in our approach by adopting an ontological model of the mechanical object [5]. The mechanical object is characterized as a collection of functional systems, i.e. sets of elementary components defined on the basis of the specific function provided by the set.

Procedural knowledge can be represented by the introduction of the *SA*–Nets* specialization of Superposed Automata Networks (SA-Nets) [6], derived from Petri Nets Theory. Some constraints of the previous formal model have been relaxed in order to fit the features of the design domain. The main role of this procedural knowledge representation is to guide the user during the design activity, pointing out possible problems due to the violation of some precedence constraint.

Experiential knowledge is represented as a specific *knowledge artifact* modeling the heuristics followed by an expert during the design of the object, and fully integrated with the other kinds of knowledge.

The chapter will focus on conceptual and computational tools for representing and integrating the three kinds of knowledge identified and how they can be implemented in effective decision support systems, with particular attention on the role of ontologies. To this aim, a case study will be presented: The IDS project [7], concerning the support of experts involved in the design and manufacturing of dies for the automotive sector.

2. Motivation and background

The development of effective software systems to support people involved in the design and manufacturing of complex products has become a very important research field. This fact is demonstrated by the growing number of Conferences and events dedicated to this topic, which presents very complex research issues. This is particularly true in the domain of mechanical industry, where people is generally involved in difficult configuration problems [8] aimed at obtaining a final product meeting marketing requirements that is also more appealing than competitors' ones in terms of price, quality and so on.

A complex mechanical product is made of hundreds and, sometimes, thousands of components, from the simplest ones (e.g. screws, screw bolts, nails and so on) to most composite one. Typically, people involved in the design of such objects exploit sophisticated Computer Aided Design (CAD) tools, like CATIA[1], Autocad[2], and so on. Unfortunately, although CAD tools are particularly suitable to check how the single components are put together from the geometrical point of view (e.g. is the screw large enough for that hole? Is that screw bolt right for the chosen screw?) they don't support experts in monitoring the project from the functional perspective (e.g. is that part correctly designed in order to properly accomplish this function?). While the former point is relatively simple to be taken into account, the latter is much more complicated to consider, since it depends on the designers' experience and knowledge.

For this reason, the configuration of complex products is very difficult from the knowledge representation point of view, and building decision support systems for designers in the mechanical industry field is not simple. In this field, three main types of information and knowledge can be recognized: geometric information (geometric representation of the model of the product in most cases the CAD model), information/knowledge about the documents used during the design process (standards, manuals, and recommendations)

---

[1] http://www.3ds.com/products/catia/welcome/

[2] http://www.autodesk.com/suites/autocad-design-suite/overview

and information/knowledge about inference rules and external program applications (calculations, simulations and so on [9]).

Knowledge Based System applications have a big potential to reduce cost and time for repetitive engineering tasks but require a relevant effort to collect and formalise the necessary knowledge in a knowledge representation scheme. In this field, generally referred to as *Engineering Design*, one of the most known examples of application to the industrial planning of complex objects has been proposed by Gero and Maher [10]. They defined a conceptual and computational approach starting from the definition of design as "a *goal-oriented, constrained, decision-making, exploration and learning activity which operates within a context which depends on the designer's perception of the context*" [11]. Their approach defines specific knowledge representation schemes (the so–called *prototypes*) for the definition of the conceptualization and ideation process generally followed by a draftsman and proposes the Case–based design paradigm to re-use previous design solutions to solve similar design problems [12].

Engineering Design can be viewed as *an articulate process composed of phases, where each phase represents a combinatorial action on the parts the composite object is constituted of.* To realize an object meeting the desired market requirements, engineering designers have to deal at the same time with different kinds of knowledge coming from different epistemological sources: "static" knowledge about objects or, Ontological Knowledge [13] (which is often represented in a declarative form), and "dynamic" knowledge about processes (which is often expressed in "procedural terms").

A number of references in literature [14–18] indicates that the competence of engineering designers is related to their ability in considering functional constraints over the parts of the objects they are designing. According to our viewpoint, this expert designers' competence gives the ability to navigate ontological and procedural knowledge, always considering different kinds of relationships among each part of the desired composite object.

The central role of heuristics in performing design tasks mainly resides in this capability to shift through different epistemological dimensions, represented by the functional and the procedural sides of knowledge. We look at design heuristics as a set of competencies, growing from experience, which bridge the gap between functional and procedural knowledge and makes designers able to articulate the design process referring to functional constraints.

Therefore the development of Knowledge Based Systems supporting engineering design activities must take into account the formal representation of both these knowledge sides [17, 18]. The conceptual framework we are proposing aims at offering to knowledge engineering discipline a theoretical structure for acquiring and representing such a knowledge.

In the following section we will take into account the role performed by ontology in filling the gap between functional and procedural knowledge representation. As observed in [10], a product design process begins with *functional* or *conceptual design*, followed by *basic design* and *detailed design*. Among these steps, functional design plays the central role in ensuring design quality and product innovativeness.

While traditional mechanical computer–aided design, based on geometric modeling, targets detailed design support (e.g. low level technical activities on the model of the designed object), innovative decision support systems should consider the entire design process, including functional design. Thus, it is crucial to represent and reason about functional requirements of design objects, a facility that traditional CAD systems do not provide. The traditional engineering design research community has widely accepted this conceptual design methodology [10]: first, a designer determines the entire function of a design object by analyzing the specifications of the product to be built. He/she then divides the function recursively into sub-functions, a process that produces a functional organization. In correspondence to each sub-function, the designer uses a catalogue to look up the most appropriate elements (a component or a set of components) that are able to perform the functional requirement. Finally, the designer composes a design solution from those selected elements. Here, function plays a crucial role, because the results of the design depend entirely on the decomposition of the function and on the designer's capability to build the appropriate object realizing that function [17, 19, 20]. As a result, a designer obtains a micro-macro hierarchy of functions that are projected on the aggregate of parts the composite objects is constituted of. Thus, when designers speak about the "function" held by an object or by one of its components, they can speak about it because they have sufficient knowledge for associating functions to a suitable object structure: this kind of knowledge is called *ontological*.

Functions are knowledge abstractions by which engineering designers conceptualize the object with specific reference to the goals for which it is designed. On the basis of what we have discussed in the previous section, ontological knowledge is put in action by designers for describing design entities in terms of *Part–Whole* relations induced by function decomposition [10]. Therefore, capturing ontological relations may on one hand enhance our representation of the engineers' cognitive structures activated during the problem solving activity, and on the other it can facilitate the development of more effective knowledge–based systems supporting it. The nature of the compositional relations, however, can widely vary. Understanding these relations allows engineers to reason about the artifacts and to make clearer the sets of functional and procedural constraints necessary to obtain a final object that meets the market requirements. Not being able to reason about the relationships that hold between different parts and the wholes they belong to can be detrimental to effective product models and design processes.

3. A knowledge management approach to KBE

Designing a complex object can be divided into two subproblems from the Knowledge Management (KM) point of view: how to represent procedural knowledge and how to represent functional knowledge. This is a general issue of the design problem, but we'll talk about a specific case in which the complex object to be configured is a mechanical component. From the functional knowledge standpoint, a mechanical component can be considered as made of different parts that can be grouped on the basis of different levels of abstraction, as shown in Figure 1.

At the *Component Level* atomic components are placed, for which no design activity or knowledge are needed. Components are used to build more complex parts of the object, that are *aggregates*. An aggregate is a composition of one or more components and can include one or more other

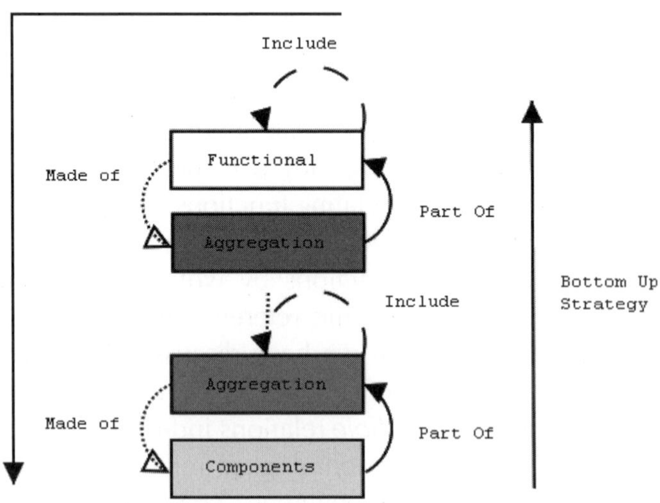

Fig. 1. A mechanical object is made of three different kind of parts, bounded by three different types of relationships.

aggregates. Although aggregates have not specific meaning from the mechanical object point of view, they are useful to provide experts with a simpler way to deal with components. The last level of abstraction is constituted by *functional* units, that are built starting from aggregates and components, but different from them represent a functional property of the under construction object. The relationships among levels can be navigated according to a bottom–up or a top–down strategy: in the former case, it is necessary to start from the component level, in the latter the first level to consider is the functional one. While the bottom–up strategy is the most used when developing a KM system for supporting the design of complex objects (e.g. a case–based reasoning system calculates the similarity between two case according to the value associated to their attributes), the top–down strategy is closer to the real way of reasoning of an expert designer than the other one. The top–down strategy is implemented in our framework by the *include* and *made–of* relationships.

Procedural knowledge is related to how taking care of design constraints in building the object: such constraints can be due to geometrical aspects (e.g. a component cannot be placed on an aggregate because of absence of space), customer requirements (e.g. don't use this type of component, use this one instead) or designer experience (e.g. the design of this functional unit influences the design of that one). This constraints can be captured by the adoption of a formalism like SA–Nets [21], that allows to manage the different steps in a synchronous or asynchronous fashion. More details about foundational issues behind our framework can be found in Ref. [22].

3.1. *Conceptual tools for functional knowledge: Ontologies*

The first shared knowledge structure allowing the contracting activity in common problem solving can be represented using the Ontology approach [23]. At a first glance, the hierarchical structural decomposition of the object (is-a, part-of relations) could represent the right structure of this kind of knowledge, because of the classificatory capabilities of the senior design professionals. The mere joining of this kind of ontological set-up with knowledge involving the functionalities (not captured by is-a, part-of relations) of the involved mechanical parts can be conceptually complicated and sometimes not feasible. A different and more suitable conceptualization has been adopted as shown in Figure 2.

The mechanical object is requested to perform different functions: Each conceptual part of the object that performs a specific function is called *Functional System*. A mechanical object can then be considered as a

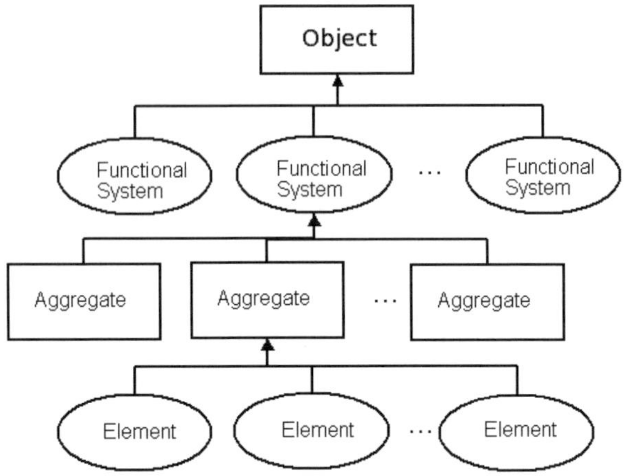

Fig. 2. Relationships between components and functional roles of object structure. Different levels of abstraction can be identified: functional systems, aggregates and atomic elements.

collection of one or more Functional Systems. Functional systems, however, can be fairly complex. Sometimes, designers conceive them as a composition of lower level *Aggregates*, which are semi-manufactured components to be grouped together for making simpler and faster the design of a Functional System. Finally, *Elements* are (atomic) elementary parts. Their role can be different according to the aggregate (and thus functional system) they belong to. An example of how this categorization can be applied in the practice will be given in Section 4.

3.2. *Conceptual tools for procedural knowledge: SA*–Nets*

The Functional Ontology introduced above clearly describes the different components of the mechanical object and their functions. The design of the single parts is governed by Procedural Knowledge. Procedural Knowledge concerns precedence constraints that must be taken into account to avoid possible mistakes in the design task. These constraints can be due to manufactures' guidelines as well as to geometric considerations.

In order to properly represent Procedural Knowledge we have adopted a specialization of Superposed Automata Nets[6] (SA-Nets), named SA*–Nets. SA–Nets are a formal conceptual and computational tool for the analysis of concurrent systems. The main idea behind the adoption of such tool in KM context is that the design of object parts can be considered as sequences of steps, which are executed both sequentially and contemporary. During this

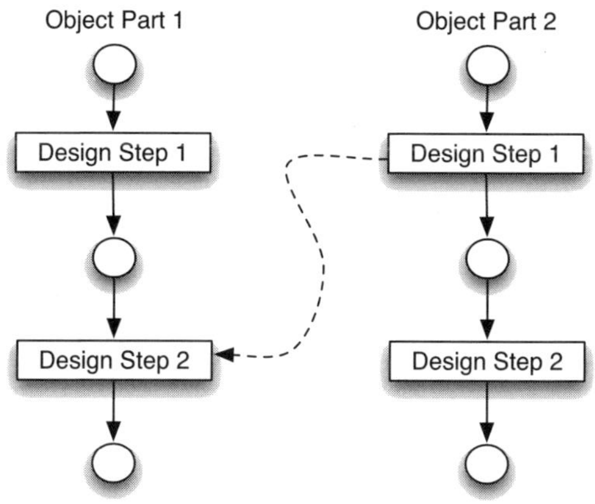

Fig. 3. The design steps of two mechanical object parts: the dashed arrow linking *design step 1* of *object part 2* and *design step 2* of *object part 1* indicates that design step 1 must be accomplished before.

process, it is possible that a design step can be influenced by the results of another one related to a different part, generating a synchronization between two distinct components: each design step can be represented by a transition in a formalism like a Petri Net. To take care of synchronizations, opportune relationships are considered (see Figure 3).

A SA*–Net can be defined as follows:

Definition 1 (SA*–Nets). *A SA*–Net is a* 4*-tuple*

$$\langle S, T, A, R \rangle$$

where:

- *S is a set of* states (*i.e. circles in Figure 3*)*;*
- *T is a set of* transitions (*i.e. rectangles in Figure 3*)*;*
- *A is a set of* arcs*, links between states and transitions of a SA*–Net* (*i.e. solid arrows in Figure 3*) *or between transitions belonging to different SA*–Nets* (*i.e. the dashed arrow Figure 3*)*;*
- *R is a set of* rules *to describe how precedence relationships among object parts are established.*

The set S contains two special states *begin* and *end*, which identify the starting and ending points of a design project. It is important to notice that states of SA*–Nets are completely different from states of Petri–Nets or SA–Nets. In fact, states in SA*–Nets allow to identify all the design steps already executed: in this sense, a marker on a state of a SA*–Net doesn't indicate the possibility for the outgoing transition to fire, but that the design step above it has been already accomplished.

Transitions represent design steps and are bounded to states above and behind them by means of arcs. There exist two particular transitions, namely *fork* and *join*, which are not design steps but are used to identify points where concurrency among distinct sequences of design steps *finish* or *begin* respectively. Arcs are not labeled and can have two semantics: they can represent a sequential flow in the execution of design step with reference to an object part or precedence constraints between two design steps that are in different SA*–Nets.

Finally, rules specify how the SA*–Net is browsed and used by the IDS system. Rules can belong to the following three categories, as shown in Figure 4:

- Rule number 1: within a SA*–Net, given an executed transition, all the transitions above it must be already visited;
- Rule number 2: if a transition T_1 of a given SA*–Net is bounded to a transition T_2 of another SA*–Net by a precedence constraint, the transition T_2 must be already visited;
- Rule number 3: if a transition T_1 is the result of a join among transitions T_2, ..., T_n, T_1 can be executed if and only if all the transitions T_2, ..., T_n have been already visited.

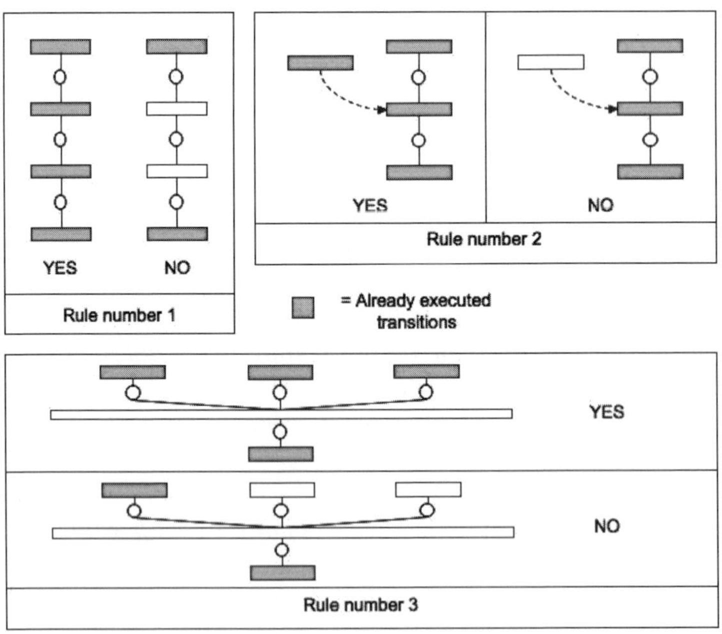

Fig. 4. A representation of the three categories of rules adopted in the framework.

Starting from the ontological representation of the object, a SA*–Net for every Functional System identified must be produced. Such net completely describes the different design steps needed to design the functional system it refers to, by means of aggregates and elements usage and configuration. The composition of all the SA*–Nets through the fork/join transitions allows the designer to give a clear and complete description of the main object design process following a bottom–up strategy.

3.3. *Conceptual tools for experiential knowledge: knowledge artifacts*

Given a complete SA*–Net, Experiential Knowledge concerns how the different design step are effectively accomplished by the designer according to his/her own design style. Each transition in the SA*–Net is then described by a group of specific *Knowledge Artifacts* (KA). Every KA specifies a set of preconditions to be verified and actions to be done. Typical actions are the evaluation of geometric parameters and suggestions about an aggregate (or element) to include in the project with respect to another one. Preconditions typically regard precedence constraints among transitions or object parts.

In Ref. [24] we find that an artifact is an object that has been intentionally produced for a specific purpose. Moreover, according to [25], an artifact is the result of a disciplined human activity, following rules and based on training and experience. As a consequence, every artifact has an author and a purpose.

Artifacts can be evaluated in terms of how their actual features match the features intended by their authors and the purposes to which they are built. Given a purpose *P*, an author *A* devises an artifact and obtains an invention, an idea or a project that describes the artifact at an abstract level. We can refer to this object, resulting from the author intellectual work, using the symbol *I*. Finally, the actual artifact *R* is used for the purpose *P*. It should be noticed that the purpose that has produced both the design of *I* and the implementation of the artifact *R* could differ from the purpose of the user of an artifact.

The artifact *R* described by *I* is the real object. The author would like *R* to have the intended features to fit the original purpose *P*. The description *I* of the artifact is clearly the result of a design process. It is a formal and abstract representation of an actual object *R*. The devised artifact needs to be implemented, in order to produce the actual artifact *R* that is going to be used.

As presented in Figure 5, *P*, *I* and *R* are related through *design*, *implementation* and *utilization*. A successful set of relationships is that in which a

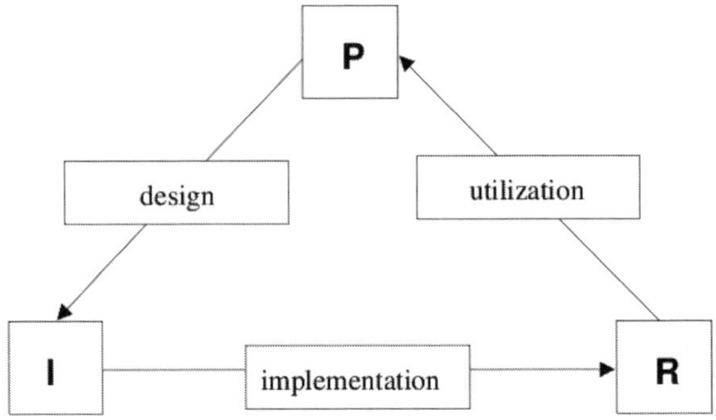

Fig. 5. Design, Implementation and Utilization of an Artifact.

design leads to an *I* that perfectly matches a given purpose *P*, whose implementation leads to an *R* that perfectly matches *I*, and such that the utilization of *R* also perfectly matches *P*.

One interesting point to be noticed is that the arrows in Figure 5 are one-to-many relations. In fact, a purpose *P* can lead to a variety of designed artifacts I_1, I_2, etc. Summarizing, an artifact is hence characterized by a particular triple (*I*, *R*, *P*), in which a design *I* is implemented as an actual object *R* that is used for a purpose *P* (which, as mentioned above, is not necessarily the purpose P_0 that led to the design of *I*). The separate elements *I*, *R* and *P* can be put together in a triple (*I*,*R*,*P*) that is the "artifact in the context" view of the artifact *R*.

Our focus is not on artifacts in general but on *KAs*, which are artifacts designed and implemented with the aim to represent expert knowledge in the mechanical object manufacturing field. For this reason, a KA suitable for the framework proposed in this chapter should be able to bind ontological description of the object (as described in Section 3.1) and procedural one (see Section 3.2). Thus, we can now define a KA for the design and manufacturing of mechanical objects as follows:

Definition 2 (Knowledge Artifact). *A Knowledge Artifact KA for the design and manufacturing of mechanical objects is a triple*

$$\langle P, I, R \rangle$$

where:

- *P is the set of* functional systems *that defines the mechanical object, as described by the functional ontology;*
- *I is a set of* design steps *to define how each functional system is projected, as described by the SA*–Net;*

- *R is a set of* conceptual tools *to represent expert knowledge involved in the definition of how each design step is accomplished by the object designer.*

In order to give a complete characterization of our KAs, the R set of the definition above should be further explained, and *Task Structures for Mechanical Object Design* (TS-MODE) will be briefly introduced to this aim.

A TS–MODE is a specialization of a Task Structure, a knowledge representation tool introduced by Chandrasekaran [26], which has widely influenced the development of knowledge engineering methodologies like CommonKADS [27] in the recent past. According to its definition, a Task Structure should concern a portion of the knowledge model, giving a synthetic description of inputs, outputs and a body describing the problem solving strategy to get outputs from inputs. In our framework, a TS–MODE is used to specify a design step involved in the definition of a functional system, as shown in Figure 6.

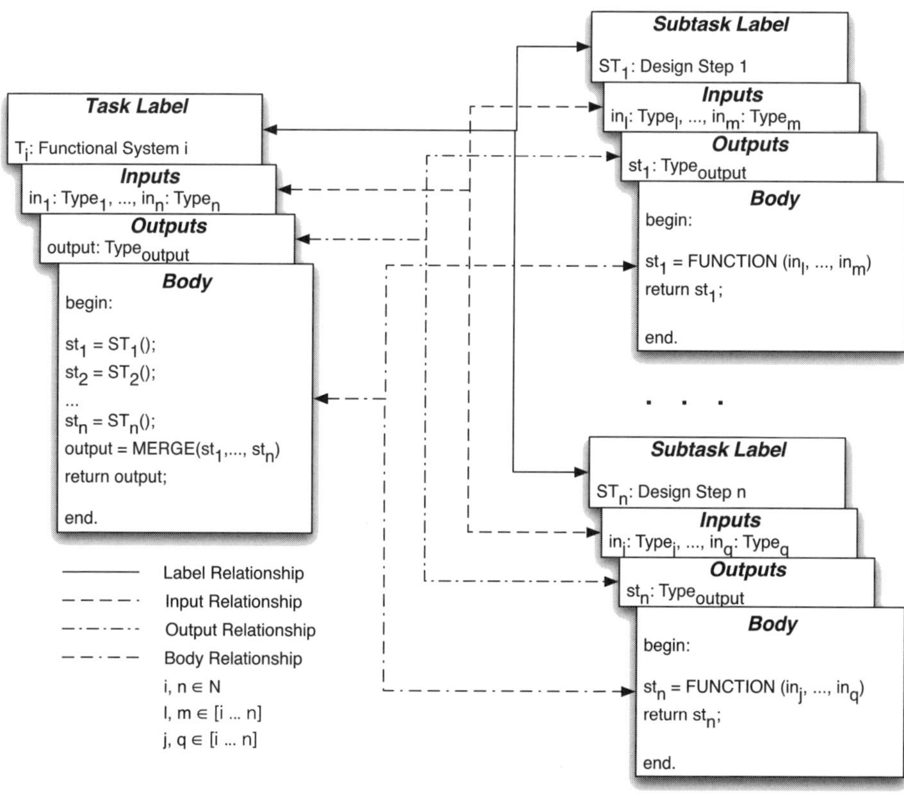

Fig. 6. A sketch of TS-MODE representation.

Definition 3 (TS–MODE). *A TS–MODE is a 4-tuple*

$$\langle L, I, O, B \rangle$$

where:

L is the label of the task, i.e. the name of the functional system or design step it refers to;
I is a set of inputs, i.e. values that must be used in the body to obtain expected results;
O is the output of the task, i.e. a value representing the expected result of the knowledge model part defined by the task;
B is the body of the task, i.e. a set of instructions (e.g. rules of rule–based system) specifying the problem solving strategy adopted to obtain expected results form given inputs.

In case of precedence constraints between two design steps, the TS–MODE representing the influenced task will contain a call to the TS–MODE representing the other task. Moreover, a distinction between *task* and *subtask* has been made: while a task is the representation of a functional system, a subtask is a representation of a part of that functional system, i.e. a given design step. In other words, while the output of the functional system is effectively returned by the task body, a subtask calculates a partial value that is necessary to obtain the output. A subtask is identified in the task body as a procedure call. In this way, it is possible to give a clear and understandable structure to the knowledge model involved in the design of a functional system, since it is possible to reuse the code for a subtask within more than one task. As highlighted in Figure 6, subtasks' inputs are subsets of the task input set, and the task output is the result of a MERGE function that exploits the partial results elaborated by subtasks.

3.4. *Computational tools for acquisition and representation of functional knowledge: NavEditOW*

In the last years both the scientic and the industrial communities recognized the role of semantics for knowledge management, access and exchange. Semantic based approaches have been applied e.g. to information retrieval, system integration and knowledge sharing structured as semantic knowledge bases. A lot of research has been carried out, a great number of theoretical results have been achieved (see e.g., [28, 29]) and a number of applications have been developed [30]. OWL has become a standard language for defining ontologies, providing a common way to automatically process and integrate information available on the Web. OWL allows defining ontologies constituted by classes, properties and instances.

Despite these efforts and enhancements, a number of open problems still prevent semantic based technologies from being effectively exploited by end users; end users in fact cannot be assumed to have formal skills that are required nowadays to interact with semantic KBs, with respect to both the contribution to the KBs growth (i.e. its update and maintenance) and the access to the KBs content on the basis of its semantics (i.e. through query and navigation).

For this reason, the development of systems that improve the access to ontological KBs, in both the updating and the retrieval and discovery of in-formation phases, is a challenging topic in order to meet knowledge management systems users perspective. In order to develop the user interface, many ontology editors and visualization tools have been investigated. In our opinion, these applications are critical, since the diffusion of Semantic Based Knowledge Management Systems and more generally Semantic Web applications depends on the availability of convenient and exible tools for editing, browsing and querying ontologies.

Before developing a new system, we have analyzed the principal tools of this area. One of the most popular ontology editor is Protègè. It is a free, open source ontology editor and knowledge-based framework. A detailed description of Protègè is out of the scope of this chapter and can be found e.g. in Ref. [31]. Protègè allows editing of ontologies expressed in OWL. Indeed, Protègè is one of the best OWL editors, but its user interface is too complex for a user with no experience of ontological languages and lacks some useful functions like the inspection of the elements (e.g. via hyperlinks) and comfortable edit/visualization facilities for the individuals.

An interesting Web-based OWL ontology exploration tool is OntoXpl, which is described in [32]. In particular, an interesting feature of OntoXpl is the visualization facility for individuals that can be displayed as a tree whose nodes are individuals and arc are properties. This kind of visualization is suitable for A-Boxes with many individuals. OntoXpl also supports the inspection of the ontology elements via hyperlinks. Swoop [33] is a hypermedia inspired ontology editor that employs a web-browser metaphor for its design and usage. All ontology editing in Swoop is done inline with the HTML renderer (using color codes and font styles to emphasize changes); it also provides a querying interface for ontologies.

NavEditOW (see Figure 7) allows exploring the concepts and their relational dependencies as well as the instances by means of hyperlinks; moreover, it provides a front–end to query the repository with the SPARQL query

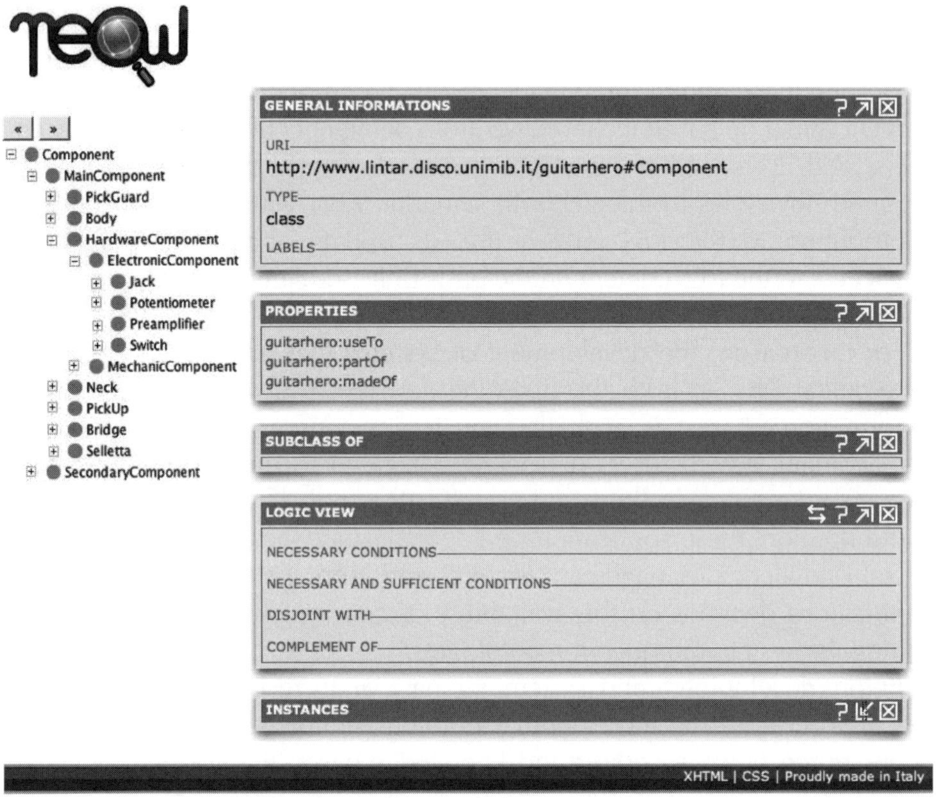

Fig. 7. The NavEditOW interface.

language. The main functionalities offered by NavEditOW are the navigation, editing and querying of OWL ontologies through a web–based interface. With the ontology navigation interface the users can view ontology individuals and their properties and browse their properties via hyperlinks. Browsing the ontology is essential for the user in order to explore the available information and it also helps not expert users to deepen their search requirements, when they don't start from any particular requirement in mind [34].

3.5. *Computational tools for acquisition and representation of procedural knowledge: SA*–Net Manager*

The implementation of SA*–Nets is obtained exploiting XML language: opportune Data Type Definitions (DTD) have been defined in order to represent how a given SA*–Net should be designed for a specific domain.

In this way, the development of a decision support system to deal with procedural knowledge becomes easier: the DTD acts as guide to procedural knowledge acquisition and representation. Figure 8 shows the DTD definition:

```
<?xml version="1.0" encoding="UTF-8"?>
<!ELEMENT reti (rete)+>
<!ELEMENT rete (start,stati,transizioni,vincoli*,end)>
<!ATTLIST rete
    id       ID        #REQUIRED
    tipo     (SE|TR|DP)    #REQUIRED>
<!ELEMENT start (stato)>
<!ELEMENT stati      (stato)+>
<!ELEMENT stato      EMPTY>
<!ATTLIST stato
    id       ID        #REQUIRED>
<!ELEMENT statoref   EMPTY>
<!ATTLIST statoref
    target   IDREF     #IMPLIED>
<!ELEMENT transizioni    ((transizione|transizioneref)+,(fork,join)*)>
<!ELEMENT fork   (entranti,uscenti)+>
<!ATTLIST fork
    id       ID        #REQUIRED
    link     IDREF     #REQUIRED>
<!ELEMENT join   (entranti,uscenti)+>
<!ATTLIST join
    id       ID        #REQUIRED
    link     IDREF     #REQUIRED>
<!ELEMENT transizione    (nome,entranti,uscenti)>
<!ATTLIST transizione
    id       ID        #REQUIRED
    tipo     (rossa|verde)    #REQUIRED>
<!ELEMENT transizioneref EMPTY>
<!ATTLIST transizioneref
    target   IDREF     #IMPLIED>
<!ELEMENT nome       (#PCDATA)>
<!ELEMENT entranti   (stato|statoref)+>
<!ELEMENT uscenti    (stato|statoref)+>
<!ELEMENT vincoli    (vincolo)+>
<!ELEMENT vincolo((transizione|transizioneref),(transizione|transizioneref),descrizione)>
<!ATTLIST vincolo
    id       ID        #REQUIRED>
<!ELEMENT descrizione    (#PCDATA)>
<!ELEMENT end    (stato)>
```

Fig. 8. The DTD for SA*–Net implementation: the code is in Italian.

The line number 2 in the figure describes the element at lower level, that is *reti* (i.e. *nets*) and can contain an arbitrary number of *rete* (i.e. *net*) components, as specified by the usage of + symbol.

The lines from number 3 to number 39 defines the structure of a *rete* element, according to Definition 1, which are the set S of states (i.e. *stati* in the figure), the set T of transitions (i.e. *transizioni* in the figure) and the set A of arcs (i.e. *vincoli* in the figure). Moreover, an opportune identifier *ID* and a *type* (i.e. *tipo* in the figure) are bounded to each net. The type allows specifying what kind of mechanical object that net is referred to. Finally, two special states, namely *start* and *end,* to identify where the procedural knowledge representation begins and terminate respectively, and two special transitions, namely *fork* and *join,* to identify the generation of possible sub–nets related to the representation of concurrent design steps are also included in the SA*–Net representation. The attributes characterized by the presence of the keyword *#REQUIRED* are mandatory.

For each transition some important information must be specified: the *name* (i.e. *nome* on line 24 in the figure) of the transition, the set states from which an arc starts to enter that transition (i.e. *entranti* on line 24 in the figure), the set of states to which an arc enters starting from the transition (i.e. *uscenti* on line 24 in the figure) and the *type* (i.e. *tipo* on line 27 in the figure) of the transitions which can be red (i.e. *rossa* on line 27 in the figure) or green (i.e. *verde* on line 27 in the figure), depending on the level of the SA*–Net under consideration in the design: a red transition is referred to a whole Functional System while a green transition concerns a single design step.

In order to manage properly Procedural Knowledge involved in the design of mechanical object, the DTD briefly introduced above is not sufficient. Thus, an opportune computational tool has been developed that has been called *SA*–Manager.*

The SA*–Manager is a collection of JAVA classes working on instances of SA*–Nets defined according to the DTD and implementing the functionalities for supporting the decision making process of expert designers, namely:

- *nextStep*: the aim of this functionality is to suggest which is the next design step that should be accomplished by the user. To this scope, a SA*–Net is browsed starting from the last point to create a set of potentially executable transitions. Then, the designer can choose on of them being sure that doing that step will not affect negatively the rest of the project, living the SA*–Net in a consistent global state.
- *procedureAnalysis*: this functionality allows the user verifying if the current state of the project is consistent or not with reference to the

procedural knowledge represented by the SA*–Net. This function can be launched whenever during the project, being sure that SA*–Manager will be able to detect if any design step with a precedence constraint with respect to the current was not conducted in the right way.
- *projectProcedureAnalysis*: this function is very similar to the procedure-Analysis one, with the difference that it involves a complete check of the whole project from the current state up to the beginning rather than focusing only on one specific design step as the checking starting point.

The SA*–Manager must browse an instance of SA*–Net to work properly: in particular, in the case of nextStep, the net is browsed on the basis of a top–down strategy (from the start state forward to the end state), while the procedureAnalysis and the projectProcedureAnalysis are based on a bottom–up approach (from the end state back to the start state. To accomplish its tasks, the SA*–Manager implements the rules described before by the Definition 1 and shown in Figure 4.

Figure 9 shows the content of the package for SA*–Manager implementation. The four classes on the right allows implementing the SA*–Net DTD. The three classes on the left, instead, allow the loading of a specific SA*–Net concerning the procedural knowledge involved in the design of a mechanical object (i.e. the *SAloader* class in the figure), the checking for constraint violations (i.e. the *Checker* class in the figure) and, finally, the effective managing of the net by means of the three functionalities described above (i.e. the *SAManager* class in the figure).

4. A case study: Supporting the design of dies for stamping

In this section we want illustrate a successful case study of decision support systems concerning experts involved in the design and manufacturing of dies for car body production, that operates within Fontana Pietro S.p.A.[3] (FP). The system name is *Intelligent Design System* (IDS), and it has been designed and implemented exploiting the conceptual and computational framework described above.

4.1. *The die for car bodies: A complex mechanical product*

Fontana Pietro S.p.A. is leader in engineering and manufacturing of dies for the deformation of sheet metal, in particular for the automotive sector.

[3] www.fontana-group.com

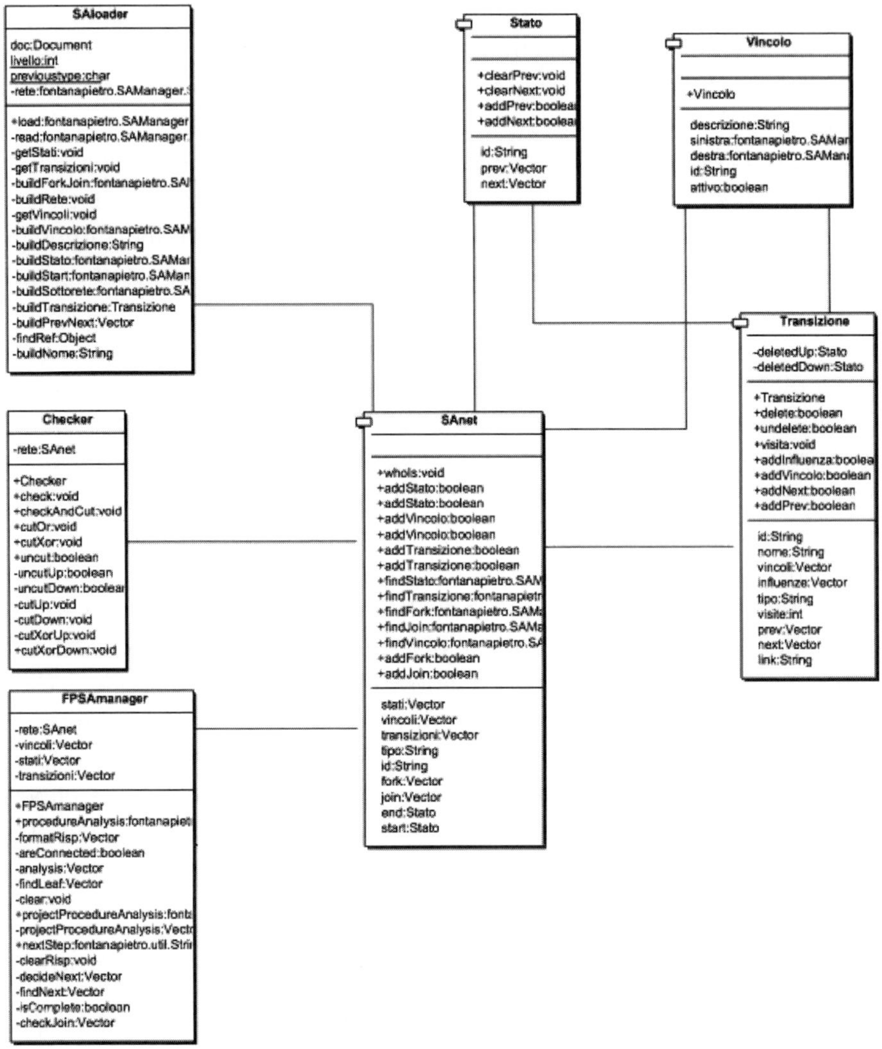

Fig. 9. The SA*–Manager package: on the right, the four classes to implement the SA*–Net DTD, on the left the three classes to implement the SA*–Manager tool.

The enterprise is divided into Business Units: FP Engineering, FP Dies Manufacturing, FP Pressing, FP Assembling.

FP Dies Manufacturing, FP Pressing and FP Assembling are devoted to manufacturing and delivering of dies; FP Engineering aims at the design of the product, through the adoption of opportune technologies (e.g. CAD) and tools, in particular CATIA V5[4].

[4] http://www.3ds.com/products/catia/portfolio/catia-v5/

A die is a very complex mechanical product, composed of a hundreds of parts with different functions that must be put together into a unique and homogeneous steel fusion. Each die is the result of a complex design and manufacturing process involving many professionals. Moreover, it is important to notice that more dies are necessary to produce a car body, each one having precise and distinct roles within the whole process.

The car body is the result of a multi–step process in which a thin sheet metal is passed through different kinds of presses, each one equipped with a specific die. Four main kinds of dies can be identified:

- *Forming die*: it provides the sheet metal with the final morphology of the car body die;
- *Cutting die*: it cuts away the unnecessary parts of the sheet metal;
- *Boring die*: it makes holes in the sheet metal, in order to make it lighter without side–effects on its performance;
- *Bending die*: it is responsible for the bending of some unnecessary parts that the Cutting die is not able to eliminate from the sheet metal.

These dies are basically made of pig iron melts on which other elements can be added according to the function (e.g. blades in Cutting dies). Moreover, holes are generally made on the melt in order to make the die lighter without hindering its functionalities.

In the IDS project only the Forming die has been considered, that is made of of four main components: A Forming die is composed of a two main components (upper and lower shoe, respectively) that are fixed to and moved by the press in order to provide the desired final morphology to sheet metal. The main components responsible for the forming operation are the *punch*, the *binder* and the *die seat*, which are placed in the lower shoe (see Figure 10). Punch is the die component responsible for providing the sheet metal with the required aspect. Its geometry is designed according to the car body part (e.g. door, trunk, and so on) to be produced by it. The binder is the component of the die that allows the sheet metal to be perfectly in contact with the punch, by blocking the sheet against the upper shoe before the punch is pushed on it. Finally, the die seat contains both the punch and the binder and allows the die to be fixed to the press. The upper shoe of the die contains only a negative copy of the punch, usually called matrix.

4.2. *The die from the designer perspective*

Since the die is an object made of hundreds of parts, each one to be properly designed, the perception of the space where the design activity is

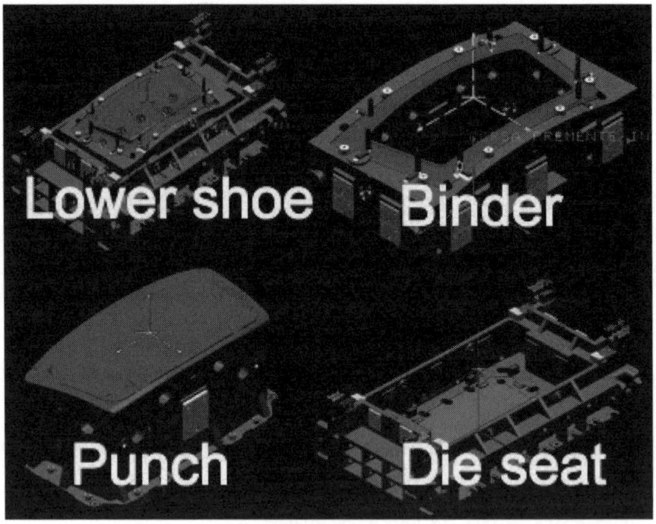

Fig. 10. *A 3D Model of a Die.*

conducted has a significant influence on the practical aspects of the design process. This induces frequent changes in the set of decisional steps this activity is made of.

Given these changes, the designer is capable to recognize the role of an object and the meaning of actions which can be accomplished on it quite instantaneously, within functional contexts which often result to be tacit and intrinsic in the design operations.

In other words, understanding the function of a given die component together with the capability to recognize the set of constraints coming from both customer (i.e. automotive industries) requirements and geometric rules about the die affects the decision making process.

Without a deep analysis of the functionalities a designer implicitly assigns to each die part, and the relationships among them, it would be impossible to capture properly the structure of designer mind activities which characterize the design and manufacturing of a die. Moreover, also the dynamic of processes involved in die design are complex, since it is characterized by sequences of activities on the different functional elements that compose the die, according to a strategy that is specific for every die to be manufactured.

Anyway, the heuristics lying under these activities don't prescribe the existence of a unique way to intend the decision making process (see Figure 11), but they indicate only a reasonable sequence of actions to accomplish the design task with the minimum risk of side–effects. Every designer generates a conceptualization of the die as a collection of parts

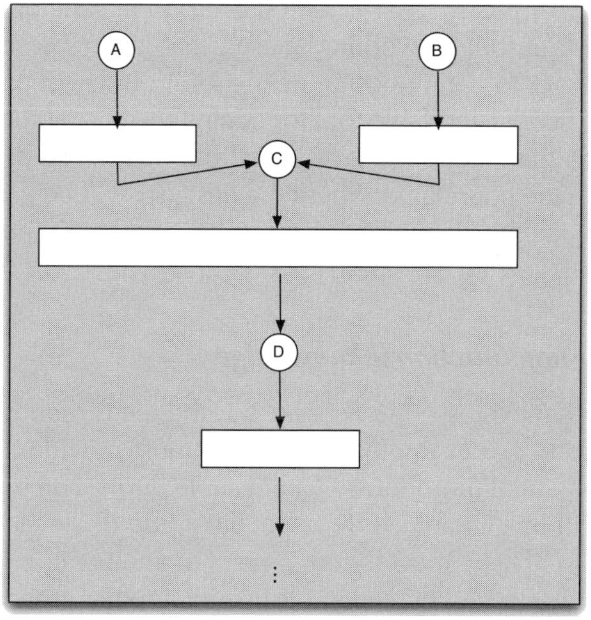

Fig. 11. A sample of procedural model of the design process. Circles represent the design step related to an object or a functional group, rectangles define functions on specific die parts. The model specifies which elements must be designed before (e.g. B must be designed before C).

each one delivering a specific functionality. This conceptualization emerges from practical experience by working on the field as well as from formal competencies reflecting engineering studies (e.g. geometrical aspects), which put together allow the designer to decide the way to conduce the different steps of a project.

It doesn't exist a well defined set of rules to do this operation: every designer follows guidelines reflecting his/her own style, evaluating step–by–step if there are possible constraints that cannot be violated. In other words, the designer follows directives about what cannot be done and his/her creativity about what can be done. This means that two designers could take different decisions about the same design step, producing as a result two morphologically different dies with the same effectiveness from the functional point of view, that is the shape to give to the sheet metal.

Such kind of design activity can be conceived as a problem solving strategy where the designer must generate innovative hypothesis at each decisional step to solve configuration problems that depend on an overall conceptualization of the object to manufacture.

Supporting this typically goal–oriented decision making process concerns the management of routine working phases, that is to represent the process activities necessary to define design heuristics, in order to provide the user with a clear and understandable tool for tracing the conceptual relationships among die parts that cannot be considered during a given design step. This means to define the boundaries where the designer will be enabled to apply his/her own style: the definition of these boundaries is the essence of a Knowledge Management System to support creativity in this field [9].

4.3. *Representing functional knowledge*

According to what expressed in Section 3.1, the die is requested to perform different functions. For example, forming die must provide the sheet metal with the desired initial morphology (changeable during some next step), and this function will be guaranteed by a specific group of die elements. But the forming die must also be moved from a press to another one, and the *movement–ability function* will be accomplished by another group of parts. Each conceptual part of the die that performs a specific function is a *Functional System* (see Section 3.1). Each Functional System in the IDS ontology is characterized by a label that specifies the function it is referred to: For example, the label *Fixing System* will be used to identify the Functional System necessary to guarantee the correct mounting of the die on the press.

As previously introduced (see Section 3.1 again), designers often conceive Functional Systems as the composition of lower level *Aggregates*, that can be grouped together in order to make simpler and faster the design of a Functional Systems, as well as reused on different Functional Systems. For example, the Aggregate *formaggella*[5] is used to identify a semi–manufactured part (similar to a piece of Swiss Emmental cheese) that is useful both in the design of the Fixing System (i.e. to maintain the right distance between the die and the press it will be mounted on) and in the design of the Moving System (i.e. to maintain the right distance between the die and the sheet metal during the different steps of elaboration).

Finally *Elements* are instead (atomic) elementary parts (screws, for instance). Their role can be different according to the Aggregate (and thus Functional System) they are related to.

This categorization is fundamental for all the Knowledge Representation choices, being the main ontological conceptualization of the domain, permitting IDS to represent a die on the basis of the function it will perform

[5]This Italian term is typical of IDS designers and cannot be translated into English language.

(according to the designer way of thinking) rather than of the elementary parts it is made up of (the vision of a CAD system like CATIA).

4.4. *Representing procedural knowledge*

Each functional unit described in the ontology should be designed according to a specific set of *procedural constraints* to be represented in the proper knowledge representation schema. In the IDS system, the SA*–Net formalism has been used to model the relationships existing across the different components of die ontology.

Figure 12 shows a sample SA*–Net, where it is represented a sketch of a die part (i.e. die seat, punch, binder or matrix) as a set of descriptive transitions (*DESCRIPTION LEVEL* in the figure) having the name of a functional system defined by the die ontology. Each descriptive transition is linked to one or more design transitions (*DESIGN LEVEL* in the figure) allowing to define how that functional system is configured. Design transitions permit to describe aggregates and elementary parts of the die ontology.

Unlike traditional SA–Nets, SA*–Nets are characterized by a semantic completely defined by its transitions; in fact, while in the SA–Nets nodes act as *tokens*, with the consequence that a transition can be activated if and only if all its entering nodes are marked, in the SA*–Net the only function of a node is to trace the next part of the die to be designed. In this way, a designer

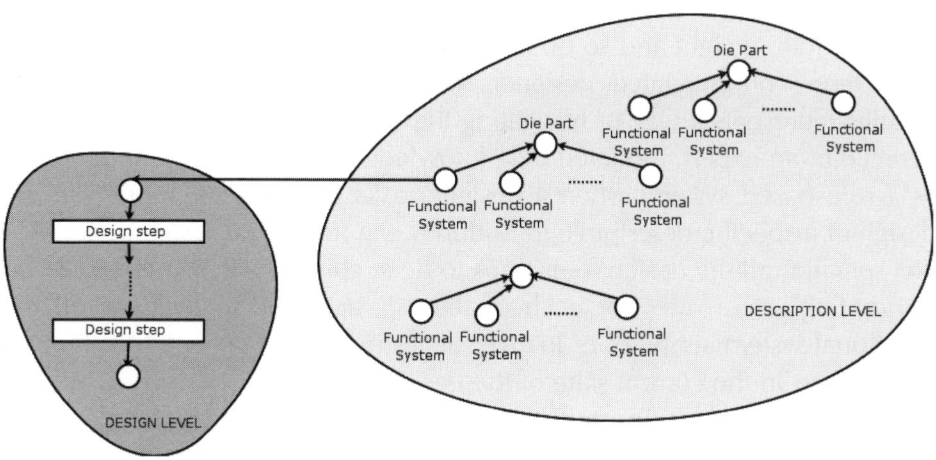

Fig. 12. A SA*–Net has two classes of transitions, descriptive transitions and design transitions.

can decide which part to define, being sure that the system will be able to support him/her in the execution of all the steps necessary to complete the chosen part of the die.

Since the set of design activities is composed of a number of steps that are not necessarily sequentially ordered, the SA*–Nets are provided with syntactic elements to manage sequential, concurrent and binding processes: A *sequential process* is a collection of design steps that must be necessarily accomplished according to a sequential order; A *concurrent process* is a collection of design steps that can be executed at the same time; A *binding process* is a collection of design steps belonging to *different* descriptive transitions where the execution of the transitions must preserve specific precedence constraints.

Four SA*–Nets have been designed and implemented in IDS, one for each part of the die: Die Seat net, Matrix net, Binder net and Punch net. These SA*–Nets have been implemented according to the DTD described in Section 3.5.

4.5. *Representing experiential knowledge*

Finally, a very important aspect of the die design decision making process captured by the IDS system is the possibility for an expert designer to exploit his/her own experience to execute a specific task by means of an opportune knowledge artifact.

SA*–Nets are able to capture procedural aspects in the design of a functional system, but they cannot be used to evaluate its parameters and geometric features. The configuration of a functional system in terms of height, width, weight and so on is made in the IDS system through a set of rules representing related designers competence. In other words, a set of rules represents a way of navigating the SA*–Nets according to the competence of an expert, modeled by a knowledge artifact that is implemented as a rule–based system: when a designer asks IDS to be supported in the design of a specific descriptive transition (i.e. a functional system), the SA*–Net specifies all the design transitions to be accomplished. Moreover, a corresponding set of rules for each of them is activated to evaluate all the functional system attributes or to give suggestions about the right position for a given part in the current state of the design.

Initialization values are startup information about the project (e.g. who is the customer, what kinds of presses the die will be mounted on and their dimensions, and so on). Such information can induce modifications in the specification of the design transition: for example, a customer could impose

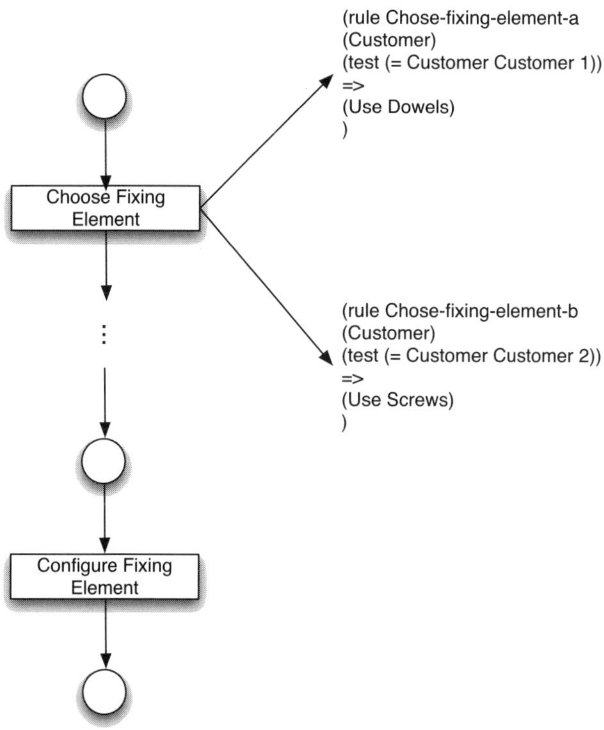

Fig. 13. The same design step could be specified by different group of rules according to different preconditions. Here, the choice about the use of dowels or screws in building the Fixing System depends on the name of the customer. On the right, how to represent constraints between design transitions in the corresponding rules.

to designers the use of dowels instead of screws in the definition of Fixing System. This fact would be represented in the IDS system by the definition of two distinct rules, as shown in Figure 13.

Preconditions in the left hand side of a rule can also be the specification of a constraint between a binding process and another design step. In this case, the binding process should have been executed before the other in order to generate useful information for the second one (e.g. the dimension of a hole is useful for choosing the right screw). An example of this kind of constraints is the creation of an object of the ontology: the binder is typically designed after the punch because its width and length are equal to the ones of the punch. Thus, there is a constraint between the punch and binder SA*–Nets such as the one shown in Figure 14. When the designer is going to define the binder width and length, the existence of a constraint involving the corresponding design transitions coming from the punch SA*–Net is

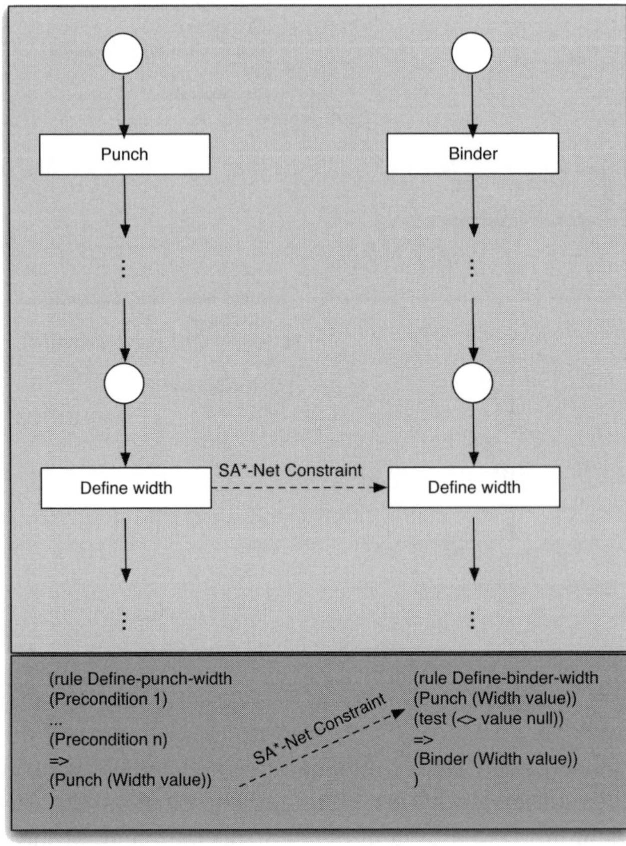

Fig. 14. How to represent constraints between design transitions in the corresponding rules.

detected. This constraint is specified by a rule through the specification of a test about the precedent evaluation of punch width and length. If the test is satisfied (i.e. there exists an ontology element named punch that has been created as a consequence of the punch descriptive transition in the punch SA*–Net whose width value is different from null) the binder width can be evaluated by IDS. Otherwise, the user will be notified about the need for executing the define width design transition in the punch SA*–Net before proceeding with the binder.

5. Conclusions

This chapter has presented an overview of available approaches to Knowledge–Based Engineering, a discipline that aims at supporting the design and manufacturing of mechanical objects. While most of such approaches has been traditionally led to the CAD/CAM/CAE areas, in the last years many benefits have been obtained from the integration with Knowledge Management methodologies, devoted to support designers through the development of knowledge models of their decision making processes rather than the typical evaluation of geometric constraints supplied by CAD softwares.

Anyway, the development of KBE systems is not simple, due to the heterogeneous nature of knowledge involved, that is typically divided into three categories: functional, procedural and experiential knowledge. This Chapter has presented a summarization of five years research in this area, with the definition of a clear and complete conceptual and computational framework to make simpler this hard activity, starting from the identification of some important connections among these knowledge kinds.

The framework is based on the definition of functional ontology as a mean to characterize a mechanical object from the standpoint of function to supply rather than the components it must be made of, that is the CAD approach. Doing so, also the attempt to model the procedural knowledge as a sequential and/or concurrent set of activities to be accomplished in the design task becomes simpler. Procedural knowledge is modeled in the framework through the exploitation of SA*–Nets which allow the system to take care of precedence constraints among the different design steps notifying the user when any constraint violation is detected. Finally the notion of Knowledge Artifact has been introduced to unify Functional and Procedural knowledge representation with the support of competencies and experience owned by the designer.

This framework has been widely adopted in decision support systems with the aim to help designers of mechanical objects in their activities: in this Chapter, the IDS system has been introduced for historical reasons (the IDS project has been the starting point of the approach development). Anyway, a couple of more recent systems have been successfully realized applying the same ideas, namely the *Terra Modena*[35] and the *Guitar Hero*[36] projects, concerning the supermotard bike and electric guitar design and manufacturing domains respectively, which are not included in this work: The heterogeneity of systems implemented according to the framework presented here is a first important proof of its effectiveness.

References

1. Oldham, K, S Kneebone, M Callot, A Murton and R Brimble. Moka a methodology and tools oriented to knowledge-based engineering applications. MOKA Project web site, available at http://www.kbe.coventry.ac.uk/moka.

2. Sriram, R and *et al.*, (1989). *Knowledge-based system application in engineering design Research at MIT* (MIT press).
3. Scrivener, S. A. R, W Tseng and L Ball. (2002). The impact of functional knowledge on sketching. In eds. T. Hewett and T. Kavanagh, *Proceedings of the 4th International Conference on Creativity and Cognition (C&C 2002),* New York. ACM Press.
4. Friedland, P. (1981). Acquisition of procedural knowledge from domain experts. In *Proceedings of International International Joint Conference on Artificial Intelligence (IJCAI 81),* pp. 856–861. Morgan-Kaufmann Publishers.
5. Colombo, E, G Colombo and F Sartori (2005). Managing functional and ontological knowledge in the design of complex mechanical objects. In *AI*IA,* pp. 608–611.
6. Girault, C and W Reisig, (eds.), (1982). *Application and Theory of Petri Nets,* Vol. 52, *Informatik-Fachberichte.* Springer. ISBN 3-540-11189-1.
7. Bandini, S. and F Sartori (2006). Industrial mechanical design: The ids case study. In ed. J. Gero, *Proceedings of 2nd International Conference on Design Computing and Cognition.* Springer-Verlag.
8. Puppe, F. (1996) *A Systematic Introduction to Expert Systems* (Springer–Verlag, Berlin).
9. Brown, DC, MB Waldron and H Yoshikawa (eds.), (1992). *Intelligent Computer Aided Design, Proceedings of the IFIP WG 5.2 Working Conference on Intelligent Computer Aided Design (IntCAD91), Columbus, OH, USA, 30 September – 3 October 1991,* Vol. B-4, *IFIP Transactions.* North-Holland. ISBN 0-444-81560-0.
10. Gero, J and ML Maher (1997). A framework for research in design computing. In *15th ECAADE–Conference Proceedings.*
11. Gero, JS (1990). Design prototypes: A knowledge representation schema for design, *AI Magazine.* **11**(4), 26–36. ISSN 0738-4602.
12. Maher, ML, B Balanchandran and DM Zhang (1995). *Case-based Reasoning in Design.* (Lawrence Erlbaum Associates).
13. Guarino, N (1998). Some ontological principles for designing upper level lexical resources. In *Proceedings of the First International Conference on Lexical Resources and Evaluation,* Granada, Spain.
14. Deng, Y (2002). Function and behaviour representation in conceptual mechanical design, *Artificial Intelligence Engineering Design Analysis Manufacturing.* **16**, 343–362.
15. Kitamura, Y, T Sano K Namba and R Mizoguchi (2002). A functional concept ontology and its application to automatic identification of functional structures, *Advanced Engineering Informatics.* **16**(2), 145–163.

16. Bracewell, R and K Wallace (2001). Designing a representation to support function-means based synthesis of mechanical design solutions. In *Proceedings of ICED 01.*
17. Umeda, Y and *et al.*, (1996). Supporting conceptual design based on the function-behavior-state modeler, *Artificial Intelligence for Engineering Design, Analysis and Manufacturing.* **10**, 275–288.
18. Umeda, Y and T Tomiyama (1997). Functional reasoning in design, *IEEE Expert: Intelligent Systems and Their Applications.* **12**(2), 42–48. ISSN 0885-9000.
19. Pahl, G and W Beitz (1988). *Engineering Design — A systematic Approach.* (The Pitman Press).
20. Chandrasekaran, B, AK Goel and Y Iwasaki (1993). Functional representation as design rationale, *IEEE Computer.* **26**(1), 48–56.
21. Simone, C (1993). Computer-supported cooperative work, petri nets and related formalisms. In *Proceedings of Workshop on Petri Nets,* Chicago, USA, (June 22).
22. Bandini, S, G Colombo and F Sartori (2005). Towards the integration of ontologies and sa–nets to manage design and engineering core knowledge. In eds. M-A Sicilia, SS Alonso, E Garcia-Barriocanal and JJ Cuadrado-Gallego, *Proceedings of the 1st International Workshop on Ontology, Conceptualization and Epistemology for Software and System Engineering (ONTOSE 05), Alcalà de Henares, Madrid, June 9–10,* Vol. 143. CEUR-WS. available at http://ftp.informatik.rwth-aachen.de/publications/CEUR-WS/Vol-143/.
23. Guarino, N and R Poli (1995). Formal ontology in conceptual analysis and knowledge representation, *International Journal of Human and Computer Studies.* **43**(5/6).
24. Hilpinen, R (1998). "artifact". The Stanford Encyclopedia of Philosophy (fall 2004 Edition), Edward N. Zalta (ed.).
25. Michelis, GD (1998). *Aperto, moteplice, continuo.* (Dunod, Milano).
26. Chandrasekaran, B (1990). Design problem solving: A task analysis, *AI Magazine.* **11** (4), 59–71.
27. Akkermans, H *et al.*, (1994). Commonkads: A comprehensive methodology for KBS development, *IEEE Expert.* pp. 28–37.
28. Sure, Y, S Staab and R Studer (2004) On-to-knowledge methodology (OTKM). In eds. S. Staab and R. Studer, *Handbook on Ontologies,* International Handbooks on Information Systems, pp. 117–132. Springer. ISBN 3-540-40834-7.
29. Hustadt, U, B Motik and U Sattler (2005). Data complexity of reasoning in very expressive description logics. In *Proceedings of 19th International International Joint Conference on Artificial Intelligence (IJCAI 81),* pp. 466–471. Morgan-Kaufmann Publishers.

30. Broekstra, J, A Kampman and FV Harmelen (2003). Sesame: An architecture for storing and querying rdf data and schema information. In *Spinning the Semantic Web*, pp. 197–222. MIT Press.
31 Knublauch, H, MA Musen and AL Rector (2004). Editing description logic ontologies with the protègè owl plugin. In *Description Logics, CEUR Workshop 104*. Morgan-Kaufmann Publishers.
32. Haarslev, V, Y Lu and N Shiri (2004). Ontoxpl — intelligent exploration of owl ontologies in web intelligence. In *Proceedings of the 2004 IEEE/WIC/ACM International Conference on Web Intelligence*, pp. 624–627. EEE Computer Society.
33. Radicioni, DP and V Lombardo (2005). A csp approach for modeling the hand gestures of a virtual guitarist. In *AI*IA*, pp. 470–473.
34. Ram, S and G Shankaranarayanan (1999). Modeling and navigation of large in-formation spaces: A semantics based approach. In *Proceedings of the 32nd Annual Hawaii International Conference on System Sciences*, pp. 157–168. EEE Computer Society.
35. Colombo, G, A Mosca, M Palmonari and F Sartori (2007). An upper-level functional ontology to support distributed design. In eds. D. Micucci, F. Sartori, and M. A. Sicilia, *Ontose 07*. Centro Copie Bicocca. ISBN 978-88-900910-1.
36. Bandini, S, A Bonomi and F Sartori (2008). Guitar hero, a knowledge–based system to support creativity in the design and manufacturing of electric guitars. In eds. J Gero and AK Goel, *Dcc 08*, pp. 181–200. Springer. ISBN 978-1-4020-8727-1.

CHAPTER III.6

METADATA AND ONTOLOGIES FOR EMERGENCY MANAGEMENT

Leopoldo Santos-Santos* and Tomás Aguado-Gómez

CIS Program Office, Emergency Military Unit (UME)
Base Aérea de Torrejón de Ardoz A-2 km.22,5, Madrid
**lsantos@et.mde.es*

During last five years we have given a jump forward in the field of emergency management and therefore in the way of focusing the solution. At present, we are including ontologies and metadata for developing this kind of systems, and also there are big efforts to standardize the way that emergencies are communicated and coordinated.

This chapter describes the state of art and efforts to standardize this field.

1. Introduction

In the last years, recent disasters have forced the authorities and governments of the whole world to create structures able to manage this kind of events. Unfortunately, we have a lot examples like, in the USA, the 9/11 terrorist attacks on the World Trade Center and the devastation caused by hurricane Katrina in New Orleans, in Europe, the 11 March 2004 Madrid train bombings (also known as 11/3 and in Spanish as 11-M) or the 7 July 2005 London bombings (also called the 7/7 bombings) and the floods in Central Europe during 2005, in Asia the tsunami of 2004, or the hurricanes that raze Center America. These disasters have provoked the reaction and the search of technological solutions that allow to be anticipated or at least to coordinate the different agencies and services that work to relieve the effects of these kinds of events.

There is a lot of literature in the area of Emergency Management Systems and they can refer to these systems with different names like Disaster Management Systems, Emergency Management Systems, Emergency Response Management

Systems,[1] Crisis Management Systems, Crisis Information Management Systems[2] and also Critical Incident Management Systems (CIMS) with the same acronym that the previous one.

Specific kind of emergency management systems are the directed ones to manage the critical infrastructures. But all of them can be named Emergency Management Systems (EMS). The important concept underlies these different names is the idea of a framework which define common messages formats, showing alerts and warnings, communicating resources position, reporting about the activities of these resources, showing the situation awareness, evaluating course of action and helping in decision support to the person in charge of the emergency.

After a brief description of the different technologies involved in EMS, this chapter will try to reflect the efforts of the scientific community to solve the interoperability needs of these systems by means of metadata and ontologies.

1.1. *Emergency domain*

There are many types of events like, floods, earthquakes, hurricanes, forest fire, terrorist attacks, nuclear accidents, chemical or biological accidents, etc. In our approach, we try to think in an Emergency as a system and classify in domains, in other systems as sectors.

In Canada [21], they have grouped infrastructures into ten key sectors: energy and utilities, communication and information technology, finance, healthcare, food, water, transportation, safety, government and manufacturing. In US [11], they have classified the infrastructures into 13 individual sectors: agriculture, food, water, public health, emergency services, government, defense industrial base, information and telecommunication, energy, transportation, banking and finance, chemical industry and postal and shipping.

In order to evaluate the range of an emergency and the necessary resources to manage it in an effective form is necessary to develop a systemic analysis of all the possible natural, infrastructure and organizational sectors (affected domains) that could turn affected by a risk specified in one of the domains

[1] Brooks distinguish between Emergency Response Management Systems (ERMS) and Emergency Response Systems Management (ERSM) in http://ontolog.cim3.net/cgi-bin/wiki.pl?ConferenceCall_2007_01_25#nidSH5.

[2] Crisis Management Information Systems (CIMS). R. Iannella describes a framework about CIMS in [40].

of risk. According to UME responsibilities in Spain, we have done the following classification:

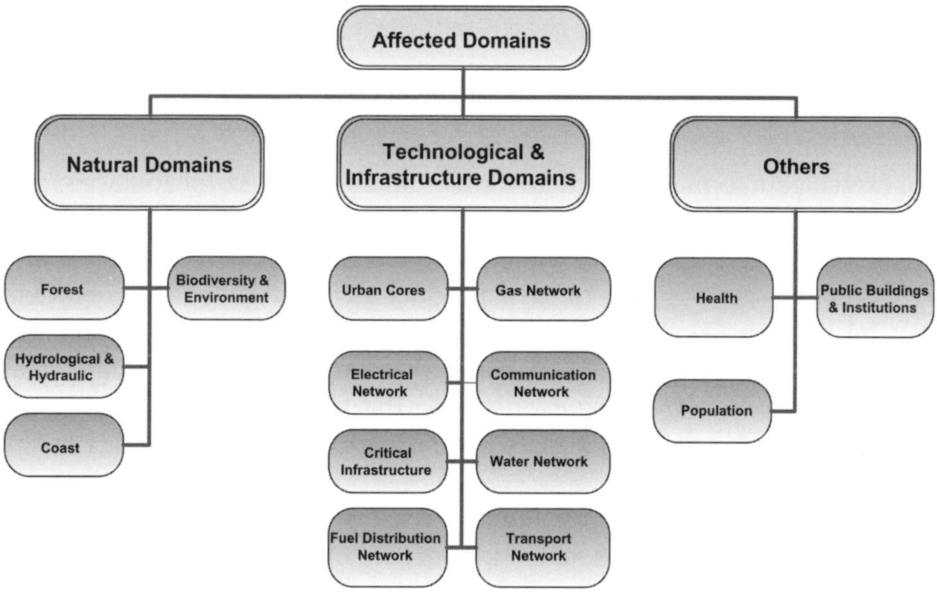

Fig. 1. Affected domains in UME.

The risks can be also divided in natural like fires, floods, earthquakes, tsunamis, big snowfalls and other adverse meteorological phenomena, technological risks like chemical, biological, nuclear, environment pollution, and others risks like terrorists attacks.

1.2. *Emergency management phases*

The Emergency Management Systems divide this process into several phases. According to Corina Warfield[3] and Valeria Hwacha in [49], we can find four different phases. *The Mitigation Phase* is concerned with minimizing the effects of possible disasters and preparing the community to effectively confront a disaster. *The Preparedness Phase* focuses on the elaboration of the plans, exercises and warnings trying to put into practice the procedures and mechanisms to be used. *The Response Phase* manages the effects of the

[3] "The Disaster Management Cycle". Available at http://www.gdrc.org/uem/disasters/1-dm_cycle.html.

disaster and takes the mobilization of resources as an aim to face to the emergency. Finally, *the Recovery Phase* tries to take to a situation of normality where the domains are affected by the emergency.

Sanderson [37] proposes to divide it in six phases from the CIS[4] point of view:

- Phase 1 — *A priori*: This phase is actually before the accident, when the relevant organizations — in cooperation with the authorities — will exchange information on data formats and any shared vocabularies, and make agreements on procedures and working methods. This phase can be called *Coordination* or *Establishment of Service.*
- Phase 2 — *Briefing*: This phase starts once an accident has been reported. The briefing involves gathering of information about the disaster, e.g., weather, location, number of people involved, and facilities in the area.
- Phase 3 — *Bootstrapping the network*: This phase takes place at the rescue site, and involves devices joining and registering as nodes in the network on arrival.
- Phase 4 — *Running of the network*: This is the main phase during the rescue operation. Events that may affect the middleware services include nodes joining and leaving the network and network partitions and merges. Information is collected, exchanged and distributed.
- Phase 5 — *Closing of the network*: At the end of the rescue operation all services must be terminated and the operations must be archived.
- Phase 6 — *Post processing*: After the rescue operation it could be useful to analyze resource use, user movements, and how and what type of information was shared, to gain knowledge for future situations. In different systems this phase is called *Lessons Learnt.*

2. How we are using the technology in disasters and emergencies

There is a small revision of which Technologies are we using and how they can be applied into EMS.

2.1. *SOA*

At present, the most practical way to interconnect different systems is by using a Service-Oriented Architecture (SOA) with the nodes of different systems connected one-by-one by a client–server relationship. The web services

[4] CIS: Communication and Information Systems.

technology is the base to implement SOA, and this web services are software applications which can be discovered, described an accessed with XML and different web protocols through intranets, extranets and Internet.

2.1.1. *CAP y EDXL*

One of the first organizations that have tried to describe events related to emergencies and disasters is Organization for the Advancement of Structured Information Standards (OASIS) (http://www.oasis-open.org). The result of this initiative is Common Alert Protocol (CAP),[5] an OASIS standard adopted September 30, 2005. In July 2008, the Department of Homeland Security (DHS) through Federal Emergency Management Agency (FEMA) announced its intention to adopt during the first quarter of calendar year 2009, an alerting protocol in line with CAP as the standard for the Integrated Public Alert and Warning System (IPAWS).

CAP is a data interchange standard for alerting and event notification applications. At the end is a XML file which can function as a standalone protocol or a payload for other messages like Emergency Data Exchange Language (EDXL).

EDXL is a broad initiative to create an integrated framework for a wide range of emergency data exchange standards to support operations, logistics, planning and finance. This message comprises four components:

(a) EDXL Distribution Element (EDXL-DE)[6]: This is the most mature of OASIS family of standards (was approved on 1 May 2006) and the purpose is to facilitate the routing of any properly formatted XML and work as a container providing the information to route payloads, such as CAP.
(b) EDXL Hospital AVailability Exchange (EDXL-HAVE): This message is still in draft[7] version and the primary purpose is to communicate the status of a hospital, its services and its resources. These include bed capacity and availability, emergency department status, available service coverage, and the status of a hospital.s facility and operations.
(c) EDXL Resource Message (EDXL-RM): The current draft[8] works with 16 different messages and the primary purpose is to manage (covering from the

[5] Common Alerting Protocol, v. 1.1 OASIS Standard CAP-V1.1, October 2005.
[6] Emergency Data Exchange Language (EDXL) Distribution Element, v. 1.0 OASIS Standard EDXL-DE v1.0, 1 May 2006.
[7] Emergency Data Exchange Language (EDXL) Hospital AVailability Exchange (HAVE) Version 1.0 Public Review Draft 05, 04 March 2008.
[8] Emergency Data Exchange Language Resource Messaging (EDXL-RM) 1.0 Public Review Draft 02, 31 January 2008.

offering, requesting, requisitioning, committing up to the releasing) resources needed in an emergency.

(d) EDXL Reference Information Model (EDXL-RIM): The purpose of the EDXL-RIM specification is to provide a high-level, abstract, information model for the family of EDXL specifications. At present, there is no public specification.

Iannella Robinson and Rinta-Koski [40] shows the relationship between the EDXL and other interoperability standards in terms of their roles.

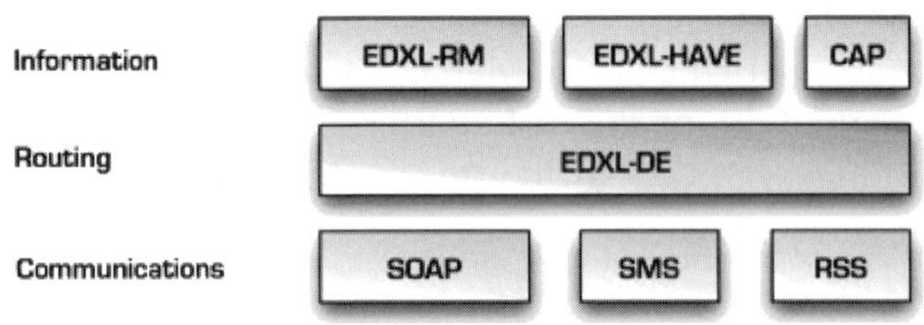

Fig. 2. CIMS interoperability layers.

2.1.2. *TSO (Tactical Situation Object)*

Also the European Union through an European Commission initiative named also OASIS (**O**pen **A**dvanced **S**ystem for d**IS**aster & emergency management, http://www.oasis-fp6.org) and the sixth framework project have tried to develop standards for this kind of events. In this framework project was defined the TSO.[9]

2.1.3. *CESAR (Coordination of Emergencias and Tracking[10] of Activities and Resources)*

CESAR is a initiative from UME[11] based on TSO but including symbology associated to events, resources and missions. Also we have suited the Data Dictionary taking into account how are managed this kind of situations in Spain, by different regional and state agencies.

[9] Definition of the OASIS Tactical Situation Object and the current version of this protocol is 1.4 from 10 /08/2006.

[10] Tracking in spanish is Seguimiento.

[11] UME is the acronym for Emergency Military Unit. This unit was created in 2006 by Spanish Government to manage Crisis related with emergencies.

2.2. *GIS*

Geographical Information Systems (GIS) have become essential in the management of critical situations where it is imperative to count on summarized, precise and spatially located information.

Either talking about military operations or emergency management, the need to know not only our resources and their capacities, but their location too, is crucial to manage them in an effective way. The spatial representation of this information together with the boundaries and events that define the current emergency makes possible an efficient management of the emergency, which could save lives or be critical infrastructures.

The information geographical component in the scope of an EMS is important because it complements and spatially contextualizes the alphanumerical data managed by the system. New relationships arise between the components of our ontology based on their spatial connection. For example, one of the most important facts to define the emergency level would be its location and its proximity to other entities, for example critical infrastructures like Nuclear Plants, Natural resources, Schools, Hospitals, etc.

Thus GIS help to assess the current situation:

- Emergency groups would be usually unfamiliar with the terrain they are operating in.
- Would help to correlate apparently disconnected events.
- Identify potentially risky situations on their first stages.
- Identify patterns in the development of similar emergencies.
- Spatial data fusion.

2.2.1. *Spatial information sharing*

Emergency management involves multiple domains, jurisdictions and systems. Each of them could have its own way of managing spatial data and that is where information sharing and ontologies play their role.

Emergency Management Units usually depend on third party entities information to count on detailed information to operate in the scope of the emergency.

A major emergency involves multiple domains managed by different entities. Those entities are not forced to share their information, thus Emergency Management Units need to create ad hoc agreements with each organization, and there is no standard way of communicating such events and resources information.

The need of integrating and sharing data is where Ontologies try to fix the problems appeared in this environment full of heterogeneous services. As described in [40], Ontologies could be used to implement a dynamic search engine of GIS Services.

The geospatial data exchanged with other entities for the UME to operate in an efficient way should be:

- **TIMELY**
  Emergency management information has an extremely low life time, thus UME should be able to receive the information coming from other organizations as soon as possible. This could be achieved via prearranged technical agreements.
- **ACCURATE**
  The quality of the information falls on third party organizations side. However, this quality should be improved by the use of ontologies and intelligent reasoning over them.
- **COMPATIBLE**
  This capacity is achieved by the use of CESAR data exchange format. The use of temporal translating engines to integrate non-standard protocols should always be considered as provisional.
- **ACCESIBLE**
  The entire data exchange model is based on the infrastructure of the RENEM (National Network for Emergency Management).

One of the key concepts aimed to facilitate and coordinate the exchange and share of spatial data in the terms exposed above, is the Spatial Data Infrastructure (SDI). SDI cover all the user needs related to the distribution of spatial data within an organization, encompassing users, data, networks, spatial data standards, security policies, etc.

SDI's applied to emergency management pose great advantages as stated in [18]:

- Effective dispersion of the large amount of spatial data needed across all the SDI.
- Dynamic spatial data regarding the evolution of events in the scope of an emergency is the most important data during response time; SDI's would enable fast sharing of this kind of information.
- Sharing data implies higher quality data, as all the stakeholders related to emergency management cooperate to complete it.

- Cost reduction.
- Common contingency plans across all the emergency management stakeholders.
- When information is shared between several emergency management institutions common, coherent, summarized information could be provided with very little effort improving the trust that citizens have on it.

Several initiatives have been carried out related to GIS and SDI's applied to Emergency Management:

- Geographical Data Infrastructure for Emergency Management (GDI4DM[12]).
- Geo-Information for risk Management (PREVIEW[13]).
- ORCHESTRA. This project already has a published Ontology Access Interface[14] to solve the problems stated in this chapter.
- INSPIRE.[15] European Directive aimed to blend and homogenize geographical information across Europe through the implementation of an European SDI.
- Global Monitoring for Environment and Security (GMES[16]).
- Department of Homeland Security (DHS) Geospatial Data Model.
- DHS endorsed standards.[17]

Two approaches to solve the heterogeneity problem could be followed, INSPIRE tries to achieve a common SDI at a higher level so semantic interoperability is possible. On the other hand, the DHS tries to achieve semantic interoperability using a low level common Geospatial Data Model aimed to achieve interoperability between all the Emergency Management Units.

One of the challenges of the INSPIRE directive is to achieve a common spatial data conceptual model for all the different domains. The GeoDatabases INSPIRE tries to link have different origins, missions, scopes, representations and semantics.

The use of ontologies in INSPIRE has been proposed to provide semantic interoperability between all the data sources affected by the directive [28].

---

[12] http://www.gdi4dm.nl/

[13] http://www.preview-risk.com/site/FO/scripts/myFO_accueil.php?lang=EN

[14] http://www.eu-orchestra.org/docs/OA-Specs/Ontology_Access_Service_Specification_v2.1-ETHZ-IITB.pdf

[15] http://inspire.jrc.ec.europa.eu/

[16] http://www.gmes.info/

[17] http://www.fgdc.gov/standards/projects/FGDC-standards-projects/fgdc-endorsed-standards

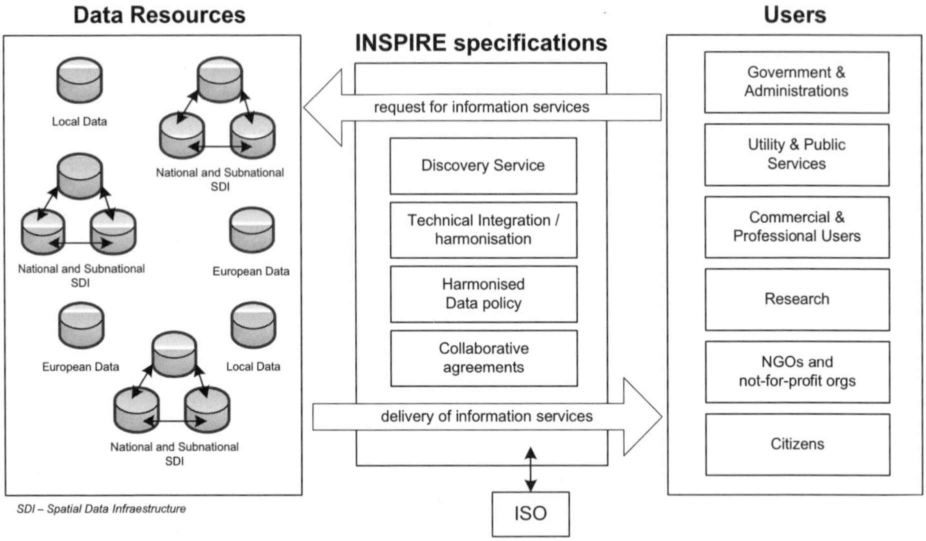

Fig. 3. INSPIRE high level project Informatión Flow.[18]

But ontologies are useless without a common and coherent metadata definition.

In order to allow ontologies to perform semantic search across several services, correct descriptions (known as metadata) should be defined and published. Ontologies should take into account high level differences, like language independency for data dictionary and so on.

Several initiatives have been carried out to enable spatial data sharing at a lower level that is sharing the same data model. The DHS Geospatial Data Model is based on Open Geospatial Consortium (OGC[19]) standards, and it has become a standard itself.

The main aim of the System is to provide a common, standard and extensible basis for all the members involved in Emergency Management.

The initiative does not only define the model, but its associated metadata too analyzing the following aspects[20] which could be used to build higher level ontologies:

- Identification. Not only the ID but the geographical scope, restrictions, origin, etc.

[18] http://snig.igeo.pt/Inspire/documentos/Consulta_Internet/INSPIRE-InternetConsultation-Phase1.pdf
[19] http://www.opengeospatial.org/standards
[20] http://www.fgdc.gov/metadata/documents/workbook_0501_bmk.pdf

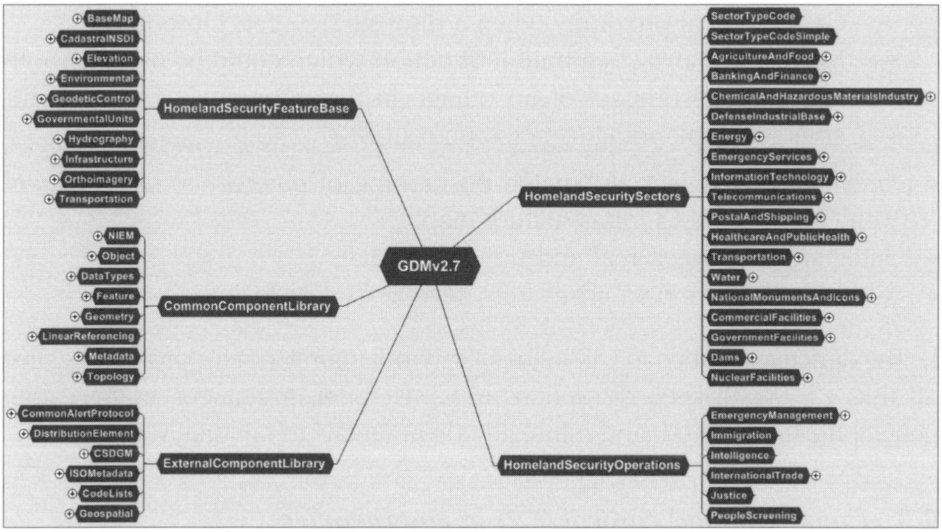

Fig. 4. DHS geospatial data model GML implementation guide.[21]

- Data Quality. This field is important because crucial decisions are based on the accuracy of the data.
- Spatial Data organization. Information related to the model used to represent the Spatial Data.
- Spatial Reference. Specific coordinate system and datum used to represent data.
- Entity and Attribute Definition. Metadata directly related to the kind of information represented (roads, wind direction, temperature, flooded area).
- Distribution. Origin, available formats.

2.2.2. *GIS and Critical Infrastructure Protection (CIP)*

Although CIP will be analyzed on subsequent chapters, it is important to present the benefits that GIS Systems provide to CIP as exposed in [12] GIS gives the following benefits related to CIP protection:

- Enables information sharing in common locations.
- Information requirements related to disasters have usually spatial attributes.

[21] http://www.fgdc.gov/participation/working-groups-subcommittees/hswg/subgroups/info-content-sg/documents/DHS-GDM-v1.1.pdf

- GIS gives a built in risk analysis:
  - Geographical proximity when a disaster area gets close to a CI.
  - Network Analysis is a built in function which could be used for both risk analysis (impact of an outage in a gas pipeline, etc.) and for emergency planning (evacuation routes).
- Integration between automated positioning of emergency management vehicles and the CI infrastructure map.
- Integration between real and simulated data.
- New intelligence data arises from several CI data fusion.

The directives related to CIP in the US[22] work mainly not to "protect" against all risks CI, but to keep disruptions in CI as "brief, infrequent, manageable, geographically isolated, and minimally detrimental" to national welfare.

2.3. *Command and control (C2) in emergencies*

Once you receive information about an emergency using CAP or CESAR, the system has to represent the information in a GIS to get the emergency Situational Awareness (SAW) in order to practice C2 of the emergency. The problem arises when you receive a big amount of heterogeneous data from different sources or sensors and it is difficult to reach common situation awareness because some sensors report duplicated information but using different data and the number of relations among these data is potentially infinite. In this context, the user has to define which relations are important according to the mission. At this point, we have to solve an Information Fusion problem.

2.3.1. *Context or situation awareness*

In [9], Matheus *et al.* explain that "maintaining a coherent *situation awareness* (SAW) concerning all units operating in a region of interest (e.g., battlefield environment, emergency disaster scene, counter-terrorism event) is essential for achieving successful resolution of an evolving situation. They call this process of achieving SAW, *situation analysis*. This information is provided by sensors (humans or equipments). Although knowledge of the objects and their current attributes are essential, and help us to build the SAW, also is important the relations among the objects that are relevant to the current operation". For example, in emergencies is important to know

[22] http://fas.org/irp/offdocs/pdd/pdd-63.htm

that exist a fire (or a flood) but also that taking into account the speed of propagation due to factors like wind or type of combustible, can be a critical infrastructure or population in the axis of progression of this fire, and this information is provided by another sensor (in this case can be a simulator).

SAW is an important notion used in data fusion, in fact is the aim of level 2 in JDL model. The concept of "levels", speaking about data fusion, was defined by the well-known JDL[23] Model [6] (see Fig. 5). The meaning of level is defined as follow:

- Level 0: Signal/Feature Assessment — estimation and prediction of signal or feature states.
- Level 1: Entity Assessment — estimation and prediction of entity parametric and attributive states (i.e., of entities considered as individuals).
- Level 2: Situation Assessment — estimation and prediction of the structures of parts of reality (i.e., of relations among entities and their implications for the states of the related entities). This level is important to build the situation awareness.
- Level 3: Impact Assessment — estimation and prediction of the utility/cost of signal, entity or situation states — including predicted impacts given a system's alternative courses of action.

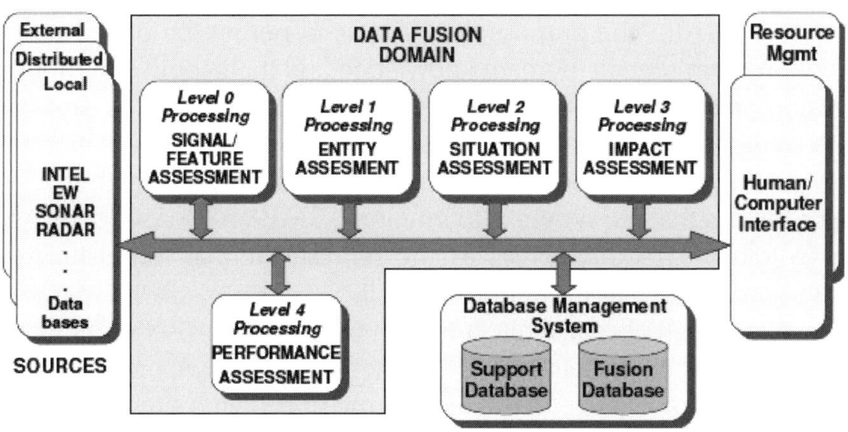

Fig. 5. Recommended revised data fusion model in [13].

[23]The origin came from the Data Fusion Group of the US Joint Directors of Laboratories (JDL) and was proposed in 1985 and published in 1988. After that JDL model has suffer two major revisions, the first in 1998 [] (A.N. Steinberg, 2008) and in 2004 [3] (J. Llinas, 2004). Currently the name of the group is DFIG (Data Fusion Information Group).

- Level 4: Performance Assessment — estimation and prediction of a system's performance as compared to given desired states and measures of effectiveness.

Others authors have included a level 5 for User Refinement as you can read in [13], [16], [15], [30] and [14] giving ideas about how users can interact with information fusion systems mainly to obtain decision support.

Once we have clarified some details about data fusion and situation awareness, it is important to distinguish the different kind of ontologies that we can use. As it is mentioned in [43], we have to take into account that ontologies may exist at many levels of abstraction and they group into three broad categories: Upper, Mid-level and Domain ontologies. Besides the definitions this paper includes a brief explanation of the following upper ontologies: SUMO, CyC and DOLCE. Also it evaluates these ontologies using criteria like licensing schema, structure, maturity and others like granularity and security.

At this moment, there are several approaches to develop an ontology-driven SAW.[24]

- SAWA (Situation Awareness Assistant) [10].
- Situation Ontology [44]

2.3.1.1. SAWA (Situation Awareness Assistant)

As is cited in [10], "the purpose of SAWA is to permit the offline development of problem specific domain knowledge and then apply it at runtime to the fusion and analysis of level-2 data. Domain knowledge is captured in SAWA using formal ontologies. The user controls the system situation monitoring requirements by specifying "standing relations", i.e., high-level relations or queries that the system is to monitor". SAWA have developed a SAW Core Ontology [10] that serves as the representational foundation of all domain knowledge that is built on top of it.

The SAWA High-Level Architecture has two aspects: a set of offline tools for Knowledge Management and a Runtime System of components for applying the domain knowledge to the monitoring of evolving situations.

SAWA is built with OWL and SWRL on top. Also they built a set of tools in order to make work easier with SWRL like a rule editor (RuleVISor, it also

[24]There are other approaches of ontologies not specifically for SAW, like SOUPA (Standard Ontology for Ubiquitous and Pervasive Applications) [19], CONON [50], and CoBrA [20] more centered in pervasive computing applications. In [33], you can find a comparison of these approaches.

assists with the generation of Jess rules), a consistency checker (ConsVISor) looking for semantic inconsistencies, and a GUI among others.

As we can see in [10], a Situation consists of Objects and Relations and a Goal (standing relation). Objects have AttributeTuples that are associated with specific Attributes and a collection of AttributeValues defined according to ExternalEvents. Relations are realized through RelationTuples that connect pairs of Objects with RelationValues defining by the firing of Rules.

2.3.1.2. Situation ontology

Due to the complexity of pervasive computing environments, it is impossible to enumerate all possible contexts and situations in a single ontology, then Situation Ontology [44] only models the upper ontology for context and situation by defining a set of core classes and relations using OWL DL to model context and situation in a hierarchical way such that the specifications for context and situation can be easily shared and reused among multiple entities. Designers can use various OWL ontology inferences over Situation Ontology like *RACER* or *Pellet.*

As mention in [44], "the contexts in our OWL-based situation ontology are aggregated as situations and complicate situations are composed of simple situations in a hierarchical structure to facilitate the sharing and reusing of context and situation knowledge since the semantics of context/situation specification can be clearly understood by all entities in the system. The hierarchical structure of situation ontology can be roughly divided to two layers: context layer and situation layer. By separating context layer and situation layer, we separate the context acquisition and processing from the situation evaluation, which gives a clearer view of SAW and facilitates SAW development."

The use of hierarchical situation ontology facilitates sharing and reusing of situation information, and can be easily extended with domain specific knowledge.

In [34], we can find several lessons learned which should be useful for developing ontology-driven information systems. They propose in this paper a domain-independent software architecture based on core ontology for situation awareness taking into account reusability and scalability.

Some authors [29] are using a new concept called Situation Theory Ontology (STO). The concepts expressed in OWL and the ones expressed using rules together form a formal ontology for situation awareness and both make STO. Using their own words "the field of situation awareness needs a unifying framework that would play the role of a common theory integrating various research efforts".

As mention Baumgartner *et al.* [35], ontology-driven SAW systems are still in their infancy, but you can find several scenarios in this document, one related with Road Traffic Management.

2.3.2. *Decision making in crisis operations*

The process comprises three levels: situation awareness, situation understanding and decision-making process which is based on level 3 data fusion (threat or impact assessment).

In [7], Steinberg presents ideas in estimating and predicting threat relationships and situations and he explains the difference between threat and impact (more broadened the last one). "Threat Assessment involves assessing situations to determine whether adversarial events are either occurring or expected". Speaking about emergencies, threat/impact assessment involves the following functions:

- Threat Event Prediction: Determining likely threat events (emergency situations): who, what, where, when, why, how.
- Indications and Warning: Recognition that an emergency is imminent or under way.
- Threat Entity Detection & Characterization: Determining the identities, attributes, composition, location/track, activity capability, intent of entities involved in a potential or current attack.
- Emergency (or Threat Event) Assessment:
  - Responsible parties (country, organization, individuals, etc.) and emergency roles.
  - Affected critical nodes.
  - Intended effect (future affected critical nodes in other domains).
  - Threat capability.
  - Force composition, coordination & tactics (goal and plan decomposition) to relieve the effects of the emergency.
- Consequence Assessment: Estimation and prediction of event outcome states and their cost/utility to the responsible parties, to affected parties or to the system user. These can include both intended and unintended consequences.

The results of this process (Threat/Impact Assessment) will be information useful for Decision Making. One of the first questions to appear is the choice

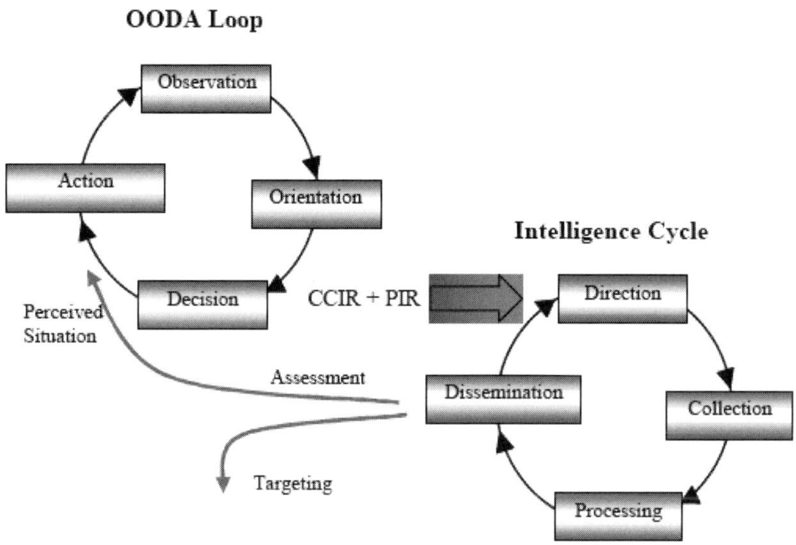

Fig. 6. Intelligence cycle interfacing with OODA loop [22].

of the model on whom there is going to be based the decision making process. There are several models in [1] and [48]:

1. Observe–Orient–Decide–Act (OODA) loop: (also known as Boyd's model[25]) is usually the model of decision-making process in military situations. This is used together with the intelligence cycle as you can see in Fig. 6.
2. Simon's model: "Simon's model was presented in 1979, but his original work did not include implementation, which has been added later. The classic Simon's problem solving model comprises three well-known phases: the Intelligence Phase, wherein the decision maker looks for indications that a problem exits, the Design Phase, wherein the alternatives are formulated and analyzed, and finally the Choice Phase, wherein one of the alternatives is selected and implemented".
3. Albert's and Hayes Model: "This model more explicitly defines the entire process of decision making and lays emphasis on information as a resource, the value of information towards decision making and defines collaboration as an important aspect towards sound decision making".

[25] Boyd was US Air Force fighter pilot and OODA is a model of decision-making created from observing jet fighter pilots in combat (Korean and Vietnam wars). With the time was adopted by other military services.

Once we have decided which model is adapted to our problem, we have to solve it. In [2], we have an example of Simon's model where domain knowledge is represented by ontologies and it is used for humanitarian logistics in emergency situations.

The adopted solution in [2] consists in a knowledge-based model of the user problem including an "ontology management for identification and definition of the problem, context management for organizing contextual information, and constraint satisfaction for problem solving". To take into account several constraints use the mechanism of Object-Oriented Constraint Networks (OOCN) and to solve them use Constraint Satisfaction Problem (CSP), and finally relate constraints with full first-order logics that is used in ontologies. In Fig. 7, we can see the conceptual framework of context-driven information integration for operational decision making.

In agreement with Simon's model, Smirnov *et al.* have taken into account two stages: a preliminary stage and a decision making stage. "The *preliminary stage* is responsible for preparedness of a decision support system to make decisions. Activities carried out at this stage are creation of semantics models for components of a decision support system information sources, domain knowledge representing the area of interests, and users), accumulating domain knowledge, and linking of domain knowledge to the environment sources (sensors, Web-sites, databases, etc.)" and the main component of the decision support system is an ontology-based representation of semantics of the problem.

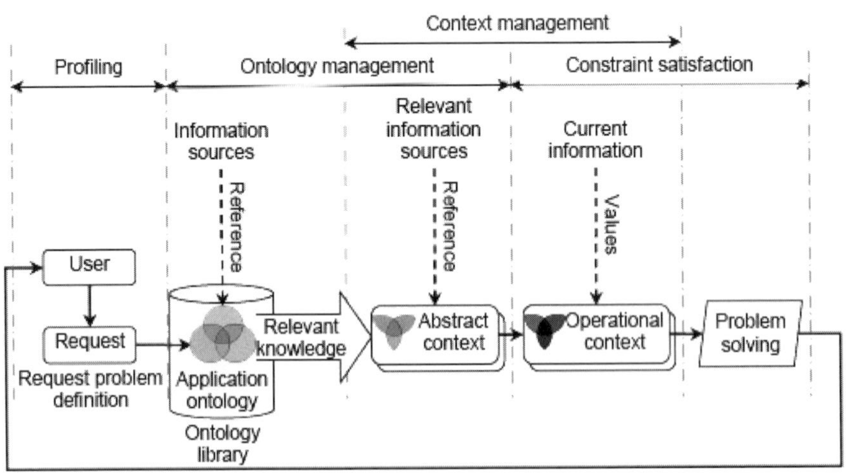

Fig. 7. Conceptual framework of context-driven information integration for operational decision making [3].

The second stage is called the *decision making stage* and it "deals with integration of information and knowledge relevant to the problem, problem description and solving". For this stage, the starting point is the user request in a free text form which is submitted to a recognition process to extract the relevant knowledge that in turn will be integrated using a mechanism of ontology-driven knowledge using consistency checking. The idea is to match the request vocabulary and the vocabulary of the ontology library. For problem description and solving they use a model called constraint satisfaction problem (CSP).[26]

The scenario described, in the preliminary stage select sources (transport infrastructures, meteorological information, etc.) and their information will be used by the decision support system but using real-time information from the selected sources.

In [3], Smirnov *et al.* propose an integrated framework for intelligent support for distributed operational decision making, and in Fig. 8 we can see this architecture. In [4], we can see an ontology editor with an example of

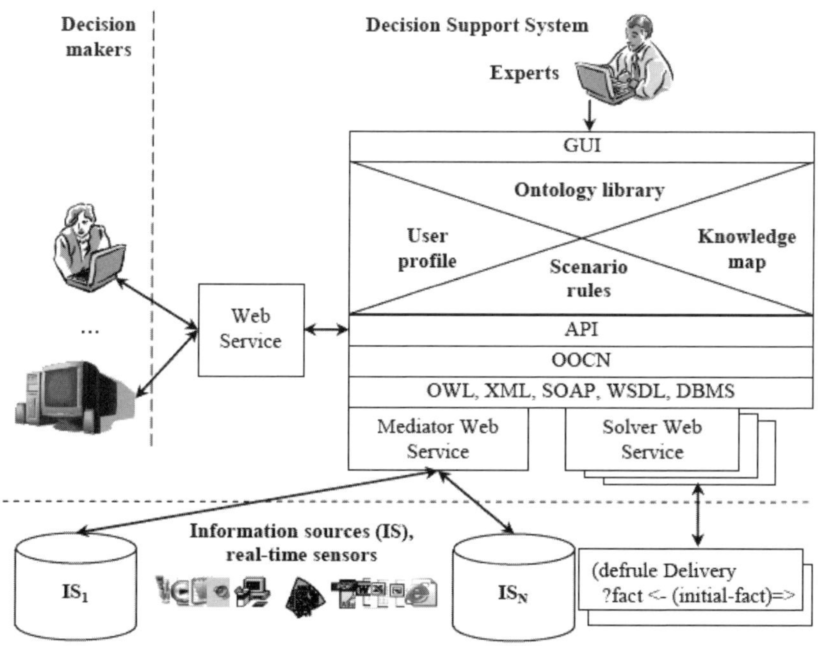

Fig. 8. Decision support system architecture described in [3].

[26]CSP model consists of three parts: a set of variables; for each variable, a set of possible values (its domain); and a set of constraints restricting the values that the variables can be simultaneously assigned. In [23], you can find more information about CSP.

indication of information source and the specification of a constraint, and in a taxonomy view of domain constituent of an abstract context (an example of a fire). We can see how to use the ontology as a sort of information filter, integrating information and knowledge that are relevant for a particular decision situation.

Independently of the model, it is important to identify the types of decisions for identifying the information that commanders need to support decision-making. In [25], Pauftz *et al.* show some key classes of decision types:

- Decisions related to classification and identification of threats.
- Decisions related to optimizing unit movement paths over a specified area.
- Decisions related to assessment of the health and status of the units.
- Decisions related to timing of action.
- Decisions related to threat and risk avoidance through appropriate resource allocation.

2.3.3. *Metadata and meta-information in command and control*

We can take advantage of metadata as a point of support to solve information fusion problem. It is important to recognize that for making good decisions we need information and also others parameters that provide quality about that information (parameters like recency, reliability, uncertainty, etc.). It is also important to distinguish between metadata and meta-information. According to [26], "are *characteristics or qualifiers* of data and information in some particular context, respectively. Metadata may be used in a variety of computational systems for filtering, managing, and processing data before it becomes an input to a decision-making process. Meta-information can be thought of as the qualifications or characteristics of that functional information that allows operators to correctly interpret that functional information as needed (e.g., this information is too old to be pertinent to my current situation)". In [25], Pauftz *et al.* has centered in meta-information (e.g., uncertainty, recency, pedigree), and its impact in situation awareness and decision-making processes. One of the most important aspects of these works is to visualize meta-information, not only uncertainty,[27] and how different types of meta-information influence the decision-making process.

In [25], Pauftz *et al.* identified the main types of meta-information that impact the decision-making process and important implications for

[27]You can find a weather forecast system displaying a managing uncertainty in [41]. Another example is a flood forecasting system [27] based also on uncertainty.

development of C2 support systems. This document explain a methodology based on *Cognitive Systems Engineering* (CSE)[28] to identify cognitive tasks and the impacts of meta-information in the decision-making process and how to visualize it. The examples presented in this paper highlight the potential impact of meta-information on decision-making and point to implications for future development of C2 support systems.

As show the Fig. XX-3 you can have several design recommendations for C2 decision-support systems taking into account data, metadata information and meta-information.

One example of an EMS where we can apply metadata in a different context from decision-making is [37] where we can find three kinds of metadata. The first category is related with information structure and content description metadata; this category addresses information item contents, structure and localization. The second kind, semantic metadata, covers concepts and relations in a domain, providing a semantic context. The third class of metadata is profile and context metadata, and this class of metadata includes profiles for users and devices, and context-related information, typically including location, time and situation. In [38], you can see another example.

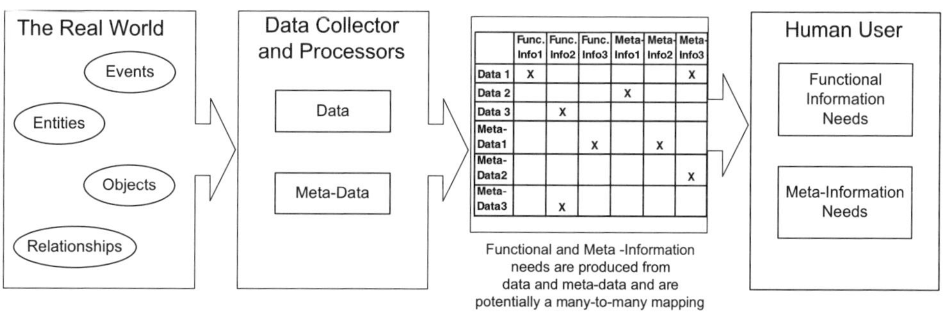

Fig. 9. Distinguishing among data, meta-data, information and meta-information in [26].

2.4. *Critical Infrastructure Protection (CIP)*

An appropriate definition taken from [42] might be this: A critical infrastructure is an array of assets and systems that, if disrupted, would threaten national security, economy, public health and safety, and way of life.

---

[28]As mention in [25], CSE is a methodology for defining aspects of human reasoning and behavior to aid system design.

In Canada, recent events [21] have realized the importance of Critical Infrastructure Protection and these have been grouped into 10 key sectors: energy and utilities, communication and information technology, finance, healthcare, food, water, transportation, safety, government and manufacturing.

In US [11], infrastructures have been classified into 13 individual sectors: agriculture, food, water, public health, emergency services, government, defense industrial base, information and telecommunication, energy, transportation, banking and finance, chemical industry and postal and shipping.

But more important is that the infrastructures in itself are the two types of knowledge within the critical infrastructure domain [42]. The first is the behaviors of a CI system when it is studied as a stand-alone system, which is called the intra-domain interdependencies. The second one is related to the interdependencies among domains, which is called the cross-domain interdependencies.

2.4.1. *Types of interdependencies*

Therefore and according to [11] interdependencies can be of different types:

- **Physical or Functional Interdependencies**: This is a requirement, often engineering reliance between components in order to operate properly.
- **Informational Interdependency**: An informational interdependency is an informational or control requirement between components. An example is a system that monitors or control another system, where the control system can fail.
- **Geospatial Interdependency**: A geospatial interdependency is a relationship that exists entirely because of the proximity of components.
- **Policy/Procedural Interdependency**: This relationship exists among entities due to policy or procedure that relates a state or event change in one infrastructure sector component to a subsequent effect on another component.
- **Societal Interdependency**: Societal interdependencies or influences refer to the effects that an infrastructure event may have on societal factors such as public opinion, public confidence, fear and cultural issues.

In [36], Svendsen and Wolthusen define a single node as you can see in Fig. 10.

2.4.2. *Ontology-based information systems for critical infrastructures*

2.4.2.1. GenOM

In words of McNally, Lee, Yavagal and Xiang [42], Generic Object Model (GenOM) is a knowledge representation and management tool that aids the design and development of software applications by using object-oriented technologies.

As shown in Fig. 10, a domain-specific application is built on top of the GenOM foundation layer, while GenOM itself serves as an integrated environment to create, edit browse, search and maintain various types of objects in the application domain model. An application domain model is represented by class, property, feature and instance objects in GenOM knowledge base which is also the rule base. The inference model provides a rule engine that can infer relationships in the object model hierarchy. The viewpoints model provides a way to identify and incorporate different views or perspectives of the domain model. The visualization model provides a mechanism to visualize the object model hierarchy. The collaboration model supports various mechanisms that facilitate collaborative domain model construction through semantic integration of knowledge from multiple domain experts. In addition, GenOM provides mechanisms for mediating, mapping and integrating different levels of knowledge representation of domain-specific objects.

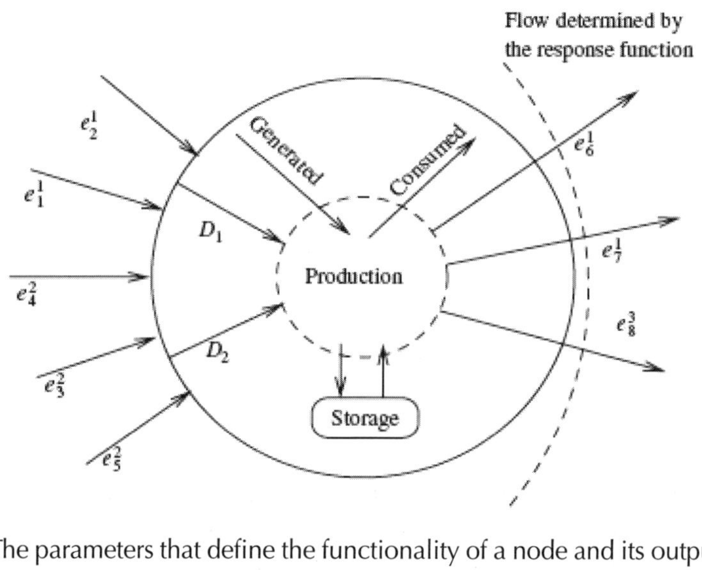

Fig. 10. The parameters that define the functionality of a node and its outputs in [36].

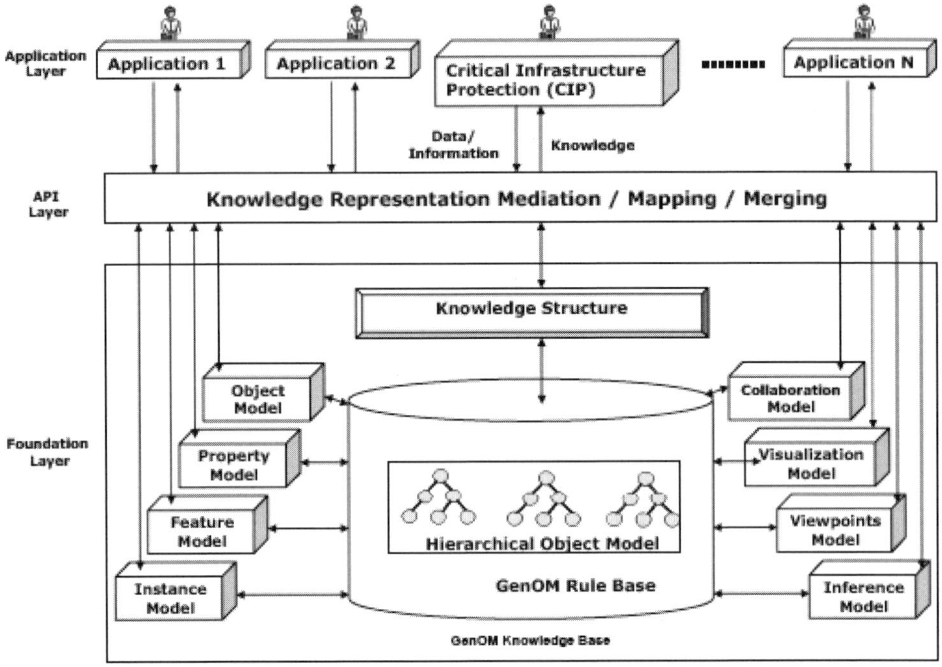

Fig. 11. GenOM conceptual architecture in [45].

As it is mentioned in [46], the requirements repository used in DITSCAP[29] Automation Tool is built upon the GenOM.

3. Modeling and simulation of EMS using ontologies

As we have seen, EMS depends on several kind of information systems, such as alerts management systems, command and control systems, geographical information systems, decision making support systems and also modeling and simulation systems.

In [31], Park and Fishwick, indicate "A model is a simplified representation of the real entity in order to increase our understanding of that entity. Modeling is the process of making the model". In their article addresses the problem of different models that can be interconnected within the same 3D space through effective ontology construction and human interaction techniques.

The most difficult thing is to get a validated model. Once you get it, to build a simulator is easier (compared with the model). As it is said in [32],

[29] DISTCAP: *Department of Defense (DoD) Information Technology Security Certification and Accreditation Process* (DITSCAP), that is a standard certification and accreditation (C&A) process for information systems that comprises the Defense Information Infrastructure (DII).

"the conceptual modeling of the domain for such systems is challenging" and they state several reasons. One reason is that disaster management is inherently multidisciplinary and complex. Another reason is that EMS deals with a large, complex system of interconnected systems with physical and social interdependencies. In this paper, they present various models proposed for modeling of systems in general or disaster management in particular".

In [39], Kruchten *et al.* "brings human into the loop and distinguish between the physical and social interdependencies between infrastructures, where the social layer deals with communication and coordination among the representatives (either humans or intelligent agents) of the various critical infrastructures. They are developing two tools using the model: a disaster simulator and a disaster querying system. As is reflected in Fig. 12, the overall structure of a complete disaster simulator follows directly from the structure of their model:

1. The disaster visualization: It is based on GIS systems that integrates all the data.
2. The physical simulator: It represents the state of all physically related elements.
3. The communication and coordination simulator: It models the human in the loop aspects.
4. The disaster scripter: This component allows the description of a disaster.

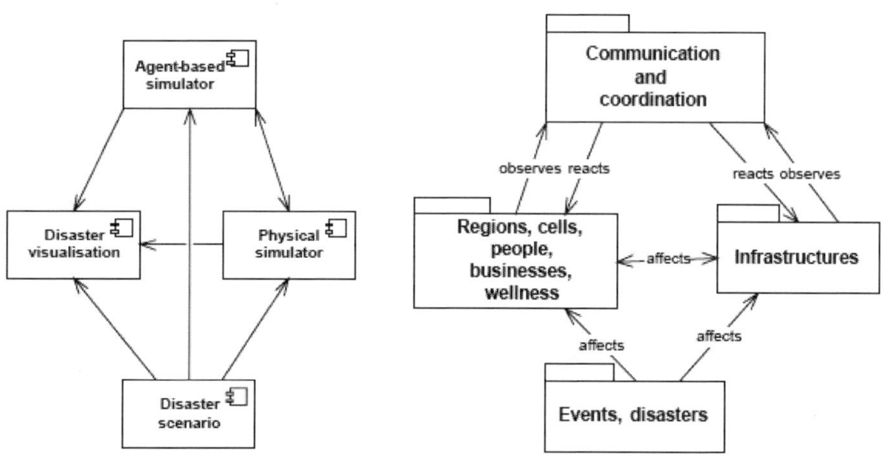

Fig. 12. The structure of the simulator is matching the model structure in [39].

In [9], Matheus *et al.* express a formal approach to reason about situations using an ontology that would satisfy several requirements. "First it needed to be able to represent objects and relationships as well as their evolution over time. Second, we wanted it to be able to express essentially any "reasonable" evolution of objects and relationships (although possibly only approximately). Third, the design needed to be economical so as to ultimately permit its implementation in a working system". In this paper, we can see a simple Battlefield scenario and how the SAW ontology was extended by subclassing a small number of core classes.

Another issue to take into account is the simulation system interoperability an according to [8] the current paradigm that identifies two models: Distributed Interactive Simulation[30] (DIS) and High Level Architecture[31] (HLA). "In both cases, HLA and DIS, the information exchange model used is a model of its own resulting from consensus between the participating systems. Every system agrees to map their information exchange to these information exchange model". Tolk and Turnitsa propose to capture the information exchange requirements using appropriate metadata in such a way that ontological means can be applied to unambiguously identify exchangeable information. In [31], we can see an example of a scene ontology for a reconnaissance mission (the battlefield scene[32] has a F15, a UAV, and a JSTARS), including the first-order logic rules for creating interaction models used for an individual object and an overall scene domain. The tools employed for the implementation are Protégé ontology editor, Semantic Web Rule Language (SWRL), and RACER along with Protégé to verify the ontology for a certain scene domain.

4. Conclusions

There are many knowledge areas involved in the construction of an EMS. This chapter has attempted to show that for all these fields there are ontologies applied at a practical or theoretical level, although most of them are now emerging as a result of the need, inter alia, of interoperability between different systems and domains.

All the aspects related to EMS development have been covered, with the aim of drawing a state-of-the-art view of applied ontologies to the field of emergency management.

[30] DIS is specified by IEEE1278.

[31] HLA is specified by IEEE1516.

[32] This can be also an emergency scene changing these planes by a helicopter used for air traffic control, a plane with water for a fire and a communications vehicle.

As it has been analyzed in this chapter, ontologies and the systems developed to be used in EMS should adapt dynamically to the real-time and challenging scenarios of an emergency, where all the stakeholders need updated information as fast as possible. Few years ago this was almost impossible, but as semantic web has evolved, new technologies have arisen to solve the ontological needs related to interoperate between different domains, languages.

Most of the research analyzed in this chapter is on early stages, and both the benefits and limits of ontology application in EMS is vast and yet to be defined.

References

1. Bordetsky, A and H Friman (2007). Case-studies of decision support models for collaboration in tactical mobile environments. In *Proceedings of the 12th International Command and Control Research Technology Symposium*, Newport.
2. Smirnov, A, M Pashkin, N Shilov, T Levashova and A Krizhanovsky (2005). Ontology-driven information integration to operational decision support. In *Proceedings of the 8th International Conference on Information Fusion (IF 2005)*, Philadelphia, USA.
3. Smirnov, A, M Pashkin, N Shilov, T Levashova and A Krizhanovsky (2006). Intelligent support for distributed operational decision making. In *Proceedings of the 9th International Conference on Information Fusion. Florence*, Italy, 10–13 July, IEEE electronic proceedings.
4. Smirnov, A, M Pashkin, N Shilov, T Levashova and A Kashevnik (2007). Context-aware operational decision support. *Information Fusion, 2007 10th International Conference*, pp. 1–8, 9–12 July 2007.
5. Steinberg, AN, CL Bowman and FE White (1998). Revisions to the JDL data fusion model. Presented at the Joint NATO/IRIS Conference, Quebec, October.
6. Steinberg, AN and CL Bowman (2004). Rethinking the JDL data fusion levels. In *Proceedings of the National Symposium on Sensor and Data Fusion*, John Hopkins Applied Physics Laboratory.
7. Steinberg, AN (2005). An approach to threat assessment. In *Proceedings of the FUSION 2005 — 8th International Conference on Multisource Information Fusion*, Philadelphia.
8. Tolk, A and CD Turnitsa (2007). Conceptual modeling of information exchange requirements based on ontological means. In *Proceedings of the Winter Simulation Conference*, SG Henderson, B Biller, M-H Hsieh, J Shortle, JD Tew and RR Baron (eds.). Piscataway, New Jersey: Institute of Electrical and Electronics Engineers, Inc.

9. Matheus, CJ, MM Kokar and K Baclawski (2003). A core ontology for situation awareness. In *Proceedings of the Sixth International Conference on Information Fusion*, 545–552.
10. Matheus, CJ, MM Kokar, K Baclawski, J Letkowski, C Call, M Hinman, J Salerno and D Boulware (2005). SAWA: An assistant for higher-level fusion and situation awareness. In *Proceedings of SPIE Conference on Multisensor, Multisource Information.* 2005 *Fusion: Architectures, Algorithms, and Applications 2005, Orlando, Florida, USA*, BV Dasarathy (ed.), Vol. 5813, 75–85, March.
11. Dudenhoeffer, DD, MR Permann, S Woolsey, R Timpany, C Miller, A McDermott and M Manic (2007). Interdependency modeling and emergency response. In *Proceedings of the 2007 Summer Computer Simulation Conference*, San Diego, California, 16–19 July.
12. Fletcher, DR (2002). The role of geospatial technology in critical transportation infrastructure protection: A research agenda.
13. Blasch, E (2006). Sensor, user, mission (SUM) resource management and their interaction with level 2/3 Fusion. In *Information Fusion, 2006 9th International Conference*, pp. 1–4, 10–13 July.
14. Blasch, E, I Kadar, J Salerno, MM Kokar, S Das, GM Powell, DD Corkill and EH Ruspini (2006). Issues and challenges in knowledge representation and reasoning methods in situation assessment (Level 2 Fusion). In *SPIE Proc*eedings, Vol. 6235, I Kadar (ed.), Orlando, Fl April.
15. Blasch, E and S Plano (2002). JDL level 5 fusion model: User refinement issues and applications in group tracking. *SPIE*, Vol. 4729, *Aerosense*, 270–279.
16. Blasch, E and S Plano (2005). DFIG level 5 (user refinement) issues supporting situational assessment reasoning. In *Information Fusion, 2005 8th International Conference*, Vol. 1, pp. xxxv–xliii, 25–28 July.
17. Klien, E and M Lutz (2006). Ontology based discovery of GIS. An application in disaster management. W Kuhn (ed.).
18. Snoeren, G, S Zlatanova, J Crompvoets and H Scholten (2007). Spatial Data Infrastructure for emergency management: The view of the users.
19. Chen, H, F Perich, T Finin and A Joshi (2004). SOUPA: Standard ontology for ubiquitous and pervasive applications. *The First International Conference on Mobile and Ubiquitous Systems (MobiQuitous 2004).*
20. Chen, H, T Finin and A Joshi (2003). Using OWL in a Pervasive Computing Broker. Workshop on Ontologies in Open Agent Systems, AAMAS.
21. Kim, HM, M Biehl and JA Buzacott (2005). M-ci2: Modelling cyber interdependencies between critical infrastructures. In 3*rd IEEE International Conference on Industrial Informatics (INDIN'05)*, pp. 644–648, August.
22. Biermann, J, L de Chantal, R Korsnes, J Rohmer and Ç Ündeger (2004). "From unstructured to structured information in military intelligence: Some steps to Improve Information Fusion". SCI Panel Symposium, London, 25 to 27 October.

23. Bowen, J (2002). Constraint processing offers improved expressiveness and inference for interactive expert systems. *International Workshop on Constraint Solving and Constraint Logic Programming*, pp. 93–108.
24. Llinas, J, C Bowman, G Rogova, A Steinberg, E Waltz and F White (2004). Revisiting the JDL Data Fusion Model II. In *The 7th International Conference on Information Fusion*, Stockholm, Sweden, June.
25. Pfautz, J, A Fouse, M Farry, A Bisantz and E Roth (2007). Representing meta-information to support C2 decision making. In *International Command and Control Research and Technology Symposium (ICCRTS).*
26. Pfautz, J, E Roth, A Bisantz, G Thomas-Meyers, J Llinas and A Fouse (2006). The role of meta-information in C2 decision-support systems. In *Proceedings of Command and Control Research and Technology Symposium*, San Diego, CA.
27. Beven, K, R Romaniwicz, F Pappenberger, P Young and M Werner (2005). The uncertainty cascade in flood forecasting. In *Advances and Implementation of Flood Forecasting Technology*, P Balbanis, D Lambroso and P Samuels (eds.). ACTIF: Tromso.
28. Bernard, L, A Annoni, I Kanellopoulos, M Millot, J Nogueras-Iso, J Nowak and K Toth (2005). What technology does INSPIRE need? — Development and research requirements. In *Proceedings of the 8th AGILE conference on geographic information science.*
29. Kokar, MM, CJ Matheus and K Baclawski (2009). Ontology-based situation awareness. *Information Fusion*, 10(1), *Special Issue on High-level Information Fusion and Situation Awareness*, pp. 83–98, January.
30. Nilsson, M (2008). Characterising user interaction to inform information-fusion-driven decision support. In *Proceedings of the 15th European Conference on Cognitive Ergonomics: The Ergonomics of Cool interaction*, Funchal, Portugal, 16–19 September.
31. Park, M and PA Fishwick (2005). Integrating dynamic and geometry model components through ontology-based inference. *Simulation*, 81(12), 795–813.
32. Sotoodeh, M and P Kruchten (2008). An ontological approach to conceptual modeling of disaster management. In *2nd Annual IEEE Systems Conference*, Montreal.
33. Baumgartner, N, W Retschitzegger (2006). A survey of upper ontologies for situation awareness. In *Proceedings of Knowledge Sharing and Collaborative Engineering.*
34. Baumgartner, N, W Retschitzegger and W Schwinger (2008). A software architecture for ontology-driven situation awareness. In *Proceedings of the 2008 ACM Symposium on Applied Computing*, Fortaleza, Ceara, Brazil, 16–20 March. SAC '08. New York, NY: ACM.
35. Baumgartner, N, W Retschitzegger and W Schwinger (2008). Application scenarios of ontology-driven situation awareness systems.

36. Svendsen, NK and SD Wolthusen (2007). Connectivity models of interdependency in mixed-type critical infrastructure networks. *Information Security Technical Report,* 12(1), 44–55.
37. Sanderson, N, V Goebel and E Munthe-Kaas (2005). Metadata management for ad-hoc InfoWare — a rescue and emergency use case for mobile ad-hoc scenarios. In *International Conference on Ontologies, Databases and Applications of Semantics (ODBASE05),* Cyprus, November 2005. In *LNCS 3761,* SB Heidelberg (ed.), pp. 1365–1380.
38. Sanderson, N, V Goebel and E Munthe-Kaas (2006). Ontology based dynamic updates in sparse mobile ad-hoc networks for rescue scenarios. In *Mobile Data Management, 2006. MDM 2006. 7th International Conference,* 10–12 May.
39. Kruchten, P, C Woo, K Monu and M Sotoodeh (2008). A conceptual model of disasters encompassing multiple stakeholder domains. *International Journal of Emergency Management,* 5(1), 25–56.
40. Iannella, R, K Robinson and O Rinta-Koski (2007). Towards a framework for crisis information management systems (CIMS). In *Proceedings of the 14th Annual Conference of The International Emergency Management Society (TIEMS),* Trogir, Croatia, 5–8 June.
41. Lefevre, R, J Pfautz and K Jones (2005). Weather forecast uncertainty management and display. In *Proceedings of 21st Int'l Conf. on Interactive Information Processing Systems (IIPS) for Meteorology, Oceanography, and Hydrology,* San Diego, CA.
42. McNally, RK, S-W Lee, D Yavagal and W-N Xiang (2007). Learning the critical infrastructure interdependencies through an ontology-based information system. *Environment and Planning B: Planning and Design,* 34, 1103–1124.
43. Semy, SK, MK Pulvermacher and LJ Obrst (2004). Toward the use of an upper ontology for U.S. government and military domains: An evaluation. *MITRE Technical Report 04B0000063,* September.
44. Yau, SS and J Liu (2006). Hierarchical situation modeling and reasoning for pervasive computing. *Software Technologies for Future Embedded and Ubiquitous Systems, 2006 and the 2006 Second International Workshop on Collaborative Computing, Integration, and Assurance. SEUS 2006/WCCIA 2006. The Fourth IEEE Workshop,* 27–28 April.
45. Lee, SW and D Yavagal (2004). GenOM user's guide. *Technical Report,* Dept. of Software and Information Systems, UNC Charlotte.
46. Lee, SW, G-J Ahn and RA Gandhi (2005). Engineering information assurance for critical infrastructures: The DITSCAP automation study. In *Proceedings of the Fifteenth Annual International Symposium of the International Council on Systems Engineering (INCOSE '05),* — Systems Engineering: Bridging Industry, Government, and Academia, Rochester, NY, 10–15 July.

47. El-Diraby, TE (2006). Infrastructure development in the knowledge city. *Lecture Notes in Computer Science*, 4200/2006, 175–185.
48. Grant, TJ and BM Kooter (2005). Comparing OODA & other models as operational view C2 architecture. In *Proceedings of the 10th International Command and Control Research Technology Symposium*, McLean, VA. USA, June.
49. Hwacha, V (2005). Canada's experience in developing a national disaster mitigation strategy. *Mitigation and Adaptation Strategies for Global Change*, 10, 507–523.
50. Wang, XH, DQ Zhang, T Gu and HK Pung (2004). Ontology based context modeling and reasoning using OWL. In *Pervasive Computing and Communications Workshops, 2004. Proceedings of the Second IEEE Annual Conference*, 18–22, 14–17 March.

CHAPTER III.7

METADATA AND ONTOLOGIES FOR TOURISM

Dimitris Kanellopoulos

Department of Mathematics, University of Patras
GR-265 00 Patras, Greece
d_kan2006@yahoo.gr

This chapter focuses on recent research on metadata models and ontologies for tourism. In particular, it presents various ontologies for the tourism domain and research efforts related to semantic metadata models applied to the tourism industry. In this chapter we describe ontologies for tourist destinations, hotels, restaurants, museums, airlines etc. and their related research projects. We survey the current state of semantic web technologies research applied to the tourism domain and identify significant emerging trends and techniques.

1. Introduction

The tourism industry is a consumer of a diverse range of information [1]. Information and communication technologies (ICTs) play a critical role for the competitiveness of tourism organizations and destinations. According to Staab and Werthner [2], ICTs are having the effect of changing: (a) the ways in which tourism companies contact their business — reservations and information management systems; (b) the ways tourism companies communicate; how customers look for information on and purchase travel goods and services. Moreover, Staab and Werthner [2] state, "in the tourism industry, the supply and demand sides form a worldwide network, in which tourism product's generation and distribution are closely worked together. Most tourism products (e.g., hotel rooms or flight tickets) are time-constrained and non-stockable. The tourism product is both 'perishable' and 'complex' and itself is a bundle of basic products aggregated by intermediaries. Consequently, basic products must have well-defined interfaces with respect to consumer needs, prices or distribution channels. In addition, a tourism product cannot be tested and controlled in advance. During decision-making, only an abstract model of the product (e.g., its description) is available". In addition we believe that the tourism industry has a heterogeneous nature and a strong small and medium-sized enterprises (SMEs) base. In the tourism industry one of the main challenges is to find, integrate and process all the tourism-related information on the Web. Since most of the Web content is primarily designed to be understood by humans, software agents can parse web page only in a structure dimension. Moreover, software agents cannot automatically process data from a particular tourism website without understanding its semantic. The semantic Web solves this problem as it extends the current Web using semantic annotation techniques. "The Semantic Web is an extension of the current Web in which information is given well-defined meaning, better enabling computers and people to work in cooperation" [3]. The semantic Web instead of trying to understand text, it attaches additional information to it that semantically marks the information found in the Web. This additional information is called *metadata*. The semantic Web involves low intelligent techniques and applications that exploit such metadata in order to achieve the global information interoperability vision for the Web [4].

1.1. *Metadata for tourism*

Metadata are data that provide additional information about other data. For example, the title of a web page can be metadata about the webpage. An example of metadata is the timetable for the availability of an offered tourism product that a web-based tourism information system provides. The current official World Wide Web Consortium (W3C) language for describing metadata for the Web is Resource Description Framework (RDF) (http://www.w3.org/RDF/). RDF is a data model that permits the declaration of additional information (or properties) about existing web resources, e.g., web pages, web services, etc. The main construct of RDF is the *statement*, which asserts a property value for a resource and is composed by a *subject* (the resource for which the property value is asserted for), a *predicate* (which is the name of the property) and an *object* (which is the value of the property for the specific resource subject). The basic building block in RDF is an object-property-value triple, commonly written as `P(O,V)`. That is, an object `O` has property `P` with value `V`. So, for example, the object `Job001821` could have property `Title` with value `Tourist_Agent`: `Title(Job001821, Tourist_Agent)`.The objects about which RDF reasons are also referred to as resources (web pages or part of pages, but can be anything).

e-Tourism is an early adopter of the semantic Web technologies, which are increasingly changing the nature of and processes in the tourism industry [5]. e-Tourism is defined as the use of ICTs in the tourism industry. It involves the buying and selling of tourism products and services via electronic channels, such as the Internet, cable TV, etc. e-Tourism includes all Intranet, Extranet and Internet applications as well as all the strategic management and marketing issues related to the use of technology. ICTs include the entire range of electronic tools, which facilitate the operational and strategic management of organizations by enabling them to manage their information, functions and processes, as well as to communicate interactively with their stakeholders for achieving their mission and objectives. Currently, e-Tourism makes use of (syntactic) web technology for tours, infrastructure, related interesting information such as public transport, timetables, weather, online reservation etc. The major barriers using the syntactic Web are:

- Creating complex queries involving background knowledge on tourism issues.
- Solving ambiguities and synonyms.
- Finding and using web services for tourism.
- Besides, the characteristics of the tourism product require information on the consumers' and suppliers' sides, involving high information search costs and causing informational market imperfections. These outcomes sequentially lead to the establishment of specific product distribution information and value-adding chains.

Given such a framework, Staab and Werthner [2] state that intelligent information systems should:

- Be heterogeneous, distributed, and cooperative.
- Enable full autonomy of the respective participants.
- Support the entire consumer life cycle and all business phases.
- Allow dynamic network configurations.
- Provide intelligence for customers (tourists) and suppliers as well as in the network.
- Be scalable and open.
- Focus on mobile communication enabling multi-channel distribution.

1.2. *Ontologies*

Ontologies constitute the main element of the semantic Web and provide conceptual models for interpreting the information provided by web pages. An ontology is a common vocabulary of basic concepts in the domain and relations among them. It is a formal explicit description of concepts (classes) in a domain, properties of each concept describing various features and attributes of the concept, and restrictions (axioms) on the concept properties. An ontology together with a set of individual instances of classes constitutes a knowledge base. An ontology is made up of the following parts:

- *Classes and instances*: For example an ontology modeling the tourism domain may contain classes such as "hotel" or "attraction". An ontology for the travel domain might contain concepts such as "tourist destination" and "means of transportation" and relationships between the terms. Usually instances are used to model elements and belong to classes. For example, the instance "Parthenon" belongs to the class "attraction". Classes are usually organized in a hierarchy of subclasses. For example, the concept "man" can be defined as a sub-class of an existing concept "person" in WordNet vocabulary (http://wordnet.princeton.edu/). If class A is a subclass of class B, instances of class A also belong to class B.
- *Properties* establish relationships between the concepts of an ontology. For example, the property "BelongTo" associates an object with its owner it belongs to.

The simplest type of ontologies is called *taxonomies* and they are made up of a hierarchy of classes representing the relevant concepts in the domain. To develop an ontology, we usually follow four steps: (a) we define classes, (b) we arrange the classes in a taxonomic (subclass-superclass) hierarchy, (c) we define concept properties (slots) and describe allowed values for them, and finally (d) we fill in the values for concept properties for instances. When we are designing an ontology, it is important to include synonyms and part-of-speech information for concepts as well as other particular information. For example, if our ontology will be used to assist in Natural Language Processing (NLP) of web documents, it may be important to include synonyms for concepts in the ontology. In another example, if a "hotel ontology" will be used to help travelers make a room reservation, we need to include pricing information and availability.

Using ontologies, users and software agents can share common understanding of the structure of information. The last decade, there are several web sites that contain tourism information or provide e-tourism services. Some of these web sites share and publish the same underlying ontology of the terms they all use. Consequently, software agents can extract and aggregate information from these different websites. This aggregated information can be used by software agents to answer user queries or as input to other intelligent applications. Ontologies enable reuse of domain knowledge as some of them represent notions that are too common in various other domains [6]. Consequently, researchers in different research fields can simply reuse these ontologies for their domains. From another perspective, ontologies make domain assumptions explicit. It is very beneficial to make explicit domain assumptions underlying an implementation because we can change easily these assumptions, if our knowledge about the domain changes. Using ontologies, we can also separate domain knowledge from the operational knowledge. For example, we can describe a task of reasoning (algorithm) to a required specification and implement an application program that executes this task independent of the domain knowledge (i.e., knowledge terms). Computational processes and agents interpret semantic content and derive consequences from the information they collect. Semantic annotation of tourism multimedia content enables the deployment of intelligent applications in the tourism domain that could reason over multimedia metadata. For example, using the semantic markup for the *Official Travel's* web page reporting travel characteristics, a software agent could learn that the *Current tourist destination* is *London*. The software agent might further learn from the *Official destination board of London* website's semantic markup that all travels to London are obtained using the *'British Airways' airlines.* Combining the two pieces of information, the agent could infer that this travel to London will be achieved using the British Airways airlines. Using ontologies, we can analyze domain knowledge by specifying terms declaratively and analyze them formally. So, we can reuse and extend existing ontologies.

1.3. *Intelligent software agents*

The semantic Web includes intelligent software agents, which "understand" semantic relationships between web resources and seek relevant information as well as perform transactions for users. Intelligent agents can provide various tourism products and services into an integrated tourism package, which can be personalized to tourist's needs. A variety of traveler, hotel, museum and other software agents can enhance the tourism marketing and management reservation processes [7,8]. There are many research prototypes of intelligent travel support systems based on software agent technology [9]. Traveler software agents can assist travelers in finding sources of tourism products and services and in documenting and archiving them. A set of agents can be deployed for various tasks including: tracking visitor schedules, monitoring meeting schedules, and monitoring user's travel plans. For example, if the user specifies the travel itinerary and his/her required services, then a set of information agents can be spawned to perform the requested monitoring activities [9]. An additional capacity of the semantic Web is realized, when intelligent agents extract information from one application and subsequently utilize the data as input for further applications [8]. Therefore, software agents can create greater capacity for large scale automated collection, processing and selective dissemination of tourism data.

2. Ontologies for Tourism

Through the use of metadata organized in numerous interrelated ontologies [10], tourism destination information can be tagged with descriptors that facilitate its retrieval, analysis, processing and reconfiguration. Tourism ontologies offer a promising infrastructure to cope with heterogeneous representations of tourism destination web resources. As we said earlier, an ontology is a conceptualization of an application domain in a human understandable and machine-readable form, and typically comprises the classes of entities, relations between entities and the axioms which apply to the entities that exist in that domain. The W3C has recently finalized the Web Ontology Language (OWL) as the standard format in which ontologies are represented online. With OWL it is possible to implement a semantic description of the tourism/travel domain by specifying its concepts and the relationships between these concepts. OWL [11] (http://www.w3.org/2004/OWL/) provides greater machine interpretability of web content than that supported by XML, RDF and RDF-schema.

Generally, existing ontologies are classified into four major categories: (1) meta-ontologies, (2) upper ontologies, (3) domain ontologies, and (4) specialized ontologies. Ontology languages such as RDF, RDFS, DAML+OIL, OWL are actually meta-ontologies themselves; and their instances are semantic web ontologies. Specialized ontologies concentrate on a set of basic and commonly used concepts, while domain ontology is the main classification. Core tourism ontologies contain knowledge about the domain of tourism and travel for developing intelligent tourism information systems.

2.1. *Upper-level ontologies*

Upper ontologies provide a high level model about the world using the ontology constructs provided by meta-ontologies.

- *Cyc* is the most comprehensive ontology, which consists of foundation ontology and several domain specific ontologies. The entire Cyc ontology containing hundreds of thousands of terms, along with millions of assertions relating the terms to each other, forming an upper ontology whose domain is all of human consensus reality. OpenCyc [12] is the open source version of the Cyc technology, the world's largest and most complete general knowledge base and commonsense reasoning engine. OpenCyc can be used as the basis of a wide variety of intelligent applications.
- *WordNet* is a general dictionary for use in Natural Language Processing (NLP) and includes general and specialized concepts, which are related to each other by other semantic relations.
- *Suggested Upper Merged Ontology (SUMO)* (http://www.ontologyportal.org) was created by an IEEE working group and is freely available. It consists of language generation templates for various languages such as German, Chinese, Italian and English.
- *The SENSUS project* (http://www.isi.edu/natural-language/projects/ONTOLOGIES.html) consists of 70,000-node taxonomy and is focusing on creating a semantic thesaurus. This thesaurus helps to understand texts and is applied to machine translation, summarization and information retrieval.

2.2. *Domain specific- travel ontologies*

A growing number of research projects are concerned with applying semantic Web technologies to the tourism industry. Tourism ontologies allow machine-supported tourism data interpretation and integration.

2.2.1. *The harmonise project*

The Harmonise (http://www.harmonise.org) is an EU *Tourism Harmonisation Network* (THN) established by the ECommerce and Tourism Research Laboratory, IFITT[1] and others. The Harmonise Ontology is specialized to

[1]The International Federation for IT and Travel & Tourism (IFITT) (http://www.ifitt.org/) is a not-for-profit organization aiming to promote international discussion about ICTs and tourism.

address interoperability problems in the area of e-tourism focusing on data exchange. The Harmonize project allows participating tourism organizations to keep their proprietary data format and use ontology mediation while exchanging information [13,14]. Harmonise is based on mapping different tourism ontologies by using a mediating ontology. Harmonise is an ontology-based mediation and harmonization tool that establishes the bridges between existing and emerging online marketplaces. This central Harmonise ontology is represented in RDF and contains concepts and properties describing tourism concepts, mainly dealing with accommodation and events.

2.2.2. *The SATINE and SWAP projects*

In the SATINE project (Semantic-based Interoperability Infrastructure for Integrating Web Service Platforms to Peer-to-Peer Networks), a secure semantics-based interoperability framework was developed for exploiting Web service platforms in conjunction with peer-to-peer (P2P) networks in the tourist industry [15]. To facilitate the service discovery and interoperability in the travel domain, Web services semantics were defined and used. In particular, semantics were used for the discovery of web service registries. In the SATINE project (IST-2104), the semantic of web service registries are exposed while service registries are connected through a P2P network. Semantics of the service registries are the semantics of Web services stored in these registries.

The EU-IST project SWAP (http://swap.semanticweb.org/) demonstrated that the power of P2P computing and the semantic Web could actually be combined to share and find "knowledge" easily with low administration efforts, while participants can maintain individual views of the world. In the travel domain, the advantages of Web semantics and P2P computing for service interoperation and discovery have been analyzed by Maedche and Staab [16].

2.2.3. *OTA specification*

Recently, the OTA[2] has developed open data transmission specifications for the electronic exchange of business information for the travel industry, including but not limited to the use of XML. The OTA members are organiza-

[2] The Open Travel Alliance (OTA) (www.opentravel.org/) is an organization that develops open data transmission specifications for the electronic exchange of business information for the travel industry, including but not limited to the use of XML.

tions that represent all segments of the travel industry, along with key technology and service suppliers. The OTA Specification defines XML Message Sets packages that contain about 140 XML Schema documents corresponding to events and activities in various travel sectors.

2.2.4. *The Mondeca tourism ontology*

Mondeca tourism ontology (http:/www.mondeca.com) includes important concepts of the tourism domain, which are defined in the World Tourism Organization (WTO) thesaurus (www.world-tourism.org) managed by the WTO. The WTO Thesaurus includes information and definitions of the topic tourism and leisure activities. The dimensions, which are defined within the Mondeca Ontology, are tourism object profiling, tourism and cultural objects, tourism packages and tourism multimedia content. The used ontology language is OWL and the ontology itself contains about 1,000 concepts.

2.2.5. *The OnTour project*

In the OnTour project, a working group at the Digital Enterprise Research Institute (DERI) deployed the *e-Tourism* ontology [17] using OWL. This ontology describes the domain of tourism and it focuses on accommodation and activities (http://e-tourism.deri.at/ont/). It is based on an international standard: the *Thesaurus on Tourism and Leisure Activities* of the World Tourism Organization [18]. This thesaurus is an extensive collection of terms related to tourism. Terms used in the tourism industry are defined in the ISO 18513 [19] standard in relation to the various types of tourism accommodation and other related services. This standard defines a common vocabulary for a better understanding between the users and providers of tourism services. The annex contains a dictionary with the equivalence between French, English, Spanish, and German.

2.2.6. *The COTRIN ontology*

A reference ontology, named Comprehensive Ontology for the Travel Industry (COTRIN) is presented in [20,21]. The objective of COTRIN ontology is the implementation of the semantic XML-based OTA specifications. Major airlines, hoteliers, car rental companies, leisure suppliers, travel agencies and others may use COTRIN to bring together autonomous and heterogeneous tourism web services, web processes, applications, data, and components residing in distributed environments. Cardoso [22] also constructed the e-tourism ontology to answer three main questions that can be asked when developing tourism applications: *what, where*, and *when*.

- *What*. What can a tourist see, visit and what can he do while staying at a tourism destination?
- *Where*. Where are the interesting places to see and visit located? Where can a tourist carry out a specific activity, such as playing golfer tennis.
- *When*. When can the tourist visit a particular place? This includes not only the day of the week and the hours of the day, but also the atmospheric conditions of the weather. Some activities cannot be undertaken if it is raining for example.

2.2.7. *The LA_DMS project*

A destination management organization (DMO) is an entity or a company that promotes a tourist destination such as to increase the amount of visitors to this destination. It uses a *destination management system* (DMS) to distribute its properties and to present the tourist destination as a holistic entity. A DMS[3] provides complete and up-to-date information on a particular tourist destination. DMSs is a perfect application area for semantic Web and P2P technologies. In DMS, data heterogeneity can be solved by providing semantic reconciliation between the different tourism information systems, with respect to a shared, conceptual reference schema: the "tourism destination" ontology. Kanellopoulos and Panagopoulos [23] developed an ontology for tourist destinations in the *LA_DMS* (Layered Adaptive semantic-based DMS based on P2P technologies) project. The aim of the LA_DMS project was to enable DMS adaptive to tourists' needs for tourist destination information. The LA_DMS system incorporates a metadata model to encode semantic tourist destination information in an RDF-based P2P network architecture. This metadata model combines ontological structures with information for tourist destinations and peers. The LA_DMS project provides semantic-based tourism destination information by combining the P2P paradigm with semantic Web technologies and Adaptive Hypermedia (AH). The model is adaptive to the user's personalization requirements (e.g., information concerning transportation, restaurants, accommodation, etc.) and it is a collection of

[3] A DMS handles both the pre-trip and post arrival information and integrates availability and booking service too. It is used for the collection, storage, manipulation and distribution of tourism information, as well as for the transaction of reservations and other commercial activities. Well-known DMSs are TISCover, VisitScotland, and Gulliver.

opinions supported by different sources of tourism destination information. In the LA_DMS framework, the semantic models of different peers (DMOs) are being aligned dynamically. The LA_DMS model supports mainly flexibility, expressivity, reusability, interoperability and standardization.

Kanellopoulos and Kotsiantis [24] proposed a semantic-based architecture in which semantic web ontology is used to model tourist destinations, user profiles and contexts. The semantic web service ontology (OWL-S) is extended for matching user requirements with tourist destination specifications at the semantic level, with context information taken into account. Semantic Web Rule Language (SWRL) (http://www.daml.org/200/11/swrl) is used for inferencing with context and user profile descriptions. Their architecture enables DMS to become fully adaptable to user's requirements concerning tourist destinations.

2.2.8. *Ontology for group package tours*

The existing tools for facilitating searches of availability of package tours do not provide intelligent matching between offered package tours and the personal requirements of the travelers. In the group package tour (GPT) domain, an intelligent web portal was proposed that helps people living in Europe to find package tours that match their personal traveling preferences [25]. For this purpose, the knowledge of the package tour domain has been represented by means of ontology. Additionally, the ontological component allows for defining an ontology-guided search engine, which provides more intelligent matches between package tours offers and traveling preferences. Common descriptors are used for offers and demands (the profile introduced by a traveler has similar attributes to the one introduced by a travel agency in an announcement of a package tour availability). This allows matching the traveler against announcement of package tour availability in a better way. Provided that the concepts "Traveler" and "GPT availability announcement" are related to the ontology by means of a common concept, namely "Profile", the search process to match suitable GPT availability announcements with a concrete traveler can be performed more efficiently by returning solely such offers as the traveler can really be interested in.

2.2.9. *The Hi-Touch project*

Semantic web methodologies and tools for intra-European sustainable tourism were developed in the Hi-Touch project [26]. These tools are used to store and structure knowledge on customers' expectations and tourism products.

The top-level classes of the *Hi-Touch* ontology are documents, objects and publication. Documents refer to any kind of documentation, advertisement, about a tourism product. Objects refer to tourism offers themselves, while a publication is a document created from the results of a query. Machines and users can process the knowledge on customers' expectations and tourism products in order to find the best matching between supply and demand. The Hi-Touch platform has already been adopted in several French regions.

2.2.10. *The TAGA ontologies*

For simulating the global travel market on the Web, a novel agent framework has been deployed, called the Travel Agent Game in Agentcities (TAGA). TAGA demonstrates Agentcities (http://www.agentcities.org) and semantic web technologies. The TAGA works on FIPA (http://www.fipa.org) compliant platforms and defines two domain ontologies to be used on simulations. The first TAGA ontology represents basic travel concepts such as itineraries, customers, travel services, and service reservations. The second ontology represents auctions, roles played by the by the participants and the protocols used. However, both ontologies due to the nature of TAGA simulations have limited scope of application. The TAGA Travel Ontology (http://taga.sourceforge.net/owl/travel.owl) provides typical concepts of traveling combined with concepts describing typical tourism activities [27].

2.2.11. *Travel ontologies*

Gordon *et al.* [28] designed a travel-related ontology for a software agent system and illustrated its RDF-based implementation. Hagen *et al.* [29] deployed the *Dynamic Tour Guide* (DTG) that computes an itinerary of a couple of hours to explore a city. DTG is a mobile agent that interrogates Tour Building Blocks (TBB) such as restaurants or potential sights, to determine current information (e.g., availability or opening hours). The profiles of the TBBs and the interests of a tourist are captured using an ontology. The DTG applies semantic matching to select TBBs according to the individual interests of a tourist and presents a tour. Based on the start point and the available time period, a heuristic approximate algorithm computes an individual tour within seconds. Semantic technology makes it possible to reuse the interests profile from one destination to the next, which will be crucial for acceptance by a broad demographic. Antoniou *et al.* [30] considered the brokering and matchmaking problem in the tourism domain, that is, how a requester's requirements and preferences can be matched against a set of offering collected by a broker. In their framework, RDF is used to represent the offerings, and a deductive logical language expresses the requirements and preferences. In addition, Antoniou *et al.* [30] used the JADE multi-agent platform in order to exploit the advantages of P2P systems (i.e., travel agencies and broker as peers) and they used the FIPA standards for agent communication and discovery.

2.2.12. *Dynamic packaging systems*

Travelers can acquire packages from a diversity of web sites. Dynamic packaging is a new technology, which enhances the online vacation planning experience. A package tour consists of transport and accommodation advertised and sold together by a vendor known as a tour operator. Tour operators provide various services like a rental car, activities or outings during the holiday. Consumers can acquire packages from a diversity of websites including online agencies and airlines. The objective of *dynamic packaging* is to pack all the components chosen by a traveler to create one reservation. Regardless of where the inventory originates, the package that is created is handled seamlessly as one transaction, and requires *only one* payment from the consumer. Cardoso and Lang [21] proposed a framework and a platform to enable dynamic packaging using semantic web technologies. A dynamic packaging application allows consumers and/or travel agents to bundle trip components. The range of products and services to be bundled is too large: guider tour, entertainment, event/festival, shopping, activity, accommodation, transportation, food and beverage etc. Figure 1 depicts the operation of a dynamic packaging tour system (DPTS).

2.2.13. *The iJADE FreeWalker guiding system*

Lam and Lee [31] created a special travel ontology by collecting and analyzing the structural information from 32 Hong Kong related travel guide websites. They implemented a tourist context-aware guiding system, iJADE FreeWalker, which is constructed by using semantic web technologies. iJADE FreeWalker (http://www.ijadk.com) integrates global position system (GPS), ontology and agent technologies to support location awareness for providing the precise navigation and to classify the tourist information for the users. The iJADE FreeWalker integrates the mobile agent technology and ontology to form an intelligent tourist guiding system. It is composed of three major components: (a) iJADE FreeWalker client, (b) GPS agent, and (c) iJADE Tourism Information Center.

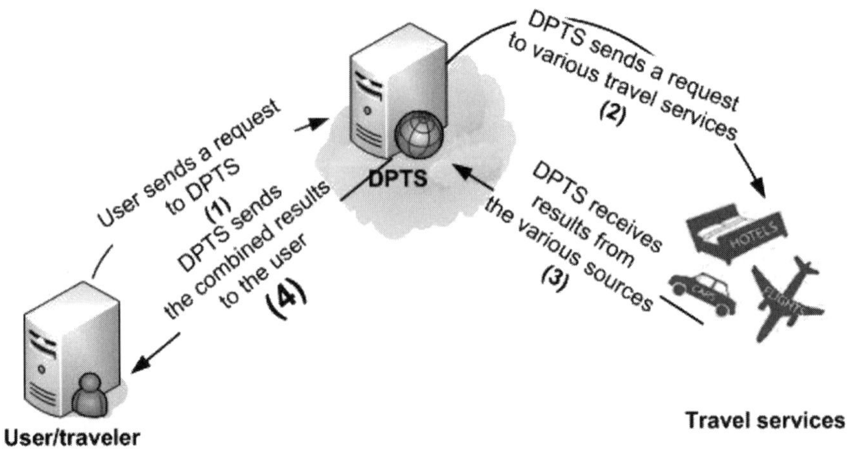

Fig. 1. The operation of DPTS [5].

2.2.14. *Air travel ontologies*

Vukmirovic *et al.* [32] created an agent-based system for selling airline tickets. Their system utilizes an air-travel ontology that matches the OTA messaging specification and satisfies procedures described in International Air Transport Association (IATA) manuals. From another perspective, Malucelli *et al.* [33] present a possible solution to the problem of lack of collaboration between different airlines, based on an electronic market. This electronic market is based on a distributed multi-agent system to help airline companies in solving unexpected operations recovery problems and matching them with potential solutions. The proposed electronic market uses ontology services allowing an airline company to access resources of other airline companies such as aircrafts and crew members. From another perpective, Kanellopoulos [34] presents an ontology-based portal, which provides intelligent matches between airline seats offers and traveling preferences. In his work [34], the knowledge of the airlines traveling domain has been represented by means of ontology, which has been used to guide the design of the application and to supply the system with semantic capabilities.

2.2.15. *Hotel ontologies: the Reisewissen project*

Niemann *et al.* [35] proposed a framework, which uses semantic web technologies to improve exploration and rating of hotels for business customers in order to reduce the search time and costs. Their framework was developed in the *Reisewissen* project (http://reisewissen.ag-nbi.de/en) and provides methods for modeling domain specific expert knowledge and integration of diverse heterogeneous data sources. Semantic technologies enable business customers to formalize their requirements and to combine them with aggregated hotel information like location of features. By this way, a selection of the hotels ranked is achieved according to the customer's requirements. Their framework includes a hotel evaluation and recommendation engine and optimizes the hotel selection process. Their proposed hotel ontology represents a wide range of hotel related information. It encompasses terms and concepts for expressing contact data (address, phone, etc.), general hotel information (number of rooms, models of payment, etc.), price information, hotel ratings and points of interest (POI) near to the hotel. In addition, their hotel ontology incorporates location-based information in the form of geo-coordinates. The Reisewissem project adopts semantic web technologies for the tourism domain. It supports the user in the choice of a hotel by selecting and ranking suitable hotels. The hotel selection and ranking is accomplished by the integration of several heterogeneous data resources into the hotel evaluation process and semantically matching the collected hotel information to the customer's individual profile [36]. The Reisewissen hotel recommendation engine is shown in Fig. 2.

Hwang *et al.* [37] constructed another hotel ontology in order customers to find a hotel with regards to some conditions such as area, room types, prices, and facilities like fitness centers, swimming pools, sauna etc. (Fig. 3).

Figure 4a shows an example of a keyword search by users' requirements from classes associated by `hasFacility` and `hasService` with search

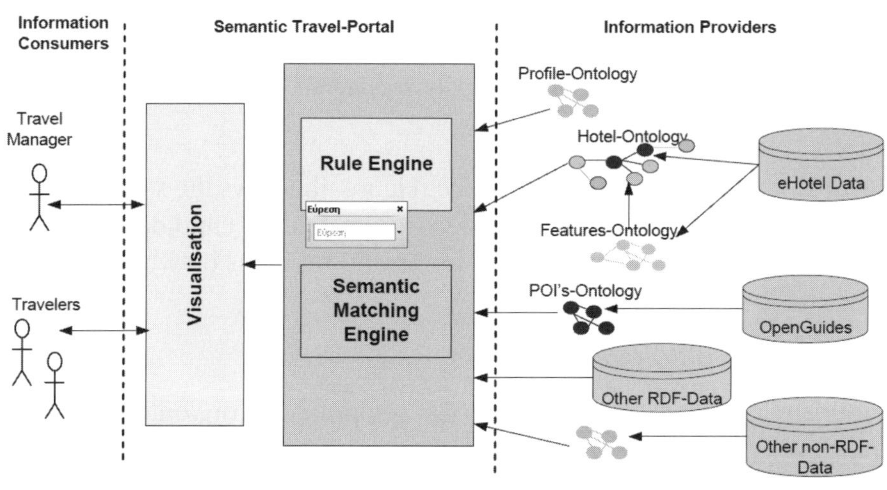

Fig. 2. The Reisewissen hotel recommendation engine [36].

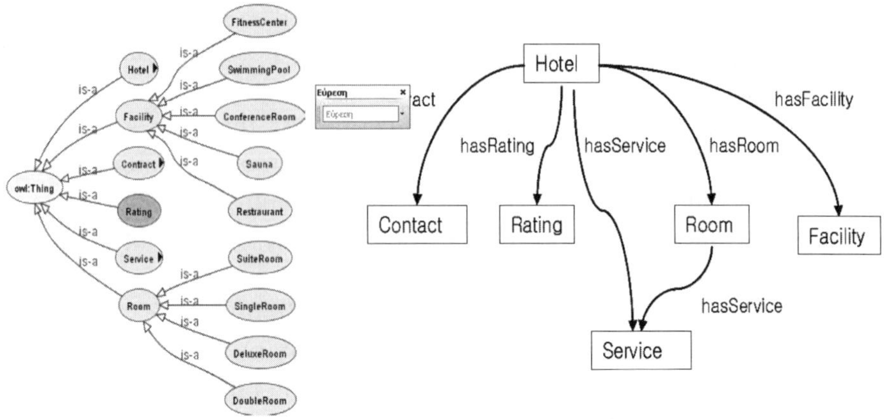

Fig. 3. The fragment of the hotel ontology and the associated classes [37].

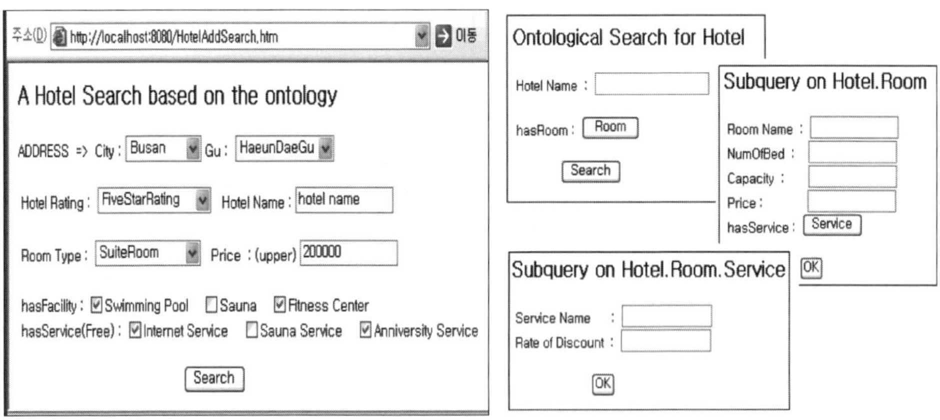

(a) (b)

Fig. 4. Ontology-based search [37].

keywords like address, rating and price. Figure 4b shows the search example by ontology browsing. To help the decision in finding candidate hotels, the search provides the hierarchy of the terms and relations between classes.

2.2.16. *Other ontologies*

A *Tourism Ontology* (http://ontobroker.semanticweb.org/ontos/comparing.html) developed by the University of Karlsruhe contains four different sub-ontologies for the tourism domain defining about 300 concepts and more than 100 relations. The EON Travelling Ontology (http://opales.ina.fr/public/

ontologies/EON-TravellingOntology-v0.2.daml) is mainly designed for the travel domain. There are also restaurant ontologies such as those found at http://e-travel.sourceforge.net/ontology/domain/index.html and http://chefmoz.org/rdf/elements/1.0/.

In the domain of coastal tourism, Badre *et al.* [38] present a communication infrastructure to improve the exchange of information and knowledge between the various scientific disciplines involved in the SYSCOLAG program (Coastal and LAGoonal SYStems in Languedoc-Roussillon area, France). In order to ensure the sharing of resources without affecting the autonomy and independence of the partners, they propose a three-level infrastructure (resources, federation and knowledge access) based on a metadata service (using ISO 19115 standard for geographic information metadata) completed by a common vocabulary (ontology).

In the domain of museums, Hyvönen *et al.* [39] present a semantic portal called *MuseumFinland* for publishing heterogeneous museum collections on the semantic Web. In their work it is shown present the semantic portal *MuseumFinland* (http://museosuomi.fi/) for publishing heterogeneous museum collections on the semantic Web. Hyvönen *et al.* [39] show how museums with their semantically rich and interrelated collection content can create a large, consolidated semantic collection portal together on the web. By sharing a set of ontologies, it is possible to make collections semantically interoperable, and provide the museum visitors with intelligent content-based search and browsing services to the global collection base. The architecture underlying MuseumFinland separates generic search and browsing services from the underlying application dependent schemas and metadata by a layer of logical rules. As a result, the portal creation framework and software developed has been applied successfully to other domains as well. MuseumFinland got the Semantic Web Challenge Award (second prize) in 2004.

2.2.17. *The implications for destination managers*

In the area of social software, we find techniques for extracting, representing and aggregating *social knowledge*. DMOs or destination managers constitute a social network as they are connected by a set of social relationships, such as co-working and information exchange. Using social network analysis [40], patterns that represent tourism destination networks and associations between destination managers can be constructed automatically. Such an analysis could yield the main groups of destination managers and identify the subgroups, the key individuals (centrality) and links between groups.

Network analysis can benefit destination managers' communities by identifying the network effects on performance and helping to devise strategies for the individual or for the community accordingly. In terms of social network analysis, the use of electronic data provides a unique opportunity to observe the dynamics of destination managers' community development. In the semantic web framework, the *Friend-of-A-Friend* project (FOAF: http://www.foaf-project.org) can represent social networks and information about people (user profiles) in a machine processable way. The FOAF project is highlighted by the following features: (a) publishing personal profile with better visibility; (b) enforcing unique person identity reference on the Web and thus supporting the merge of partial data from different sources; and (c) representing and facilitating large scale social networks on the Web. For the extraction and analysis of online social (tourism destination) networks we can use the Flink [41] system. Flink can employ semantic web technology for reasoning with "personal" destination information extracted from a number of electronic information sources including web pages, emails, etc. The acquired knowledge can be used for the purposes of social network analysis and for generating a web-based presentation of the tourism destination community. In addition, the Flink exploits FOAF documents for the purposes of social intelligence. By social intelligence, we mean the semantics-based integration and analysis of *social knowledge* extracted from electronic sources under diverse ownership or control. Flink is interesting to all destination managers, who are planning to develop systems using semantic web technologies for similar or different purposes.

3. Semantic Web services for Tourism

Semantics can be used in the discovery, composition and monitoring of tourism web services [42,43]. The semantic web services purpose is to describe web services' capabilities and content in a computer-interpretable language and improve the quality of existing tasks, including web services discovery, invocation, composition, monitoring, and recovery. They have major impact on industries as they allow the automatic discovery, composition, integration, orchestration, and execution of inter-organization business logic, making the Internet become a global common platform [44,45].

3.1. *Ontological description of web Services*

Web Service Modeling Ontology [46] (WSMO) and OWL-S (http://www.daml.org/services/owls/1.1B/) can provide the infrastructure for ontological description of tourism web services. Especially, WSMO can describe semantic web services to solve the integration problem. The WSMO describes all relevant aspects related to services with the ultimate goal of enabling the automation of the tasks involved in integration of web services. These tasks are: discovery, selection, composition, mediation, execution, monitoring, etc. WSMO has its conceptual basis in the *Web Service Modeling Framework* [47] (WSMF) refining and extending this framework and developing a formal ontology and set of languages. The OWL-S is an ontology for service description based on the OWL. It can facilitate the design of semantic web services and can be considered as "a language for describing services, reflecting the fact that it provides a standard vocabulary that can be used together with the other aspects of the OWL description language to create service descriptions". The OWL-S ontology consists of the following three parts:

- A *service profile* for advertising and discovering services;
- A *process model* that describes the operation of a service in detail;
- The *grounding* that provides details on how to interoperate with a service, via messages.

4. Conclusions

In this chapter, we presented some work of various projects on identifying tourism domain ontologies. According to Staab and Werthner [2], the semantic web technology has an enormous potential for e-Tourism by providing: (1) integration and interoperability, (2) personalized and context-aware recommendations, (3) semantically enriched information searching, and (4) internationalization. Staab and Werthner [2] state that the requirements of intelligent tourism information systems will raise a number of important technical research issues such as: (1) semantic interoperability and mediated architectures; (2) e-business frameworks supporting processes across organizations; (3) mobility and embedded intelligence; (4) natural multilingual interfaces and novel interface technologies; (5) personalization and context-based tourism services; (6) information-to-knowledge transformations — data mining and knowledge management. In addition, we believe [8] that two great challenges are going to emerge: (1) creating a social ontology for destination managers that would allow classifying complex, social relationships along several dimensions; (2) finding patterns for identifying these relationships using electronic data. As DMOs or destination managers' lives become even more accurately traceable through ubiquitous computers, the opportunities for social science based on electronic data will only become more prominent.

References

1. Buhalis, D and P O'Connor (2005). Information communication technology — revolutionising tourism. *Tourism Recreation Research*, 30(3), 7–16.
2. Staab, S and H Werthner (2002). Intelligent systems for tourism. *IEEE Intelligent Systems*, 17(6), 53–55.
3. Berners-Lee, T, J Hendler and O Lassila (2001). The Semantic Web. *Scientific American*, 284(5), 34–43.
4. Kanellopoulos, D and S Kotsiantis (2007). Semantic Web: A state of the art survey. *International Review on Computers and Software,* 2(4), 428–442.
5. Kanellopoulos, D (2009). Intelligent technologies for tourism. In Second Edition of the *Encyclopedia of Information Science and Technology,* M Khosrow-Pour (ed.), pp. 2141–2146. Idea Group Inc.
6. Chandrasekaran, B, JR Josephson and VR Benjamins (1999). What are ontologies, and why do we need them? *Intelligent Systems and Their Applications,* 14(1), 20–26.
7. Paprzychi, M, A Gilbert and M Gordon (2002). Knowledge representation in the agent-based travel support system. *LNCS 2457,* pp. 232–241. Berlin: Springer.
8. Kanellopoulos, D (2006). The advent of semantic Web in tourism information systems. *Tourismos: An International Multidisciplinary Journal of Tourism,* 1(2), 75–91.
9. Camacho, D, D Borrajo and J Molina (2001). Intelligent travel planning: a multiagent planning system to solve web problems in the e-tourism domain. *Autonomous agents and multi-agent systems,* 4(4), 387–392.
10. Mizoguchi, R (2004). Ontology engineering environments. In *Handbook on ontologies,* S Staab and R Studer (eds.), pp. 275–298. Berlin: Springer.
11. Dean, M and G Schreiber (eds.) (2004). OWL Web ontology language reference, *W3C recommendation.* 10 February.
12. OpenCyc v. 1.0 (2006). Available at http://www.opencyc.org/.
13. Dell' Erba, M (2004). Exploiting semantic Web technologies for data interoperability. *AIS SIGSEMIS Bulletin,* 1(3), 48–52.
14. Fodor, O and H Werthner (2005). Harmonise — A step towards an interoperable e-tourism marketplace. *International Journal on Electronic Business,* 9(2), 11–39.
15. Dogac, A, Y Kabak, G Laleci, S Sinir, A Yildiz, S Kirbas and Y Gurcan (2004). Semantically enriched Web services for the travel industry. *ACM Sigmod Record,* 33(3), 21–27.
16. Maedche, A and S Staab (2003). Services on the move: Towards P2P-enabled semantic Web services. In *Proceedings of information and communication technologies in tourism 2003, ENTER 2003,* pp. 124–133. Helsinki: Springer.

17. Prantner, K (2004). *OnTour: The Ontology*. DERI Innsbruck, Austria. Available at http://e-tourism.deri.at/ont/docu2004/OnTour%20-%20The%20Ontology.pdf.
18. World Tourism Organisation (WTO) (2002). Thesaurus on tourism and leisure activities of the World Tourism Organization. Available at http://www.world-tourism.org.
19. ISO (2003). ISO 18513: Tourism services — Hotel and other types of tourism accommodation — Terminology. Available at http://www.iso.org/en/CatalogueDetailPage.CatalogueDetail?CSNUMBER=31812.
20. Cardoso, J (2006). Developing dynamic packaging systems using semantic web technologies. *Transactions on Information Science and Applications,* 3(4), 729–736.
21. Cardoso, J and C Lange (2007). A framework for assessing strategies and technologies for dynamic packaging applications in e-Tourism. *Information Technology & Tourism,* 9(1), 27–44.
22. Cardoso, J (2006). Developing an OWL ontology for e-Tourism. In *Semantic Web Services, Processes and Applications,* Vol. 3, pp. 247–282. US: Springer.
23. Kanellopoulos, D and A Panagopoulos (2008). Exploiting tourism destinations' knowledge in an RDF-based P2P network. *Network and Computer Applications,* 31(2), 179–200.
24. Kanellopoulos, D and S Kotsiantis (2007). A semantic-based architecture for intelligent destination management systems. *International Journal of Soft Computing,* 2(1), 61–68.
25. Kanellopoulos, D (2008). An ontology-based system for intelligent matching of travelers' needs for group package tours. *International Journal of Digital Culture and Electronic Tourism,* 1(1), 76–99.
26. Hi-Touch Working Group (2003). Semantic Web methodologies and tools for intra-European sustainable tourism. Available at http://www.mondeca.com/articleJITT-hitouch-legrand.pdf/ [accessed on 10 January 2004].
27. Bachlechner, D (2004). Ontology collection in view of an e-tourism portal. Technical report, Digital Enterprise Research Institute (DERI), Innsbruck.
28. Gordon, M, A Kowalski, Paprzycki, T Pelech, M Szymczak and T Wasowicz (2005). Ontologies in a travel support system. *In Internet 2005,* DJ Bem *et al.* (eds.), Technical University of Wroclaw Press, pp. 285–300.
29. Hagen, K, R Kramer, M Hermkes, B Schumann and P Mueller (2005). Semantic matching and heuristic search for a dynamic tour guide. In *Information and Communication Technologies in Tourism 2005,* AJ Frew, M Hitz, P O'Connor (eds.). New York: Springer.
30. Antoniou, G, T Skylogiannis, A Bikakis and N Bassiliades (2005). A semantic brokering system for the tourism domain. *Journal of Information Technology & Tourism,* 7(3–4), 183–200.

31. Lam, THW and RST Lee (2007). iJADE FreeWalker — An intelligent ontology agent-based tourist guiding system. *Studies in Computational Intelligence (SCI)*, 72, 103–125. Verlag Berlin, Heidelberg: Springer.
32. Vukmirovic, M, M Szynczak, M Gawinecki, M Ganza and M Paprzycki (2007). Designing new days for selling airline tickets. *Informatica*, 31, 93–104.
33. Malucelli, A, A Castro and E Oliveira (2006). Crew and aircraft recovery through a multiagent airline electronic market. In *Proceedings of IADIS International Conference e-Commerce*.
34. Kanellopoulos, D (2008). An ontology-based system for intelligent matching of travellers' needs for airline seats. *International Journal of Computer Applications in Technology*, 32(3), 194–205.
35. Niemann, M, M Mochol and R Tolksdorf (2008). Enhancing hotel search with semantic web technologies. *Journal of Theoretical and Applied Electronic Commerce Research*, 3(2), 82–96.
36. Garbers, J, M Nieman and M Mochol (2006). A personalized hotel selection engine, *3rd European Semantic Web Conference* (ESWC 2006), Budra, Monterego, 11th–14th June 2006.
37. Hwang, H-S, K-S Park and C-S Kim (2006). Ontology-based information search in the real world using web services. In *ICCSA 2006, LNCS* 3982, M Gavrilova *et al.* (eds.), pp. 125–133. Berlin, Heidelberg: Springer-Verlag.
38. Badre, J, T Libourel and P Maurel (2005). A metadata service for integrated management of knowledges related to coastal areas. *Multimedia Tools and Applications*, 25, 419–429.
39. Hyvönen, E, E Mäkelä, M Salminen, A Valo, K Viljanen, S Saarela, M Junnila, S Kettula (2005). Museum Finland — Finnish museums on the semantic web. *Journal of Web Semantics*, 3(2–3), 224–241.
40. Wasserman, S, K Faust, D Iacobucci and M Granovetter (1994). *Social Network Analysis: Methods and Applications*. Cambridge University Press.
41. Mika, P (2005). Flink: Semantic web technology for the extraction and analysis of social networks. *Journal of Web Semantics*, 3(1), 211–213.
42. Sycara, K, M Paolucci, A Ankolekar and N Srinivasan (2003). Automated discovery, interaction and composition of semantic web services. *Journal of Web Semantics*, 1, 27–46.
43. Ouzzani, M and A Bouguettaya (2004). Efficient access to web services. *IEEE Internet Computing*, 8(2), 34–44.
44. McIlraith, S, T Cao Son and H Zeng (2001). Semantic web services. *IEEE Intelligent Systems*, March/April 2001, 46–53.
45. Cardoso, J (2004). Semantic web processes and ontologies for the travel industry. *AIS SIGSEMIS Bulletin*, 1(3), 25–28.

46. Roman, D, U Keller, H Lausen, J Bruijn, R Lara, M Stollberg, A Polleres, C Feier, C Bussler and D Fensel (2005). Web service modeling ontology. *Applied Ontology*, 1, 77–106.
47. Fensel, D and C Bussler (2002). The web service modeling framework WSMF. *Electronic Commerce Research and Applications*, 1(2), 1–33.

CHAPTER III.8

METADATA STANDARDS AND ONTOLOGIES FOR MULTIMEDIA CONTENT

Tobias Bürger

PAYBACK GmbH
Theresienhöhe 12
80339 München, Germany
tobias@tobiasbuerger.com

Michael Hausenblas

Digital Enterprise Research Institute, National University of Ireland,
Lower Dangan, Galway, Ireland
michael.hausenblas@deri.org

This chapter provides an overview of the current state of the art in the area of metadata for multimedia content, focusing on existing metadata standards, vocabularies and ontologies for the description of multimedia content. We introduce the most important metadata standards for images, video, audio and 3D content and provide an overview of recent proposals for vocabularies and ontologies for the semantic description of multimedia content. We introduce typical scenarios in which they are used and outline their actual uses. We conclude the survey with an analysis of open issues and possible directions for future research.

1. Introduction

Multimedia content is a predominant part of our daily lives. It is consumed and produced in huge amounts in different forms and via different channels every day: video is broadcasted over TV, audio is broadcasted via radio, graphical advertisements are published in newspapers and displayed on any imaginable place in cities or beyond. Furthermore multimedia content is increasingly consumed and produced for the Web. Additionally to the growing amount and diversity of multimedia content a shift has happened: While professionally produced content is still prominent, also end users increasingly produce and share huge amounts content, which is a part of the Web 2.0 phenomena.

In the last decades much research has been done on how to organise or annotate these vast amounts of multimedia content to enable better search and reuse of content. Due to its intrinsic nature, the multimedia research faced some hard challenges which were mainly due to the Semantic Gap which commonly refers to the large gulf between automatically extractable low-level features and high-level semantics which are typically derived based on the background of a human being [1]. As multimedia content in retrieval and organization scenarios cannot be treated equally as text for which indexes can be automatically generated, there is an evident need to describe and preserve the aspects of multimedia content ranging from contextual properties like what the content is about, what is depicted in it, how and under which circumstances it can be used and who owns the rights on the content to its intrinsic constituents like color histograms or motion vectors.

As multimedia content is a very broad concept and its types range from still images to complex 3D animations, different requirements for multimedia standards and description schemes are given which is why different standards emerged for different types, for different domains and and also for different usage scenarios. Furthermore the shift from professionally to user generated content demands for different description facilities as the needs in professional environments are very different to the needs of home users in tagging scenarios like, e.g., on social media sharing sites like Flickr[1].

This chapter acknowledges the growth in the amount of content, its growth in diversity, growth in usage scenarios and the continuous shift from professionally to user generated content. By that it presents a wide range of multimedia metadata standards, description schemes and vocabularies which range from traditional multimedia metadata standards over multimedia ontologies to folksonomies and vocabularies used to describe multimedia content on the Web.

Besides the discussion of traditional metadata standards we put an additional focus on recent trends in the area of multimedia ontologies which are increasingly being built and used to overcome the commonly known drawbacks of existing multimedia metadata standards for the descriptions of the semantics of multimedia content [2, 3].

---

[1] http://www.flickr.com

This chapter is organized as follows: First, a classification schema for different types of multimedia metadata is introduced in Sec. 2. Secondly, (traditional) multimedia metadata formats are introduced in Sec. 3. Section 4 gives an introduction to multimedia ontologies and provides an overview of the most prominent ones. Section 5 introduces Web 2.0 based organization and description schemes like folksonomies and simple vocabularies. Finally we conclude the chapter with a discussion of future research challenges in Section 6.

2. Classification and types of multimedia metadata formats

There is a multitude of possibilities to classify multimedia metadata formats, depending on scope, format, coverage, granularity and other aspects. Taking [4] as a starting point, we will classify and discuss multimedia metadata formats along two orthogonal dimensions:

1. Modality and content-type, and
2. Application domain.

While the former focuses on the question "which media type or which modality which included in the media type is covered", the latter captures its potential application area.

Following [5] we understand that there are different types of metadata (administrative, descriptive, etc.) and the metadata format itself can have different scopes and may differ in terms of level of granularity or level of formality. We furthermore separate the discussion of multimedia metadata formats according to their representation type: Section 3 discusses XML and non-XML based formats and Sec. 4 discusses formats based on Semantic Web representation languages like RDF, RDF(S), or OWL which are introduced in chapter "C_II_2. Ontology languages" in this volume.

3. Multimedia metadata formats

3.1. *Multimedia metadata for the description of still images*

3.1.1. *Exchangeable image file format (EXIF)*

A widely deployed metadata format for digital images is the Exchangeable Image File Format (Exif)[2]. The standard "specifies the formats to be used for images and sounds, and tags in digital still cameras and for other systems

[2] http://www.digicamsoft.com/exif22/exif22/html/exif22_1.htm

handling the image and sound files recorded by digital cameras". The so called Exif header carries the metadata for the captured image or sound.

The metadata fields which the Exif standard provides, cover metadata related to the capture of the image and the situation of the capturing. This includes metadata related to the image data structure (such as height, width, orientation), capturing information (e.g., rotation, exposure time, flash), recording offset (for example image data location or bytes per compressed strip), image data characteristics (e.g., transfer function, color space transformation), as well as general fields (e.g., image title, copyright holder, manufacturer). Metadata elements pertaining to the image are stored in the image file header and are identified by unique tags, which serve as an element identifier. Exif is widely used on Web 2.0 platforms such as Flickr and APIs to retrieve and query Exif data are available.[3]

3.1.2. *Visual resource association (VRA) core*

Visual Resource Association (VRA) Core 4.0[4] is a data standard for the cultural heritage community that was developed by the Visual Resources Association's Data Standards Committee. It consists of a metadata element set (units of information such as title, location, date, etc.), as well as an initial blueprint for defining how those elements can be hierarchically structured. VRA Core makes a logical distinction between a record describing a work such as a painting and a recording describing an image documenting that work (for example a digital image of the painting).

Similar to Dublin Core, VRA Core refers to terms in their vocabularies as elements, and it also use qualifiers to refine elements. Some of the general elements of VRA Core have direct mappings to comparable fields in Dublin Core. Furthermore, both vocabularies are defined in a way that abstracts from implementation issues and underlying serialization languages. VRA Core provides an XML schema; though not as widely spread as, for example, Exif, there are (for educational purposes) example usages available.[5]

3.1.3. *NISO Z39.87*

The NISO Z39.87 standard[6] defines a set of over 120 metadata elements for digital raster images to enable users to develop, exchange, and interpret

[3] http://sourceforge.net/projects/libexif

[4] http://www.vraweb.org/projects/vracore4/

[5] http://gort.ucsd.edu/escowles/vracore4/

[6] http://www.niso.org/standards/resources/Z39-87-2006.pdf

digital image files. The standard defines a set of metadata fields which cover a wide spectrum: These include basic image parameters, image creation, imaging performance assessment, or image history. The standard is intended to facilitate the development of applications to validate, manage, migrate, and otherwise process images of enduring value in applications such as large-scale digital repositories or digital asset management systems. The element dictionary has been designed to facilitate interoperability between systems, services, and software as well as to support the long-term management and continuing access to digital image collections; an XML schema for the dictionary[7] and mappings to Exif and DIG35 are available.[8]

3.1.4. *DIG35*

The DIG35 specification[9] includes a "standard set of metadata for digital images promoting interoperability and extensibility, as well as a uniform underlying construct to support interoperability of metadata between various digital imaging devices". The following blocks are defined by the standard:

- **Basic image parameter** to specify general information about the image, such as file name, format and size.
- **Image creation parameter** to specify information related to the creation of the image such as information about the device used to capture the image (such as a camera or scanner), technical information about the capture condition as well as information about the software used to create the image.
- **Content description metadata** to provide fine grain information about the depicted content. The modeling capabilities in this part go far beyond basic keywords and allow detailed modeling of depicted persons and objects, locations or events using domain specific ontologies. DIG35 allows to relate descriptions to parts of images via the definition of regions or splines.
- **History metadata** which holds information about the creation and customizations performed to the image and information about previous versions of the metadata set.
- **IPR metadata** can be used to protect the image and to preserve both moral — and copyrights.

---

[7] http://www.loc.gov/standards/mix/
[8] http://www.oclc.org/programs/ourwork/past/automaticexposure/ae_appendix2_2003.pdf
[9] http://www.i3a.org/resources/dig35/

3.2. *Multimedia metadata for the description of audio content*

3.2.1. *ID3*

ID3[10] is a metadata container which is used to embed metadata within an MP3 audio file. It allows to state information about music tracks including the title, artist, album, etc. The ID3 specification aims to address a broad spectrum of metadata (represented in so-called "frames") ranging from encryption, over a list of involved people, lyrics, musical group, relative volume adjustment to ownership, artist, and recording dates. Additionally, users can define their own properties if needed. Furthermore, a list of 79 genres (ranging from Blues to Hard Rock) is defined by ID3. The format is widely used and supported by a number of tools and libraries such as ID3Lib[11].

3.2.2. *Musicbrainz XML metadata format (MMD)*

The MusicBrainz XML Metadata Format (MMD)[12] is an XML based document format to represent music metadata. The official format description is a Relax NG schema. The core set of the standard is capable of expressing basic music related metadata such as artist, album, track, etc. The predetermined use of MMD is in the MusicBrainz Web service which provides access to MusicBrainz[13] an open music database on the Web. However, it may be useful for other applications, too.

3.3. *Multimedia metadata for the description of audio visual content*

3.3.1. *MPEG-7*

The ISO MPEG-7 standard [6, 7], formally named "Multimedia Content Description" is an exhaustive standard for the description of multimedia content of any type. The objective of the standard is to enable efficient search, filtering and browsing of multimedia content. Possible applications are in the areas of digital audiovisual libraries, electronic news media and interactive TV. MPEG-7 provides standardized description schemes that enable the creation of descriptions of material that are directly linked with the essence to support efficient retrieval. The audiovisual information can be represented in various forms of media, such as

---

[10] http://www.id3.org/
[11] http://id3lib.sourceforge.net/
[12] http://musicbrainz.org/doc/MusicBrainzXMLMetaData
[13] http://musicbrainz.org/

pictures, 2D/3D models, audio, speech, and video. Because MPEG7 was developed to be universally applicable, it is independent of how the content is coded or stored.

Most notably MPEG-7 standardizes so-called "description tools" for multimedia content: It standardizes ways to define multimedia descriptors (Ds), description schemes (DSs) and the relationships between them: escriptors are used to represent the specific media features, respectively the low level features such as visual features (e.g., texture, camera motion) or audio features (e.g., melody), while description schemes refer to more abstract description entities (usually a set of related descriptors) and semantic meaning of content. These description tools as well as their relationships are represented using the Description Definition Language (DDL), a core part of the language. The W3C XML Schema recommendation has been adopted as the most appropriate schema for the MPEG-7 DDL, adding a few extensions (array and matrix data types) in order to satisfy specific MPEG-7 requirements. MPEG-7 descriptions can be serialized as XML or in a binary format defined in the standard.

The MPEG-7 standard (Version 2) is structured into the following parts [8]:

- **MPEG-7 Systems**: The tools needed to prepare MPEG-7 descriptions for efficient transport and storage and the terminal architecture.
- **MPEG-7 Description Definition Language (DDL)**: The language for defining the syntax of the *MPEG-7 Description Tools* and for defining new *Description Schemes (DS)*.
- **MPEG-7 Visual**: The *Description Tools* dealing with (exclusively) *visual descriptions.* This part consists of basic structures and descriptors that cover basic visual features such as color, texture, shape, motion, localization and face recognition.
- **MPEG-7 Audio**: The *Description Tools* dealing with (exclusively) *audio descriptions.* This part consists of both low level features for describing audio content such as spectral, parametric, and temporal and high level features such as sound recognition, indexing etc.
- **MPEG-7 Multimedia Description Schemes**: The *Description Tools* dealing with generic features and multimedia descriptions. It provides amongst other things description schemes for: Content description, content management, content organization, navigation & access and user interaction.
- **MPEG-7 Reference Software**: A software implementation of relevant parts of the MPEG-7 standard with normative status.
- **MPEG-7 Conformance Testing**: Guidelines and procedures for testing conformance of MPEG-7 implementations.

- **MPEG-7 Extraction and use of descriptions**: Informative material (in the form of a technical report) about the extraction and use of some of the *Description Tools.*
- **MPEG-7 Profiles and levels**: Provides guidelines and standard profiles.
- **MPEG-7 Schema Definition**: Specifies the schema using the DDL.

3.3.2. *Advanced authoring format (AAF)*

The Advanced Authoring Format (AAF) [9] is a cross-platform file format for the interchange of data between multimedia authoring tools. AAF supports the encapsulation of both metadata and essence (the raw content). The object-oriented AAF object model allows for extensive timeline-based modeling of compositions (i.e., motion picture montages), including transitions between clips and the application of effects (e.g., dissolves, wipes, flipping). Furthermore, AAF supports storing event-related information (e.g., time-based user annotations and remarks) or specific authoring instructions.

AAF files are fully agnostic as to how essence is coded and served as a wrapper for any kind of essence coding specification. In addition to the means to describe the current location and characteristics of essence clips, AAF also supports descriptions of the entire provenance chain for a piece of essence, from its current state to the original storage medium, possibly a tape (identified by tape number and time code), or a film (identified by an edge code for example). The AAF data model and essence are independent of the specificities of how AAF files are stored on disk. The most common storage specification used for AAF files is the Microsoft Structured Storage format, but other storage formats (e.g., XML) can be used.

3.3.3. *Material exchange format (MXF)-dms-1*

The Material Exchange Format (MXF) is a streamable file format optimized for the interchange of material for the content creation industries. MXF is a wrapper/container format intended to encapsulate and accurately describe one or more "clips" of audiovisual essence (video, sound, pictures, etc.). This file format is essence-agnostic, which means it should be independent of the underlying audio and video coding specifications in the file. The MXF format embeds the necessary information in the header of a file which includes the duration, required codecs, time-line complexity of the encoded information or further key characteristics which are necessary to know to allow its interchange.

Structural Metadata is used to describe different essence types and their relationship along a timeline. The structural metadata defines the synchronization of different tracks along a timeline. It also defines picture size, picture rate, aspect ratio, audio sampling, and other essence description parameters. The MXF structural metadata is derived from the AAF data model. Next to the structural metadata described above, MXF files may contain descriptive metadata which is metadata created during production or planning of production. Possible information can be about the production, the clip (e.g., which type of camera was used) or a scene (e.g., the actors in it). DMS-1 (Descriptive Metadata Scheme 1) [10] is an attempt to standardize such information within the MXF format. Furthermore DMS-1 is able to interwork as far as practical with other metadata schemes, such as MPEG-7, TV-Anytime, etc. and Dublin Core.

3.3.4. *MPEG-A*

MPEG-A [11] is a recent addition to a sequence of standards that have been developed by the MPEG group. This new standard was developed by selecting existing technologies from all published MPEG standards and combining them into so-called "Multimedia Application Formats" (MAFs). MPEG-A aims to supports a fast track to standardization by selecting readily tested and verified tools taken from the MPEG body of standards (MPEG-1,-2,-4,-7 or -21) and combining them to form a MAF. This approach builds on the toolbox approach of existing MPEG standards: Hence, a MAF is created by cutting horizontally through all MPEG standards, selecting existing parts and profiles as appropriate for the envisioned application. Thus, ideally, a MAF specification consists of references to existing profiles within MPEG standards. If MPEG cannot provide a needed piece of technology, then additional technologies originating from other organizations can be included by reference in order to facilitate the envisioned MAF.

Currently a set of MAFs exist, e.g., the Music Player MAF [12], the Photo Player MAF[14], the Open Access MAF[15], an e-Learning MAF [13] and others.[16]

3.4. ***Domain specific metadata formats***

Multimedia content is an integral part in many different domains which often provide their own standards to cover domain- or application specific needs. For example, in the news domain a set of standards exist: This includes the

[14] http://www.chiariglione.org/mpeg/technologies/mpa-pp/index.htm
[15] http://or.ldv.ei.tum.de/
[16] Further MAFs are summarized at http://maf.nist.gov/

News Architecture for G2-Standards[17] developed by the International Press Telecommunication Council (IPTC) whose goal is to provide a single generic model for the exchange of all kinds of newsworthy information, thus providing a framework for a future family of IPTC news exchange standards. This family includes NewsML-G2, SportsML-G2, EventsML-G2, ProgramGuideML-G2 or a future WeatherML. All are XML-based languages used for describing not only the news content (traditional metadata), but also their management, packaging, or related to the exchange itself (transportation, routing).

Further, there are many in-house formats used by different broadcasters to organize their archives or to exchange information about programs and streamed content. This includes for example the TVAnytime format[18] which allows the controlled delivery of multimedia content to a user's digital video recorder by means of Electronic Program Guides (EPG).

There are many more domains where multimedia content and its descriptions play a vital role which includes the domain of E-Learning which most prominently developed the Learning Object Metadata (LOM) standard [14] or the archival domain in which a set of standards for the description and preservation of content have been defined such as the Open Archival Information System (OAIS) reference model [15] or the Metadata Encoding and Transmission Standard (METS) [16]. We refer the interested reader according to the chapters in this book (*cf. III.2. Metadata and ontologies for e-learning,* chapter *III.1. Metadata and ontologies for librarianship,* or chapter *III.12. Metadata and ontologies for long-term preservation*).

3.5. *Container formats*

In this section, multimedia specific container formats like MPEG-21, SMIL and Adobe XMP are discussed. Other container formats like METS [16], IMS Content Packaging [17] or the OAI-ORE model [18] which also include multimedia specific parts are discussed in chapter *III.2. Metadata and ontologies for e-learning* and chapter *III.1. Metadata and ontologies for librarianship* in this volume.

3.5.1. *MPEG-21*

MPEG-21 [19] aims at defining a framework for multimedia delivery and consumption which supports a variety of businesses engaged in the trading of digital

[17] http://www.iptc.org/newsml/

[18] http://www.tv-anytime.org/

objects which offers users transparent and interoperable consumption and delivery of rich multimedia content. The MPEG-21 has been built on its previous coding and metadata standards (MPEG-1, -2, -4 and -7) such that it links these together to produce a protectable universal package for collecting, relating, referencing and structuring multimedia content for the consumption by users.

MPEG-21 is based on two essential concepts: The "Digital Item" — a fundamental unit of distribution and transaction and the concept of "Users" interacting with these items. The standard consists of 19 parts, including the following key parts:

- **Digital Item Declaration (DID)**: The DID part describes a set of abstract terms and concepts to form a useful model for defining *Digital Items.* The DID model defines digital items, containers, fragments or complete resources, assertions, statements and annotations of digital items.
- **Digital Item Identification and Description (DII)**: The DII part deals with the unique identification of complete or partial *Digital Items* by encapsulating Uniform Resource Identifiers into the *Identification DS.* It also enables the identification of *Digital Items* via a registry authority.
- **Intellectual Property Management and Protection (IPMP)**: This part deals with the management and protection of intellectual property within MPEG-21.
- **Rights Expression Language (REL):** The REL enables the declaration of rights and permissions using the terms as defined in the Rights Data Dictionary. An MPEG REL grant consists of: the principal to whom the grant is issued; the right that the grant specifies; the resource to which the right in the grant applies and the condition that must be met before the right can be exercised.
- **Rights Data Dictionary (RDD)**: The RDD comprises a set of uniquely identified terms to support the REL. RDD is designed to support mapping and transformation of metadata from the terminology of one namespace into that of another namespace.
- **Digital Item Adaptation (DIA)**: This part enables adaptation of digital content to preserve quality of user experience taking care of user, terminal or network characteristics.
- **Digital Item Processing (DIP)**: DIP was motivated by the need to make DIDs active as these are just declarative and provide no usage instructions. DIP should improve the processing of Digital Items by providing tools that allow users to add functionality to a DID. DIP specifies so called *Digital Item Methods (DIM)* using the *Digital Item Method Language (DIML).*

- **Fragment Identification (FI)** specifies a syntax to identify fragments of MPEG data types.

3.5.2. *The synchronized multimedia integration language (SMIL)*

The Synchronized Multimedia Integration Language (SMIL)[19] is a W3C standard that enables the integration of independent multimedia objects such as text, audio, graphics or videos into a synchronized multimedia presentation. Within this presentation, an author can specify the temporal coordination of the playback, the layout of the presentation and hyperlinks for single multimedia components. The SMIL recommendation contains elements to control the animation, the content, the layout, the structure and timing and transition issues of a presentation. Using SMIL authors are able to declaratively describe interactive multimedia presentations. An author can describe the temporal behavior of a multimedia presentation, associate hyperlinks with media objects and describe the layout of the presentation on a screen.

The main characteristics of SMIL are:

(1) The synchronization in SMIL: SMIL enables the control of the spatial layout and the time frame of a multimedia presentation based on a common time line.
(2) SMIL is declarative: SMIL does not specify the events that show or hide objects, but specifies an amount of objects and their synchronization.
(3) SMIL is integrative: SMIL enables referential integration of media objects.

SMIL presentations are created from one or more components that all are accessible via URIs and which may be of different media type (video, audio, text). These components can be spatially and timely positioned and their appearance can be manipulated in different forms. For that, the standard includes different media composition and transformation capabilities, e.g. visual transparency, visual deformations, color effects, audio track manipulation or sound effects. The current version of SMIL is SMIL 3.0[20]. SMIL 2.1 added mobile support to SMIL 2.0 and extends some of the modules defined in SMIL 2.0. SMIL 3.0 added a new media type called *smilText, smilState* to provide more detailed control over the presentation flow and *SMIL Timesheets* to be able to provide external timing information for a SMIL presentation.

---

[19] http://www.w3.org/AudioVideo/
[20] More information available at http://www.w3.org/TR/SMIL3/

3.5.3. *Adobe extensible metadata platform (XMP)*

The Adobe XMP specification *standardizes the definition, creation, and processing of metadata by providing a data model, storage model (serialization of the metadata as a stream of XML), and formal schema definitions (predefined sets of metadata property definitions that are relevant for a wide range of applications). XMP makes use of RDF in order to represent the metadata properties associated with a document* [20]. Adobe XMP is a method and format for expressing and embedding metadata in various multimedia file formats. It provides a basic data storage platform as well as a serialization format for expressing metadata in RDF [20], provides storage mechanisms for different media types [21] and defines a basic set of schemas for managing multimedia (versioning, media management, etc.) [22].

The most important components of the specification are the data model and the defined (and extensible) schemas. The data model is a subset of the RDF data model. Most notably it provides support for different metadata properties which are associated with a resource and which consist of a property name and a property value. Properties can be structured, qualified, and language specific. Furthermore, XMP support the definition of schemas to be used to describe resources. Schemas consist of predefined sets of metadata property definitions that are relevant for a wide range of applications varying from media management, versioning and specific schemas that Adobe uses within its tools. Schemas are essentially collections of statements about resources which are expressed using RDF. It is possible to define new external schemas, extend the existing ones or add some if necessary. The XMP specification already includes the following schemas: the Dublin Core Schema, the XMP Basic Schema, the XMP Rights Management Schema, the XMP Media Management Schema, the XMP Basic Job Ticket Schema, the XMP Paged-Text Schema and the XMP Dynamic Media Schema. Furthermore, more specialized schemas are provided such as the Adobe PDF schema, the Photoshop schema, the Camera Raw schema, or the EXIF schemas. Additionally the IPTC defined a XMP schema for IPTC metadata.[21]

4. Multimedia ontologies

As defined by Gruber [23], an ontology is an explicit specification of a (shared) conceptualization. The term ontology has been in use for many centuries and ontologies are widely used in applications related to information integration, information retrieval, knowledge management or in the Semantic Web.

[21] http://www.iptc.org/IPTC4XMP/

Ontologies are usually used to establish a common understanding of a domain and to capture domain knowledge. This is usually done by modeling basic terms and relations which hold between terms, and by providing rules stating restrictions on the usage of both terms and relations. Ontologies are widely discussed in chapter *Methodologies for the Creation of Semantic Data* in this volume.

By using multimedia ontologies, recent research initiatives in the multimedia domain try to overcome the commonly known drawbacks of existing multimedia metadata standards for the descriptions of the semantics of multimedia content (*cf.* [24–28]). The existing multimedia ontologies were mostly designed to serve one or more of the following purposes [29]:

(1) **Annotation**, which is in most cases motivated by the need to have high-level summarizations of the content of multimedia items
(2) **Automated semantic analysis**, i.e., to support the analysis of the semantics and syntax of the structure and content of multimedia items
(3) **Retrieval**, i.e., to use rich formal descriptions to enable context-based retrieval and recommendations to users. The use of semantics enables automatic matching of content properties with user properties
(4) **Reasoning**, i.e., the application of reasoning techniques to discover previously unknown facts of multimedia content or to enable question answering about properties of the content.
(5) **Personalized Filtering**, i.e., the delivery of multimedia content according to user-, network- or device-preferences.
(6) **Meta-Modeling**, i.e., to use ontologies or rules to model multimedia items and associated processes.

In the following, we will introduce a variety of multimedia ontologies which have been built over the past years. First, we introduce ontologies which are based on the MPEG-7 standard in Sec. 4.1, subsequently we introduce ontologies for the description of still images (*cf.* Sec. 4.2), for audio (*cf.* Sec. 4.3), for audiovisual content (*cf.* Sec. 4.4), and for 3D content (*cf.* Sec. 4.5). Finally, we describe a set of domain- and application specific multimedia ontologies in Sec. 4.6.

4.1. *MPEG-7 ontologies*

As introduced in Sec. 3.3.1, MPEG-7 is an ISO/IEC standard for the structural and semantic description of multimedia content. One drawback of MPEG-7 is that its XML Schema based approach has led to a high degree of complexity and ambiguity of semantic descriptions as identified and discussed in [30–32].

The last years of multimedia semantics research brought up a considerable amount of approaches that deal with the augmentation or reformulation of MPEG-7 (*cf.* [24, 25, 27, 28, 33, 34]), all of which take different approaches to overcome the identified drawbacks: A more or less purist approach where whole MPEG-7 documents are transformed to OWL [34], an integrated approach that integrates OWL in MPEG-7 [33], a layered approach that uses each vocabulary in its appropriate realm [24], or a highly formalized approach which remodels MPEG-7's multimedia content structure and content description capabilities using ontology design patterns from DOLCE and by that aligns multimedia descriptions to a foundational ontology [28].

In the following, we will introduce the most sophisticated approaches all of which are having a large coverage of the MPEG-7 standard.

4.1.1. *Hunter's MPEG-7 ontology*

The first MPEG-7 ontology has been provided by Jane Hunter in 2001 [33]. An early version of the ontology has been created manually and reflected a 1:1 translation from MPEG-7 to RDF Schema. An OWL Full version of the ontology has later been aligned to the foundational ABC ontology. Hunter's ontology mainly covers the decomposition schemes defined in the MPEG-7 MDS part and the structural description of different media types and their features. Hunter's ontology can be used to decompose audiovisual material, it allows to specify visual descriptors and can integrate domain ontologies to formally express depiction of domain specific instances in images or videos. Other semantic relations as defined by MPEG-7 can also be used to attach domain ontologies.

Extensions to the Hunter's ontology are reported in [35].

4.1.2. *The rhizomik MPEG-7 ontology*

The Rhizomik ontology [34], which is available in OWL Full and OWL DL, has been created fully automatically using a generic XML Schema to OWL mapping approach. Thus it consequently covers the whole MPEG-7 standard. This approach most notably allows to reuse existing MPEG-7 descriptions available in XML fully automatically.

4.1.3. *The DS-MIRF MPEG-7 ontology*

The DS-MIRF ontology [27] also fully captures the MPEG-7 multimedia description schemes (MDS) and the MPEG-7 classification schemes. The

DS-MIRF ontology has been built manually and was implemented in OWL-DL. It most notably makes use of datatype definitions from an MPEG-7 file using an external XML Schema. A mapping ontology is utilized to store correspondences between the XML Schema and the OWL ontology and that captures some semantics of the XML Schema which are not representable in OWL (like sequencing of elements).

Domain knowledge can be integrated in an MPEG-7 description by the creation of subclasses of the semantic base types which are defined in the MPEG-7 standard such as events or agents. Furthermore relationship types as defined by MPEG-7 can be used to specify relations between objects or agents depicted in an audiovisual resource.

4.1.4. *The COMM ontology*

The "Core Ontology of MultiMedia" (COMM) [28] is an OWL DL ontology which is based on a re-engineering approach of the semantics of the MPEG-7 standard. As such it is not aligned to the XML Schema as defined by the MPEG-7 standard but is based on ontology design patterns which are defined in the DOLCE foundational ontology. COMM extends these pattern as multimedia description patterns to describe concepts defined by MPEG-7. Most notably COMM defines patterns for the decomposition and annotation of multimedia content (the decomposition, content and media and semantic media annotation patterns), and basic patterns to represent digital data and algorithms. COMM most notably represents the structural and the semantic content description parts of MPEG-7.

A comparison of the MPEG-7 ontologies which we presented above is given in [32]. The comparison includes a comparative example showing the use of the different ontologies and discusses pros and cons of each approach. Further approaches which partly model the MPEG-7 standard or were influenced by the standard are introduced in Secs. 4.4.1, 4.4.2, 4.6.2, and 5.3. Another approach that partly represents MPEG-7 visual descriptors was introduced in the SmartMedia ontology as described in [36].

4.2. *Multimedia ontologies for the description of still images*

4.2.1. *The DIG35 ontology*

The DIG35 ontology[22] is a formal representation of the DIG35 metadata standard for the description of digital still images (*cf.* Sec. 3.1.4). The standard

[22] http://multimedialab.elis.ugent.be/users/gmartens/Ontologies/DIG35

defines five metadata blocks and one additional common block containing fundamental metadata types and fields which are referred by the other blocks. While each block is logically separated, formal relations may exist between the blocks. The DIG35 standard as introduced in Sec. 3.1.4 is defined in different parts covering basic image parameter, image creation parameter, content description (who, what, when and where) metadata, image history, or IPR metadata.

The DIG35 ontology consists of set of small ontologies including ontologies for each of the listed parts above and additionally more general purpose ontologies for the description of persons, locations, events, or date and time.

4.2.2. *EXIF ontologies*

There are currently two ontologies available that provide an encoding of the basic Exif metadata tags in a more formal ontology. EXIF includes — as introduced in Sec. 3.1.1 — basic data about the camera with which a picture has been shot, technical information, information relating to image data structure or image data characteristics (such as chromaticity, color space information), and other tags to describe the copyright holder, artist, or bibliographic information like the title of the image.

The first ontology which formally represents the Exif data is the Kanzaki OWL-DL ontology[23] in which all EXIF tags are defined as OWL properties. This ontology has been adopted by the W3C Semantic Web Best Practices group.

Another Exif ontology in RDF(S) is provided by Norm Walsh.[24]

4.2.3. *PhotoRDF*

PhotoRDF [37] has been developed by the W3C in order to define a basic set of standardized categories and labels for personal photo collections. The goal of PhotoRDF was to define a very simple but useable standard which covers central aspects of photos and which can be used to exchange descriptions between different photo organization tools. It defines three different sub schemas, namely a Dublin Core, a technical and a content schema each containing a small amount of properties. Dublin Core is used to specify general descriptions like the title, creator or the creation date of the photo. The technical schema contains some of the EXIF properties (*cf.* Secs. 3.1.1

[23] http://www.kanzaki.com/ns/exif
[24] http://nwalsh.com/java/jpegrdf/

and 4.2.2) and the content schema contains a few keywords which can be used to describe the depicted content in the subject field of Dublin Core.

4.2.4. *Further ontologies*

Mindswap Digital Media Ontology The "Mindswap Digital Media Ontology"[25] [38, 39] defines basic concepts to describe still and moving images and parts therein. The ontology is rather simple and defines concepts like *image, video, video frame, region,* as well as relations such as *depicts* or *regionOf* which hold between regions and the image or the image/region and a domain specific concept.

Core Image Region Ontology The core image region ontology [40] is an OWL-DL ontology which defines spatial relations. It includes concepts like *background, left/right of, next to,* etc. By importing domain specific ontologies, the ontology can be used to annotate images.

Descriptive Vocabulary for Image Structure The "Descriptive Vocabulary for Image Structure" [41] is an effort to provide a commonly agreed vocabulary that can be used to describe the internal structure of images across domains. The ontology includes elements to describe the spatial distribution of objects and includes concepts like *General-part, Extremity, Inside-of, On, Vertical, Horizontal.* The ontology is assumed to be used across domains and to support interoperability between content based image retrieval approaches that could use the ontology as a shared vocabulary to issue queries across systems.

4.3. *Multimedia ontologies for the description of audio content*

4.3.1. *The music ontology*

The "Music Ontology" (MO)[26] [42] provides means to formally describe music related information on the Web. The MO can be used to describe musical metadata (e.g., editorial information), cultural metadata (e.g., musical genres and social networking information) and content-based information. The MO is organized in three levels with increasing complexity. Level 1 provides a vocabulary for simple editorial information (tracks/artists/releases, etc.), level 2 provides a vocabulary for expressing the music creation workflow (composition, arrangement, performance, recording, etc.), and level 3 provides a vocabulary for complex event decomposition which includes

[25] http://www.mindswap.org/2005/owl/digital-media
[26] http://musicontology.com/

information like the description of melody lines or fine grained descriptions of concerts or other events.

The MO is built on top of the Timeline[27], Events[28], the FOAF [29] and the Functional Requirements for Bibliographic Records (FRBR) ontology.[30] The MO is built around the core concepts such as *MusicalWork, MusicArtist, MusicGroup,* and *Performance.* It provides vocabularies to describe music related information in the three levels and also offers anchor points to use more detailed specifications.

4.3.2. *The music recommendation ontology*

The "Music Recommendation Ontology" (MRO)[31] defines basic properties of musical artists and music titles as well as some low-level audio descriptors (e.g., tonality or rhythm). It allows to describe musical items as well as relationships between musical items, other items or musical artists (e.g., one artist is influenced by another or one musical item is a cover song of another musical item, etc.). The MRO can be mapped to MusicBrainz as described in [34]. Most notably the MRO is used for social music recommendation which combines metadata-, social- and content-based filtering as described in [43].

4.3.3. *Kanzaki's music vocabulary*

The scope of the "Kanzaki Music Vocabulary" (KMV)[32] is to describe classical music and different types of performances. It provides classes and individuals to describe different artist types, instruments, events, and information about musical scores.

4.4. *Multimedia ontologies for the description of audio visual content*

4.4.1. *The BOEMIE ontology*

The BOEMIE ontology[33] is designed to enable multimedia reasoning and by that to infer high-level semantics from low-level features. It is being applied

[27] http://purl.org/NET/c4dm/timeline.owl
[28] http://purl.org/NET/c4dm/event.owl
[29] http://xmlns.com/foaf/0.1/
[30] http://vocab.org/frbr/core
[31] http://foafdevel.searchsounds.net/music-ontology/foafing-ontology-0.3.rdf
[32] http://www.kanzaki.com/ns/music
[33] http://repository.boemie.org/ontology_repository_tbox/

in the domain of athletic events and can be used to spatially decompose a multimedia document and to attach low- and high-level descriptors to parts of a document. The ontology consists of a set of subontologies centered around the *Multimedia Content Ontology* (MCO) and the *Multimedia Descriptor Ontology* (MDO). The MCO provides means to describe the structure of multimedia documents, including the representation of the different types of multimedia content and their decomposition. The MDO addresses the descriptors that are used to describe various visual and audio low-level descriptors. Both ontologies were influenced by the MPEG-7 standard: the MDO contains the complete set of visual and audio descriptors from MPEG-7 enriched with formal axioms to capture their semantics. The MCO is built based on the MPEG-7 Media Description Schemes (MDS); it contains the complete MDS whose semantics is captured using formal axioms.

The BOEMIE ontology is built on top of a core ontology which is based on SUMO[34], DOLCE[35] and WordNet[36] and includes additional domain-specific extension to describe athletic events (the Athletic Events Ontology) or geographic information (the Geographic Ontology). The MCO and MDO ontologies are described in [44] and the domain-specific extension are described in [45].

4.4.2. *The ACEMEDIA ontologies*

The ACEMEDIA ontologies[37] [25, 46] were developed in the European project ACEMEDIA[38] in order to support annotation and reasoning on multimedial content. The ontologies are built on top of a core ontology which is based on a lightweight version of the DOLCE foundational ontology and extends DOLCE's region concept branch in order to describe topological and directional relations between regions of different types like 2D or 3D regions. Topological relations describe possible overlaps between regions while spatial relations describe how visual segments are placed and related to each other. On top of that is the Visual Descriptor ontology (VDO) which models the MPEG-7 visual descriptors as described in Sec. 4.1. The VDO is used to describe visual characteristics of multimedia content. Further the Multimedia Description Scheme (MDS) ontology models basic entities from the MPEG-7

[34] http://www.ontologyportal.org/
[35] http://www.loa-cnr.it/DOLCE.html
[36] http://wordnet.princeton.edu/
[37] http://www.acemedia.org/aceMedia/files/resource/aceMedia-KIv2-2007-08-30.zip
[38] http://www.acemedia.org

MDS as described in Sec. 4.1. Further Visual Descriptor Extractor (VDE) ontologies describe how to extract visual descriptors in particular application domains. The project provided conceptualizations for the Formula-1 and tennis domain as described in [47].

The ontologies are particularly used to support multimedia reasoning, i.e., to infer annotations for multimedia content based on previous annotations and based on low-level feature descriptions as explained in [47].

4.4.3. *The interactive media manager metadata model*

The "Interactive Media Manager (IMM) Metadata Model" has been implemented by Microsoft to support media- and most notably video management and workflow support in the Interactive Media Manger[39]. The model consists of two ontologies: the IMM Core and the IMM Full ontology. The IMM Core ontology contains basic metadata and the essential classes which are needed for the IMM workflow support. The IMM Full ontology provides a full set of metadata and classes to support the management of videos in the IMM.

The IMM metadata model which has been published in late 2008 is based on the MPEG-21 DID abstract model (*cf.* Sec. 3.5.1). The IMM metadata model does not fully reflect the MPEG-21 DID model, however is based on its core elements: The central elements of the DID model are items which are deployed in containers and which are described via descriptions or annotated via annotations. The IMM metadata model defines different item types like Audio- or Videoitems which may contain resources which are bound to physical files and which additionally contain (technical) descriptions about these resources. Descriptions and annotations can be bound to fragments of resources using anchors.

The IMM model is extensible and most notably can be augmented with domain or media specific descriptors for media items.

4.5. *Ontologies for 3D content*

4.5.1. *The AIM@SHAPE virtual human ontology*

The "AIMSHAPE ontology for virtual humans" (VHO)[40] [48] defines concepts, relations and axioms for the semantic descriptions of virtual humans, which are, as defined in [49], graphical representations of human beings that can be used in virtual environments (like games, online shops, virtual worlds,

[39] http://www.microsoft.com/resources/mediaandentertainment/solutions_imm.mspx
[40] http://www.aimatshape.net/resources/aas-ontologies/virtualhumansontology.owl/view

etc). The VHO is part of an ontology framework and is layered on top of an ontology for feature representation of virtual humans which itself is layered on top of the graphical representation of the virtual humans itself. This layering makes the reconstruction of the graphical representation of virtual humans based on the semantic descriptions possible.

The ontology covers provenance data (like the creation or adaptation history), feature descriptions of the VHs (like does the model represent an artificial person or a real person, the representation of the body, available animations, etc.), descriptions of the available animations and animation algorithm needs, and the interaction of the VH with other objects.

VHs can be described using the following central concepts:

- **Geometry**: A VH can have a geometry description which reflects his physical visual representation. This may include body shape descriptors which include vertices, edges, scales and descriptors for accessoirs supporting the same primitives.
- **Animation**: An animation description for a VH covers body animations and facial animation which are both based on structural descriptors as defined in the VH geometry part.
- **Morphology**: The morphology concept defines properties like age, weight or size of the VH.
- **Behavior**: A VH might have associated behavior descriptors which includes individual descriptors about his personality or cultural background and behavior controllers which allow to adapt his emotional state and individuality.

The VH ontology is amongst others used for character retrieval and to support shape extraction and analysis.

4.5.2. *The SALERO virtual character ontology*

The SALERO Virtual Character Ontology (SVCO) [50] which is available in OWL DL and WSML DL [51] is based on the AIM@SHAPE VH ontology (*cf.* Sec. 4.5.1). It consists of the SALERO Virtual Character Core (SVCC) — ontology and the SALERO Annotations (SA) ontology.

The SVCC ontology extends the AIM@SHAPE VH ontology at several points. Most notably it adds a set of individual descriptors which can be used in the VH ontology to define the behavior of a character. The SVCC ontology adds a set of descriptors to specify the personality of a character such as his demographics, his abilities, his social behavior or his role in a media production. The individual descriptors which can be used to express the personality of a character are based on the *General User Model Ontology* (GUMO) [52] which has been extended to cover properties of fictive, non-human characters. Furthermore the relation between a character and another character in a story can be expressed and its relation to the target audience.

The SVCO is inteded to be used in retrieval and to support the exchange of models between different applications.

4.6. *Domain and application specific multimedia ontologies*

In this section, we introduce some domain-specific multimedia ontologies that have been developed to acknowledge domain specific multimedia document requirements in biology or medicine (*cf.* Sec. 4.6.1, and the cultural heritage domain (*cf.* Sec. 4.6.2). Furthermore, we report on ontologies for the generation of multimedia presentations in Sec. 4.6.3. Further ontologies which are not covered in this section are reported in the media domain [53].

4.6.1. *Multimedia ontologies for biology*

4.6.1.1. The medical image domain ontology

The intention of the Medical Image Domain (MID) ontology [54] is to support the interpretation of mammography images enabled through reasoning. The ontology consists of a domain ontology for breast imaging reporting which provides the concepts used for indexing the semantic content of textual descriptions which are provided along with mammography images, and a visual ontology which provides the concepts and properties for indexing the visual content of the images.

The domain ontology (the American College of Radiology (ACR) ontology) is based on the Breast Imaging Reporting and Data System (BI-RADS) standard which provides terminonoloy to describe mammography features and their assessment. The visual ontology is based on the ACEMEDIA Visual Descriptor Ontology (VDO) which is explained in Sec. 4.1. The VDO ontology has been transferred to OWL-DL and has further been extended by basic descriptors for color or texture and by more specific visual descriptors for, e.g., the description of different types of 3D shapes.

Both ontologies are used to describe mammography images: the VDO ontology to provide a visual description and the ACR ontology to describe associated reports. The ACR ontology and the BI-RADS standard respectively have concepts to describe shapes which are mapped to the descriptors from VDO to establish the connection between ACR and VDO.

4.6.1.2. The imageStore ontology

The intention of the ImageStore (IS) ontology is to provide a means to describe images of biological research relevance [55]. The IS ontology is used to align and integrate descriptions in the BioImage database, a database with scientific images, with domain-specific ontologies like the GeneOntology[41] or the taxonomy of biological specifies[42]. It is used to annotate images with information on the biological species, experimental procedures and image processing applied and details of the image itself. Furthermore, it is used to provide descriptions of interpretations of the depicted content and keeps track of people and institutions involved.

The IS ontology uses a subset of the class model of AAF to describe media objects and uses a subset of MPEG-7 to describe multimedia content. Furthermore, it includes a domain-specific ontology to describe scientific experiments.

The IS ontology is used in the BioImage database to provide its structure and to annotate images. The BioImage database itself is centered around the notion of studies, each of which may contain a set of 2D, 3D images or videos. The images are described on a low level using MPEG-7 descriptors and furthermore are annotated with facts (i.e., what is depicted and what can be objectively observed) and interpretations (i.e., subjective statements about the raw facts).

Further work in the biological domain is reported by the Woundontology consortium[43] which aims to provide a set of ontologies to support analysis of wound images.

4.6.2. *Multimedia ontologies for cultural heritage*

4.6.2.1. VRA core ontologies from VUA/SIMILE

The VRA Core model [56] (VC) — as introduced in Sec. 3.1.2 — has been designed by the Visual Resource Association (VRA) which is an organization combines institutions that host collections of images and other representations of works of art. Most notably the VC distinguishes between a work of

---

[41] http://www.geneontology.org
[42] http://www.ncbi.nlm.nih.gov/Taxonomy
[43] http://www.woundontology.com/

visual art, which ranges from paintings to complex artistic installations, and an image depicting this work.

Additionally, the model defines elements to describe both record types and a set of qualifiers to describe these elements in more detail. Each element is described with its qualifiers and corresponding Dublin Core elements. The elements in the core model include: Record type, type, title, measurements, material, technique, creator, date, location, ID number, style/period, culture, subject, relation, description, source, rights.

Two formalized versions of the VC were proposed: The first from the Vrije Universiteit Amsterdam (VUA), the other by the SIMILE group at MIT.

The VUA ontology[44] [57] is available as RDF(S) and OWL Full. This ontology defines three classes: *vra:VisualResource*, which is always the domain of all defined properties, and its subclasses *vra:Work* and *vra:Image*. For each element of the VC a property is defined and additionally a subproperty for each qualifier.

The SIMILE VRA Core ontology[45] defines a set of classes to represent images, works which are sublcasses of records, entities and corporations. Both elements and qualifiers are modeled as properties. The SIMILE VRA Core is formalized using RDF(S).

MPEG-7 Extensions to CIDOC-CRM In [58], Jane Hunter describes the combination of CIDOC-CRM[46] which is a domain-specific ontology which can be used to describe any objects in museum ranging from paintings to installations, and the MPEG-7 ontology she developed and which is described in Sec. 4.1.

The CIDOC-CRM ontology is an intra-institutional ontology which intends to cover the documentation effort to describe collections held in museums. This includes the detailed description of individual items within collections, groups of items and collections as a whole. Furthermore, the ontology is especially covering contextual information which includes historical, geographical or theoretical background not specific to a particular domain. CRM defines the following top-level classes: *Temporal Entity, Time-Span, Place, Dimension, Persistent Item* which are further refined by the ontology. The connection to multimedia objects is established via the *Persistent Item* class which contains Information Objects which might be *Visual Items*. The MPEG-7 ontology extends the *Information Object* class with a subclass Multimedia Content which includes the MPEG-7 multimedia segment class hierarchy. Further, the

---

[44] http://www.w3.org/2001/sw/BestPractices/MM/vra-conversion.html
[45] http://simile.mit.edu/2003/10/ontologies/vraCore3
[46] http://cidoc.ics.forth.gr/

is ComposedOf-property of CIDOC-CRM is extended with sub-properties like *is TemporallyComposedOf* and *is SpatiallyComposedOf*. Finally, it adds multimedia specific descriptors via the newly created *AudioFeature* and VisualFeature classes and further extensions to specify formatting properties.

Further, work has been reported in [59] in which the authors use a reduced core set of CIDOC CRM,[47] the *CIDOC CRM Core*, to annotate media objects in combination with the Getty Art and Architecture Thesaurus (AAT).[48]

4.6.3. *Ontologies for multimedia presentation generation*

4.6.3.1. The SWeMPS ontology

The SWeMPS ("Semantic Web enabled Multimedia Presentation System") ontology[49] [60] provides a high-level formalization for an intelligent multimedia generation process based on the standard reference model for intelligent multimedia presentation systems (IMPSS) which is presented in [61]. Its intention is to guide an application realizing the IMPSS model using Semantic Web technologies.

The SWeMPS ontology has three core concepts: *Subject, Resource*, and *Service*, each of which are associated with metadata and described via specialized ontologies. These concepts represent the core entities involved in a multimedia generation process: concepts may be addressed in the multimedia presentation (i.e., about what the presentation should be), the resources represent those concepts and the services provide additional computational capabilities such as mediating between two different ontologies or transformation of resources, etc.

The SWeMPS ontology makes use of the XYZ ontology which is presented in Sec. 4.6.3 and further domain ontologies which are used in the metadata about either subject, resource or services.

4.6.3.2. The XYZ ontology

The *XYZ ontology*[50] as presented in [60] is an OWL Full ontology which is based on the XYZ multimedia model [62]. The XYZ model allows the hierarchical specification of a multimedia document using a tree of presentation elements and bindings between these elements. A presentation element can

[47] http://cidoc.ics.forth.gr/working_editions_cidoc.html
[48] http://www.getty.edu/research/conducting_research/vocabularies/aat/about.html
[49] http://page.mi.fu-berlin.de/nixon/swemps/swemps.owl
[50] http://page.mi.fu-berlin.de/nixon/swemps/xyz.owl

be an operand element to specify relations between the presentation elements or fragments which encapsulate reusable pieces of the multimedia document. Fragments can be atomic media objects or complex media objects depending on their granularity.

5. Lightweight vocabularies and folksonomies

This section covers lightweight approaches to describe multimedia content on the Web. This includes so-called syndication formats (*cf.* Sec. 5.1), vocabularies to describe multimedia content inline of HTML pages (*cf.* Sec. 5.2) and approaches that employ tagging to organize multimedia content (*cf.* Sec. 5.3).

5.1. *Syndication formats*

Syndication formats such as Really Simple Syndication (RSS)[51] or ATOM [63] are successfully applied on the Web in order to push contents to end users by the means of news feeds.

5.1.1. *MediaRSS*

MediaRSS[52] is a widely used RSS dialect defined by Yahoo for syndicating multimedia files in RSS feeds. While the standard RSS 2.0 format supports the syndication of audio and image files, MediaRSS extends it towards video files. As such it is most notably being used in podcasting.

MediaRSS supports the descriptions of media objects and their grouping into similar elements. It supports basic metadata for media objects including technical metadata like format, bitrate, duration, size but also other metadata types like rating schemes, rights, classification, and basic descriptive information.

5.1.2. *TXFeed*

TXFeed[53] is a syndication format based on the ATOM publishing protocol which can be used to describe video feeds. It is very similar to MediaRSS but provides more detailed sub-schemas for the description of technical aspects such as the codec being used. Further it offers detailed controlled

[51] http://www.rssboard.org/rss-specification
[52] http://search.yahoo.com/mrss
[53] http://transmission.cc/xmlns

vocabularies for the description of genre of a video or contributors based on the MARC standard.[54] Another difference is the explicit distinction between video, metadata and subtitle databases and its support for inclusion of information by reference.

5.2. *Microformats and vocabularies to embed metadata in HTML*

This section introduces vocabularies for the embedding of metadata into (X) HTML pages via so-called microformats[55] or RDFa [64]. The idea of both formats is to add semantic descriptions of content to websites by embedding additional information into normal websites using predefined attributes. While microformats define their own tags, RDFa makes use of existing HTML attributes to embedded RDF into HTML. Both endeavors acknowledge the rise of user generated content and the need to deploy metadata for the content in conventional HTML pages.

5.2.1. *hMedia microformat*

Microformats are a means to define classes of attributes which can be used to semantically markup pieces of content on Web pages using a set of defined attributes such as @class or @rel. The hMedia microformat[56] has been designed to identify semantic information about multimedia resources which are embedded in websites. It covers a wide range of basic properties of multimedia objects which are agnostic to specific media types. This includes descriptive information, as well as rights or evaluative information like reviews.

5.2.2. *RDFa deployed multimedia metadata (Ramm.x)*

Ramm.x[57] [65] provides a small, but extensible vocabulary for marking up multimedia resources and to embed semantic metadata inside of HTML using RDFa. RDFa is a serialization syntax for the RDF data model. It defines how an RDF graph is embedded in an (X)HTML page using a set of defined attributes such as @about, @rel, @instanceof, and others. Ramm.x further enables the hooking of existing multimedia metadata formats into the

---

[54] http://www.loc.gov/marc/
[55] http://microformats.org/about/
[56] http://wiki.digitalbazaar.com/en/Media_Info_Microformat
[57] http://rammx.joanneum.at

Semantic Web by linking existing descriptions represented in a multimedia metadata format and referencing services capable of transforming (parts of) the descriptions to RDF.

Ramm.x aims at enabling existing multimedia metadata formats to enter the Semantic Web. It targets at self-descriptive media asset descriptions allowing to apply the follow-your-nose principle to gather more information about media assets using GRDDL [66] transformations of existing "traditional" metadata formats.

5.2.3. *Media RDF vocabularies*

The "Media RDF vocabularies" are a set of minimal vocabularies to be used with RDFa to embed semantic descriptions in (X)HTML pages. The set consists of vocabularies to markup media in general[58], audio-[59], or video-files.[60]

All formats have been based on a minimally shared subset of media content descriptions. Each vocabulary reuses terms from Dublin Core[61] or the Dublin Core Terms subset.[62] Furthermore the vocabularies make use of the Commerce vocabulary[63] which defines basic terms to mark up licenses, rights or cost related information.

5.2.4. *Reusable intelligent content objects (RICO)*

The RICO model [67] has been built to support the reuse of multimedia content on the Web. RICO provides a conceptual model to describe, annotate, and represent multimedia resources on the Web. The model implements a multimedia resource-centric view of conventional Web pages, thus being equally applicably to multimedia content published within Web pages (e.g., images embedded in news stories), to social media, or to professional media licensing sites. It is implemented as a set of Semantic Web ontologies and uses RDFa to mark up multimedia resources inline of HTML pages. By using semantic metadata referencing formal ontologies, RICO not only provides a basis for the uniform annotation and description of multimedia

---

[58] http://purl.org/media
[59] http://purl.org/media/audio
[60] http://purl.org/media/video
[61] http://dublincore.org/
[62] http://dublincore.org/documents/dcmi-terms/
[63] http://purl.org/commerce

resources on the Web, but also enables intelligent multimedia retrieval features such as automatic reasoning about the contents and structure of multimedia resources and their usage conditions.

The conceptual model of RICO consists of a data model to describe multimedia content and associated descriptions and a metadata model to mark up multimedia content on the Web. The intention of the RICO data model is to lay a graph over multimedia resources published on the Web, to link descriptions contained in Web pages, as well as other metadata, to these resources, and to type descriptive information. It is based on the MPEG-21 Digital Item abstract model (see *cf.* Sec. 3.5.1). The RICO metadata model support technical features, rights, classification, relational, or evaluative metadata and supports so-called authorative and non-authorative metadata sets to distinguish between metadata contributed by the author and other users on the Web.

Both the data model and the metadata model are realised by a set of ontologies to mark up multimedia content. The descriptions according to the ontologies are embedded in HTML pages based on the ramm.x model (*cf.* Sec. 5.2.2).

5.3. *Tagging and folksonomies*

Tagging and folksonomies have become popular with the advent of Web 2.0 which marked a turn towards more user interaction on the Web. Tagging is a means with a low-entry barrier for end users to organize their content and thus very popular and widely used. Folksonomies are defined as *the result of personal free tagging of information and objects (anything with a URL) for one's own retrieval. The tagging is done in a social environment (shared and open to others). The act of tagging is done by the person consuming the information.*[64] Free tagging of multimedia is supported on many different websites that host multimedia content, such as Flickr, YouTube, or Slideshare. More advanced forms of tagging are supported by Flickr which supports so called machine tags.[65] Machine tags or triple tags, as they are sometimes called, consist of a namespace declaration and a property/value — pair to assign more semantics to tags.

To combine tagging with more richer knowledge structures seems to be a viable way to overcome the commonly known problems of tagging like synonyms, spelling errors or other effects which can be frequently observed.

[64] http://vanderwal.net/folksonomy.html
[65] http://www.machinetags.org/wiki/

Therefore, researchers began to investigate the derivation of more richer semantic structures from tags and folksonomies [68, 69] or more richer forms of tagging based on MPEG-7 semantic basetypes [70].

6. Conclusions

It is commonly acknowledged that reliable metadata is essential to support different actions in the lifecycle of multimedia metadata like search & retrieval, management, repurposing, or use [4]. This chapter presented a wide range of multimedia metadata standards and multimedia ontologies whose intention is to support more efficient management, annotation, and retrieval of multimedia content and to overcome some of the drawbacks of traditional multimedia standards: Existing multimedia metadata standards such as MPEG-7 can be used to annotate but keep a certain amount of ambiguity amongst these annotations. It is well-known that MPEG-7 allows variability in the syntactic representation of multimedia descriptions which may cause interoperability issues. A second problem of standards like MPEG-7 is their complexity which up to now hindered its wide adoption beyond the academic community.

The problem with all metadata standards is the creation of metadata adhering to these standards without which management and retrieval is not possible. This is especially true for multimedia content for which automatic metadata generation, covering high level and abstract features, does not work on a large scale. Ongoing research as presented in the chapter *II.5. Methodologies for the Creation of Semantic Data* in this volume discusses these issues and investigates incentives on how to motivate end users to contribute a critical mass of annotations.

On the end user side of the spectrum, Web 2.0 based knowledge structures were investigated as a solution for the management of the huge amounts of user generated content created by the means of tagging. But again the problems associated with tagging are manifold; there are open issues, such as consistency among tags, reconciliation of tags, and how to associate tags with parts of the tagged content. Solutions to overcome these drawbacks use controlled tags, structured tags, or tag recommendations.

For advanced scenarios more requirements have to be fulfilled, which cannot be solely solved by traditional or Web 2.0 based approaches and which make more formalized descriptions of content necessary. This is why some researchers investigated the deployment of multimedia content together with more richer knowledge structures in order to realize advanced retrieval scenarios across different sites.

Two ongoing issues related to the description of multimedia content on the Web are currently being researched in the W3C Video Activity[66] which (1) aims to develop a core multimedia ontology to describe video on the Web covering central aspects of different metadata standards with the aim to increase interoperability, and (2) investigates solution for the addressing of temporal and spatial fragments in videos and images using URIs.

Reference

1. Smeulders, A, M Worring, S Santini, A Gupta and R Jain (2000). Content-based image retrieval at the end of the early years. *IEEE Transactions on Pattern Analysis and Machine Intelligence,* 22(12), 1349–1380.
2. van Ossenbruggen, J, F Nack and L Hardman (2004). That obscure object of desire: Multimedia metadata on the web, part 1. *IEEE MultiMedia,* 11(4), 38–48. ISSN 1070-986X,. doi: http://doi.ieeecomputersociety.org/10.1109/MMUL.2004.36.
3. Nack, F, J van Ossenbruggen and L Hardman (2005). That obscure object of desire: Multimedia metadata on the web, part 2. *IEEE MultiMedia,* 12(1), 54–63. ISSN 1070-986X. doi: http://doi.ieeecomputersociety.org/10.1109/MMUL.2005.12.
4. Smith, JR and P Schirling (2006). Metadata standards roundup. *IEEE MultiMedia,* 13 (2), 84–88.
5. Baca, M (2008). *Introduction to Metadata.* Getty Publication.
6. Nack, F and AT Lindsay (1999). Everything you wanted to know about MPEG-7 (Part I). *IEEE Multimedia,* 6(3), 65–77.
7. Nack, F and AT Lindsay (1999). Everything you wanted to know about MPEG-7 (Part II). *IEEE Multimedia,* 6(4), 64–73.
8. Martinez, M (2004). Mpeg-7 overview. Available at http://www.chiariglione.org/mpeg/standards/mpeg-7/mpeg-7.htm.
9. AAFM (2005). AAF Association. Available at http://www.aafassociation.org.
10. SMPTE (2004). Material exchange format (mxf) — descriptive metadata scheme-1 (standard) smpte 380m. Available at http://www.pro-mpeg.org/publicdocs/mxf.html.
11. Chang, W (2004). Mpeg-a multimedia application format overview and requirements (v.2). Available at http://www.chiariglione.org/mpeg/standards/mpeg-a/mpeg-a.htm.
12 Quackenbush, S (2005). Mpeg music player maf. Available at http://www.chiariglione.org/mpeg/technologies/mpa-mp/index.htm.
13. Lee, S, S Yang, YM Ro and HJ Kim (2006). e-learning media format for enhanced consumption on mobile application. *In Proceedings of the 1st International Workshop on Semantic-Enhanced Multimedia Presentation Systems (SEMPS-2006).*

[66] http://www.w3.org/2008/01/video-activity.html

14. Hodgins, W and E Duval (2002). Draft standard for learning object metadata. Technical report, Learning Technology Standards Committee, IEEE.
15. CCSDS (2002). Reference model for an open archival information system (oais). Blue Book 1, Consultative Committee for Space Data Systems (CCSDS), CCSDS Secretariat Program Integration Division (Code M-3) National Aeronautics and Space Administration Washington, DC 20546, USA.
16. METS Editorial Board (2007). Metadtata encoding and transmission standard: Primer and reference manual version 1.6. Available at http://www.loc.gov/standards/mets/METS%20Documentation%20final%20070930%20msw.pdf.
17. IMS Global Learning Consortium (2001). Ims content packaging xml binding — version 1.1.2 — final specication.
18. Lagoze, C and HV de Sompel (2007). Compound information objects: The oai-ore perspective. Available at http://www.openarchives.org/ore/documents/CompoundObjects-200705.html.
19. Bormans, J and K Hill (2002). Mpeg-21 overview v.5. Available at http://www.chiariglione.org/mpeg/standards/mpeg-21/mpeg-21.htm.
20. Adobe (2008). Xmp specication — part 1, data and serialization models. Available at http://partners.adobe.com/public/developer/en/xmp/sdk/XMPspecification.pdf.
21. Adobe (2008). Xmp specication — part 3, storage in files. Available at http://partners.adobe.com/public/developer/en/xmp/sdk/XMPspecification.pdf.
22. Adobe (2008). Xmp specication — part 2, standard schemas. Available at http://partners.adobe.com/public/developer/en/xmp/sdk/XMPspecification.pdf.
23. Gruber, TR (1993). A translation approach to portable ontology specications. *Knowledge Acquisition,* 5(2), 199–220.
24. Troncy, R (2003). Integrating structure and semantics into audio-visual documents. In KSD Fensel and J Mylopoulos (eds.), *The Semantic Web — Proceedings ISWC'03,* (2003). Vol. 2870, *Lecture Notes in Computer Science.*
25. Bloehdorn, S, K Petridis, C Saathoff, VTN Simou, Y Avrithis, S Handschuh, I Kompatsiaris, S Staab and MG Strintzis (2005). Semantic annotation of images and videos for multimedia analysis. In *Proc. of the 2nd European Semantic Web Conference (ESWC 2005), Heraklion, Greece, May 2005.*
26. Troncy, R, W Bailer, M Hausenblas, P Hofmair and R Schlatte (2006). Enabling multimedia metadata interoperability by defining formal semantics of mpeg-7 profiles. In *Proceedings of the 1st International Conference on Semantics And Digital Media Technology (SAMT 06).*
27. Tsinaraki, C, P Polydoros and S Christodoulakis (2007). Interoperability support between mpeg-7/21 and owl in ds-mirf. *Transactions on Knowledge and Data Engineering (IEEE-TKDE).* **Special Issue on the Semantic Web Era**.

28. Arndt, R, R Troncy, S Staab, L Hardman and M Vacura (2007). Comm: Designing a well-founded multimedia ontology for the web. In *The Semantic Web — Proceedings of ESWC 2007*. Springer.
29. Eleftherohorinou, H, V Zervaki, A Gounaris, V Papastathis, Y Kompatsiaris and P Hobson (2006). Towards a common multimedia ontology framework. Technical report, ACEMEDIA.
30. Troncy, R and J Carrive (2004). A reduced yet extensible audio-visual description language. In *DocEng '04: Proceedings of the 2004 ACM symposium on Document engineering*, pp. 87–89, New York, NY, USA. ACM. ISBN 1-58113-938-1. doi: http://doi.acm.org/10.1145/1030397.1030415.
31. Celma, O, S Dasiopoulou, M Hausenblas, S Little, C Tsinaraki and R Troncy (2007). Mpeg-7 and the semantic web. Available at http://www.w3.org/2005/Incubator/mmsem/XGR-mpeg7/.
32. Troncy, R, O Celma, S Little, R Garcia and C Tsinaraki (2007). Mpeg-7 based multimedia ontologies: Interoperability support or interoperability issue? In *Proceedings of the 1st Workshop on Multimedia Annotation and Retrieval enabled by Shared Ontologies (MARESO '07).*
33. Hunter, J (2001). Adding multimedia to the semantic web — building an mpeg-7 ontology. In *Proceedings of the 1st International Semantic Web Working Symposium (SWWS 2001),* Stanford, USA, 30 July – 1 August 2001.
34. Garcia, R and O Celma (2005). Semantic integration and retrieval of multimedia metadata. In *Proceedings of 4rd International Semantic Web Conference. Knowledge Markup and Semantic Annotation Workshop,* Galway, Ireland.
35. Laura Hollink, MW and A Schreiber (2005). Building a visual ontology for video retrieval. In *Proceedings of the 13th ACM International Conference on Multimedia.*
36. Oberle, D, A Ankolekar, P Hitzler, P Cimiano, M Sintek, M Kiesel, B Mougouie, S Baumann, S Vembu, M Romanelli, P Buitelaar, R Engel, D Sonntag, N Reithinger, B Loos, H-P Zorn, V Micelli, R Porzel, C Schmidt, M Weiten, F Burkhardt and J Zhou (2007). Dolce ergo sumo: On foundational and domain models in the smartweb integrated ontology (swinto). *Web Semant,* 5(3), 156–174. ISSN 1570-8268. doi: http://dx.doi.org/10.1016/j.websem.2007.06.002.
37. W3C (2002). Describing and retrieving photos using rdf and http. W3C Note 19 April 2002. Available at http://www.w3.org/.
38. Halaschek-Wiener, C, A Schain, J Golbeck, M Grove, B Parsia and J Hendler (2005). A flexible approach for managing digital images on the semantic web. In *Proceedings of the 5th International Workshop on Knowledge Markup and Semantic Annotation (SemAnnot 2005).*
39. Halaschek-Wiener, C, J Golbeck, A Schain, M Grove, B Parsia and J Hendler (2006). Annotation and provenance tracking in semantic web photo libraries. In *Provenance and Annotation of Data.* Springer.

40. Noia, TD, ED Sciascio, FM Donini, F di Cugno and E Tinelli (2005). Non-standard inferences for knowledge-based image retrieval. In *Proceedings of the 2nd European Workshop on the Integration of Knowledge, Semantic and Digital Media Techniques*, pp. 191–195. IEE Press.
41. Beebe, C (2007). Bridging the semantic gap: Exploring descriptive vocabulary for image structure. In *Poster Proceedings of the Second International Conference on Semantics and Digital Media (SAMT 2007).*
42. Raimond, Y, S Abdallah, M Sandler and F Giasson (2007). The music ontology. In *Proceedings of the International Conference on Music Information Retrieval.*
43. Celma, O (2006). Foafing the music bridging the semantic gap in music recommendation. In *Proceedings of the 5th International Semantic Web Conference (ISWC) 2006.*
44. Dasiopoulou, S, K Dalakleidi, G Stoilos, V Tzouvaras and Y Kompatsiaris (2008). Multimedia content and descriptor ontologies final version. Project Deliverable D3.8 from 28/07/2008, BOEMIE.
45. Dalakleidi, K, C Evangelou, S Dasiopoulou and V Tzouvaras (2008). Domain ontologies — version 2. Project Deliverable D3.5 from 21/08/2007, BOEMIE.
46. Petridis, K, I Kompatsiaris, MG Strintzis, S Bloehdorn, S Handschuh, S Staab, N Simou, V Tzouvaras and Y Avrithis (2004). Knowledge representation for semantic multimedia content analysis and reasoning. *In Proceedings of the 1st European Workshop for the Integration of Knowledge, Semantics and Digital Media Technology (EWIMT 2004), London, UK, 25–26 November 2004.*
47. Simou, N, C Saathofi, S Dasiopoulou, E Spyrou, N Voisine, V Tzouvaras, I Kompatsiaris, Y Avrithis and S Staab (2005). An ontology infrastructure for multimedia reasoning. In *Proceedings of the International Workshop on Very Low Bitrate Video Encoding '05 (VLBV 2005),* Sardinia, Italy, 15–16 September 2005.
48. Gutierrez, M, A Garcia Rojas, D Thalmann, F Vexo, L Moccozet, N Magnenat-Thalmann, M Mortara and M Spagnuolo (2007). An ontology of virtual humans: Incorporating semantics into human shapes. *The Visual Computer.* 23(3), 207–218.
49. Garcia-Rojas, A, D Thalmann, F Vexo, L Moccozet, N Magnenat-Thalmann, M Spagnuolo and M Gutierrez (2005). An Ontology of Virtual Humans: Incorporating Semantics into Human Shapes. In *The 2nd European Workshop on the Integration of Knowledge, Semantics and Digital Media Technology (EWIMT 2005),* pp. 7–14.
50. Bürger, T, P Hofmair and G Kienast (2008). The salero virtual character ontology. In *Proceedings of the First Workshop on Semantic 3D Media, co-located with SAMT 2008,* 3–5 December, 2008.
51. de Bruijn, J (2008). The wsml specification, wsmo deliverable d16, wsml working draft 2008-08-08. Available at http://www.wsmo.org/TR/d16/, year = 2008, month = August.

52. Heckmann, D, E Schwarzkopf, J Mori, D Dengler and A Kroener (2007). The user model and context ontology gumo revisited for future web 2.0 extensions. In *Proceedings of the International Workshop on Contexts and Ontologies: Representation and Reasoning (C&O:RR) Collocated with the 6th International and Interdisciplinary Conference on Modelling and Using Context (CONTEXT-2007).*
53. Hausenblas, M (2008). Non-linear interactive media productions. *Multimedia Systems Special Issue on Canonical Processes of Media Production,* 14(6), 405–413.
54. Golbreich, C (2006). Combining content-based retrieval and description logics reasoning. In *Proccedings of the 1st International Workshop on Semantic Web Annotations for Multimedia (SWAMM),* May 22, 2006, *Edinburgh, Scotland.*
55. Catton, C, S Sparks and D Shotton (2006). The imagestore ontology and the bioimage database: Semantic web tools for biological research images. In *Proceedings of the First Jena User Conference (JUCS).*
56. VRA Data Standards Committee (2002). Vra core categories, version 3.0. Available at http://www.vraweb.org/vracore3.htm.
57. van Assem, M (2005). Rdf/owl representation of vra, draft 16 january 2005. Available at http://www.w3.org/2001/sw/BestPractices/MM/vra-conversion.html.
58. Hunter, J (2002). Combining the cidoc crm and mpeg-7 to describe multimedia in museums. In *Proceedings of Museums on the Web, Boston,* April, 2002.
59. Sinclair, P, M Addis, F Choi, M Doerr, P Lewis and K Martinez (2006). The use of crm core in multimedia annotation. In *Proceedings of the First International Workshop on Semantic Web Annotations for Multimedia (SWAMM).*
60. Nixon, L (2005). Integrating knowledge, semantics and digital media into the multimedia generation process. In *Proceedings of the 2nd European Workshop on the Integration of Knowledge, Semantic and Digital Media, London,* November 2005.
61. Bordegoni, M, G Faconti, S Feiner, MT Maybury, T Rist, S Ruggieri, P Trahanias and M Wilson (1997). A standard reference model for intelligent multimedia presentation systems. *Computer Standards Interfaces,* 18(6–7), 477–496. ISSN 0920-5489. doi: http://dx.doi.org/10.1016/S0920-5489(97)00013-5.
62. Boll, S and W Klas (2001). Zyx: A multimedia document model for reuse and adaptation. *IEEE Transactions on Knowledge and Data Engineering,* 13(3), 361–382.
63. Nottingham, M and R Sayre (2005). The atom syndication format, request for comments 4287. Available at http://tools.ietf.org/html/rfc4287.
64. Adida, B and M Birbeck (2008). Rdfa primer, w3c working group note 14 october 2008. Available at http://www.w3.org/TR/xhtml-rdfa-primer/.

65. Hausenblas M, W Bailer, T Bürger and R Troncy (2007). Ramm.x: Deploying multimedia metadata on the semantic web. In *Proceedings of SAMT 2007,* 4–7 December, Genova, Italy, 2007.
66. Connolly, D (2007). Gleaning resource descriptions from dialects of languages (grddl), w3c recommendation 11 September 2007. Available at http://www.w3.org/TR/grddl/.
67. Bürger, T (2008). Towards increased reuse: Exploiting content related and social features of multimedia content on the semantic web. In *Proceedings of the Workshop on Interacting with Multimedia Content on the Web (IMC-SSW), co-located with SAMT 2008,* 3–5 December Koblenz, Germany, 2008.
68. Schmitz, P (2006). Inducing ontology from ickr tags. In *Proceedings of the Collaborative Web Tagging Workshop (WWW 06).* Available at http://www.rawsugar.com/www2006/22.pdf.
69. Sigurbjörnsson, B and R van Zwol (2008). Flickr tag recommendation based on collective knowledge. In *WWW '08: Proceeding of the 17th international conference on World Wide Web,* pp. 327–336, New York, NY, USA, (2008). ACM.
70. Klamma, R, M Spaniol and D Renzel (2007). Community-Aware Semantic Multimedia Tagging — From Folksonomies to Commsonomies. In *Proceedings of I-Media' 07, International Conference on New Media Technology and Semantic Systems,* J.UCS (Journal of Universal Computer Science) Proceedings, K Tochtermann, H Maurer, F Kappe and A Scharl (eds.), pp. 163–171. Springer-Verlag.

CHAPTER IV.1

TECHNOLOGIES FOR METADATA INTEGRATION AND INTEROPERABILITY

Ricardo Eito-Brun

Universidad Carlos III de Madrid
Departmento Biblioteconomía y Documentación
C/Madrid, 126-28903 Madrid, Spain
reito@bib.uc3m.es

Libraries and information services face the need of dealing with a growing number of metadata schemas. The use of metadata in libraries is not only restricted to resource description; other key activities like resource preservation and the maintenance of complex digital objects also requires the use of additional metadata schemas. In addition, we need to consider the availability of information gateways and databases using heterogeneous metadata. This chapter provides an overview of the different aspects involved in metadata integration and interoperability, from technical aspects related to the capability of exchanging metadata records across heterogeneous systems, to semantic-related issues related to the capability of establishing equivalences between the metadata managed by the different applications. Relevant projects executed in the last years (CORES, Schemas, etc.) and the role of standards like RDF, RDF Schemas or SPARQL in metadata interoperability projects is also described.

1. Introduction

The wide spread of the Internet and the World Wide Web brought the opportunity to distribute information beyond traditional limits, and technologies like http, html, xml and web services have removed the constraints to reach a previously inaccessible universe of data and knowledge.

Metadata, usually defined as "structured data about data", consist of properties and attributes about entities (usually documents) that support data access and management processes. Typical actions like document retrieval, preservation or data processing depend on the availability of previously assigned metadata.

Metadata take different forms: The most frequently used consist of a set of properties common to objects of the same type. These properties are shared by all the instances of this type of objects. Values are assigned to these properties for specific instances to obtain a surrogate or summary representation of them. These surrogates are then used to represent the instances in the above-mentioned information management processes.

But metadata also refers to other data we can store and manage about objects, as the relationship that an object maintains with other entities and the subject it is about. These are also part of the set of properties or characteristics that we need to keep as part of a metadata schema.

The use of metadata is part of the regular activities traditionally carried on by professionals working on information management. Although research on metadata has been reinforced since the invention of the World Wide Web, librarians and archivists have accumulated a prior, wide experience on these activities.

Today, information professionals have to deal with a complex ecosystem of metadata systems. Some of them have different purposes and designed by different people to achieve similar objectives.

These metadata schemas are usually the basis for information retrieval services and IT systems that give access to information. As a result, end-users need to deal with information services understanding "different metadata languages". This constitutes a handicap to users (both humans and software-agents).[1] The availability of different implementations of metadata — even for the same type of objects, information resources and purposes — raised the need of searching for metadata interoperability solutions.

2. Levels of interoperability

Metadata interoperability and integration requirements have to be analyzed from different points of view. First of all, we need to review technical aspects related to the way software applications and information services exchange and transfer metadata; in addition, it is necessary to ensure that metadata are

[1] One of the most interesting areas of studies in the last years is the development of software agents with the capability of working as intermediaries between an end-user and a set of disparate information services. The software agent will have the capability of searching and gathering information from different information services (probably based on different metadata schemas) and collect a single, consolidated list of results that are presented to the end user.

exchanged using a common syntax to make possible their automated processing. A third level of integration — more complex to achieve — refers to semantic compatibility of the metadata, that is to say, the equivalences that can be established between metadata from different vocabularies or schemas that have the same (or a similar) meaning. These levels of compatibility are described in the following sections.

2.1. *Technical interoperability*

Technical communication and transfer is the first point we need to deal with to achieve the interoperability between information services. It refers to the capability to exchange information through a network — usually the Internet — between disparate information services. In the last years, Web-based standardization initiatives from the W3C have produced technical solutions based on the use of the http communication protocol and the exchange of messages codified in XML. *XML-based web services* and *Services-Oriented Architectures* (*SOA*) are the terms used to refer to information systems compliant with the interoperability capabilities proposed by these W3C standards.

The term web service is usually applied to any function or service that an organization provides to their users or patrons through the web. In the IT context, this term has a more precise meaning. In a glossary published by the W3C [2], it is said to refer to: *"a software system designed to support the interoperability between computers connected to a network. One web service has an interface described in a computer-processable format. Other systems can interact with the web service through the sending of SOAP messages through HTTP serialized as XML"*.

Another definition taken from the W3C specification defines a web service as a "software application identified by an URI (Universal Resource Identifier), whose interfaces can be defined, described and discovered by means of XML, and that support the interaction with other application through the sending of XML messages through the Internet communication protocols".

Web services are today the preferred approach to develop distributed software applications [3]. Their characteristics can be summarized as follows:

(i) The exchange of messages (requests and responses) is done through the web using the HTTP protocol.
(ii) XML is used to encode the messages exchanged between computers and software applications.

(iii) Web services can be accessed through a URL.
(iv) Web services do not provide a user interface. They will be always invoked by a software application (the consumer of the service), and the results will be provided in XML format, so they can be reformatted or reprocessed with different purposes.
(v) W3C has published specifications to standardize the implementation and deployment of web services. The most important are *Service Oriented Application Protocol* (*SOAP*) and *Web Services Description Language* (*WSDL*), widely supported by the IT industry.

The application of the web-service model is not restricted to a specific area, and it can be applied in any scenario that requires the interaction of software systems. As a W3C standard, web services are independent of specific suppliers, and facilitate the interaction between information systems based on non-compatible platforms and technologies.

Regarding the W3C standardization, the main specifications for web services are SOAP and WSDL specifications:

- SOAP establishes the standard method to request the execution of the web service to a remote application, and the way to encode and transfer the results obtained after their execution.[2]
- WSDL indicates how to describe web services in a standardized way, so clients or consumer applications know how to invoke the services to the hosting applications.

In SOAP, the execution of web services is based on the exchange of XML messages between the client and the host application. The XML message specifies the web service to be executed and the necessary parameters.

As an example, in the context of an information retrieval application, the host application could offer a web service to search a database. To invoke

[2]The current version of the SOAP specification is 1.2. It is made up of four W3C recommendations, published as independent documents:

- *SOAP Version 1.2 Part 0: Primer*. This is a tutorial providing a description of the web services concept. It is available at http://www.w3.org/TR/soap12-part0/
- *SOAP Version 1.2 Part 1: Messaging Framework*. It describes the format of the messages to get exchanged to invoke services and codify the answers. It is a normative document available at http://www.w3.org/TR/soap12-part1/
- *SOAP Version 1.2 Part 2: Adjuncts*. It defines the data types that can be used to indicate which kind of parameters are sent when invoking a remove web service. It is available at http://www.w3.org/TR/soap12-part2/
- *SOAP Version 1.2 Specification Assertions and Test Collection*.

this service, consumer applications should send a SOAP XML message containing parameters that identify the database name, the query, username and password. The answer generated as a result of the execution of the web service shall also be sent to the client application in the form of an XML message containing, for example, the list of records retrieved from the database.

SOAP messages can be seen as envelopes that contain data about the operation we want to execute, or the results of its execution (in SOAP we have two types of messages: requests and responses). Below we include an example of a SOAP message extracted from the *SOAP Version 1.2: Primer*.

```
<?xml version='1.0' ?>
<env:Envelope xmlns:env="http://www.w3.org/2003/05/
  soap-envelope">
<env:Body>
   <p:itinerary
      xmlns:p="http://travelcompany.example.org/
      reservation/travel">
   <p:departure>
         <p:departing>New York</p:departing>
         <p:arriving>Los Angeles</p:arriving>
         <p:departureDate>2001-12-14</p:departureDate>
   </p:departure>
   <p:return>
      <p:departing>Los Angeles</p:departing>
      <p:arriving>New York</p:arriving>
      <p:departureDate>2001-12-20</p:departureDate>
   </p:return>
  </p:itinerary>
 </env:Body>
</env:Envelope>
```

The SOAP message includes a root element called <Envelope> (in the example, elements from the SOAP specification are preceded by the env prefix). The <Envelope> element can include an optional element, <Header>, and a mandatory element called <Body> that will contain the specific details about the requests or the answer.

It can be noticed that the rest of the elements within the <Body> element are not SOAP elements, but taken from different namespaces [27] represented by the q and p aliases. This feature characterizes SOAP messages: The data transferred to the application hosting the web service can contain any markup not defined as part of the SOAP specification. Of course this markup must be understandable by the target application, as it must extract and process these data to know which operation is being requested.

Regarding the transfer of the SOAP messages, the standard gives several choices: http, SMTP, FTP, etc., although http is the preferred one. SOAP specification provides additional capabilities, like the possibility of annexing files in different formats to the messages, or encoding security data as part of the headers.

From an interoperability point of view, the main advantage of SOAP is the fact of being a platform independent standard, which facilitates building interfaces between applications (we just need to implement the capability of understanding and processing SOAP requests). Of course, the details about the methods that can be invoked, their parameters, etc., are application-dependent, and must be known in advance in order to articulate a solution based on this technology. To facilitate that, the W3C has also developed a complimentary specification, WSDL.

WSDL provides a normalized way to describe web services. Its purpose is to give to the client applications all the details needed to interact with a remote web service. WSDL documents shall provide the access point for the web service (usually a URL where the requests have to be sent), the name of the methods or operations that can be requested and the parameters that these operations expect to receive.

Although SOAP-based web services are widely implemented and supported to build technical interoperability solutions, this is not the only solution at our disposal. RESTful web services are another alternative successfully adopted, and they are gaining more and more attention. They are based on one method widely used to exchange requests between browsers and web servers through the Web: the addition of parameters to the URL of a remove web page. This is the method used by search engines to receive requests, and it is known as *http GET requests*. In fact, we could say that the target web page implements a service or functionality, and that the parameters needed to call these functionality are attached to the page's URL after the ? character. Each parameter has a name and a value that are written in the URL, separated by the equal character. If more than one parameter is attached, they are separated by the & character.

For example, when running a search in Altavista we will see that the URL that is being requested to the server is similar to the following one:

http://www.altavista.com/web/results?itag=ody&q=CQL+AGENCY+LIBRARY&kgs=1&kls=0.

We can appreciate that the sign ? is added to the page URL, followed by a set of parameters: `itag` param with the *ody* value, q param with the

CQL+AGENCY+LIBRARY value, etc. When the target web server receives this request, it extracts the parameters and processes them to provide an answer.

In addition to http GET it is also possible to use http POST. This method also sends parameters to the target web server, but they are not attached to the URL, but included as part of the header of the http requests. This has one advantage over http GET: longer values can be assigned to the parameters.[3] In any case, the results obtained by the server are sent back to the client in the form of XML data.

Both *http GET* and *http POST* approaches are widely used today as an easier alternative to SOAP, and a distinction is made between SOAP-based and RESTful web services (the last term used to refer to the sending of requests through http GET and http POST).

2.2. *Syntactical interoperability*

Technical interoperability refers to the capability of exchanging requests and responses between information services and applications. In our area of interest these requests and responses are aimed to exchange metadata about information resources. On the basis of this capability, information services must also be able to use a common syntax to codify these metadata (whether exchanged via SOAP, Restful web services or any other method).

Syntactical interoperability is assured by the use of a common syntax to codify and transfer data. Today, the preferred approach is the use of markup languages, and more specifically XML [24]. This markup language provides a way to codify documents and data containing markup. The purpose of markup is to differentiate the data contained within documents. XML establishes a syntax widely supported by software applications, and it has been massively adopted by agencies involved in the design and maintenance of metadata schemas (Library of Congress, Dublin Core Metadata Initiative, Society of American Archivists, etc.).

Today we have at our disposal different XML schemas for the principal metadata systems. These XML schemas are files where the structure of metadata records is declared [25]. XML schemas specify which tags are allowed in a specific type of document or metadata record, their order, how they must be nested, etc. Different XML schemas shall define different tags depending on the type of information they are expected to record, but the use of a common syntax provides one important advantage: the same tools can be used to process any XML document, regardless the fact of being based on different

[3] In addition, in *http GET* is difficult to indicate the character set of the parameters. In the case of http POST this data can be indicated as part of the http request header.

XML schemas. This simplifies the work of metadata implementers, and provides an additional level of compatibility between systems.

Among the tools we can use to process XML documents, *extensible Style sheet Language Transformations* (XSLT) [26] style sheets are the most relevant for metadata interoperability.

XSLT is a W3C specification that describes an XML-based language to write transformations between documents. An XSLT style sheet takes one (or more) XML documents as an input and generates one (or more) XML documents as an output after applying some transformation rules. The resulting document(s) will usually contain different tags. By applying XSLT, it is possible to convert one XML document based on a specific schema (for example MARCXML) into another document containing the same data but based on another schema (e.g., EAD).

XSLT can include commands to make complex processing with the data contained in the input documents. Functions to process substrings, concatenate element values or complete mathematical operations are part of this specification. It is also possible to filter items, change the order in which they appear, or merging several documents to generate a unique document as a result. All these features make XSLT a powerful tool that improves the interoperability between information systems supporting XML. XSLT has also been widely used to generate user-friendly displays of XML documents, usually by transforming them into HTML.

XSLT capabilities give the choice of creating cross-walks between XML schemas and ensure that metadata codified as XML can be easily converted into an equivalent record based on other schema as long as a mapping or equivalence between both schemas has been previously defined. Of course, this translation will be effective if a semantic compatibility can be established between the elements managed by these schemas.

2.3. *Semantic interoperability*

Having the capability of exchanging messages and data between information services and a common syntax to encode metadata records are the foundations to achieve interoperability. But this is not enough. As explained in the previous section, an additional work has to be done to identify which metadata are semantically equivalent in different schemas.

This is the final step to achieve real compatibility between information services. When we are querying two different databases, which are the fields/metadata we need to search to be sure we are getting consistent results?

In the metadata interoperability research, "metadata crosswalks" refer to the equivalences between pairs of metadata schemas. These crosswalks correlate the metadata items or elements defined in a specific schema with those in another.

St. Pierre [10] defines a crosswalk as *"a set of transformations applied to the content of elements in a source metadata standard that result in the storage of appropriately modified content in the analogous elements of a target metadata standard"*. This author also proposed the use of formal models to define crosswalks (practical experiences on the use of formal models to encode crosswalks were completed as part of the OCLC Metadata Switch Project [12]).

Well-known examples of these crosswalks are those defined by the *Library of Congress* between MARCXML, Dublin Core and MODS, the *Getty Museum,* the *Canadian Heritage Information Network* or UKOLN [17]. GODBY also described an OCLC project that codified crosswalks using METS and defined XSLT transformations between metadata schemas.

Unfortunately, conceptual mapping between metadata schemas need to be done in an ad-hoc basis, identifying which items (or combination of items) are actually equivalent to those used in the other schemas. This analysis can find situations where it is not possible to establish a correspondence between one metadata item in a specific schema and the items available in the others. To deal with these cases and ensure a minimum level of semantic compatibility, an interesting approach is to establish a basic core of elements that should be mapped *at least.* This approach was the basis of the Dublin Core metadata schema [20]. This system proposed a basic set of metadata elements (known as the core and consisting of 15 items) that were considered the basic set of metadata that should be recorded about a resource [21]. Metadata implementers were given the choice of extending this core with additional properties as needed; at the same time, a minimum level of compatibility was ensured as long as the implementation provided the equivalent items to those defined in the "core".

This approach — with some variations — has been followed in different initiatives. For example, OAI (to which we will refer later) defined a basic record structure with metadata from the Dublin Core; *Search/Retrieve URL* (SRU) established profiles or basic set of access points to which queries could be directed [1].

3. Metadata and the identification of information resources

One critical aspect in metadata management is the method used to identify information resources. Information resources need to be uniquely identified in order to provide descriptions about them. In addition, in some cases metadata about objects have been used as a way to identify resources (usually to solve problems and restrictions related to access to electronic resources).

Web-based resources volatility is one of the main problems in the access to electronic information, as web links and URLs are based on the physical location of the resource in the target web server. For example, a URL like the following:

http://www.uc3m.es/cources/resources_e.pdf

refers to one file with name `resources_e.pdf hosted in the` `www.uc3m.es` web server, and more specifically, in the folder named `courses`. If the website administrator renames this folder or moves the file to a different location within the website, the links pointing to this resource will stop working and will be broken.

To solve this issue, different approaches have been proposed to ensure that electronic resources have a unique, global identifier in the web. An identifier that is not changed and do not depend on the physical location of the resource. These identifiers are a building block in most of the metadata management projects, as it is necessary to have a unique identity for resources. The most important approaches are DOI (Digital Object Identifiers), PURL and OpenURL.

3.1. *DOI (Digital Object Identifiers)*

The purpose of DOI is to assign a unique, persistent, global identifier to any electronic resource. Persistent resources are those that do not change and do not depend on the physical location of the document within a web server. The origin of DOI is a program of the Corporation for National Research Initiatives (CNRI) named Handle System, started in 1997. DOI work as follow:

- Electronic documents are assigned a unique, global and persistent identifier known as DOI. This identifier shall be used when linking to the electronic resources instead of their URLs.
- When a third party wants to create a link to the resource to which the DOI has been assigned, this DOI shall be used. The link shall be similar to the following one: http://dx.doi.org/10.1038/35057062.

DOI-based links have three parts:

- The first one refers to an intermediate server, "DOI registry" or "handle system". In the example, the name of this handle server is `dx.doi.org`.

- After the name of the handle system, there is a prefix that identifies the entity publishing the electronic resource. In the example, the prefix is `10.1038`.
- Finally, there is a suffix that identifies the electronic resource within the full set of documents made available by the publisher. In this example, this suffix is `35057062`.
- Links pointing to a DOI do not redirect to the web server where the document is hosted. Instead, the request is redirected to the intermediate server. This server shall receive and process the request to obtain the physical location (URL) that corresponds to the DOI that is being requested.
- The intermediate server can obtain the actual URL corresponding to the resource because it has access to a database where this information is stored. In the DOI model, publishers are responsible of keeping this information updated (as they publish documents in the web, they will facilitate the DOIs and the corresponding URLs of their documents to the intermediate server). If the URL changes, publishers are responsible for updating this information in the DOI registry.
- Finally, the intermediate server will redirect the user to the publisher's website where the document is hosted. The document shall be displayed.

In the linking model based on URLs, if the URL changes all the pages containing links to it should be updated to avoid broken links. If DOIs are assigned to documents, third-parties will use this persistent identifier in their links. If the publisher needs to change the physical location of the resource, this change has to be notified to the intermediate server, and none of the pages containing links to this resource need to be updated.[4]

Currently, DOIs are used by the main publishers of academic contents. Databases from *Springer, Elsevier* o *McGraw-Hill,* are displaying the DOIs assigned to their articles as part of the metadata they provide.

3.2. *PURL (Persistent URL)*

This is an *Online Computer Library Center* (OCLC) initiative to solve the problems due to the volatility of web links. Not as popular as DOI, it also

[4] Further details about DOI can be obtained in the website of the International DOI Foundation, http://www.doi.org, where the list of agencies authorized to assign identifiers to publishers is included. We remind that the allocation of identifiers to specific documents is responsibility of the publishers and content providers.

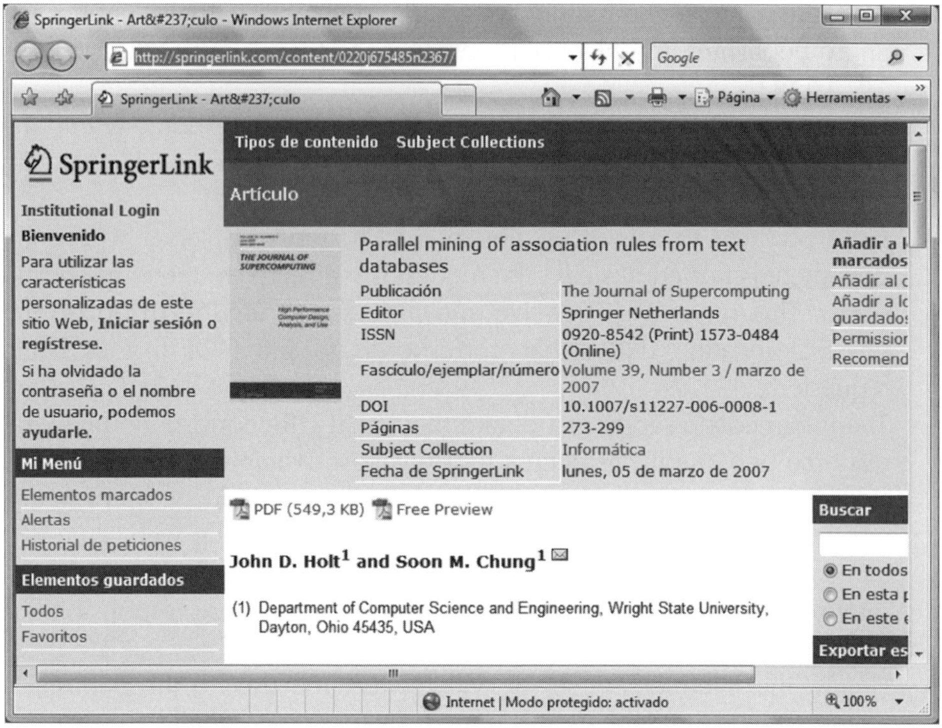

Fig. 1. Use of DOIs in Springer databases as part of articles' metadata.

requires the availability of an intermediate server in charge of solving link requests, translating a persistent URL to an actual URL and redirecting users to this one. PURL identifiers were used in the *OCLC's Internet Cataloguing Project.*[5]

3.3. *CrossRef project*

CrossRef is not a technical approach for the identification of resources, but a project launched by big editorial companies to facilitate the creation of hypertext links between their publications. Participants included companies within the *Science, Technology and Medicine* (STM) area, where an article usually contains several references and links to articles from other publishers.

CrossRef was initially based in a project of John Wiley & Sons, Academic Press and the International DOI Foundation (IDF). CrossRef participants

[5] OCLC distributes the software to enable an intermediate PURL server. At the moment of writing this chapter, the software was freely available at the following URL: http://www.oclc.org/research/projects/purl/download.htm

include publishers within the Publishers International Linking Association (PILA) association: about 148 publishers managing more than 6,000 journals, as well as libraries and library consortia.

Participation in CrossRef can be described as follows:

- Publishers need a method to refer to articles (both those published in their own journals, and those published by other parties). DOI was adopted for this purpose.
- A centralized database is needed to locate the DOIs assigned to articles. In this database, it is possible to locate, for example, one article published in a specific volume and issue of a journal.
- Publishers keep this database updated, storing the basic metadata about the articles, their DOIs and the URLs needed to solve the DOI.

The next diagram summarizes how CrossRef works:

Any publisher or library can be part of this project to take advantage of this centralized database. For publishers, the main advantage of being involved in *CrossRef* is a wider visibility to their publications; if other publishers can make links to their contents, the probability of researches accessing their contents becomes higher.

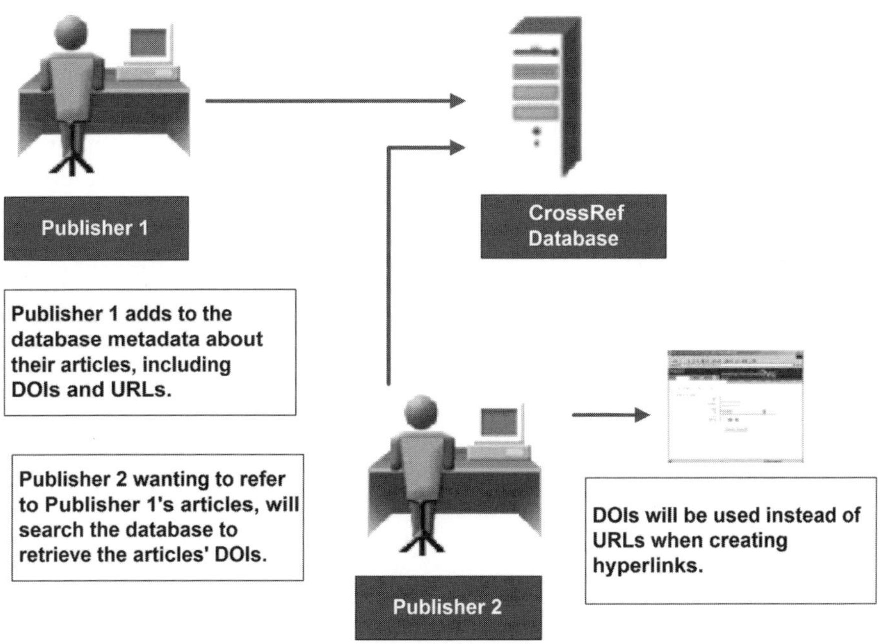

Fig. 2. CrossRef schema.

3.4. *OpenURL*

The third technical approach related to resource identification and metadata management and interoperability is the OpenURL and the software applications called *link resolvers*. This standard and the related software applications were designed to solve a specific problem in the access to electronic resources. Some electronic resources — mainly the electronic journals — are distributed through different databases or packages. Even the same e-journal can be distributed as part of different packages by the same publisher, distributor, or aggregator. It is also possible to find a more complex scenario where one provider gives access to the full-text of the e-journal, while another one just provides access just to references and abstracts. It is also possible that different types of users have different access rights to the e-journal through distinct gateways or databases.

In this scenario the issue of the "appropriate copy" raises. This refer to the fact that as users can access the same resource through different databases and gateways, it is necessary to direct them to the most appropriate copy of the resource in which they are interested.

Another issue that OpenURL technology and linking resolution servers try to solve is the navigation and browsing between heterogeneous e-resources. Usually, libraries subscribe access to databases that contain just the metadata and the abstracts of articles about a specific knowledge area. But the library can also be subscribed to the full-text of some of the journals referenced in these databases. From an end-user perspective, it should be possible to access the full-text of the subscribed articles from the list of results provided by the reference databases, at the click of a mouse, without having to annotate the details, connecting to the full-text journal, running an additional search, etc.

Having disparate sources for electronic resources (gateways, aggregators, and publishers giving access to full-text journals) translate into additional difficulties for end-users to access contents. Things will be better if end-users could navigate between the different e-resources subscribed by the library without the need of log-out, log-in, and repeat searches.

In 1999, H. Van de Sompel, from the Gantt University (Belgium), started the development of a computer-based solution to solve these problems. The proposed solution was a piece of software that worked as an intermediary between:

- the information services containing the references to the articles and
- those services giving access to the full-text of the articles, or any other related service (for example, to check the availability of printed copies of the journal within the library).

This software was called "link resolution server" or Institutional Service Component. It received requests coming from end-users. These requests meant: Which services are available for this article I am interested in? Is there any subscription where I can access the full text of this article? Is it available as part of the hard-copy collection of journals in my library?

To answer these requests, the link resolver needed to check the information in an internal database to show users a web page listing all the services related to this specific article. This result page provided links to, for example: (a) gateways, databases or any other service subscribed by the library where the full-text of the article could be downloaded; (b) the signature of the hard-copy of the journal in the Library (if available) or (c) one form where the article could be requested by interlibrary loan.

The development from H. Van de Sompel evolved into a software application called *SFX*, that was later acquired by the *ExLibris* company, who is now in charge of their maintenance and evolution. This model is also implemented and supported by other software providers.

Link resolver technology is based on the interaction of the following components:

- Online information service from which users can request information to the link resolver about the services available for a specific publication or article.

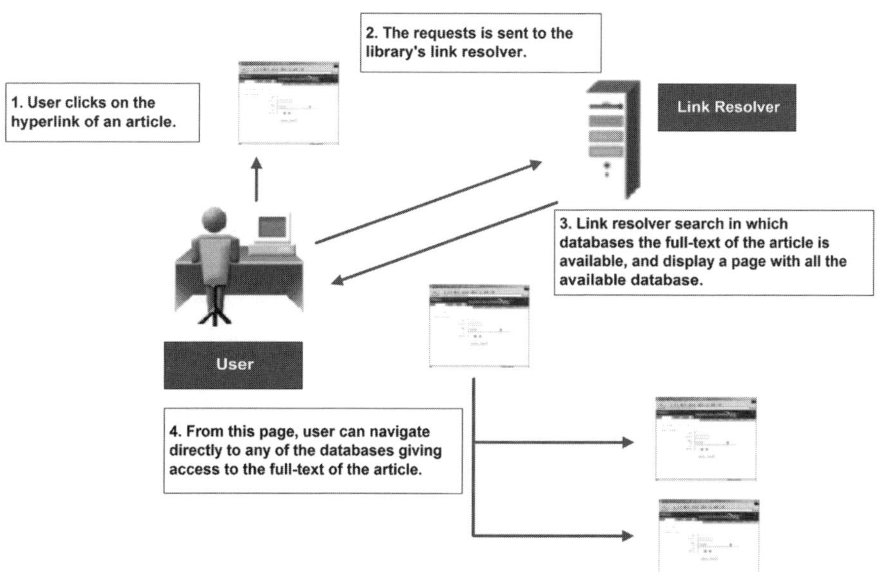

Fig. 3. OpenURL schema.

- One link resolver that receives the requests, identifies the services available for any given reference and generates a web page with the results.
- One database where the link resolver can access the list of services available for each publication. This database is usually a part of the link resolver software.
- Several online information services that provide access to the services identified by the link resolver.

Requests to the link resolver are always sent through the *Hypertext Transfer Protocol* (http) protocol. The diagram below shows the interaction between these components:

This solution deals with information systems integration through metadata exchange. This is the point where the OpenURL standard comes into place, as it provides a method to transfer metadata about a specific object through the web. OpenURL is used to transfer metadata about the article the user is interested in, from the reference databases to the link resolver. OpenURL was designed in 1999. In 2001 is was proposed to National Information Standards Organization (NISO) for standardization, and in 2005 it was approved as the Z39.88 standard.

For example, if we are searching a database, we find a reference to an article written by *Antonio Gomez in Revista de Documentación Científica*, Vol. 10, Issue 3, and we want to check the availability of its full-text in any of the databases subscribed by our library, we will activate a link to send to the link resolver the article metadata. These metadata are codified in the format established by the OpenURL standard. This is similar to a standard URL, with the difference that instead of containing paths and file names, it contains metadata. The following are examples of OpenURLs where this can be appreciated:

```
http://sfxserver.uni.edu/sfxmenu?issn=12345678&date=1998&
  volume=12&issue=2&spage=134
http://sfxserver.uni.edu/sfxmenu?id=doi:123/345678
```

In both cases, requests are sent to a link resolver available at the URL: http://sfxserver.uni.edu.

The first OpenURL requests to the link resolver the set of services available for an article published in the Vol. 12 (1998), Issue 2 of a journal with ISSN 12345678, and that starts at page 134. The URL includes all the metadata needed to identify the exact article within the journal. In the second example, the DOI is used to request to the link resolver the services available for the article with this DOI.

Link resolvers are software applications that have to be installed as part of the library IT infrastructure (it is also possible to work with hosted link resolvers). Today this technology is widely supported by providers of library software and electronic resources, with working applications like WebBridge (Innovative Interfaces), Sirsi Resolver (Sirsi-Dynix), SFX (ExLibris), LinkSource (EBSCO), LinkSolver (Ovid), TOUR (TDNet), etc.

Besides setting up a link resolver, the information services the users interact with must give the choice of linking to the link resolver from their search result pages. For example, each retrieved article should provide a hyperlink pointing to the link resolver installed at the library. These links must be compliant with the OpenURL specification.

Currently, most information service providers and databases give libraries the possibility of customizing search result pages to point to link resolvers: The Gale Group, GoogleScholar, JSTOR, ISI Web of Knowlege, OCLC FirstSearch, Innovative Innopac Millenium, Elsevier, Dialog, EBSCO Publishing, SCOPUS, Ei Village, OVID, Swets Information Services, Oxford University Press, Chemical Abstracts Services, etc., support this feature.

Finally, the link resolver has to know how to build the URLs that are shown to the end-users after "resolving" the requests; the set of links pointing to the services available for the library users. OpenURL is not used for this purpose, and link resolvers must be configured according to the specific set up facilitated by information service providers.

4. Technical interoperability approaches

From a technical perspective, metadata interoperability in the global context of the web is supported by technologies like SOAP and RESTful web services. In both cases, these are general approaches for application interoperability. We can find solutions specifically developed for libraries based on these approaches. This section provides an overview of the most relevant initiatives: SRU from the Library of Congress, and the *Open Archives Initiative — Protocol for Metadata Harvesting* (OAI-PMH). The work completed by NISO in the area of federated searching is also included in this section.

4.1. *Web-service approach: SRU*

The use of XML within libraries is not restricted to the codification of electronic documents and metadata records. As explained in Sec. 2.1, XML-based web services are the preferred approach to achieve interoperability between software applications in the web. SRU technical protocol is the result of the evolution of the Z39.50 standard.

This protocol defines how two computers connected to the web have to interact in an information retrieval process; the messages that the client computer has to send to the server, the answers to these requests and the encoding to be used to serialize these messages.

SRU was developed in the context of the *Z39.50 International Next Generation* (ZING) initiative, to adapt Z39.50 to the web.

Z39.50-2003 Information Retrieval: Application Service Definition and protocol Specification is a widely implemented standard published by American National Standards Institute (ANSI). Its equivalent ISO standard is ISO 23950:1998, Information and Documentation — Information Retrieval. Its development started at the beginning of the '80. In the USA, the Linked System Project (LSP) designed a protocol for information retrieval from databases hosted by OCLC, Library of Congress, Western Library Network (WLN) and Research Library Group (RLG) that was approved in 1988 as an American standard (version 1 of Z39.50). A similar project was developed in Europe, Search and Retrieval (SR), whose results were published in 1993 as ISO 10162 and ISO 10163-1 [4].

Z39.50 provides a model for the information retrieval process between two computer systems: one acting as the Client or *source* and another one as the Server or *target*. The standard establishes the requests that the Client can send to the server and the answers to be provided. For each activity in the information retrieval process (establishing a connection, sending queries, sending results, closing the connection, etc.) the structure, contents and format of the messages are defined by the standard. Z39.50 [22] has played a key role in the automation of libraries, as it enabled librarians to search catalogs hosted by other libraries that run software from other vendors using a single interface (the Z39.50 client). To make this possible, companies developing library software had to implement the capability of understanding Z39.50 requests as part of their software applications.

The generalization of the Web brought the need of analyzing which changes were needed to adapt Z30.50 to the web technologies and standards. ZING project was launched in 2001 with this purpose, under the leadership of the *Library of Congress* and contributions from *OCLC*, Oxford University, Liverpool University, *IndexData* and the *Koninklijke Bibliotheek* from Netherlands.

ZING developed three research lines: the SRU *and Search/Retrieve Web Service* (SRW) protocols and the *Common Query Language* (CQL).

SRU and SRW described the information retrieval process between two computers, the services to be provided by the server and the structure and content of the messages to be exchanged. SRU can be seen as equivalent to Z39.50 in its purpose and in the underlying model; the main differences are the use of the http protocol and XML messages in the new proposal. The responses containing search results were sent in XML format, and it was possible to use different metadata schemas like Dublin Core, MARCXML, etc.

CQL was the query language that established the syntax to be used in queries embeded in SRU and SRW requests. CQL[6] support different types of queries:

- **Simple queries** that contains one term or sentence, optionally truncated.
- **Booleans** that combine terms with the AND, OR and NOT operators.
- **Proximity** for retrieving records that contain terms separated by at most a specific number of words, sentences or paragraphs.
- **Qualified search** for restricting the query to specific fields, metadata items or indexes.

Other initiatives were developed as part of ZING, like *Z39.50 Object Oriented Model* (ZOOM) or ZeeRex. ZOOM specified Application Programming Interfaces (APIs) for building Z39.50 applications. *Z39.50 Explain Explained and Re-Engineered in XML* (ZeeRex) *was started in* 2002 to simplify the Explain operation in Z39.50 (used to provide descriptions of information retrieval services).

The first version of SRW, SRU and CQL was published in November 2002; they were under tests for a period of nine months. Version, 1.1 was published in February 2004 and version 1.2 in 2007.

Today, the protocol is still valid although its terminology has changed. ZING and SRW are no longer used and SRU refers to both protocol variants (the one based on REST and the one based on SOAP). For the latter, the documentation refers to "SRU via HTTP SOAP". In addition, since 2007 the evolution of SRU is linked to *OASIS Search Web Services Technical Committee,* focused on the development of version 2.0. This version will be a binding of SRU to an Abstract Protocol Definition that provides a model for search and retrieve services over the web. Another protocol, OpenSearch, is also in the

[6] CQL specification establishes three conformance levels for applications, depending on the features supported. Level 0 just requires software applications to interpret queries with one or more terms; level 1 requires the understanding of boolean operators and qualified searches; level 2 requires support to all the features defined in the CQL specification.

scope of this committee activity. Standardization is expected to be ready at the end of 2009.

4.2. *SRU operations*

SRU declares a set of operations that are part of a standard information retrieval process. These are:

- `SearchRetrieve` — indicates how queries have to be sent from the Client application to the remote server, and how to send the retrieved records.
- `Scan` — to search the indexes managed by the server, and get the number of documents or records available for a specific term or name.
- `Explain` — to obtain information about the server characteristics, its database and the metadata schemas the server will use to send the answers.

For these services, requests and response messages are defined. As part of these messages, parameters shall be included. As an example, the following fragment corresponds to an SRU over SOAP message requesting the *SearchRetrieve* operation to a remote server.

```
<SOAP:Envelope
xmlns:SOAP="http://schemas.xmlsoap.org/soap/envelope/">
   <SOAP:Body>
      <SRW:searchRetrieveRequest xmlns:SRW="http://www.
        loc.gov/srw">
         <SRW:version>1.1</SRW:version>
         <SRW:query>(dc.author exact "unamuno")
      </SRW:query>
         <SRW:startRecord>1</SRW:startRecord>
         <SRW:maximumRecords>10</SRW:maximumRecords>
         <SRW:recordSchema>info:srw/schema/mods
      </SRW:recordsSchema>
      </SRW:searchRetrieveRequest>
   </SOAP:Body>
</SOAP:Envelope>
```

The requests contain SRU specific data like the version of the protocol in use, the query, number of records to be retrieved, and the metadata schema in which the results have to be provided.

The same requests using SRU (without SOAP) will be similar to this one:

```
http://z3950.loc.gov:7090/voyager?version=1.1&operation=search
Retrieve&query=unamuno&maximumRecords=10&recordSchema=mods
```

The answer to the previous requests would be, in both cases, an XML document containing metadata about the retrieved records.

SRU is not linked to a specific metadata standard, and that the results can be provided in any metadata schema according to the user requests and the server supported capabilities. The picture below shows an example of SRU search results.

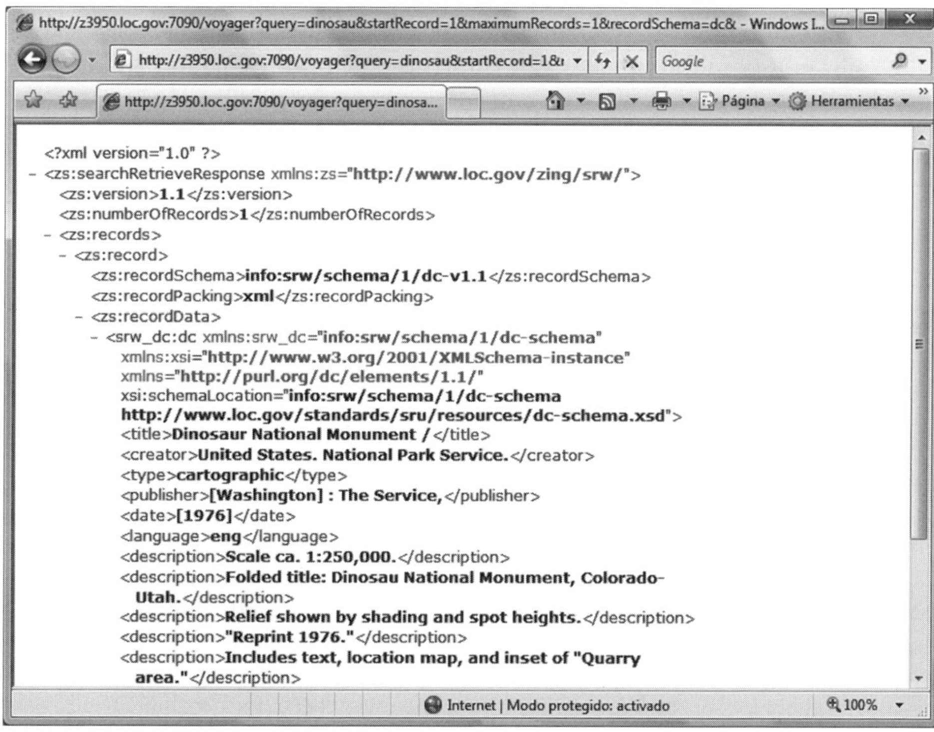

Fig. 4. SRU sample search results in XML format.

4.3. *OAI-PMH (Open Archives Initiative — Protocol for Metadata Harvesting)*

An assessment of current approaches designed for metadata interoperability (aggregation, collection, search, etc.) would show that OAI-PMH is the most used technical solution.

OAI-PMH is a technical protocol designed to automate the recollection (harvesting) of metadata records about resources distributed in the web. OAI-PMH makes use of HTTP as transfer protocol and XML to encode metadata in an easy to process format.

This technical protocol is part of the Open Archives Initiative (OAI).[7] OAI defines itself as an "initiative to develop and promote standards for the interoperability, to facilitate the efficient diffusion of content". The idea behind this technical protocol is to enable the sharing of metadata records between organizations using automated, unattended processes.

OAI-PMH is the basis of some repositories known as "open archives". An open archive is a database that gives access to metadata about electronic resources. Usually, these databases are the result of the cooperation between different organizations, and they provide access the metadata created by different centers (although the repository is centrally managed by a single organization). In open archives, authors can easily publish their contributions, avoiding the time-consuming review process that characterize academic journals.

The first stable version of the OAI-PMH protocol was 2.0, available since June 2002 (the first version was published in January 2001, and it was based on an existing protocol called *Dienst* [5]). The protocol establishes a set of requests and responses to collect metadata records in an automated way, and the method to encode metadata.[8]

One of the technical foundations of the OAI-PMH [23] protocol is the approach used to achieve the integration of metadata. Instead of using a distributed search approach (as the one proposed, for example, in Z30.50),

---

[7] The origin of OAI was a meeting held in Santa Fe (Nuevo México) between 21st and 22th October 1999. The meeting was organised by three researchers working at *Los Alamos Nacional Laboratory* (USA): *Paul Ginsparg, Rick Luce* y *Herbert Van de Sompel*[6].

The purpose of this meeting was to discuss with experts the possibility of integrating the information available in different repositories of e-prints (contributions and text not formally published yet but exchanged between academics and researchers). The capability of aggregating the contributions spread through these repositories will give a higher visibility to them, as end-users would not need to search repositories one after another to obtain comprehensive results. After this meeting, in 2000 the *Digital Library Federation,* the *Coalition of Networked Information* and the *National Science Foundation* started supporting this initiative [7, 8]. OAI standardization work also includes the development of Object Reuse and Exchange (OAI-ORE) for the description and exchange of aggregated web resources; OAI-ORE makes use of RDF).

[8] In the meeting held at Santa Fe, a metadata system based on XML with name *Open Archives Metadata Set* (OAMS) was adopted, although it was later replaced by non-qualified Dublin Core. OAMS included nine elements: *title, Date of Accession, DisplayID, FullID, Author, Abstract, Subject, Comment* and *Date of Discovery.* A DTD was designed for this metadata schema.

a metadata harvesting process that collected metadata from web servers and aggregated them into a centralized database was considered more suitable. The harvester regularly checks the URLs of the remote site where metadata records are stored as part of an XML file (that can be generated on the fly after reception of the request from the harvester). The protocol supports two criteria to filter metadata records: (a) last modification date (to ensure that only those records created or modified since the last interaction between the harvester and the server are collected) and (b) sets, used to classify metadata records by subject, or by any other criteria.

Once downloaded, the XML file can be processed to extract the metadata and write them in the database. The agency managing the central database shall provide a search interface for end-users. The approach proposed by OAI-PMH is characterized by its simplicity, and this is with no doubt one of the reason for its widen adoption and success.

In the OAI-PMH protocol, XML is used to transfer the responses from the websites providing the metadata records to the harvester. The requests from the harvester to the sites providing metadata records are sent as http GET requests.

The protocol defines six operations or "verbs": Identify, ListMetadataFormats, ListSet, ListIdentifiers, ListRecords y GetRecord.

The first one — Identify — requests a description of the repository. ListMetadataFormats requests the list of metadata formats that the data provider supports (Dublin Core, MARCXML, etc.). ListSets can be used to requests the sets managed by the data provider to classify metadata records. ListIdentifiers requests the header of the metadata records (not the full record), ListRecords requests a full set of metadata records (filtered by date or by set) and GetRecord retrieves a specific record.

The following is an example of a ListRecords requests:

```
http://www.proveedordatos.com/oai-
script?verb=ListRecords&metadataPrefix=oai_dc&set=biology
```

And the corresponding answer:

```
<?xml version="1.0" encoding="UTF-8"?>
<OAI-PMH
xmlns="http://www.openarchives.org/OAI/2.0/"
xsi:schemaLocation="http://www.openarchives.org/OAI/2.0/
http://www.openarchives.org/OAI/2.0/OAI-PMH.xsd">
   <responseDate>2002-06-01T19:20:30Z</responseDate>
   <request verb="ListRecords"
```

```
            from="1998-01-15"
            metadataPrefix="oai_rfc1807">
    </request>
    <ListRecords>
        <record>
        <header>
            <identifier>oai:arXiv.org:hep-th/9901001</
              identifier>
            <datestamp>1999-12-25</datestamp>
            <setSpec>physics:hep</setSpec>
            <setSpec>math</setSpec>
        </header>
        <metadata>
            <rfc1807>
              <bib-version>v2</bib-version>
              <id>hep-th/9901001</id>
              <entry>January 1, 1999</entry>
              <title>Investigations of Radioactivity</title>
              <author>Ernest Rutherford</author>
              <date>March 30, 1999</date>
            </rfc1807>
        </metadata>
    </record>
</ListRecords>
/OAI-PMH>
```

To conclude this section, we will remark that the collected metadata records contain one header and one element that enclose the metadata codified in a specific metadata vocabulary. The protocol makes mandatory the support to simple *Dublin Core,* but this is not the only choice available. Other metadata schemas like *rfc1807*, MARC XML or an adaptation of MARC known as *oai_marc* could also be used,[9] although in practical terms, Dublin Core is the preferred choice [18].

4.4. *NISO metadata search initiative*

In 2006, NISO published the results of its *Metadata Search Initiative* (started in 2003) and a guide for implementers of a technical protocol for searching

[9] rfc1807, published by the *Internet Engineering Task Force (IETF)* was presented in June 1995 to codify bibliographic descriptions of technical reports. This protocol was used in one of the predecessors of OAI, the D*ienst* protocol. In the case of the *oai_marc*, it was publsihed by OAI to support the codification of records in MARC in June 2002. This alternative is expected to be replaced by the MARCXML schema from the *Library of Congress.*

remote, web-based resources. This protocol, *Metadata XML Gategay* (MXG) was based on the Library of Congress SRU. The objective of this initiative was to standardize the transfer of metadata between federated search applications and content providers. Federated search tools receive a query from the user, forward it to several content providers and — once they get the results — show them in an aggregated, single list. Following SRU, the protocol proposed by NISO did not restrict the use of metadata schemas (any schema could be used to transfer the results from the content providers to the metasearch application).

5. Semantic interoperability approaches

The final step toward achieving full interoperability between information services is concerned with the semantic layer of metadata. This section describes key projects and initiatives developed in this area: Schemas, CORES and OCLC Metadata Switch Project. The selected initiatives and their conclusions are fully representative of the main concerns in the metadata research community and practitioners.

5.1. *Schemas and CORES*

These are two closely related projects in the area of metadata interoperability. Schemas was launched in 2000 as a two-year effort. Participants included companies like PricewaterhouseCoopers Luxembourg (PwC), the Hungarian research institute MTA SZTAKI , UKOLN (based on the University of Bath[10]) and the research organization Fraunhofer-Gesellschaft.

One of its objectives was the creation of an online registry where software developers and practitioners could easily locate existing metadata schemas and reuse them in their own development and projects. Through this registry, it would be possible to identify schemas already designed for different purposes, gain the attention of the user community, leverage and promote their use. Sharing the recommendations on how a specific schema had been used in different scenarios was also part of the information that Schemas wanted to provide.

The metadata registry was planned to include the customizations that practitioners made on available metadata schemas. These customizations usually consisted the merging of metadata elements taken from different schemas, on the addition of new elements, and resulted in "application profiles".

[10] UKOLN is funded by the Library and Information Commission, the Joint Information Systems Committee (JISC) of the Higher Education Funding Councils.

From a conceptual perspective, one of the major achievements of Schemas was the preparation of a glossary that clarified the meaning of some key terms usually found in metadata management and research initiatives.

The glossary proposed the term "namespace" to refer to the document or specification were the metadata terms and the vocabulary of a particular schema were declared. Namespaces defined the element set accepted by the metadata system, their identifiers, definition and the relationships between them.

The glossary also made a distinction between the terms *schemas* and *schemes*. For schemas, different usages were reported, that ranged from a "*set of terms that compose a metadata system*" (its vocabulary), to the use of a specific encoding method to serialize metadata records. In the case of schemes, it was proposed to designate the set of values accepted for specific elements.

Another important term defined in the Schemas glossary was "application profiles". Profiles referred to the customization made by an organization on an existing metadata schema to facilitate its use in a specific context. Profile are needed as, in some situations, a single schema cannot provide answers to all the requirements for a particular application. Profiles should contain usage notes, recommendations on the use of metadata elements and the list of values accepted for them.[11]

Schemas developed a set of recommendations to formally document metadata profiles using RDF schemas, as having a common set of guidelines will make easier to publish and integrate profiles within the metadata registry. The use of RDF to express metadata profiles made possible the harvesting of metadata profiles in an unattended, fully automated way (similar to OAI). The use of RDF was also proposed to codify the characteristics of metadata schemas or namespaces, and a detailed business case was completed for the Dublin Core metadata schema.

The implementation of the metadata registry and related tools was partially achieved. It was based on one tool already developed by the OCLC — *Extensible Open RDF (EOR) Toolkit* — and the work completed by a previous initiative called DESIRE.[12] This implementation served as a proof-of-concept of the different aspects under discussion.

[11] The definition provided in the Schemas documentation for a profile defines this as an "schema consisting of data elements drawn from one or more namespaces optimized for a particular local application [...] It draws on existing namespaces and introduces no new data elements".

[12] DESIRE registry can still be checked at http://desire.ukoln.ac.uk/registry/. This was one of the first relevant initiatives aimed to provide a technical implementation of a repository for metadata schemas. It even included the possibility of creating crosswalks among schemas.

Schemas was continued by *CORES — A Forum on Shared Metadata Vocabularies.* CORES started in May 2002 with a planned duration of 15 months. The same as Schemas, it was developed in the context of the *European Commission's IST Program* in the area of metadata interoperability.

CORES objective was "building semantic bridges between metadata standards within the framework of the Semantic Web" and "create consensus on the means to share semantics to enable existing standards to work together in an integrated, machine-understandable Semantic Web environment" [14]. To achieve this, CORES established a Standards Interoperability Forum that started its activity with a meeting held on Brussels on 18 November 2002. Inputs to this meeting were the results of a survey where representatives from major metadata initiatives participated: DCMI, MARC21, ONIX, DOI, IEEE/Learning Object Metadata, OASIS, GILS, mpeg-7, etc. The most relevant conclusion from this meeting — known as the CORES Resolution [15] — was the recognition of the need of having a method to uniquely identify metadata elements in the global context of the Web. URIs was the chosen method.[13] The use of URIs prevents any ambiguity in the naming of resources and metadata.

The CORES Resolution was a two pages-document. It stated:

"The meeting achieved consensus on a resolution to assign unique identifiers to metadata elements as a useful first step towards the development of mapping infrastructures and interoperability services. The participants agreed to promote the implementation of this consensus in their standards communities and beyond".

The resolution also included some clarifications, like the fact URIs should also be used to identify metadata schemas and even the values assigned to metadata elements, and that these URIs do not need to correspond to actual locations in the web.[14]

---

[13] URI are uniquely, global identifiers assigned to both resources and properties. An URI is similar to a URL; the main difference is that URIs do not refer to an actual, existing locations in the Web; they are just identifiers allocated to items.

[14] The text of the clarifications is extracted below:

"This resolution promotes the use of URIs for identifying metadata elements. However, there is no expectation that these URIs will be used to represent those elements within particular application environments — e.g., to include them in instance metadata records or use them in SQL queries. Rather, the intent is to offer a common citation mechanism usable, when needed, for purposes of interoperability across standards.

While the resolution focuses on the identification of individual metadata elements, URIs should also be used to identify other relevant entities at various levels of granularity, such as sets of elements (schemas) and the terms and sets of controlled vocabularies of metadata

The identification of metadata elements by URIs ensures language independency, as translations into different languages can be assigned to these URIs at the user-interface level.

The development of CORES also included the creation of a metadata registry where organizations could declare metadata vocabularies, schemas and profiles. The registry was completed at the beginning of 2003, and it is still currently accessible at the web site of one of the partners, Sztaki, at the URL:

http://cores.dsd.sztaki.hu/

Registry enables browsing and searching metadata vocabularies, element definitions, encoding methods, data about the agencies in charge of their maintenance, and project specific profiles and adaptations. One tool was developed — *Schema Creation and Registration Tool* — that supported the metadata schema registration process.

CORES can be seen as an evolution of Schemas. One of the principal conclusions from these early projects is the fact that metadata integration needs to achieve compatibility not only at the semantic level, but also at the grammatical level. This refers to the underlying data model on which the metadata schema is based. Usually, integration and interoperability is planned in an ad-hoc basis, thinking in the integration of pairs of metadata vocabularies known in advance, by identifying equivalences between the terms used in each metadata schema. In these ad-hoc projects, there is no need of analyzing additional details about the grammatical compatibility between the schemas. Establishing the common foundations — a common grammar — between metadata systems would be a factor that will improve our capability of defining equivalences between disparate metadata systems [13]. This can be understood better if we think in the complex, nested structure of most XML documents. To identify equivalences between these XML document types a detailed knowledge of their structure is needed; a detailed knowledge that — in turn — has to be embedded in the software applications that will process these transformations. In an ideal scenario, the metadata elements from different systems — as well as their relationships — would be codified in a generic way, based on a common grammar or abstract model. This can be partly achieved with the use of the Resource Description Framework (RDF) specification. The Schemas project clearly identified the

---

values. Deciding which of its own entities are important or salient enough to be assigned URIs is the prerogative of a particular Standards-Developing Organization.

This resolution specifies the use of URIs as identifiers with no requirement or expectation that those URIs will reference anything on the World Wide Web, such as documentation pages or machine-understandable representations of metadata elements."

restrictions of ad-hoc interoperability approaches for achieving scalable metadata interoperability. RDF, described in a later section of this chapter, provides these foundations and a generic model to express metadata about any type of entity/object. RDF model also shares the feature identified by the CORES Resolution: having a unique, global identifier for metadata terms based on URIs. If we had the capability of expressing any existing metadata schema in RDF, the chances for integrating and exchanging these metadata will be improved.

5.2. *OCLC metadata switch project*

The third project we need to mention is the Metadata Switch Project developed by the OCLC. Probably, it would be better to describe it as a program, as it dealt with several aspects related to metadata management and resource description in a global, web-based, context.

Metadata Switch Project was proposed as an answer to the challenges raised in a new scenario; a scenario where libraries were using a growing number of metadata schemas to describe different types of materials. The need of merging or aggregating metadata coming from disparate sites and based on different cataloging and classification practices were other factors motivating its development [11]. Its objectives and goals have been described in different references: "*look at constructing experimental modular services that add value to metadata, and at exposing this functionality as web services*" [9] and "*create a collection of Web services that perform key tasks required for the management of the digital library — such as Web page harvesting, automatic subject assignment, and the standardization of terminology and proper names*" [17].

The result of this project was a set of related, web-based services providing advanced functions to libraries, like metadata schema transformations and terminology services [19]. For example, web services were built to transform a metadata record encoded in a particular schema into an equivalent record based on another metadata system (e.g., from MARCXML to Dublin Core). Other web-services were built to translate subject heading between different languages, obtain class numbers for a specific web page, or get the class number from a Classification System that would be equivalent to a specific subject heading.

To deal with metadata translation, a two paths approach was proposed. The first one was based on a direct translation between metadata schemas using XSLT transformations. *Metadata & Transmission Encoding Schema* (METS) — a Library of Congress standard for encoding digital objects) was proposed to encode the equivalences between metadata items in both schemas. The second approach was designed for more complex scenarios where it was not possible to establish direct equivalences between tags (this happens, for example, when dealing with MARC records). For these cases, it was proposed to: (a) complete a syntactical normalization of the input records, (b) complete a translation of the metadata items into an interoperable core based on MARC, and (c) translate the resulting record from this interoperable core into the target schema and syntax.

This set of functions was based on the use of the XML-based web services, described in a previous section of the chapter. Metadata Switch Project is one of the most interesting efforts, from a practical point of view, to explore how libraries could take advantage of web-services to enhance their capability to interoperate and exchange metadata.

6. Abstract models for metadata interoperability: RDF and SPARQL

To conclude this chapter, we need to refer to Resource Description Framework (RDF) and SPARQL. This is in line with one of the conclusions mentioned in previous sections: The need of having a common grammar or abstract model between metadata schemas.

6.1. *RDF (Resource Description Framework)*

RDF is today the most relevant standard for web-based metadata exchange and integration, at least from a theoretical point of view. Developed by the W3C as one of the pillars of the semantic web initiative [30], it is briefly defined as "*a language for representing information about resources in the World Wide Web*". RDF was proposed in 1997 as a means to codify and transfer metadata about resources across the web. The first version of this specification was published in two documents: (a) RDF Model and Syntax, usually referred to as RDF MS and (b) RDF Schema, referred to as RDFS [32]. After a period of revision, the RDF specification was reviewed and a different set of documents were released.

RDF establishes a model for declaring metadata about resources, and it is close to the abstract model or grammar we referred before when analyzing Schemas and CORES conclusions. In RDF, metadata records consist of triples, each triple containing a subject, a predicate and an object. The subject refers to the resource for which metadata are provided, the predicate to one property of this resource (the metadata element) and the object is the value assigned to this property. It is possible to have several triples referring to the same resource (one for each metadata element or property that is being stored).

RDF also uses the term *statements* to refer to triples, so this language is sometimes described as a means to "formalize statements about resources".

The specification is toughly related to a graphical representation, where triples are displayed as graphs where resources (subjects) and property values (objects) are displayed as nodes (drawn as ovals or squares) and predicates (properties) are displayed as arcs (directed arrows going from the resource to the property value).

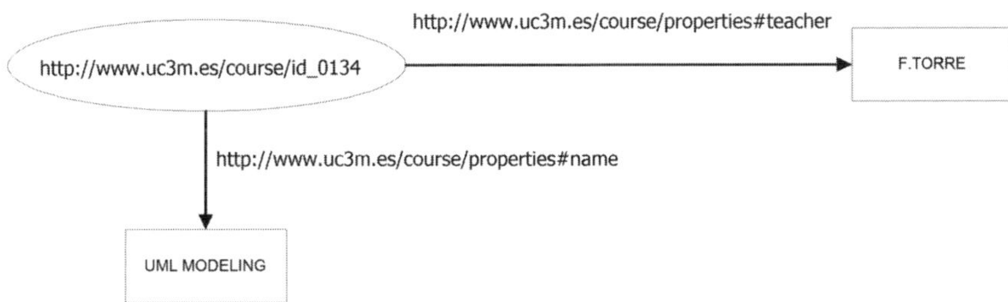

Fig. 5. Basic diagram showing two RDF statements.

The picture above shows a couple of statements or metadata triples. The subject of these statements is the resource identified by the URI http://www.uc3m.es/course/id_0134; the properties or metadata elements recorded for this resource are identified by the URIs:

`http://www.uc3m.es/course/properties#name and`
`http://www.uc3m.es/course/properties#teacher.`

Finally, the values assigned to these properties are represented by the squares containing the literals "UML Modeling" and "F. Torre".

The object (property value) of RDF statements may be a literal (string, integer, etc.) or a reference to another resource. In the first case, a distinction is made between typed literals (those having one datatype defined in the XML Schema specification like xsd:integer, xsd:string, etc.) and plain literals (those for which no data type is indicated). The value of a predicate can also consist of an XML fragment. In the case of predicates having a resource as their value, the graph will show the property's value as an oval, and additional statements can be declared for it.

An example of this is provided in Fig. 6. The value of the *trainer* property is now a reference to another resource, and additional statements are also provided for this one.

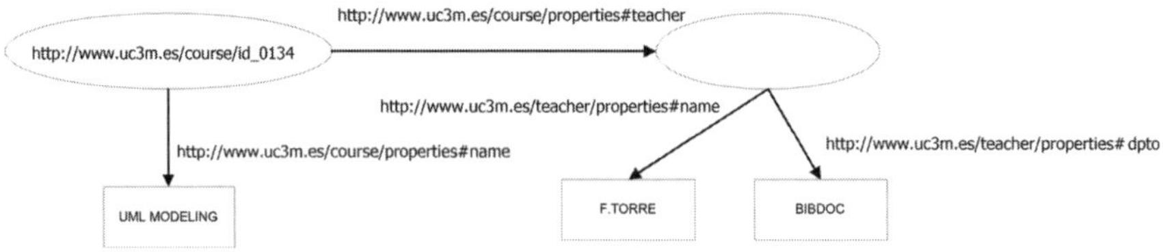

Fig. 6. Basic diagram showing two RDF statements, one having as an object another resource.

Graphs are not the only method available to represent RDF statements. Another approach uses single lines for each triple, where the subject, predicate and object are written separated by blank spaces, like in the following example (we can see that URIs are written within angle brackets and that the data type allocated to the object is indicated with a reference to an XSD data type):

```
<http://www.example.org/staffid/85740>
<http://www.example.org/terms/age>
"27"^^<http://www.w3.org/2001/XMLSchema#integer>
```

RDF does not declare specific metadata elements to describe resources, but a framework that can be used to declare and codify any kind of metadata, possible taken from other schemas. This raises some questions about RDF: how are resources and properties identified? Which kind of properties and metadata elements can be used in RDF triples? How are these RDF triples/statements serialized for storage, transport, etc.?

RDF makes use of URIs to identify both resources (the subjects of statements) and resource properties (the predicates of the statements). As previously stated, URIs ensure the uniqueness of resources and properties, and avoid issues due to name collisions if two organizations use the same name for different properties in their metadata schemas.[15]

As said before, RDF specification does not establish a closed set of metadata or resource properties, like Dublin Core and most of metadata schemas.

[15] RDF permits resources having no URIs (for example, because it is not known at the moment of representing the metadata). This is the case of the anonymous resources. In RDF, it is possible to make statements about anonymous resources, and no major differences exists between how they are managed (the only difference is that there is no URI allocated to them, so software applications for RDF shall implement some kind of process for the automatic generation of a IDs for anonymous resources). In the graphical representation of RDF statements, anonymous resources are represented by means of empty ovals or blank nodes containing no URI inside.

RDF is open and gives the choice of using any metadata element as the predicate of the statements. This is similar to the flexibility provided by XML, where we can choose the tags to be included in our documents. RDF documents containing statements will use different properties as predicates depending on the kind of resource the statement is about. In the W3C documentation we can find examples of RDF documents that make use of different metadata vocabularies in their statements: Dublin Core, PRISM, FOAF, etc.

To ensure consistency in the statements made in an RDF document (for example, to apply those properties that are valid for a specific type of resource), the RDF specification includes RDF Schemas.

RDF Schemas provide a way for declaring a vocabulary containing the terms (types of resources, properties or valid predicates, etc.) that can be used in RDF statements. A RDF Schema is described as a "light ontology development language", as it provides a basic set of constructs to define classes, their properties and the range and domain of these properties. These are the kind of constraints that can be declared in RDF Schemas.

6.2. *Serialization of RDF*

W3C specifications for RDF include the serialization of statements as XML documents, to support their storage, transfer and processing.[16]

The selection of XML as serialization method was a natural choice, mainly if we consider the role of RDF in the transfer and exchange of metadata across the Web and the treatment that software agents are expected to do from these metadata in the Semantic Web scenario.

As a summary, RDF statements in XML — from now on RDF/XML [31] — are enclosed in XML documents having a root element called <rdf:RDF>. This root element will contain the set of statements or triples. There will be one or more <rdf:Description> elements, one for each resource that is being described (this resource is the subject of the statements).

The <rdf:Description> element shall be accompanied by an *about* attribute that takes as a value the URI identifying the resource (except in the case of the anonymous ones); this element will also contain within its open and closing tags one XML element for each property or metadata element. The name of these XML elements will be the qualified name (or URI) of the

[16]The first version of the specification contained in the method to serialize RDF as XML data in the RDF Model and Syntax document. In the last review of this specification, a separate document was published describing how to represent RDF statements in this way.

properties, and will be different depending on the metadata system being used, as shown in the example below:

```
<?xml version="1.0"?>
<rdf:RDF
xmlns:rdf="http://www.w3.org/1999/02/22-rdf-syntax-ns#"
xmlns:contact="http://www.w3.org/2000/10/swap/pim/
contact#">
   <rdf:Description about="http://www.w3.org/People/EM/">
      <contact:fullName>Eric Miller</contact:fullName>
      <contact:mailbox rdf:resource="mailto:em@w3.org"/>
      <contact:personalTitle>Dr.</contact:personalTitle>
   </rdf:Description>
</rdf:RDF>
```

The serialization of the RDF statements in XML must make use of XML namespaces, as the resulting documents combine tags from different vocabularies:

(a) Elements and attributes taken from the RDF vocabulary like <rdf:RDF>, <rdf:Description>, etc., that are qualified by the http://www.w3.org/1999/02/22-rdf-syntax-ns# prefix (abbreviated with the rdf alias) and
(b) Elements that refer to resource properties, that are taken from other metadata schemas.

Properties (or predicates) that takes one literal as a value, will contain this literal between their start and ending tags, being possible to add an xml:lang attribute to indicate the language of the text. When the properties take an URIRef as a value, the element corresponding to the predicate shall be empty and include an rdf:resource attribute. The value of this attribute will be the URI of the resource (see example below).

```
<?xml version="1.0"?>
<rdf:RDF
xmlns:rdf="http://www.w3.org/1999/02/22-rdf-syntax-ns#"
xmlns:dc="http://purl.org/dc/elements/1.1/"
xmlns:exterms="http://www.example.org/terms/">
   <rdf:Description rdf:about="http://example.org/index.
     html">
      <exterms:date >August 16, 1999</exterms: date>
      <dc:language>en</dc:language>
      <dc:creator rdf:resource="http://example.
```

```
    org/1230"/>
  </rdf:Description>
</rdf:RDF>
```

Another constructs used in RDF are containers. They are usually applied for multivalued properties. RDF establishes three kind of containers: rdf:Bag, rdf:Seq and rdf:Alt. The first one refers to a set of values with no order; in the second case, the values grouped within the container have a significant order; rdf:Alt, refers to values that represent choices or alternatives (for example, different translations of the abstract of a document).

Values within a container are identified by an <rdf:LI> element. Predicates containing a set of values will have a rdf:type attribute that will take as a value the type of the container (rdf:Bag, rdf:Seq, etc.).

RDF provides additional constructs, like the collections (to enumerate the whole set of values within a list) or reification (used to record statements about statements, e.g., the person who made the statement, the date and time when it was stated, etc.). Additional terms — with their corresponding XML elements and attributes are defined to handle these cases.

6.3. *Encoding of RDF schemas*

RDF Schemas gives the capability of fixing the vocabulary and the terms that can be used in RDF statements, the type of resources and properties we can use. The XML elements used when serializing RDF in XML shall be taken from one of these schemas. RDF Schemas specification explains how to declare these vocabularies.

The main construct in RDF Schema are the classes. One class corresponds to an abstraction representing instances of the same type that are characterized by a common set of properties. This is a similar concept to the classes used in object-oriented programming, with the difference that just properties (and no methods or operations) are defined in RDF Schemas.

Classes can be hierarchically arranged, and one class can be declared as a subclass of an existing one. The subclass shall inherit the properties assigned to its parent class.

Besides defining classes, RDF Schemas shall define properties. Properties will have a name, a range and a domain. The domain of one property corresponds to the classes that can make use of this property. Domain indicates which properties or metadata element can be used when describing particular types of resources. The range of the properties indicates which values can be assigned to the property. The range can be an XML Schema data type or an existing class.

The following fragment from an RDF Schema shows the definition of three classes (book, author, publisher) and two properties assigned to the book class: written_by and isbn. The values for the first property must be an instance of the author class. The value of the isbn property must be any string.

```
<?xml version="1.0"?>
<rdf:RDF
xmlns:rdf="http://www.w3.org/1999/02/22-rdf-syntax-ns#"
xmlns:rdfs="http://www.w3.org/2000/01/rdf-schema#"
xml:base="http://library.org/ ">
   <rdfs:Class rdf:ID="book"/>
   <rdfs:Class rdf:ID="author"/>
   <rdfs:Class rdf:ID="publisher"/>
   <rdf:Property rdf:ID="written_by ">
      <rdfs:domain rdf:resource="#book"/>
      <rdfs:range rdf:resource="#author "/>
   </rdf:Property>
   <rdf:Property rdf:ID="isbn ">
      <rdfs:domain rdf:resource="#book "/>
      <rdfs:range rdf:resource="&xsd;string"/>
   </rdf:Property>
</rdf:RDF>
```

Although RDF Schema provides a way to define metadata vocabularies, the restrictions of this language have been highlighted mainly when compared with other ontology languages like OWL or DAML+OIL.

One point to remark before completing this summary is the differences between RDF Schemas and XML Schemas. Despite their expected similarity, RDF statements are not based on the elements and attributes defined in XML Schemas, and they are totally independent specifications.

There is one similarity as long as XML documents based on XML schemas also contains metadata about information resources. But the main purpose of XML Schemas is to declare the allowed tags for a specific document type, their order and how they must be nested. RDF Schemas declare types of resources and the properties that are applicable to them.

Of course it is possible to process an XML Schema or document, extract and collect tag-delimited metadata and build RDF statements into a separate RDF/XML document. These transformations are feasible and easy to do.

The additional value of RDF becomes clear when dealing with metadata systems or vocabularies that are defined in a conceptual plane and do not provide encoding or serialization methods (usually in the form of XML schemas). This happened, for example, with Dublin Core, where a vocabulary or set of metadata terms was declared, but it was not tied to a particular encoding schema or representation. RDF is an excellent alternative to encode metadata. Usage of RDF has plenty of advantages, it requires metadata from different sources to be exchanged between software applications (for example, to be aggregated on a common database). These applications need to understand and process different types of metadata, and a common framework for encoding and transferring them is clearly needed.

6.4. *SPARQL query language*

SPARQL is a complimentary specification developed by the W3C to query RDF repositories. This specification defines a query language to gather information from collections of RDF statements. In the target vision of the Semantic Web, different repositories and databases shall expose metadata to software agents who will access and collect them to serve different purposes. RDF is the main standard to serialize these metadata and to enable metadata exchange. But this scenario needs another piece to fully realize its potential: a query language to filter the data needed by consumer applications. The role of SPARQL in metadata integration is expected to be more and more important, as indicated in the same specification: "*SPARQL can be used to express queries across diverse data sources, whether the data is stored natively as RDF or viewed as RDF via middleware*".

SPARQL has been developed by the RDF Data Access Working Group (DAWG) within W3C. This specification provides a query language for RDF [33], one access protocol to transport queries [34] and an XML-based format for sending the results of queries [35]. SPARQL has separate specifications for each of these parts (all of them reached the Recommendation status on 15 January 2008).

Several "query modes" are supported:

- **SELECT** that returns data from the RDF statements bounded or associated to specific variables. It is possible to say that this query mode returns the results in the form of a "table of variables".
- **CONSTRUCT** that returns an RDF graph as a result, with the subset of statements matching the query conditions. Results for CONSTRUCT queries are serialized as RDF/XML documents.
- **ASK** returns a boolean value indicating whether there is at least one statement within the RDF repository matching the query.
- **DESCRIBE** returns RDF graph that describes the resources matching the query.

SPARQL's SELECT mode presents strong similarities with the SQL language designed for accessing relational databases. As an example, an SPARQL query includes the SELECT, FROM and WHERE clausules that are also found in SQL queries.

SPARQL binds the data retrieved from the RDF graph to named variables. This list of variables included in the SELECT clausule would be the equivalent to column names appearing in the SELECT part of an SQL query. Variables have a name, and at query execution they are bound to the actual data retrieved from the RDF repository. The data from the RDF repository can correspond to resource URIs, property names (also URIs) or property values (that is to say, an SPARQL query can retrieve the subject, the predicate or the object of RDF statements).

In the query mode, retrieved results will include one or more "solutions". A basic example is given below:

```
SELECT ?title
WHERE
{
<http://www.uc3m.es /text1>
<http://purl.org/dc/elements/1.1/title> ?title .
}
```

This query is just requesting the value assigned to the http://purl.org/dc/elements/1.1/title property for the resource identified by the http://www.uc3m.es/text1 URI. The query defines one variable called title (varible names are always preceeded by the ? or $ signs), that is bounded (in the WHERE clause) to the object of those statements whose subject and predicate are equal to the values entered in the query (URIs are written within angle brackets).

SPARQL queries can be understood as graph patters. The query is in fact a "graph pattern" that includes one or more "triple patterns". Each triple pattern shall indicate which statements have to be selected from the full graph made up of all the statements within the RDF repository.

Variables can also be bounded to the subjects or predicates of statements. For example, the following query:

```
SELECT ?resourceURI, ?author
WHERE
{
?resourceURI <http://purl.org/dc/elements/1.1/creator>
  ?author .
}
```

shall retrieve the resources' URI and the values of the http://purl.org/dc/elements/1.1/creator predicate from all the statements within the RDF repository.[17] When asking for predicates, query results will retrieve only those statements for which the requested predicate has been stated.

SPARQL queries can be more complex and retrieve several metadata values for the resources. To do that, we just need to add additional conditions to the WHERE clause and the corresponding variables to the SELECT:

```
SELECT ?resourceURI, ?author ?title
WHERE
{
?resourceURI <http://purl.org/dc/elements/1.1/creator>
?author ?resourceURI <http://purl.org/dc/elements/1.1/
title> ?title .
}
```

The previous query retrieves the URI of the resources having both http://purl.org/dc/elements/1.1/creator and http://purl.org/dc/elements/1.1/title predicates, as well as the values assigned to these metadata. If we want to retrieve the resources having both properties, but also those having just one of them — for example, just the http://purl.org/dc/elements/1.1/creator, we can make use of the OPTIONAL keyword:

```
SELECT ?resourceURI, ?author ?title
WHERE
{
?resourceURI <http://purl.org/dc/elements/1.1/creator>
  ?author .
OPTIONAL ?resourceURI <http://purl.org/dc/elements/1.1/
  title> ?title .
}
```

This query indicates that having the http://purl.org/dc/elements/1.1/title property is not mandatory, and that resources havig only the http://purl.org/dc/elements/1.1/creator property must be retrieved too.

[17] One feature we can apply to make SPARQL statements less verbose are the prefixes. Prefixes are alias assigned to XML namespaces used in the URIs of metadata properties. The prefix has to be declared at the beginning of the query and then it can be used instead of the full qualified name of predicates.

To retrieve information from statements matching one of several conditions, the UNION operator is defined:

```
SELECT ?x ?title ?creator
WHERE {   { ?x <http://purl.org/dc/elements/1.1/title>
?title }
UNION
{ ?x <http://purl.org/dc/elements/1.1/creator> ?creator } }
```

Results shall include here the URIs of resources having a http://purl.org/dc/elements/1.1/title or a http://purl.org/dc/elements/1.1/creator property (and not only those having both of them).[18]

SPARQL queries can also include filters to refine the conditions that statements need to fulfill to be retrieved. Following SPARQL terminology, it is said that "filters are used to restrict the solutions returned by the query". Filters shall be added to the WHERE part, and expressed with regular expressions as defined in XQuery 1.0 and XPath 2.0. Below there are some examples:

```
SELECT ?title
WHERE {   ?x <http://purl.org/dc/elements/1.1/title> ?title
FILTER regex(?title, "UC3M")
}

SELECT ?title ?date
WHERE {   ?x <http://purl.org/dc/elements/1.1/date> ?date .
?x <http://purl.org/dc/elements/1.1/ title> ?title .
FILTER (?date < 2009/07/22)
}
```

The first query will retrieve the values of the http://purl.org/dc/elements/1.1/title predicate of all the statements that contain the UC3M term in this property value.[19]

[18] Query results can contain blank nodes; their names will include the "_:" prefix followed by a blank node label generated by the software application.

[19] Filters in SPARQL queries can compare property values with integers, decimals, booleans, strings or dates. The data type of these values used in filters can be included in the query, applying this syntax: "targetValue"^^xsd:datatype, where targetValue is the value we want to compare with those of the bounded variables, and xsd:datetype will be replaced by the namespace of XML Schemas and one data type valid in the XML Schemas specifications. For example: "3"^^xsd:integer.

The second one retrieves the values of the http://purl.org/dc/elements/1.1/title and http://purl.org/dc/elements/1.1/date predicates for all the resources having statements for both predicates, and having a value in the http://purl.org/dc/elements/1.1/date predicate before the date 22 July 2009.

The previous examples have shown the basic structure of SPARQL queries and how to use the SELECT and WHERE. As stated, queries can also include a FROM part. This part shall be used to indicate with RDF document (or data set) has to be searched. The data set concept has a wider scope than one RDF document, as it has to be understood as a collection of RDF statements. This part of the query is mandatory as it is assumed that the target repository shall have a default data set to which queries are directed. The FROM clause can include references to more than one RDF document; in these cases, the queries shall be run against the data set obtained after merging the statements within these documents.

SPARQL includes additional features also found in the SQL language. For example, the ORDER BY keyword can be added to the query to requests the ordering of results by the value of a specific variable(s) in the SELECT part, in ascending or descending order. The DISTINCT keyword can be added just after SELECT to indicate that duplicate solutions must not be included in the results. It is also possible to limit the number of solutions to be retrieved by means of the LIMIT keyword (to be written after the WHERE clause).

The characteristics previously described about filters are equally applicable to the rest of the query modes supported by SPARQL (and not only in the SELECT mode).

As mentioned at the beginning of this subsection, SPARQL is made up of three specifications. One of them defines the format in which the results of query using the SELECT or ASK modes have to be presented. This will be an XML document similar to the next example:

```
<?xml version="1.0"?>
   <sparql xmlns="http://www.w3.org/2005/sparql-
 results#">
      <head>
         <variable name="title"/>
         <variable name="creator"/>
      </head>
      <results>
         <result>
           <binding name="title">
             <literal>Analsys of literary trends</literal>
           </binding>
```

```
            <binding name="creator">
               <literal>F. Torres</literal>
            </binding>
          </result>
        <result>
          <binding name="title">
            <literal>Bibliometric analysis </literal>
          </binding>
          <binding name="creator">
            <literal>J. Bustamante</literal>
          </binding>
        </result>
    </results>
 </sparql>
```

The result to a query in ASK mode shall include just one value, true or false, depending on the assessment of the query against the set of RDF statements. The results for queries using the CONSTRUCT and DESCRIBE modes do not follow this structure, as they return RDF graphs.

7. Conclusions

In the previous sections, an overview of the main achievements in the way toward metatada interoperability has been provided. The main standards and initiatives of value for metadata integration has been described, presented in three levels of "interoperability needs": technical communication and transference of metadata records, syntactic compatibility and semantic equivalences. For the technical transference of metadata we have at our disposal well-founded and proven technologies like web services, web protocols, and specific developments and standards have been proposed for libraries (like SRU or OAI-PMH). The need of having a common syntax to encode metadata also is solved by the general adoption of the XML standard. Semantic integration is the area where additional efforts are needed. Although crosswalks have already been designed for the principal metadata schemas, the possibility of adapting current metadata schemas to the Semantic Web requirements, and leverage current efforts on metadata development to achieve a higher level of compatibility and integration between information services requires an on-going effort from librarians and information professionals. Features of incipient (from the point of view of the professional practice) standards like RDF, RDF(S) and SPARQL have been described as a first step to analyze the opportunities open by these standards.

References

1. Search/Retrieve Web Service Version 1.1: SRW/U and CQL Version 1.1 Specifications Released. OASIS Cover Pages. Available at http://xml.coverpages.org/SRWv11.html.
2. Candella, P (2003). W3C Glossary and Dictionary. Available at http://www.w3.org/2003/glossary/.
3. Cordeiro, M and J Carvalho (2002). Web services: What they are and their importance for libraries. *VINE*, 32(4), 46–62.
4. Taylor, S (2003). A quick guide to Z39.50. *Interlending & Document Supply*, 31(1), 25–30.
5. Harrison, T, M Nelson and M Zubair (2003). The Dienst-OAI Gateway. In *Proceedings of the 2003 Joint Conference on Digital Libraries (JCDL'03)*, 309–311.
6. Sompel, H and C Lagoze (2000). The santa fe convention of the open archives initiative. *D-Lib Magazine*, 6(2). Available at http://www.dlib.org/dlib/february00/vandesompel-oai/02vandesompel-oai.html.
7. Lagoze, C and H Sompel (2001). The open archives initiative: Building a low-barrier interoperability framework. In *Proceedings on ACM/IEEE Joint Conference on Digital Libraries*, 54–62.
8. Lagoze, C and H Sompel (2003). The making of the open archives initiative protocol for metadata harvesting. *Library Hi Tech*, 21(2), 118–128.
9. Dempsey, L and R Heery (1998). Metadata: A current view of practice and issues. *Journal of Documentation*, 54(2), 145–172.
10. St. Pierre, M and WP LaPlant. Issues in crosswalking content metadata standards. Available at http://www.niso.org/publications/white_papers/crosswalk/.
11. Tennant, R (2004). A bibliographic metadata infrastructure for the 21st century. *Library Hi Tech*, 22(2), 175–181.
12. Lagoze, C, J Hunter and D Brickley (2000). An event-aware model for metadata interoperability. *Lecture Notes in Computer Science*. Available at http://www.cs.cornell.edu/lagoze/papers/ev.pdf.
13. Nilson, M and P Johnston. Towards an interoperability framework for metadata standards. Available at http://www.dublincore.go.kr/dcpapers/pdf/2006/Paper39.pdf.
14. Heery, R *et al.* (2003). Metadata schema registries in the partially Semantic Web: The CORES experience. Available at http://dcpapers.dublincore.org/ojs/pubs/article/viewArticle/729.
15. Baker, T and M Dekkers (2003). Identifying metadata elements with URIs: The CORES resolution. *D-Lib Magazine*, 9(7/8).
16. Baker, T and G Salokhe (2002). The SCHEMAS forum — A retrospective glossary. Available at http://www.schemas-forum.org/info-services/d74.htm.

17. Godby, CJ, D Smith and E Childress (2003). Two paths to interoperable metadata. Available at http://www.oclc.org/research/publications/archive/2003/godby-dc2003.pdf.
18. Ward, J (2004). Unqualified Dublin Core usage in OAI-PMH data providers. *OCLC Systems & Services*, 20(1), 40–47.
19. Vizine-Goetz, D, *et al.* (2004). Vocabulary mapping for terminology services. *Journal of Digital Information*, 4(4). Available at http://journals.tdl.org/jodi/article/viewArticle/114.
20. DCMI (2000). Dublin Core Qualifiers. Dublin Core Metadata Initiative. Available at http://www.dublincore.org/documents/2000/07/11/dcmes-qualifiers/.
21. DCMI (2006). Dublin Core Metadata Element Set, Version 1.1. Dublin Core Metadata Initiative. Available at http://dublincore.org/documents/dces/.
22. NISO (1995). *ANSI/NISO Z39.50-1995. Information Retrieval (Z39.50): Application Service Definition and Protocol Specification.* Bethesda, MD: NISO Press. Available at http://lcweb.loc.gov/z3950/agency.
23. OAI (2004). The open archives initiative protocol for metadata harvesting: Protocol version 2.0. Open archives initiative. Available at http://www.openarchives.org/OAI/openarchivesprotocol.html.
24. W3C (1998). Extensible Markup Language (XML) 1.0: W3C Recommendation. 10 February 1998. Available at http://www.w3.org/TR/1998/REC-xml-19980210.
25. W3C (2004). XML Schema Part 0 Primer: W3C Recommendation. 28 October 2004. Available at http://www.w3.org/TR/xmlschema-0/.
26. W3C (2007). XSL Transformations (XSLT) Version 2.0: W3C Recommendation. 23 January 2007. Available at http://www.w3.org/TR/xslt20/.
27. W3C (2006). Namespaces in XML 1.0 (Second Edition): W3C Recommendation. 16 August 2006. Available at http://www.w3.org/TR/xml-names.
28. W3C (2007). SOAP Version 1.2 Part 0: Primer: W3C Recommendation. 27 April 2007. Available at http://www.w3.org/TR/soap12-part0/.
29. W3C (2007). SOAP Version 1.2 Part 2: Adjuncts: W3C Recommendation. 27 April 2007. Available at http://www.w3.org/TR/soap12-part2/.
30. W3C (2004). Resource Description Framework (RDF): Concepts and Abstract Syntax, W3C Recommendation. 10 February 2004. Available at http://www.w3.org/TR/rdf-concepts/.
31. W3C (2004). RDF/XML Syntax Specification (Revised), W3C Recommendation. 10 February 2004. Available at http://www.w3.org/TR/rdf-syntax-grammar/.
32. W3C (2004). RDF Vocabulary Description Language 1.0: RDF Schema, W3C Recommendation. 10 February 2004. Available at http://www.w3.org/TR/rdf-schema/.

33. W3C (2008). SPARQL Query Language for RDF, W3C Recommendation. 15 January 2008. Available at http://www.w3.org/TR/rdf-sparql-query/.
34. W3C (2008). SPARQL Protocol for RDF, W3C Recommendation. 15 January 2008. Available at http://www.w3.org/TR/rdf-sparql-protocol/.
35. W3C (2008). SPARQL Query Results XML Format, W3C Recommendation. 15 January 2008. Available at http://www.w3.org/TR/rdf-sparql-XMLres/.

CHAPTER IV.2

TECHNOLOGIES FOR METADATA EXTRACTION

Koraljka Golub*, Henk Muller† and Emma Tonkin‡

UKOLN — The University of Bath
BA2 7AY, Bath, United Kingdom
University of Bristol, United Kingdom
**k.golub@ukoln.ac.uk*
†henkm@cs.bris.ac.uk
‡e.tonkin@ukoln.ac.uk

The chapter examines two major themes in the area of metadata extraction — formal metadata extraction and subject metadata extraction. The focus of the chapter is on textual documents, with references provided to the multimedia. Approaches to each of the two major themes are presented and discussed, with examples from the area of document classification and metadata extraction from preprints; however, analogous methods exist for use on other types of digital object, and are referenced where relevant. Suggestions are provided in which circumstances and context of use which approaches are most suitable. The chapter concludes with the thought that, owing to recognized evaluation issues, evaluation should be a major future research question in this area.

1. Introduction

Automated metadata extraction has been a challenging research issue for several decades now, major motivation being the high cost of manual metadata creation. The interest has especially grown in the 1990s when the number of digital documents started to increase exponentially. Because of the vast amount of available documents it was recognized that established objectives of bibliographic systems could be left behind [63], and that automated means could be a solution to preserve them (p. 30).

This chapter focuses on the problems underlying automated metadata extraction. We discuss methods for metadata extraction that are applicable to various forms of digital objects, and provide examples in the area of textual documents. Two major themes in the area of metadata extraction are discussed in particular, namely formal metadata extraction and subject metadata extraction.

The chapter is structured as follows: background information with definitions and document landscape are given in Sec. 2; then, formal metadata extraction with its sources of metadata, techniques, methods and evaluation are presented and discussed in Sec. 3; further, approaches to subject metadata extraction and evaluation issues are dealt with in Sec. 4; finally, concluding remarks with issues for the future are provided in Sec. 5.

2. Background

Metadata creation involves identifying elements of a document recognized as important for the purpose of document discovery and use. Traditionally, in, for example, libraries and indexing and abstracting services, this has been referred to as cataloging or bibliographic description. Metadata creation results in metadata records (or catalog or bibliographic records), which are commonly used as document surrogates — that is, records that represent a document. Information systems that make use of metadata records do so for two major reasons: digital objects, especially videos and images, are more easily described, indexed and searched *via* an accompanying metadata record than *via* direct analysis; furthermore, metadata records are generally expected to contain a high standard of descriptive information about various facets of the document, much of which is external to the digital object itself, but is the result of interpretation.

In the literature, two types of metadata creation are often distinguished: formal, and subject. In library catalogs, formal metadata creation is prescribed by International Standard Bibliographic Description (ISBD) rules and typically involves the following elements: title, responsibilities, edition, material or type, publication, production, distribution, physical description (e.g., number of pages in a book or number of CDs issued as a unit), series, notes area, identifiers (e.g., ISBN, ISSN) and terms of availability. Subject metadata creation shares essentially similar processes to those referred to as subject classification or indexing [39] and implies determination of a document's topics and choosing terms to best represent those topics. These terms can be from a controlled vocabulary (e.g., classification schemes, thesauri, subject heading systems) or freely assigned ones. Freely assigned terms can be manually assigned but can also refer to automated full-text indexing. The debate between using the former versus the latter is more than a century old but the literature acknowledges the need for both [56].

Automated metadata creation implies that the relevant processes are conducted mechanically — human intellectual processes are replaced by, for example, statistical and computational techniques. There is an intermediate approach, which can be referred to as machine-aided subject indexing or partially-automated metadata creation. Here, metadata creation is supported by mechanical means to the greatest extent possible, while final decision is left to human intellect. For example, a system could provide an appropriately tailored form for the document, or automatically fill in available form of elements with generated metadata and highlight elements which remain incomplete.

Manual metadata creation is often considered to be an expensive process, particularly when experts must be paid to generate records instead of requesting and using user-contributed metadata. Actual time taken varies greatly by domain and purpose. For example, self-archiving of an preprint to an institutional repository has been estimated to take five and a half minutes as a median average [10], requiring input of a simple metadata record comprising author, title, publication, date, etc. Creating a full bibliographic record for an information system requiring careful analysis and thorough representation usually requires much more time and effort.

Automated metadata generation is expected to play a role in reducing the metadata generation bottleneck [46]. For example, the process of depositing digital objects is rendered longer and more interactive where metadata input is required. A portion of the metadata of relevance to a given digital object can be retrieved either directly from the object itself, or from other information sources. Several methods of automatic metadata generation exist [22], including metadata extraction and metadata harvesting. The latter, metadata harvesting, relates to the collection and reuse of existing metadata. The former relates to various subtasks such as to the harvesting of information that is intrinsic to the digital object, to the content of the object (i.e., features of the document), and information that may be extracted based on comparison of the current document to other documents that this one is related to.

2.1. *Document landscape*

In the chapter, we focus on objects from which text may be extracted; in particular, documents such as web pages and preprints, stored in file formats such as PostScript, the Portable Document Format (PDF) and plain-text.

The wider world of multimedia is out of scope of this chapter but approaches to metadata extraction exist and we briefly mention some of them. Examples include audio recordings, including multilingual spoken word content [7,8,73]; audiovisual recordings, which may be indexed *via* several approaches, including text-to-speech software, as with Hewlett-Packard's Speechbot project [67]; still images, for which two primary approaches are identified in the literature — external metadata-based systems, and content-based image retrieval (CBIR), in which image content features are themselves used as query terms [43].

Each medium poses unique challenges. For example, audiovisual material presents a progression through time, whilst still images do not; however, a still image without accompanying audio contains very little contextual information to aid the process of analysis, other than perhaps pre-existing metadata such as EXIF produced at the time of image creation. At times, accompanying text will be available — in the case of audiovisual material, captions can be embedded along with the resource. Due to the complexity of directly analyzing still images, many services such as Google make use of the image context and index via the text surrounding the images (link text, captions, etc), but others like picsearch.com use information taken directly from the image as metadata, such as dimensions, file size, file type and color information. Researchers such as Clippingdale and Fujii [12], and Lee [41] have taken a similar approach to video indexing, and hybrid or multimodal approaches that index according to a combination of video and audio information have also been proposed [1]. IBM's 2006 Marvel search service (for local installation) uses advanced content analysis techniques for labeling and analyzing data, and provides hybrid and automated metadata tagging.

3. Formal metadata extraction

A large number of facts exist about any given digital object, all of which could be described as "metadata", but the majority of which are never collected or used. In Table 1, we list a number of different types of metadata that are commonly stored to describe different types of digital objects, along with the types of digital objects for which this information may be considered relevant. Elements marked with an "**" are intrinsic to certain document types, but are not present in all documents.

Also, many documents provide neither title nor author (for example, technical and data sheets often do not provide the author's name). This implies that the effectiveness of metadata extraction, or the relevance of

Table 1. Data types and corresponding formal metadata.

Type	Name	Example
Intrinsic	Filetype/attributes	PDF, MOV, MP3 at given bitrate and encoding
Intrinsic	File size	Size of file
Intrinsic	File checksum	32-bit CRC checksum
Intrinsic	File creation date	UNIX datestamp
Intrinsic	Resource language	e.g., Video contains audio streams in English, French and Russian.
Intrinsic**	Type of document	Preprint, technical report, magazine article, journal article, MSc thesis, homework, PowerPoint presentation, poster
Intrinsic**	Title	"A Christmas Carol"
Intrinsic**	Author(s)	Charles Dickens
Intrinsic**	Affiliation or contact details of author(s)	
Intrinsic**	Date of publication	Year, (may include month, day, and time)
Intrinsic**	Page count	
Intrinsic**	First and final page numbers	
Intrinsic**	Publisher, organization and title of collection/proceedings	
Intrinsic**	Document summary	
Intrinsic**	Document index, table of contents	
Intrinsic**	Sources cited/referenced within document/ bibliography	
Extrinsic	Theme	Poverty
Extrinsic	Related documents	Some forms of metadata explicitly encode various types of relationship between document objects

metadata extraction as an approach, depends greatly on the circumstances and context of use.

3.1. *Sources of metadata*

Many approaches to metadata extraction are based on document structure [23]. Document structure involves the use of the visual grammar of pages, for example, making use of the observation that title, author(s) and affiliation(s) generally appear in content header information. In this section, we discuss where metadata can be extracted — the next section describes methods and techniques for the actual extraction.

At least five general structures may be instrumental in metadata extraction:

- **Formatting structure:** The document may have structure imposed on it in its electronic format. For example, from an HTML document one can extract a DOM tree, and find HTML tags such as <TITLE>.
- **Visual structure:** The document may have a prescribed visual structure. For example, postscript and PDF specify how text is to be laid out on a page, and this can be used to identify sections of the text.
- **Document layout:** The document may be structured following some tradition. For example, it may start with a title, then the authors, and end with a number of references.
- **Bibliographic citation analysis:** Documents that are interlinked *via* citation linking or co-authorship analysis may be analyzed *via* bibliometric methods, making available various types of information.
- **Linguistic structure:** The document will have linguistic structure that may be accessible. For example, if the document is written in English, the authors may "conclude that xxx", which gives some meaning to the words between the conclude and the full stop.

3.1.1. *Formatting structure*

Certain document types contain structural elements with relatively clear or explicit semantics. One of the potential advantages of a language like HTML that stresses document structure over a language such as Postscript that stresses document layout, is that given a document structure it is potentially feasible to mechanically infer the meaning of parts of the document.

Indeed, if HTML is used according to modern W3C recommendations, HTML is to contain only structural information, with all design information contributed to CSS. This process of divorcing design from content began in the HTML 4.0 specification [4]. Under these circumstances, a large amount of information can potentially be gained by simply inspecting the DOM tree. For example, all headers H1, H2, H3, ... can be extracted and they can be used to build a table of contents of the paper, and find titles of sections and subsections. Similarly, the HEAD section can be dissected in order to extract the title of a page, although this may not contain the title of the document.

However, given that there are multiple ways in HTML to achieve the same visual effect, the use of the tags given above is not enforced, and indeed many WYSIWIG tools generate a <P class='header2'> tag rather than a H2 tag, making extraction of data from HTML pages in practice difficult. A technical report by Bergmark [5] describes the use of XHTML as an intermediate format for the processing of online documents into a structure, but concedes that, firstly, most HTML documents are "not well-formed and are therefore difficult to parse"; translation of HTML into XHTML resolves a proportion of these difficulties, but many documents cannot be parsed unambiguously into XHTML. A similar approach is proposed by Krause and Marx [38].

3.1.2. *Visual structure*

In contrast to HTML, other methods to present documents often prescribe visual structure rather than document structure. For example, both Postscript and PDF specify symbol or word locations on a page, and the document consists of a bag of symbols or words at specific locations. Document structure may be inferred from symbol locations. For example, a group of letters placed close together is likely to be a word, and a group of words placed on the same vertical position on the page may be part of a sentence in a western language.

The disadvantage of those page description languages is that there are multiple ways to present text, for example, text can be encoded in fonts with bespoke encodings; the encoding itself has no relation to the characters depicted, and it is the shape of the character which conveys the meaning. In circumstances like this it is very difficult to extract characters or words, but the visual structure itself can still be used to identify sections of a document. For example, Fig. 1 shows a (deliberately) pixelated image of the first page of a paper, and even without knowing anything about the particular characters, four sections can be highlighted that almost certainly contain text, authors, affiliation and abstract.

Indeed, it turns out that visual structure itself can provide help in extracting sections of an image of, for example, legacy documents that have been scanned in. However, it is virtually impossible to distinguish between author names above the title and author names below the title, if the length of the title and the length of the author block are roughly the same.

We have performed some experiments that show that we can extract bitmaps for the title and authors from documents that are otherwise unreadable — 3–6% of documents on average in a sample academic environment [66]. An approximately 80% degree of success is achievable using a simple

Fig. 1. Document's visual structure.

image segmentation approach. These images, or indeed the entire page, may alternatively be handed to OCR software such as gOCR for translation into text and the resulting text string processed appropriately. An account of the use of appearance and geometric position of text and image blocks for document analysis and classification of PDF material may be found in [48], and a rather later description of a similar "spatial knowledge" approach applied to Postscript formatted files is given by Giuffrida, Shek, and Yang [19].

Ha *et al.* [24] note that an advantage of an approach that primarily makes use of visual features is the ease of generalization to documents in languages other than English. This approach, however, focuses solely on the problem of extracting the document title.

3.1.3. *Document layout*

From both structured description languages (such as HTML) and page description languages (such as PDF) we can usually extract the text of the document. The text itself can be analyzed to identify metadata. In particular, author names usually stand out, and so do affiliations, and even the title and journal details.

The information that can be extracted from the document structure includes:

1. Title
2. Authors
3. Affiliation
4. Email
5. URL
6. Abstract
7. Section headings (table of contents)
8. Citations
9. References
10. Figure and table captions [42]
11. Acknowledgments [18]

Extracting these purely from the document structure is difficult, but together with knowledge about words likely found in, for example, author names or titles, the extraction is feasible. A detailed discussion on the methods that we use can be found later on in this paper.

3.1.4. *Bibliographic citation analysis*

There exists a widespread enthusiasm for bibliometrics as an area, which depends heavily on citation analysis as an underlying technology. Some form of citation extraction is a prerequisite for this. As a consequence, a number of methods have been identified for this approach, making use of various degrees of automation. Harnad and Carr [28] describe the use of tools from the Open Journal Project and Cogprints that can, given well-formed and correctly specified bibliographic citations, extract and convert citations from HTML and PDF.

The nature and level of interlinking between documents is a rich source for information about the relations between them. For example, a high rate of co-citation may suggest that the subject area or theme is very similar; e.g., Hoche and Flach [29] investigated the use of co-authorship information to predict the topic of scientific papers.

The harvesting of acknowledgments has been suggested as a measure for an individual's academic impact [18], but may also carry thematic information as well as information on a social-networking level that could potentially be useful for measuring points such as conflict of interest.

3.1.5. *Linguistic structure*

Finally, the document can be analyzed linguistically, inferring meaning of parts of sentences, or relationships between metadata. For example, citations in the main text may be contained within the same sentence, indicating that the two citations are likely to be related in some way. The relation may be a positive relationship or a negative relationship, depending on the text around it, e.g., "... in contrast to work by Jones (1998), work by Thomas (1999)..."

Analyzing linguistic structure depends on knowledge of the document language, and possibly on domain knowledge. Using linguistic analysis one can attempt to extract:

1. Keywords
2. Relations between citations

3.2. *Techniques and methods*

Metadata can be extracted *via* various means, for example using support vector machines upon linguistic features [25], a variable hidden Markov model [64], or a heuristic approach [5]. Ha *et al.* [24] describe an approach that makes use of the following models upon formatting information: Perceptron with Uneven Margins, Maximum Entropy (ME), Maximum Entropy Markov Model (MEMM), Voted Perceptron Model (VP), and Conditional Random Fields (CRF). Here we will begin by discussing various approaches that are useful in metadata extraction:

- **Classification**, with the example of Bayesian classification.
- **Pattern matching**, with examples of regular expressions.
- **Direct application of observed heuristics**
- **Model fitting**: where prior knowledge is available, it may be applied as domain knowledge to build a set of models for use in metadata extraction.
- **Elicitation of grammatical structure** (ideally automated). This enables probabilistic parsing. An example is provided on the basis of Hidden Markov Models. Maximum Entropy Markov Models and conditional random fields are also discussed.

The many methods available today have different uses, competences and areas of weakness so it is likely that a complete metadata extraction tool will make use of several approaches for different tasks.

3.2.1. *Bayesian classification*

A Bayesian classifier is based on prior knowledge of statistical properties of the dataset. The prior knowledge is obtained by training the Bayesian classifier on a set of manually classified data. For example, when analyzing a set of documents where one half are cooking-recipes and the other half are newspaper clippings we may find that in cooking recipes 1% of the words was "flour", whereas in the general newspaper clippings "flour" was only 0.1%, Bayesian statistics says that if we see a document with the word "flour" in it is very likely (90%) to be a cooking recipe, and not very likely (10%) to be a general newspaper clipping.

In metadata extraction Bayesian classifiers are appropriate for use in tasks such as:

- Author name extraction
- Affiliation extraction
- Publication detail extraction

Classifiers are useful in author name extraction because names are typically very different from ordinary words found in the main body of a paper. For example, "Ruud", "John", and "Canagarajah" are very likely to be names whereas "following", "classifier" and "sentence" are very unlikely to not be names. Still, there is a small, but frequently occurring, group of words that could be either. For example, "A" is a word that occurs very frequently in English text, but it could also be an initial of a name.

However, being able to classify a string to be either a name or not a name does not necessarily mean that the Author name has been extracted. In many cases names can legitimately appear elsewhere in the text. For example, we have used the names "Bayes" and "Markov" in this chapter in the context of referring to a branch of statistics and an algorithm. Even more confusing is the string "Markov" which is a proper noun (an individual's name) that is used in the text in this chapter in reference to an algorithm. Also, in papers in Arts and Literature, many names will appear that identify the subject matter rather than the author name. Thus we conclude that a Bayesian classifier can be a good basis for a metadata extractor, but if used on its own would lead to poor results.

Bayesian classifiers are one of many approaches to classification that could be used in this context. For example, Han *et al.* [25] make use of support vector machine classification. See Sec. 4 of this chapter for discussion of various approaches to subject classification in machine learning. However, the intrinsic probabilistic nature of Bayesian classification results in both a classification and a confidence measure of the classification, making it suitable for integration into a larger system.

The strength of a Bayesian classifier is that it has a strong and simple mathematical foundation, and that it is completely problem independent. When used on text, it works as well on French as Chinese text, provided that suitable training data is available.

3.2.2. *Pattern matching*

A pattern comprises a description of how to construct a sequence of characters, and by repeatedly matching the pattern over a large text, parts of the text can be classified as following the pattern. Patterns come in useful to describe entities that occur often and are more reliably identified by a pattern than by any other method.

As an example, consider the email address:

buzz.aldrin@moon.com

In order to define a pattern, we typically describe the string in terms of a regular expression. The above address could be matched with the following regular expression:

```
[^ @]*@[^ ]*
```

meaning: any sequence not comprising spaces or @-characters, followed by an @-character, followed by a sequence of characters not containing any spaces. This regular expression would also match neil.armstrong@nasa.org and it would match cakes@77 in the sentence "10 cakes@77 cents each". Patterns can be made more specific, and various languages exist to express patterns.

The weakness of patterns is that it is very difficult to build a precisely matching pattern, without missing anything out. The pattern above that matches email address will for example not match the following email "address":

{alice, bob}@malice.com

Which is a notation used on many papers to indicate that both Alice and Bob have an email address at malice.com. Although it is not hard to extend the regular expression to include spaces, it will then match much more text in front of the email address, which is undesirable. The trade-off here is one between false negatives and false positives, i.e., how often has a piece of text not been matched as an email address that should have been, and how often has a piece of text been classified as an email address that should not have been. Ideally, there are no false negatives and no false positives, but in reality it is difficult to build a system where on every 10 email addresses found at least one will not be too short or too long. This is in part a consequence of the fact that conventional notations often apply simplifications or short-cuts that are not described in a formal standard — the format of email addresses, described in RFC 2822, does not include guidance on appropriate shorthand for circumstances such as paper headers — appropriate practice is defined according to style guidelines.

Pattern matching is not limited to regular expressions. We can use a grammar to capture patterns that are more complex (and that describe, for example, the nested structure of an HTML document). A grammar comprises a set of rules, each rule describing part of the structure. For example, a simple grammar for a scientific paper might read:

document :: title authors affiliations abstract section* references
section :: number string newline paragraph*
paragraph :: sentence*

As is the case with regular expressions, it is difficult to capture all document formats using a grammar — many e-prints list affiliation per author; something that is not captured by the grammar above.

In metadata extraction patterns are typically useful to pre-classify a few bits of metadata that probably have a meaning in the metadata:

- Email addresses
- URLs
- Dates
- Numbers

We have discussed email addresses above. A URL (RFC 1738, 2396) typically starts with http:// or ftp:// and can be extracted up to the point where they have been split over multiple lines, something that happens often in citations. Dates are easily recognized because a dozen formats capture them all; the most important ones being 5/1/2008, and 5 January 2008; it is not always possible to tell which date it is (as the former could refer to either the fifth of January or the first of May, depending on the convention applied) but it is very likely to be a date. Numbers are useful to recognize because they usually refer to page numbers, volume numbers, etc.

3.2.3. *Direct application of observed heuristics*

In certain instances, the semi-structured nature of the data renders it possible to achieve reasonable accuracy in data extraction by applying a set of heuristics, rules that encompass the most commonplace structures or layouts. This is particularly common in the case of metadata extraction from HTML/XHTML documents. Here each text element is surrounded by semi-semantic markup. The aspiration is that no layout information is contained within the XHTML document itself, but within an accompanying cascading style sheet referenced by the document; however, in practice this is not always the case — and the markup used can vary greatly according to the software used to generate it. For both of these reasons, seemingly simple heuristics — such as

> *'The title tends to be at or near the top of the document and appear in a larger font than other document elements'*

can be difficult to express in terms of the simple rules or pseudocode that are often suggested, such as

> *'look for the first H1 element; if there is none, look for H2, then H3, and finally <bold>'.*

The situation is simpler when working from a plain-text document. Since there is no formatting information extant from which to work, we must rely on establishing the sequence in which elements occur. There are some conventions here that can be expressed as heuristics, such as "The title tends to appear just above the authors" names, which generally precede the "affiliation, email addresses and abstract". However, there are many valid sequences in which this information appears, depending on the template used. As a result, heuristics will provide false positives.

3.2.4. *Model fitting*

In many cases there is prior knowledge about the metadata that we want to extract, and we may wish to use this information in extracting that metadata.

For example, page numbers mostly appear at the top or bottom of the page, and each page number is usually one higher than the page number of the previous page. Similarly, citations are usually a list that contains identically formatted entries starting with one of three patterns, e.g., "[1]", "[Kirk09]", or "(Wendel and Martin, 2009)". Both use pattern matching as a first step, but then require relationships between data points in order to establish whether the extracted information is useful — in the first example there must be a numeric relationship between the matched data, in the second example there must be identical patterns used in the matching process.

Page numbers are a useful example. The pattern that we match is one of {page-boundary}[1-9][0-9]* and [1-9][0-9]*{page-boundary}, resulting in one or two matches per page of text analyzed. The model that we try and fit to this data has one unknown parameter s (the number of the start page) and then requires that for each page i ($0 = i <$ number of pages), the matched number is identical to $s + i$. For a document with p pages this will result in at most $2p$ possible values for s, and for each of those possible values the total number of candidate page numbers that agree is tallied up. If at least, say, 50% of the page numbers can be identified this way, then the start page number of this paper has been identified, and hence the end-page number can be computed.

Models like the one above need to be designed carefully — they contain many assumptions, and are therefore brittle. A first problem with the model above is acceptance of any number appearing as the first or last word on a page as a valid candidate page number, although it could be a year of publication, volume number, or indeed some numeric part of the contents that happened to be in the bottom right hand of the page. In order to filter out the years, volumes, and numerical contents we require numbers on subsequent pages to be a sequence of numbers, which will successfully isolate page numbers if the paper is more than one page long. Additionally, page numbers are often not the first or last word on a page. A title or author names may appear on the right and left hand side of the page; therefore, page numbers may be missed. The above algorithm tries to deal with that by requiring only 50% of the page numbers to agree with the model.

Even though model fitting has some weaknesses, its strength is that it allows domain knowledge to be used in extracting metadata. Template matching is a special case of model fitting. Since papers are published in only a limited number of venues — probably a few tens of thousands journals and conferences using perhaps a thousand different "style sheets" — it is possible to extract the contents of an HTML or PDF file encoded in a known template by matching it against either the visual structure or grammatical flow of content elements dictated by the template. The development by hand of a set of guidelines encompassing the majority of these "style sheets" would be an interminably long and difficult process, so techniques from machine learning are often used to solve this problem.

3.2.5. *Elicitation of grammatical structure*

3.2.5.1. Hidden Markov Models (HMMs)

The methods discussed above can determine where on a document a single word or a string of words is likely to belong. Previous examples included the problem of identifying whether a word is possibly a name, or whether a string is an email address. The Bayesian classifier assigns a probability, whereas the pattern matcher approach simply gives a binary result. In many cases, the significance of a match is determined by the context in which the classification occurs. For example, a number at the end of a citation is likely to be a publication year, and a name early on in a scientific article is likely to be an author name.

A common technique that takes context into account is the Hidden Markov Model, or HMM, described by Han *et al.* [25] as the most widely used generative learning method for representing and extracting information from sequential data. The general idea of HMM is that the problem under observation is modeled as a sequence of states. On observing an event, the state can change, and a sequence of events brings us through a sequence of states.

HMMs are therefore useful in describing systems that, although we cannot observe the underlying structure directly, generate visible patterns over time. For example, we might use a sequence of observable weather conditions to guess at the shifting state of the upper atmosphere, or model ocean currents over time by examining visible features such as sediment deposits — although these observable features are not equivalent to the hidden underlying system, they are nonetheless related.

We may describe a stream of text, by analogy, as a set of observable features that overlay a hidden underlying model, the document model. If we have removed all formatting from the document, we are left with only a long stream of text, potentially punctuated with line returns, such as:

"Confirmation-Guided Discovery of First-Order Rules PETER A. FLACH, NICOLAS LACHICHE flach@cs.bris.ac.uk lachiche@cs.bris.ac.uk Department of Computer Science, University of Bristol, United Kingdom Abstract. This paper deals with learning first-order logic rules from data lacking an..."

Underlying this is a hidden structure, a sequence of states or types; we begin at a title, give two authors' names, two email addresses, and a departmental affiliation, and then move on to the abstract.

3.2.5.2. Probabilistic parsing on the basis of a HMM

The output from the Bayesian classifier gives us a good indication as to whether a given string forms part of the title or part of a string of authors, but some terms are ambiguous, or may well appear in either context. For example, the term "Markov" may well be in a preprint title, or can be an author.

The solution to this is to create a state machine (Markov chain), in which we, as background knowledge, specify likely sequences of tokens (words). For example, a likely sequence for a scientific paper comprises a number of title tokens, followed by a newline, followed by a number of author tokens, followed by a newline, followed by a number of affiliation tokens.

Given the probabilities from the Bayesian classifier, we then examine all possible evaluations of the state machine (akin to Earley parsing [14]), and we record for each possible evaluation the likelihood of this evaluation. A very simple state-machine could be that a scientific paper is simply a Title followed by a list of Author names:

PrePrint ::= Title+ Author+

i.e., a PrePrint is one or more Title-tokens followed by one or more Author-tokens. If we apply the above grammar to the example lines on the previous page, we get 11 possible parses. These parses are (Bold denotes the title and Italics denote the author):

Confirmation-Guided Discovery *of First-Order Rules, PETER A. FLACH, NICOLAS LACHICHE*
Confirmation-Guided Discovery of First-Order *Rules, PETER A. FLACH, NICOLAS LACHICHE*
...
Confirmation-Guided Discovery of First-Order Rules, *PETER A. FLACH, NICOLAS LACHICHE*
Confirmation-Guided Discovery of First-Order Rules, **PETER A. FLACH**, *NICOLAS LACHICHE*

The likelihood of each parse is computed by multiplying the probability of each token belonging to the specific part of the document. For example, the likelihood of the first parse requires us to multiply the probability of "Confirmation" being a title with the probability of all other terms being authors, whereas the likelihood of the last parse requires us to multiply the probability of LACHICHE being an author with all other title-probabilities. The likelihood of the third parse shown above is the multiplication of the p_{title} values for the tokens "Confirmation ... Rules" with the p_{author} values of the tokens "PETER ... LACHICHE". Computing all likelihoods, it turns out that the likelihood for the third parse is much higher than the likelihood for all other parses, and hence, according to this metric this is the "right" parse.

In the process of multiplying, all probabilities that are less than a threshold are increased to the threshold; a zero-probability of the Bayesian classifier simply means that this token has not been seen in the training set in that circumstance; it does not imply that this token can never be seen as such.

The simple state machine above would fail if, for example, the first author had an initial "A"; or has a name that is part of the scientific literature. For this reason, in a full grammar one might cluster tokens according to visual mark-up, such as line breaks and large spaces before applying the grammar rules.

3.2.5.3. Related methods: MEMMs and CRFs

Han *et al.* [25] point out that HMMs are based on the assumption that features of the model they represent are not independent from each other, and that as a consequence HMMs have difficulty in exploiting regularities of a semi-structured real system. Hence, maximum entropy based Markov models and conditional random fields (CRFs) have been proposed to deal with independent features.

Maximum entropy based Markov models (MEMMs) are closely related to the classical HMM. The term "maximum entropy" as applied here is simply a way to state that the model is designed to be as general as possible — that is, the least biased estimate possible on the given information, the most non-committal with regard to missing information [33].

MEMMs differ from HMMs in that MEMMs are not simply trained on examining the output tokens themselves (i.e., the word, the Bayesian classification of the word, etc) but make use of a feature set derived from them. HMMs only look at the word itself, and do not look at the large set of ways in which that word might be described. For a single word, such a feature set might include whether it is capitalized or whether it ends in a full stop, whether it contains an @ sign, whether it is a noun, etc. There is a very large number of different possible features on a word, sentence, paragraph or page level. So MEMMs may be described as taking into account "overlapping" features. For some classes of problem, particularly those with sparse datasets on which to train, using an MEMM can be expected to improve overall performance — predictably, since the features that are examined are relatively generic. The other approach mentioned, CRFs, are sometimes described as a generalization of the HMM that, whilst flexible and powerful, are relatively conceptually complex. A good introduction to CRFs is given in [68].

3.2.6. *Integrating additional evidence*

Each piece of information that has already been collected and parsed may become a useful additional source of data. For example, extracted references may be used as an additional source of information, not only about the ways in which documents are linked, but also about the documents that we have already parsed. In many cases, information that is contained within references is not contained within the document itself — for example, the publication date of the document is often absent from the document template, as is the name of the publisher, proceedings or journal, the location of the publisher or conference, and the page numbers at which the document appears. It is possible to make use of a metadata extraction database as an ever-growing knowledge base, which is able to review and correct extracted metadata as and when further pieces of evidence about the same document become available. Therefore, metadata extraction can usefully be thought of and treated as an ongoing process of iterative information discovery, gathering and reasoning, rather than a short process of information input, filtering and output of a metadata record.

3.3. *Error propagation*

Once errors in metadata exist, they propagate in various ways; reinforcing similar errors on future preprints, introduction of seemingly unrelated extra errors, and obfuscation of the data presented to the user. Firstly, a system will normally use previous classifications in order to classify future papers. In our system, paperBase, author-names, title, abstract, and classification of previous preprints are being used to predict the classification of new preprints. Once a preprint has been misclassified, future papers may be mis-classified in a similar manner.

Secondly, a system typically uses the metadata found in preprints in order to establish connections between preprints. Connections can be made because two preprints are written by an author with the same name, because they cite each other, or because they cover a similar subject matter according to the keywords. Those connections can be used to, for example, disambiguate author identities. A missing link or an extraneous link would make the process of reasoning about clusters of related papers increasingly difficult.

Thirdly, the answers of search queries are diluted when errors are introduced. Cascading errors cause a disproportional dilution of search results. This is also true of user-contributed systems in which users may infer the use of classification terms through examining available exemplars.

When machine-generated classifications are provided, they are generally represented as unitary facts; either a document may be described *via* a keyword, or it may not. Consider the following example of a machine-generated classification:

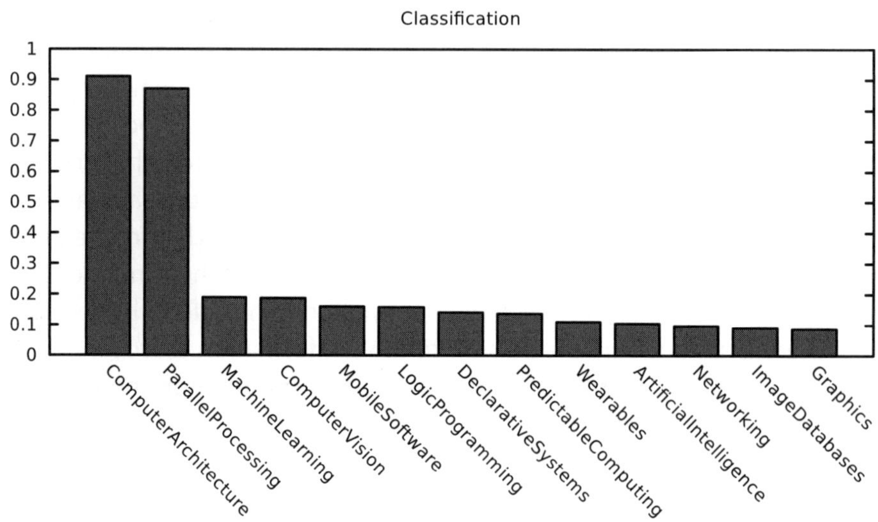

Fig. 2. A typical Bayesian classification record.

In this case, a document is considered almost certain to be about "Computer Architecture" or "Parallel Processing", and to have a diminishing likelihood of being classifiable as about "Machine Learning" or any of the other terms. In general, a threshold is placed, or the top classification accepted by default, when the result is presented, but it is this distribution that describes the paper with respect to others. The shape of this distribution is very relevant in establishing the nature and relevance of the classification. There may be no clear winner if there are many keywords with similar probability, and then our confidence in the clarity of the results may be shaken absent human evaluation of that judgment.

In the case of classifications, many options may be acceptable, but this is less the case in other situations where uncertainty exists. Consider the set of sample parses shown previously. The likelihood for the correct parse is much higher than the likelihood for all other parses. Unlike the prior example of a classification, only one of these parses can be valid. Whilst it is the most likely, we do not have total confidence in this, but we are able to generate a probability of its accuracy (our level of confidence, a value between zero and one). Hence, it is possible to provide some guidance as to the validity of this datum as a "fact" about the document.

The danger of reasoning over data in which we, or the system, have low confidence, is the risk of propagating errors. If we retain a Bayesian viewpoint, we may calculate any further conclusions on the basis of existing probabilities *via* Bayesian inference. If, however, we treat a probability as a fact and make inferences over inaccurate data without regard to degree of confidence, the result may be the production of hypotheses over which we have very little confidence indeed.

As a consequence, an extension of DC metadata to include estimates of confidence, as described in [9] is useful, as in the case of classification would be an estimate of the number of classifications considered "plausible"; the breadth or range of likely classifications, which could also be described in terms of variation or level of consistency in judgment — a similar value to that which might be generated in any other situation in which generated or contributed classifications may be treated as "votes", such as collaborative tagging systems.

If the nature and extent of the error are known, further functions that employ these values may apply this information to estimate the accuracy of the result or that of derivative functions. We note that for certain types of metadata, this problem is well-investigated. For example, author name disambiguation has received a great deal of interest in recent years, e.g., Han *et al.* [25], Han, Zha and Giles [27].

3.4. Evaluation

Once a metadata extraction system has been designed and implemented it is usually evaluated to check that it is fit for purpose. This evaluation may take a number of different forms, depending on the goal that was set. The evaluation may check that the metadata is correct — that is, little incorrect metadata is present, and/or that the metadata is complete — that is, all metadata has been filled in. Another relevant quantitative metric is the time taken to complete an extraction.

There are various methods of evaluation, some of which employ comparison against a typical manual metadata extraction process; user-studies can also be used. Many approaches depend on comparison of actual results with a set of "standard" answers — in computer science, this is often referred to as a ground truth.

The concept of a ground-truth is that there is an undisputed correct answer. Such sample data is usually created and corrected by hand. The ground truth can be used in system design, to train components of the system, like classifiers, which in some cases are trained by presentation of examples. It is also useful for measuring the performance of the system, by comparing the outcome of the metadata extraction process with the ground truth, and counting the number of errors according to an appropriate system of scoring. The ground truth is therefore often split into a training set and an evaluation set.

Since creation of a ground truth is a manual process, collecting a large ground truth is painstaking work, and often one has to compromise. One compromise is to collect a small ground truth, the other is to collect an "almost"-truth, a set of answers that is, though imperfect, fairly precise. The latter may contain typographic errors and misclassifications. This may degrade system performance if used for training. In evaluation, comparison against an incorrect ground truth will usually make the results look worse than they are. The reported error rate will comprise both human and machine errors.

Although the ground truth is a useful tool in training and evaluation it is not always the best tool for assessing the outcome. There are cases where the extracted metadata is not "right" or "wrong", but is open to interpretation. An example of this may be the subject matter of the document or in the case of very old documents it may not be established who the author of a document is, or when it was written. In this case, it is very difficult to *a priori* create a ground truth. One can ask a number of experts in the field for their input into the ground truth, and tally up votes (maybe weighted by expertise), but that does not guarantee that the ground truth is in any way complete. An extra complication is that if some of the metadata that is subjective in nature, then the interpretation of this metadata or indeed of the source of the metadata may mean that there is no fixed ground truth, but that the ground truth depends on when the document was written, or when the metadata was extracted, or when the metadata was interpreted.

To this end, another comparison method is to take the output of the metadata extraction process to a group of experts, and to ask them to assess the correctness of the data. This method has the disadvantage of requiring time from an expert panel to assess potentially a large volume of output.

The first objective metric that is important in assessing the quality of the metadata is to measure the correctness of the metadata. That is, given all the metadata that the system extracted, how much of it is actually correct metadata (compared to the ground truth or the user panel). Although it is straightforward to define when the data is correct, that is, both strings of metadata must be the same, character by character, it is much harder to define how to count errors. For example, the metadata may contain an extra space before or after the metadata, which is probably perfectly acceptable. It may contain a full stop after author initials, which is probably also acceptable. When two characters have gone missing in the title, this can be counted as one error ("the title is wrong"), two errors ("two characters are missing") or even 20 errors ("all subsequent characters are wrong").

Correct metadata is important, but not at all costs — a system can be designed to have a high degree of correctness by extracting solely metadata that the system is absolutely 100% confident about, and hence extract very little information. For this reason, a second metric that is to be satisfied is that of completeness, which measures how much of the desired metadata has actually been extracted. The idea is to extract all metadata, maybe at the cost of some of the metadata being wrong or "over-complete". As an example, extracted metadata may contain both author and editor names as authors, or it may contain title and part of the abstract as a title.

The trade-off between completeness and correctness means that one usually has to allow for a few errors, and accept that some metadata is missing. One way to represent this is to plot, for a number of parameter settings, the completeness against the correctness, and to choose a parameter setting that has an acceptable error at a satisfactory level of completeness — the level where some data needs to be added, and some errors need to be corrected. This plot is known as an Receiver Operating Curve (ROC). When an ROC curve is to be made, the system has to be tested under many different parameter settings, and one must have a ground truth to mechanically check on the number of errors.

The correctness and completeness are very close to the precision and recall in information retrieval, but they are not the same. In particular, in information retrieval the answer of the query comprises a selection from a set of all possible answers. Hence, the term precision can be defined as X/A where X is the number of answers that were useful and A is the number of answers. The recall can be defined as X/C where X is the number of answers that were useful and C is all correct answers (as stipulated by the ground truth).

Completeness and correctness look at the validity of the metadata *per se*. Another aspect of the evaluation of the complete system involves user studies, studying how all people involved rate the resulting metadata. User studies can involve professionals (digital librarians and archivists), authors of papers, and users of the metadata. Pertinent points in the development of such a system include the validity of the metadata itself, and the advantages and disadvantages, both perceived and quantitatively measured, for users in various contexts such as information retrieval, resource deposit and browsing.

4. Subject metadata extraction

4.1. *Approaches to automated subject metadata extraction*

Research related to automated subject metadata extraction is spread around a number of different areas, a most obvious one being word, term or phrase extraction. Wu and Li [70] provide an overview of keyphrase extraction for different purposes, including subject metadata derivation and automated subject classification. Automated subject metadata extraction can be also seen as what has been referred to in the literature as automated subject classification, subject indexing and text categorization, to name the few terms. All these processes are often used interchangeably and have in common one aim, and that is to automatically determine topics or subjects of a document. One can distinguish between three major approaches to automated subject classification: machine learning, clustering and string matching. In this document, machine learning refers to supervised learning, and clustering to unsupervised grouping of similar documents.

Machine learning is the most widespread approach to automated subject classification. Here documents with human-assigned classes are needed because they are then used as so-called training documents based on which characteristics of subject classes are learnt. A number of different algorithms, called classifiers, are developed to this purpose. In the following step, characteristics of documents to be classified are simply compared against the characteristics of the subject classes.

The classifiers can be based on Bayesian probabilistic learning, decision tree learning, artificial neural networks, genetic algorithms or instance-based learning — for explanation of those, see, for example, Mitchell [51]. There have also been attempts of classifier committees (or metaclassifiers), in which results of a number of different classifiers are combined to decide on a class [47]. Comparisons of classifiers can be found in Schütze, Hull, and Pedersen [57], Li and Jain [45], Yang [71], and Sebastiani [58].

The basis for these processes is representation of documents as vectors of term weights. Most representative terms are chosen for each document, and non-informative terms such as stop words are removed; this process is also conducted for computing reasons and is referred to as dimensionality reduction. The term weights can be derived using a variety of heuristic principles. For example, phrases could be given higher weight than single words; bolded terms from web pages could also be given higher weight [21]. Hypertext-specific characteristics such as headings [15], anchor words [6] and metadata [17] have been experimented with. Yang, Slattery, and Ghani [72] emphasized the importance of recognizing regularities of a web page collection when choosing a heuristic principle. For example, augmenting the document to be classified with the text of its neighbors will yield good results only if the majority in the collection has the source document and the neighbors related enough.

A major problem with machine learning is that human-classified documents are often unavailable in many subject areas, for different document types or for different user groups. If one would judge by the standard Reuters Corpus Volume 1 collection [44], some 8,000 training and testing documents would be needed per class. Because of this, approaches which diminish the need for a large number of training documents have been experimented with [6, 47, 50].

A related problem is that machine-learning algorithms perform well on new documents only if they are similar enough to the training documents. The issue of document collections was pointed out by Yang [71] who showed how similar versions of one and the same document collection had a strong impact on performance.

Finally, experiments in machine learning are largely conducted under laboratory-like, controlled conditions (see Sec. 4.2). Still, examples of its application in operative information systems exist [13, 50, 65].

Clustering is another approach to automated subject classification. Here no documents with human-assigned classes are needed — instead, documents to be classified are simply compared to each other, and the ones that are similar enough are assigned the same subject and put into the same cluster of documents (hence the name of the approach).

As in machine learning, in order to allow comparison of the documents, they are first represented by vectors, which are then compared to each other using similarity measures. Here also different heuristic principles are applied to derive the vectors as to which words or terms to use, how to extract them, which weights to assign. For example, Wang and Kitsuregawa [69] improved performance by combining terms from the web page with terms from pages pointing to it and pages leading from it. Also, different similarity measures for comparing vectors can be used, a usual one being the cosine measure.

In the following step, documents are grouped into clusters using clustering algorithms. Two different types of clusters can be constructed: partitional (or flat), and hierarchical. With partitional algorithms all clusters are determined at once. A typical example is *k*-means, in which a *k* number of clusters is first randomly generated based on an initial group of documents. Then new documents are assigned to the existing clusters, resulting in new characteristics of the clusters, requiring re-computation and rearrangement of the clusters.

In hierarchical clustering, often agglomerative algorithms are used: first, each document is viewed as an individual cluster; then, the algorithm finds the most similar pair of clusters and merges them. Similarity between documents is calculated in a number of ways. For example, it can be defined as the maximum similarity between any two individuals, one from each of the two groups (single-linkage), as the minimum similarity (complete-linkage), or as the average similarity (group-average linkage) [32, 55].

Another approach to document clustering is self-organizing maps (SOMs). SOMs are a data visualization technique, based on unsupervised artificial neural networks, that transform high-dimensional data into (usually) two-dimensional representation of clusters. For a detailed overview of SOMs, see Kohonen [37].

Since in clustering (including SOMs) clusters and their labels are produced automatically, deriving the labels is a major research challenge. In an early example of automatically derived clusters [16], which were based on citation patterns, labels were assigned manually. Today a common heuristic principle is to extract between five and ten of the most frequent terms in the centroid vector, then to drop stop-words and perform stemming, and choose the term which is most frequent in all documents of the cluster. To a limited degree, relationships between clusters are also automatically derived, which is an even more difficult problem [63]. In addition, "[a]utomatically-derived structures often result in heterogeneous criteria for category membership and can be difficult to understand" [11]. Also, clusters' labels and relationships between them change as new documents are added to the collection; unstable class names and relationships are in information systems user-unfriendly, especially when used for subject browsing.

Finally, as with machine learning, experiments are largely conducted under laboratory-like, controlled conditions (see Sec. 4.2). Still, examples of its application in operative information systems exist (e.g., Clusty for clustering search-engine results, http://clusty.com/).

String matching is the third major approach to automated subject classification. Here, matching is conducted between controlled vocabulary terms and text of documents to be classified. A major advantage of this approach is that it does not require training documents (unlike machine learning), while still maintaining a pre-defined structure (unlike clustering). Also, controlled vocabularies have the additional advantage of improving precision and recall of information retrieval. Certain controlled vocabularies will also be suitable for subject browsing. This would be less the case with automatically created classes and structures of clustering or home-grown directories not created in compliance with professional principles and standards. Yet another motivation to apply controlled vocabularies in automated subject classification is to reuse the intellectual effort that has gone into creating such a controlled vocabulary [62].

This approach does share similarities with machine learning and clustering: The pre-processing of documents to be classified includes stop-words removal; stemming can be conducted; words or phrases from the text of documents to be classified are extracted and weights are assigned to them based on different heuristical principles.

A major project involving string matching was GERHARD, a robot-generated directory of web documents in Germany [52]. The controlled vocabulary used was a multilingual version of Universal Decimal Classification (UDC) in English, German and French. GERHARD's approach included advanced linguistic analysis: from captions, stop words were removed, each word was morphologically analyzed and reduced to stem; from web pages stop words were also removed and prefixes were cut off. After the linguistic analysis, phrases were extracted from the web pages and matched against the captions. The resulting set of UDC notations was ranked and weighted statistically, according to frequencies and document structure.

Online Computer Library Center's (OCLC) project Scorpion built tools for automated subject recognition, using Dewey Decimal Classification (DDC). The main idea was to treat a document to be indexed as a query against the DDC knowledge base. The results of the "search" were treated as subjects of the document. Larson [40] used this idea earlier, for books. In Scorpion, clustering was also used, for refining the result set and for further grouping of documents falling in the same DDC class [60]. Different term weights were experimented with.

In Golub [20], building on an earlier project [3], terms from the Engineering Information thesaurus and classification scheme were matched against text of documents to be classified. Plain string-matching was enhanced in several ways, including term weighting with cut-offs, exclusion of certain terms, and enrichment of the controlled vocabulary with automatically extracted terms. The final results were comparable to those of state-of-the-art machine-learning algorithms, especially for particular classes.

Other projects include Nordic WAIS/World Wide Web Project [2], Wolverhampton Web Library (WWLib) [34] and Bilingual Automatic Parallel Indexing and Classification [53].

The three above discussed approaches are applied to textual documents. Concerning (moving) images and audio documents, according to Kirkegaard [36], this research is still in its infancy, although promising results have been achieved. The automatic approach is primarily based on computational production of numerical representations of attributes [55]. Automatic approaches can also incorporate information derived from external sources [35, 55, 59]. Further analysis of non-textual documents is out of scope of this chapter.

4.2. *Evaluation*

Various measures are used to evaluate different aspects of automated subject metadata extraction and automated subject classification [71]. Effectiveness, the degree to which correct classification decisions have been made, is often evaluated using performance measures from information retrieval, such as precision (correct positives/predicted positives) and recall (correct positives/actual positives). Efficiency can also be evaluated, in terms of computing time spent on different parts of the process. There are other evaluation measures, and new are being developed such as those that take into account degrees to which a document was wrongly categorized [13, 61]. For more on evaluation measures, see Sebastiani [58].

A major problem with evaluation as it is today is that classification results are compared against existing human-assigned classes of the used document collection. Several often ignored issues are involved and discussed below.

According to ISO standard on methods for examining documents, determining their subjects, and selecting index terms [31], manual subject indexing is a process involving three steps: (1) determining subject content of a document, (2) conceptual analysis to decide which aspects of the content should be represented, and (3) translation of those concepts or aspects into a controlled vocabulary. These steps, in particular the second one, are based on a specific library's policy in respect to its document collections and user groups. Thus, when evaluating automatically assigned classes against the human-assigned ones, it is important to know the collection indexing policies. Yang [71] claims that the most serious problem in evaluations is the lack of standard document collections and shows how different versions of the same collection have a strong impact on the performance, and other versions do not.

Another problem to consider when evaluating automated classification is the fact that certain subjects are erroneously assigned. When indexing, people make errors such as those related to exhaustivity policy (too many or too few subjects become assigned), specificity of indexing (which usually means that the assigned subject is not the most specific one available), they may omit important subjects, or assign an obviously incorrect subject [39].

In addition, it has been reported that different people, whether users or professional subject indexers, would assign different subjects to the same document. Studies on inter- and intra-indexer consistency report generally low indexer consistency [54]. Markey [49] reviewed 57 indexer consistency studies and reported that consistency levels ranged from 4% to 84%, with only 18 studies showing over 50% consistency. There are two main factors that seem to affect it:

1) Higher exhaustivity and specificity of subject indexing both lead to lower consistency, i.e., indexers choose the same first term or class notation for the major subject of the document, but the consistency decreases as they choose more subjects;
2) The bigger the vocabulary, or, the more choices the indexers have, the less likely they will choose the same terms or class notations [54].

For document collections used in evaluation it is thus important to obtain indexing policies. Also, without a thorough qualitative analysis of automatically assigned classes one cannot be sure whether, for example, the classes assigned by algorithms, but not human-assigned, are actually wrong, or if they were left out by mistake or because of the indexing policy.

Today evaluation in automated classification experiments is mostly conducted under controlled conditions, ignoring the above-discussed issues. Normally it does not involve real-life situations, subject experts or users; instead, experiments typical of laboratory information retrieval tradition are applied [30]. Or, as Sebastiani [58] puts it, "… the evaluation of document classifiers is typically conducted experimentally, rather than analytically. The reason is that … we would need a formal specification of the problem that the system is trying to solve (e.g., with respect to what correctness and completeness are defined), and the central notion … that of membership of a document in a category is, due to its subjective character, inherently nonformalizable."

5. Conclusions and outlook

The effectiveness of metadata extraction — indeed, the relevance of metadata extraction as an approach — depends greatly on the circumstances and context of use. There are many scenarios in which the methods described in this document will be inappropriate, or appropriate only in terms of a partial implementation or limited use case. Choosing the best approach to subject metadata extraction and automated classification will depend on availability of a suitable controlled vocabulary (string matching), training documents (machine learning), and purpose of the application. Clustering is least suited because automatically derived cluster labels and relationships between the clusters are often incorrect, inconsistent and hard to understand. Also, clusters change as new documents are added to the collection, which is not user-friendly either.

Practical deployment of any service or application involves a great deal of evaluation, and the results are seldom generalizable to all possible usage scenarios of that software or service. Hence, the same is true of metadata extraction. However, owing to recognized evaluation issues, it is difficult to estimate to what degree subject metadata extraction of today is applicable in operative information systems. Evaluation results depend on multiple factors, such as document collection, application context, and user tasks. It is believed that evaluation methodology of automated classification where all the different factors would be included, perhaps through a triangulation of standard collection-based evaluation and user studies, should be a major further research question.

Those with an interest in metadata extraction of any flavor are likely to benefit most from active experimentation; early deployment with the ability to opt-out, beta-testing, user evaluation and agile development are all good strategies for implementing novel methods or approaches into existing services.

References

1. Albiol, A, L Torres and EJ Delp (2004). Face recognition: When audio comes to the rescue of video. In *Proceedings of the International Workshop on Image Analysis for Multimedia Interactive Services*, Lisboa, Portugal, April 2004.
2. Ardö, A, F Falcoz, T Koch, M Nielsen and M Sandfær (1994). Improving resource discovery and retrieval on the Internet: The Nordic WAIS/World Wide Web project summary report. *NORDINFO Nytt*, 17(4), 13–28.

3. Ardö, A and T Koch (1999). Automatic classification applied to the full-text Internet documents in a robot-generated subject index. In *Proceedings of the 23rd International Online Information Meeting,* London, 239–246.
4. Austin, D, D Peruvemba, S McCarron, M Ishikawa and M Birbeck (2006). XHTML™ Modularization 1.1, W3C Working Draft. Available at http://www.w3.org/TR/xhtml-modularization/xhtml-modularization.html [last date of access 30 April 2006].
5. Bergmark, D (2000). Automatic extraction of reference linking information from online documents. CSTR 2000-1821, Cornell Digital Library Research Group.
6. Blum, A and T Mitchell (1998). Combining labeled and unlabeled data with co-training. In *Proceedings of the Workshop on Computational Learning Theory,* 99–100.
7. Brown, MG, JT Foote, GJF Jones, K Sparck Jones and SJ Young (1995). Automatic content-based retrieval of broadcast news. In *Proceedings of the third ACM international conference on Multimedia,* 35–43, San Francisco, November 1995. ACM Press.
8. Byrne, W, D Doermann and M Franz (2004). Automatic recognition of spontaneous speech for access to multilingual oral history archives. *IEEE Transactions on Speech and Audio Processing,* Special Issue on Spontaneous Speech Processing, July 2004.
9. Cardinaels, K, E Duval and HJ Olivié (2006). A formal model of learning object metadata. *EC-TEL,* 74–87.
10. Carr, L and S Harnad (2005). Keystroke economy: A study of the time and effort involved in self-archiving. Unpublished public draft. Available at http://eprints.ecs.soton.ac.uk/10688/1/KeystrokeCosting-publicdraft1.pdf.
11. Chen, H and ST Dumais (2000). Bringing order to the web: Automatically categorizing search results. In *Proceedings of the ACM International Conference on Human Factors in Computing Systems,* Den Haag, 145–152.
12. Clippingdale, S and M Fujii (2003). *Face Recognition for Video Indexing: Randomization of Face Templates Improves Robustness to Facial Expression.* Lecture Notes in Computer Science, Vol. 2849/2003. Berlin / Heidelberg: Springer.
13. Dumais, ST, DD Lewis and F Sebastiani (2002). Report on the workshop on operational text classification systems (OTC-02). *ACM SIGIR Forum,* 35(2), 8–11.
14. Earley, J (1970). An efficient context-free parsing algorithm. *Communications of the Association for Computing Machinery,* 13(2), 94–102.
15. Fürnkranz, J (2002). Hyperlink ensembles: A case study in hypertext classification. *Information Fusion,* 3(4), 299–312.
16. Garfield, E, MV Malin and H Small (1975). A system for automatic classification of scientific literature. Reprinted from *Journal of the Indian Institute of Science,* 57(2), 61–74. (Reprinted in: *Essays of an Information Scientist,* 2, 356–365).

17. Ghani, R, S Slattery and Y Yang (2001). Hypertext categorization using hyperlink patterns and metadata. In *Proceedings of the 18th International Conference on Machine Learning,* 178–185.
18. Giles, CL and ID Councill (2004). Who gets acknowledged: Measuring scientific contributions through automatic acknowledgment indexing. *PNAS,* 101(51), 17599–17604.
19. Giuffrida, G, EC Shek and J Yang (2000). Knowledge-based metadata extraction from PostScript files. In *DL '00: Proceedings of the fifth ACM conference on digital libraries,* 77–84. NY, USA: ACM. DOI: http://doi.acm.org/10.1145/336597.336639
20. Golub, K (2007). Automated subject classification of textual documents in the context of web-based hierarchical browsing. Doctoral dissertation, Lund University.
21. Gövert, N, M Lalmas and N Fuhr (1999). A probabilistic description-oriented approach for categorising web documents. In *Proceedings of the Eighth International Conference on Information and Knowledge Management,* 475–482.
22. Greenberg, J (2004). Metadata extraction and harvesting: A comparison of two automatic metadata generation applications. *Journal of Internet Cataloging,* 6(4), 59–82.
23. Greenberg, J, K Spurgin and A Crystal (2006). Functionalities for automatic metadata generation applications: A survey of metadata experts' opinions. *International Journal of Metadata, Semantics and Ontologies,* 1(1), 3–20.
24. Ha, Y, H Li, Y Cao, L Teng, D Meyerzon and Q Zheng (2006). Automatic extraction of titles from general documents using machine learning. *Information Processing and Management,* 42(5), 1276–1293.
25. Han, H, CL Giles, E Manavoglu and H Zha (2003). Automatic document metadata extraction using support vector machines. In *Proceedings of the Third ACM/IEEE-CS Joint Conference on Digital Libraries,* 37–48. New York: ACM Press.
26. Han, H, CL Giles, H Zha, C Li and K Tsioutsiouliklis (2004). Two supervised learning approaches for name disambiguation in author citations. In *Proceedings of the Fourth ACM/IEEE Joint Conference on Digital Libraries,* 296–300. New York: ACM Press.
27. Han, H, H Zha and CL Giles (2005). Name disambiguation in author citations using a K-way spectral clustering method. In *Proceedings of JCDL'2005,* 334–343.
28. Harnad, S and L Carr (2000). Integrating, navigating and analysing open Eprint archives through open citation linking (the OpCit project). *Current Science,* 79(5), 629–638.
29. Hoche, S and P Flach (2006). Predicting topics of scientific papers from co-authorship graphs: A case study. In *Proceedings of the 2006 UK Workshop on Computational Intelligence (UKCI2006),* 215–222. September 2006.

30. Ingwersen, P and K Järvelin (2005). *The Turn: Integration of Information Seeking and Retrieval in Context.* Dordrecht: Springer.
31. International Organization for Standardization (1985). *Documentation — Methods for Examining Documents, Determining their Subjects, and Selecting Index Terms: ISO 5963.* Geneva: International Organization for Standardization.
32. Jain, AK, MN Murty and PJ Flynn (1999). Data clustering: A review. *ACM Computing Surveys,* 31(3), 264–323.
33. Jaynes, ET (1957). Information theory and statistical mechanics. *Physical Review Letters,* 106, 620.
34. Jenkins, C, M Jackson, P Burden and J Wallis (1998). Automatic classification of web resources using java and Dewey Decimal Classification. *Computer Networks and ISDN Systems,* 30, 646–648.
35. Jörgensen, C (1999). Access to pictorial material: A review of current research and future prospects. *Computers and the Humanities,* 33(4), 293–318.
36. Kirkegaard, B (2008). Metadata elements preferred in searching and assessing relevance of archived television broadcast by scholars and students in media studies: Towards the design of surrogate records. Doctoral dissertation, Royal School of Library and Information Science.
37. Kohonen, T (2001). *Self-Organizing Maps,* 3rd edn. Berlin: Springer-Verlag.
38. Krause, J and J Marx (2000). Vocabulary switching and automatic metadata extraction or how to get useful information from a digital library. In *Proceedings of the First DELOS Network of Excellence Workshop on "Information Seeking, Searching and Querying in Digital Libraries".* Zurich, Switzerland.
39. Lancaster, FW (2003). *Indexing and Abstracting in Theory and Practice,* 3rd edn. London: Facet.
40. Larson, RR (1992). Experiments in automatic Library of Congress Classification. *Journal of the American Society for Information Science,* 43(2), 130–148.
41. Lee, J-H (2005). Automatic video management system using face recognition and MPEG-7 visual descriptors. *ETRI Journal,* 27(6), 806–809.
42. Liu, Y, P Mitra, CL Giles and K Bai (2006). Automatic extraction of table metadata from digital documents. In *Proceedings of the Sixth ACM/IEEE-CS Joint Conference on Digital Libraries,* 339–340.
43. Lew, MS, N Sebe, C Djeraba and R Jain (2006). Content-based multimedia information retrieval: State of the art and challenges. *ACM Transactions on Multimedia Computing, Communications, and Applications (TOMCCAP),* 2(1), 1–19.
44. Lewis, DD, Y Yang, T Rose and F Li (2004). RCV1: A new benchmark collection for text categorization research. *The Journal of Machine Learning Research,* 5, 361–397.
45. Li, YH and AK Jain (1998). Classification of text documents. *The Computer Journal,* 41(8), 537–546.

46. Liddy, ED, S Sutton, W Paik, E Allen, S Harwell, M Monsour, A Turner and J Liddy (2001). Breaking the metadata generation bottleneck: Preliminary findings. In *Proceedings of the 1st ACM/IEEE-CS joint conference on Digital libraries,* 464. Roanoke, Virginia, United States.
47. Liere, R and P Tadepalli (1998). Active learning with committees: Preliminary results in comparing winnow and perceptron in text categorization. In *Proceedings of the 1st Conference on Automated Learning and Discovery,* 591–596.
48. Lovegrove, WS and DF Brailsford (1995). Document analysis of PDF files: Methods, results and implications. *Electronic publishing,* 8(2–3), 207–220.
49. Markey, K (1984). Interindexer consistency tests: A literature review and report of a test of consistency in indexing visual materials. *Library and Information Science Research,* 6, 155–177.
50. McCallum, AK, K Nigam, J Rennie and K Seymore (2000). Automating the construction of Internet portals with machine learning. *Information Retrieval Journal,* 3, 127–163.
51. Mitchell, T (1997). *Machine Learning.* New York, NY: McGraw Hill.
52. Möller, G, K-U Carstensen, B Diekmann and H Watjen (1999). Automatic classification of the WWW using the Universal Decimal Classification. In *Proceedings of the 23rd International Online Information Meeting,* 231–238, London, 7–9 December.
53. Nübel, R, C Pease, P Schmidt and D Maas (2002). Bilingual indexing for information retrieval with AUTINDEX. In *Third International Conference on Language Resources and Evaluation,* 29th, 30th and 31st May, Las Palmas de Gran Canaria (Spain), 1136–1149.
54. Olson, HA and JJ Boll (2001). *Subject Analysis in Online Catalogs,* 2nd edn. Englewood, CO: Libraries Unlimited.
55. Rasmussen, EM (1997). Indexing images. In *Annual Review of Information Science and Technology,* ME Williams (ed.), Vol. 32, pp. 169–196. Medford, NJ: Information Today.
56. Rowley, J (1994). The controlled versus natural indexing languages debate revisited: A perspective on information retrieval practice and research. *Journal of Information Science,* 20(2), 108–119.
57. Schütze, H, DA Hull and JO Pedersen (1995). A comparison of classifiers and document representations for the routing problem. In *Proceedings of the 18th Annual International ACM SIGIR Conference on Research and Development in Information Retrieval,* Seattle, 229–237.
58. Sebastiani, F (2002). Machine learning in automated text categorization. *ACM Computing Surveys,* 34(1), 1–47.

59. Smeaton, AF (2004). Indexing, browsing, and searching of digital video. In Annual *Review of Information Science and Technology,* B Cronin (ed.), Vol. 38, 371–407. Medford, NJ: Information Today.
60. Subramanian, S and KE Shafer (1998). *Clustering.* OCLC Publications. Available at http://digitalarchive.oclc.org/da/ViewObject.jsp?objid=0000003409 [accessed on 10 June 2008].
61. Sun, A, E-P Lim and W-K Ng (2001). Hierarchical text classification and evaluation. In *ICDM 2001, IEEE International Conference on Data Mining,* 521–528.
62. Svenonius, E (1997). Definitional approaches in the design of classification and thesauri and their implications for retrieval and for automatic classification. In *Proceedings of the Sixth International Study Conference on Classification Research,* 12–16.
63. Svenonius, E (2000). *The Intellectual Foundations of Information Organization.* Cambridge, MA: MIT Press.
64. Takasu, A (2003). Bibliographic attribute extraction from erroneous references based on a statistical model. In *Proceedings of the Third ACM/IEEE-CS Joint Conference on Digital Libraries,* 49–60. New York: ACM Press.
65. Thunderstone (2005). Thunderstone's web site catalog. Available at http://search.thunderstone.com/texis/websearch [10 June 2008].
66. Tonkin, E and HL Muller (2008). Semi automated metadata extraction for preprints archives. *JCDL 2008.*
67. Van Thong, J-M, D Goddeau, A Litvinova, B Logan, P Moreno and M Swain (2000). SpeechBot: A speech recognition based audio indexing system for the web. *International Conference on Computer-Assisted Information Retrieval,* Recherche d'Informations Assistee par Ordinateur (RIAO), Paris, April 2000, 106–115.
68. Wallach, HM (2004). Conditional random fields: An introduction. Technical Report MS-CIS-04-21. Department of Computer and Information Science, University of Pennsylvania.
69. Wang, Y and M Kitsuregawa (2002). Evaluating contents-link coupled web page clustering for web search results. In *Proceedings of the Eleventh International Conference on Information and Knowledge Management,* McLean, Virginia, USA, 499–506.
70. Wu, YB and Q Li (2008). Document keyphrases as subject metadata: Incorporating document key concepts in search results. *Information Retrieval,* 11, 229–249.
71. Yang, Y (1999). An evaluation of statistical approaches to text categorization. *Journal of Information Retrieval,* 1(1/2), 67–88.

72. Yang, Y, S Slattery and R Ghani (2002). A study of approaches to hypertext categorization. *Journal of Intelligent Information Systems*, 8(2–3), 219–241.
73. Ye, R, Y Yang, Z Shan, Y Liu and S Zhou (2006). Aseks: A p2p audio search engine based on keyword spotting. In *ISM '06: Proceedings of the Eighth IEEE International Symposium on Multimedia*, 615–620. Washington, DC, USA: IEEE Computer Society. Available at http://portal.acm.org/citation.cfm?id=1194217.

CHAPTER IV.3

TECHNOLOGIES FOR METADATA AND ONTOLOGY STORAGE

Mary Parmelee* and Leo Obrst†

The MITRE Corporation
7515 Colshire Drive, McLean, VA 22102–7539, USA
**mparmelee@mitre.org*
†lobrst@mitre.org

The subject of metadata and ontology storage is broad, complex and rapidly evolving. This chapter aims to provide an overview of the kinds of technologies that are used for metadata and ontology storage as well as the methods, tools and standards for implementing those technologies. We also include a comparison matrix of metadata and ontology storage and management tools as well as a list of references for locating more information about metadata and ontology storage.

1. Introduction

This section describes the differences between metadata, ontology and related concepts as a precursor to describing the similarities and differences in technologies for managing and storing them. It also provides an overview of the structure of the chapter.

Metadata are information objects also known as elements, that are usually in the form of textual terms or phrases that describe properties of other information objects [14]. An information object can be anything from a real world object such as a vehicle, to a single piece of data, such as a vehicle identification number (VIN). Metadata are typically used for the purpose of clarifying the meaning of information objects, managing information objects, or complying with regulations that apply to them. There are two primary kinds of metadata, product metadata and content metadata. Product metadata describes information about the object as a container, while content metadata describes what is inside the container [75]. For example, if the product being described is a document about vehicles, then the product metadata might include the publication date, author name and publisher name, while the content metadata might include topic, and keywords. Metadata elements are typically organized into a controlled vocabulary for describing information objects called a metadata schema. Metadata can also describe other metadata, such as metadata that describes the metadata schemas in a metadata registry [59].

An ontology defines real world things by grouping them into categories called classes and specifying the common properties of the things in each class. Ontologies also specify relations between things as well as constraints and rules that restrict the definition of things and the relations between things [78, 79]. For example, a Vehicle ontology might define a class of things called Unicycle and specify the parts of a Unicycle as common properties, such as hasPart Wheel, hasPart Pedal, and hasPart Brake. The Vehicle ontology might also define a Person class. Then it specifies a relation between Unicycle and Person with a hasOwner relation. The Vehicle ontology could also specify a constraint that a Unicycle must have at most one wheel so that a rule engine, called an automated reasoner, could interpret that constraint and infer that if a vehicle has more than one wheel then it cannot be a Unicycle.

The previous descriptions address the categories of things that are defined in metadata schemas and ontologies. Once defined, these categories are applied to create individual information object descriptions called metadata records and ontology instance descriptions respectively. Table 1 illustrates a metadata record for the Vehicle document and an ontology instance description for a Unicycle as described in the previous examples.

Table 1. Metadata record and ontology instance.

Vehicle document metadata record	**Vehicle ontology unicycle instance description**
Product Metadata	Unicycle: 12345
— publication date: 11/14/2009	— has part: pedal
— author name: Howard Parmelee	— has part: brake
— publisher name: The Vehicle Historical Society	— has part: wheel
	— has wheel constraint ≤ 1
	— has owner: Leo Obrst
Content Metadata	
— title: 100 years of American Made Vehicles	
— topic: vehicle history	
— keywords: United States history, vehicle manufacturing	

Depending on their specific application, metadata schemas, ontologies and their individual descriptions require overlapping and sometimes completely different storage tools and methods [59, 82, 83, 102].

This chapter is organized as follows. In Section 2, we introduce metadata and ontology storage and management models and technologies, such as relational databases, object-oriented databases, and Semantic Web triple stores. In Section 3, we discuss storage and access methods, including registries, repositories, catalogues, federations, and indexes. Section 4 presents the relevant metadata and ontology standards. Section 5 provides some example metadata and ontology registries and repositories. In Section 6, we briefly describe some tools. We conclude with a chapter summary.

2. Metadata and ontology storage and management technologies

This section provides an overview and discussion of the main technologies that are used for managing and storing metadata and ontologies, including major advantages and disadvantages of using each technology for metadata management and storage. The storage technologies that are discussed in this section are relational database (RDB), object-relational database (ORDB), object oriented database (OODB), Native Extensible Markup Language (XML) database (NXDB), and triple stores.

2.1. *Relational database (RDB)*

The majority of metadata management and storage systems and many ontology management and storage systems use relational database technology. Relational databases are represented as a collection of information about data entities, stored in tabular format. An entity is a person, place, thing or event about which data is being stored. Each table is called a relation and is stored as a separate file in the database. Relations hold sets of entities that are semantically linked by their common characteristics [101].

An attribute is a characteristic or property of an entity. Each row in a relation represents an entity and each column represents an attribute of that entity. Semantic linkage within a relation is represented by the intersecting cell between an entity (row) and its characteristic or attribute (column). The intersection value represents a single characteristic of the associated entity. Relations apply no syntactic constraints to attribute order. The tabular structure of the relational database constrains semantic linkages to binary relations of primitive or atomic values. Table 2 illustrates the structural representation of a relation [101].

Table 2. The structural representation of the binary relation (cell) that is the intersection of an entity (row) and attribute (column) in a relational database.

	Attribute 1	Attribute 2
Entity 1	Value	Value
Entity 2	Value	Value

Inter-relational semantic linkages are formed by linking relations (tables) together by their unique identifiers or primary key attributes. The link typically represents a relation between relations. For example, a student relation, could be linked to a course relation by an enrolled in relation. Figure 1 depicts a relational model that links students to the courses in which they are enrolled by joining the primary keys of the Student and Course relations in an Enrolled_In relation [101].

Relational database technology has the advantage of being a mature technology that is optimized for speed, scalability and reliability. Most relational database systems have robust functionality such as security, disaster recovery, stored procedures and triggers that facilitate database operation and maintenance. However, the relational model has limited utility for representing and interpreting more complex entities and interrelations and relational

Type Key
A = Attribute: An attribute (column) in a table (relation)
CK = Compound Key: A primary key that is a combination of two or more attributes in a table
FK = Foreign Key: An attribute that references a primary key in a related table
PK = Primary Key: One or more attributes that contain a unique ID for each entity in a table

Student	Type
Student_ID	PK
First_Name	A
Last_Name	A
Major	A

Enrolled_In	Type
Student_ID	FK
Course_ID	FK
Semester	A
Enroll_Year	A

Course	Type
Course_ID	PK
Course_Name	A
Credit_Hours	A

Fig. 1. A relational model that uses primary keys to link students to the courses in which they are enrolled.

models are based on a static world view that makes it difficult to change a relational model once it has been implemented. Most of the semantics in relational models are expressed in artifacts such as logical diagrams that are designed for human consumption, or are tacit knowledge of the database designers and users.

Although there has been limited success with representing simple hierarchies and ontologies using the relational model, retrofitting the relational model to simulate the structure expressed in semi-structured metadata such as XML schemas (XSDs) or the semantics expressed in ontologies can be costly and time consuming. Except for import and export conversion, the relational technology does not support the complex objects and hierarchical structure of XML. Nor does it support the interpretation of many of the key semantic relations, constraints, and rules that ontologies need to express in order to represent the meaning of entities and their relations. Transitivity for example, is not supported and is difficult to simulate. Consequently, ontologies and metadata schemas are often stored as files called binary large objects (BLOB) in relational models and then extracted for manipulation and interpretation by external tools.

Relational database technology is an excellent choice for managing and storing simple metadata models with stable binary relations where the metadata instances can be stored as database records in a central repository. A data dictionary is an example of metadata that is conducive to relational database storage. Relational technology also performs well as a centralized repository for managing metadata schemas and ontologies as database records to be retrieved and downloaded. Oracle is an example of a relational database management system (RDBMS). For an extensive comparison of relational databases and knowledge bases, see Gardarin and Valduriez [26].

2.1.1. *Relational databases and ontologies*

Ontologies address formal vocabularies and their meanings with an explicit, expressive, and well-defined semantics, possibly machine-interpretable. Ontologies limit the possible formal models of interpretation (semantics) of those vocabularies to the set of meanings a modeler intends (i.e., close to the human conceptualization). None of the other "vocabularies," such as database schemas or object models with less expressive semantics, does that.

The approaches with less expressive semantics assume that humans will look at the "vocabularies" and supply the semantics via the human semantic interpreter (your mental model). Additionally, a developer will code programs to enforce the local semantics that the database/database management system (DBMS) cannot.

Ontologies model generic, real-world concepts and their meanings, unlike either database schemas or object models, which are typically specific to a particular set of applications and represent limited semantics. A given ontology cannot model any given domain completely. However, in capturing real world and imaginary (i.e., a theory of unicorns and other fantastic beasts) semantics, one is enabled to reuse, extend, refine, and generalize, etc., that semantic model.

Ontologies are meant to be reused; database schemas cannot be reused. A database conceptual schema might be used as the basis of an ontology; however, that would require moving from a lesser to a more expressive model, from an Entity-Relation model to a Conceptual Model (i.e., a weak ontology) to a Logical Theory (strong ontology) [77].

Often with relational databases and other non-ontological approaches to capturing the semantics of data, systems, and services, the modeling process stops at a syntactic and structural model, and even then throws the impoverished semantic model away to act as historical artifact. The rudimentary model is completely separated from the evolution of the live database, system, or service, and remains only semantically interpretable by an individual human who can read the documents, interpret the graphics, supply the real world knowledge of the domain, and understands how the database, system, or service will be implemented and used. Ontologists want to shift some of that "semantic interpretative burden" to machines and have them mimic human semantics (i.e., understand what we mean). The result would bring the machine up to the human, not force the human to the machine level.

The primary purpose of relational databases is for storage and ease of access to data, not complex use. Software applications (with the data semantics embedded in non-reusable code via programmers) and individuals must focus on data use, manipulation, and transformation, all of which require a high degree of interpretation of the data. Extending the capabilities of a database often requires significant reprogramming and restructuring of the database schema. Extending the capabilities of an ontology can be done by adding to its set of constituent relationships. In theory, this may include relationships for semantic mapping, whereas semantic mapping between multiple databases will require external applications.

2.2. *Deductive Databases*

Deductive databases [15, 56, 65] combine both rule-reasoning in the form of logic programming, along with the set-at-a-time operations of relational databases. As such, they combine the symbolic reasoning of ontologies and its rules with the efficiency of access and joinability of instance data of relational databases. As an example, the commercial tools of OntologyWorks are commercial implementations of deductive databases, and support a version of the International Standards Organization (ISO) Common Logic [13, 49]. Deductive databases, like logic programming tools in general, enable ontologies and their rules to be executed efficiently at run-time, thus providing real-time machine reasoning. See Samuel [106] for a system which combines OWL ontologies, SWRL rules, and logic programming reasoning.

2.3. *Object relational database (ORDB)*

An object relational database implements an object-oriented (OO) model in a relational database. The object is a combination of data and related code that forms the basic unit in an OO model. Objects are the instances of object classes. The OO model is a network model that forms relations between objects in a much more flexible way than a relational model. Object relational models typically leverage the relational database as a repository for storage and retrieval, but do not implement a relational model. Instead, each table typically corresponds to an object class, while its contents correspond to an object instance. Tables are then mapped to programming objects typically using object-relational mapping software. This mapping is processed in a mapping layer that transforms relational data to programming objects at runtime, thereby creating a virtual OODB [6].

The advantages of an ORDB are that it layers a much more flexible model over the Relational model while still leveraging the robust storage and retrieval capabilities of the RDBMS. The Object model is a network model that supports important OO capabilities such as encapsulation of data into complex objects, inheritance, as well as support for standard XML-based and communications protocols (e.g. HTTP) [94]. Figure 2 is a simple example of an object model that is implemented in both ORDB and OODB technologies [120].

ORDB technology is conducive to managing more complex semantics and more of the capabilities that are necessary for more robust management

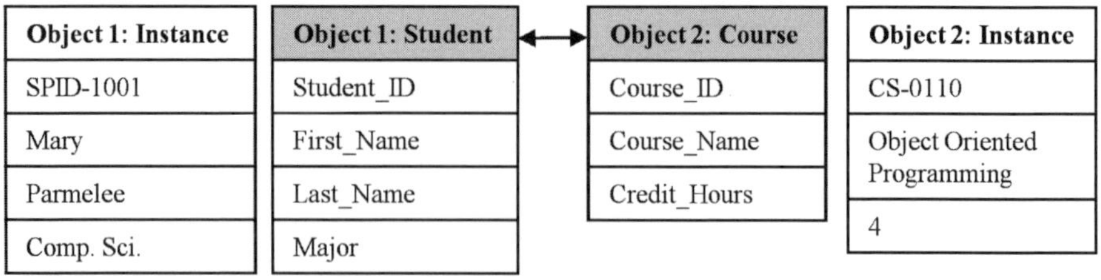

Fig. 2. ORDB Object Model

and storage of XML and ontologies. Virtuoso is an example of an object relational database management system (ORDBMS).

2.4. *Object oriented database (OODB)*

Object oriented database technology has the same advantages and functionality as the ORDB, except that objects are created and stored in their native object form, thus eliminating the overhead of relational-mapping and the mapping transformation layer of ORDB technology. However, the consequence is that much of the robust data management and storage capability that the underlying RDBMS provides for the ORDB must be recreated for the OODB. However, object-oriented databases are maturing and may eventually be the storage technology of choice for managing complex network models. Objectivity is an example of an object-oriented database management system (OODBMS) [74]. See also Kim and Lochovsky [50]; Zdonik and Maier [134].

2.5. *Native XML database (NXDB)*

The defining factors for Native XML databases are: The logical model is defined by XML, XML documents are stored in their native form, and the NXDB is agnostic to the underlying physical model [117]. This means that:

(i) the logical model is typically encoded in an XSD;
(ii) no data transform is necessary before the XML instance documents can be used;
(iii) a NXDB can be implemented using any persistent technology for storage.

Not surprisingly, NXDBs work particularly well in any environment that relies heavily on XML for processing data, which includes XML encoded metadata. Organizations, such as libraries, archives and publishing organizations whose operations are document-centric as well as organizations that rely heavily on XML for data exchange (e.g. web services) could benefit greatly from NXDB technology.

Most metadata that is implemented at the production level today is encoded in XML. Since XML is a structural, rather than a semantic meta-language, NXDB is a reasonable choice of technology for organizations that are mostly concerned with product metadata (e.g. author of an information object), and do not have a strong need for content metadata (the meaning of the information object). Semantic languages such as the Web Ontology Language (OWL) and Resource Description Framework Schema language (RDFS) are generally better suited for representing content metadata.

Since OWL and RDF are grounded in XML and can be serialized as XML, NXDB technology can be used to store, retrieve and process it as XML, which may prove to be an advantage over storing ontologies using a relational model or in flat files. However, specialized technology is required in order to be capable of interpreting the semantics that are encoded in ontologies. How semantic tools can be effectively layered over NXDB technology to enable advanced semantic capabilities is still a research question, but a system that supports scalable intelligent interaction between ontologies and their structural XML translations could provide such advanced capabilities as ontology-aware web services and ontology-aware publishing. Oracle BerkeleyDB XML and Tamino are examples of NXDBs [60, 96, 113].

2.6. *Triple and N-tuple stores*

Triple stores are stores for RDF instances, which have the following structure (for a discussion of RDF, see Section 4:

- Subject or Resource: First element of the triple. Something with a URI, a literal (string or XML datatype), or a blank node (unnamed or anonymous), the primary entity about which something is being asserted,
- Predicate or Property: Second element of the triple. An Attribute or relation, the connection between the Subject and the Object,
- Object or Resource: Third element of the triple. Something with a URI, a literal (string or XML datatype), or a blank node (unnamed or anonymous), the secondary entity about which something is being asserted, e.g., the other entity related by the Predicate/Property to the Subject. If the second element of the triple is really a relation, then the third element (object) is another entity comparable to the first element (subject), as in <John, hasFather, Henry>. If the second element is really an attribute, then the third element is an attribute value, as in <John, hasHairColor, Red> [66].

Some examples in a more perspicuous syntactic rendering are the following (there are many of these, from the canonical RDF/XML to *N-triples,* to *Notation 3,* to *Turtle* (Terse RDF Triple Notation) [131] where a Property can be either a Relation between two objects or an Attribute that holds of an object:

<Subject, Property, Object>
<Object1, Relation, Object2>
<Leo, hasColleague, Barry>

<Object1, Attribute, AttributeValue>
<Leo, hairColor, brown>

Any argument in the triple can be a URI (now, an IRI), i.e., a URI identifier or address that can be located anywhere on the Web.

Triple stores become quadruple stores or even potentially n-tuple stores because of RDF reification [127].

RDF reification is a statement about a triple. An example is the following:

Given a triple like: <Leo, hasColleague, Barry>;

then a reification is a quadruple like: <Statement1, Leo, hasColleague, Barry>; which is meant to indicate that the "statement" (a so-called *blank node* in RDF terminology or a URI) is a statement about a triple. It's typically preceded by a normal triple such as:

<John, believes, Statement1>.

Semantically, there is no *entailment* relation between the original triple and the reification of the triple, and so the reification can make no claim about the truth of the original triple, only that some statement has been made of it.

How reification is typically used, however, is as a statement about provenance, i.e., origin, lineage, or even security classification about the statement. In all cases, the interpreting engine must impose its own interpretation of that reification, which is outside of the RDF semantics. This does not mean that reification is not useful. It does mean that the interpretation of reification varies, sometimes dramatically, and semantic consistency of the interpretation cannot be guaranteed, especially across different RDF triple stores and different Semantic Web reasoning engines.

Triple (and quadruple) stores thus represent a kind of storage structure for the graph-based RDF data model, along the lines of the relational model for relational databases. Instead of SQL, however, for triple or n-tuple stores, the query language SPARQL Protocol and RDF Query Language (SPARQL) [123, 130] is used. SPARQL is a graph-based language. For a comparison of relational (tabular) SQL, tree-based XQuery for XML, and graph-based SPARQL for RDF/OWL, see Melton [63].

A given triple store can be either centralized or distributed, as can all triple stores accessible to SPARQL queries, if those triple stores are made known to the originating SPARQL query engine as an exposed SPARQL endpoint, which is a way of indexing a triple store so that it is known to a query engine [37]. However, what constitutes a SPARQL endpoint is currently ill-defined. Particular RDF triple stores attempt to define SPARQL endpoints from their perspectives, as, for example, Drupal [16].

Many triple and n-tuple stores advertise high storage sizes and various other high access, query, and load rates, some using Lehigh University Benchmark (LUBM) results [52]. Most high-end triple stores report the ability to store billions of triples, some as high as 60 billion, but these claims are not yet independently confirmed.

Some example triple stores are: OWLIM, Garlik 4Store, AllegroGraph, Jena, Sesame, Oracle 11g, Mulgara, Semantics.Server, and OpenLink Virtuoso. For a comparison of large triple (and quadruple) stores, gauged with respect to actual quoted deployments rather than predictions about scalability see, *"Large Triple Stores"* [20].

3. Metadata and ontology storage methods

Section 3 gives an overview of the main methods for metadata and ontology storage methods and relates those methods with the standards and example systems that are described in Sections 4 and 5 of this chapter.

3.1. *Embedded metadata*

Embedded metadata is encapsulated with the information object that it describes. This kind of metadata storage is most commonly used to describe the content of electronic information objects that are difficult to categorize using automated methods. For example, digital images, video, audio and to some degree, unstructured text are difficult to index, mine or otherwise categorize without human intervention.

Major software manufacturers like Microsoft and Adobe automatically embed some metadata with all word processing and image files and enable document owner to augment metadata properties manually with metadata such as subject keywords and descriptions. Adobe developed its own standard for embedded document metadata exchange called the Extensible Metadata Platform (XMP). The headers of HTML Web pages always contain at least some descriptive metadata, such as the version of HTML used, copyright and other legal rights and disclaimers, and subject keywords.

The main advantage of embedded metadata is that it makes information objects self-describing. The main disadvantage of embedded metadata is that the methods and representation of embedded metadata vary between digital media types [55].

3.2. *Catalogues*

A catalogue stores and manages the metadata records that describe information objects. The records in a metadata catalogue are akin to library catalogue cards and the information objects are akin to the books on a library shelf. A metadata catalogue contains information on how to locate the information objects that it describes, but generally it does not store those objects in their original form. Each metadata record in a metadata catalogue has a corresponding information object that it describes. Especially for large or complex metadata catalogues, the metadata records are often grouped into the categories of a classification scheme, such as the Library of Congress Subject Heading (LCSH) scheme [53]. Catalogues can store and manage metadata records about virtually anything that can be described. For example, a data catalogue stores metadata records about data objects such as unstructured documents, a metadata catalogue stores metadata records about metadata schemas, and an ontology catalogue stores metadata records about ontologies.

3.3. *Registries*

A registry is a kind of catalogue that stores and manages metadata records that have been submitted by registered users. The information objects that are being described are often called registry items [99]. Registries are typically organized around information objects (e.g. data and metadata objects) that have something in common, such as a common subject area, common owner, or common technology. The IANA Protocol Registry is an example of a data registry that is organized around the subject of Internet protocols and the Dublin Core (DC) Metadata Registry [17] is an example of a metadata registry that is organized around product metadata [17, 40, 102].

3.4. *Repositories*

Repositories differ from registries in that they store the information objects themselves, or copies thereof, rather than just the metadata that describes them. Repositories may also have both registry and repository capabilities. Repositories may be the authoritative source for the original information objects that they store or they may store copies of the information objects. Storing copies of the source information objects rather than pointing to the original source gives registry/repository administrators local control over retrieving and managing the source. However, it also creates ongoing synchronization maintenance and latency issues. The NASA SWEET ontology library is an example of a simple ontology repository storing original ontology content, while the BioPortal and Open Ontology Repository store ontology copies and have both registry and repository capability [68, 71, 87, 102].

3.5. *Distributed storage*

Distributed storage involves a network of systems called nodes that share the responsibility of storing and managing shared information. These include replication-based data archives, such as Google's Big Table [12], peer-to-peer systems such as BitTorrent, service oriented environments such as web services, and others. Distributed storage networks share information using common protocols and interfaces, such as REST and SOAP web services. The largest distributed storage system is the World Wide Web.

Distributed systems are rising in popularity as storage and processing demands increase and more systems have a need to share information. Compared to centralized systems, distributed systems enable greater storage capacity, computing power, scalability and reliability at a lower cost. Replication-based archiving, for instance, optimizes scalability and reliability by replicating data across multiple nodes. Peer-to-peer systems leverage the power of many small computers to collectively store and process huge amounts of information that would exceed the capabilities of any single system, and web services enable disparate systems to publish their information using a common protocol without reengineering their systems. The disadvantages of distributed systems are that system management issues, such as routing, searching, caching, and security must also be based on a distributed model which makes them more complex and difficult to control [8,132].

One example of distributed metadata storage application is the Lex Enterprise Vocabulary Services (LexEVS) Terminology Server. LexEVS is an implementation of the LexGrid vocabulary exchange standard. See Sections 4 and 5 of this chapter for more information on LexGrid and LexEVS.

3.6. *Federated storage*

Federated storage is a kind of distributed storage method that is made up of a union of independent peer systems who participate in a federation. Federations have agreed upon criteria such as common interfaces or protocols and integrated identity management, which are typically geared toward enabling the federation to be accessed and queried as if it were a single system. Federation participants are cooperating partners in the federation that can join or leave a federation over time [99, 102].

3.7. *Indexes*

Indexes are data structures that are created for the purpose of improving the ability of computer applications to analyze, categorize, search and retrieve digital information. Indexes are most commonly used by search engines and database applications to improve information retrieval capability. Like a book index points you to the page(s) in a book that are about the term or phrase in the index, electronic indexes organize all or part of a digital information objects' content into structures that are fast and easy to process and serve as pointers to the original information object. For example, an inverted index is a table structure that matches keywords to the information objects that contain those keywords. Search engines use inverted indexes to quickly match keywords to search terms entered by the user and then retrieve the information objects that the index has associated with those keywords. This method is much faster and more efficient than searching through every information object for the same keywords.

Table 3 illustrates a simple example of an inverted index that matches the search terms "Labrador dog breed". Given these search terms, a search engine would match the terms to the Terms column of the index and then use

Table 3. Example of an inverted index.

Terms	**Objects**
Labrador	Object 1, Object 3, Object 2
Dog	Object 2, Object 3, Object 4
Breed	Object 2
...	...

the object pointer information in the Objects column of the index to rank and display a list of search results to the user. For example, since Object 2 is the only document containing all three search terms, it might be ranked first in the list.

Metadata and ontologies can be used as keyword terms for indexing information objects and can also be indexed themselves. The National Center for Biomedical Ontology (NCBO)'s BioPortal is an example application that uses metadata and ontologies as keyword index terms and many of the metadata registries mentioned in this chapter index metadata schemas and ontologies as information objects.

3.8. *Related methods*

Many other types of applications store and make use of metadata and ontologies. Collaboration tools, Wikis, discussion lists, annotation tools, and content management systems all store and make use of metadata for information management and classification. While detailed discussion of these related applications is beyond the scope of this chapter, in general, these applications use one or more of the storage methods described in this section.

3.9. *Semantic web metadata and ontology storage methods*

This section discusses advanced applications that apply Semantic Web technologies to store and manage metadata and ontologies. These include Semantic Web registries, repositories, indexes and Wikis. Semantic Web metadata and ontology storage methods typically include:

(i) representing metadata and ontologies in a W3C standard language such as Simple Knowledge Organization System (SKOS), Web Ontology Language (OWL), or Resource Description Framework (RDF) and RDF Schema (RDFS);
(ii) storing metadata and ontologies in the form of RDF triple stores that can be queried with a Semantic Web Query language such as the SPARQL W3C standard query language;
(iii) Providing a standard Semantic Web Query interface, such as a SPARQL endpoint.

The Extended Metadata Registry (XMDR) and the National Science Digital Library (NSDL) Metadata Registry are examples of metadata registries that have implemented RDF triple stores and SPARQL query end-points.

The NSDL also uses SKOS as its vocabulary encoding language. Swoogle is an example of a Semantic Web metadata index, and Semantic Media Wiki is an example of a Semantic Web Wiki. See Section 5 of this chapter for more information about these Semantic Web applications. For more information on RDF triple stores and Semantic Web standards see Sections 2 and 4 of this chapter respectively.

4. Metadata and ontology storage and management related standards

In Section 4 we provide an overview of selected metadata and ontology storage standards. The scope of this section includes standards that directly apply to metadata, controlled vocabulary and ontology registry and repository storage management, and associated markup languages for the exchange of metadata between repositories. Content-centric metadata standards as well as standards for related tools, such as metadata harvesting standards are out of the scope of this chapter.

4.1. *ISO/IEC 11179, Information technology — Metadata registries (MDR)*

ISO 11179 is a family of metadata registry standards that is intended to provide comprehensive guidance for the systematic identification, classification, structure and naming of metadata elements in a metadata registry. The standard is divided into six parts; the following five of those apply to metadata management and storage:

Part 1: Framework — Defines the terminology used by the standard, describes the essential underlying concepts that the standard is based upon, and provides a contextual overview of Parts 2–6. Some of the most fundamental definitions of 11179 are listed below.

- Concept: a unit of knowledge created by a unique combination of characteristics
- Concept system: set of concepts structured according to the relations among them
- Conceptual model: a data model that represents an abstract view of the real world
- Relationship: connection among model elements
- Object: anything perceivable or conceivable [43]

Part 2: Classification — Defines a model for managing classification schemes. Its purpose is to associate objects with one or more concepts from one or more classification schemes. A classification scheme is considered by 11179 to be a kind of concept system [44].

Part 3: Registry metamodel — Defines an object model in Unified Modeling Language (UML), which the standard describes as a conceptual metamodel (model of models). The intention of the metamodel is to prescribe a high level information structure for metadata registries [45].

Part 5: Naming and identification principles — Provides rules and guidance for developing unique identification schemes and consistent naming conventions for "administered items" in a metadata registry. Part 5 defines an administered item as either a data element concept, conceptual domain, data element, or a value domain, which is a subset of the administered items that are defined in Part 3. Although 11179 does not specify the syntax for an administered item identifier, it requires a compound identifier that includes registry authority, data, and version identifiers. It also specifies the scope of uniqueness to be within the domain of a registry authority. For naming conventions, 11179 defines principles and best practices and provides concrete examples of applied naming conventions [47].

Part 6: Registration — The final part of the ISO/IEC 11179 standard provides procedural guidance for registering administered items in a metadata registry, including the assignment of identifiers, status levels, and product metadata. It does not distinguish between types of administered items. Part 6 necessarily covers some administrative tasks and roles with respect to maintaining an administrative item once it is registered and it specifies the kinds of operational procedures that organizations need to define for registry administration. It also defines a subset of metadata attributes that apply to all types of administered items and assigns Metadata attributes in ISO/IEC 11179–3 and specifies the "conditionality" of each attribute (e.g. required, optional, etc.) [48].

ISO 11179 is a mature standard that meets the needs for the majority of metadata that organizations currently store and manage in a metadata registry. With careful application, it could also be used to classify ontologies as administered items in a metadata registry. However, a more stringent approach to semantics would be required in order for the 11179 to specify the description of ontologies at the same level of granularity that it has prescribed for metadata without loss of fidelity. The ISO 11179 notions of fundamental concepts such as "conceptual model" and "object" apply to metadata systems from an object oriented perspective. They overlap with, but don't quite match similar ontological notions. The semantics in 11179 are intended for human interpretation, while the semantics of ontologies are intended for machine interpretation. The latter requires a stricter interpretation of semantics and knowledge representation. The 11179 Joint Technical Committee is currently investigating potential expansion of the 11179 standard to include ontologies. Lawrence Berkeley Laboratories has developed an ISO 11179 reference application called the Extended Metadata Registry (XMDR) as a test bed for improving semantic representation in 11179 compliant registries. Modifications and extensions to 11179 that prove to be useful will be proposed as updates to the standard. For a description of the XMDR project, see Section 5 of this chapter.

4.2. *ISO 16642 terminological markup framework: A model for controlled vocabularies TMF*

The TMF provides a generic information structure for managing multilingual controlled vocabularies. This simple hierarchical structure could be applied to any vocabulary, including metadata schemas, which at their core are controlled vocabularies. The TMF specifies a simple hierarchical containment structure with metadata description at each level. There are four main container levels. From outside in they are: terminology collection, terminological entry, language, and term. Each vocabulary is a terminology collection. Within each terminology collection are one or more terminological entries. A terminological entry is a container for a set of multilingual synonyms. Within each terminological entry is one or more language containers, within each language container are one or more term containers. Nested metadata descriptors can be associated with any of the four levels. Figure 3 illustrates an example of a simple vocabulary using the TMF structure [41, 58].

This structure has proven to be useful for facilitating interoperability and for establishing multilingual metadata registries. When applied in a metadata registry context, this structure could store mappings between metadata schemes, classification systems, data dictionaries and controlled vocabularies. It could also be used to facilitate language translation as well as reuse of metadata elements in application profiles.

4.3. *ISO 30042: Term base eXchange*

The Term Base eXchange (TBX) standard is a standard markup language for exchanging structured terminological data that was developed as an

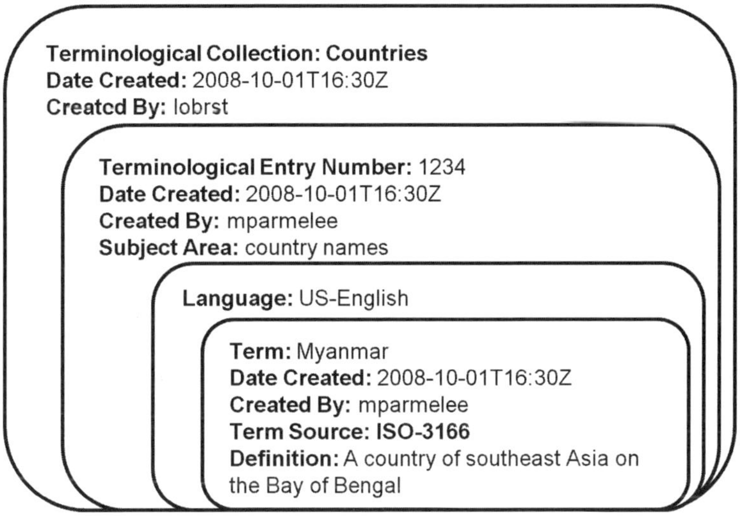

Fig. 3. Terminology Markup Framework Example.

international standard by the Localization Industry Standards Association (LISA). The TBX is a terminological markup language (TML) as defined in the ISO 16642 TMF standard (see Section 4.2). It includes a core structure and an eXtensible Constraint Specification (XCS) that specifies the data-categories and constraints of an application specific TML. TBX provides a default TML that is encoded in XML and RELAX NG. TBX takes this modular approach to provide flexibility at the implementation level to accommodate a wide variation of data-categories [42, 57].

Although TBX was originally designed to exchange controlled vocabularies for the purpose of supporting the localization industry, it is a mature standard with a simple and flexible structure that could be the basis for exchange of metadata or controlled vocabularies. Like ISO 11179 its application scope is up to and including controlled vocabularies, and can handle basic classification of ontologies. However, it is not robust enough to describe the detailed structure or semantics of ontologies.

4.4. *American national standards institute/National information standards organization (ANSI/NISO) Z39*

The Z39 family of standards is written for and maintained by the library science community. Two of those standards apply to metadata and controlled vocabulary management and storage. They are Z39.19 and Z39.50.

4.4.1. *ANSI/NISO Z39.19 Guidelines for the construction, format, and management of controlled vocabularies*

Although its main focus is on controlled vocabulary development, Z39.19 also addresses functional requirements for the management and storage of controlled vocabularies. These requirements can be found in Sections 9, 10, 11 and Appendix A of Z39.19–2005. Section 9 addresses user interface and display of controlled vocabularies. Section 10 is about interoperability of controlled vocabularies. Section 11 covers controlled vocabulary construction, testing, and maintenance and management. Finally Appendix A is a summarized list of functional requirements in a tabular format [3].

4.4.2. *ANSI/NISO Z39.50–2003 (ISO 23950): Information retrieval application service definition and protocol specification*

Maintained by the Library of Congress, Z39.50 defines a client-server application protocol for the search and retrieval of information in remote databases. Many application profiles for Z39.50 are widely used by organizations such as libraries, universities, government agencies, and content management and publishing industries. Application profiles are standards compliant specifications that are designed for a specific area of application (e.g. library applications). The **W**ide **A**rea **I**nformation **S**erver (WAIS) application profile is probably the most well known Z39.50 application profile [54]. The Zthes specifications are application profiles for Z39.50 and Z39.19 [134]. The Synaptica Taxonomy Manager is a controlled vocabulary management system that is an implementation of the Zthes application profile.

4.5. ***OASIS electronic business XML (ebXML) registry standards***

The ebXML registry and repository standards consist of a pair of standards; the ebXML Registry Information Model (ebRIM) and the ebXML Registry Services and Protocols (ebRSP) Version 3.0. The ebXML registry standards define a detailed specification for a web service-enabled XML metadata registry and repository and its services. Although the specifications were originally designed for the ebXML metadata standard, their application actually has a broader scope as implied by the following ebXML standard definition of an ebXML registry:

"an information system that securely manages any content type and the standardized metadata that describes it. The ebXML Registry provides a set of services that enable sharing of content and metadata between organizational entities in a federated environment" [99, 100].

4.5.1. *ebXML registry information model (ebRIM)*

The ebRIM is a set of 8 information models that together define the classes and relationships that represent registry object metadata. Registry objects are metadata objects that describe repository items and are stored in a metadata registry. Repository items are the metadata artifacts that are managed by a metadata registry and stored in a metadata repository. The ebRIM consists of the following information models:

(i) Core Information Model: describes a set of commonly used information model classes.
(ii) Association Information Model: describes the association class to relate any two registry objects instances. A registry object instance is a single version of a registry object.
(iii) Classification Information Model: describes how a registry object is classified by a classification node in a classification scheme.
(iv) Provenance Information Model: describes the classes that enable the tracking of the responsible parties for creating, publishing and maintaining a registry object or repository item.
(v) Service Information Model: describes the service description classes. It is broad description that encompasses many kinds of services besides web services.
(vi) Event Information Model: describes the registry Event Notification classes.
(vii) Cooperating Registries Information Model: describes classes for federated registries.
(viii) Access Control Information Model: describes classes for control of access to registry objects and repository items [99].

4.5.2. *ebXML registry services and protocols (ebRSP) version 3.0*

The ebRSP is a comprehensive specification for metadata registry services and protocols. It describes a high level N-tier registry architecture, including a registry and repository, authorization, authentication, service, and client layers. It provides detailed message exchange protocols including binding for registry service interfaces, lifecycle management, query, and event notification. It also describes content management services, such as content validation and cataloguing, and publishing of a content management service. The ebRSP defines use cases for federated metadata registries (cooperating registries) and provides the required federated metadata for information exchanges among members of a federation. Finally, the ebRSP defines a registry security specification and provides a Security Assertion Markup Language (SAML) registry profile [100].

The ebXML community also provides an open source reference application called freebXML Registry, as well as XML schemas, Web Service Description Language (WSDL) service interface definitions, and SQL code for defining the ebXML database [18].

4.6. *Java API for XML registries (JAXR)*

JAXR provides a standard Java API for XML Registries. JAXR defines an XML registry as "an enabling infrastructure for building, deploying, and discovering web services". The current version of the JAXR specification includes detailed bindings between the JAXR information model and both the ebXML Registry and the UDDI Registry v2.0 specifications [114].

4.7. *The extensible markup language (XML)*

The XML family of specifications is commonly used for metadata exchange. The markup language is a subset of the ISO 8879:1986 Standard Generalized Markup Language (SGML) that was designed to enable user defined web processable tagging that functions similar to HTML. XML has expanded to a wide variety of related standards, including XML Schema language for defining valid XML documents, the XPath XML Query language, and the Schematron pattern assertion language [124].

4.8. *Semantic web standards*

The building blocks of the Semantic Web are often depicted as a stack of interrelated technology standards [66], as Figure 4 shows.

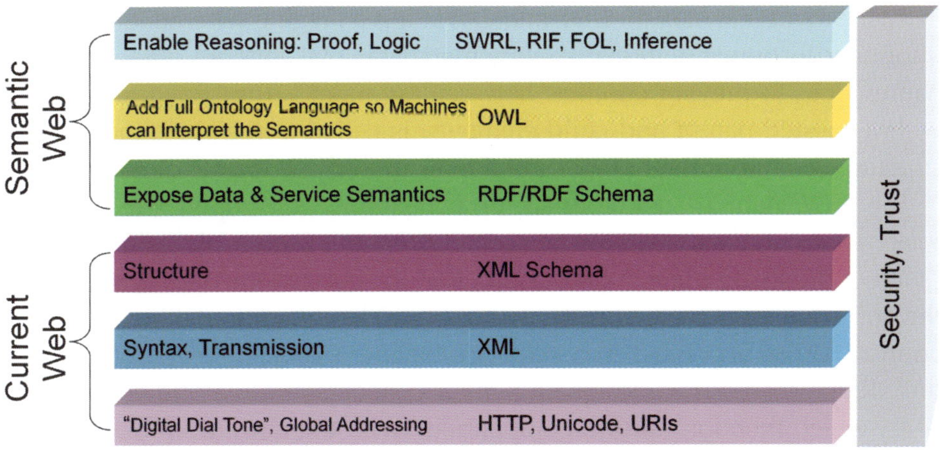

Fig. 4. The Semantic Web Stack: One View.

While different versions of the Semantic Web stack exist, for this chapter's purposes, the above model is used as a guideline. This chapter concentrates on RDF, OWL, and rules that enable automated reasoning/proof (the upper three levels in the above diagram) and repositories that can contain semantic content expressed in the Semantic Web languages.

What the Semantic Web stack enables is this: ontologies can be built to describe and represent information content on the Web. Each ontology item can be associated with a Uniform Resource Identifier (URI). A URI is in essence a hierarchical naming scheme that acts as an addressing mechanism. It can refer to anything: a resource, a person, organization, or concept. It need not be directly retrievable over the Web. A Uniform Resource Locator (URL) is a kind of URI that provides location information that allows a resource to be accessed and retrieved by some mechanism. The HTTP URL, e.g. http://www.google.com, is a specific kind of URL used to access web pages on the World Wide Web via the HTTP protocol. A file URL specifies the location of a file in a computer or network directory. The Internationalized Resource Identifier (IRI) generalizes the URI, which is based on ASCII, to a character set based on Unicode, thus enabling the use of names in other natural languages based on different alphabets.

Unicode (ISO 10646) is a standard for representing language characters and other ideograms as codes and streams of bytes that can be correctly processed by a computer. A repository must store and retrieve information in Unicode properly — typically in UTF-8.

XML provides syntax for RDF and OWL. It is a tagging scheme for marking information content with explanatory metadata. XML tags are organized into namespaces to prevent conflicts between tag names. The structure of XML, with its nested parent and child elements, is called a tree since the nesting structure resembles the branches of a tree.

The *RDF* data model consists of collections of 3-tuples (i.e., triples) relating two concepts with some named property. Each triple is in the form "subject predicate object" and asserts that the subject-concept is related to the object-concept by the predicate-concept. Here the term "object" has the connotation of an object in a sentence having a subject-verb-object structure. RDF uses URIs to designate named concepts and may be encoded in XML, which therefore allows compatibility with the current Web. RDF can express primitive class and property hierarchies and relationships. The structure of RDF is formally called a graph, since the pattern of links between resources resembles that of a network.[a]

RDF Schema[b] (RDFS) provides a means to define simple ontologies, i.e., to declare RDF resource classes and properties and the relationships between these properties and other resources. Comparing RDFS to RDF instances is analogous to comparing an XML Schema to an XML document.

OWL is a language for expressing more complicated ontologies. An ontology organizes the world into classes (i.e., categories of things such as countries), specific individuals (i.e., instances that belong to the classes, such as the United States), relations that can link instances to each other (such as the United States *has-diplomatic-relations-with* Australia, the Middle East *includes* Jordan), and properties, relations, or attributes (such as population, area, Gross National Product). OWL has an XML presentation syntax, uses the semantics of RDF and RDFS, and extends these.[c] OWL primarily uses RDF as the representation of instances of OWL classes and properties.

Rules specify constraints on classes, relations, and properties. They thereby constrain how new classes, relations, and properties are defined, prevent contradictory information from being added to a knowledge base,

[a] For comparison, XML Schema models (Document Object Model (DOM, etc.) are based on trees, a data structure in computer science that is simpler than a graph.

[b] "Schema" is actually a misnomer and owes more to the groups who originally defined RDFS, who were more conversant in database technology. A better term for RDF Schema would be "RDF Ontology Language."

[c] In fact, because there are some rather esoteric issues involving the semantics of RDFS, only OWL Full, the most complex of the three dialects or levels of OWL, can preserve all of the semantics of RDF/S.

and enable discovery of new information without explicitly asserting the information. Examples of common rules are 1) a rule that prevents a "child" from being its own "parent", and 2) a rule that says a "parent" of a "parent" that has a "child" is a "grandparent." The de facto standard Semantic Web Rule Language (SWRL) is an example of a language for expressing rules and is based on OWL [33]. There is an emerging W3C standard for rules called the Rule Interchange Format (RIF), which will probably supersede SWRL.

Finally, *security and trust* apply to all levels in the stack, and so are represented as a vertical rectangle on the right side of the stack. Trust requires [76]:

- **Identity:** Knowing that the person, agent, organization, software application, or Semantic Web ontology is who they say they are; digital signatures, PKI, etc., help establish this,
- **Credibility, Trustworthiness:** knowing that the Semantic Web artifact was created by a reputable agent, organization, i.e., one that has a reputation for quality, truth, response to customers, commitment to error correction, and adherence to self-advertised use and intent policies,
- **Proof:** being able to prove that the response you, your agent, or your inference engine is given to a query, function call, or service request on the Semantic Web is indeed true, and correctly follows; an explanation or trace that ensures this,
- **Security and Privacy:** being able to ensure that access to your property and to the rights you grant are strictly enforced at the sufficient granularity of detail you or your policy requires.

Although there are emerging standards for trust and security, due to space limitations we cannot address them in this chapter. The remainder of Section 4 provides a brief introduction to RDF, OWL, and rules.

4.8.1. *The resource description framework (RDF) and RDF schema (RDFS)*

RDF is an XML-based language for describing resources. It is a World Wide Web Consortium (W3C) standard. A resource in RDF can be anything that exists. An RDF description is one or more statements about a resource. RDF statements are called triples, because they are composed of three parts called the Subject, Predicate and Object because they roughly correspond to a subject predicate and object of a sentence. RDF Schema is a vocabulary description language that is layered over RDF. It defines a schema for creating RDF vocabularies. The RDFS data model is an object oriented model that enables the description of classes of resources and their properties, thus providing a language for constructing simple ontologies of Web resources [14].

4.8.2. *Simple knowledge organization system (SKOS)*

SKOS is an RDF application that is a recent W3C standard for describing the structure and content of classification systems, such as thesauri, taxonomies, and controlled vocabularies [129]. The main advantage of SKOS for metadata registries and repositories is that it encodes classification schemes in the same triple-based syntax as ontologies. Therefore, ontologies, controlled vocabularies and other metadata could be managed with the same set of RDF-centric tools.

4.8.3. *The web ontology language (OWL)*

OWL is layered over RDFS and enables greater machine interpretability of semantics than RDFS. OWL builds on and extends RDFS semantics to provide additional vocabulary and formal semantics. OWL 1.0 and 1.1 have three sublanguages: OWL Lite, OWL DL (Description Logic), and OWL Full. These are increasingly more expressive, meaning that each is capable of representing more robust semantics [2].

OWL 2.0 (OWL 2) is a Proposed W3C Recommendation (22 Sept 2009) [76, 129]. It's compatible with OWL 1, but provides some new features, such as:

- Increased datatype c\overage: Designed to take advantage of the new datatypes and clearer explanations available in XSD 1.1 (not yet a recommendation)
- Syntactic Sugar for more easily saying things in OWL, such as expressing disjoint classes, negative object properties, local reflexivity for properties, property-qualified cardinality restrictions, etc.
- New constructs that increase expressivity, including "declarations", which signals that an entity is part of the vocabulary of an ontology or that a specific individual is a named individual
- Simple meta-modeling capabilities such as "punning", which allows different uses of the same term and an individual
- Extended annotation capabilities, including annotating specific OWL entities, and annotations for axioms and ontologies

OWL 2 profiles are similar to the dialects of OWL 1, but have undergone more vigorous description; currently three profiles are defined: OWL 2 EL for applications with ontologies that define very large numbers of classes and properties; OWL 2 QL, which focuses on sound and complete query answering in LOGSPACE for UML, Entity-Relation, and database applications; and OWL 2 RL, for applications needing scalable reasoning with robust expressive power such as in rule-based systems (like Description Logic Programming [106] and RDFS-represented systems requiring additional expressiveness [126].

4.8.4. *Rules, proof, and the rule interchange format (RIF)*

Specifying rules semantically is powerful, and promotes reuse. In a database, rules are either embedded in the data model itself and various queries and views over this data, or embedded in procedural code in applications that support and use the database. The rules are tied to a particular database schema. Semantically-specified rules tie rules to an ontology.

Rules are also very closely associated with *proof*, i.e., rules require a proof mechanism to realize their value. In fact, a class of rules, inference rules, are directly associated with proof insofar as those inference rules license valid deductions as steps in an automated proof. Modus Ponens is one type of inference rule. *Consequence* is the proof relation that allows a valid consequence to be drawn from the given premises, as in a proof based on the logical proof pattern called Modus Ponens (which uses an implication $P \rightarrow Q$):

$$\frac{\begin{array}{l} P \rightarrow Q \\ P \end{array}}{Q} \qquad \text{Modus Ponens}$$

In general, a rule represented as an implication should be considered just another kind of operator in an ontology/knowledge representation language, i.e., there is no difference in kind between implication and any other logical connective. In fact $P \rightarrow Q$ is logically equivalent to $P \vee Q$. So if negation and disjunction are present in a logical system, implication is not needed except as a convenience. That's the simplest notion of rule. However, the real notion of rule is a proof or inference rule, i.e., a consequence relation, where premises are needed (i.e., class or property level assertions, or facts, as instantiated predicates are called) along with the implication, and then the inference rule applies, logically validating the conclusion. In logic programming (which refers to Horn Logic, a syntactic restriction of first-order logic, and thus also Prolog and Datalog[d]), the actual basic inference rule used is Selective Linear Definite clause (SLD) resolution [10].[e]

The user interest groups concerned with rule languages have come typically from a variety of backgrounds: those concerned with business rules for data and enterprise models, technologists working with logic programming and logical ontologies, and developers using expert systems.

RIF [76, 128] RIF is a rule language based on XML syntax. RIF provides multiple versions, called dialects:

- **Core:** the fundamental RIF language, and a common subset of most rule engines (It provides "safe" positive Datalog with builtins)
- **BLD (Basic Logic Dialect):** adds to Core: logic functions, equality in the then-part, and named arguments (This is positive Horn logic, with equality and builtins)
- **PRD (Production Rules Dialect):** adds a notion of forward-chaining rules, where a rule fires and then performs some action, such as adding more information to the store or retracting some information (This is comparable to production rules in expert systems, sometimes called condition-action, event-condition-action, or reaction rules) (see Forgy [23]).

RIF really represents a stack partially parallel to the Semantic Web stack depicted above, since some aspects of the RIF are not compatible with OWL. However, space limitations preclude a discussion of these differences.

4.9. *Emerging, defacto, and other standards*

There are many other standards relevant to our discussion of metadata and ontology repositories. Some of these are emerging and de facto standards. Others are miscellaneous applicable standards. These standards include those for: 1) mapping between content languages (knowledge representation languages) or between models; 2) establishing metadata for registration of ontologies into repositories; and 3) de facto candidate upper or foundational ontologies to assist in establishing semantic interoperability among domain,

[d] Horn Logic is a logic based on "Horn Clauses" is the foundation of the Prolog logic programming language. See http://en.wikipedia.org/wiki/Horn_clause. Datalog is a subset of Prolog, primarily distinguished from Prolog by not allowing function symbols, but there are also other restrictions, such as requiring stratification. See http://en.wikipedia.org/wiki/Datalog. and http://en.wikipedia.org/wiki/Prolog.

[e] See Brewka (1996), and http://en.wikipedia.org/wiki/SLD_resolution.

utility, reference, and application ontologies. The following sections briefly describe some of these standards.

4.9.1 *Standards for mapping between content (knowledge representation) languages or between models*

The issue of how to relate elements in one content (knowledge representation) language or knowledge classification scheme (i.e., ontology, taxonomy, or thesaurus) to others in a repository is one that is very salient in multiple communities today. For example, it is also an issue that is the topic of the Open Management Group's (OMG) Ontology Definition Metamodel (ODM) [91], and the ISO/IEC 19763 Metamodel Framework (Framework for Metamodel Interoperability, MMF) [42, 45, 46] The ODM standard establishes metamodels for RDF, OWL, ISO Common Logic, and Topic Maps. In addition, the standard specifies a mapping from UML to OWL, a mapping from Topic Maps to OWL, and a mapping of RDFS and OWL to Common Logic.

The ISO/IEC 19763.4 Metamodel Framework for Interoperability (MFI) — Part 4: Metamodel for Model Mapping [46] establishes a metamodel for registering rules of transformation between different models or objects registered according to ISO/IEC 19763-2: Core Model, i.e., the standard for specifying the core model required to describe metamodel elements, prospectively also for a registry of such metamodels.

4.9.2. *Standards for establishing metadata for registration of ontologies in repositories*

Metadata must be kept on items such as metadata schemas, controlled vocabularies, and ontologies that are entered into repositories. These metadata identify the salient information associated with the schemas, vocabularies, and ontologies, such as important date-times, representation languages, and many other items. Two standards that address these issues for ontologies include ISO/IEC 19763-3: Metamodel for Ontology Registration [45] and the Ontology Metadata Vocabulary (OMV) [28, 29]. The latter, for example, differentiates the following metadata that should be captured for ontologies (Figure 5) [28].

Two examples of defacto registry model standards that are designed for metadata schemas and controlled vocabularies are the Object Management Group (OMG)'s Terminology Query Services specification and the Mayo Clinic Division of Biomedical Informatics' LexGrid Model. The LexGrid Model is a simplified derivation of the OMG's Terminology Query Services

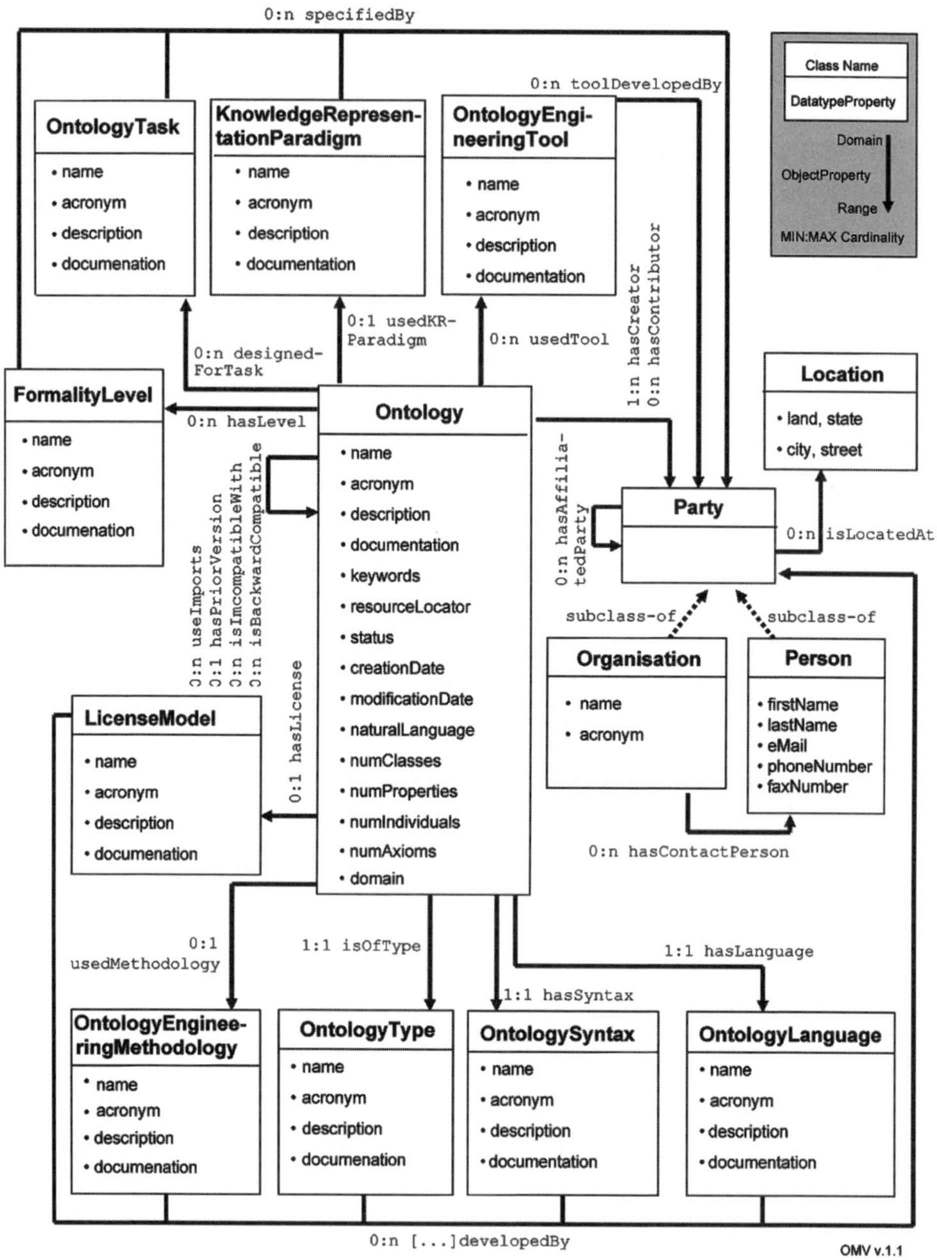

Fig. 5. OMV: Ontology Metadata Vocabulary's Ontology.

model [70]. It specifies a standard vocabulary format and core vocabulary management model that is designed to accommodate a wide range of what LexGrid calls "lexical resources". These include, controlled vocabularies, metadata schemas and to a limited extent, ontologies. LexGrid aims to enable a common set of lexical resource metadata, tools and APIs for accessing distributed lexical resources in many source formats. Source encoding formats that LexGrid currently supports are the Open Biomedical Ontologies (OBO), Web Ontology Language (OWL), and the Unified Medical Language System (UMLS) Rich Release Format (RRF). The National Cancer Institutes' LexEVS Terminology Server (see Section 5.4 of this chapter) is an example of a system that is an implementation of LexGrid compliant services [69].

In addition, the Ontology Summit 2007: Ontology, Taxonomy, Folksonomy: Understanding the Distinctions [85] established a number of dimensions that enable diverse semantic models such as ontologies, taxonomies, and folksonomies to be compared and thus partially mapped to each other. These included both semantic and pragmatic dimensions, as shown in Figure 6 from [86]: expressiveness, structure, granularity, intended use, automated reasoning, prescriptive vs. descriptive disposition, and governance.

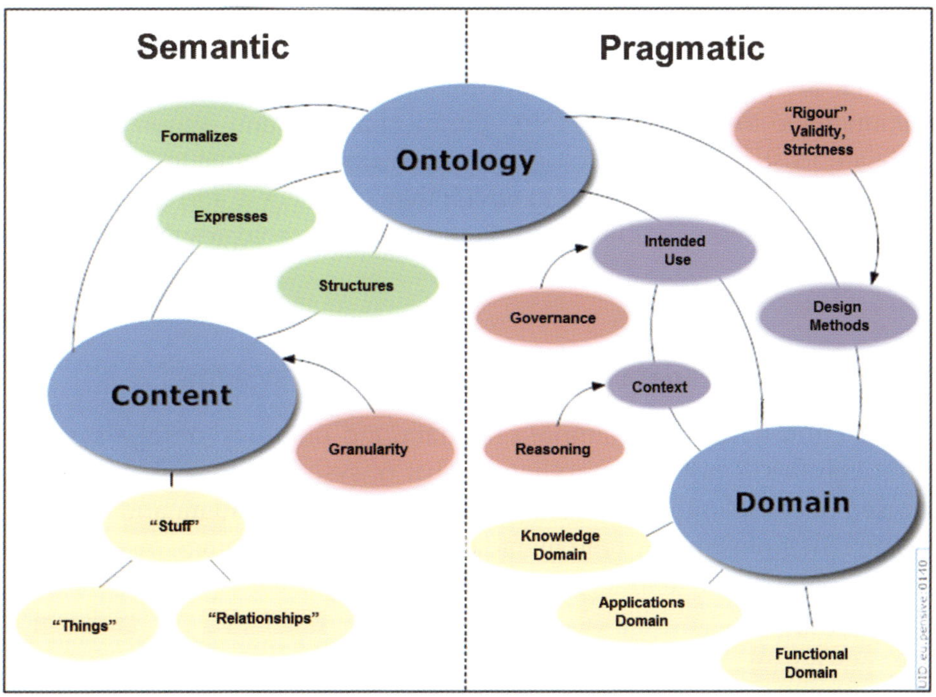

Fig. 6. Ontology Dimensions Map (from Ontology Summit 2007).

4.9.3 *Upper or foundational ontology standards*[f]

There have been a number of ongoing initiatives to define a standard upper ontology. Two initiatives that began in the early 2000s and ended within the past five years were the IEEE Standard Upper Ontology Working Group (SUO WG) and Wonder Web. IEEE SUO WG was a standards effort operated under the IEEE Standards Association and sponsored by the IEEE Computer Society Standards Activities Board. IEEE SUO WG proposed three candidate upper ontologies, namely Suggested Upper Merged Ontology (SUMO), Upper Cyc Ontology (UCO) and Information Flow Framework (IFF).

WonderWeb was a project consortium of universities and Industry, working in cooperation with the DARPA DAML program and the W3C. WonderWeb defined a library of foundational ontologies that cover a wide range of application domains. This library is intended to be used as a basis for the development of more detailed domain ontologies. Currently three modules exist: DOLCE, OCHRE, and BFO [62, 109]. In addition, there have been proposed other upper (foundational) ontologies, including Generalized Ontological Language (GOL)/General Formal Ontology (GFO) [30, 31].

For comparisons of upper ontologies, see Grenon [27], Semy, Pulvermacher, Obrst [110]; and Mascardi, Cordi, Rosso [61]. There was also an effort in 2006 by the Ontolog Forum called the Upper Ontology Summit, at which many major upper ontology developers signed a joint communiqué to agree "to develop the mechanisms and resources needed to relate existing upper ontologies to each other in order to increase the ability to reuse the knowledge to which they give access and thereby facilitate semantic interoperability among those other ontologies that are linked to them" [80].

5. Example metadata and ontology storage systems

This section describes example metadata and ontology storage systems. Although this is not a comprehensive list of systems, these systems were chosen because together they represent advanced metadata and ontology storage methods, most of the metadata and ontology storage methods and technologies, and standards that are described in Section 4 of this chapter.

[f] This section was adapted from Obrst (2010).

5.1. *The open ontology repository (OOR)*

The Open Ontology Repository (OOR) [87, 92]. effort began as the focus of Ontology Summit 2008: Toward an Open Ontology Repository [5, 87]. Its mission is:

- Establishing a hosted registry-repository,
- Enabling and facilitating open, federated, collaborative ontology repositories, and
- Establishing best practices for expressing interoperable ontology and taxonomy work in registry-repositories where "an ontology repository is a facility where ontologies and related information artifacts can be stored, retrieved and managed" [87].

The OOR has established a sandbox for federated repository components to participate in (http://oor-01.cim3.net/). Currently, this includes the National Center for Biomedical Ontologies' BioPortal [71]. The OOR's approach and architecture are documented at the OOR Web site [92].

5.2. *The extended metadata registry (XMDR)*

The Extended Metadata Registry (XMDR) is a prototype metadata registry that was designed as a test bed for the purpose of improving the ability of the 11179 metadata registry standards to support semantics. The XMDR project is based at the Lawrence Berkeley National Laboratory and is supported by a consortium of organizations such as the National Science Foundation (NSF), Department of Defense (DoD), and the Environmental Protection Agency (EPA), the National Cancer Institute NCI, and the National Biological Information Infrastructure (NBII). The goal of the XMDR is to investigate implementations of semantic extensions to the 11179 standards and then propose revisions to the standards based on the outcome of those investigations. XMDR use cases describe such advanced capabilities as semantic disambiguation and harmonization, semantic normalization of vocabularies as well as stored semantic mappings of interrelationships between vocabularies [51].

The XMDR prototype metadata registry ingests, transforms and indexes vocabularies as well as provides a mechanism to query vocabulary content by vocabulary, or across vocabularies. A key capability of the current XMDR prototype is the ability to store mappings between vocabularies. These mappings are also managed as lexical resources and can be searched and retrieved as such. The current version 0.6 includes a core software release that can be used to build an OWL/RDF-based metadata registry and a 11179 software release that consists of the software components that can be used to build an ISO/IEC 11179 compliant metadata registry. The core software includes scripts for loading data into the registry, REST APIs, and a web-based search interface. OWL/RDF metadata can be retrieved using a SPARQL endpoint or text search.

The XMDR currently contains indexes of a number of standard and common vocabularies that it calls "concept systems", including the Adult Mouse Anatomical Dictionary, the Defense Technology Information Center Thesaurus (DTIC)_Thesaurus 1.0, the International Standards Organization 2 letter country codes (ISO3166) and currency codes currency codes (ISO4217), and the Standard Industrial Classification System SIC codes. Many other vocabularies have been proposed or are planned for future inclusion in the XMDR [51].

5.3. *Dublin core (DC) metadata registry*

The Dublin Core Metadata Registry is an early example of a metadata registry. It is an open-source project that was developed by the OCLC Office of Research in conjunction with Dublin Core Metadata Initiative Registry Community. The Dublin Core Metadata Registry contains authoritative metadata about DCMI metadata elements and related vocabularies including some translations of definitions and usage comments into other languages. The registry uses an open source web-enabled relational database that is accessible from the DCMI Web site as well as REST and SOAP service interface.

5.4. *LEX enterprise vocabulary services (LexEVS) terminology server*

The LexEVS Terminology Server is an open source terminology management system that implements the LexGrid Model and associated LexBIG services. LexEVS provides access to controlled vocabularies that are associated with the National Cancer Institute's NCI Enterprise Vocabulary Services (EVS) project. The EVS Terminology Server is a Java application that includes: a Java API, REST/HTTP and SOAP Web service interfaces, and a distributed LexBIG interface based on the LexGrid 2009/01 data model that provides remote access to the native LexEVS API [69].

5.5. *BioPortal*

BioPortal is a Web-based ontology storage and management application that is funded by the National Institutes of Health (NIH) and led by the National Center for Biomedical Ontology (NCBO). BioPortal has similar capabilities as the XMDR prototype and is a more mature than XMDR. Using only their web browser, BioPortal users can browse, search and visualize ontologies in multiple formats including standards such as OWL, RDF, the National Library of Medicine's Rich Resource Format (RRF) and LexGrid XML.

BioPortal also has a rich collaboration capability. Users can annotate ontologies at the term level. BioPortal annotations are used to rate ontologies and add reviews, map terms between ontologies, propose new terms or term modifications, and upload images as term descriptors. Annotations are browsable through the Portal application, accessible via Web services, and users can subscribe to an RSS feed for notification of new annotations. Users can also post information about projects that are using ontologies that are managed in the BioPortal [71].

BioPortal has a layered architecture that uses an object-relational database (ORDB) for storage and Mayo Clinic's LexGrid along with Protégé for managing ontologies and terminologies of different formats [73]. Recently, BioPortal added a resource annotator that automatically tags biological resources with ontology terms and then indexes those resources to those ontologies [71].

5.6. *The national science digital library (NSDL) metadata registry*

The NSDL Metadata Registry was originally built to support the National Science Digital Library (NSDL). It was funded by the National Science Foundation for its first three years and is now available as an open metadata registry. It was an early adopter of the W3C Simple Knowledge Organization System standard. The registry is currently encoded in SKOS and includes a SPARQL end point. Future plans include leveraging semantic technologies to automate the creation and maintenance of schemas and application profiles, and for mapping relationships among terms and concepts in registered metadata schemes [72].

5.7. *Environmental protection agency (EPA) system of registries*

The EPA System of Registries (SoR) is a Web portal application that was designed to serve as a resource for facilitating the understanding of environmental terminology and data that is used by the EPA. The SoR is divided into 6 component registries each containing metadata that serves a different functional area.

- The System Inventory Services Registry stores metadata about EPA Systems, applications, their data models and data sets.
- The Data Registry Service manages the metadata for environmental data maintained in EPA and partner systems. It contains definitions, sources, usage information, valid values, and examples of data elements, code sets, and standards used in EPA systems.
- The Substance Registry Services (SRS) manages the vocabulary and metadata of the substances that EPA tracks and regulates. It links substance by synonym and identifies which synonyms are used in which EPA systems. The SRS contains metadata about chemicals and biological organisms, their physical properties and associated metadata [19].
- The Reusable Component Registry Service contains metadata about reusable web services, schemata, code blocks, data models, and templates.
- Terminology Repository Services is a terminology management tool that contains a repository of environmental terms, and metadata that defines relationships between terms, term definitions, and other term descriptors. It also includes a tool for the creation and management of controlled vocabularies such as glossaries and thesauri.
- The Facility Registry System (FRS) is a database that contains data and metadata that identifies the name, location, owner or manager, and associated metadata descriptors of the air, water and waste facilities that are subject to EPA regulation or tracking.
- These registries use a variety of storage and management methods and software including the Synaptica Taxonomy Manager for the terminology services (which employs ANSI Z39 terminology standards), and mostly relational database technology for storage. The registries are in different stages of developing web services and common tools for the distributed stewardship, consumption and reuse of registry metadata [19].

5.8. *Semantic Media Wiki (SMW)*

Semantic Media Wiki (SMW) uses embedded metadata storage methods to extend the open source MediaWiki application. The semantic annotations that SMW embeds in wiki pages enable the software to function like a database. Semantic annotations are used to enhance the ability to search, organize, edit, display and browse through wiki pages. Wiki pages make heavy use of hyperlinks to interconnect their concepts between pages. SMW extends these hyperlinks with annotations that describe the relationship that is stated in the wiki text and implied by the hyperlink. For example, if a wiki page about a movie contains a hyperlinked name of its starring actor, SMW enables the link to be annotated with a "starring actor" property that describes the relationship of the actor to the movie. SMW calls these "typed links". SMW can reason over these typed links to enable advanced query and aggregation of wiki content and can export the typed links to OWL/RDF XML format for use with Semantic Web tools. SMW is funded and developed by the Institute for Applied Computer Science and Formal Description Methods (AIFB) of University of Karlsruhe, Germany [122].

5.9. *Swoogle*

Swoogle is a Semantic Web search engine research project that is led by the ebiquity research group in the Computer Science and Electrical Engineering Department at the University of Maryland, Baltimore County (UMBC). Swoogle does not store its source ontologies, rather it crawls the World Wide Web for publicly accessible vocabulary documents that are encoded in the W3C standard Resource Description Framework syntax and creates semantic indexes of those documents for the purpose of search and retrieval. Swoogle is a Java application that stores its indexes in a MySQL database. Swoogle also provides web services and a Web enabled search interface that is modelled after the Google™ search engine. Swoogle currently indexes over three million RDF documents [121].

5.10. *NASA ontology sharing web sites*

The National Aeronautical and Space Administration (NASA) Jet Propulsion Laboratory (JPL) has published a library of publicly available OWL ontologies, as part of the Semantic Web for Earth and Environmental Terminology (SWEET) project [68]. Planetont.org is community and forum for sharing earth science related ontologies that is funded by NASA and is affiliated with the SWEET project. Both Planetont.org and the SWEET ontologies are stored as files in a web-enabled relational database and published online as a list of OWL files.

6. Metadata and ontology storage and management tools

In Section 6 we list a sampling of existing metadata and ontology management and storage tools. We separated the list into two categories: metadata-related

Table 4. A list of metadata and controlled vocabulary storage-related tools. They are categorized by the technology, standards, and whether they are free, commercial or open source. Table key: C/F/O = commercial (C), free (F), open source (O). See the chapter references for more information on metadata and ontology storage-related tools.

Tool name	C/F/O	Storage technology	Encoding standards
ASG-Rochade Metadata Repository [4]	C	RDBMS	XML
ebXML Registry-Repository [18]	FO	ORDBMS, Distributed DBMS	XML, ebRIM, ebRSP
Fedora Repository [21, 22]	FO	Middleware, Triple Store, RDBMS	XML, RDF
InfoLibrarian Universal MetaMart™ Metadata Repository [34, 35]	C	Middleware, RDBMS	XML
Informatica PowerCenter Advanced Edition Metadata Manager [36]	C	Middleware, RDBMS	N/A
MarkLogic Server [60]	C	Native XML	XML
MetaMatrix MetaBase Repository [103]	C	Middleware, RDBMS	XML
Objectivity/DB® [74]	C	OODBMS, Distributed DBMS	N/A
Open Harmonize [7]	FO	Distributed	WebDAV
Oracle Berkeley DB XML [96]	FO	Native XML	XML
Oracle Repository [97]	C	RDBMS	N/A
SAS® Metadata Server [107]	C	File Server	XML
SDL MultiTerm [111]	C	Middleware, Native XML, ORDBMS	XML
SchemaLogic [108]	C	ORDBMS	XML
Synaptica Taxonomy Manager [116]	C	Middleware, RDBMS	Zthes, SKOS, RDF,OWL
SuperLuminate [115]	FO	RDBMS	XML
Tamino [113]	C	Native XML	XML

tools and ontology-related tools. These are illustrated in Tables 4 and 5 respectively. The rationale for the separation is to separate by major functional division. While there is some overlap in functionality between the two lists, in general metadata-related tools are useful for traditional metadata management and simple ontology storage and retrieval. They are not designed for processing, managing and interpreting the semantics of ontologies. The ontology-related list is a more specialized set of tools that offer more robust functionality for managing ontologies and are compatible with ontology-related standards and tools.

Table 5. A list of ontology storage-related tools. They are categorized by the technology, native encoding, method, standards, and whether they are free, commercial or open source. Table key: C/F/O = commercial (C), free (F), open source (O). See the references section for information on metadata and ontology storage-related tools.

Tool name	C/F/O	Storage technology	Encoding standards
AllegroGraph RDFStore™ [24]	C	Triple Store	RDF
Anzo Semantic Server/Open Anzo [11, 90]	C/FO	Triple Store	RDF
Asio Parliament [9]	CO	Triple Store	RDF, OWL
Boca [39]	FO	Triple Store	RDF
eXtensible Knowledge Server (XKS™) [88]	C	Deductive Database	Common Logic
Jena [32]	FO	Middleware, Triple Store	RDF, OWL
Knoodl [104]	C	Wiki, Triple Store	RDF, OWL
Metatomix [64]	C	Middleware, Triple Store	RDF
Mulgara Semantic Store [67]	FO	Triple Store	RDF, OWL
Oracle Spatial 11g RDFDB [98]	C	Triple Store	RDF
OWLIM Semantic Repository [89]	FO	Triple Store	RDF, OWL
Semantic Media Wiki [122]	FO	Wiki, RDBMS	RDF
Seamark Navigator [112]	C	Middleware, RDBMS	RDF, OWL
Semantics. Server 1.0 [38]	C	Triple Store	RDF, OWL
Sesame [1]	FO	Middleware/Triple Store	RDF
Thetus Publisher [118]	C	Middleware/	RDF/OWL
TopBraid Suite [119]	C	Middleware/	RDF/OWL/XML
Virtuoso Universal Server [93]	C	ORDBMS/Native XML/Triple Store	XML/SOAP/ WSDL/ RDF

Although several kinds of related tools, such as metadata harvesters and reasoners are mentioned in this chapter, only metadata and ontology storage management systems are listed in this section. Compiling a list of related tools is beyond the scope of this chapter [25].

7. Chapter summary

This chapter focused on the storage and management technologies relevant to metadata schemes and ontologies. It discussed the different kinds of models and approaches used for metadata and ontology storage and access, and provided an overview of the appropriate standards. It described metadata and ontology storage and management technologies including relational databases; object-oriented and graph-structured databases; as well as Semantic Web and other logic-based technologies. The kinds of metadata and ontology storage mechanisms addressed included registries, repositories, catalogues, federations, and other forms. Prominent existing examples of registries and repositories were also discussed.

We intended to provide the reader with a solid introduction to the issues, methods, and technologies involved in metadata and ontology storage and management. We hope that this foundation may serve as sound technical guidance to those who develop strategies or select particular storage and access methods for their own future organizational or community needs.

Acknowledgments

The views expressed in this paper are those of the authors alone and do not reflect the official policy or position of The MITRE Corporation or any other company or individual.

References

1. Aduna (OpenRDF community), *Sesame*, http://www.openrdf.org/
2. Allemang D. and Hendler, *Semantic Web for the Working Ontologist*, 294–300 (2008).
3. American National Standards Institute/National Information Standards Organization (ANSI/NISO) Z39.19 — *Guidelines for the Construction, Format, and Management of Monolingual Controlled Vocabularies*, http://www.niso.org/kst/reports/standards?step=2&gid=&project_key=7cc9b583cb5a62e8c15d3099e0bb46bbae9cf38a (2005).
4. ASG, *ASG-Rochade Metadata Repository*, http://www.asg.com/products/product_details.asp?code=ROC (2009).
5. Baclawski, Kenneth, Todd Schneidery, *The Open Ontology Repository Initiative: Requirements and Research Challenges*, Workshop on Collaborative Construction, Management and Linking of Structured Knowledge (CK 2009), ISWC 2009, Chantilly, VA (2009).
6. Barry, Douglas K., *Transparent persistence in object-relational mapping*, http://www.service-architecture.com/object-relational-mapping/articles/transparent_persistence.html (2009).
7. Bell, M *Open Harmonize*, http://sourceforge.net/projects/openharmonise/

8. Bettati, Riccardo, *Introduction to Distributed Systems and Distributed OSs*, University of Texas A&M, Course CPSC662, http://faculty.cs.tamu.edu/bettati/Courses/662/2007A/Slides/Handouts/hINTRO.pdf (2007).
9. Bolt, Beranek and Newman (BBN), *Asio Parliament*, http://bbn.com/technology/knowledge/parliament (2009).
10. Brewka, Gerhard, ed., *Principles of Knowledge Representation*, Stanford, CA: Center for the Study of Language and Information (CSLI), and The European Association for Logic, Language, and Information (FoLLI) (1996).
11. Cambridge Semantics, *Anzo Data Collaboration Server*, http://www.cambridgesemantics.com/products/anzo_data_collaboration_server (2009).
12. Chang, Fay *et al.*, *Bigtable: A Distributed Storage System for Structured Data*, Google, Inc, OSDI'06: Seventh Symposium on Operating System Design and Implementation, Seattle, WA (2006).
13. Common Logic Standard site, http://cl.tamu.edu/ (2009).
14. Daconta M, Obrst L. and Smith K., *The Semantic Web: The Future of XML, Web Services, and Knowledge Management*, John Wiley, Inc. (2003).
15. Das, Subrata Kumar, *Deductive Databases and Logic Programming*, Workingham, England and Reading, MA: Addison-Wesley (1992).
16. Drupal.org, *DRUPAL RDF SPARQL Endpoint*, http://drupal.org/project/sparql_ep, (2009).
17. Dublin Core Metadata Initiative Recommendation, *Dublin Core Metadata Element Set, Version 1.1*, http://dublincore.org/documents/dces/ (2008).
18. ebXML Community, *ebXML Registry-Repository*, http://ebxmlrr.sourceforge.net/wiki/index.php/Overview (2009).
19. Environmental Protection Agency (EPA), *EPA System of Registries*, http://iaspub.epa.gov/sor_internet/registry/sysofreg/home/overview/home.do (2009).
20. European Semantic Web Group, European Semantic Web Conference (ESWC), *Large Triple Stores*, http://esw.w3.org/topic/LargeTripleStores (2009).
21. Fedora Commons, *Fedora Respository*, http://fedora-commons.org/confluence/display/FCR30/Fedora+Repository (2009).
22. Fedora Commons, *Fedora Tutorial #1 Introduction to Fedora, Fedora 3.0*, http://fedoracommons.org/confluence/download/attachments/4718930/tutorial1.pdf?version=1&modificationDate=1218459761506 (2008).
23. Forgy, Charles, *Rete: A Fast Algorithm for the Many Pattern/Many Object Pattern Match Problem*, Artificial Intelligence 19, 17–37 (1982).
24. Franz Inc., *AllegroGraph RDFStore™*, http://www.franz.com/agraph/allegrograph/ (2009)
25. Friedman, Ted, *et al.*, *Gartner Magic Quadrant for Data Integration Tools*, Gartner RAS Core Research Note G00160825 (2008).

26. Gardarin, Georges, Valduriez, Patrick, *Relational Databases and Knowledge Bases*, Reading, MA: Addison-Wesley (1989).
27. Grenon, P., *BFO in a nutshell: A bi-categorial axiomatization of BFO and comparison with DOLCE*, Technical Report, IFOMIS, University of Leipzig (2003).
28. Haase, Peter, *OMV Ontology Metadata Vocabulary*, April 10, 2008, Ontology Summit 2007, http://ontolog.cim3.net/file/work/OpenOntologyRepository/2008-04-10_Ontology-of-Ontologies/OMV-Ontology-Summit--PeterHaase_20080410.ppt (2008).
29. Hartmann, Jens, Raul Palma, York Sure, *OMV–Ontology Metadata Vocabulary*, http:// oyster.ontoware.org/oyster/omv-iswc.pdf (2007).
30. Heller, B. and Herre, H., *Ontological Categories in GOL [Generalized Ontological Language]*, 57–76, Axiomathes 14, (2004).
31. Herre, H., B. Heller, P. Burek, R. Hoehndorf, F. Loebe, and H. Michalek, *General formal ontology (GFO) — Part I: Basic principles*, Technical Report 8, Onto-Med, University of Leipzig (2006).
32. Hewlett Packard (HP) Labs, *Jena*, http://www.hpl.hp.com/semweb/ (2009).
33. Horrocks, Ian, Peter F. Patel-Schneider, Harold Boley, Said Tabet, Benjamin Grosof, Mike Dean, *SWRL: A Semantic Web Rule Language Combining OWL and RuleML*, W3C Member Submission. http://www.w3.org/Submission/SWRL/ (2004).
34. InfoLibrarian Corporation, *InfoLibrarian Universal MetaMart™ Metadata Repository*, http://www.infolibcorp.com/Metadata%20Repository.html (2009).
35. InfoLibrarian Corporation, *InfoLibrarian™ Desktop Express*, http://www.infolibcorp.com/ (2009).
36. Informatica Corp, *Informatica PowerCenter Advanced Edition Metadata Manager*, http://www.informatica.com/products_services/powercenter/editions/advanced_edition/Pages/advanced_edition_metadata_manager.aspx (2009).
37. Institute of Applied Informatics and Formal Description Methods (AIFB), semanticweb.org, *SPARQL Endpoint*, http://semanticweb.org/wiki/SPARQL_endpoint (2009).
38. IntelliDimension, *Semantics. Server*, http://www.intellidimension.com/products/semantics-server/ (2009).
39. International Business Machines (IBM) Advanced Technology group, *Boca*, http://ibm-slrp.sourceforge.net/wiki/index.php/BocaUsersGuide-2.x (2009).
40. Internet Assigned Numbers Authority (IANA), *Protocol Registries*, http://www.iana.org/protocols/ (2009).
41. International Standards Organization (ISO) 16642:2003, *Computer applications in terminology — Terminological markup framework*, http://www.iso.org/iso/iso_catalogue/catalogue_tc/catalogue_detail.htm?csnumber=32347 (2003).

42. International Standards Organization (ISO), *ISO 30042:2008 Systems to manage terminology, knowledge and content — TermBase eXchange (TBX)* (2008).
43. International Standards Organization/International Electrotechnical Commission (ISO/IEC), *ISO/IEC 19763-1 Metamodel Framework for Interoperability (MFI)*, http://standards.iso.org/ittf/PubliclyAvailableStandards/c035347_ISO_IEC_11179-1_2004(E).zip (2004).
44. International Standards Organization/International Electrotechnical Commission (ISO/IEC), *ISO/IEC 19763-2, Information technology — Metamodel framework for interoperability (MFI) Part 2: Core model*, http://standards.iso.org/ittf/PubliclyAvailableStandards/c035347_ISO_IEC_11179-2_2005(E).zip (2005).
45. International Standards Organization/International Electrotechnical Commission (ISO/IEC), *ISO/IEC 19763-3: Metamodel for ontology registration*, Final Committee Draft (FCD): http://standards.iso.org/ittf/PubliclyAvailableStandards/c035347_ISO_IEC_11179-3_2003(E).zip (2003).
46. International Standards Organization/International Electrotechnical Commission (ISO/IEC), *ISO/IEC 19763-4: Metamodel for model mapping*, Final Committee Draft 2 (FCD2): http://standards.iso.org/ittf/PubliclyAvailableStandards/c035346_ISO_IEC_11179-4_2004%28E%29.zip (2004).
47. International Standards Organization/International Electrotechnical Commission (ISO/IEC), *ISO/IEC 19763-5: Naming and identification principles*, http://standards.iso.org/ittf/PubliclyAvailableStandards/c035347_ISO_IEC_11179-5_2005(E).zip (2005).
48. International Standards Organization/International Electrotechnical Commission (ISO/IEC), *ISO/IEC 19763-6, Registration*, http://standards.iso.org/ittf/Publicly-AvailableStandards/c035347_ISO_IEC_11179-6_2005(E).zip (2005).
49. International Standards Organization/International Electrotechnical Commission (ISO/IEC), *ISO/IEC 24707 — Common Logic*, http://metadata-stds.org/24707/index.html (2007).
50. Kim, Won, Lochovsky, Frederick ed., *Object-Oriented Concepts, Databases, and Applications*, Reading, MA: Addison-Wesley (1988).
51. Lawrence Berkeley Laboratory, *Extended Metadata Registry (XMDR)*, https://xmdr.org/ (2009).
52. Lehigh University, *Lehigh University Benchmark* (LUBM), http://swat.cse.lehigh.edu/projects/lubm/ (2009).
53. Library of Congress, *Library of Congress Subject Headings (LCSH)*, http://id.loc.gov/authorities/search/ (2009).
54. Library of Congress International Standards Maintenance Agency, *Z39.50: Information Retrieval Application Service Definition and Protocol Specification*, http://www.loc.gov/z3950/agency/document.html (2003).

55. Lilley, Chris, *Not Just Decoration: quality graphics for the Web,* Fourth International World Wide Web Conference (WWW4), http://www.w3.org/Conferences/WWW4/Papers/53/gq-meta.html (1995).
56. Liu, Mengchi, *Deductive Database Languages: Problems and Solutions,* ACM Computing Surveys, V. 31:1, pp. 27–62 (1999).
57. Localization Industry Standards Association, *Termbase Exchange Standard,* http://www.lisa.org/TBX-Specification.33.0.html (2008).
58. Lorraine Laboratory of IT Research and its Applications, *Terminology Markup Framework* Webpage, http://www.loria.fr/projets/TMF/ (2009).
59. Marco D. Jennings M., *Universal Meta Data Models,* John Wiley & Sons (2004).
60. MarkLogic, *MarkLogic Server,* http://www.marklogic.com/information/xml-server.html (2009).
61. Mascardi, Viviana, Valentina Cordì, Paolo Rosso, *A Comparison of Upper Ontologies.* Technical Report DISI-TR-06-21, http://www.disi.unige.it/person/MascardiV/Download/DISI-TR-06-21.pdf (2006).
62. Masolo, C., Borgo, S., Gangemi, A., Guarino, N., Oltramari, A. *WonderWeb Deliverable D18 Ontology Library* (final), December 31 (2003).
63. Melton, James, *SQL, XQuery, and SPARQL,* www.w3.org/2006/Talks/0301-melton-query-langs.pdf] (2006).
64. Metatomix, *Metatomix Semantic Middleware,* http://www.metatomix.com/360solutions/data/index.php (2009).
65. Minker, Jack, ed., *Foundations of Deductive Databases and Logic Programming,* Los Altos, CA: Morgan Kaufman Publishers, Inc. (1988).
66. MITRE Corporation internal report, *RDF/OWL Repositories* (2006).
67. Mulgara Community, *Mulgara Semantic Store,* http://www.mulgara.org/ (2009).
68. National Aeronautical and Space Administration (NASA), Jet Propulsion Laboratory (JPL), *Semantic Web for Earth and Environmental Terminology (SWEET) Ontologies,* http://sweet.jpl.nasa.gov/ontology/ (2009).
69. National Cancer Institute (NCI), caBIG Knowledge Center, *LexBig and LexEVS,* https://cabig-kc.nci.nih.gov/Vocab/KC/index.php/LexBig_and_LexEVS (2009).
70. National Cancer Institute (NCI), caBIG Knowledge Center, *LexGrid,* https://cabig-kc.nci.nih.gov/Vocab/KC/index.php/LexGrid (2009).
71. National Center for Biomedical Ontology, *BioPortal,* http://bioontology.stanford.edu/BioPortal (2009).
72. National Science Digital Library (NSDL), *NSDL Metadata Registry,* http://metadataregistry.org/ (2009).
73. Noy, Natalya F., *et al., BioPortal: ontologies and integrated data resources at the click of a mouse,* Nucleic Acids Research, 1–4 (2009).
74. Objectivity, Inc., *Objectivity/DB®,* http://www.objectivity.com/ (2009).
75. Obrst, L., *Metadata and its Return On Investment (ROI): A White Paper,* MITRE report, 3 (2002).

76. Obrst, Leo, *Information Semantics 101: Semantics, Semantic Models, Ontologies, Knowledge Representation, and the Semantic Web.* Ontologies for the Intelligence Community (OIC) Tutorial, George Mason University, Fairfax, VA (2009).
77. Obrst, Leo, *Ontological Architectures, Chapter 2 in Part One: Ontology as Technology* in the book: TAO — Theory and Applications of Ontology, Volume 2: The Information-science Stance, Michael Healy, Achilles Kameas, Roberto Poli, eds. Forthcoming, Springer (2010).
78. Obrst, L., and H. Liu, *Knowledge Representation, Ontological Engineering, and Topic Maps*, chapter in XML Topic Maps: Creating and Using Topic Maps for the Web, Jack Park, ed., Addison-Wesley (2002).
79. Obrst, L., H. Liu, and R. Wray, *Ontologies for Corporate Web Applications*, Artificial Intelligence Magazine, special issue on Ontologies, American Association for Artificial Intelligence, Chris Welty, ed. (2003).
80. Obrst, Leo, Patrick Cassidy, Steve Ray, Barry Smith, Dagobert Soergel, Matthew West, Peter Yim, *The 2006 Upper Ontology Summit Joint Communiqué*, Journal of Applied Formal Ontology. Volume 1: 2 (2006).
81. Online Computer Library Center (OCLC), *The Dublin Core Metadata Registry*, http://dcmi.kc.tsukuba.ac.jp/dcregistry/pageDisplayServlet?page=about.xsl (2009).
82. Online Computer Library Center (OCLC), Preservation Metadata Implementation Strategies Working Group, *Implementing Preservation Repositories For Digital Materials: Current Practice And Emerging Trends In The Cultural Heritage Community* (2004).
83. Online Computer Library Center (OCLC), Preservation Metadata Implementation Strategies Working Group, *PREMIS Data Dictionary for Preservation Metadata, v. 2* (2008).
84. Ontolog Community, *Ontology Summit 2006: the Upper Ontology Summit*, NIST, Gaithersburg, MD, http://ontolog.cim3.net/cgi-bin/wiki.pl?UpperOntologySummit, March 15 (2006).
85. Ontolog Community, Ontology Summit 2007: *Ontology, Taxonomy, Folksonomy: Understanding the Distinctions*, NIST, Gaithersburg, MD, http://ontolog.cim3.net/cgi-bin/wiki.pl?OntologySummit 2007, April 23–24 (2007).
86. Ontolog Community, Ontology Summit 2007, *Ontology Dimensions Map*, http://ontolog.cim3.net/cgi-bin/wiki.pl?OntologySummit2007_Frameworks-ForConsideration/DimensionsMap (2007).
87. Ontolog Community, Ontology Summit 2008, *Toward an Open Ontology Repository*, NIST, Gaithersburg, MD, http://ontolog.cim3.net/cgi-bin/wiki.pl?OntologySummit2008, April 28–29 (2008).
88. OntologyWorks, *eXtensible Knowledge Server (XKS™)*, http://www.ontology-works.com/products/xks (2009).

89. Ontotext, *OWLIM Semantic Repository,* http://www.ontotext.com/owlim/ (2009).
90. Open Anzo Community, *Open Anzo,* http://www.openanzo.org/ (2009).
91. Open Management Group (OMG) Ontology Definition Model (ODM). 2009. http://www.omg.org/spec/ODM/1.0/. Version 1 (2009).
92. *The Open Ontology Repository (OOR),* http://ontolog.cim3.net/cgi-bin/wiki.pl?OpenOntologyRepository (2009).
93. OpenLink Software, *Virtuoso Universal Server Platform,* http://virtuoso.openlinksw.com/ (2009).
94. OpenLink Software, *Virtuoso Universal Server Platform Online Documentation,* http://docs.openlinksw.com/virtuoso/ (2009).
95. OpenLink Software, *Virtuoso Universal Server Platform, Open Source Edition* http://virtuoso.openlinksw.com/dataspace/dav/wiki/Main/VOSIntro (2009).
96. Oracle, *Oracle Berkeley DB XML, http://www.oracle.com/database/berkeley-db/xml/index.html* (2009).
97. Oracle, *Oracle Enterprise Repository, http://www.oracle.com/technologies/soa/enterprise-repository.html* (2009).
98. Oracle, *Oracle Spatial 11g RDFDB,* http://www.oracle.com/technology/tech/semantic_technologies/index.html (2009).
99. Organization for the Advancement of Structured Information Standards (OASIS), *ebXML Registry: Information Model (RIM),* http://www.oasis-open.org/committees/regrep/documents/2.0/specs/ebrim.pdf (2005).
100. Organization for the Advancement of Structured Information Standards (OASIS) ebXML *ebXML Registry Services,* http://www.oasis-open.org/committees/regrep/documents/2.0/specs/ebrs.pdf (2005).
101. Parmelee, Mary, *Design For Change: Ontology-Driven Knowledgebase Applications For Dynamic Biological Domains,* University of North Carolina at Chapel Hill, School of Information and Library Science, Masters Paper (2002).
102. Parmelee, Mary, Deborah Nichols, Leo Obrst, *A Net-Centric Metadata Framework for Service Oriented Environments,* International Journal of Metadata, Semantics and Ontologies (IJMSO), 250–260, 2009 — Vol. 4, No. 4 (2009).
103. Redhat, JBoss Enterprise Data Services Platform, *MetaMatrix MetaBase Repository,* http://www.jboss.com/products/platforms/dataservices/ (2009).
104. Revelytix, *Knoodl,* http://www.revelytix.com/knoodl.php (2009).
105. Richardson, James *et al., Gartner, Magic Quadrant for Business Intelligence Platforms,* Gartner RAS Core Research Note G00163529 (2009).
106. Samuel, Ken, Leo Obrst, Suzette Stoutenberg, Karen Fox, Paul Franklin, Adrian Johnson, Ken Laskey, Deborah Nichols, Steve Lopez, and Jason Peterson, *Applying Prolog to Semantic Web Ontologies & Rules: Moving Toward*

Description Logic Programs, The Journal of the Theory and Practice of Logic Programming (TPLP), Massimo Marchiori, ed., Cambridge University Press, pp. 301–322, Volume 8, Issue 03 (May 2008).

107. SAS, *SAS® Metadata Server,* http://www.sas.com/technologies/bi/appdev/base/metadatasrv.html (2009).
108. SchemaLogic, *SchemaServer,* http://www.schemalogic.com/ (2009).
109. Schneider, L., *How to build a foundational ontology: The object-centered high level reference ontology OCHRE,* in A. Günter, R. Kruse, and B. Neumann, editors, Proceedings of the 26th Annual German Conference on AI, KI 2003: Advances in Artificial Intelligence, volume 2821 of Lecture Notes in Computer Science, pages 120–134, Springer (2003).
110. Semy, S., Pulvermacher, M. and L. Obrst. 2005, *Toward the Use of an Upper Ontology for U.S. Government and U.S. Military Domains: An Evaluation,* MITRE Technical Report, MTR 04B0000063 (2005).
111. SDL TRADOS, *SDL TRADOS MultiTerm,* http://www.sdl.com/en/products/terminology-management/ (2009).
112. Siderean, *Seamark Navigator,* http://www.siderean.com/products_suite.aspx (2009).
113. SoftwareAG, *Tamino,* http://www.softwareag.com/us/products/wm/tamino/default.asp (2009).
114. Sun Developer Network, *Java API for XML Registries (JAXR),* http://java.sun.com/webservices/jaxr/overview.html (2009).
115. SuperLuminate, *SuperLuminate Data Dictionary,* http://www.superluminate.com/main.php?main_p_sl.html (2009).
116. Synaptica LLC, *Synaptica Taxonomy Manager,* http://www.synapticasoftware.com/Synaptica_Software/Home.html (2009).
117. *The XML:DB Initiative, http://xmldb-org.sourceforge.net/legal.html* (2009).
118. Thetus, *Thetus Publisher, http://www.thetus.com/publisher.html* (2009).
119. Top Quadrant, *TopBraid Suite,* http://www.topquadrant.com/products/TB_Suite.html (2009).
120. United States Department of Transportation Federal Highway Administration Office of Asset Management, *Data Integration Glossary* (2001)
121. University of Maryland Baltimore County (UMBC), Computer Science and Electrical Engineering Department, ebiquity research group, *Swoogle Semantic Web Search,* http://swoogle.umbc.edu/index.php?option=com_swoogle_manual&manual=faq (2009).
122. Wikimedia Foundation, *Semantic Media Wiki,* http://semantic-mediawiki.org/wiki/Help:Introduction_to_Semantic_MediaWiki (2009).
123. Wikipedia, *SPARQL,* http://en.wikipedia.org/wiki/SPARQL (2009).
124. Wikipedia, *XML,* http://en.wikipedia.org/wiki/XML (2009).

125. World Wide Web Consortium (W3C), *OWL 2.0*, http://www.w3.org/TR/2009/PR-owl2-new-features-20090922 (2009).
126. World Wide Web Consortium (W3C), *OWL Profiles*, http://www.w3.org/TR/2009/PR-owl2-profiles-20090922/ (2009).
127. World Wide Web Consortium (W3C), *Resource Description Framework (RDF) Semantics*, W3C Recommendation http://www.w3.org/TR/rdf-mt/ (2004).
128. World Wide Web Consortium (W3C), *Rule Interchange Format (RIF)*, http://www.w3.org/2005/rules/wiki/RIF_Working_Group (2009).
129. World Wide Web Consortium (W3C), *SKOS — Simple Knowledge Organization System Reference*, http://www.w3.org/TR/2009/REC-skos-reference-20090818/ (2009).
130. World Wide Web Consortium (W3C), *SPARQL Query Language for RDF*, http://www.w3.org/TR/rdf-sparql-query/ (2008).
131. World Wide Web Consortium (W3C), *Turtle* (*Terse RDF Triple Notation*), http://www.w3.org/TeamSubmission/turtle/ (2008).
132. Yianilos, Peter N., Sobti , Sumeet, *The Evolving Field of Distributed Storage*, IEEE INTERNET COMPUTING, September/October 2001, http://computer.org/internet/ (2001).
133. Zdonik, Stanley B., Maier, David, ed., *Readings in Object-Oriented Database Systems*, San Mateo, CA: Morgan Kaufman (1990).
134. *Zthes*, http://zthes.z3950.org/ (2006).